BOOKS BY THE AUTHOR

A Glossary to A Course in Miracles

A Glossary to A Course of Love

ACIM Lesson Journal: Volume I, II & III

Christ Illuminates The Bible: Volume I & II

53 Miracle Principles

Metaphors With Vision

Egoic Traps To Be Avoided

The Alchemical Power Of Light

Copyright

Published by: C. Know Be-Create
Email: contact@cknowbecreate.com
Interior Design by: Boris Stromar, Nadia Abaneeva
Cover Design by: Calvin Kwon
Editing by: Michael Ireland

Be-Create, C. Know, 2019 – *A Glossary to A Course in Miracles*

ISBN: 978-164516410-4

10 9 8 7 6 5 4 3 2 1
1. A Course in Miracles 2. Non-dual Thought 3. Spirituality

First Edition
Printed in the United States of America

WE SINCERELY...

Appreciate all our relations for being our teachers.

Pray these ideas benefit you as much as they did us.

Encourage you to read this material with an open mind.

Benefit from you extending these ideas to others.

Give freely because The Path has been given freely to us.

Offer you all of our books free on Kindle.

Dedicate all proceeds of printed books to translation.

Enjoy receiving your feedback and suggestions.

Ask you to leave comments for this book on Amazon.

MANY BLESSINGS!

A GLOSSARY TO A COURSE IN MIRACLES

A facilitator for reading *A Course in Miracles*,
and allowing its ideas to become your reality.

C. Know Be-Create

TABLE OF CONTENTS

Introduction

Containing nearly 500 terms with cited definitions, *A Glossary to A Course in Miracles* is currently the most extensive *A Course in Miracles* glossary. The definitions are divided into three categories: Dictionary, Ego, and Holy Spirit. Words listed in the Ego and Holy Spirit categories have corresponding synonyms listed beside them—and only those mentioned in *ACIM* have been included.

In order to integrate the teachings of *A Course in Miracles* (also referred to as *ACIM* or the *Course*) accurately, you must regard the words of the *Course* in the same sacred light as the Holy Spirit does. To embrace the true meaning of each term, you must relinquish all your worldly understandings of (and any personal connotations you hold about) any of these words or terms. Reinterpreted, each word becomes a miracle that will bring you closer to your Divine Self.

You are entitled to miracles. You can acquire Vision. Be determined to see things differently and the Real World will arise. Heaven is a choice and reaching it is a matter of being willing to reach it. Effort is not required. We give thanks to Christ for sharing clear Vision with us, unveiling the Celestial Order always and in all ways. You are closer to eternity, perfection, and unconditional love than you may realize. Walking the *ACIM* path is *"...a journey without distance to a goal that has never changed."* T8.VI.51.2

Dictionary

These entries provide a conventional definition and pronunciation of each term. Excerpts from widely accepted and understood definitions are included. This will aid in understanding the difference between conventional versus *ACIM* meanings.

Synonyms

The *Course* equates many words to have the same meaning. Each term frequently has other terms as synonyms. This is a powerful tool for unifying meaning, which in turn corrects perception. Only literal synonyms contained in the *Course* have been included.

ACIM definitions

The *Course* frequently gives uncommon meanings to common words. It addresses both the separated and unified mind throughout, emphasizing the difference. A clear distinction is provided, namely ego and Holy Spirit. For simplicity purposes, the first letter of all definitions is lowercase (including proper names), as many definitions are not complete sentences taken from the *Course*. For conjunctive terms (linked words such as teacher/ student or cause/effect), you will find that both terms are defined in the same sentence(s).

Boldface

Bold type identifies terms defined within the glossary. Only when the word appears exactly as the glossary term itself, the font is changed to bold.

Prioritization

Terms are listed in alphabetical order. Definitions under each term are presented in order of appearance in *ACIM*. A filtration process has eliminated repetitive ideas.

CITATIONS

Citations from *A Course in Miracles-Original Edition*, Course in Miracles Society (Third Printing, 2012) & *Supplements to A Course in Miracles,* Foundation for Inner Peace (Second Printing, 1996) appear after each definition in italics. Each citation begins with a letter, which denotes the particular volume of the *Course* and supplements. The format is expressed as follows:

INTRODUCTION:	I-paragraph.sentence
TEXT:	T-chapter.section.paragraph.sentence
WORKBOOK:	W-part(I or II).lesson.paragraph.sentence
	W-part(I or II).section.paragraph.sentence
EPILOGUE:	E-paragraph.sentence
MANUAL:	M-section.paragraph.sentence
PSYCHOTHERAPY:	P-chapter.section.paragraph.sentence
SONG OF PRAYER:	S-chapter.section.paragraph.sentence

ABILITIES

DICTIONARY: *possession* of the *means* or skill to do something.

EGO

~   abilities which **man** possesses are only shadows of his real strengths and that the intrusion of the ability to perceive, which is inherently judgmental, was introduced only after the **separation.** *T-3.VII.51.1*

~   abilities began with the **ego**, which perceived them as potentials for excelling. This is how the **ego** still perceives them and uses them. *T-7.IV.21.5:6*

~   all their harmfulness lies in its **judgment.** *T-9.III.11.5*

HOLY SPIRIT;   *potentials*

~   abilities are potentials, not accomplishments. Your abilities are totally useless in the presence of God's accomplishments and also of yours. Accomplishments are results which **have** been achieved. When **they** are perfect, abilities are meaningless. *T-6.V.52.2:5*

~   dealing with abilities, where degree of development is meaningful. This does not mean that what the ability is used for is necessarily either limited or divided. Yet one **thing** is certain—abilities are potentials for **learning**, and **you will** apply them to what **you want** to learn. *T-7.IV.21.1:3*

~   **he** can use them only for **healing.** *T-7.V.35.2*

~   all their helpfulness lies in the **judgment** of the **Holy Spirit.** *T-9.III.11.6*

~   **you** cannot **see** your abilities, but **you gain confidence** in their existence as **they** enable **you** to act. And the results of your actions **you** can **see.** *T-11.VIII.62.6:7*

ACCEPTANCE

DICTIONARY: *agreement with or **belief** in an **idea**, opinion, or explanation.*

EGO

~   **man** is very fearful of everything **he** has perceived but has refused to accept. **He** believes that, because **he** has refused to accept it, **he** has lost control over it. *T-3.VIII.64.1:2*

ACCUSE

DICTIONARY: *claim that (someone) has done something wrong.*

EGO

~   to accuse is not to **understand.** *T-14.II.7.6*

~   accusation is a bar to **love.** *T-27.III.13.3*

~   damaged bodies are accusers. *T-27.III.13.3*

ACKNOWLEDGMENT

|əkˈnäləjmənt|

DICTIONARY: *acceptance of the **truth** or existence of something.*

HOLY SPIRIT

~ your acknowledgment of your **Father** is the acknowledgment of yourself as **you** are. *T-9.XI.10.1.4*

~ to acknowledge Him is to deny all that **you** think **you** know. *T-16.III.16.6*

ADJUSTMENT

|əˈjəstmənt|

DICTIONARY: *the process of adapting or becoming used to a new **situation**.*

EGO; *change*

~ the **belief** in **sin** is an adjustment. And an adjustment is a **change**; a **shift** in **perception** or a **belief** that what was so before has been made different. Every adjustment is therefore a distortion and calls upon defenses to uphold it against **reality**. **Knowledge** requires no adjustment and in **fact** is lost if any **shift** or **change** is undertaken. For this reduces it at once to mere **perception**—a **way** of looking in which **certainty** is lost and **doubt** has entered. To this impaired **condition** are adjustments necessary because **they** are not true. *T-20.IV.16.1:6*

~ adjustments of any kind are of the **ego**. For it is the ego's fixed **belief** that all relationships depend upon adjustments to **make** of them what it would **have** them be. *T-20.IV.17.1:2*

~ fearful thoughts of those who would adjust themselves to a **world** made fearful by their adjustments. *T-20.IV.19.6*

ADVANCE

|ədˈvans|

DICTIONARY: *move forward, typically in a purposeful **way**.*

EGO

~ **you** cannot distinguish between advance and retreat. Some of your greatest advances **you have** judged as failures, and some of your deepest retreats **you have** evaluated as success. *T-18.VI.41.5:6*

ADVICE

|ədˈvīs|

DICTIONARY: *guidance or recommendations concerning prudent **future** action, typically given by someone regarded as knowledgeable or authoritative.*

EGO

~ forgetfulness and **sleep** and even **death** become the ego's best advice for how to deal with the perceived and harsh intrusion of **guilt** on **peace**. *T-13.IV.35.1*

ALLIANCE

DICTIONARY: *a **union** or association formed for mutual benefit.*

EGO

~ perceiving something alien to itself in your **mind**, the **ego** turns to the **body**, not the **mind**, as its ally, because the **body** is not **part** of you. This makes the **body** the ego's friend. It is an alliance frankly based on **separation**. If **you** side with this alliance, **you will** be afraid, because **you** are siding with an alliance of **fear**. *T-6.V.48.5:8*

~ angry alliances, born of the **fear** of loneliness and yet dedicated to the continuance of loneliness, **they seek** relief from **guilt** by increasing it in the other. For **they** believe that this decreases it in them. *T-15.VIII.73.3:4*

HOLY SPIRIT

~ without your alliance in your own **destruction**, the **ego** could not hold **you** to the **past**. *T-16.VIII.72.6*

ALONE

DICTIONARY: *having no one else **present**; on one's own.*

EGO;   *guilty*

~ **you** communicate with no one, and **you** are as isolated from **reality** as if **you** were alone in all the **universe**. In your **madness**, **you** overlook **reality** completely, and **you see** only your own split **mind** everywhere **you** look. **God** calls **you** and **you** do not hear, for **you** are preoccupied with your own **voice**. And the **vision** of **Christ** is not in your **sight**, for **you** look upon yourself alone. *T-12.V.38.3:6*

~ nor **will they see** Him alone, for **He** is no more alone than **they** are. *T-12.V.44.3*

~ in **sleep you** are alone, and your **awareness** is narrowed to yourself. And that is why the nightmares come. **You dream** of isolation because your eyes are closed. *T-12.VI.56.4:6*

~ **we** cannot sing redemption's hymn alone. *T-12.VII.76.1*

~ **you** cannot **see** alone. *T-14.IV.31.1*

~ it is **impossible** to **remember God** in **secret** and alone. *T-14.VI.55.1*

~ **you** think **you** know Him not only because, alone, it is **impossible** to know Him. *T-14.VII.75.2*

~ to be alone is to be guilty. For to **experience** yourself as alone is to deny the **oneness** of the **Father** and his Son and thus to **attack reality**. *T-15.VI.46.6:7*

~ alone does neither **have** it. So must it remain useless to both. *T-25.VI.40.2:3*

~ **you** cannot crucify yourself alone. *T-27.I.1.5*

~ this **world** is but the **dream** that **you** can be alone and think without affecting those apart from you. To be alone must mean **you** are apart, and if **you** are, **you** cannot but be sick. This seems to prove that **you** must be apart. *T-28.VIII.64.2:4*

~ **you** do not **see** how limited and weak is your allegiance and how frequently **you have** demanded that **love** go away and leave **you** quietly alone in "**peace**." *T-29.II.7.5*

~ while **you** still insist on leading or on following, **you** think **you** walk alone with no one by your side? This is the road to nowhere, for the **light** cannot be given while **you** walk alone, and so **you** cannot **see** which **way** **you** go. And thus there is **confusion** and a **sense** of endless doubting as **you** stagger back and forward in the **darkness** and alone. *T-31.II.25.3:5*

~ **you** could never be released alone. *W-pI.132.19.2*

HOLY SPIRIT

~ once **they have** chosen what **they** cannot complete alone, **they** are no longer alone. *T-6.V.69.6*

~ by accepting the **Atonement** for yourself, **you** are deciding against the **belief** that **you** can be alone, thus dispelling the **idea** of **separation** and affirming your true identification with the whole **Kingdom** as literally **part** of you. *T-7.IX.90.3*

~ the **Kingdom** cannot be found alone, and **you** who are the **Kingdom** cannot find yourselves alone. *T-8.IV.21.6*

~ alone **we** can do **nothing**, but together our wills fuse into something whose **power** is far beyond the **power** of its separate parts. By not **being** separate, the **Will** of **God** is established in ours and as ours. This **will** is invincible, because it is undivided. *T-8.V.36.2:4*

~ the whole **power** of God's Son lies in all of us, but not in any of us alone. **God** would not **have** us be alone, because He does not **will** to be alone. That is why He created His Son and gave him the **power** to create with Him. *T-8.VI.49.4:6*

~ **you** cannot hear the **Voice** for **God** in yourself alone because **you** are not alone. And His **answer** is only for what **you** are. *T-8.XI.112.3:4*

~ **atonement** is for all, because it is the **way** to **undo** the **belief** that anything is for **you** alone. *T-9.III.9.1*

~ it is not true that **you** can **make** decisions by yourself or for yourself alone. *T-13.VIII.73.3*

~ for no one alone can judge the **ego** truly. Yet when two or more **join** together in searching for **truth**, the **ego** can no longer defend its lack of content. The **fact** of **union** tells them it is not true. *T-14.VI.54.5:7*

~ remembering Him **means you** are not alone and willing to **remember** it. *T-14.VI.55.2*

~ it is not His **Will** to be **alone**. And neither is it yours. *T-25.III.20.12:13*

~ and so **you** walk toward **Heaven** or toward **hell**, but not **alone**. *T-25.VI.41.3*

ALTAR |ˈôltər|

DICTIONARY: *a table or flat-topped block used as the focus for a religious ritual, especially for making sacrifices or offerings to a deity.*

EGO; *beliefs, devotions.*

~ and at its altar it demands **you** lay all of the things it bids **you** get, leaving **you** no **joy** in them. *T-12.VII.68.11*

~ **you have** not left open and unoccupied the altar where the gifts belong. Where **they** should be, **you have** set up your idols to something else. *T-21.III.22.2:3*

HOLY SPIRIT

~ the **Spirit**, not the **body**, is the altar of **truth**. *T-1.I.20.1*

~ the inestimable **value** of the altar itself. It was created perfect and is entirely worthy of receiving **perfection**. *T-2.II.51.2:3*

~ these altars are not things; **they** are devotions. *T-5.IV.26.4*

~ the altar is perfectly clear in **thought**, because it is a **reflection** of perfect **Thought**. It sees only brothers, because it sees only in its own **light**. *T-7.V.29.9:10*

~ only at the altar of **God will you** find **peace**. And this altar is in **you**, because **God** put it there. *T-9.IX.84.1:2*

~ at the altar of **God**, the holy **perception** of God's Son becomes so enlightened that **light** streams into it, and the **Spirit** of God's Son shines in the **Mind** of the **Father** and becomes one with it. *T-11.VII.60.2*

~ the altar to your **Father** is as pure as **He** Who raised it to Himself. *T-13.IV.28.7*

~ no altar stands to **God** without His Son. And **nothing** brought there that is not equally worthy of both but **will** be replaced by gifts wholly acceptable to **Father** and to Son. *T-14.IV.33.3:4*

~ **god** has not left His altar, though His worshiper placed other Gods upon it. *T-14.V.40.8*

~ no one but seeks to draw to it the worshippers of what **he** placed upon it, making it worthy of their **devotion**. *T-20.III.7.3*

~ come before each other's holy altar where the **strength** and **freedom** wait. *T-20.III.15.5*

~ as **you** look upon each other, **you will see** an altar to your **Father**, holy as **Heaven**, glowing with radiant purity and sparkling with the shining lilies **you** laid upon it. *T-20.IX.70.4*

ANALYZE

|ˈanl͟ˌīz|

DICTIONARY: *examine methodically and in detail the constitution or structure of (something, especially information), typically for purposes of explanation and interpretation.*

EGO

~ to analyze **means** to separate out. The attempt to **understand** totality by breaking it up is clearly the characteristically contradictory approach of the **ego** to everything. *T-10.VI.53.2:3*

~ the **study** of the **ego** is not the **study** of the **mind**. In **fact**, the **ego** enjoys the **study** of itself and thoroughly approves the undertakings of students who would analyze it, approving its importance. *T-14.VI.53.6:7*

ANGEL

|ˈānjəl|

DICTIONARY: *a spiritual **being** believed to act as an attendant, agent, or **messenger** of God, conventionally represented in human **form** with wings and a long robe.*

HOLY SPIRIT

~ around **you** angels hover lovingly, to keep away all darkened thoughts of **sin** and keep the **light** where it has entered in. *T-26.X.83.1*

~ say His **name**, and **you** invite the angels to surround the ground on which **you** stand and sing to **you** as **they** spread out their wings to keep **you** safe and shelter **you** from every worldly **thought** that would intrude upon your **holiness**. *W-pI.183.2.2*

~ **you** do not walk **alone**. God's angels hover close and all about. *W-p2.EPILOGUE.6.5:6*

ANGER

DICTIONARY: *a strong feeling of annoyance, displeasure, or hostility.*

EGO; *blessing*

~ anger always involves **projection** of **separation**, which must ultimately be accepted as entirely one's own responsibility. *T-6.II.1.2*

~ anger cannot occur unless **you** believe that **you have** been attacked, that [the **attack** was unjust, and] **you** are in no **way** responsible. *T-6.II.1.3*

~ **projection means** anger, anger fosters assault, and assault promotes **fear.** *T-6.II.6.3*

~ whenever **you** become angry with a **brother**, for whatever **reason**, **you** are believing that the **ego** is to be saved and to be saved by **attack.** *T-11.IV.26.1*

~ it is **impossible** for the **ego** to enter into any **relationship** without anger, for the **ego** believes that anger makes friends. *T-15.VIII.66.1*

~ the more anger **you** invest **outside** yourself, the safer **you** become. *T-15.VIII.68.6*

~ anger takes many forms, but it cannot long deceive those who **will** learn that **love** brings no **guilt** at all, and what brings **guilt** cannot be **love** and must be anger. All anger is **nothing** more than an attempt to **make** someone feel guilty. *T-15.VIII.74.2:3*

~ when **you** are angry, is it not because someone has failed to fill the **function you** allotted him? *T-29.V.28.1*

~ having projected his anger onto the **world, he** sees **vengeance** about to strike at him. *W-pI.22.1.2*

~ for **threat** brings anger, anger makes **attack** seem reasonable, honestly provoked, and righteous in the **name** of self defense. *W-pI.153.2.2*

~ anger recognizes a **reality** that is not there, yet is the anger certain **witness** that **you** do believe in it as **fact.** **Now** is escape **impossible** until **you** see you have responded to your own **interpretation** which **you** have projected on an **outside world.** *M-17.9.7:8*

~ anger but screeches, "**guilt** is real." *M-18.3.1:2*

~ who sees anger as justified in any **way** or any circumstance proclaims that **peace** is meaningless and must believe that it cannot **exist.** *M-20.3.4*

~ returning anger, in whatever **form, will** drop the heavy curtain once again, and the **belief** that **peace** cannot **exist will** certainly return. **War** is again accepted as the one **reality.** *M-20.4.2:3*

HOLY SPIRIT

~ without **projection** there can be no anger. *T-7.IX.82.1*

~ anger is never justified. *T-30.VII.70.1*

~ the anger may take the **form** of any reaction ranging from mild irritation to rage. *W-pI.21.2.3*

~ anger in response to perceived **magic** thoughts is the basic **cause** of **fear.** *M-17.5.1*

~ if anger comes from an **interpretation** and not a **fact**, it is never justified. *M-17.8.6*

~ every **time you** feel a stab of anger, realize **you** hold a sword above your head. And it **will** fall or be averted as **you** choose to be condemned or free. Thus does each one who seems to tempt **you** to be angry represent your **savior** from the prison-house of **death.** *W-pI.192.9.4:6*

~ anger makes no **sense.** *W-p2.249.1.1*

~ anger is insane. *W-p2.360.5.4*

~ if a **magic thought** arouses anger in any **form**, God's **teacher** can be sure that he is strengthening his own **belief** in **sin** and has condemned himself. *M-17.1.6*

~ no one can be angry at a **fact**. *M-17.4.1*

~ it may be merely slight irritation, perhaps too mild to be even clearly recognized. Or it may also take the **form** of intense rage accompanied by thoughts of violence, fantasized or apparently acted out. It does not matter. All of these reactions are the same. *M-17.4.4:7*

~ anger recognizes a **reality** that is not there, yet is the anger certain **witness** that **you** do believe in it as **fact**. **Now** is escape **impossible** until **you see you have** responded to your own **interpretation** which **you have** projected on an **outside world**. Let this grim sword be taken from **you now**. *M-17.9.7:9*

~ god's teachers' major **lesson** is to learn how to react to **magic** thoughts wholly without anger. Only in this **way** can **they** proclaim the **truth** about themselves. *M-18.2.1:2*

ANSWER ⎮ˈansər⎮

DICTIONARY: *a **thing** said, written, or done to deal with or as a reaction to a **question**, statement, or **situation**.*

EGO

~ the **ego** is the questioning compartment in the post-**separation** psyche which **man** created for himself. It is capable of asking valid questions but not of perceiving valid answers because these are cognitive and cannot be perceived. *T-3.VI.41.1:2*

~ the **ego** has never given **you** a sensible answer to anything. *T-8.III.9.4*

~ an answer which demands the slightest **loss** to anyone has not resolved the **problem** but has added to it and made it greater, harder to resolve, and more **unfair**. *T-25.X.80.3*

~ **within** the **world** the answers merely raise another **question**, though **they** leave the first unanswered. *T-27.V.43.4*

HOLY SPIRIT; *right answer, **teacher**.*

~ since the **Holy Spirit** answers truly, **He** answers for all **time**, which **means** that **everyone** has the answer **now**. *T-6.V.47.6*

~ his Answer is your **Teacher**. *T-6.V.56.11*

~ the **Holy Spirit** is the Answer. **He** is the Answer to everything, because **He** knows what the answer to everything is. *T-8.IX.80.1:2*

~ the very **fact** that one has asked the **Holy Spirit** for anything **will** ensure a response. *T-8.XI.109.2*

~ no response given by the **Holy Spirit will** ever be one which would increase **fear**. It is possible that His answer **will** not be heard at all. It is **impossible**, however, that it **will** be lost. There are many answers which **you have** already received but **have** not yet heard. Assure **you** that **they** are waiting for **you**. *T-8.XI.109.3:7*

~ the answer to all prayers lies in them. **You will** be answered as **you** hear the answer in **everyone**. *T-8.XI.113.6:7*

~ it is an exalted answer because of its **Source**, but the **Source** is true and so is Its answer. *T-9.VII.58.7*

~ the **Holy Spirit will** answer every specific **problem** as long as **you** believe that problems are specific. His answer is both many and one, as long as **you** believe that the one is many. *T-10.VIII.80.5:6*

~ his answer is the **release** from **fear**. *T-10.VIII.83.1*

~ **he** could but answer your insane **request** with a sane answer which would abide with **you** in your **insanity**. [And this **He** did. No one who hears His answer but **will give** up **insanity**.] For His answer is the reference point beyond illusions from which **you** can look back on them and **see** them as insane. *T-12.III.22.6:9*

~ his sane answer tells **you** that what **you have** offered yourself is not true. *T-12.V.39.5*

~ in Him **you** are answered by His **peace**. *T-12.VI.53.6*

~ the **Holy Spirit will** not **delay** at all in answering your every **question** what to do. **He** knows. And **He will** tell **you** and then do it for **you**. *T-13.IX.92.4:6*

~ the answer is given. **Seek** not to answer it, but merely **receive** the answer as it is given. *T-18.V.36.2:3*

~ what **God** gave Answer to is answered and is gone. *T-26.VI.32.7*

~ applies to all its forms. God's answer is eternal, though it operates in **time** where it is needed. *T-26.VIII.49.2:3*

~ the **laws** of **time** do not affect its workings. It is in this **world**, but not a **part** of it. For it is real and dwells where all **reality** must be. *T-26.VIII.49.4:6*

~ **god** must **have** given **you** a **way** of reaching to another state of **mind** in which the answer is already there. *T-27.V.37.3*

~ an **honest** answer asks no **sacrifice** because it answers questions truly asked. *T-27.V.42.1*

~ answers which **will** solve your problems because **they** stand apart from them, and **see** what can be answered—what the **question** is. *T-27.V.43.3*

~ for this one answer takes away the **cause** of every **form** of sorrow and of **pain**. The **form** affects His answer not at all, for **He** would **teach you** but the single **cause** of all of them, no matter what their **form**. *T-27.IX.87.3:4*

~ the answer **will** be true because of Whom **you ask**. *W-pI.72.15.3*

~ god's answer cannot **fail**. *W-pI.80.4.2*

~ **he** has one answer to appearances regardless of their **form**, their size, their depth, or any attribute **they** seem to **have**. *W-pI.99.7.3*

~ **ask** and expect an answer. *W-pI.106.10.1*

~ answer, clear and plain, beyond **deceit** in its simplicity. *W-pI.122.6.6*

~ **everyone** is answered by His **Voice**. *W-pII.267.1.7*

~ the instant the **idea** of **separation** entered the **Mind** of God's Son, in that same instant was God's Answer given. In **time** this happened very long ago. In **reality** it never happened at all. *M-2.2.6:8*

~ the one answer to **sickness** of any kind is **healing**. The one answer to all illusions is **truth**. *M-8.6.7:8*

~ and **He will** send His Answer through the **therapist** who best can serve His Son in all his **present** needs. *P-2.V.6.7*

~ there is Something in him that **will** tell **you**, if **you** listen. And that is the answer; listen. Do not demand, do not decide, do not **sacrifice**. Listen. What **you** hear is true. *P-3.I.2.3:7*

~ **you will receive** a specific answer if such is your **need**. *S-1.I.2.1*

~ **you** cannot be asked to accept answers which are beyond the **level** of **need** that **you** can recognize. *S-1.I.2.5*

~ it is not the **form** of the **question** that matters, nor how it is asked. The **form** of the answer, if given by **God**, **will** suit your need as **you see** it. *S-1.I.2.6:7*

ANTI-CHRIST

|ˈan(t)ē ˌkrīst′|

DICTIONARY: *a personal opponent of* **Christ** *expected to appear before the end of the* **world**.

EGO

~   all forms of anti-**Christ** oppose the **Christ** and fall before His face like a dark **veil** which seems to shut you off from Him, **alone** in **darkness**. *T-29.IX.54.5*

~   anti-**Christ** becomes more powerful than **Christ** to those who **dream** the **world** is real. *W-pI.137.6.2*

HOLY SPIRIT

~   this is the anti-**Christ**—the strange **idea** there is a **power past** omnipotence, a place beyond the infinite, a **time** transcending the eternal. *T-29.IX.57.1*

APOCALYPSE

|əˈpäkə ˌlips|

DICTIONARY: *the complete final* **destruction** *of the* **world**, *especially as described in the biblical book of* **Revelation**.

HOLY SPIRIT

~   the first **step** toward **freedom** must entail a sorting out of the false from the true. This is a process of division only in the constructive **sense** and reflects the true **meaning** of the Apocalypse. **Man will** ultimately look upon his own **creations** and **will** to preserve only what is **good**, just as **God** Himself looked upon what **He** had created and knew that it was **good**. *T-2.VI.109.5:7*

APPEARANCE

|əˈpirəns|

DICTIONARY: *impression given by someone or something, although this may be misleading*.

EGO

~   **they** but obscure **reality**, and **they** bring **fear** because **they hide** the **truth**. *T-30.V.53.3*

~   **you** think that some appearances are real and not appearances at all. *T-30.VII.75.3*

~   some appearances are harder to look **past** than others are. *T-30.VII.75.4*

~   if one appearance must remain apart from **healing**, one **illusion** must be **part** of **truth**. *T-30.VII.76.3*

~   ancient lessons that **you** taught yourself about the sinfulness in **you**. *T-31.II.23.1*

HOLY SPIRIT

~   appearances deceive because **they** are appearances and not **reality**. *T-30.V.53.1:2*

~   appearances can but deceive the **mind** that wants to be deceived. *T-30.V.54.1*

~   there can be no appearance that cannot be overlooked. *T-30.VII.74.4*

~   there cannot be appearances which **have** replaced the **truth** about God's Son. *T-30.VII.76.8*

~   appearances deceive but can be changed. *T-30.IX.89.1*

~   appearances are shown to be unreal because **they change**. *T-30.IX.90.9*

~   there is no false appearance but **will** fade if **you request** a **miracle** instead. *T-30.IX.94.5*

- ~ no appearance but **will** turn to **truth** before the eyes of **you** who **rest** in **God**. *W-pI.109.3.5*
- ~ appearances cannot intrude on **you**. *W-pI.109.4.4*
- ~ appearances cannot replace the **truth**. *W-pI.110.3.1*

APPETITE
|ˈapəˌtīt|

DICTIONARY: *a natural **desire** to satisfy a bodily **need**, especially for food.*

EGO

- ~ all appetites are "getting" mechanisms, representing the ego's **need** to confirm itself. *T-4.III.32.5*
- ~ bodily appetites are not physical in origin. *T-4.III.32.7*

HOLY SPIRIT

- ~ the pull of **God** Himself can hardly be equated with the pull of human appetites. By perceiving them as the same, the **ego** attempts to save itself from **being** swept away, as it would surely be in the presence of **knowledge**. *T-4.IV.46.2:3*

APPRECIATION
|əˌprēSHēˈāSH(ə)n|

DICTIONARY: *the recognition and enjoyment of the **good** qualities of someone or something.*

EGO

- ~ **you** cannot **love** what **you** do not appreciate, and **fear** makes appreciation **impossible**. *T-6.II.24.1*

HOLY SPIRIT

- ~ only one equal **gift** can be offered to the equal Sons of **God**, and that is full appreciation. *T-6.V.64.4*
- ~ the appreciation of **wholeness** comes only through **acceptance**. *T-10.VI.53.2*
- ~ only appreciation is an appropriate response to your **brother**. **Gratitude** is due him for both his loving thoughts and his appeals for **help**, for both are capable of bringing **love** into your **awareness** if **you** perceive them truly. *T-11.II.6.6:7*

ARK OF PEACE
A Course in Miracles Term

HOLY SPIRIT

- ~ the ark of **peace** is entered two by two, yet the beginning of another **world** goes with them. Each **holy relationship** must enter **here** to learn its **special function** in the Holy Spirit's **plan**, **now** that it shares His **purpose**. And as this **purpose** is fulfilled, a new **world** rises in which **sin** can enter not, and where the **Son of God** can enter without **fear**, and where **he** rests a while to forget imprisonment and to **remember freedom**. *T-20.V.33.5:7*
- ~ except **you** be there, **he** is not complete. And it is his **completion** that **he** remembers there. *T-20.V.33.9:10*
- ~ the whole new **world** rests in the hands of every two who enter **here** to **rest**. *T-20.V.34.3*

ARMY

DICTIONARY: *a large number of people or things, typically formed or organized for a particular **purpose**.*

EGO

~ the army of the powerless is weak indeed. It has no weapons, and it has no **enemy**. Yes, it can overrun the **world** and **seek** an **enemy**. But it can never find what is not there. Yes, it can **dream** it found an **enemy**, but this **will shift** even as it attacks, so that it runs at once to find another and never comes to **rest** in victory. And as it runs, it turns against itself. *T-21.VIII.73.1:6*

ARROGANT

DICTIONARY: *having or revealing an exaggerated **sense** of one's own importance or **abilities**.*

EGO

~ any attempt **you make** to correct a **brother means** that **you** believe **correction** by **you** is possible, and this can only be the arrogance of the **ego**. *T-9.II.7.8*

~ arrogance is the **denial** of **love**, because **love** shares and arrogance withholds. As long as both appear to **you** to be desirable, the **concept** of **choice**, which is not of **God**, **will** remain with **you**. *T-9.XI.106.3:4*

~ it is only arrogance that would deny the **power** of your **will**. *T-22.VII.60.2*

~ arrogance to think your **little** errors cannot be undone by Heaven's **justice**. *T-25.X.78.1*

~ but it is arrogant to lay aside the **power** that **He** gave and choose a **little** senseless **wish** instead of what **He** wills. *T-26.VIII.65.3*

~ only in arrogance could **you** conceive that **you** must **make** the **way** to **Heaven** plain. *T-31.VI.65.1*

~ arrogance which says that **we** are sinners, guilty and afraid, ashamed of what **we** are. *W-pI.152.10.1*

~ only the **ego** can be arrogant. *W-pI.152.9.2*

~ the arrogant must cling to words, afraid to go beyond them to **experience** which might affront their stance. *W-pI.186.5.5*

HOLY SPIRIT; *denial* of *love*

~ to accept your littleness is arrogant, because it **means** that **you** believe your evaluation of yourself is truer than God's. *T-9.VII.57.9*

~ it is not arrogant to be as **He** created **you** or to **make** use of what **He** gave to **answer** all His Son's mistakes and set him free. *T-26.VIII.65.2*

~ arrogance makes an **image** of yourself that is not real. *W-pI.186.6.1*

~ arrogance opposes **truth**. *W-pII.319.1.2*

~ **where** there is no arrogance, the **truth will** come immediately and fill up the space the **ego** left unoccupied by lies. *W-pII.319.1.3*

16

ASK

DICTIONARY: *say something in* **order** *to obtain an* **answer** *or some information.*

EGO; *taking*

~ **you** believe that asking is taking, and **you** do not perceive it as sharing. *T-10.VIII.81.1*

~ to ask that what is false be true can only **fail**. *W-pI.200.3.4*

~ if **he** asks for the **impossible**, if **he** wants what does not **exist** or seeks for illusions in his heart, all this becomes his own. The **power** of his **decision** offers it to him, as **he** requests. Herein lie **hell** and **Heaven**. *M-21.3.4:6*

~ to ask for the specific is much the same as to look on **sin** and then forgive it. *S-1.I.4.2*

HOLY SPIRIT

~ **we** do not ask for what **we** do not **have**. **We** merely ask for what belongs to us, that **we** may recognize it as our own. *W-pI.107.8.6:7*

~ **you** do not ask too much of **life**, but far too **little**. *W-pI.133.2.1*

~ to ask for what **you have** already must succeed. *W-pI.200.3.3*

~ ask and **you have** received, for **you have** established what it is **you want**. *S-1.II.2.6*

ATHEIST

DICTIONARY: *a person who disbelieves or lacks* **belief** *in the existence of* **God** *or Gods.*

EGO

~ if, then, a **mind** believes that its **will** is different from His, it can only decide either that there is no **God** or that **God's Will** is fearful. The former accounts for the atheist and the latter for the **martyr**. Martyrdom takes many forms, the category including all doctrines which hold that **God** demands sacrifices of any kind. *T-8.X.97.2:4*

~ the atheist believes **he** is **alone**. *T-8.X.97.5*

~ both really **fear** abandonment and retaliation, but the atheist is more reactive against abandonment and the **martyr** against retaliation. *T-8.X.97.6*

~ the atheist maintains that **God** has left him, but **he** does not care. **He will**, however, become very fearful and hence very angry if anyone suggests that **God** has not left him. *T-8.X.98.1:2*

ATONEMENT

DICTIONARY: *reparation or expiation for* **sin**.

EGO

~ neurotic **guilt** feelings are a device of the **ego** for "atoning" without sharing and for asking pardon without **change**. The **ego** never calls for real Atonement and cannot tolerate **forgiveness**, which is **change**. *T-5.VI.48.4:5*

~ **you** cannot dispel **guilt** by making it real and then atoning for it. This is the ego's **plan**, which it offers instead of dispelling it. The **ego** believes in atonement through **attack**, **being** fully committed to the insane notion that **attack** is **salvation**. *T-11.X.98.1:3*

~ **vengeance** becomes your **substitute** for Atonement, and the escape from **vengeance** becomes your **loss.** *T-16.VIII.74.7*

~ our **plan** for the escape from **guilt** has been to bring Atonement to it and **make salvation** fearful. *T-18.V.38.3*

~ no one accepts Atonement for himself who still accepts **sin** as his **goal. You have** thus not met your one responsibility. Atonement is not welcomed by those who prefer **pain** and **destruction.** *T-18.VIII.63.4:6*

~ to the **ego sin means death**, and so Atonement is achieved through murder. *T-19.V.56.3*

HOLY SPIRIT; *way to* **peace**, *act of* **love**, *final demonstration, final* **miracle**, *perfect* **lesson**, *total commitment,* **God's Word**, *remedy,* **defense**, *one* **need**, *device.*

~ "atoning" really **means** "undoing." *T-1.I.30.2*

~ the **purpose** of the Atonement is to restore everything to **you**, or rather to restore it to your **awareness.** *T-1.I.31.1*

~ atonement is the natural profession of the Children of **God.** *T-1.I.34.3*

~ the Atonement restores the **Soul** to its proper place. *T-1.I.46.7*

~ atonement undoes all errors in this respect and thus uproots the real **source** of **fear.** *T-1.I.53.1*

~ the Atonement is the only **defense** which cannot be used destructively. That is because, while **everyone** must eventually **join** it, it is not a device which was generated by **man.** The Atonement principle was in effect long before the Atonement itself began. The principle was **love**, and the Atonement itself was an act of **love.** Acts were not necessary before the **separation** because the **time**-space **belief** did not **exist.** It was only after the **separation** that the **defense** of Atonement and the necessary conditions for its fulfillment were planned. *T-2.II.36.1:6*

~ his **choice** could not, however, turn it into a weapon of **attack**, which is the inherent characteristic of all other defenses. The Atonement thus becomes the only **defense** which is not a two-edged sword. *T-2.II.37.3:4*

~ the Atonement actually began long before the **crucifixion.** *T-2.II.38.1*

~ a split-proof device which could be used only to heal. *T-2.II.39.2*

~ the Atonement was built into the space-**time belief** in **order** to set a **limit** on the **need** for the **belief** and ultimately to **make learning** complete. The Atonement is the final **lesson.** *T-2.II.39.3:4*

~ the Atonement is the device by which **he** can free himself from the **past** as **he** goes ahead. It undoes his **past** errors, thus making it unnecessary for him to keep retracing his steps without advancing to his return. In this **sense** the Atonement saves **time** but, like the **miracle** which serves it, does not abolish it. As long as there is **need** for Atonement, there is **need** for **time.** Until the Atonement is finished, its various phases **will** proceed in **time**, but the whole Atonement stands at time's end. At this point, the **bridge** of the return has been built. *T-2.II.41.1:6*

~ the Atonement can only be accepted **within you.** *T-2.II.44.1*

~ the Atonement belongs at the center of the inner **altar**, where it undoes the **separation** and restores the **wholeness** of the **mind.** *T-2.II.46.1*

~ the Atonement is the only **gift** that is worthy of **being** offered to the **altar** of **God.** *T-2.II.51.1*

~ the Atonement **plan** is to **undo error** at all levels. *T-2.III.53.1*

~ it **will** inevitably be expressed in whatever **way** is most helpful to the receiver[, not the giver]. *T-2.III.59.2*

~ pragmatic steps in the larger process of accepting the Atonement as the remedy. *T-2.V.82.3*

~ perfect **love** is the Atonement. *T-2.V.86.1*

~ the **crucifixion** did not establish the Atonement. The **resurrection** did. *T-3.III.11.2:3*

~ the Atonement too is totally without symbolism. It is perfectly clear because it exists in **light**. Only man's attempts to shroud it in **darkness have** made it inaccessible to the unwilling and ambiguous to the partly willing. The Atonement itself radiates **nothing** but **truth**. It therefore epitomizes harmlessness and sheds only **blessing**. It could not do this if it arose from anything but perfect **innocence**. **Innocence** is wisdom because it is unaware of **evil**, which does not **exist**. It is, however, perfectly aware of everything that is true. *T-3.III.17:2:9*

~ atonement is thus the perfect **lesson**. It is the final demonstration that all of the other lessons which **I** taught are true. *T-3.III.18.3:4*

~ the Atonement was an act based on true **perception**. **I** cannot choose for **you**, but **I** can **help you make** your own right **choice**. *T-3.VI.49.5:6*

~ the Atonement is the guarantee of the safety of the **Kingdom**. *T-5.VI.47.1*

~ the Atonement cannot be understood except as a pure act of sharing. That is what is meant when **we** said it is possible even in this **world** to listen to one **voice**. *T-5.VI.50.4:5*

~ the **purpose** of the Atonement is to save the **past** in purified **form** only. *T-5.VII.69.3*

~ atonement is the one **need** which in this **world** is universal. *T-6.III.29.5*

~ by accepting the Atonement for yourself, **you** are deciding against the **belief** that **you** can be **alone**, thus dispelling the **idea** of **separation** and affirming your true identification with the whole **Kingdom** as literally **part** of **you**. *T-7.IX.90.3*

~ atonement is no more separate than **love**. Atonement cannot be separate, because it comes from **love**. *T-9.II.76:7*

~ the Atonement is a **lesson** in sharing, which is given **you** because **you have** forgotten how to do it. *T-9.III.11.1*

~ atonement is for all, because it is the **way** to **undo** the **belief** that anything is for **you alone**. *T-9.III.9.1*

~ the Atonement is the **way** to **peace**. *T-9.VI.39.5*

~ the Atonement was not the price of our **wholeness**, but it was the price of your **awareness** of your **wholeness**. *T-11.V.42.1*

~ atonement **will** radiate from your **acceptance** of it for yourself to **everyone** the Holy Spirit sends **you** for your **blessing**. *T-11.VIII.61.5*

~ the Atonement is but the **way** back to what was never lost. *T-11.IX.84.8*

~ accepting the Atonement teaches **you** what **immortality** is, for by accepting your guiltlessness, **you** learn that the **past** has never been, and so the **future** is needless. *T-11.X.97.1*

~ the Atonement has always been interpreted as the **release** from **guilt**. *T-12.II.8.1*

~ atonement brings a re-evaluation of everything **you** cherish, for it is the **means** by which the **Holy Spirit** can separate the false and the true, which **you have** accepted into your minds without distinction. *T-13.III.14.1*

~ the **purpose** of Atonement is to dispel illusions, not to establish them as real and then forgive them. *T-13.IV.25.6*

~ the Atonement was established as the **means** of restoring guiltlessness to the **mind** which has denied it and thus denied **Heaven** to itself. Atonement teaches **you** the true **condition** of the **Son of God**. It does not **teach you** what **you** are or what your **Father** is. *T-14.I.3.2:4*

~ the circle of Atonement has no end. And **you will** find ever-increasing **confidence** in your safe inclusion in what is for all in **everyone you** bring **within** its safety and its perfect **peace**. *T-14.II.11.6:7*

~ the Atonement does not **make** holy. **You** were created holy. It merely brings unholiness to **holiness**, or what **you** made to what **you** are. *T-14.V.38.1:3*

~ the Atonement offers **you** God. *T-14.V.40.5*

19

~ atonement teaches **you** how to escape forever from everything that **you have** taught yourselves in the **past** by showing **you** only what **you** are **now**. *T-14.VII.60.1*

~ the Atonement is in **time** but not for **time**. **Being** in **you**, it is eternal. What holds remembrance of **God** cannot be bound by **time**. *T-15.III.16.1:3*

~ real Atonement which would heal and the ego's "atonement" which would destroy. *T-16.VIII.79.1*

~ atonement centers on the **past**, which is the **source** of **separation**, and where it must be undone. *T-17.IV.20.6*

~ atonement cannot come to those who think that **they** must first atone, but only to those who offer it **nothing** more than simple willingness to **make way** for it. *T-18.V.36.6*

~ if **you** already understood the **difference** between **truth** and **illusion**, the Atonement would **have** no **meaning**. The **holy instant**, your **holy relationship**, the Holy Spirit's **teaching**, and all the **means** by which **salvation** is accomplished would **have** no **purpose**. *T-18.VI.41.2:3*

~ it is extremely **difficult** to reach Atonement by fighting against **sin**. [Enormous **effort** is expended in the attempt to **make** holy what is hated and despised.] Nor is a lifetime of contemplation and long periods of meditation aimed at detachment from the **body** necessary. All such attempts **will** ultimately succeed because of their **purpose**. Yet the **means** are tedious and very **time** consuming, for all of them look to the **future** for **release** from a state of **present** unworthiness and inadequacy. *T-18.VIII.66.7:11*

~ beside each of **you** is one who offers **you** the chalice of Atonement, for the **Holy Spirit** is in him. *T-19.V.102.1*

~ accepting the Atonement for yourself **means** not to **give** support to someone's **dream** of **sickness** and of **death**. It **means** that **you share** not his **wish** to separate and let him turn illusions on himself. Nor do **you wish** that **they** be turned instead on **you**. Thus **have they** no effects. And **you** are free of dreams of **pain** because **you** let him be. *T-28.V.37.1:5*

~ atonement remedies the strange **idea** that it is possible to **doubt** yourself and be unsure of what **you** really are. *W-pI.139.6.1*

~ atonement **teach** and demonstrates the **oneness** of God's Son is unassailed by his **belief** he knows not what **he** is. *W-pI.139.9.3*

~ atonement heals with **certainty** and cures all **sickness**. *W-pI.140.4.1*

~ atonement does not heal the sick, for that is not a cure. It takes away the **guilt** that makes the **sickness** possible. And that is cure indeed. For **sickness now** is gone, with **nothing** left to which it can return. *W-pI.140.4.4:7*

~ atonement corrects illusions, not the **truth**. Therefore it corrects what never was. Further, the **plan** for this **correction** was established and completed simultaneously, for the **Will** of **God** is entirely apart from **time**. So is all **reality**, **being** of Him. *M-2.2.2:5*

~ atonement is for **you**. Your **learning** claims it, and your **learning** gives it. The **world** contains it not, but learn this **course** and it is yours. *M-13.8.7:9*

~ atonement **means correction**, or the undoing of errors. When this has been accomplished, the **teacher of God** becomes a **miracle** worker by definition. His sins **have** been forgiven him, and **he** no longer condemns himself. *M-18.5.6:8*

~ **healing** and Atonement are not related; **they** are identical. There is no **order** of difficulty in miracles, because there are no degrees of Atonement. It is the one complete **concept** possible in this **world**, because it is the **source** of a wholly unified **perception**. Partial Atonement is a meaningless **idea**, just as **special** areas of **hell** in **Heaven** is inconceivable. Accept Atonement, and **you** are healed. Atonement is the **word** of **God**. *M-22.1.1:6*

~ the offer of Atonement is universal. It is equally applicable to all individuals in all circumstances. And in it is the **power** to heal all individuals of all forms of **sickness**. *M-22.6.1:3*

- atonement is received and offered. Having been received, it must be accepted. It is in the receiving, then, that **healing** lies. *M-22.6.11:13*
- atonement might be equated with total escape from the **past** and total lack of interest in the **future**. *M-24.6.3*

ATTACK

|əˈtak|

DICTIONARY: *an aggressive and violent action against a person or place.*

EGO;   *power, grandeur, salvation, best defense.*

- if **you** attack **error** in one another, **you will hurt** yourself. **You** cannot recognize each other when **you** attack. Attack is always made on a **stranger.** *T-3.V.36.1:3*
- what **man** perceives as its attack is merely his own vague recognition of the **fact** that it can always be remembered, never having been destroyed. *T-3.VI.47.6*
- assault can ultimately be made only on the **body.** *T-6.II.7.1*
- those who communicate **fear** are promoting attack, and attack always breaks **communication**, making it **impossible.** *T-6.V.65.8*
- if it is not relinquished entirely, it is not relinquished at all. *T-7.VII.54.4*
- those who attack do not know **they** are blessed. **They** attack because **they** believe **they** are deprived. *T-7.VIII.77.5:6*
- attack could never promote attack unless **you** perceived it as a **means** of depriving **you** of something **you** **want.** *T-7.VIII.78.1*
- attack is always physical. *T-8.VII.53.1*
- to attack is to separate. *T-8.VII.64.1*
- when **you** attack, **you** are denying yourself. **You** are specifically **teaching** yourself that **you** are not what **you** are. *T-9.IX.71.1:2*
- **you** always attack yourself. *T-9.IX.71.5*
- the **ego** always attacks on behalf of **separation.** *T-10.VI.46.1*
- attack makes **guilt** real, and if it is real, there is no **way** to overcome it. *T-11.X.99.3*
- **everyone you** attack keeps it and cherishes it by holding it against **you.** Whether **he** does this or does it not **will make** no **difference; you will** think **he** does. *T-13.VIII.69.5:6*
- whom **you** attack **you** cannot **want** to heal. *T-21.VIII.77.3*
- **you** do not **see** that every **sin** and every **condemnation** which **you** perceive and justify is an attack upon your **Father.** *T-22.II.61.3*
- it seems safer to attack another or yourself than to attack the great **Creator** of the **universe**, whose **power** **you** know. *T-22.VII.61.7*
- only the different can attack. So **you** conclude because **you** can attack **you** must be different. *T-22.VII.63.1:2*
- **you will fear** what **you** attack. *T-23.I.2.4*
- **you** attack only in **self defense.** *T-23.III.29.9*
- attack in any **form** is equally destructive. Its **purpose** does not **change.** Its sole intent is murder. *T-23.IV.41.3:5*
- attack makes **Christ** your **enemy** and **God** along with Him. *T-25.VI.38.1*

~ thus does **he fear** his own attack but sees it at another's hands. As **victim, he** is **suffering** from its effects but not their **cause**. *T-28.III.22.7:8*

~ attack is a response to **function** unfulfilled as **you** perceive the **function**. *T-29.V.27.1*

~ his own attack is thus perceived as **self-defense**. *W-pI.22.1.3*

~ it is surely obvious that if **you** can be attacked, **you** are not invulnerable. **You see** attack as a real **threat**. That is because **you** believe that **you** can really attack. And what would **have** effects through **you** must also **have** effects on **you**. *W-pI.26.1.1:4*

~ because your attack thoughts **will** be projected, **you will fear** attack. And if **you fear** attack, **you** must believe that **you** are not invulnerable. Attack thoughts therefore **make you** vulnerable in your own **mind**, which is where the attack thoughts are. Attack thoughts and **invulnerability** cannot be accepted together. **They** contradict each other. *W-pI.26.2.1:5*

~ if attack thoughts must entail the **belief** that **you** are vulnerable, their effect to weaken **you** in your own eyes. Thus **they have** attacked your **perception** of yourself. And because **you** believe in them, **you** can no longer believe in yourself. *W-pI.26.3.2:4*

~ in every attack **you call** upon your own **weakness**. *W-pI.62.3.1*

~ **i** try to attack only when **I** am afraid, and only when **I** try to attack can **I** believe that my eternal safety is threatened. *W-pI.87.5.3*

~ for **threat** brings **anger, anger** makes attack seem reasonable, honestly provoked, and righteous in the **name** of **self defense**. *W-pI.153.2.2*

~ no one attacks without intent to **hurt**. *W-pI.170.1.1*

~ to defend from **fear** is to attack. *W-pI.170.2.1*

~ first, it is obvious ideas must leave their **source**. For it is **you** who **make** attack and must **have** first conceived of it. Yet **you** attack **outside** yourself and separate your **mind** from him who is to be attacked with perfect **faith** the split **you** made is real. *W-pI.170.5.2:4*

~ to attack another is but to attack yourself. *W-pI.196.1.2*

~ attack can enter only if **perception** of separate goals has entered. *M-17.3.3*

HOLY SPIRIT; *self attack, separate.*

~ all attack is **self**-attack. It cannot be anything else. Arising from your own **decision** not to be what **you** are, it is an attack on your identification. Attack is thus the **way** in which your identification is lost because, when **you** attack, **you** must **have** forgotten what **you** are. And if your **reality** is God's, when **you** attack **you** are not remembering Him. This is not because **He** is gone, but because **you** are willing actively not to **remember** Him. *T-9.IX.72.1:7*

~ no one can **will** to destroy himself. When **you** think **you** are attacking yourself, it is a sure sign that **you** hate what **you** think **you** are. And this, and only this, can be attacked by **you**. *T-9.IX.74.3:5*

~ to attack what **you have** created is **impossible**. *T-9.VIII.64.1*

~ all attack which **you** perceive is in your own **mind** and nowhere else, **you will** at last **have** placed its **source**, and where it began it must end. *T-11.IV.34.4*

~ if **you** did not feel guilty, **you** could not attack, for **condemnation** is the root of attack. It is the **judgment** of one **mind** by another as unworthy of **love** and deserving of **punishment**. But herein lies the split. *T-11.X.85.1:3*

~ **you** cannot attack yourself, for without **guilt**, attack is **impossible**. *T-11.X.99.6*

~ **you** must attack yourself first, for what **you** attack is not in others. Its only **reality** is in your own **mind**, and by attacking others, **you** are literally attacking what is not there. *T-12.V.35.6:7*

~ attack **will** always yield to **love** if it is brought to **love**, not hidden from it. *T-14.III.17.2*

~ but **you will** not **remember** this while **you** believe attack of any kind **means** anything. It is unjustified in any **form** because it has no **meaning**. The only **way** it could be justified is if each one of **you** were separate from the other, and all were separate from your **Creator**. For only then would it be possible to attack a **part** of the **creation** without the whole, the Son without the **Father**, and to attack another without yourself or **hurt** yourself without the other feeling **pain**. *T-22.VII.62.2:5*

~ attack is neither safe nor dangerous. It is **impossible**. *T-22.VII.62.8:9*

~ because **you** are not different, **you** cannot attack. *T-22.VII.63.4*

~ the **purpose** of attack is in the **mind**, and its effects are felt but where it is. *T-24.V.36.5*

~ attack and **sin** are bound as one **illusion**, each the **cause** and aim and justifier of the other. Each is meaningless **alone**, but seems to draw a **meaning** from the other. Each depends upon the other for whatever **sense** it seems to **have**. And no one could believe in one unless the other were the **truth**, for each attests the other must be true. *T-25.VI.37.3:6*

~ attack has **power** to **make** illusions real. Yet what it makes is **nothing**. *T-30.V.53.5:6*

~ attack has no foundation. *T-30.VII.70.2*

~ if **you** did not believe that **you** deserved attack, it never would occur to **you** to **give** attack to anyone at all. *T-31.III.27.7*

~ without attack thoughts **I** could not **see** a **world** of attack. *W-pI.55.4.2*

~ **we** must replace attack with **acceptance**. *W-pI.72.11.2*

ATTRACTION |əˈtrakSH(ə)n|

DICTIONARY: *the action or **power** of evoking interest, **pleasure**, or liking for someone or something.*

EGO

~ the **ego** really believes that it can get and keep by making guilty. This is its one attraction; an attraction so weak that it would **have** no hold at all, except that no one recognizes it. For the **ego** always seems to attract through **love** and has no attraction at all to anyone who perceives that it attracts through **guilt**. *T-15.VIII.66.3:5*

~ the **ego** always seems to attract through **love** and has no attraction at all to anyone who perceives that it attracts through **guilt**. *T-15.VIII.66.5*

~ the attraction of **guilt** opposes the attraction of **God**. *T-15.IX.90.2*

HOLY SPIRIT

~ the attraction of **love** for **love** remains irresistible. *T-11.IX.83.5*

~ the attraction of **light** must draw **you** willingly, and willingness is signified by giving. *T-12.VI.56.2*

~ his attraction for **you** remains unlimited. *T-15.IX.90.3*

ATTRACTION TO GUILT   *A Course in Miracles Term*

EGO

~ the **attraction** of **guilt** opposes the **attraction** of God. *T-15.IX.90.2*

~ the **attraction** of **guilt** is found in **sin**, not **error**. **Sin will** be repeated because of this **attraction**. *T-19.IV.25.1:2*

~ the **attraction** of **guilt** produces **fear** of **love**. *T-19.V.49.1*

~ where the **attraction** of **guilt** holds sway, **peace** is not wanted. *T-19.V.59.2*

~ such is guilt's **attraction**. **Here** is **death** enthroned as **savior**; **crucifixion** is **now redemption**, and **salvation** can only mean **destruction** of the **world**, except yourself. *T-24.V.34.6:7*

HOLY SPIRIT;   *fear*

~ in the **holy instant**, **guilt** holds no **attraction**, since **communication** has been restored. *T-15.VIII.77.5*

~ in any single instant, the **attraction** of **guilt** would be experienced as **pain** and **nothing** else and would be avoided. It has no **attraction now**. Its whole **attraction** is imaginary and therefore must be **thought** of in the **past** or in the **future**. *T-18.VIII.65.5:7*

~ the fierce **attraction** which **guilt** holds for **fear** is wholly absent from love's gentle **perception**. *T-19.V.51.1*

~ the **attraction** of **guilt** is only **fear**. *T-22.II.8.6*

~ there can be no **attraction** of **guilt** in **innocence**. *T-23.I.4.2*

AUTHORITY PROBLEM   *A Course in Miracles Term*

EGO

~ **you** still believe **you** are images of your own **creation**. *T-3.IX.77.7*

~ money is but one of its many reflections and is a reasonably representative example of the kind of thinking which stems from it. *T-4.II.5.3:4*

~ authority **problem** which, because it accepts the one inconceivable **thought** as its premise, can only produce ideas which are inconceivable. *T-4.II.6.3*

~ the authority **problem** as involving the **concept** of usurping God's **power**. The **ego** believes that this is what **you** did because it believes it is **you**. *T-5.VII.61.3:4*

~ the authority **problem** remains the only **source** of perceived **conflict**, because the **ego** was made out of the **wish** of God's Son to **father** Him. The **ego**, then, is **nothing** more than a delusional system in which **you** made your own **father**. *T-10.I.2.3:4*

~ the **illusion** of the autonomy of the **body** and its ability to overcome loneliness is but the working of the ego's **plan** to establish its own autonomy. *T-15.VIII.76.1*

~ **desire** to create your own **Creator** and be **father** and not son to Him. *T-21.III.25.4*

HOLY SPIRIT;   *"root of all defense", "root of all evil."*

~ is always because **he** believes **he** is the author of himself, projects his **delusion** onto others, and then perceives the **situation** as one in which people are literally fighting him for his authorship. This is the fundamental **error** of all those who believe **they have** usurped the **power** of **God**. *T-3.VIII.66.5:6*

~ the **belief** is very frightening to them but hardly troubles God. **He** is, however, eager to **undo** it, not to punish His **Children**, but only because **He** knows that it makes them unhappy. Souls were given their true Authorship, but men preferred to be anonymous when **they** chose to separate themselves from their Author. The **word** "authority" has been one of their most fearful symbols ever since. Authority has been used for great cruelty because, **being uncertain** of their true Authorship, men believe that their **creation** was anonymous. This has left them in a position where it sounds meaningful to consider the possibility that **they** must **have** created themselves. *T-3.VIII.67.1:6*

- all **fear** comes ultimately and sometimes by **way** of very devious routes from the **denial** of Authorship. The offense is never to **God**, but only to those who deny Him. To deny His Authorship is to deny themselves the **reason** for their own **peace**, so that **they see** themselves only in pieces. This strange **perception** is the authority **problem**. *T-3.VIII.70.4:7*

- **you** cannot resolve the authority **problem** by depreciating the **power** of your minds. *T-3.IX.73.1*

- only in this **world** is the **idea** of an authority **problem** meaningful. *T-3.IX.80.10*

AWAKEN

|əˈwākən|

DICTIONARY: *make someone aware of (something) for the first **time**.*

EGO

- what **you** seem to wake to is but another **form** of this same **world you see** in dreams. *T-18.III.19.2*

HOLY SPIRIT; *joining*

- awakening runs easily and gladly through the **Kingdom** in **answer** to the **call** of **God**. This is the natural response of every **Son of God** to the **Voice** of his **Creator**. *T-8.IV.15.5:6*

- waking is joining. *T-8.IX.82.6*

- whenever **you** wake dispiritedly, it was not of the **Holy Spirit**. Only when **you** awaken joyously **have you** utilized **sleep** according to the **Holy Spirit**'s **purpose**. *T-8.IX.83.4:5*

- as **you** awaken other minds to the **Holy Spirit** through Him and not yourself, **you will understand** that **you** are not obeying the **laws** of this **world**, but that the **laws you** are obeying work. *T-9.IV.29.1*

- when **you** awake in Him **you will** know your **magnitude** by accepting His limitlessness as yours. *T-9.V.34.8*

- **holy Spirit** teaches **you** to awaken others. As **you see** them waken, **you will** learn what waking **means**. *T-9.V.35.2:3*

- the instant **you** waken, **you** know that everything that seemed to happen did not happen at all. *T-9.VIII.65.6*

- **you will** awaken to your own **call**, for the **Call** to awake is **within** you. If **I** live in you, **you** are awake. *T-10.VII.67.1:2*

- **i will** awaken **you** as surely as **I** awakened myself, for **I** awoke for you. *T-11.III.20.2*

- awakening unto **Christ** is following the **laws** of **love** of your **free will** and out of **quiet** recognition of the **truth** in them. *T-12.VI.56.1*

- **you will** first **dream** of **peace** and then awaken to it. *T-12.VII.67.1*

- the **Holy Spirit will teach you** to awaken unto us and to yourself. *T-12.VII.75.5*

- the **miracle** does not awaken **you** but merely shows **you** who the dreamer is. *T-28.III.19.1*

- **you** cannot wake yourself. Yet **you** can let yourself be wakened. *T-29.IV.22.1:2*

- **you** cannot **dream** some dreams and wake from some, for **you** are either sleeping or awake. *T-29.V.25.7*

- one either sleeps or wakens. There is **nothing** in between. *W-pI.140.2.6:7*

AWARENESS

DICTIONARY: *knowledge or perception of a situation or fact.*

EGO

~ **death** wishes do not **kill** in the physical **sense**, but **they** do **kill** spiritual awareness. All destructive thinking is dangerous. *T-2.V.91.2:3*

~ **nothing** that **you have** refused to accept can be brought into awareness. It does not follow that it is dangerous, but it does follow that **you have** made it dangerous. *T-3.VIII.64.4:5*

~ your awareness is narrowed to yourself. *T-12.VI.56.4*

HOLY SPIRIT

~ the **miracle** is an expression of an inner awareness of **Christ**. *T-1.I.72.1*

~ everything that results from accurate spiritual awareness is merely channelized toward **correction**. *T-2.III.68.2*

~ as Freud correctly pointed out, what **you have** repressed can retain a very active **life** beyond your awareness. *T-4.IV.45.4*

~ the **wholeness** of the **Kingdom** does not depend on your **perception**, but your awareness of its **wholeness** does. It is only your awareness which needs protection since your **being** cannot be *assailed. T-6.V.93.2*

~ his perceptions are your natural awareness. *T-10.VII.61.4*

~ to perceive truly is to be aware of all **reality** through the awareness of your own. *T-12.VI.45.1*

~ yet this awareness and this **memory** can arise across the threshold of the unconscious only where all barriers to **truth have** been removed. *M-26.1.3*

AWE

DICTIONARY: *a feeling of reverential respect mixed with **fear** or wonder.*

EGO; *worship*

~ awe **will** be confused with **fear**, and the **experience will** be more traumatic than beatific. *T-3.I.3.1*

~ awe is an inappropriate response to miracles. *T-1.I.76.1*

~ awe implies inequality. *T-1.I.78.2*

HOLY SPIRIT; *worship*

~ awe is a proper reaction in the Presence of your **Creator**. *T-3.I.2.3*

~ awe is not an appropriate reaction to me because of our inherent equality. *T-3.I.2.6*

~ awe should be reserved for **revelation**, to which it is perfectly and correctly applicable. It is not appropriate for miracles because a state of awe is worshipful. It implies that one of a lesser **order** stands before a greater one. This is the case only when a **Soul** stands before its **Creator**. Souls are perfect **creations** and **experience** awe only in the Presence of the **Creator** of **perfection**. *T-1.I.77.2:6*

~ equals cannot be in awe of one another because awe implies inequality. *T-1.I.78.2*

BARGAIN

DICTIONARY: *an agreement between two or more parties as to what each party **will** do for the other.*

EGO

~ to believe that it is possible to get much for **little** is to believe that **you** can bargain with **God**. *T-8.XI.11:7.2*

~ to bargain is to set a **limit**, and any **brother** with whom **you have** a limited **relationship you hate**. **You** may attempt to keep the bargain in the **name** of "fairness," sometimes demanding **payment** of yourself, perhaps more often of the other. *T-21.IV.29.3:4*

~ **you make** a bargain that **you** cannot keep. *T-29.VII.39.2*

~ your **will** is lost to **you** in this strange bartering, in which **guilt** is traded back and forth and grievances increase with each exchange. *W-pI.73.3.1*

~ **you have** made a thousand losing bargains at the least. *W-pI.98.5.4*

~ **they** are not like to the gifts the **world** can **give**, in which the giver loses as **he** gives the **gift**; the taker is the richer by his **loss**. These are not gifts, but bargains made with **guilt**. *W-pI.105.1.4:5*

~ and **you will seek** to rid yourself of **guilt** in further bargains which can **give** no hope, but only greater **pain** and **misery**. *S-2.II.6.3*

HOLY SPIRIT;   *limit*

~ to **gain you** must **give**, not bargain. To bargain is to **limit** giving, and this is not **God's Will**. *T-7.II.4.3:4*

~ **he** makes no bargains. *T-21.IV.37.3*

~ **here** is an offer guaranteeing **you** your full **release** from **pain** of every kind and **joy** the **world** does not contain. **You** can exchange a **little** of your **time** for **peace** of **mind** and **certainty** of **purpose** with the **promise** of complete success. And since **time** has no **meaning**, **you** are **being** asked for **nothing** in return for everything. **Here** is a bargain that **you** cannot lose. And what **you gain** is limitless indeed! *W-pI.98.6.1:5*

BATTLE

DICTIONARY: *a lengthy and **difficult conflict** or struggle.*

EGO

~ the "battle for **survival**" is **nothing** more than the ego's struggle to preserve itself and its **interpretation** of its own beginning. *T-4.III.35.3*

~ the **war** against yourself is but the battle of two illusions, struggling to **make** them different from each other in the **belief** the one which conquers **will** be true. *T-23.II.12.1*

~ illusions battle only with themselves. **Being** fragmented, **they fragment**. *T-23.II.13.4:5*

~ one **illusion** about yourself can battle with another, yet the **war** of two illusions is a state where **nothing** happens. There is no victor, and there is no victory. *T-23.II.13.8:9*

~ the **ego** does constant battle with the **Holy Spirit** on the fundamental **question** of what your **function** is. So does it do constant battle with the **Holy Spirit** about what your happiness is. It is not a two-way battle. The **ego** attacks and the **Holy Spirit** does not respond. *W-pI.66.2.1:4*

HOLY SPIRIT

~ no one finds himself ravaged and torn in endless battles which **he** himself perceives as wholly without **meaning**. *T-13.IV.35.5*

~ one **illusion** about yourself can battle with another, yet the **war** of two illusions is a state where **nothing** happens. There is no victor, and there is no victory. *T-23.II.13.8:9*

~ what is born of **nothing** cannot win **reality** through battle. *T-23.II.14.7*

~ battle is not real and easily escaped. *T-23.V.51.7*

~ bodies may battle, but the clash of forms is meaningless. *T-23.V.51.8*

~ it is over when **you** realize it never was begun. *T-23.V.51.9*

~ there is no battle which must be prepared, no **time** to be expended, and no plans that **need** be laid for bringing in the new. There is an ancient battle **being** waged against the **truth**, but **truth** does not respond. *T-31.II.13.3:4*

~ forget the battle. Accept it as a **fact**, and then forget it. Do not **remember** the **impossible** odds against **you**. Do not **remember** the immensity of the "**enemy**," and do not think about your frailty in comparison. Accept your **separation**, but do not **remember** how it came about. Believe that **you have** won it, but do not retain the slightest **memory** of Who your great "**opponent**" really is. Projecting your "forgetting" onto Him, it seems to **you He** has forgotten too. *M-17.6.5:11*

BATTTLEGROUND

|ˈbadl ˌground|

DICTIONARY: the **piece** of ground on which a **battle** is or was fought.

Ego

~ there is no safety in a battleground. *T-23.IV.46.5*

~ from **within** it, **you** can find no safety. *T-23.IV.46.7*

~ **here** in the midst of it, it does seem real. **Here you have** chosen to be **part** of it. **Here** murder is your **choice**. Yet from above, the **choice** is miracles instead of murder. *T-23.V.51.3:6*

~ everything fought for on the battleground is of the **body**—something it seems to offer or to own. *T-23.V.55.3*

BEHAVIOR

|bəˈhāvyər|

DICTIONARY: the **way** in which one acts or conducts oneself, especially toward others.

Ego;   *response to motivation*

~ behavior is response. *T-1.I.62.3*

~ all behavior is essentially motivated by needs, but behavior itself is not a divine attribute. *T-1.I.90.5*

~ the **body** is the mechanism for behavior. *T-1.I.90.6*

~ as long as a **man** believes in what his physical **sight** tells him, all his corrective behavior **will** be misdirected. *T-2.III.68.5*

~ behavior is erratic until a firm commitment to one or the other is made. *T-3.IV.25.5*

~ when their behavior is unstable **they** are disagreeing with God's **idea** of the **creation**. *T-3.VII.53.4*

~ "reliable behavior" is a meaningful **perception** as far as **ego** thinking goes. However, "valid behavior" is an expression which is inherently contradictory, because validity is an end and behavior is a **means**. *T-4.III.37.3:4*

~ much of the ego's strange behavior is directly attributable to its definition of **guilt**. *T-12.II.4.1*

HOLY SPIRIT; *response to motivation*

~ those who perceive and acknowledge that **they have** everything **have** no **need** for driven behavior of any kind. *T-1.I.58.5*

~ men can learn to improve their behavior and can also learn to become better and better learners. *T-2.II.40.1*

~ this is controlled by me automatically as soon as **you** place what **you** think under my **guidance.** *T-2.IV.74.3*

~ **you** cannot **change** your **mind** by changing your behavior. *T-4.IV.57.1*

~ any **decision** of the **mind will** affect both behavior and **experience.** What **you will**, **you** expect. *T-5.VIII.70.4:5*

~ all behavior teaches the beliefs which motivate it. *T-6.II.23.2*

~ behavior is not the **level** for either teaching or **learning.** This must be so, since **you** can act in accordance with what **you** do not believe. *T-7.VI.40.4:5*

BEING |ˈbēiNG|

DICTIONARY: *the nature or essence of a person.*

EGO

~ in being there is no **difference** between "having" and "being" as there is in existence. In the state of being, the **mind** gives everything always. *T-4.VIII.99.6:7*

~ at this point, the equality of "having" and "being" is not yet perceived. Until it is, "having" appears to be the **opposite** of "being." Therefore, the first **lesson** seems to contain a **contradiction** since it is being learned by a conflicted **mind.** *T-6.V.73.1:3*

~ our very being seems to **change** as **we experience** a thousand shifts in mood, and our emotions raise us high indeed or dash us to the ground in hopelessness. *W-pI.186.8.5*

HOLY SPIRIT; *knowledge of God, having, teaching, **learning**, projecting, hearing.*

~ against this **sense** of temporary existence the **Soul** offers **you** the **knowledge** of permanence and unshakable being. *T-4.IV.48.6*

~ it is a state in which the **mind** is in **communication** with everything that is real, including the **Soul.** *T-4.VIII.98.4*

~ in being there is no **difference** between "having" and "being" as there is in existence. In the state of being, the **mind** gives everything always. *T-4.VIII.99.6:7*

~ being **alone** lives in the **Kingdom**, where everything lives in **God** without **question.** *T-6.V.51.5*

~ the **Voice** for **God** speaks only for **belief** beyond **question**, which is the **preparation** for being without **question.** *T-6.V.91.3*

~ being is never threatened. *T-6.IV.40.3*

~ all being is in Him who is all Being. *T-7.V.38.5*

~ being is in infinity. *T-7.IX.90.5*

~ being must be extended. That is how it retains the **knowledge** of itself. *T-7.X.92.6:7*

~ the **Soul** yearns to **share** its being as its **Creator** did. Created by sharing, its **will** is to create. It does not **wish** to contain **God** but to extend His Being. The **extension** of God's Being is the Soul's only **function.** *T-7.X.93.1:4*

~ being is known by sharing. *T-7.XII.113.3*

BELIEF

|bə'lēf|

DICTIONARY: *an **acceptance** that a statement is true or that something exists.*

EGO; *secret enemies of **peace***

~ people prefer to believe that their thoughts cannot exert real control, because **they** are literally afraid of them. *T-2.V.90.3*

~ the belief that **God** rejected **man** and forced him out of the **Garden of Eden**. It is also responsible for the **fact** that **you** may believe from **time** to **time** that **I** am misdirecting **you**. *T-3.III.16.2:3*

~ it is the belief that conflicting interests are possible, and therefore **you have** accepted the **impossible** as true. *T-7.V.28.4*

~ beliefs of the **ego** cannot be shared, and this is why **they** are unreal. *T-9.IV.21.1*

~ if **you** believe the **holy instant** is **difficult** for **you**, it is because **you have** become the arbiter of what is possible and remain unwilling to **give** place to One Who knows. The whole belief in orders of difficulty in miracles is centered on this. *T-18.V.40.3:4*

~ the belief that **you** could **give** and get something else, something **outside** yourself, has cost **you** the **awareness** of **Heaven** and the **loss** of your **Identity**. *T-18.VII.50.3*

~ each is united, a complete **thought system**, but totally disconnected to each other. *T-19.II.8.4*

~ thus is the joining of **mind** and **body** an inescapable belief of those who **value sin**. *T-21.IV.38.6*

~ beliefs **will** never openly **attack** each other, because conflicting outcomes are **impossible**. But an unrecognized belief is a **decision** to **war** in **secret**, where the results of **conflict** are kept unknown and never brought to **reason** to be considered sensible or not. *T-24.II.4.1:2*

~ all that can be denied is their **reality**, but not their outcome. *T-24.II.4.8*

~ the fixed belief that there is **reason** to uphold pursuit of what has always failed on grounds that it **will** suddenly succeed and bring what it has never brought before. *T-25.III.14.3*

~ all belief in **sin**, in **power** of **attack**, in **hurt** and **harm**, in **sacrifice** and **death**. *T-26.VII.44.5*

~ belief that your thoughts **have** no effect. *W-pI.16.1.1*

~ the beliefs of the **world** tell us that what **God** would **have** us do is **impossible**. *W-pI.45.4.4*

~ insane belief that it is **hell** in place of **Heaven** that **you** choose. *W-pI.73.9.6*

~ what **you** think **you** are is a belief to be undone. *W-pI.91.8.2*

~ the belief **you** are a **body** calls for **correction**, being a mistake. *W-pI.91.8.4*

~ magical beliefs that come from the conviction **you** are a **body** and the body's eyes can **see**. **You** also believe the body's **brain** can think. *W-pI.92.2.1:2*

~ these are beliefs so firmly fixed that it is **difficult** to **help you see** that **they** are based on **nothing**. *W-pI.93.2.1*

~ these weird beliefs **He** does not **share** with **you**. This is enough to prove that **they** are wrong, but **you** do not perceive that this is so. *W-pI.93.3.3:4*

~ heavy load **you** laid upon yourself with the insane belief that **sin** is real. *W-pI.101.9.2*

~ **you** operate from the belief **you** must protect yourself from what is happening because it must contain what threatens **you**. *W-pI.135.2.2*

~ these mad beliefs can **gain** unconscious hold of great intensity and grip the **mind** with terror and anxiety so strong that it **will** not relinquish its ideas about its own protection. *W-pI.138.8.1*

~ belief in **sin**, which made the **world** seem ugly and unsafe, attacking and destroying, dangerous in all its ways, and treacherous beyond the hope of **trust** and the escape from **pain**. *W-pII.ST361.1.5*

~ belief that, to be safe, one must control the unknown. *P-2.V.1.3*

~ belief that there are forces to be overcome to be alive at all. And next, it seems as if these forces can be held at bay only by an inflated **sense** of self that holds in **darkness** what is truly felt, and seeks to raise illusions to the **light**. *P-2.V.1.5:6*

HOLY SPIRIT; *ego function*

~ **you** believe in what **you value**. *T-2.II.18.3*

~ **thought** and belief combine into a **power** surge that can literally move mountains. *T-2.V.90.1*

~ all beliefs are real to the believer. *T-3.IX.74.6*

~ **god** and His **creations** are beyond belief, because **they** are beyond **question**. *T-6.V.91.2*

~ belief does not require **vigilance** unless it is conflicted. *T-7.VII.61.3*

~ when **you** believe something, **you have** made it true for **you**. *T-7.VII.61.7*

~ whatever these beliefs may be, **they** are the premises which **will** determine what **you** accept into your **mind**. *T-7.X.99.5*

~ to believe is to accept and to side with. To believe is not to be credulous but to accept and appreciate. *T-8.XI.115.2:3*

~ **holy Spirit** judges every belief **you** hold in terms of where it comes from. If it comes from **God**, **He** knows it to be true. If it does not, **He** knows that it is meaningless. *T-9.VI.44.8:10*

~ for **you will** believe in what **you** manifest, and as **you** look out, so **will you see** in. *T-11.VIII.65.7*

~ no belief is neutral. Every one has the **power** to dictate each **decision you make**. *T-24.I.2.3:4*

~ let us be glad that **you will see** what **you** believe, and that it has been given **you** to **change** what **you** believe. *T-31.III.31.1*

~ **you will** identify with what **you** think **will make you** safe. Whatever it may be, **you will** believe that it is one with **you**. *W-pII.ST261.5.1:2*

~ all beliefs that lead to progress should be honored. *M-24.6.11*

~ nor is belief in **God** a really meaningful **concept**, for **God** can be but known. Belief implies that unbelief is possible. *P-2.II.4.4:5*

BELIEF SYSTEM

DICTIONARY: *a set of principles or tenets which together **form** the basis of a **religion**, philosophy, or moral code.*

EGO

~ **you have** built your whole insane **belief** system because **you** think **you** would be helpless in God's Presence, and **you** would save yourself from His **love** because **you** think it would crush **you** into nothingness. *T-12.III.14.1*

HOLY SPIRIT

~ **you** cannot evaluate an insane **belief** system from **within** it. Its own range precludes this. **You** can only go beyond it, look back from a point where **sanity** exists, and **see** the **contrast**. Only by this **contrast** can **insanity** be judged as insane. *T-9.VI.43.1:4*

~ it has been recognized that if **they** were brought together their joint **acceptance** would become **impossible**. But if one is kept in **darkness** from the other, their **separation** seems to keep them both alive and equal in their **reality**. Their joining thus becomes the **source** of **fear**, for if **they** meet, **acceptance** must be withdrawn from one of them. *T-14.IV.27.4:6*

~ **you** cannot **have** them both, for each denies the other. Apart, this **fact** is lost from **sight**, for each in a separate place can be endowed with firm **belief**. Bring them together, and the **fact** of their complete incompatibility is instantly apparent. One **will** go because the other is seen in the same place. *T-14.IV.28.1:4*

BIRTH |bərTH|

DICTIONARY: *the beginning or coming into existence of something.*

EGO

~ this beginning is always associated with physical birth, because no one maintains that the **ego** existed before that point in **time**. The religiously ego-oriented believe that the **Soul** existed before and **will** continue to **exist** afterwards, after a temporary lapse in **ego life**. Some actually believe that the **Soul will** be punished for this lapse, even though in **reality** it could not possibly know anything about it. *T-4.III.35.4:6*

HOLY SPIRIT;   *continuing*

~ real birth is not a beginning; it is a continuing. *T-5.VI.47.6*

~ to be born again is to let the **past** go and look without **condemnation** upon the **present**. *T-12.VI.47.5*

~ each instant is a clean, untarnished birth, in which the **Son of God** emerges from the **past** into the **present**. *T-15.II.9.4*

~ **time** appointed not his destiny nor set the hour of his birth and **death**. *T-29.VII.39.12*

~ the birth of **Christ** is **now**, without a **past** or **future**. *W-p2.308.1.6*

~ there is no **past** nor **future**, and the **idea** of birth into a **body** has no **meaning** either once or many times. *M-24.1.2*

BLAME |blām|

DICTIONARY: *responsibility for a fault or wrong.*

EGO

~ any **concept** of "**punishment**" involves the **projection** of blame and reinforces the **idea** that blame is justified. The **behavior** that results is a **lesson** in blame. *T-6.II.23.2*

~ as blame is withdrawn from without, there is a strong tendency to harbor it **within**. *T-10.V.34.5*

~ if your brothers are **part** of **you** and **you** blame them for your **deprivation, you** are blaming yourself. And **you** cannot blame yourself without blaming them. *T-10.V.35.1:2*

~ or has your **appreciation** flickered and grown dim in what seemed to be the **light** of the mistakes? **You** are **now** entering upon a campaign to blame each other for the discomfort of the **situation** in which **you** find yourselves. *T-17.VI.53.8:9*

HOLY SPIRIT

~ as blame is withdrawn from without, there is a strong tendency to harbor it **within**. It is **difficult** at first to realize that this is exactly the same **thing**, for there is no distinction between **within** and without. *T-10.V.34.5:6*

~ if your brothers are **part** of **you** and **you** blame them for your **deprivation, you** are blaming yourself. And **you** cannot blame yourself without blaming them. *T-10.V.35.1:2*

~ blame must be undone, not re-allocated. Lay it to yourself and **you** cannot know yourself, for only the **ego** blames at all. **Self**-blame is therefore **ego** identification and as strong an **ego defense** as blaming others. *T-10.V.35.3:5*

~ the blameless cannot blame. *W-pI.60.2.2*

BLESSING ⎮ˈblesiNG⎮

DICTIONARY: *a beneficial **thing** for which one is grateful; something that brings well-**being**.*

EGO

~ whenever **you** deny a blessing to a **brother, you will** feel deprived. *T-7.VIII.70.1*

~ **anger** is its blessing. *T-15.VIII.74.1*

~ if **you** shrink from blessing **will** the **world** indeed seem fearful, for **you have** withheld its **peace** and comfort, leaving it to die. *T-27.VI.47.3*

HOLY SPIRIT

~ **you** go with my blessing and for my blessing. Hold it and **share** it, that it may always be ours. *T-5.VI.58.4:5*

~ what is truly blessed is incapable of giving rise to **guilt** and must **give** rise to **joy**. This makes it invulnerable to the **ego** because its **peace** is unassailable. It is invulnerable to disruption because it is whole. *T-5.VII.60.1:3*

~ **you** do not **need** God's blessing since that **you have** forever, but **you** do **need** yours. *T-7.VIII.73.1*

~ blessing is the **opposite** of **sacrifice**. *T-7.X.92.5*

~ **you** can learn to bless and cannot **give** what **you have** not. If, then, **you** offer blessing, it must **have** come first to yourself. *T-13.VI.48.3:4*

~ **you** can learn to bless and cannot **give** what **you have** not. If, then, **you** offer blessing, it must **have** come first to yourself. And **you** must also **have** accepted it as yours. *T-13.VI.48.3:5*

~ the One Who blesses **you** loves all the **world** and leaves **nothing within** the **world** that could be feared. *T-27.VI.47.2*

~ **being** blessed, **you will** bring blessing. *T-27.VI.48.2*

~ we offer blessing to all things, uniting lovingly with all the **world**, which our **forgiveness** has made one with us. *W-pII.283.2.2*

~ i would bless the **world** by looking on it through the eyes of **Christ**. *W-pII.304.1.5*

BLIND

|blīnd|

DICTIONARY: *lacking **perception**, **awareness**, or discernment.*

EGO

~ the **world** the sightless "**see**" must be imagined, for what it really looks like is unknown to them. **They** must infer what could be seen from evidence forever indirect. *T-21.II.3.1:2*

~ the blind become accustomed to their **world** by their adjustments to it. **They** think **they** know their **way** about in it. **They** learned it, not through joyous lessons, but through the stern necessity of limits **they** believed **they** could not overcome. *T-21.II.6.1:3*

~ **they** hold those lessons dear and cling to them because **they** cannot **see**. **They** do not **understand** the lessons keep them blind. This **they** do not believe. And so **they** keep the **world they** learned to "**see**" in their imagination, believing that their **choice** is that or **nothing**. **They hate** the **world they** learned through **pain**. And everything **they** think is in it serves to remind them that **they** are incomplete and bitterly deprived. *T-21.II.6.4:9*

~ thus **they** define their **life** and where **they** live, adjusting to it as **they** think **they** must, afraid to lose the **little** that **they** have. *T-21.II.7.1*

~ **they** try to reach each other, and **they** fail and **fail** again. And **they** adjust to loneliness. *T-21.II.7.3:4*

HOLY SPIRIT

~ to open the eyes of the blind is the Holy Spirit's **mission**, for He knows that **they have** not lost their **vision** but merely **sleep**. *T-11.VII.56.2*

~ **guilt** makes **you** blind, for while **you see** one spot of **guilt within** you, **you will** not **see** the **light**. *T-13.III.17.1*

~ and **now** the blind can **see**, for that same **song they** sing in honor of their **Creator** gives **praise** to them as well. The blindness which **they** made **will** not withstand the **memory** of this **song**. *T-21.II.12.1:2*

BODY

|ˈbädē|

DICTIONARY: *the physical structure of a person or an animal, including the bones, flesh, and organs.*

EGO;   *instrument, instruments of **separation**, instrument of **vengeance**, the ego's friend, ego's **idol**, great seeming betrayer of **faith**, isolated speck of **darkness**, engine of **destruction**, tiny spot of senseless mystery, hidden **secret** room, **prison**-house, **home** of **madness**, guilt's **messenger**, mechanism for **behavior**, protector, tiny fence, chosen **home**, chosen weapon, Lord of the **mind**, **savior**, **Son of God**.*

~ the body can act erroneously, but this is only because it is responding to mis-**thought**. The body cannot create, and the **belief** that it can, a fundamental **error**, produces all physical symptoms. *T-2.III.53.5:6*

~ the body does not learn any more than it creates. As a **learning device**, it merely follows the **learner**, but if it is falsely endowed with **self**-initiative, it becomes a serious obstruction to the very **learning** it should facilitate. *T-2.III.66.1:2*

~ the body is not capable of understanding. *T-3.III.23.4*

~ the ability to perceive made the body possible because **you** must perceive something and with something. *T-3.VI.46.1*

~ the **ego** uses the body for **attack**, for **pleasure**, and for **pride**. The **insanity** of this **perception** makes it a fearful one indeed. *T-6.V.65.3:4*

~ if **you** use the body for **attack**, it is harmful to **you**. *T-8.VII.55.1*

~ regarding the body as an end, the **ego** has no real use for it because it is not an end. *T-8.VIII.71.4*

~ the **ego**, however, establishes it as an end because as such it **will** lose its true **function**. *T-8.VIII.75.2*

~ the body is the **symbol** of the **ego**. *T-15.IX.86.3*

~ the **union** of bodies thus becomes the **way** in which **you** would keep minds apart. For bodies cannot forgive. **They** can only do as the **mind** directs. *T-15.VIII.75.8:10*

~ the body is emphasized, with **special** emphasis on certain parts, and used as the standard for comparison for either **acceptance** or rejection of suitability for acting out a **special form** of **fear**. *T-18.I.3.7*

~ **you have** identified with this **thing you hate**, the instrument of **vengeance** and the perceived **source** of your **guilt**. *T-18.VII.54.7*

~ the body is a **limit** imposed on the universal **communication** which is an eternal property of **mind**. *T-18.VII.56.3*

~ what plans do **you make** that do not involve its comfort or protection or enjoyment in some **way**? This makes it an end and not a **means** in your **interpretation**, and this always **means you** still find sin attractive. *T-18.VIII.63.2:3*

~ it is only the **awareness** of the body that makes **love** seem limited. For the body is a **limit** on **love**. The **belief** in limited **love** was its origin, and it was made to **limit** the unlimited. *T-18.IX.71.1:3*

~ the body **will** remain guilt's **messenger** and **will** act as it directs as long as **you** believe that **guilt** is real. *T-18.X.89.1*

~ the body **will** seem to be sick, for **you have** made of it an "**enemy**" of **healing** and the **opposite** of **truth**. *T-19.II.4.6*

~ under fear's orders, the body **will** pursue **guilt**, serving its master whose **attraction to guilt** maintains the whole **illusion** of its existence. This, then, is the **attraction** of **pain**. Ruled by this **perception**, the body becomes the servant of **pain**, seeking it dutifully and obeying the **idea** that **pain** is **pleasure**. It is this **idea** that underlies all of the ego's heavy investment in the body. *T-19.V.72.2:5*

~ dedicated to **death**, a **symbol** of corruption, a **sacrifice** to **sin**, offered to **sin** to feed upon and keep itself alive—a **thing** condemned, damned by its maker, and lamented by every mourner who looks upon it as himself. *T-19.V.81.2*

~ homeless, the **ego** seeks as many bodies as it can collect to place its idols in and so establish them as temples to itself. *T-20.VII.48.7*

~ the body is an isolated speck of **darkness**; a hidden **secret** room, a tiny spot of senseless mystery, a meaningless enclosure carefully protected, yet hiding **nothing**. *T-20.VII.49.2*

~ this is the **temple** dedicated to no relationships and no return. *T-20.VII.50.5*

~ the body is the ego's **idol**; the **belief** in **sin** made flesh and then projected outward. *T-20.VII.55.1*

~ what seems to be a wall of flesh around the **mind**, keeping it prisoner in a tiny spot of space and **time**. *T-20.VII.55.2*

~ the body is the sign of **weakness, vulnerability**, and **loss of power**. *T-20.IX.71.1*

~ only bodies can be separate and therefore unreal. *T-21.VII.61.4*

~ the **home of madness** cannot be the **home** of **reason**. *T-21.VII.61.5*

~ frail and helpless in its own **defense**. It was conceived to **make you** frail and helpless. *T-24.V.35.2:3*

~ **here** is an **image** that **you want** to be yourself. It is the **means** to **make** your **wish** come true. *T-24.VIII.70.5:6*

~ behold the body, and **you will** believe that **you** are there. And everybody that **you** look upon reminds **you** of yourself—your sinfulness, your **evil**, and above all, your **death**. *T-25.II.5.3:4*

~ it is always an attempt to **limit loss**. The body is itself a **sacrifice**—a giving up of **power** in the **name** of saving just a **little** for yourself. *T-26.I.1.4:5*

~ this separating off is symbolized in your **perception** by a body which is clearly separate and a **thing** apart. Yet what this **symbol** represents is but your **wish** to be apart and separate. *T-26.VIII.54.3:4*

~ a broken body shows the **mind** has not been healed. *T-27.III.16.8*

~ this body, purposeless **within** itself, holds all your memories and all your hopes. *T-27.VII.56.1*

~ the body is the central figure in the dreaming of the **world**. There is no **dream** without it, nor does it **exist** without the **dream**, in which it acts as if it were a person, to be seen and be believed. It takes the central place in every **dream**, which tells the story of how it was made by other bodies, born into the **world outside** the body, lives a **little** while and dies, to be united in the dust with other bodies dying like itself. In the brief **time** allotted it to live, it seeks for other bodies as its friends and enemies. Its safety is its main concern. Its comfort is its guiding **rule**. It tries to look for **pleasure** and avoid the things that would be hurtful. Above all, it tries to **teach** itself its pains and joys are different and can be told apart. *T-27.IX.77.1:8*

~ it does not know what seeing is, what listening is for. It is as **little** able to perceive as it can judge or **understand** or know. Its eyes are blind; its ears are deaf. It cannot think, and so it cannot **have** effects. *T-28.VI.50.6:9*

~ a **symbol** for the limitations which **you want** your **mind** to **have** and see and keep. *T-28.VII.56.10*

~ **you** send it forth to **seek** for **separation** and to be a separate **thing**. And then **you hate** it, not for what it is, but for the uses **you have** made of it. *T-28.VII.56.2:3*

~ it sees and acts for **you**. It hears your **voice**. And it is frail and **little** by your **wish**. It seems to punish **you** and thus deserve your hatred for the limitations which it brings to **you**. *T-28.VII.56.6:9*

~ the body, **innocent** of any **goal**, is your excuse for variable goals **you** hold and force the body to maintain. *T-29.II.8.1*

~ the body can appear to **change** with **time**, with **sickness** or with **health**, and with events that seem to alter it. Yet this but **means** the **mind** remains unchanged in its **belief** of what the **purpose** of the body is. *T-29.III.16.7:8*

~ this is the **purpose he** bestows upon the body—that it **seek** for what **he** lacks and **give** him what would **make** himself complete. *T-29.VIII.44.4*

~ some **hate** the body and try to **hurt** and humiliate it. Others **love** the body and try to glorify and exalt it. *W-pI.72.8.2:3*

~ the body's **suffering** is a mask the **mind** holds up to **hide** what really suffers. It would not **understand** it is its own **enemy**, that it attacks itself and wants to die. It is from this your law's would save the body. It is for this **you** think **you** are a body. *W-pI.76.5.4:7*

~ defend the body, and **you have** attacked your **mind**. For **you have** seen in it the faults, the weaknesses, the limits, and the lacks from which **you** think the body must be saved. *W-pI.135.10.1:2*

~ yet it is not the body that can **fear**, nor be a **thing** to **fear**. It has no **need** but those which **you** assign to it. It needs no complicated structures of **defense**, no **health**-inducing medicine, no care, and no concern at all. *W-pI.135.6.1:3*

~ it is your **mind** which gave the body all the functions that **you see** in it and set its **value** far beyond a **little** pile of dust and water. *W-pI.135.7.5*

~ thus is the body stronger than the **truth**, which asks **you** live but cannot overcome your **choice** to die. And so the body is more powerful than everlasting **life**. *W-pI.136.10.1:2*

~ the body is the instrument the **mind** made in its striving to deceive itself. Its **purpose** is to strive. *W-pII.ST251.2.1:2*

~ the body is a fence the **Son of God** imagines **he** has built to separate parts of his **Self** from other parts. It is **within** this fence, **he** thinks **he** lives, to die as it decays and crumbles. For **within** this fence **he** thinks that **he** is safe from **love**. Identifying with its safety, **he** regards himself as what his safety is. *W-pII.ST261.1.1:4*

~ made to be fearful, must the body serve the **purpose** given it. *W-pII.ST261.3.3*

HOLY SPIRIT; *communication medium,* **dream,** **means** *for return to* **sanity,** **temple,** *ego's* **home,** *ego's* **symbol,** **limit** *on* **love,** *meaningless enclosure,* **belief** *in* **sin** *made flesh, mechanism for* **behavior,** **learning device,** *instrument the* **mind** *made.*

~ the body, if properly understood, shares the **invulnerability** of the **Atonement** to two-edged application. This is not because the body is a **miracle** but because it is not inherently open to misinterpretation. The body is merely a **fact** in human **experience.** Its **abilities** can be and frequently are over-evaluated. *T-2.III.56.1:4*

~ **god** did not **make** the body because it is destructible and therefore not of the **Kingdom.** The body is the **symbol** of what **you** think **you** are. It is clearly a **separation** device and therefore does not **exist.** *T-6.V.62.1:3*

~ the **Holy Spirit,** as always, takes what **you have** made and translates it into a **learning device** for **you.** *T-6.V.62.4*

~ the **Holy Spirit** sees the body only as a **means** of **communication** and because communicating is sharing, it becomes **communion.** *T-6.V.65.5*

~ the body is **nothing** more than a framework for developing **abilities.** It is therefore a **means** for developing potentials. *T-7.VI.39.1:2*

~ use it only to reach the minds of those who believe **they** are bodies and **teach** them through the body that this is not so. *T-8.VII.55.2*

~ in the **service** of uniting, it becomes a beautiful **lesson** in **communion,** which has **value** until **communion** is. *T-8.VII.55.4*

~ the **Holy Spirit** does not **see** the body as **you** do, because **He** knows the only **reality** anything can **have** is the **service** it can render **God** on behalf of the **function He** has given it. *T-8.VII.55.6*

~ body becomes for **you** a **means** which **you give** to the **Holy Spirit** to use on behalf of **union** of the **Sonship.** *T-8.VII.56.5*

~ only a **means** by which the **part** of the **mind you have** separated from your **Soul** can reach beyond its distortions and return to the **Soul.** *T-8.VII.61.5*

~ the **Holy Spirit** teaches **you** to use your body only to reach your brothers, so **He** can **teach** His **message** through **you.** *T-8.VIII.79.1*

~ the only **value** which the body has is to enable **you** to bring your brothers to the **bridge** with **you** and to be released together there. *T-16.VII.63.5*

~ the body was not made by **love.** Yet **love** does not condemn it and can use it lovingly, respecting what the **Son of God** has made and using it to save him from illusions. *T-18.VII.52.7:8*

~ **love** does not condemn it and can use it lovingly, respecting what the **Son of God** has made and using it to save him from illusions. *T-18.VII.52.8*

~ at no single instant does the body **exist** at all. It is always remembered or anticipated, but never experienced just **now.** Only its **past** and **future make** it seem real. *T-18.VIII.65.1:3*

~ the body cannot heal because it cannot **make** itself sick. It needs no **healing.** Its **health** or **sickness** depends entirely on how the **mind** perceives it and the **purpose** which the **mind** would use it for. *T-19.II.3.1:3*

~ it has no feeling. It transmits to **you** the feelings that **you** want. Like any **communication** medium, the body receives and sends the messages that it is given. It has no feeling for them. All of the feeling with which **they** are invested is given by the sender and the receiver. *T-19.V.73.3:7*

38

- body incorruptible and perfect as long as it is useful for your holy **purpose**. *T-19.V.8.2.1*

- the exaltation of the body is given up in favor of the **Spirit**, which **you love** as **you** could never **love** the body. *T-19.V.9.4.4*

- the body is merely neutral. It is not **sinful**, but neither is it **sinless**. As **nothing**, which it is, the body cannot meaningfully be invested with attributes of **Christ** or of the **ego**. *T-20.VIII.6.1.4:6*

- the body does not separate **you** from your **brother**. *T-21.VII.6.3.1*

- bodies **have** no **goal**. *T-24.V.3.5.5*

- of itself the body can do **nothing**. *T-24.V.3.5.10*

- it is a **picture** of a body still, for what **you** really are cannot be seen nor pictured. Yet this one has not been used for **purpose** of **attack** and therefore never suffered **pain** at all. It witnesses to the eternal **truth** that **you** cannot be **hurt** and points beyond itself to both your **innocence** and his. *T-27.II.5.6:8*

- the Holy Spirit's **picture** changes not the body into something it is not. It only takes away from it all signs of accusation and of blamefulness. Pictured without a **purpose**, it is seen as neither sick nor well, nor bad nor **good**. *T-27.II.10.3:5*

- it has no **life**, but neither is it dead. It stands apart from all **experience** of **fear** or **love**. For **now** it witnesses to **nothing** yet, its **purpose being** open and the **mind** made free again to choose what it is for. **Now** is it not condemned, but waiting for a **purpose** to be given that it may fulfill the **function** that it **will receive**. *T-27.II.10.7:10*

- your body can be **means** to **teach** that it has never suffered **pain** because of him. And in its **healing** can it offer him mute testimony of his **innocence**. It is this testimony which can speak with **power** greater than a thousand tongues. For **here** is his **forgiveness** proved to him. *T-27.III.1.7:4*

- it takes no sides and judges not the road it travels. It perceives no **gap** because it does not **hate**. *T-28.VII.5.5.7:8*

- it can be seen as not your **home** but merely as an aid to **help you** reach the **home** where **God** abides. *T-28.VIII.6.2.6*

- the body thinks no thoughts. It has no **power** to learn, to pardon, nor enslave. It gives no orders that the **mind need** serve nor sets conditions that it must obey. It holds in **prison** but the willing **mind** that would abide in it. It sickens at the bidding of the **mind** that would become its prisoner. And it grows old and dies because that **mind** is sick **within** itself. *T-31.III.29.2:7*

- it is the body that is **outside** us and is not our concern. To be without a body is to be in our natural state. *W-pI.72.10.2:3*

- a **mind** and body cannot both **exist**. **Make** no attempt to reconcile the two, for one denies the other can be real. If **you** are physical, your **mind** is gone from your **self-concept**, for it has no place in which it could be really **part** of **you**. If **you** are **Spirit**, then the body must be meaningless to your **reality**. *W-pI.96.4.1:4*

- the body is in **need** of no **defense**. This cannot be too often emphasized. It **will** be strong and healthy if the **mind** does not abuse it by assigning it to roles it cannot fill, to purposes beyond its scope, and to exalted aims which it cannot accomplish. *W-pI.135.8.1:3*

- the thoughts in **need** of **healing**, and the body **will** respond with **health** when **they have** been corrected and replaced with **truth**. This is the body's only real **defense**. *W-pI.135.11.1:2*

- its only **purpose being now** to bring the **vision** of what **you experience** this day to **light** the **world**. *W-pI.157.6.1*

- the **time will** come when **you will** not return in the same **form** in which **you now** appear, for **you will have** no **need** of it. *W-pI.157.8.1*

39

~ and it becomes perfect in the ability to serve an undivided **goal**. In **conflict** free and unequivocal response to **mind** with but the **thought** of **freedom** as its **goal**, the body serves, and serves its **purpose** well. Without the **power** to enslave, it is a worthy servant of the **freedom** which the **mind within** the **Holy Spirit** seeks. *W-pI.199.6.4:6*

~ but **we** can **change** the **purpose** which the body **will** obey by changing what **we** think that it is for. *W-pII.ST261.3.5*

~ the body is the **means** by which God's Son returns to **sanity**. Though it was made to fence him into **hell** without escape, yet has the **goal** of **Heaven** been exchanged for the pursuit of **hell**. *W-pII.ST261.4.1:2*

~ **now** is the body holy. **Now** it serves to heal the **mind** that it was made to **kill**. *W-pII.ST261.4.4:5*

~ the existence of the **world** as **we** perceive it depends on the body **being** the **decision**-maker. Terms like "instincts," "reflexes" and the like represent attempts to endow the body with non-mental motivators. Actually, such terms merely state or describe the **problem**. **They** do not **answer** it. *M-5.4.7:10*

~ what **you** use the body for, it **will** become to **you**. *M-12.5.1*

~ use it to bring the **word** of **God** to those who **have** it not, and the body becomes holy. Because it is holy it cannot be sick, nor can it die. When its usefulness is done, it is laid by, and that is all. *M-12.5.4:6*

~ who transcends the body has transcended limitation. *M-23.3.10*

~ the body is not cured. It is merely recognized as what it is. Seen rightly, its **purpose** can be understood. *P-2.IV.11.3:5*

~ the body can be healed as an effect of true **forgiveness**. *S-3.I.3.1*

BORDERLAND |ˈbôrdərˌland|

DICTIONARY: *an area of overlap between two things.*

HOLY SPIRIT;   *meeting place*

~ there is a borderland of **thought** which stands between this **world** and **Heaven**. It is not a place, and when **you** reach it is apart from **time**. **Here** is the meeting-place where thoughts are brought together—where conflicting values meet and all illusions are laid down beside the **truth** where **they** are judged to be untrue. This borderland is just beyond the gate of **Heaven**. **Here** is every **thought** made pure and wholly simple. **Here** is **sin** denied and everything that is received instead. *T-26.IV.19.3:8*

~ **salvation** is a borderland where place and **time** and **choice have meaning** still, and yet it can be seen that **they** are temporary, out of place, and every **choice** has been already made. *T-26.IV.20.6*

~ this is the borderland between the worlds, the **bridge** between the **past** and **present**. **Here** the **shadow** of the **past** remains, but still a **present light** is dimly recognized. *T-26.VI.40.8:9*

~ **salvation** is the borderland between the **truth** and **illusion**. *W-pI.99.2.3*

BRAIN |brān|

DICTIONARY: *an organ of soft nervous tissue contained in the skull of vertebrates, functioning as the coordinating center of sensation and intellectual and nervous activity.*

EGO

~ the brain cannot interpret what your **vision** sees. *T-22.II.6.7*

~ the brain interprets to the **body**, of which it is a **part**. But what it says, **you** cannot **understand**. Yet **you** have listened to it. And long and hard **you** tried to **understand** its messages. **You** did not realize it is **impossible** to **understand** what fails entirely to reach **you**. *T-22.II.6.9:13*

HOLY SPIRIT

~ **you** also believe the body's brain can think. If **you** but understood the nature of **thought**, **you** could but laugh at this insane **idea**. It is as if **you thought you** held the match that lights the sun and gives it all its warmth or that **you** had the **universe** imprisoned in your hand, securely bound until **you** let it go. Yet this is no more foolish than to believe the body's eyes can **see**, the brain can think. *W-pI.92.2.2:5*

BRANCH IN THE ROAD   *A Course in Miracles Term*

HOLY SPIRIT

~ for **now** if **you** go straight ahead, the **way you** went before **you** reached the branch, **you will** go nowhere. The whole **purpose** of coming this far was to decide which branch **you will** take **now**. The **way you** came no longer matters. It can no longer serve. No one who reaches this far can **make** the wrong **decision**, but **he** can **delay**. And there is no **part** of the **journey** that seems more hopeless and futile than standing where the road branches and not deciding on which **way** to go. *T-22.V.58.3:8*

~ it is but the first few steps along the right **way** that seem hard, for **you have** chosen, although **you** still may think **you** can go back and **make** the other **choice**. *T-22.V.59.1*

~ all roads that lead away from what **you** are will lead **you** to **confusion** and **despair**. *T-31.V.41.5*

BRIDGE |brij|

DICTIONARY: *something that is intended to reconcile or **form** a connection between two things.*

HOLY SPIRIT;   *transition*

~ **you will** cross the bridge in perfect safety, translated quietly from **war** to **peace**. *T-16.V.31.6*

~ the bridge that leads to **union** in yourself must lead to **knowledge**, for it was built with **God** beside **you** and **will** lead **you** straight to Him, where your **completion** rests wholly compatible with His. *T-16.V.39.1*

~ the **Holy Spirit** is the bridge to Him, made from your willingness to unite with Him and created by His **joy** in **union** with **you**. *T-16.V.41.2*

~ the bridge that **He** would carry **you** across lifts **you** from **time** into **eternity**. *T-16.V.42.4*

~ the bridge itself is **nothing** more than a transition in your perspective of **reality**. On this side, everything **you see** is grossly distorted and completely out of perspective. What is **little** and insignificant is magnified, and what is strong and powerful cut down to littleness. In the transition there is a period of **confusion** in which a **sense** of actual disorientation seems to occur. *T-16.VII.64.1:4*

~ the new perspective **you will gain** from crossing over **will** be the understanding of where **Heaven** is. *T-16.VII.68.1*

~ the bridge between that **world** and this is so **little** and so easy to cross that **you** could not believe it is the meeting place of worlds so different. Yet this **little** bridge is the strongest **thing** that touches on this **world** at all. *T-17.III.8.4:5*

~ **god** builds the bridge, but only in the space left clean and vacant by the **miracle**. *T-28.IV.33.1*

~ across this bridge, as powerful as **Love** Which laid Its **blessing** on it, are all dreams of **evil** and of hatred and **attack** brought silently to **truth**. *W-pI.134.11.1*

~ **christ's vision** is the bridge between the worlds. And in its **power** can **you** safely **trust** to carry **you** from this **world** into one made holy by **forgiveness**. *W-pI.159.5.1:2*

~ across the bridge that **He** provides are dreams all carried to the **truth**, to be dispelled before the **light** of **knowledge**. *W-pII.ST281.1.3*

BROTHER

|ˈbrəT͟Hər|

DICTIONARY: *a fellow human **being**.*

EGO; *enemy, a "hateful-**love**," guide to **pain**.*

~ **you will** react to your brothers as though **they** were someone else, and this **will** surely prevent **you** from perceiving them as **they** are. *T-12.IV.27.5*

~ for **you** do not respond to what a brother really offers **you**, but only to the particular **perception** of his **offering** by which the **ego** judges it. *T-14.VI.52.6*

~ the **ego** would **limit** your **perception** of your brothers to the **body**. *T-15.IX.85.1*

~ **you** can **make** a brother what **he** is not because **you** would **have** him so. *T-15.VI.56.6*

~ it is **impossible** to overestimate your brother's **value**. Only the **ego** does this, but all it **means** is that it wants the other for itself and therefore values him too **little**. What is inestimable clearly cannot be evaluated. *T-20.VI.39.1:3*

~ the **veil** that hides the **gift** hides him as well. **He** is the **gift**, and yet **he** knows it not. *T-20.VI.43.6:7*

~ it is **impossible** to **see** your brother as **sinless** and yet to look upon him as a **body**. *T-20.VIII.61.1*

~ **you** are his **enemy** in specialness. *T-24.II.8.4*

~ not one **sin you** see in him but keeps **you** both in **hell**. *T-24.VII.53.4*

~ your brother is a **symbol** for a "hateful-**love**" a "weakened-**power**" and above all, a "living-**death**." And so **he** has no **meaning** to **you**, for **he** stands for what is meaningless. **He** represents a double **thought**, where half is canceled out by the remaining half. *T-27.IV.30.1:3*

~ sometimes a friend, perhaps, provided that your separate interests made your friendship possible a **little** while. But not without a **gap** between **you**, lest **he** turn again into an **enemy**. *T-29.I.3.5:6*

~ **he** is afraid to walk with **you** and thinks perhaps a bit behind, a bit ahead, would be a safer place for him to be. *T-31.II.23.3*

~ **you** never **hate** your brother for his sins, but only for your own. Whatever **form** his sins appear to take, it but obscures the **fact** that **you** believe them to be yours and therefore meriting a "just" **attack**. *T-31.III.26.5:6*

~ when **you call** upon a brother, it is to his **body** that **you make** appeal. His. *W-pI.184.8.4:5*

~ his **unity** is twice denied, for **you** perceive him separate from **you**, and **he** accepts this separate **name** as his. *W-pI.184.8.7*

~ your brother is your "**enemy**" because **you** see in him the rival for your **peace**, a plunderer who takes his **joy** from **you** and leaves **you nothing** but a black **despair** so bitter and relentless that there is no hope remaining. *W-pI.195.3.1*

HOLY SPIRIT; *friend, perfect **gift**, mirror, **savior**, co-**creator**, guide to **peace**.*

~ **salvation** is of your brother. The **Holy Spirit** extends from your **mind** to his and answers **you**. *T-8.XI.112.1:2*

~ **you** perceive a brother only as **you** see him **now**. His **past** has no **reality** in the **present**, and **you** cannot **see** it. Your **past** reactions to him are also not there, and if it is to them that **you** react **now**, **you** see but an **image** of him which **you** made and cherish instead of him. *T-12.VI.45.3:5*

~ his errors are all **past**, and by perceiving him without them, **you** are releasing him. And since his **past** is yours, **you share** in this **release**. *T-12.VI.49.2:3*

~ in timeless **union** with them is your continuity, unbroken because it is wholly shared. *T-12.VI.52.3*

~ when **you have** seen your brothers as yourself, **you will** be released to **knowledge**, having learned to free yourself of Him Who knows of **freedom**. *T-13.II.8.1*

~ and **you will see** it with them. Because **you** taught them gladness and **release**, **they will** become your teachers in **release** and gladness. *T-13.VII.59.8:9*

~ in the **light** of your **forgiveness**, **he will remember** who **he** is and forget what never was. *T-19.V.65.3*

~ the lamp is lit in both of **you** for one another. And by the hands that gave it to each other shall both of **you** be led **past fear** to **love**. *T-20.III.15.6:7*

~ your brother's **body** is as **little** use to **you** as it is to him. When it is used only as the **Holy Spirit** teaches, it has no **function**, for minds **need** not the **body** to communicate. *T-20.VI.41.1:2*

~ your holy brother, **sight** of whom is your **release**, is no **illusion**. *T-20.VIII.65.7*

~ as **you** look upon the **change** in him, it **will** be given **you** to **see** it in yourself. *T-21.III.19.9*

~ desiring to look upon their brothers in **holiness**, the **power** of **belief** and **faith** goes far beyond the **body**, supporting **vision**, not obstructing it. *T-21.IV.36.3*

~ neither your brother nor yourself can be attacked **alone**. But neither can accept a **miracle** instead without the other **being** blessed by it and healed of **pain**. *T-21.VII.64.9:10*

~ beyond his errors is his **holiness** and your **salvation**. **You** gave him not his **holiness** but tried to **see** your sins in him to save yourself. And yet his **holiness** is your **forgiveness**. *T-22.IV.36.5:7*

~ your brother is your friend because his **Father** created him like **you**. There is no **difference**. *T-24.II.8.9:10*

~ all that is real proclaims his sinlessness. *T-24.V.38.6*

~ **he** is your **savior** from the dreams of **fear**. **He** is the **healing** of your **sense** of **sacrifice** and **fear** that what **you have will** scatter with the wind and turn to dust. In him is your assurance **God** is **here** and with **you now**. *T-24.VII.49.2:4*

~ his errors cannot withhold God's **blessing** from himself nor **you** who **see** him truly. *T-24.VII.56.2*

~ **he** is the mirror of yourself wherein **you see** the **judgment you have** laid on both of **you**. The **Christ** in **you** beholds his **holiness**. Your specialness looks on his **body** and beholds him not. *T-24.VII.56.6:8*

~ what is **within** your brother still contains all of **creation**, everything created and creating, born and unborn as yet, still in the **future** or apparently gone by. What is in him is changeless. *T-24.VIII.63.2:3*

~ the **holiness** in **you** belongs to him. And by your seeing it in him, returns to **you**. All of the tribute **you have** given specialness belongs to him and thus returns to **you**. *T-24.VIII.63.4:6*

~ **nothing** due him is not due to **you**. *T-24.VIII.63.9*

~ **he** has no **need** but this—that **you** allow him **freedom** to complete the task **God** gave to him. *T-25.VI.41.6*

~ and as **he** is in **Heaven**, so must **he** be eternally and everywhere. **He** is the same forever—born again each instant, untouched by **time**, and far beyond the reach of any **sacrifice** of **life** or **death**. *T-26.II.8.1:2*

~ one is given **you** to **see** in him his perfect sinlessness. *T-26.III.15.6*

~ **dream** softly of your **sinless** brother, who unites with **you** in holy **innocence**. And from this **dream**, the Lord of **Heaven will** Himself **awaken** His beloved Son. **Dream** of your brother's kindnesses instead of dwelling in your dreams on his mistakes. Select his thoughtfulness to **dream** about instead of counting up the hurts **he** gave. Forgive him his illusions and **give** thanks to him for all the helpfulness **he** gave. And do not brush aside his many gifts because **he** is not perfect in your dreams. *T-27.VIII.75.1:6*

~ **share** not in his **illusion** of himself, for your **identity** depends on his **reality**. Think rather of him as a **mind** in which illusions still persist, but as a **mind** which brother is to **you**. *T-28.V.39.2:3*

~ it is his **reality** that is your brother, as is yours to him. Your **mind** and his are joined in brotherhood. His **body** and his dreams but seem to **make** a **little gap**, where yours **have** joined with his. The **voice you** hear in him is but your own. *T-28.V.39.5:8*

~ be certain, if **you** do your **part, he will** do his, for **he will join you** where **you** stand. *T-28.V.41.1*

~ **join** not your brother's dreams but **join** with him, and where **you join** His Son, the **Father** is. *T-28.V.46.1*

~ and **now** is **God** forgiven, for **you** chose to look upon your brother as a friend. *T-30.III.37.8*

~ your brother has a changelessness in him beyond **appearance** and deception both. *T-30.IX.90.3*

~ **you** are free to learn of him and learn of him anew. **Now** is **he** born again to **you**, and **you** are born again to him without the **past** that sentenced him to die, and **you** with him. **Now** is **he** free to live, as **you** are free because an ancient **learning** passed away and left a place for **truth** to be reborn. *T-31.I.12.7:9*

~ **he** is asking what **will** come to **you** because **you see** an **image** of yourself and hear your **voice** requesting what **you want**. *T-31.III.17.14*

~ this brother neither leads nor follows us but walks beside us on the selfsame road. **He** is like us, as near or far away from what **we want** as **we will** let him be. **We make** no gains **he** does not **make** with us, and **we** fall back if **he** does not **advance**. *T-31.II.20.2:4*

~ in his progress do **you** count your own. *T-31.II.20.5*

~ because **he** is your equal in God's **love, you will** be saved from all appearances and **answer** to the **Christ** Who calls to **you**. *T-31.II.21.1*

~ **you have** come with but one **purpose**—that **you** both may learn **you love** each other with a brother's **love**. And as a brother, must his **Father** be the same as yours, as **he** is like yourself. *T-31.II.24.5:6*

~ next to **you** is One Who holds the **light** before **you** so that every **step** is made in **certainty** and sureness of the road. *T-31.II.25.7*

~ **he** Who travels with **you** has the **light**. *T-31.II.25.9*

~ should one brother dawn upon your **sight** as wholly worthy of **forgiveness**, then your **concept** of yourself is wholly changed. *T-31.VII.69.5*

~ no longer did **you** choose that **you** should be the sign of **evil** and of **guilt** in him. And as **you** gave your **trust** to what is **good** in him, **you** gave it to the **good in you**. *T-31.VII.69.7:8*

~ **you** recognize your brother as yourself and thus do **you** perceive that **you** are whole. *W-pI.159.2.3*

~ and **you will** know **you have** forgiven me if **you** behold your brother in the **light** of **holiness**. **He** cannot be less holy than can **I**, and **you** cannot be holier than **he**. *W-pII.288.2.2:3*

~ **i** never **see** my brother as **he** is, for that is far beyond **perception**. What **I see** in him is merely what **I wish** to **see** because it stands for what **I want** to be the **truth**. *W-p2.335.1.2:3*

CALL

DICTIONARY: *a cry made as a summons or to attract someone's attention.*

EGO

~ **they hate** the call that would **awaken** them. *T-24.IV.32.5*

~ **you** had been deceived by forms the call was hidden in. *T-31.I.8.6*

HOLY SPIRIT; . *call to joy*

~ the call to return is stronger than the call to depart, but it speaks in a different **way**. *T-5.IV.23.7*

~ **you** could not control your joyous response to the call of **love** if **you** heard it, and the whole **world you** think **you** control would vanish. *T-12.III.13.3*

~ it can never be that His Son called upon Him and remained unanswered. His call to **you** is but your call to Him. *T-12.VI.53.4:5*

~ a call for **help** is given **help**. *T-14.VI.51.13*

~ the ancient clarion call of **life**. This call has **power** far beyond the weak and miserable cry of **death** and **guilt**. *T-27.III.18.2:3*

~ the Call to **healing**, and the Call to heal. *T-28.VIII.61.2*

~ and never does a call remain unheard, misunderstood, nor left unanswered in the selfsame tongue in which the call was made. *T-31.I.8.3*

~ soft, eternal calling. *T-31.I.8.8*

~ the Call is universal. It goes on all the **time** everywhere. It calls for teachers to speak for it and redeem the **world**. Many hear it, but few **will answer**. But it is all a matter of **time**. **Everyone will answer** in the end, but the end can be a long, long **way** off. It is because of this that the **plan** of the teachers was established. Their **function** is to save **time**. Each one begins as a single **light**, but with the Call at its center, it is a **light** that cannot be limited. And each one saves a thousand years of **time** as the **world** judges it. To the Call itself, **time** has no **meaning**. *M-1.2.4:14*

CALM

DICTIONARY: *the absence of violent or confrontational activity **within** a place or group.*

HOLY SPIRIT

~ the certain are perfectly calm, because **they** are not in **doubt**. *T-7.V.30.6*

~ calm **within**, where in holy stillness dwells the living **God you** never left and Who never left **you**. *T-18.II.8.2*

~ **quiet** calm which liberates **you** from the **world** and lets **you** stand apart in **quiet** and in **peace** [unlimited]. *T-29.IX.53.7*

~ **nothing** can intrude upon the eternal calm of the **Son of God**. *W-pI.50.2.5*

CAUSE

DICTIONARY: *a person or thing that gives rise to an action, phenomenon, or* **condition***.*

HOLY SPIRIT

~ cause is one. *T-13.VIII.72.5*

~ what never was is causeless and is not there to **interfere** with **truth**. There is no cause for faithlessness, but there is a Cause for **faith**. That Cause has entered any **situation** which shares Its **purpose**. *T-17.VIII.71.6:8*

~ a **future** cause as yet has no effects. And therefore must it be that if **you fear**, there is a **present** cause. And it is this that needs **correction**, not a **future** state. *T-26.IX.71.6:8*

~ cause so ancient that it far exceeds the span of **memory** which your **perception** sees. *T-28.II.7.9*

~ its consequences **will** indeed seem new because **you thought** that **you** remembered not their Cause. *T-28.II.8.4*

~ and **you** are Its effects, as changeless and as perfect as Itself. Its **memory** does not lie in the **past** nor await the **future**. It is not revealed in miracles. **They** but remind **you** that It has not gone. When **you** forgive It for your sins, It **will** no longer be denied. *T-28.II.9.5:9*

~ his Cause is Its effects. *T-28.II.14.5*

~ its effects are changelessly eternal, beyond **fear**, and **past** the **world** of **sin** entirely. *T-28.II.14.7*

~ the cause of **healing** is the only Cause of everything. It has but one effect. *T-28.III.18.3:4*

~ and **you will** not **see** the many gains your **choice** has offered **you**. Yet though **you** do not **see** them, **they** are there. Their cause has been effected, and **they** must be **present** where their cause has entered in. *T-29.III.10.6:8*

~ there is no cause beyond yourself that can reach down and bring oppression. No one but yourself affects **you**. *W-pI.190.5.3:4*

~ his **love** is Cause of everything beyond all **fear** and thus forever real and always true. *M-17.9.13*

CAUSE/EFFECT

EGO

~ **cause** and effect are very clear in the ego's **thought system** because all your **learning** has been directed towards establishing the **relationship** between them. *T-16.IV.22.6*

~ the **purpose now** becomes to keep obscure the **cause** of the effect and **make** effect appear to be a **cause**. This seeming independence of effect enables it to be regarded as standing by itself and capable of serving as a **cause** of the events and feelings its maker thinks it causes. *T-21.III.25.2:3*

~ the Son is the effect, whose **Cause he** would deny. And so **he** seems to be the **cause**, producing real effects. **Nothing** can **have** effects without a **cause** and to confuse the two is merely to **fail** to **understand** them both. *T-21.III.25.6:8*

~ effects are seen as separate from their **source** and seem to be beyond **you** to control or to prevent. What is thus kept apart can never **join**. *T-26.VIII.59.6:7*

~ without the **cause** do its effects seem serious and **sad** indeed. Yet **they** but follow. And it is their **cause** which follows **nothing** and is but a jest. *T-27.IX.84.5:7*

~ effect and **cause** are first split off and then reversed, so that effect becomes a **cause**; the **cause**, effect. *T-28.III.23.7*

~ it seems to **you** that other people are apart from **you** and able to behave in ways which **have** no bearing on your thoughts, nor theirs on [yourself]. Therefore your attitudes **have** no effect on them, and their appeals for **help** are not in any **way** related to your own. *W-pI.126.2.2:3*

HOLY SPIRIT

~ "**Cause**" is a term properly belonging to **God**, and "Effect," which should also be capitalized, is His Son. *T-2.V.9:7.3*

~ **cause** and effect are one, not separate. *T-26.VIII.60.1*

~ nor **will** the **cause** be changed by seeing it apart from its effects. The **cause** produces the effects which then bear **witness** to the **cause** and not themselves. *T-27.VIII.66.2:3*

~ in gentle laughter does the **Holy Spirit** perceive the **cause** and looks not to effects. *T-27.IX.85.1*

~ **you** judge effects, but **He** has judged their **cause**. And by His **judgment** are effects removed. *T-27.IX.85.4:5*

~ remembering a **cause** can but produce illusions of its presence, not effects. *T-28.I.1.9*

~ new effects of **cause** accepted **now**, with consequences **here**. *T-28.II.7.7*

~ without a **cause** there can be no effects, and yet without effects there is no **cause**. The **cause** a **cause** is made by its effects; the **Father** is a **father** by His Son. Effects do not create their **cause**, but **they** establish its causation. *T-28.III.16.1:3*

~ if it has no **cause**, it has no **purpose**. **You** may **cause** a **dream**, but never **will you give** it real effects. *T-28.III.21.2:3*

~ the **function** of causation is to **have** effects. And where effects are gone, there is no **cause**. *T-28.III.26.2:3*

~ what **you desire**, **you will see**. Such is the real law of **cause** and effect as it operates in the **world**. *W-pI.20.5.5:6*

~ thinking and its results are really simultaneous, for **cause** and effect are never separate. *W-pI.19.1.4*

~ place **cause** and effect in their true sequence in one respect, and the **learning will** generalize and transform the **world**. *M-5.7.4*

~ **cause** and effect but replicate **creation**. Seen in their proper perspective, without distortion and without **fear**, **they** re-establish **Heaven**. *M-5.7.10:11*

CERTAINTY |ˈsərtntē|

DICTIONARY: *firm conviction that something is the case.*

EGO;   *cloak*

HOLY SPIRIT;   *strength*

~ to know is to be certain. *T-3.V.30.3*

~ certainty is **strength**. *T-3.V.30.5*

~ the Bible instructs **you** to "know yourself" or be certain. Certainty is always of **God**. *T-3.V.35.1:2*

~ certainty does not require action. *T-3.V.35.6*

~ certainty is of **God** for **you**. *T-6.V.93.6*

~ **inspiration** is of the **Spirit**, and certainty is of **God** according to His **laws**. Both, therefore, come from the same **Source**, [because] **inspiration** comes from the **Voice** for **God**, and certainty comes from the **laws** of **God**. *T-7.V.33.2:3*

~ the stillness of your certainty of Him and of yourself is **home** to both of **you**, who dwell as one and not apart. *T-23.II.16.1*

~ there is a **way** of finding certainty right **here** and **now**. Refuse to be a **part** of fearful dreams whatever **form they will** take, for **you will** lose **identity** in them. *T-28.V.38.1:2*

~ certainty and **quiet calm** which liberates **you** from the **world** and lets **you** stand apart in **quiet** and in **peace** [unlimited]. *T-29.IX.53.7*

~ sureness is not required to **receive** what only your **acceptance** can bestow. *W-pI.165.4.8*

~ how **happy** to be certain! *W-pI.98.2.1*

~ certainty that has been born of **truth**. *W-pI.107.9.1*

CHAIN

|CHān|

DICTIONARY: *a connected flexible series of metal links used for fastening or securing objects and pulling or supporting loads.*

EGO

~ **faith** can keep the **Son of God** in chains as long as **he** believes **he** is in chains. *T-21.IV.31.3*

~ chains which bar the door to **freedom**. *W-pI.128.5.4*

~ and learn the fragile nature of the chains that seem to keep the **knowledge** of yourself apart from your **awareness**. *W-pI.139.13.3*

HOLY SPIRIT

~ the heavy chains which seem to bind them unto **despair they** do not **see** as **nothing** until **you** bring the **light** to them. And then **they see** the chains **have** disappeared, and so **they** must **have** been **nothing**. *T-13.VII.59.6:7*

~ when **he** is released from them, it **will** be simply because **he** no longer believes in them, withdrawing **faith** that **they** can hold him and placing it in his **freedom** instead. *T-21.IV.31.4*

~ each **thing you value here** is but a chain that binds **you** to the **world**, and it **will** serve no other end but this. *W-pI.128.2.1*

CHANGE

|CHānj|

DICTIONARY: *the act or instance of making or becoming different.*

EGO

~ change is always fearful to **the separated ones** because **they** cannot conceive of it as a change towards **healing** the **separation**. **They** always perceive it as a change towards further **separation** because the **separation** was their first **experience** of change. *T-4.II.7.6:7*

~ the changes the **ego** seeks to **make** are not really changes. **They** are but deeper shadows, or perhaps different cloud patterns. *P-2.I.2.6:7*

HOLY SPIRIT; *illusion*

~ change in motivation is a change of **mind**, and this **will** inevitably produce fundamental change, because the **mind** is fundamental. *T-6.V.7.2.2*

~ change is an **illusion**, taught by those who could not **see** themselves as **guiltless**. There is no change in **Heaven** because there is no change in **God**. *T-15.II.11.5:6*

~ if the change be real and not imagined, illusions must **give way** to **truth** and not to other dreams that are but equally unreal. This is no **difference**. *T-22.III.18.9:10*

~ to change is to attain a state unlike the one in which **you** found yourself before. *T-29.III.16.3*

~ there is no change in **immortality**, and **Heaven** knows it not. Yet **here** on earth it has a double **purpose**, for it can be made to **teach** opposing things. And **they** reflect the **teacher** who is **teaching** them. *T-29.III.16.4:6*

~ change is the greatest **gift God** gave to all that **you** would **make** eternal, to ensure that only **Heaven** would not pass away. *T-29.VII.40.7*

~ **learning** is all that causes change. And so the **body**, where no **learning** can occur, could never change unless the **mind** preferred the **body** change in its appearances to suit the **purpose** given by the **mind**. For it can learn, and there is all change made. *T-31.III.29.8:10*

~ **you have** made no changes in yourself which **have reality**, nor changed the **universe** so that what **God** created was replaced by **fear** and **evil**, **misery** and **death**. *W-pI.110.1.3*

~ what is unalterable cannot change. *W-pI.136.12.7*

CHANNEL ⎸ˈCHanl⎸

DICTIONARY: *a medium for **communication** or the passage of information.*

HOLY SPIRIT

~ **god** has only one channel for **healing**, because He has but one Son. *T-9.IX.76.1*
~ his channels of reaching out cannot be wholly closed and separated from Him. *T-13.V.42.3*

CHAOS ⎸ˈkāˌäs⎸

DICTIONARY: *complete disorder and **confusion**.*

EGO

~ chaos and consistency cannot coexist for long, since **they** are mutually exclusive. *T-6.V.87.7*

~ your Gods do not bring chaos; **you** are endowing them with chaos and accepting it of them. *T-9.X.89.3*

~ from the **belief** in **sin**, the **faith** in chaos must follow. It is because it follows that it seems to be a logical conclusion—a valid **step** in ordered **thought**. The steps to chaos do follow neatly from their starting point. Each is a different **form** in the progression of truth's reversal, leading still deeper into terror and away from **truth**. *T-23.III.39.1:4*

~ only chaos rules a **world** which represents chaotic thinking, and chaos has no **laws**. *W-pI.53.3.3*

~ **you** look on chaos and proclaim it as yourself. *W-pI.191.2.5*

HOLY SPIRIT

~ the chaotic is without **meaning**, because it is without **God**. *T-9.X.88.9*

~ chaos is lawlessness and has no **laws**. To be believed, its seeming **laws** must be perceived as real. Their **goal** of **madness** must be seen as **sanity**. *T-23.III.33.3:5*

CHARITY

DICTIONARY: *kindness and tolerance in judging others.*

EGO

~ the **ego** literally lives by comparisons. This **means** that equality is beyond its grasp and charity becomes **impossible**. The **ego** never gives out of abundance, because it was made as a **substitute** for it. *T-4.III.32.1:3*

~ when **you** "forgive"; a **sin** there is no **gain** to **you** directly. **You give** charity to one unworthy merely to point out that **you** are better, on a higher plane than **he** whom **you** forgive. **He** has not earned your charitable tolerance, which **you** bestow on one unworthy of the **gift** because his sins **have** lowered him beneath a true equality with **you**. **He** has no claim on your **forgiveness**. It holds out a **gift** to him but hardly to yourself. *W-pI.126.3.1:5*

HOLY SPIRIT

~ charity is a **way** of perceiving the **perfection** of another even if **he** cannot perceive it himself. *T-2.III.69.6*

~ charity lies **within** the human limitations, though toward its higher levels. *T-2.III.71.1*

CHILD

DICTIONARY: *a young human **being** below the age of puberty or below the legal age of majority.*

EGO

~ those who lack wisdom are children. *T-6.V.60.1*

~ children do confuse **fantasy** and **reality**, and **they** are frightened, because **they** do not know the **difference**. *T-6.V.60.3*

~ their minds are trapped in their **brain**, and its powers decline if their bodies are **hurt**. **They** seem to **love**, yet **they** desert and are deserted. **They** appear to lose what **they love**, perhaps the most insane **belief** of all. And their bodies wither and gasp and are laid in the ground and seem to be no more. Not one of them but has **thought** that **God** is cruel. *T-11.X.86.7:11*

~ the **dream** of **judgment** is a children's game in which the child becomes the **father**, powerful, but with the **little** wisdom of a child. What hurts him is destroyed; what helps him, blessed. Except **he** judges this as does a child, who does not know what hurts and what **will** heal. And bad things seem to happen, and **he** is afraid of all the **chaos** in a **world he** thinks is governed by the **laws he** made. *T-29.X.66.4:7*

HOLY SPIRIT

~ the Children of **God** are entitled to perfect comfort, which comes from a **sense** of perfect **trust**. Until **they** achieve this, **they** waste themselves and their true creative powers on useless attempts to **make** themselves more comfortable by inappropriate **means**. But the real **means** is already provided and does not involve any **effort** at all on their **part**. Their egocentricity usually misperceives this as personally insulting, an **interpretation** which obviously arises from their misperception of themselves. *T-2.II.50.1:4*

~ **nothing** made by a Child of **God** is without **power**. *T-3.IX.72.7*

~ if **they ask** someone **they trust** for the real **meaning** of what **they** perceive and are willing to let their interpretations go in favor of **reality**, their **fear** goes with them. *T-10.VIII.88.2*

~ **fear** lies not in **reality**, but in the minds of children who do not **understand reality**. It is only their lack of understanding which frightens them, and when **they** learn to perceive truly, **they** are not afraid. *T-10.VIII.89.2:3*

- the Children of **Heaven** live in the **light** of the **blessing** of their **Father** because **they** know that **they** are **sinless**. *T-14.I.3.1*

- **little** children, **innocent** of **sin**. *T-21.V.48.3*

- children of **peace**, the **light** has come to **you**. The **light you** bring **you** do not recognize, and yet **you will remember**. *T-22.VII.56.1:2*

- there is a Child in **you** Who seeks His Father's house and knows that **He** is alien **here**. This Childhood is eternal, with an **innocence** that **will** endure forever. Where this Child shall go is holy ground. It is His **holiness** that lights up **Heaven** and that brings to earth the pure **reflection** of the **light** above, wherein are earth and **Heaven** joined as one. *W-pI.182.4.3:6*

- it is this Child in **you** your **Father** knows as His own Son. It is this Child Who knows His **Father**. He desires to go **home** so deeply, so unceasingly, His **voice** cries unto **you** to let Him **rest** a while. He does not **ask** for more than just a few instants of respite—just an **interval** in which He can return to breathe again the holy air that fills His Father's house. You are His **home** as well. He **will** return. But **give** Him just a **little time** to be Himself **within** the **peace** that is His **home**, resting in silence and in **peace** and **love**. *W-pI.182.5.1:7*

- this Child needs your protection. He is far from **home**. He is so **little** that He seems so easily shut out, His tiny **Voice** so readily obscured, His calls for **help** almost unheard amid the grating sounds and harsh and rasping noises of the **world**. Yet does He know that in **you** still abides His sure protection. **You will fail** Him not. He **will** go **home**, and **you** along with Him. *W-pI.182.6.1:6*

- this Child is your **defenselessness**, your **strength**. He trusts in **you**. He came because He knew **you** would not **fail**. He whispers of His **home** unceasingly to **you**. For He would bring **you** back with Him, that **He** Himself might stay and not return again where **He** does not belong and where **He** lives an outcast in a **world** of alien thoughts. His **patience** has no limits. He **will** wait until **you** hear His gentle **Voice within you**, calling **you** to let Him go in **peace** along with **you** to where **He** is at **home** and **you** with Him. *W-pI.182.7.1:7*

CHOICE |CHois|

DICTIONARY: *an act of selecting or making a **decision** when faced with two or more possibilities.*

EGO

- choosing **means** divided **will**. *T-5.IV.23.2*

- but **conflict** enters the instant the choice seems to be one between illusions, for this choice does not matter. Where one choice is as dangerous as the other, the **decision** must be one of **despair**. *T-16.V.34.8:9*

- a senseless wandering, without a **purpose** and without accomplishment of any kind, is all the other choice can offer **you**. *T-24.VII.57.2*

- what **you** would choose between is not a choice and gives but the **illusion** it is free, for it **will have** one outcome either **way**. Thus is it really not a choice at all. *T-31.II.15.1:2*

- there is no choice at all **within** the **world**. *T-31.IV.35.8*

- **you have** no choice, and **you** can but decide how **you** would choose the better to deceive yourself again. *T-31.IV.40.2*

- what **I have** chosen to **see** has cost me **vision**. *W-pI.52.5.4*

- first, if **you** choose a **thing** that **will** not last forever, what **you** chose is valueless. *W-pI.133.7.1*

- if **you** feel any **guilt** about your choice, **you have** allowed the ego's goals to come between the real alternatives, and thus **you** do not realize there are but two. And the alternative **you** think **you** chose seems fearful and too dangerous to be the nothingness it actually is. *W-pI.133.12.2:3*

52

~ choice is the obvious escape from what appears as opposites. *W-pI.138.3.1*

~ **you** think a thousand choices are confronting **you** when there is really only one to **make**. *W-pI.138.4.1*

~ chooses **nothing** as a **substitute** for everything. *M-13.4.10*

Holy Spirit

~ the **truth** is that **you** are responsible for what **you** think because it is only at this **level** that **you** can **exercise** choice. *T-2.IV.73.7*

~ "many are called, but few are chosen" should read, "All are called, but few choose to listen. Therefore, **they** do not choose right." *T-3.VI.49.7:8*

~ the "chosen ones" are merely those who choose right sooner. This is the real **meaning** of the celestial speed-up. *T-3.VI.50.1:2*

~ littleness and **glory** are the choices open to your striving and your **vigilance**. **You will** always choose one at the expense of the other. *T-15.IV.22.6:7*

~ your choice is your evaluation of yourself. *T-15.IV.23.1*

~ there is no **conflict** in the choice between **truth** and **illusion**. *T-16.V.34.6*

~ on the **voice you** choose to hear and on the sights **you** choose to **see**, depends entirely your whole **belief** in what **you** are. *T-21.VI.49.9*

~ a choice made with the **power** of **Heaven** to uphold it cannot be undone. *T-22.V.39.3*

~ **perception** rests on choosing; **knowledge** does not. *T-25.IV.25.1*

~ that there is choice is an **illusion**. *T-26.IV.23.4*

~ **you** can **make** a simple choice that **will** forever place **you** far beyond deception. *T-30.V.54.2*

~ there is a choice which **you have power** to **make** when **you have** seen the real alternatives. *T-31.IV.40.1*

~ what can think has choice and can be shown that different thoughts **have** different consequence. *T-31.V.56.5*

~ in that choice are false distinctions gone, illusory alternatives laid by, and **nothing** left to **interfere** with **truth**. *T-31.VIII.91.3*

~ in this choice is **everyone** made free. *T-31.VIII.94.7*

~ the choice is not whether to **see** the **past** or the **present**: it is whether to **see** or not. *W-pI.52.5.3*

~ **attack** and grievances are not there to choose. *W-pI.88.2.3*

~ the real and the unreal are all there is to choose between, and **nothing** more than these. *W-pI.130.5.6*

~ the **laws** which govern choice **you** cannot **make**, no more than **you** can **make** alternatives from which to choose. The choosing **you** can do; indeed **you** must. *W-pI.133.4.1:2*

~ there is no **compromise** in what your choice must bring. It cannot **give you** just a **little**, for there is no in-between. Each choice **you make** brings everything to **you** or **nothing**. Therefore, if **you** learn the tests by which **you** can distinguish everything from **nothing**, **you will make** the better choice. *W-pI.133.6.1:4*

~ **i** can elect to **change** all thoughts that **hurt**. *W-pII.284.1.7*

CHRIST

DICTIONARY: *the title, also treated as a **name**, given to **Jesus** of Nazareth.*

EGO

~   christ is invisible to **you** because of what **you have** made visible to yourselves. *T-11.IX.82.7*

HOLY SPIRIT;   *Son of God, the Self the Sonship shares, God's Son as He Created Him, my Self, Creation, extension of love, link.*

~   christ-control can take over everything that does not matter, while Christ-**guidance** can direct everything that does if **you** so choose. *T-2.IV.72.3*

~   the first coming of Christ is just another **name** for the **creation.** *T-4.V.66.1*

~   christ is at God's **altar,** waiting to **welcome** His Son. *T-10.V.36.1*

~   christ is the **Son of God** who lives in his **Creator** and shines with His **glory.** Christ is the **extension** of the **love** and the loveliness of **God,** as perfect as his **Creator** and at **peace** with Him. *T-10.V.37.4:5*

~   christ does rise above the **ego** and all its works and ascends to the **Father** and His **Kingdom.** *T-10.VII.59.7*

~   **learning** of Christ is easy, for to perceive with Him involves no strain at all. His perceptions are your natural **awareness,** and it is only distortions which **you** introduce that tire **you.** *T-10.VII.61.4:5*

~   to Christ it is given to be like the **Father.** *T-10.VII.68.9*

~   christ is his **healing** and yours. Christ is the **Son of God,** who is in no **way** separate from His **Father,** whose every **thought** is as loving as the **Thought** of His **Father** by which **He** was created. *T-10.VIII.84.2:3*

~   **nothing** can withstand the **love** of Christ for His **Father** or His Father's **love** for Him. *T-11.III.19.5*

~   christ has placed the **Atonement** on the **altar** for **you.** *T-11.IV.35.2*

~   christ has never slept. *T-11.VII.58.4*

~   every **Child of God** is one in Christ, for his **Being** is in Christ as Christ's is in **God.** Christ's **love** for **you** is His **love** for His **Father.** *T-11.VII.59.1:2*

~   the blamelessness of Christ is the proof that the **ego** never was and can never be. *T-11.X.90.4*

~   **he** is the Holy Spirit's manifestation, looking always on the **real world** and calling forth its witnesses and drawing them unto **you.** For **He** loves what **He** sees **within you,** and **He** would extend it. And **He will** not return unto the **Father** until **He** has extended your **perception** even unto Him. And there **perception** is no more, for **He** has returned **you** to the **Father** with Him. *T-12.V.42.5:8*

~   the Christ revealed to **you now** has no **past,** for **He** is changeless, and in His changelessness lies your **release.** For if **He** is as **He** was created, there is no **guilt** in Him. No cloud of **guilt** has risen to obscure Him, and **He** stands revealed in **everyone you** meet because **you see** Him through Himself. *T-12.VI.47.2:4*

~   christ is still there, although **you** know Him not. His **Being** does not depend upon your recognition. **He** lives **within you** in the **quiet present** and waits for **you** to leave the **past** behind and enter into the **world** **He** holds out to **you** in love. *T-12.VII.63.7:9*

~   christ **will** always offer **you** the **Will** of God in recognition that **you share** it with Him. *T-12.VII.64.7*

~   **nothing** can keep from **you** what Christ would **have you see.** His **Will** is like His **Father's,** and **He** offers mercy to every **Child of God,** as **He** would **have you** do. *T-13.IV.28.8:9*

~   those who are joined in Christ are in no **way** separate. For Christ is the **Self** the **Sonship** shares, as **God** shares His **Self** with Christ. *T-15.VI.54.10:11*

~ christ knows of no **separation** from His **Father**, who is His one **relationship**, in which **He** gives as His **Father** gives to Him. *T-15.IX.82.7*

~ the **time** of Christ is the **time** appointed for the **gift** of **freedom**, offered to **everyone**. *T-15.X.94.6*

~ **he** comes demanding **nothing**. No **sacrifice** of any kind of anyone is asked by Him. In His Presence, the whole **idea** of **sacrifice** loses all **meaning**. For **He** is **Host** to God. *T-15.XI.102.3:6*

~ the **time** of Christ is meaningless apart from **joy**. *T-15.XI.108.3*

~ **we** are deprived of **nothing**? Such is the **message** of the **time** of Christ. *T-15.XI.108.5:6*

~ **he** would bring **peace** to **everyone**, and how can **He** do this except through you? *T-19.V.41.8*

~ behold your Friend, the Christ Who stands beside **you**. *T-19.V.103.1*

~ a slain Christ has no **meaning**. But a risen Christ becomes the **symbol** of the Son of God's **forgiveness** of himself; the sign **he** looks upon himself as healed and whole. *T-20.I.1.4:5*

~ christ comes to what is like Himself; the same, not different. For **He** is always drawn unto Himself. *T-22.II.15.1:2*

~ the **love** of Christ **will light** your faces and shine from them into a darkened **world** that needs the **light**. And from this holy place **He will** return with **you**, not leaving it nor **you**. **You will** become His messengers, returning Him unto Himself. *T-22.V.40.7:9*

~ the Christ in **you** is very still. **He** looks on what **He** loves and knows it as Himself. And thus does **He** rejoice at what **He** sees because **He** knows that it is one with Him and with His **Father**. *T-24.VI.40.1:3*

~ the Christ in **you** is very still. **He** knows where **you** are going, and **He** leads **you** there in **gentleness** and **blessing** all the **way**. His **love** for **God** replaces all the **fear you thought you** saw **within** yourself. His **holiness** shows **you** Himself in him whose hand **you** hold and whom **you** lead to Him. And what **you see** is like yourself. *T-24.VI.40.1:5*

~ the Christ in **you** looks only on the **truth** and sees no **condemnation** that could **need forgiveness**. **He** is at **peace** because **He** sees no **sin**. *T-24.VI.42.2:3*

~ **he** is your eyes, your ears, your hands, your feet. *T-24.VI.42.5*

~ christ has no **doubt**, and from His **certainty** His **quiet** comes. **He will** exchange His **certainty** for all your doubts if **you** agree that **He** is one with **you** and that this **Oneness** is endless, timeless, and **within** your grasp because your hands are His. **He** is **within you**, yet **He** walks beside **you** and before, leading the **way** that **He** must go to find Himself complete. His quietness becomes your **certainty**. *T-24.VI.48.3:6*

~ the Christ in **you** can **see** your **brother** truly. *T-24.VII.58.7*

~ out of His lack of **conflict** comes your **peace**. And from His **purpose** comes the **means** for effortless accomplishment and **rest**. *T-24.VII.61.6:7*

~ the Christ in **you** inhabits not a **body**. Yet **He** is in **you**. *T-25.I.1.1:2*

~ christ is **within** a frame of **holiness** whose only **purpose** is that **He** may be made manifest to those who know Him not, that **He** may **call** to them to come to Him and **see** Him where **they thought** their bodies were. *T-25.I.1.8*

~ **nothing** that the **body** says or does but makes Him manifest. To those who know Him not, it carries Him in **gentleness** and **love** to heal their minds. *T-25.I.3.5:6*

~ for the **mind** is His. And so it must be yours. His **holiness** directs the **body** through the **mind** at one with Him. *T-25.II.4.3:5*

~ christ and His **Father** never **have** been separate, and Christ abides **within** your understanding in the **part** of **you** that shares His Father's **Will**. *T-25.II.8.4*

~ christ stands before **you** both each **time you** look on one another. *T-25.VI.38.9*

~ when **He** has appeared to **you, you will** be certain **you** are like Him, for **He** is the changeless in your **brother** and in **you.** *T-30.IX.93.9*

~ the Christ in **you** remembers **God** with all the **certainty** with which **He** knows His **love.** *T-31.I.9.3*

~ christ calls to all with equal tenderness, seeing no leaders and no followers and hearing but one **answer** to them all. Because **He** hears one **Voice, He** cannot hear a different **answer** from the one **He** gave when **God** appointed Him His only Son. *T-31.II.21.5:6*

~ he would not leave one **source** of **pain unhealed** nor any **image** left to **veil** the **truth.** [He would remove all **misery** from **you,** whom **God** created altars unto **joy.**] **He** would not leave **you** comfortless, **alone** in dreams of **hell,** but would **release** your minds from everything that hides His face from **you.** His **holiness** is yours because **He** is the only **power** that is real in **you.** His **strength** is yours because **He** is the **Self** that **God** created as His only Son. *T-31.VIII.87.3:7*

~ he will be your **savior** from all idols **you have** made. For when **you** find Him **you will understand** how worthless are your idols and how false the images which **you** believed were **you.** *W-pI.110.10.2:3*

~ him **within you** Who is Christ in **you,** the **Son of God** and **brother** to the world—the **savior** who has been forever saved, with **power** to save whoever touches Him however lightly, asking for the **word** that tells him **he** is **brother** unto Him. *W-pI.110.8.2*

~ christ cannot **doubt** Himself. The **Voice** of **God** can only honor Him, rejoicing in His perfect, everlasting sinlessness. *W-pI.151.8.2:3*

~ christ beholds no **sin** in anyone, and in His **sight** the **sinless** are as one. Their **holiness** was given by His **Father** and Himself. *W-pI.159.4.4:5*

~ christ has dreamed the **dream** of a forgiven **world.** *W-pI.159.10.4*

~ christ has come to search the **world** for what belongs to Him. His **vision** sees no strangers, but beholds His own and joyously unites with them. **They** see Him as a **stranger,** for **they** do not recognize themselves. Yet as **they give** Him **welcome, they remember.** And **He** leads them gently **home** again where **they** belong. *W-pI.160.9.1:5*

~ not one does **He** forget. Not one **He** fails to **give you** to **remember** that your **home** may be complete and perfect as it was established. **He** has not forgotten **you.** But **you will** not **remember** Him until **you** look on all as **He** does. *W-pI.160.10.1:4*

~ he looks **past time** and sees **eternity** as represented there. **He** hears the sounds the senseless busy **world** engenders, yet **He** hears them faintly, for beyond them all **He** hears the **song** of **Heaven** and the **Voice** of **God** more clear, more meaningful, more near. *W-pI.164.1.4:5*

~ the **world** fades easily away before His **sight.** *W-pI.164.2.1*

~ christ answers for **you,** echoing your **Self,** using your **voice** to **give** His glad consent, accepting your deliverance for **you.** *W-pI.164.2.6*

~ he has **need** of your most holy **mind** to save the **world.** *W-pI.164.8.4*

~ christ has called **you** friend and **brother. He** has even come to **you** to **ask** your **help** in letting Him go **home** completed and completely. **He** has come as does a **little child** who must beseech his **father** for protection and for **love. He** rules the **universe,** and yet **He** asks unceasingly that **you** return with Him and take illusions as your Gods no more. *W-pI.182.11.2:5*

~ to **everyone** who lives **will** Christ yet come, for **everyone** must live and breathe in Him. His **Being** in His **Father** is secure because Their **will** is one. *W-pI.197.7.3:4*

~ christ is God's Son as **He** created Him. **He** is the **Self we share,** uniting us with one another and with **God** as well. **He** is the **Thought** Which still abides **within** the **Mind** That is His **Source. He** has not left His holy **home** nor lost the **innocence** in which **He** was created. **He** abides unchanged forever in the **Mind** of God. *W-pII.ST271.1.1:5*

~ christ is the **link** that keeps **you** one with **God** and guarantees that **separation** is no more than an **illusion** of **despair**. For hope forever **will** abide in Him. Your **mind** is **part** of His and His of yours. **He** is the **part** in which God's **Answer** lies, where all decisions are already made and dreams are over. **He** remains untouched by anything the body's eyes perceive. For though in Him His **Father** placed the **means** for your **salvation**, yet does **He** remain the **Self** Who, like His **Father**, knows no **sin**. *W-pII.ST271.2.1:6*

~ it is **impossible** to **share** a **goal** not blessed by Christ, for what is unseen through His eyes is too fragmented to be meaningful. *P-2.II.6.7*

~ the **psychotherapist** becomes his **patient**, working through other patients to express his thoughts as **he** receives them from the **Mind** of Christ. *P-2.III.4.6*

~ only Christ forgives, knowing His sinlessness. His **vision** heals **perception** and **sickness** disappears. *P-2.VII.3.3:4*

~ his constancy remains in tranquil silence and in perfect **peace**. **He** does not know of shadows. *S-2.I.6.6:7*

~ christ is for all because **He** is in all. It is His face **forgiveness** lets **you see**. It is His face in which **you see** your own. *S-2.II.7.7:9*

~ **he** knows the **need**; the **question** and the **answer**. **He** will say exactly what to do, in words that **you** can **understand** and **you** can also use. Do not confuse His **function** with your own. **He** is the **Answer**. **You** the one who hears. *S-2.III.5.6:10*

~ **he will** be heard by anyone who calls upon His **Name**, and places his **forgiveness** in His hands. *S-2.III.6.6*

~ **forgiveness** has been given Him to **teach**, to save it from **destruction** and to **make** the **means** for **separation**, **sin** and **death** become again the holy **gift** of **God**. **Prayer** is His Own right Hand, made free to save as true **forgiveness** is allowed to come from His eternal **vigilance** and **Love**. *S-2.III.6.7:8*

~ **he will** not leave **you** comfortless, nor **fail** to send His angels down to **answer you** in His Own **Name**. *S-2.III.7.5*

CHRIST'S VISION   *A Course in Miracles Term*

EGO

~ the **vision** of **Christ** is not in your **sight**, for **you** look upon yourself **alone**. *T-12.V.38.6*

~ christ's **vision** is their "**enemy**" for it sees not what **they** would look upon, and it would show them that the specialness **they** think **they see** is an **illusion**. *T-24.III.16.6*

HOLY SPIRIT

~ christ's eyes are open, and **He will** look upon whatever **you see** with **love** if **you** accept His **vision** as yours. *T-11.VII.56.4*

~ through the eyes of **Christ**, only the **real world** exists and can be seen. *T-11.VIII.72.7*

~ beyond this **darkness** and yet still **within you** is the **vision** of **Christ**, who looks on all in **light**. Your **vision** comes from **fear**, as His from **love**. And **He** sees for **you** as your **witness** to the **real world**. *T-12.V.42.2:4*

~ through Christ's **vision He** beholds Himself. And seeing what **He** is, **He** knows His **Father**. Beyond your darkest dreams, **He** sees God's **guiltless** Son **within you**, shining in perfect radiance, which is undimmed by your dreams. And this **you will see** as **you** look with Him, for His **vision** is His **gift** of **love** to **you**, given Him of the **Father** for **you**. *T-12.V.43.3:6*

~ christ's **vision** is His **gift** to **you**. His **Being** is His Father's **gift** to Him. *T-13.II.6.6:7*

~ the **vision** of **Christ** is given the very instant that it is perceived. *T-13.VII.63.3*

~ the **vision** of **Christ** is not for Him **alone** but for Him with **you**. *T-14.IV.30.7*

~ in Christ's **sight**, the **world** and God's **creation** meet, and as **they** come together, all **perception** disappears. His kindly **sight** redeems the **world** from **death**. For **nothing** that **He** looks on but must live, remembering the **Father** and the Son; **Creator** and **creation** unified. *W-pII.271.1.3:5*

CHRISTMAS |ˈkrisməs|

DICTIONARY: *the annual Christian festival celebrating Christ's **birth**, held on December 25 in the Western Church.*

HOLY SPIRIT;   *state of **mind***

~ christmas is not a **time**; it is a state of **mind**. *T-4.IV.41.7*

~ in this season (Christmas), which celebrates the **birth** of **holiness** into this **world**. *T-15.IV.29.1*

~ the sign of Christmas is a star, a **light** in **darkness**. *T-15.XI.102.1*

CHURCH |CHərCH|

DICTIONARY: *a building used for public Christian worship.*

HOLY SPIRIT

~ the inappropriate emphasis men **have** put on beautiful church buildings is a sign of their **fear** of **Atonement** and their unwillingness to reach the **altar** itself. *T-2.II.45.6*

~ only **you** can be the foundation of God's church. A church is where an **altar** is, and the presence of the **altar** is what makes it a church. Any church which does not inspire **love** has a hidden **altar** which is not serving the **purpose** for which **God** intended it. *T-6.II.12.1:3*

CLARITY |ˈklerədē|

DICTIONARY: *the quality of **being** certain or definite.*

EGO

~ clarity of **thought** cannot occur under conditions of vacillation. Unless a **mind** is fixed in its **purpose**, it is not clear. *T-5.IX.85.5:6*

HOLY SPIRIT;   *the state of **light***

~ clarity literally **means** the state of **light**. *T-5.IX.85.7*

~ clarity undoes **confusion** by definition. *T-10.VI.41.2*

~ the simple is merely what is easily understood, and for this it is apparent that it must be clear. *T-17.VII.57.3*

CLOUDS

DICTIONARY: *a large cloud formation considered in terms of its visual effect.*

EGO; *heavy-seeming barrier, dark clouds of **guilt**, heavy clouds of complication, clouds of **complexity**, heavy clouds of **doubt**, misty clouds.*

~ if **you see** it **now** in your delusions, it has not gone from **you**, although it is not there. *T-12.VI.47.7*

~ heavy clouds of complication which were made to keep the **problem** unresolved. *T-27.VIII.63.3*

~ the clouds seem to be the only **reality**. **They** seem to be all there is to **see**. *W-pI.69.5.2:3*

~ **you have** never found anything in the cloud patterns **you** imagined that endured or that **you** wanted. *W-pI.70.12.6*

HOLY SPIRIT; *foolish cobwebs*

~ the cloud which obscures God's Son to **you** is the **past**, and if **you** would **have** it **past** and gone, **you** must not **see** it **now**. *T-12.VI.47.6*

~ dark clouds of **guilt**, no more impenetrable and no more substantial. **You will** not bruise yourself against them in traveling through. *T-18.X.92.1:2*

~ beneath them is a **world** of **light** whereon **they** cast no shadows. Their shadows lie upon the **world** beyond them, still further from the **light**. Yet from them to the **light** their shadows cannot fall. *T-18.X.92.3:5*

~ clouds cannot stop **you**. *W-pI.69.6.4*

COMMUNICATION

DICTIONARY: *the successful conveying or sharing of ideas and feelings.*

EGO

~ the **ego** is thus against communication except in so far as it is utilized to establish separateness rather than to abolish it. *T-4.VIII.95.2*

~ its communication is controlled by its **need** to protect itself, and it **will** disrupt communication when it experiences **threat**. *T-4.VIII.95.4*

~ a medium of communication **will** lose its usefulness if it is used for anything else. *T-8.VII.63.5*

~ **you** communicate with no one, and **you** are as isolated from **reality** as if **you** were **alone** in all the **universe**. *T-12.V.38.3*

~ **you** may believe **you want** it broken, and this **belief** does **interfere** with the deep **peace** in which the sweet and constant communication which **God** would **share** with **you** is known. *T-13.V.42.2*

~ **you** taught yourselves the most unnatural habit of not communicating with your **Creator**. *T-13.VIII.82.1*

~ it is **impossible** to recognize perfect communication while breaking communication holds **value** to **you**. *T-15.V.42.2*

~ to be with a **body** is not communication. *T-15.VIII.75.1*

~ **you** believe that to communicate is to **make** yourself **alone**. *T-15.VIII.75.4*

~ the **limit** on communication cannot be the best **means** to expand communication. Yet the **ego** would **have you** believe that it is. *W-pI.72.2.4:5*

HOLY SPIRIT; *creation, salvation.*

~ existence as well as **being** rests on communication. *T-4.VIII.98.1*

~ communication is perfectly direct and perfectly united. It is totally without strain, because **nothing** discordant ever enters. *T-7.III.18.7:8*

~ only minds communicate. *T-7.VI.40.1*

~ **healing** is the Holy Spirit's **form** of communication and the only one **He** knows. *T-7.VI.41.2*

~ to communicate with **part** of **God** Himself is to reach beyond the **Kingdom** to its **Creator** through His **Voice**, which **He** has established as **part** of you. *T-8.VII.57.9*

~ to communicate is to **join**. *T-8.VII.64.1*

~ his remaining communication **link** with all His Children joins them together and them to Him. *T-9.IX.76.2*

~ the Communication **Link** which **God** Himself placed **within you**, joining your minds with His, cannot be broken. *T-13.V.42.1*

~ **god** can communicate only to the **Holy Spirit** in your **mind**. *T-14.II.4.3*

~ for what is not in communication with the **Mind** of **God** has never been. Communication with **God** is **life**. **Nothing** without it is at all. *T-14.II.4.5:7*

~ the Holy Spirit's **function** is entirely communication. **He** therefore must remove whatever interferes with it in **order** to restore it. *T-14.III.23.1:2*

~ communication between what cannot be divided cannot cease. *T-14.IV.34.5*

~ as **God** communicates to the **Holy Spirit** in **you**, so does the **Holy Spirit** translate His communications through **you** so **you** can **understand** them. **God** has no **secret** communications, for everything of Him is perfectly open and freely accessible to all, **being** for all. *T-14.VI.56.1:2*

~ the willingness to communicate attracts communication to it and overcomes loneliness completely. *T-15.VIII.78.2*

~ **he** has kept this **channel** open to **receive** His communication to **you** and yours to Him. **God** does not **understand** your **problem** in communication, for **He** does not **share** it with **you**. It is only **you** who believe that it is understandable. *T-15.IX.83.5:7*

~ communication must be unlimited in **order** to **have meaning**, and deprived of **meaning**, it **will** not satisfy **you** completely. Yet it remains the only **means** by which **you** can establish real relationships. *T-15.IX.86.5:6*

~ communication remains unbroken, even if the **body** is destroyed, provided that **you see** not the **body** as the necessary **means** of communication. *T-15.XI.107.2*

~ communication embraces everything, and in the **peace** it re-establishes, **love** comes of itself. *T-15.XI.108.2*

~ communication is internal. [It is not made up of different parts which reach each other.]. *T-18.VII.56.4:6*

COMMUNION

|kə'myoonyən|

DICTIONARY: *the sharing or exchanging of intimate thoughts and feelings, especially when the exchange is on a mental or spiritual **level**.*

EGO

~ egocentricity and communion cannot coexist. Even the terms are contradictory. *T-2.II.50.5:6*

HOLY SPIRIT; *Holy Communion*

~ the **Soul** never loses its communion with **God**. *T-1.I.45.1*

~ communion, not **prayer**, is the natural state of those who know. *T-3.VII.60.4*

~ i do not **want** to **share** my **body** in communion, because that is to **share nothing**. [Would **I** try to **share** an **illusion** with the most holy children of a most holy **Father**?] Yet **I** do **want** to **share** my **mind** with you, because **we** are of One **Mind** and that **Mind** is ours. *T-7.VI.51.7:8*

~ communion is another kind of **completion** which goes beyond **guilt** because it goes beyond the **body**. *T-19.V.58.4*

~ **we** are there together in the **quiet** communion in which the **Father** and the Son are joined. *T-19.V.66.3*

~ our communion, where **we** are joined already. *T-19.V.67.5*

COMPLETION |kəm'plēSH(ə)n|

DICTIONARY: *the state of being finished.*

EGO

~ to the **ego**, completion lies in triumph and in the **extension** of the "victory" even to the final triumph over **God**. In this it sees the ultimate **freedom** of the **self**, for **nothing** would remain to **interfere** with it. This is its **idea** of **Heaven**. From this it follows that **union**, which is a **condition** in which the **ego** cannot **interfere**, must be **hell**. *T-16.VI.47.5:8*

~ to think **you** could be satisfied and **happy** with so **little** is to **hurt** yourself, and to **limit** the happiness that **you** would **have** calls upon **pain** to fill your meager store and **make** your lives complete. This is completion, as the **ego** sees it. *T-19.V.58.1:2*

~ to **seek** a **special** person or a **thing** to add to **you** to **make** yourself complete can only mean that **you** believe some **form** is missing. And by finding this, **you will** achieve completion in a **form you** like. *T-30.IV.40.3:4*

HOLY SPIRIT; *function*

~ there is complete **forgiveness here**, for there is no **desire** to exclude anyone from your completion in sudden recognition of the **value** of his **part** in it. *T-15.VIII.78.3*

~ your completion is God's, whose only **need** is to **have you** be complete. For your completion makes **you** His in your **awareness**. And **here** it is that **you experience** yourself as **you** were created and as **you** are. *T-15.VIII.78.5:7*

~ across the **bridge** is your completion, for **you will** be wholly in **God**, willing for **nothing special** but only to be wholly like unto Him, completing Him by your completion. *T-16.V.38.1*

~ the abode of **peace** and perfect **holiness**. Only there is the completion of **God** and of His Son established forever. *T-16.V.38.2:3*

~ in your completion lies the **memory** of His **wholeness** and His **gratitude** to **you** for His completion. *T-16.V.40.11*

~ your completion lies in **truth** and nowhere else. *T-16.V.40.4*

~ to **everyone Heaven** is completion. There can be no disagreement on this, because both the **ego** and the **Holy Spirit** accept it. **They** are, however, in complete disagreement on what completion is and how it is accomplished. *T-16.VI.47.1:3*

~ the **Holy Spirit** knows that completion lies first in **union** and then in the **extension** of **union**. *T-16.VI.47.4*

~ **communion** is another kind of completion which goes beyond **guilt** because it goes beyond the **body.** *T-19.V.58.4*

~ what is His is yours because in your completion is His Own. *T-24.VI.47.2*

~ the complete can be a **part** of God's completion. *T-29.VI.33.3*

~ completion is the **function** of God's Son. **He** has no **need** to **seek** for it at all. *T-30.IV.42.1:2*

COMPLEXITY |kəmˈpleksədē|

DICTIONARY: *the state or quality of being intricate or complicated.*

EGO

~ complexity is of the **ego** and is **nothing** more than the ego's attempt to obscure the obvious. *T-15.V.39.5*

~ complexity is not of **God.** *T-26.IV.18.1*

~ all this complexity is but a desperate attempt not to recognize the **problem** and therefore not to let it be resolved. *W-pI.79.6.1*

HOLY SPIRIT;   *screen of smoke*

~ let not the **form** of the **decision** deceive you. Complexity of **form** does not imply complexity of content. It is **impossible** that any **decision** on earth can **have** a content different from just this one simple **choice.** *W-pI.64.6.4:6*

~ complexity is **nothing** but a screen of smoke which hides the very simple **fact** that no **decision** can be **difficult.** *W-pI.133.13.3*

COMPROMISE |ˈkämprəˌmīz|

DICTIONARY: *an agreement or a settlement of a dispute that is reached by each side making concessions.*

EGO

~ to compromise is to accept but **part** of what **you want**—to take a **little** and **give** up the **rest.** *T-23.IV.43.2*

~ compromise is the **belief salvation is impossible.** It would maintain **you** can **attack** a **little, love** a **little,** and know the **difference.** Thus it would **teach** a **little** of the same can still be different, and yet the same remain intact as one. *T-23.IV.43.6:8*

HOLY SPIRIT

~ there is no compromise possible between everything and **nothing.** *T-2.V.100.1*

~ there is no compromise. **You** are your **Self** or an **illusion.** *T-2.V.100.1:2*

~ **mistake** not truce for **peace,** nor compromise for the escape from **conflict.** To be released from **conflict means** that it is over. *T-23.IV.46.1:2*

~ **teacher of God,** your one assignment could be stated thus: accept no compromise in which **death** plays a **part.** *M-27.7.1*

COMPULSION

|kəmˈpəlSHən|

DICTIONARY: *an irresistible urge to behave in a certain **way**, especially against one's conscious wishes.*

EGO

~ repetition compulsions can be endless unless **they** are given up by an act of **will**. *T-4.I.4.1*

~ human living has indeed been needlessly wasted in a repetition compulsion. It reenacts the **separation**, the **loss** of **power**, the foolish **journey** of the **ego** in an attempt at reparation, and finally the **crucifixion** of the **body** or **death**. *T-4.II.3.4:5*

CONCEPT

|ˈkänˌsept|

DICTIONARY: *an abstract **idea**; a general notion.*

EGO

~ concepts are learned. **They** are not natural. Apart from **learning, they** do not **exist**. **They** are not given, and **they** must be made. Not one of them is true, and many come from feverish imaginations, hot with hatred and distortions born of **fear**. What is a concept but a **thought** to which its maker gives a **meaning** of his own? Concepts maintain the **world**. But **they** cannot be used to demonstrate the **world** is real. For all of them are made **within** the **world**, born in its **shadow**, growing in its ways, and finally "maturing" in its **thought**. **They** are ideas of idols painted with the brushes of the **world**, which cannot **make** a single **picture** representing **truth**. *T-31.V.49.1:10*

~ a concept of the **self** is meaningless, for no one **here** can **see** what it is for and therefore cannot **picture** what it is. *T-31.V.50.1*

~ something must **have** done the **learning** which gave rise to them. *T-31.V.55.3*

~ the concept of the **self** has always been the great preoccupation of the **world**. And **everyone** believes that **he** must find the **answer** to the riddle of himself. *T-31.V.56.1:2*

~ the concept of the **self** embraces all **you** look upon, and **nothing** is **outside** of this **perception**. *T-31.V.57.7*

~ **you will make** many concepts of the **self** as **learning** goes along. Each one **will** show the changes in your own relationships as your **perception** of yourself is changed. *T-31.V.58.1:2*

~ in this world's concepts are the guilty "bad;" the "**good**" are **innocent**. *T-31.VII.68.5*

~ the concept of yourself which **now you** hold would guarantee your **function here** remain forever unaccomplished and undone. And thus it dooms **you** to a bitter **sense** of deep depression and futility. *T-31.VII.73.1:2*

~ the concept of the **self** stands like a shield, a silent barricade before the **truth**, and hides it from your **sight**. All things **you see** are images because **you** look on them as through a barrier which dims your **sight** and warps your **vision**, so that **you** behold **nothing** with **clarity**. *T-31.VII.74.1:2*

HOLY SPIRIT

~ there can be no concept that can stand for what **you** are. *T-31.V.57.2*

~ **where** concepts of the **self have** been laid by is **truth** revealed exactly as it is. *T-31.V.59.4*

~ no concept of yourself **will** stand against the **truth** of what **you** are. *T-31.VI.66.1*

~ concepts are not **difficult** to **change**. One **vision**, clearly seen, that does not fit the **picture** as it was perceived before **will change** the **world** for eyes that learn to **see**, because the concept of the **self** has changed. *T-31.VI.66.3:4*

~ concepts are needed while **perception** lasts, and changing concepts is salvation's task. *T-31.VII.68.3*

CONDEMNATION

⎰ˌkändəmˈnāSH(ə)n⎱

DICTIONARY: *the action of condemning someone to a **punishment**; sentencing.*

EGO

~ for the **idea** of **guilt** brings a **belief** in condemnation of one by another, projecting **separation** in place of **unity**. You can condemn only yourself, and by so **doing**, **you** cannot know that **you** are God's Son. **You have** denied the **condition** of his **Being**, which is his perfect blamelessness. *T-11.X.94.3:5*

~ no one who condemns a **brother** can **see** himself as **guiltless** in the **peace** of **God**. *T-13.IV.30.7*

~ when anyone is seen as losing, **he** has been condemned. *T-25.X.80.8*

~ only the **self**-accused condemn. *T-31.III.26.1*

~ **you** condemn only yourself. *W-pI.46.1.5*

~ condemn and **you** are made a prisoner. *W-pI.198.2.1*

HOLY SPIRIT; *the root of **attack***

~ condemnation is unreal, and it must be unreal since it is a **form** of **attack**, then it can **have** no results. *T-8.VII.63.3*

~ condemnation is not of **God**. Therefore, it is not true. No more are any of the results of your condemnation. *T-8.VII.67.4:6*

~ **he will teach you** how to **see** yourself without condemnation by **learning** how to look on everything without it. Condemnation **will** then not be real to **you**, and all your errors **will** be forgiven. *T-9.II.8.8:9*

~ **you** are condemning yourself and must therefore regard yourself as inadequate. *T-9.VI.78.42.6*

~ there is no condemnation in the Son, for there is no condemnation in the **Father**. *T-10.V.38.2*

~ to condemn is thus **impossible** in **truth**. What seems to be its influence and its effects **have** not occurred at all. Yet must **we** deal with them a while as if **they** had. *W-pI.198.2.5:7*

~ there is no condemnation in him. **He** is perfect in his **holiness**. **He** needs no thoughts of mercy. *W-pI.198.14.1:3*

CONDITION

⎰kənˈdiSH(ə)n⎱

DICTIONARY: *a state of affairs that must **exist** or be brought about before something else is possible or permitted.*

EGO

~ the fear-prone condition in which **attack** is always possible. *T-3.VI.42.4*

~ **self** esteem is always vulnerable to stress, a term which actually refers to a condition in which the **delusion** of the ego's **reality** is threatened. This produces either **ego** deflation or **ego** inflation, resulting in either withdrawal or **attack**. *T-4.III.31.5:6*

~ whose **Will** is that **you** know Him. Therefore, **you** must be **guiltless**. Yet if **you** do not accept the necessary conditions for knowing Him, **you have** denied Him and do not recognize Him, though **He** is all around **you**. **He** cannot be known without His Son, whose guiltlessness is the condition for knowing Him. *T-14.I.1.1:4*

~ **darkness** cannot be seen, for it is **nothing** more than a condition in which seeing becomes **impossible**. *T-14.VII.61.2*

HOLY SPIRIT

~ your **will** is the **means** by which **you** determine your own condition. *T-8.V.31.2*

64

~ **they** do not wait upon your willingness for what **they** are. Your willingness is needed only to **make** it possible to **teach you** what **they** are. *T-18.V.35.4:7*

~ **peace** and **guilt** are both conditions of the **mind** to be attained. And these conditions are the **home** of the **emotion** which called them forth and therefore is compatible with them. *T-19.V.69.9:10*

CONFIDENCE |ˈkänfədəns|

DICTIONARY: *the feeling or **belief** that one can rely on someone or something; firm **trust**.*

HOLY SPIRIT

~ confidence cannot develop fully until mastery has been accomplished. *T-2.V.104.1*

~ when **you** lack confidence in what someone **will** do, **you** are attesting to your **belief** that **he** is not in his right **mind**. This is hardly a **miracle**-based frame of reference. It also has the disastrous effect of denying the creative **power** of the **miracle**. *T-3.IV.27.5:7*

~ the recognition of your own frailty is a necessary **step** in the **correction** of your errors, but it is hardly a sufficient one in giving **you** the confidence which **you need** and to which **you** are entitled. **You** must also **gain** an **awareness** that your confidence in your real **strength** is fully justified in every respect and in all circumstances. *W-pI.47.7.1:2*

~ anticipation plays no **part** at all, for **present** confidence directs the **way**. *W-pI.135.17.5*

CONFLICT |ˈkänˌflikt|

DICTIONARY: *an incompatibility between two or more opinions, principles, or interests.*

EGO

~ the alternating investment in the two types or levels of **perception** is usually experienced as conflict for a long **time** and can become very acute. *T-2.II.48.6*

~ the **ego** always tries to preserve conflict. *T-7.IX.84.1*

~ those who are in conflict are not peaceful. *T-8.I.1.8*

~ the **ego** believes in "solving" conflict through fragmentation and does not perceive the **situation** as a whole. Therefore, it seeks to split off segments of the **situation** and deal with them separately. *T-17.VII.62.9:10*

~ and **fear will** reign in **madness** and **will** seem to **have** replaced **love** there. This is the conflict's **purpose**. And to those who think that it is possible, the **means** seem real. *T-23.II.8.10:12*

~ conflict is fearful, for it is the **birth** of **fear**. *T-23.II.14.6*

HOLY SPIRIT;   *the root of all **evil**, **choice** between illusions, **sleep**.*

~ **intrapersonal** conflict arises from the same basis as interpersonal conflict. One **part** of the psyche perceives another **part** as on a different **level** and does not **understand** it. *T-3.VI.42.1:2*

~ conflict can seem to be interpersonal, but it must be **intrapersonal** first. *T-7.III.12.5*

~ conflict cannot be projected, precisely because it cannot be fully shared. *T-7.IX.85.1*

~ conflict is the root of all **evil**, for **being blind**, it does not **see** whom it attacks. Yet it always attacks the **Son of God**, and the **Son of God** is **you**. *T-10.IV.23.7:8*

~ the real conflict **you experience**, then, is between the ego's idle wishes and the **Will** of **God**, which **you share.** *T-10.VI.44.5*

~ the seeming conflict between **truth** and **illusion** can only be resolved by separating yourself from the **illusion** and not from **truth.** *T-16.IV.24.10*

~ yet the retreat to **death** is not the end of conflict. Only God's **Answer** is its end. *T-19.V.84.3:4*

~ **you** cannot be in conflict. *T-23.II.13.7*

~ conflict must be between two forces. It cannot **exist** between one **power** and nothingness. There is **nothing you** could **attack** that is not **part** of **you.** And by attacking it, **you make** two illusions of yourself in conflict with each other. *T-23.II.14.1:4*

~ to be released from conflict **means** that it is over. *T-23.IV.46.2*

~ it is conflict that makes **choice** [complex]. *T-26.IV.18.7*

~ in conflict there can be no **answer** and no resolution, for its **purpose** is to **make** no resolution possible and to ensure no **answer will** be plain. A **problem** set in conflict has no **answer**, for it is seen in different ways. And what would be an **answer** from one point of view is not an **answer** in another **light. You** are in conflict. *T-27.V.36.2:5*

~ conflict has no limited effects. *T-27.V.36.6*

~ without illusions, conflict is **impossible.** *W-pI.74.2.5*

~ conflict must be resolved. It cannot be evaded, set aside, denied, disguised, seen somewhere else, called by another **name**, nor hidden by **deceit** of any kind if it would be escaped. It must be seen exactly as it is, where it is **thought** to be, in the **reality** which has been given it, and with the **purpose** that the **mind** accorded it. For only then are its defenses lifted and the **truth** can shine upon it as it disappears. *W-pII.333.1.1:4*

~ no one at one with himself can even conceive of conflict. *M-4.12.3*

~ conflict is the inevitable result of **self**-deception. *M-4.12.4*

CONFUSION |kənˈfyo͞oZHən|

DICTIONARY: *lack of understanding; uncertainty.*

EGO

~ the endless speculation about the **meaning** of **mind** has led to considerable confusion because the **mind** is confused. *T-3.VI.41.3*

~ a separated or divided **mind** must be confused; it is **uncertain** by definition. It has to be in **conflict** because it is out of accord with itself. *T-3.VI.41.5:6*

~ confusion interferes with **meaning** and therefore prevents the **learner** from appreciating it. *T-7.III.18.2*

~ a conflicted **teacher** is a poor **teacher** and a poor **learner**. His lessons are confused, and their transfer **value** is severely limited by his confusion. *T-7.IX.85.3:4*

~ **you have** carried the ego's reasoning to its logical conclusion, which is total confusion about everything. *T-7.X.98.1*

~ confusion is the **cause** of the whole **idea** of **sacrifice.** *T-7.XI.101.6*

~ the **ego** is expert only in confusion. It does not **understand** anything else. As a **teacher**, then, it is totally confused and totally confusing. *T-8.III.8.6:8*

66

~ confusion is not limited. If it occurs at all, it **will** be total. *T-26.XI.85.5:6*

~ confused **perception will** block **knowledge**. *T-26.XI.85.9*

HOLY SPIRIT

~ only One-Mindedness is without confusion. *T-3.VI.41.4*

~ there is no confusion in the **Kingdom**, because there is only one **meaning**. *T-7.III.18.3*

~ all confusion comes from not extending **life**, since that is not the **Will** of your **Creator**. *T-7.VIII.75.5*

~ there is no confusion in the **mind** of a **Son of God** whose **will** must be the **Will** of the **Father**, because the Father's **Will** is His Son. *T-7.XI.105.11*

~ in the transition there is a period of confusion in which a **sense** of actual disorientation seems to occur. But **fear** it not, for it **means nothing** more than that **you have** been willing to let go your hold on the distorted frame of reference which seemed to hold your **world** together. *T-16.VII.64.4:5*

~ there **will** be some confusion every **time** there is a **shift**, but be **you** thankful that the **learning** of the **world** is loosening its grasp upon your **mind**. And be **you** sure and **happy** in the **confidence** that it **will** go at last and leave your **mind** at **peace**. *T-31.V.58.3:4*

CONSCIOUSNESS ˈkän(t)SHəsnəs

DICTIONARY: *the fact of awareness by the mind of itself and the world.*

EGO

~ consciousness was the first split that **man** introduced into himself. *T-3.VI.40.1*

~ consciousness is correctly identified as the domain of the **ego**. *T-3.VI.40.3*

~ all forms of **sickness**, even unto **death**, are physical expressions of the **fear** of awakening. **They** are attempts to reinforce unconsciousness out of **fear** of consciousness. *T-8.IX.82.2:3*

HOLY SPIRIT; *domain of the ego*

~ the conscious **level** is in between and reacts to either sub-or **superconscious** impulses in varying ratios. Consciousness is the **level** which engages in the **world** and is capable of responding to both. Having no impulses from itself and **being** primarily a mechanism for inducing response, it can be very wrong. *T-1.I.36.3:5*

~ consciousness is the state which induces action. *T-1.I.38.4*

~ consciousness is thus the **level** of **perception** but not of **knowledge**. *T-3.VI.39.5*

~ in our **picture** of the psyche, there is an unconscious **level** which properly consists only of the **miracle** ability and which should be under my direction. There is also a conscious **level**, which perceives or is aware of impulses from both the unconscious and the **superconscious**. Consciousness is thus the **level** of **perception** but not of **knowledge**. *T-3.VI.39.3:5*

~ the **Soul** knows that the consciousness of all its brothers is included in its own, as it is included in **God**. *T-7.X.92.1*

~ unconsciousness is **impossible**. *T-8.IX.83.8*

CONSISTENCE

|kən'sistəns|

DICTIONARY: *conformity in the application of something, typically that which is necessary for the sake of* **logic**, *accuracy, or fairness.*

EGO

~ when **you** are inconsistent, **you will** not always **give** rise to **joy** and so **you will** not always recognize. *T-9.V.32.3*

~ his consistency. *T-9.V.32.3*

HOLY SPIRIT; *understanding*

~ **healing** itself is consistence since only consistence is **conflict**-free, and only the **conflict**-free are whole. *T-7.VI.44.3*

~ understanding **means** consistence because **God means** consistence. *T-7.VI.46.5*

CONTRADICTION

|ˌkäntrəˈdikSH(ə)n|

DICTIONARY: *the statement of a position* **opposite** *to one already made.*

EGO

~ the **ego** is a contradiction. *T-4.II.8.4*

~ for contradiction is the **way we make** what **we** perceive and what **we** think is real. *W-pI.138.1.3*

HOLY SPIRIT

~ there is no contradiction in what **holiness** calls forth. *T-14.V.45.2*

~ **god** made no contradictions. What denies its own existence and attacks itself is not of Him. **He** did not **make** two minds, with **Heaven** as the glad effect of one and earth the other's sorry outcome that is Heaven's **opposite** in every **way**. *W-pI.131.8.2:4*

~ there is no contradiction to the **truth**. *W-pI.138.4.7*

~ **god** sees no contradictions. Yet His Son believes **he** sees them. Thus **he** has a **need** for One Who can correct his erring **sight** and **give** him **vision** that **will** lead him back to where **perception** ceases. *W-pI.193.2.1:3*

CONTRAST

|ˈkänˌtrast|

DICTIONARY: *the state of* **being** *strikingly different from something else, typically something in juxtaposition or close association.*

EGO

~ the contrast between what is true and what is not is perfectly apparent, yet **you** do not **see** it. *T-13.VII.56.6*

HOLY SPIRIT

~ only by this contrast can **insanity** be judged as insane. *T-9.VI.43.4*

~ the **Holy Spirit** points quietly to the contrast, knowing that **you will** finally let Him judge the **difference** for **you**, allowing Him to demonstrate which must be true. *T-13.V.38.4*

~ **you have need** of contrast only **here**. Contrast and differences are necessary teaching aids, for by them **you** learn what to avoid and what to **seek**. When **you have** learned this, **you will** find the **answer** that makes the **need** for any differences disappear. *T-13.V.40.2:4*

~ the **Holy Spirit** must **teach** through comparisons and uses opposites to point to **truth**. *T-16.VIII.75.2*

CORRECTION |kəˈrekSH(ə)n|

DICTIONARY: *a **change** that rectifies an **error** or inaccuracy.*

EGO

~ the ego's opposition to correction leads to its fixed **belief** in **sin** and disregard of errors. It looks on **nothing** that can be corrected. *T-22.IV.30.6:7*

~ correction, to a **mind** so split, must be a **way** to punish sins **you** think are yours in someone else. *T-27.III.23.3*

~ thus does **he** become your **victim**, not your **brother**, different from **you** in that **he** is more guilty, thus in **need** of your correction as the one more **innocent** than **he**. *T-27.III.23.4*

~ **correction you** would do must separate, because that is the **function** given it by **you**. *T-27.III.24.1*

~ what **you** would correct is only half the **error**, which **you** think is all of it. Your brother's sins become the central target for correction, lest your errors and his own be seen as one. *T-27.III.25.3:4*

~ in this **interpretation** of correction, your own mistakes **you will** not even **see**. The focus of correction has been placed **outside** yourself on one who cannot be a **part** of **you** while this **perception** lasts. *T-27.III.26.1:2*

HOLY SPIRIT;   *forgiveness, pardon.*

~ correction belongs at the **thought level**. *T-2.III.61.2*

~ the correction is therefore a matter of your **will**, because its presence shows that **you have** raised the unimportant to a higher **level** than it warrants. *T-2.IV.72.6*

~ correction belongs only at the **level** where **creation** is possible. The term does not mean anything at the **symptom level**, where it cannot work. The correction of **fear** is your responsibility. *T-2.IV.75.2:4*

~ the true corrective procedure is to recognize **error** temporarily but only as an indication that immediate correction is mandatory. This establishes a state of **mind** in which the **Atonement** can be accepted without **delay**. *T-2.V.99.8:9*

~ all forms of correction (or **healing**) rest on this fundamental correction in **level perception**. *T-3.II.5.2*

~ correcting **perception** is merely a temporary expedient. *T-4.VII.81.1*

~ correction is of **God**, who does not know of arrogance. *T-9.II.79*

~ correction is for all who cannot **see**. *T-11.VII.56.1*

~ for every **learning** that would **hurt you, God** offers **you** correction and complete escape from all its consequences. *T-16.VI.57.5*

~ when correction is completed, **time** is **eternity**. *T-19.IV.28.9*

~ correction cannot be accepted or refused by **you** without your **brother**. **Sin** would maintain it can. *T-21.VII.60.1:2*

~ correction is not your **function**. It belongs to One Who knows of fairness, not of **guilt**. If **you** assume correction's **role, you** lose the **function** of **forgiveness**. *T-27.III.22.1:3*

~ correction is but to forgive and never to **accuse**. *T-27.III.22.4*

~ correction is the same as pardon, then **you** also know the Holy Spirit's **mind** and yours are one. *T-27.III.24.2*

~ correction is the **function** given both, but neither one **alone**. And when it is fulfilled as shared, it must correct mistakes in both of **you**. It cannot leave mistakes in one **unhealed** and set the other free. That is divided **purpose** which cannot be shared, and so it cannot be the **function** which the **Holy Spirit** sees as His. *T-27.III.27.1:4*

~ correction process—the reversal of the thinking of the **world**. *W-pI.11.1.1*

~ one **Thought**, completely unified, **will** serve to unify all **thought**. This is the same as saying one correction **will** suffice for all correction or that to forgive one **brother** wholly is enough to bring **salvation** to all minds. *W-pI.108.5.1:2*

~ correction of a lasting nature—and only this is true correction—cannot be made until the **teacher of God** has ceased to confuse **interpretation** with **fact** or **illusion** with **truth**. *M-18.1.1*

COURSE |kôrs|

DICTIONARY: *a series of lectures or lessons in a particular subject, typically leading to a qualification.*

Ego

~ **you** are afraid of it. *T-10.VI.47.1*

~ **you** must, then, believe that by not **learning** the course, **you** are protecting yourself. *T-12.II.7.6*

~ the ego's whole continuance depends on its **belief you** cannot learn this course. *T-22.IV.30.1*

~ **you** would oppose this course because it teaches **you you** are alike. *T-24.II.10.6*

~ this course appear to **rest salvation** on a whim. *W-pI.134.1.2*

~ **you** may believe this course requires **sacrifice** of all **you** really hold dear. *M-13.6.1*

Holy Spirit;   *guide to behavior*

~ a **self-study** course for retraining the **mind** that is spiritual, rather than religious, in its perspective. *T-F.4.1*

~ this is a course in **mind training**. *T-3.I.1.1*

~ that the basic concepts referred to in this course are not matters of degree. Certain fundamental concepts cannot be meaningfully understood in terms of coexisting polarities. *T-3.IV.25.1:2*

~ the whole **purpose** of this course is to **teach you** that the **ego** is unbelievable and **will** forever be unbelievable. *T-7.IX.90.1*

~ the **purpose** of this course is to learn what **you** are. *T-8.X.91.2*

~ its **purpose** is the escape from **fear**. *T-8.XI.107.4*

~ this course is a guide to **behavior**. **Being** a very direct and very simple **learning situation**, it provides the Guide who tells **you** what to do. If **you** do it, **you will see** that it works. Its results are more convincing than its words. *T-9.IV.29.5:8*

~ this is not a course in the play of ideas, but in their practical application. *T-10.VIII.80.3*

~ **we** are therefore embarking on an organized, well-structured, and carefully planned program aimed at **learning** how to offer to the **Holy Spirit** everything **you** do not **want**. *T-11.III.23.1*

~ its **goal** for **you** is happiness and **peace**. *T-12.II.71*

~ this is a course on **love** because it is about **you**. *T-12.IV.23.2*

- this course **will teach you** what **you** are, restoring to **you** your **identity**. *T-14.VI.57.4*

- this course is not beyond immediate **learning** unless **you** prefer to believe that what **God** wills takes **time**. *T-15.V.35.1*

- the **reason** why this course is simple is that **truth** is simple. *T-15.V.39.4*

- this is a course in how to know yourself. *T-16.IV.24.1*

- the **decision** whether or not to listen to this course and follow it is but the **choice** between **truth** and **illusion**. For **here** is **truth** separated from **illusion** and not confused with it at all. *T-16.VI.57.6:7*

- **here** is the ultimate **release** which **everyone will** one day find in his own **way**, at his own **time**. **We** do not **need** this **time**. **Time** has been saved for **you** because **you** are together. This is the **special means** this course is using to save **you time**. **You** are not making use of the course if **you** insist on using **means** which **have** served others well, neglecting what was made for **you**. *T-18.VIII.68.1:5*

- this course **will** lead to **knowledge**, but **knowledge** itself is still beyond the scope of our **curriculum**. *T-18.XI.95.1*

- **being** so simple and direct, this course has **nothing** in it that is not consistent. The seeming inconsistencies or parts **you** find more **difficult** than others are merely indications of areas where **means** and end are still discrepant. And this produces great discomfort. This **need** not be. This course requires almost **nothing** of **you**. It is **impossible** to imagine one that asks so **little** or could offer more. *T-20.VIII.58.3:8*

- **we have** repeated how **little** is asked of **you** to learn this course. It is the same small willingness **you need** to **have** your whole **relationship** transformed to **joy**; the **little gift you** offer to the **Holy Spirit** for which **He** gives **you** everything; the very **little** on which **salvation** rests; the tiny **change** of **mind** by which the **crucifixion** is changed to **resurrection**. *T-21.III.13.1:2*

- it is so simple that it cannot **fail** to be completely understood. Rejected yes, but not ambiguous. And if **you** choose against it **now**, it **will** not be because it is obscure, but rather that this **little** cost seemed in your **judgment** to be too much to pay for **peace**. *T-21.III.13.3:5*

- this is a course in **cause** and not effect. *T-21.VIII.77.8*

- of all the messages **you have** received and failed to **understand**, this course **alone** is open to your understanding and can be understood. This is your **language**. *T-22.II.10.1:2*

- this course **will** be believed entirely or not at all. For it is wholly true or wholly false and cannot be but partially believed. *T-22.III.22.4:5*

- this course is easy just because it makes no **compromise**. Yet it seems **difficult** to those who still believe that **compromise** is possible. *T-23.IV.44.1:2*

- motivation for this course is the attainment and the keeping of the state of **peace**. *T-24.I.1.1*

- to learn this course requires willingness to **question** every **value** that **you** hold. Not one can be kept hidden and obscure but it **will** jeopardize your **learning**. *T-24.I.2.1:2*

- the principle that **justice means** no one can lose is crucial to this course. *T-25.X.82.6*

- nor is it necessary **we** dwell on anything that cannot be immediately grasped. *T-26.IV.19.2*

- this course **will teach you** only what is **now**. *T-26.VI.39.2:3*

- the **laws** of **healing** must be understood before the **purpose** of the course can be accomplished. *T-26.VIII.47.2*

- this course attempts to **teach** no more than that the **power** of **decision** cannot lie in choosing different forms of what is still the same **illusion** and the same **mistake**. *T-31.IV.40.3*

- a unified **thought system** in which **nothing** is lacking that is needed, and **nothing** is included that is contradictory or irrelevant. *W-pI.42.9.2*

~ when **you fail** to comply with the requirements of this course, **you have** merely made a **mistake**. This calls for **correction** and for **nothing** else. *W-pI.95.10.3:4*

~ a major **learning goal** this course has set is to reverse your view of giving, so **you** can **receive**. *W-pI.105.3.3*

~ there is no **world**! This is the central **thought** the course attempts to **teach**. *W-pI.132.7.1:2*

~ this course does not attempt to take from **you** the **little** that **you have**. It does not try to **substitute** utopian ideas for satisfactions which the **world** contains. *W-pI.133.2.3:4*

~ but **knowledge** is beyond the goals **we seek** to **teach within** the framework of this course. *W-pI.138.5.4*

~ this course removes all doubts which **you have** interposed between Him and your **certainty** of Him. **We** count on **God** and not upon ourselves to **give** us **certainty**. And in His **name we practice** as His **word** directs **we** do. His sureness lies beyond our every **doubt**. His **love** remains beyond our every **fear**. The **thought** of Him is still beyond all dreams and in our minds according to His **Will**. *W-pI.165.7.6:11*

~ how extremely different the goals this course is advocating are from those **you** held before. *W-pI.181.4.2*

~ this course was sent to open up the path of **light** to us, and **teach** us, **step** by **step**, how to return to the eternal **Self we thought we** lost. *W-pI.Rev V.7.4*

~ this course is a beginning, not an end. *W-pII.E.1.1*

~ emphasizes that to **teach** is to learn, so that **teacher** and **learner** are the same. It also emphasizes that **teaching** is a constant process—it goes on every moment of the day and continues into sleeping thoughts as well. *M-I.1.5:6*

~ the **purpose** of the course might be said to provide **you** with a **means** of choosing what **you want** to **teach** on the basis of what **you want** to learn. *M-I.2.5*

~ there is a course for every **teacher of God**. The **form** of the course varies greatly. So do the particular **teaching** aids involved. But the content of the course never changes. Its central theme is always, "God's Son is **guiltless**, and in his **innocence** is his **salvation**." It can be taught by actions or thoughts, in words or soundlessly, in any **language** or in no **language**, in any place or **time** or manner. *M-I.3.1:6*

~ duration is not the major concern. *M-16.4.4*

~ forgive the **world**, and **you will understand** that everything which **God** created cannot **have** an end, and **nothing He** did not create is real. In this one sentence is our course explained. *M-20.5.7:8*

~ our course is not concerned with any **concept** that is not acceptable to anyone, regardless of his formal beliefs. His **ego will** be enough for him to cope with, and it is not **part** of wisdom to add sectarian controversies to his burdens. *M-24.3.4:5*

~ this course aims at a complete reversal of **thought**. *M-24.4.1*

~ the emphasis of this course always remains the same—it is at this moment that complete **salvation** is offered **you**, and it is at this moment that **you** can accept it. *M-24.6.1*

~ in some cases, it may be helpful for the **pupil** to read the manual first. Others might do better to begin with the **workbook**. Still others may **need** to start at the more abstract **level** of the **text**. *M-29.1.5:7*

~ it is the practical with which this course is most concerned. If **you have** made it a habit to **ask** for **help** when and where **you** can, **you** can be confident that wisdom **will** be given **you** when **you need** it. *M-29.5.7:8*

~ levels of **teaching** the universal course is a **concept** as meaningless in **reality** as is **time**. The **illusion** of one permits the **illusion** of the other. *M-3.3.1:2*

CREATION

DICTIONARY: *the action or process of bringing something into existence.*

EGO

~ **you have** chosen, therefore, to create unlike Him, and **you have** made **fear** for yourselves. *T-4.II.16.2*

~ to establish your personal autonomy, **you** tried to create unlike your **Father**, believing what **you** made to be capable of **being** unlike Him. *T-10.VIII.71.6*

~ thus is creation seen as not eternal, and the **Will** of God open to opposition and defeat. *T-19.III.18.5*

~ an attempt to wrest creation away from **truth** and keep it separate. *T-19.III.20.5*

HOLY SPIRIT; *sum of all **God's thoughts**, **Will** of **God**, **truth**, ability to accept **truth**, sharing, **communication**, extension, will, your **gift**, first coming of **Christ**, Holy **Son of God**, divine abstraction.*

~ in the creation, **God** projected His creative ability from Himself to the Souls **He** created, and **He** also imbued them with the same loving **will** to create. *T-2.I.5.2*

~ his **will** to create was given him by his own **Creator**, Who was expressing the same **will** in His creation. Since creative ability rests in the **mind**, everything that **man** creates is necessarily a matter of **will**. *T-2.V.105.3:4*

~ creation and **communication** are synonymous. *T-4.VIII.97.2*

~ divine Abstraction takes **joy** in application, and that is what creation **means**. *T-4.VIII.99.4*

~ real creation gives everything, since it can create only like itself. *T-4.VIII.99.5*

~ **god** created His Sons by extending His **Thought** and retaining the extensions of His **Thought** in His **Mind**. *T-6.III.32.1*

~ creation is without **limit**. *T-6.V.95.11*

~ the creative **power** of both **God** and His **creations** is limitless. *T-7.I.1.1*

~ to create is to **love**. *T-7.I.3.3*

~ to create like Him is to **share** the perfect **love He** shares with **you**. *T-7.II.6.1*

~ every **part** of creation is of one **order**. *T-7.V.34.3*

~ creating is the **opposite** of **loss**. *T-7.X.92.5*

~ what **God** and His Sons create is eternal, and in this and this only is their **joy**. *T-8.VI.43.9*

~ therefore **you** can create as **He** did, and your **dissociation will** not alter this. *T-9.V.34.2*

~ the **Sonship** must create as one, **you remember** creation whenever **you** recognize **part** of creation. *T-9.V.34.4*

~ the law of creation is that **you love** your **creations** as yourself because **they** are **part** of **you**. Everything that was created is therefore perfectly safe, because the **laws** of **God** protect it by His **Love**. *T-9.VIII.64.3:4*

~ creation is perfectly lawful. *T-9.X.88.9*

~ creation shares **power** and never usurps it. *T-9.IX.77.7*

~ if creation is sharing, it cannot create what is unlike itself. It can **share** only what it is. *T-9.XI.97.4:5*

~ creation is your **will** because it is His. *T-10.II.13.10*

~ creation is not of **you**. *T-11.VI.46.5*

~ **suffering** is not of His creation. Having given **you** creation, **He** could not take it from **you**. *T-12.III.22.4:5*

~ creation cannot be interrupted. *T-13.II.3.4*

73

~ creating is **being** in **Heaven.** *T-13.VIII.66.2*

~ creation is the natural **extension** of perfect purity. *T-14.II.7.4*

~ everything **God** created knows its **Creator**. For this is how creation is accomplished by the **Creator** and by His **creations**. In the holy meeting place are joined the **Father** and His **creations**, and the **creations** of His Son with them together. *T-14.IV.36.7:9*

~ the **miracle** of creation has never ceased, having the holy stamp of **immortality** upon it. *T-14.VII.71.7*

~ **nothing God** created is apart from happiness, and **nothing God** created but would extend happiness as its **Creator** did. *T-17.V.27.6*

~ if creation is **extension**, the **Creator** must **have** extended Himself. *T-19.IV.31.2*

~ creation is the **means** for God's **extension**, and what is His must be His Son's as well. *T-23.V.49.5*

~ what **God** creates has no alternative. *T-24.I.2.8*

~ what **God** created cannot be attacked, for there is **nothing** in the **universe** unlike itself. *T-24.II.6.1*

~ the **Father** keeps what **He** created safe. **You** cannot touch it with the false ideas **you** made because it was created not by **you.** *T-24.VIII.66.1:2*

~ what **God** creates is safe from all corruption, unchanged and perfect in **eternity.** *T-25.III.17.8*

~ in joyous **answer will** creation rise **within you** to replace the **world you see** with **Heaven**, wholly perfect and complete. *T-26.VIII.56.2*

~ such is creation's law—that each **idea** the **mind** conceives but adds to its abundance, never takes away. *T-26.VIII.60.3*

~ unweakened **power** with no **opposite** is what creation is. For this there are no symbols. *T-27.IV.32.4:5*

~ the circle of creation has no end. Its starting and its ending are the same. But in itself it holds the **universe** of all creation, without beginning and without an end. *T-28.III.16.6:8*

~ fatherhood is creation. *T-28.III.17.1*

~ creation proves **reality** because it shares the **function** all creation shares. *T-28.VI.52.1*

~ creation gives no separate person and no separate **thing** the **power** to complete the **Son of God**. *T-30.IV.41.9*

~ **nothing** in God's creation is affected in any **way** by this **confusion** of mine. *W-pI.52.2.6*

~ creation is eternal and unalterable. *W-pI.93.7.4*

~ creation knows no **opposite**. *W-pI.138.1.4*

~ for in creation are all minds as one. *W-pI.139.12.2*

~ creation merely waits for your return to be acknowledged, not to be complete. *W-pI.192.2.5*

~ creation cannot even be conceived of in the **world**. It has no **meaning here. Forgiveness** is the closest it can come to earth. For **being Heaven**-borne, it has no **form** at all. Yet **God** created One Who has the **power** to translate into **form** the wholly formless. *W-pI.192.3.1:5*

~ creation is the sum of all **God's thoughts**, in number infinite and everywhere without all **limit**. Only **Love** creates and only like Itself. *W-pII.ST321.1.1:2*

~ creation is the **opposite** of all illusions, for creation is the **truth**. Creation is the holy **Son of God**, for in creation is His **Will** complete in every aspect, making every **part** container of the whole. Its **oneness** is forever guaranteed inviolate, forever held **within** His holy **will** beyond all possibility of **harm**, of **separation**, imperfection, and of any spot upon its sinlessness. *W-pII.ST321.3.1:3*

~ creation leans across the bars of **time** to lift the heavy burden from the **world**. *S-3.IV.9.1*

CREATIONS
|krē ˈāSH(ə)n|

DICTIONARY: *a **thing** that has been made or invented.*

EGO

~ **you** believe that the sick things which **you have** made are your real creations, because **you** believe that the sick images **you** perceive are the Sons of **God**. *T-9.XI.105.6*

~ a **mind within** a **body** and a **world** of other bodies, each with separate minds, are your "creations". *T-28.III.18.6*

HOLY SPIRIT

~ your creations belong in **you**, as **you** belong in **God**. *T-7.I.3.1*

~ god's creations **have** always been, because **He** has always been. Your creations **have** always been, because **you** can create only as **God** creates. *T-7.I.3.7:8*

~ **they** are there as **part** of your own **being**, because your fulfillment includes them. The creations of every **Son of God** are yours since every **creation** belongs to **everyone**, **being** created for the **Sonship** as a whole. *T-7.X.95.5:6*

~ your creations are the logical outcome of His premises. *T-7.X.99.1*

~ your creations are your **gift** to the **Holy Trinity**, created in **gratitude** for your **creation**. **They** do not leave **you**, any more than **you have** left your **Creator**, but **they** extend your **creation** as **God** extended Himself to **you**. *T-8.VI.45.3:4*

~ your creations **love you** as your **Soul** loves your **Father** for the **gift** of **creation**. *T-8.VI.45.7*

~ in your open **mind** are your creations, in perfect **communication** born of perfect understanding. *T-9.V.37.4*

~ **you will** find your creations because **he** created them with **you**. *T-9.V.37.8*

~ your creations add to Him as **you** do, but **nothing** is added that is different, because everything has always been. *T-9.VIII.60.4*

~ your creations establish your fatherhood in **Heaven**. *T-13.II.9.1*

~ god is no **image**, and His creations, as **part** of Him, hold Him in them in **truth**. **They** do not merely reflect **truth**, for **they** are **truth**. *T-14.V.45.6:7*

~ the **will** of your creations calls to **you** to **share** your **will** with them. *T-15.IX.80.8*

~ **they will** take the place of what **you** took in to replace them. **They** are quite real as **part** of the **Self you** do not know. And **they** communicate to **you** through the **Holy Spirit**, and their **power** and **gratitude** to **you** for their **creation they** offer gladly to your **teaching** of yourself, who is their **home**. **You** who are **host** to **God** are also **host** to them. *T-16.IV.25.6:9*

~ your creations are holding out their hands to **help you** cross and **welcome** them. For it is **they you seek**. **You seek** but for your own **completion**, and it is **they** who render **you** complete. *T-16.V.37.1:3*

~ your **relationship** with them is without **guilt**, and this enables **you** to look on all your brothers with **gratitude** because your creations were created in **union** with them. **Acceptance** of your creations is the **acceptance** of the **oneness** of **creation**, without which **you** could never be complete. *T-16.V.37.5:6*

~ the Son's creations are like his Father's. Yet in creating them, the Son does not delude himself that **he** is independent of his **Source**. *T-21.III.27.1:2*

~ my creations, children of my **Will**. *W-pII.253.1.6*

CREATOR

DICTIONARY: *a person or **thing** that brings something into existence.*

EGO

~ if **you** think what **you** made can tell **you** what **you** see and feel and place your **faith** in its ability to do so, **you** are denying your Creator and believing that **you** made yourself. For if **you** think the **world you** made has **power** to **make you** what it wills, **you** are confusing Son and **Father**, effect and **Source**. *T-21.III.26.4:5*

~ **here** is the self-made "**savior**," the "creator" who creates unlike the **Father** and which made His Son like to itself and not like unto Him. *T-24.III.14.4*

HOLY SPIRIT; *benign Creator, perfect creator, Prime Creator, Creator of **life**, Creator of the **universe**, Creator of **reality**, Creator of infinity.*

~ he is the Prime Creator, because He created His co-creators. *T-7.II.7.6*

~ because your Creator creates only like Himself, **you** are like Him. *T-8.III.14.6*

~ your **Father** is your Creator, and **you** are like Him. *T-10.IV.27.7*

~ **nothing** created not by your Creator has any influence over **you**. And if **you** think what **you have** made can tell **you** what **you** see and feel and place your **faith** in its ability to do so, **you** are denying your Creator and believing that **you** made yourself. *T-21.III.26.3:4*

~ a co-creator with the **Father** must **have** a Son. Yet must this Son **have** been created like Himself. A perfect **being**, all-encompassing and all-encompassed, **nothing** to add and **nothing** taken from—not born of size nor weight nor **time** nor held to limits or uncertainties of any kind. **Here** do the **means** and end unite as one, nor does this one **have** any end at all. *T-24.VIII.68.1:4*

~ a creator wholly unlike his **creation** is inconceivable. *W-pI.72.4.6*

~ what **He** creates is not apart from Him, and nowhere does the **Father** end, the Son begin as something separate from Him. *W-pI.132.13.4*

CRUCIFIXION

DICTIONARY: *the execution of a person by nailing or binding them to a cross.*

EGO; *redemption*

~ if the crucifixion is seen from an upside-down point of view, it does appear as if **God** permitted and even encouraged one of his Sons to suffer because **he** was **good**. *T-3.III.11.6*

~ this particularly unfortunate **interpretation**, which arose out of the combined misprojections of a large number of my would-be followers, has led many people to be bitterly afraid of **God**. This particularly anti-religious **concept** enters into many religions, and this is neither by chance nor by coincidence. *T-3.III.12.1:2*

~ terrible misperception that **God** Himself persecuted His own Son on behalf of **salvation**. *T-3.III.13.4*

~ **you** are free to crucify yourself as often as **you** choose. *T-4.I.4.4*

~ if **you** interpret the crucifixion in any other **way**, **you** are using it as a weapon for assault rather than as the **call** for **peace** for which it was intended. *T-6.II.19.1*

~ the crucifixion is the **symbol** of the **ego**. *T-12.II.6.1*

~ **you** are not afraid of crucifixion. Your real terror is of **redemption**. *T-12.III.11.2:3*

- crucifixion is always the ego's aim. It sees as guilty, and by its **condemnation**, it would **kill**. *T-14.II.14.6:7*

- the crucified **give pain** because **they** are in **pain**. *T-19.V.109.3*

- it is indeed but **you** your **mind** can try to crucify. *W-pI.196.12.5*

HOLY SPIRIT; *symbol* *of the* *ego,* *teaching* *device, extreme example.*

- the only **message** of the crucifixion was that **we** can overcome the cross. *T-4.I.4.3*

- it was not a **form** of **punishment**. **Nothing**, however, can be really explained in negative terms only. There is a positive **interpretation** of the crucifixion which is wholly devoid of **fear** and therefore wholly benign in what it teaches if it is properly understood. The crucifixion is **nothing** more than an extreme example. Its **value**, like the **value** of any **teaching** device, lies solely in the kind of **learning** it facilitates. It can be and has been misunderstood. *T-6.II.4.3:8*

- the crucifixion was the last foolish **journey** that the **Sonship need** take and that it should mean **release** from **fear** to anyone who understands it. *T-6.II.5.2*

- the real **meaning** of the crucifixion lies in the apparent intensity of the assault of some of the Sons of **God** upon another. This, of **course**, is **impossible** and must be fully understood as an impossibility. In **fact** unless it is fully understood as only that, **I** cannot serve as a real model for **learning**. *T-6.II.6.4:6*

- my one **lesson**, which I must **teach** as I learned, is that no **perception** which is out of accord with the **judgment** of the Holy Spirit can be justified. I undertook to show this was true in a very extreme case merely because it would serve as a **good teaching** aid to those whose temptations to **give** in to **anger** and assault would not be so extreme. *T-6.II.15.2:3*

- the crucifixion cannot be shared because it is the **symbol** of **projection**. *T-6.II.16.4*

- the **message** of the crucifixion was, "**Teach** only **love**, for that is what **you** are". *T-6.II.17.1*

- just as all **behavior** teaches the beliefs which motivate it. The crucifixion was a complex of behaviors arising out of clearly opposed **thought** systems. As such, it [is] the perfect **symbol** of **conflict** between the **ego** and the **Son of God**. *T-6.II.23.2:4*

- in crucifixion is **redemption** laid, for **healing** is not needed where there is no **pain** or **suffering**. *T-26.VIII.64.1*

CURRICULUM |kəˈrikyələm|

DICTIONARY: *the subjects comprising a **course** of **study** in a school or college.*

EGO

- a meaningful curriculum cannot be inconsistent. If it is planned by two teachers, each believing in diametrically opposed ideas, it cannot be integrated. If it is carried out by these two teachers simultaneously, each one merely interferes with the other. This leads to fluctuation, but not to **change**. *T-8.II.6.2:5*

- whenever the reaction to **learning** is depression, it is only because the **goal** of the curriculum has been lost **sight** of. *T-8.VII.60.6*

- every legitimate teaching aid, every real **instruction**, and every sensible guide to **learning will** be misinterpreted. For **they** are all for **learning** facilitation, which this strange curriculum **goal** is against. *T-11.VI.49.4:5*

- the curriculum **you have** chosen is against **love** and amounts to a **course** in how to **attack** yourself. *T-11.VI.50.1*

- the curriculum that **you** set up is therefore determined exclusively by what **you** think **you** are and what **you** believe the **relationship** of others is to **you**. *M-1.2.1*

~ **everyone** who follows the world's curriculum, and **everyone here** does follow it until **he** changes his **mind**, teaches solely to convince himself that **he** is what **he** is not. Herein is the **purpose** of the **world**. *M-1.4.3*

HOLY SPIRIT

~ the **Holy Spirit** has taken very diversified areas of your **learning** and has applied them to a unified curriculum. *T-7.IV.22.6*

~ the **goal** of the curriculum, regardless of the **teacher you** choose, is know thyself. *T-8.IV.20.1*

~ the Holy Spirit's curriculum is never depressing, because it is a curriculum of **joy**. *T-8.VII.60.5*

~ the curriculum is totally unambiguous because the **goal** is not divided, and the **means** and the end are in complete accord. *T-11.VI.52.3*

~ there is no **conflict** in this curriculum, which has one aim however it is taught. Each **effort** made on its behalf is offered for the single **purpose** of **release** from **guilt** to the eternal **glory** of **God** and His **creation**. *T-14.II.10.3:4*

~ **we** are not inconsistent in the thoughts that **we present** in our curriculum. *W-pI.156.2.1*

~ as the **course** emphasizes, **you** are not free to choose the curriculum or even the **form** in which **you will** learn it. **You** are free, however, to decide when **you want** to learn it. And as **you** accept it, it is already learned. *M-2.3.6:8*

~ **forgiveness** is the final **goal** of the curriculum. It paves the **way** for what goes far beyond all **learning**. The curriculum makes no **effort** to exceed its legitimate **goal**. *M-4.24.9:11*

~ our curriculum trains for the relinquishment of **judgment** as the necessary **condition** of **salvation**. *M-9.2.7*

~ the aim of our curriculum, unlike the **goal** of the world's **learning**, is the recognition that **judgment** in the usual **sense** is **impossible**. *M-10.3.1*

~ there is no program, for the lessons in the curriculum **change** each day. *M-16.1.2*

~ **we need** a many-faceted curriculum, not because of content differences but because symbols must **shift** and **change** to suit the **need**. *M-23.7.6*

~ the curriculum is highly individualized. And all aspects are under the Holy Spirit's particular care and **guidance**. *M-29.2.6:7*

DARKNESS

DICTIONARY: *the partial or total absence of **light**.*

EGO

~ it has **power** only because the **Son of God** gave **power** to it. *T-11.III.15.2*

~ **you** cannot **see** in darkness. Yet in the darkness in the private **world** of **sleep**, **you** see in dreams, although your eyes are closed. And it is **here** that what **you see you** made. But let the darkness go, and all **you** made **you will** no longer **see**, for **sight** of it depends upon denying **vision**. *T-12.V.41.1:4*

~ choose to bring this darkness with **you**, and by holding it in your minds, **see** it as a dark cloud that shrouds your brothers and conceals their **reality** from your **sight**. *T-12.VI.46.5*

~ and by not dispelling darkness, **he** became afraid of darkness and of **light**. *T-13.VIII.70.5*

~ it is only in darkness and in ignorance that **you** perceive the frightening, and **you** shrink away from it to further darkness. And yet it is only the hidden that can terrify, not for what it is, but for its hiddenness. The obscure is frightening because **you** do not **understand** its **meaning**. *T-14.III.16.3:5*

HOLY SPIRIT;   *lack of **light**, own imagining.*

~ by perceiving **light**, darkness automatically disappears. *T-1.1.57.2*

~ whenever **light** enters darkness, the darkness is abolished. *T-2.V.99.4*

~ no darkness abides anywhere in the **Kingdom**, but your **part** is only to allow no darkness to abide in your own **mind**. *T-6.III.38.4*

~ in the darkness **you have** obscured the **glory God** gave **you** and the **power He** bestowed upon His **guiltless** Son. *T-14.IV.32.1*

~ darkness cannot be seen, for it is **nothing** more than a **condition** in which seeing becomes **impossible**. *T-14.VII.61.2*

~ let the darkness be dispelled by Him Who knows the **light** and lays it gently in each **quiet** smile of **faith** and **confidence** with which **you** bless each other. *T-22.VII.59.11*

~ to reach **light** is to escape from darkness. *W-pI.44.6.2*

~ darkness cannot obscure the **glory** of the **Son of God**. *W-pI.94.2.5*

~ and then **step** back to darkness, not because **you** think it real, but only to proclaim its unreality in terms which still **have meaning** in the **world** which darkness rules. *W-pI.184.10.3*

DEATH

DICTIONARY: *the action or **fact** of dying or **being** killed; the end of the **life** of a person or organism.*

EGO;   *the end, lack, **treasure**, victory, triumph.*

~ death wishes do not **kill** in the physical **sense**, but **they** do **kill** spiritual **awareness**. All destructive thinking is dangerous. Given a death **wish**, a **man** has no **choice** except to act upon the **thought** or behave contrary to it. *T-2.V.91.2:4*

~ death is an attempt to resolve **conflict** by not willing at all. Like any other **impossible** solution which the **ego** attempts, it **will** not work. *T-6.V.61.6:7*

~ **remember**, then, that whenever **you** look without and react unfavorably to what **you see**, **you have** judged yourself unworthy and **have** condemned yourself to death. The death penalty is the ego's ultimate **goal**, for it fully believes that **you** are a criminal, as deserving of death as **God** knows **you** are deserving of **life**. The death penalty never leaves the ego's **mind**, for that is what it always reserves for **you** in the end. Wanting to **kill you** as the final expression of its feeling for **you**, it lets **you** live but to await death. It **will** torment **you** while **you** live, but its hatred is not satisfied until **you** die. For your **destruction** is the one end toward which it works, and the only end with which it **will** be satisfied. *T-11.VIII.74.1:6*

~ the **goal** of death, which it craves for **you**, leaves it unsatisfied. No one who follows the ego's teaching is without the **fear** of death. *T-15.II.4.3:4*

~ the **ego** teaches thus: Death is the end as far as hope of **Heaven** goes. Yet because **you** and itself cannot be separated, and because it cannot conceive of its own death, it **will** pursue **you** still because **guilt** is eternal. Such is the ego's version of **immortality**. And it is this the ego's version of **time** supports. *T-15.II.5.2:5*

~ so does the **ego** find the death it seeks, returning it to **you**. *T-19.V.76.6*

~ made by the **ego**, its dark **shadow** falls across all living things because the **ego** is the "**enemy**" of **life**. *T-19.V.77.9*

~ death is the result of the **thought we call** the **ego**. *T-19.V.79.8*

~ the arrogance of **sin**, the **pride** of **guilt**, the sepulcher of **separation**—all are **part** of your unrecognized dedication to death. *T-19.V.81.5*

~ death is seen as safety, the great dark **savior** from the **light** of **truth**, the **answer** to the **Answer**, the silencer of the **Voice** that speaks for **God**. *T-19.V.84.2*

~ the thoughts that seem to **kill** are those which **teach** the thinker that **he** can be killed. And so **he** dies because of what **he** learned. **He** goes from **life** to death, the final proof **he** valued the inconstant more than constancy. *T-21.IX.85.3:5*

~ death demands **life**, but **life** is not maintained at any cost. *T-25.VIII.62.3*

~ in death **alone** are opposites resolved, for ending opposition is to die. And thus **salvation** must be seen as death, for **life** is seen as **conflict**. To resolve the **conflict** is to end your **life** as well. *W-pI.138.7.3:5*

~ death is a **thought** which takes on many forms, often unrecognized. It may appear as sadness, **fear**, anxiety, or **doubt**; as **anger**, faithlessness, and lack of **trust**; concern for bodies, envy, and all forms in which the **wish** to be as **you** are not may come to tempt **you**. All such thoughts are but reflections of the worshiping of death as **savior** and as giver of **release**. *W-pI.163.1.1:3*

~ it **will** never **fail** to take all **life** as hostage to itself. *W-pI.163.3.4*

~ it says but this: "**Here** lies a **witness God** is dead." *W-pI.163.5.3:4*

~ in this **world** there appears to be a state that is life's **opposite**. **You call** it death. *W-pI.167.2.1:2*

~ the **idea** of death takes many forms. It is the one **idea** which underlies all feelings that are not supremely **happy**. It is the alarm to which **you give** response of any kind that is not perfect **joy**. All sorrow, **loss**, anxiety, and **suffering** and **pain**, even a **little** sigh of weariness, a slight discomfort or the merest frown, acknowledge death. And thus deny **you** live. *W-pI.167.2.3:7*

~ death is the **thought** that **you** are separate from your **Creator**. It is the **belief** conditions **change**, emotions alternate because of causes **you** cannot control, **you** did not **make**, and **you** can never **change**. It is the fixed **belief** ideas can leave their **source** and take on qualities the **source** does not contain, becoming different from their own origin, apart from it in kind as well as distance, **time**, and **form**. *W-pI.167.4.1:3*

~ your **judgment** sees but death as the inevitable end of **life**. *M-11.2.5*

~ death is the central **dream** from which all illusions stem. *M-27.1.1*

~ **where** there is death is **peace impossible**. *M-27.2.8*

~ the "**reality**" of death is firmly rooted in the **belief** that God's Son is a **body**. *M-27.5.1*

~ death is cruel in its frightened eyes and takes the **form** of **punishment** for **sin**. *S-3.II.5.1*

HOLY SPIRIT; *form of unconsciousness, **illusion**, central **dream**, symbol of the fear of God, reward, nothing.*

~ there is no death. *T-1.1.65.4*

~ **nothing** is accomplished through death because death is **nothing**. *T-6.V.61.2*

~ death is not your Father's **Will** nor yours, and whatever is true is the **Will** of the **Father**. *T-11.V.41.2*

~ while it could perhaps be argued that death suggests there was **life**, no one would claim that it proves there is **life**. *T-12.IV.25.2*

~ death yields to **life** simply because **destruction** is not true. *T-14.III.19.1*

~ no one can die for anyone, and death does not atone for **sin**. *T-19.V.57.4*

~ no one can die unless **he** chooses death. What seems to be the **fear** of death is really its **attraction**. *T-19.V.77.4:5*

~ the appeal of death is lost forever as love's **attraction** stirs and calls to **you**. *T-19.V.94.5*

~ **god** Himself, who knows that death is not your **will**, must say, "Thy **will** be done" because **you** think it is. *T-24.IV.30.8*

~ there is no death because the living **share** the **function** their **Creator** gave to them. Life's **function** cannot be to die. It must be life's **extension**, that it be as one forever and forever without end. *T-29.VII.41.8:10*

~ decisions are continuous. **You** do not always know when **you** are making them. *T-30.II.2.1:2*

~ **misery** and death do not exist. *W-pI.110.2.1*

~ the dead arise when **you** let thoughts of **life** replace all thoughts **you** ever held of death. *W-pI.132.9.3*

~ **god** made not death. Whatever **form** it takes must therefore be **illusion**. *W-pI.163.8.6:7*

~ there is no death because an **opposite** to **God** does not **exist**. There is no death because the **Father** and the Son are one. *W-pI.167.1.6:7*

~ it is but an **idea**, irrelevant to what is seen as physical. *W-pI.167.3.2*

~ death cannot come from **life**. *W-pI.167.5.1*

~ the **thought** of death is not the **opposite** to thoughts of **life**. *W-pI.167.8.3*

~ what dies was never living in **reality** and did but mock the **truth** about myself. *W-pII.248.1.6*

~ decisions are of the **mind**, not of the **body**. If **sickness** is but a faulty **problem**-solving approach, it is a decision. And if it is a decision, it is the **mind** and not the **body** that makes it. *M-5.4.4:6*

~ **you see** in death escape from what **you** made. But this **you** do not **see**—that **you** made death, and it is but **illusion** of an end. Death cannot be escape, because it is not **life** in which the **problem** lies. **Life** has no **opposite**, for it is God. **Life** and death seem to be opposites, because **you have** decided that death ends **life**. *M-20.5.2:6*

~ **god** says there is no death. *M-11.2.5*

~ death is the **symbol** of the **fear** of God. *M-27.3.1*

~ the grimness of the **symbol** is enough to show it cannot co-**exist** with God. *M-27.3.3*

~ what seems to die has but been misperceived and carried to **illusion**. *M-27.7.3*

~ there is a kind of seeming death that has a different **source**. It does not come because of hurtful thoughts and raging **anger** at the **universe**. It merely signifies the end has come for usefulness of **body** functioning. And so it is discarded as a **choice**, as one lays by a garment **now** outworn. *S-3.II.1.8:11*

~ this is what death should be; a **quiet choice**, made joyfully and with a **sense** of **peace**, because the **body** has been kindly used to **help** the **Son of God** along the **way he** goes to God. **We** thank the **body**, then, for all the **service** it has given us. But **we** are thankful, too, the **need** is done to walk the **world** of limits, and to reach the **Christ** in hidden forms and clearly seen at most in lovely flashes. **Now we** can behold Him without blinders, in the **light** that **we have** learned to look upon again. *S-3.II.2.1:4*

~ **we call** it death, but it is liberty. It does not come in forms that seem to be thrust down in **pain** upon unwilling flesh, but as a gentle **welcome** to **release**. If there has been true **healing**, this can be the **form** in which death comes when it is **time** to **rest** a while from labor gladly done and gladly ended. **Now we** go in **peace** to freer air and gentler climate, where it is not hard to **see** the gifts **we** gave were saved for us. *S-3.II.3.1:4*

~ this gentle passage to a higher **prayer**, a kind **forgiveness** of the ways of earth, can only be received with thankfulness. Yet first true **healing** must **have** come to bless the **mind** with loving pardon for the sins it dreamed about and laid upon the **world**. **Now** are its dreams dispelled in **quiet rest**. **Now** its **forgiveness** comes to heal the **world** and it is ready to depart in **peace**, the **journey** over and the lessons learned. *S-3.II.4.1:4*

~ death is **reward** and not a **punishment**. *S-3.II.5.5*

~ nor **will** death any more be feared because it has been understood. *S-3.III.6.5*

DECEIT |dəˈsēt|

DICTIONARY: *the action or **practice** of deceiving someone by concealing or misrepresenting the **truth**.*

EGO

~ and **being** deceived in yourself, **you** are deceived in your **Father** in Whom no deceit is possible. *T-10.VIII.84.5*

~ **you** can be deceived only in yourself. *T-10.VIII.90.2*

~ the **self**-deceiving must deceive, for **they** must **teach** deception. *M-I.5.2*

HOLY SPIRIT

God *is not deceived in* you*. T-10.VIII.90.2*

~ the **Holy Spirit**, who **will teach you** that, as **part** of God, deceit in **you** is **impossible**. When **you** perceive yourself without deceit, **you will** accept the **real world** in place of the false one **you have** made. And then your **Father will** lean down to **you** and take the last **step** for **you** by raising **you** unto Himself. *T-10.VIII.90.3:5*

DECISION |dəˈsiZHən|

DICTIONARY: *a conclusion or resolution reached after consideration.*

EGO

~ **will** oppose your free decision at every possible moment and in every possible **way**. *T-5.VIII.72.8*

~ the ego's decisions are always wrong, because **they** are based on a complete fallacy which **they** were made to uphold. *T-5.VIII.74.2*

~ whenever **you** decide to **make** decisions for yourself, **you** are thinking destructively, and the decision **will** be wrong. It **will hurt you** because of the **concept** of decision which led to it. It is not true that **you** can **make** decisions by yourself or for yourself **alone**. *T-13.VIII.73.1:3*

~ every decision **you** undertake **alone** but signifies that **you** would define what **salvation** is and what **you** would be saved from. *T-13.VIII.77.3*

~ only your own volition seems to **make** deciding hard. *T-13.IX.92.3*

~ it has been your decision to **make** everything that is natural and easy for **you impossible**. *T-18.V.40.1*

~ decisions which can be made and then unmade and made again. *T-21.VIII.81.4*

~ if **you** feel yourself unwilling to sit by and **ask** to **have** the **answer** given **you**. This **means you have** decided by yourself and cannot **see** the **question**. *T-30.II.10.3:4*

~ and these decisions are made unaware to keep them safely undisturbed, apart from **question** and from **reason** and from **doubt**. *W-pI.138.8.3*

~ decide against Him, and **you** choose **nothing** at the expense of the **awareness** of everything. *M-13.8.3*

HOLY SPIRIT

~ when **you make** a decision of purpose, then, **you have** made a decision about your **future effort**, a decision which **will** remain in effect unless **you change** the decision. *T-4.VI.78.4*

~ wrong decisions **have** no **power**, because **they** are not true. *T-8.IV.23.9*

~ the **power** of decision is all that is yours. What **you** can decide between is fixed because there are no alternatives except **truth** and **illusion**. *T-13.VIII.68.3:4*

~ every decision is made for the whole **Sonship**, directed in and out and influencing a constellation larger than anything **you** ever dreamed of. *T-13.VIII.73.5*

~ his decisions are reflections of what **God** knows about **you**, and in this **light**, **error** of any kind becomes **impossible**. *T-13.VIII.80.2*

~ all **knowledge** lies behind every decision which the **Holy Spirit** makes for **you**. *T-13.VIII.80.3*

~ all decisions become as easy and as right as breathing. *T-13.IX.92.1*

~ the **power** of decision, which **you** made in place of the **power** of **creation, He** would **teach you** how to use on your behalf. *T-14.III.20.6*

~ every decision which **you make** stems from what **you** think **you** are and represents the **value** that **you** put upon yourself. *T-15.IV.24.3*

~ be **happy**, and **you** gave the **power** of decision to Him Who must decide for **God** for **you**. This is the **little gift you** offer to the **Holy Spirit**, and even this **He** gave to **you** to **give** yourself. *T-21.III.17.6:7*

~ a decision is a conclusion based on everything that **you** believe. It is the outcome of **belief** and follows it as surely as does **suffering** follow **guilt** and **freedom** sinlessness. *T-23.I.2.5:6*

~ your decisions come from your beliefs. *T-24.I.2.10*

~ yet **will you** choose in countless situations and through **time** which seems to **have** no end until the **truth** be your decision. *T-24.VII.55.2*

~ the **truth** makes no decisions, for there is **nothing** to decide between. *T-26.IV.18.10*

~ having decided that **you** do not like the **way you** feel, what could be easier than to continue with, And so **I** hope **I have** been wrong. This works against the **sense** of opposition and reminds **you** that **help** is not **being** thrust upon **you** but is something that **you want** and that **you need**, because **you** do not like the **way you** feel. *T-30.II.18.1*

~ **you** cannot **make** decisions by yourself. *T-30.II.29.3*

~ your **judgment** has been lifted from the **world** by your decision for a **happy** day. *T-30.II.32.7*

~ decide for **truth**, and everything is yours. *T-30.IV.38.10*

~ each decision that **you make** is one between a **grievance** and a **miracle**. *W-pI.78.1.1*

~ decisions are the outcome of your **learning**, for **they rest** on what **you have** accepted as the **truth** of what **you** are and what your needs must be. *W-pI.138.5.6*

~ the **power** of decision is our own. *W-pI.152.8.2*

~ decide for **God**, and everything is given **you** at no cost at all. *M-13.8.2*

DEFENSE

|dəˈfensˈdēˌfens|

DICTIONARY: *the action of defending from or resisting **attack.***

EGO; ***attack, secret** magic wand.*

~ the defenses which **man** can choose to use constructively or destructively were not enough to save him. *T-2.II.37.1*

~ a two-**way** defense is inherently weak precisely because it has two edges and can turn against the **self** very unexpectedly. *T-2.II.42.7*

~ when defenses are disrupted, there is a period of real disorientation accompanied by **fear**, **guilt**, and usually vacillations between anxiety and depression. *T-2.II.43.3*

~ it believes that the best defense is **attack** and wants **you** to believe it. *T-6.V.48.3*

~ the whole defense system which the **ego** evolved to protect the **separation** from the **Holy Spirit**. *T-17.V.30.1*

~ only illusions **need** defense because of **weakness**. *T-22.VI.45.8*

~ consider what the **ego** wants defenses for—always to justify what goes against the **truth**, flies in the face of **reason**, and makes no **sense**. *T-22.VI.46.1*

~ an invitation to **insanity** to save **you** from the **truth**. *T-22.VI.46.3*

~ **belief** in **sin** needs great defense and at enormous cost. All that the **Holy Spirit** offers must be defended against and sacrificed. *T-22.VI.46.5:6*

~ it gives illusions full **reality** and then attempts to handle them as real. It adds illusions to illusions, thus making **correction** doubly **difficult**. *W-pI.135.1.2:3*

~ defenses are the plans **you** undertake to **make** against the **truth**. Their aim is to select what **you** approve and disregard what **you** consider incompatible with your beliefs of your **reality**. *W-pI.135.18.1:2*

~ defense is frightening. It stems from **fear**, increasing **fear** as each defense is made. **You** think it offers safety. Yet it speaks of **fear** made real and terror justified. *W-pI.135.4.1:4*

~ the aim of all defenses is to keep the **truth** from **being** whole. The parts are seen as if each one were whole **within** itself. *W-pI.136.2.4:5*

~ defenses are not unintentional nor are **they** made without **awareness**. **They** are **secret magic** wands **you** wave when **truth** appears to threaten what **you** would believe. **They** seem to be unconscious but because of the rapidity with which **you** choose to use them. *W-pI.136.3.1:3*

~ defensiveness is **weakness**. It proclaims **you have** denied the **Christ** and come to **fear** His Father's **anger**. *W-pI.153.7.1:2*

HOLY SPIRIT

~ withdrawal is properly employed in the **service** of withdrawing from the meaningless. It is not a device for escape, but for consolidation. *T-2.II.27.1:2*

~ defenses are not **being** disrupted but reinterpreted, even though **you** may **experience** it as the same **thing**. In the reinterpretation of defenses, only their use for **attack** is lost. Since this **means they** can be used only one **way, they** become much stronger and much more dependable. **They** no longer oppose the **Atonement** but greatly facilitate it. *T-2.II.43.4:7*

~ the best defense, as always, is not to **attack** another's position but rather to protect the **truth**. *T-3.III.13.1*

~ the **Holy Spirit** uses defenses on behalf of **truth** only because **you** made them against it. His **perception** of them, according to His **purpose**, merely changes them into a **call** for what **you have** attacked with them. *T-14.IV.28.10:11*

~ what needs no protection does not defend itself. *T-14.IV.28.7*

~ defense is of your making. **God** knows it not. *T-14.IV.28.8:9*

~ defenses, like everything **you** made, must be gently turned to your own **good**, translated by the **Holy Spirit** from **means** of **self-destruction** to **means** of preservation and **release**. *T-14.IV.29.1*

~ the **truth** itself needs no defense, but **you** do **need** defense against your own **acceptance** of the **gift** of **death**. *T-17.V.36.2*

~ your defense must **now** be undertaken to keep **truth** whole. *T-17.V.36.4*

~ the **power** of **Heaven**, the **love** of **God**, the tears of **Christ**, and the **joy** of His eternal **Spirit** are marshaled to defend **you** from your own **attack**. *T-17.V.36.5*

~ what merely is needs no defense and offers none. *T-22.VI.45.7*

~ **you** are the strong ones in this seeming **conflict**. And **you** need no defense. Everything that needs defense **you** do not **want**, for anything that needs defense **will** weaken **you**. *T-22.VI.45.10:12*

~ **you need** no defense. Everything that needs defense **you** do not **want**, for anything that needs defense **will** weaken **you**. *T-22.VI.45.11:12*

~ your **present trust** in Him is the defense which promises a **future** undisturbed, without a trace of sorrow and with **joy** which constantly increases as this **life** becomes a **holy instant**, set in **time** but heeding only **immortality**. *W-pI.135.20.1*

~ without defenses, **you** become a **light** which **Heaven** gratefully acknowledges to be its own. *W-pI.135.21.1*

~ **we need** no defense because **we** are created unassailable. *W-pI.153.9.1*

~ your defenses **will** not work, but **you** are not in danger. **You have** no **need** of them. Recognize this, and **they will** disappear. *M-16.6.11:13*

DEFENSELESSNESS
|dəˈfensləs|

DICTIONARY: *without **defense** or protection; totally vulnerable.*

HOLY SPIRIT; *strength*

~ our defenselessness is all that is required for the **truth** to dawn upon our minds with **certainty**. *W-pI.135.22.3*

~ defenselessness is all **you** need to **give** Him in return. *W-pI.153.21.5*

~ defenselessness is **strength**. It testifies to recognition of the **Christ** in **you**. Perhaps **you will** recall the **course** maintains that **choice** is always made between His **strength** and your own **weakness** seen apart from Him. Defenselessness can never be attacked because it recognizes **strength** so great **attack** is folly or a silly game a tired **child** might play when **he** becomes too sleepy to **remember** what **he** wants. *W-pI.153.6.1:4*

~ in defenselessness **we** stand secure, serenely certain of our safety **now**, sure of **salvation**; sure **we will** fulfill our chosen **purpose** as our ministry extends its holy **blessing** through the **world**. *W-pI.153.9.3*

~ it is not danger that comes when defenses are laid down. It is safety. It is **peace**. It is **joy**. And it is **God**. *M-4.17.11:15*

DELAY

|də'lā|

DICTIONARY: *make (someone or something) late or slow.*

EGO

~ delay is of the **ego**, because **time** is its **concept**. Delay is obviously a **time idea**. *T-5.VI.36.1:2*

~ it is tragic in **time**. *T-5.VIII.71.3*

~ it is in your **power** in **time** to delay the perfect **union** of the **Father** and the Son. *T-15.X.92.1*

~ delay is senseless, and the "reasoning" which would maintain effects of **present cause** must be delayed until a **future time** is merely a **denial** of the **fact** that consequence and **cause** must come as one. *T-26.IX.76.6*

HOLY SPIRIT

~ the **mind** then realizes with increasing **certainty** that delay is only a **way** of increasing unnecessary **pain**, which it **need** not tolerate at all. *T-2.II.49.7*

~ the **Atonement** can be accepted without delay. *T-2.V.99.9*

~ delay does not matter in **eternity**. *T-5.VIII.71.3*

~ **you** can delay the **completion** of the **Kingdom**, but **you** cannot introduce the **concept** of assault into it. *T-5.VIII.78.5*

~ delay of **joy** is needless. **God** wills **you** perfect happiness **now**. *T-9.VI.38.7:8*

~ **you** can delay this **now** but only a **little** while. *T-16.III.16.10*

~ delay **will hurt you now** more than before only because **you** realize it is delay and that escape from **pain** is really possible. *T-16.VII.65.6*

DELUSION

|də'looZHən|

DICTIONARY: *an idiosyncratic **belief** or impression that is firmly maintained despite **being** contradicted by what is generally accepted as **reality** or rational argument, typically a **symptom** of mental disorder.*

EGO

~ **dissociation** is not a solution; it is a delusion. The delusional believe that **truth will** assail them, and so **they** do not **see** it, because **they** prefer the delusion. Judging **truth** as something **they** do not **want**, **they** perceive deception and block **knowledge**. *T-8.V.35.7:9*

~ the delusional believe that **truth will** assail them, and so **they** do not **see** it, because **they** prefer the delusion. *T-8.V.35.8*

~ **they** do not **rest** on their own foundation. In concealment **they** appear to do so, and thus **they** seem to be **self**-sustained. This is the fundamental **illusion** on which **they rest**. For beneath them and concealed as long as **they** are hidden is the loving **mind** that **thought** it made them in **anger**. *T-12.III.16.1:4*

~ to oppose the pull or the **Will** of **God** is not an ability but a real delusion. The **ego** believes that it has this ability and can offer it to **you** as a **gift**. **You** do not **want** it. It is not a **gift**. It is **nothing** at all. *T-7.V.37.1:5*

87

~ the delusional can be very destructive, for **they** do not recognize that **they have** condemned themselves. **They** do not **wish** to die, yet **they will** not let **condemnation** go. And so **they** separate into their private worlds, where everything is disordered and where what is **within** appears to be without. Yet what is **within they** do not **see**, for the **reality** of their brothers **they** cannot **see**. *T-12.V.36.1:4*

~ if **he** is **guiltless** and in **peace** and sees it not, **he** is delusional and has not looked upon himself. *T-13.IV.30.8*

~ **healing pain** is not accomplished by delusional attempts to enter into it and lighten it by sharing the delusion. *T-16.I.1.6*

~ the core of the **separation** delusion lies simply in the **fantasy** of **destruction** of love's **meaning**. *T-16.VI.57.1*

~ what could be more unstable than a tightly-organized delusional system? Its seeming stability is its pervasive **weakness**, which extends to everything. The variability which the **little** remnant induces merely indicates its limited results. *T-19.V.47.4:6*

DENIAL |dəˈnīəl|

DICTIONARY: *the action of declaring something to be untrue.*

EGO; *defense*

~ denial is not a purely negative device; it results in positive **miscreation**. *T-2.II.22.3*

~ what **you** deny **you** lack, not because it is lacking, but because **you have** denied it in another and are therefore not aware of it in **you**. *T-7.VIII.72.6*

~ delusional attempt of the **mind** to deny itself and escape the penalty of denial. It is not an attempt to relinquish denial but to hold on to it. *T-11.X.85.5:6*

~ to deny is the **decision** not to know. *T-13.VI.49.5*

~ if **you have** and **give** and are everything, and all this has been denied, your **thought system** is closed off and wholly separated from the **truth**. *T-13.VI.50.2*

~ anything **you** deny which **He** knows to be true, **you have** denied yourself. *T-13.VI.52.2*

~ when **you** deny his right to everything, **you have** denied your own. **You** therefore **will** not recognize the things **you** really **have**, denying **they** are there. *W-pI.133.8.2:3*

~ deny **we** were created in His **Love**, and **we** deny our **Self**, to be unsure of who **we** are, of who our **Father** is, and for what **purpose we have** come. *W-pII.276.1.6*

HOLY SPIRIT; *powerful protective device*

~ this is the proper use of denial. It is not used to **hide** anything but to correct **error**. It brings all **error** into the **light**, and since **error** and **darkness** are the same, it corrects **error** automatically. True denial is a powerful protective device. **You** can and should deny any **belief** that **error** can **hurt you**. This kind of denial is not a concealment device but a **correction** device. The "right **mind**" of the mentally healthy depends on it. *T-2.II.19.1:7*

~ denial of **error** is a powerful **defense** of **truth**. *T-2.II.22.1*

~ in the **service** of the "right **mind**," the denial of **error** frees the **mind** and reestablishes the **freedom** of the **will**. *T-2.II.22.6*

~ my use of **projection**, which can also be yours, is not based on faulty denial. It does involve, however, the very powerful use of the denial of errors. *T-2.II.23.4:5*

~ flight from **error** is perfectly appropriate. *T-2.II.30.2*

~ it has no **power** in itself, but **you** can **give** it the **power** of your **mind**, whose **power** is without **limit** of any kind. If **you** use it to deny **reality**, **reality** is gone for **you**. *T-7.VIII.70.7:8*

~ yet denial is a **defense**, and so it is as capable of **being** used positively as it is of **being** used destructively. Used negatively it **will** be destructive because it **will** be used for **attack**, but in the **service** of the **Holy Spirit**, [the law becomes as beneficent as all of the **laws** of **God**. Stated positively,] the law requires **you** to recognize only **part** of **reality** to appreciate all of it. *T-7.VIII.71.2:4*

~ **remember** that what **you** deny, **you** must **have** known. And if **you** accept denial, **you** can accept its undoing. *T-9.XI.98.5:6*

~ denial is as total as love. **You** cannot deny **part** of yourself because the remainder **will** seem to be unintegrated and therefore without **meaning**. *T-10.III.18.1:2*

~ to deny **meaning** must be to **fail** to **understand**. *T-10.III.18.4*

~ the out of **mind** is out of **sight** because what is denied is there but is not recognized. *T-12.VII.63.6*

~ it is **impossible** to deny the **Source** of effects so powerful **they** could not be of **you**. *T-14.VII.75.4*

~ it is denial of illusions that calls on **truth**, for to deny illusions is to recognize that **fear** is meaningless. *T-22.II.14.6*

~ your denial made no **change** in what **you** are. *W-pI.139.5.2*

~ what has not been denied is surely there if it be true, and can be surely reached. *W-pI.189.9.5*

DEPENDENCE |dəˈpendəns|

DICTIONARY: *the state of relying on or **being** controlled by someone or something else.*

EGO

~ the **ego** sees all dependency as threatening and has twisted even your longing for **God** into a **means** of establishing itself. *T-10.VI.45.8*

HOLY SPIRIT

~ unless **you** fully recognize your complete dependence on **God**, **you** cannot know the real **power** of the Son in his true **relationship** with the **Father**. *T-11.88.6*

~ yours is the independence of **creation**, not of autonomy. Your whole creative **function** lies in your complete dependence on **God**. *T-10.VI.45.1:2*

~ **god** is as dependent on **you** as **you** are on Him because His autonomy encompasses yours and is therefore incomplete without it. *T-10.VI.51.1*

DEPRIVATION |ˌdeprəˈvāSH(ə)n|

DICTIONARY: *the lack or **denial** of something considered to be a necessity.*

EGO

~ **projection**, to the **Holy Spirit**, is the law of **extension**. To the **ego**, it is the law of deprivation. It therefore produces abundance or scarcity, depending on how **you** choose to apply it. *T-7.IX.83.1:3*

~ if your brothers are **part** of **you** and **you** blame them for your deprivation, **you** are blaming yourself. *T-10.V.35.1*

~ **you have** believed that to **ask** for **guidance** of the **Holy Spirit** is to **ask** for deprivation. T-10.VIII.82.2

~ deprivation breeds **attack, being** the **belief** that **attack** is justified. T-15.XI.105.6

~ **you** think He would deprive **you** for your **good**. But "**good**" and "deprivation" are opposites and cannot meaningfully **join** in any **way**. T-21.IV.39.3-4

~ **sacrifice** and deprivation are paths which lead nowhere, choices for defeat, and aims which **will** remain **impossible**. W-pI.155.7.2

HOLY SPIRIT

~ no one is deprived or can deprive. T-28.IV.36.4

~ **i** cannot suffer any **loss** or deprivation or **pain** because of who **I** am. W-pI.58.6.4

~ deprivation cannot cut him off from God's sustaining **love** and from his **home**. W-pI.165.6.6

DESIRE |də'zī(ə)r|

DICTIONARY: *a strong feeling of wanting to have something or wishing for something to happen.*

EGO

~ any desire which stems from the **ego** is a desire for **nothing** and to **ask** for it is not a **request**. It is merely a **denial** in the **form** of a **request**. T-8.X.100.2-3

HOLY SPIRIT;   *request, asking for.*

~ **nothing** is **difficult** that is wholly desired. To desire wholly is to create, and creating cannot be **difficult** if **God** Himself created **you** as a **creator**. T-6.V.80.3-4

~ if to desire wholly is to create, **you will have** willed away the **separation**, returning your **mind** simultaneously to your **Creator** and your **creations**. T-9.VIII.67.1

~ for **you** desire the only **thing you** ever had or ever were. T-18.IV.27.15

~ in your desire lies its accomplishment. T-18.IV.28.2

~ no **little**, faltering footsteps that **you** may take can separate your desire from His **Will** and from His **strength**. T-18.IV.28.4

~ **vision** adapts to **wish**, for **sight** is always secondary to desire. T-20.VIII.62.6

~ **faith** and desire go hand in hand, for **everyone** believes in what **he** wants. T-21.III.23.6

~ desire what **you will**, and **you will** look on it and think it real. T-21.IX.84.6

~ what **you** desire **you** receive. T-21.IX.88.2

~ desire is a **request**, an asking for, and made by one whom **God** Himself **will** never **fail** to **answer**. T-21.IX.88.6

~ what happens is what **I** desire. W-p2.253.1.3

DESPAIR

DICTIONARY: *the complete **loss** or absence of hope.*

EGO; *bleak despair, icy hopelssness.*

~ through this despair **you** travel **now**, yet it is but **illusion** of despair. *T-24.III.25.3*

~ despite your hopes and fancies, always does despair result. *T-25.III.12.5*

~ men despair because the savior's **vision** is withheld, and what **they see** is **death**. *T-31.VII.82.2*

~ concern may take the **form** of depression, worry, **anger**, a **sense** of imposition, **fear**, foreboding, or preoccupation. *W-pI.26.6.2*

~ the unforgiving **mind** is in despair, without the prospect of a **future** which can offer anything but more despair. Yet it regards its **judgment** of the **world** as irreversible and does not **see** it has condemned itself to this despair. *W-pI.121.5.1:2*

~ watch despair snatch from your fingers every scrap of hope, leaving **you nothing** but the **wish** to die. *W-pI.191.3.4*

~ **i** sought for many things and found despair. *W-p2.251.1.1*

HOLY SPIRIT

~ **grandiosity** is always a cover for despair. *T-9.VII.49.1*

~ if **you** are willing to look upon your **grandeur**, **you** cannot despair, and therefore **you** cannot **want** the **ego**. *T-9.VII.53.2*

~ the unreal **world** is a **thing** of despair, for it can never be. *T-11.IX.83.3*

~ his **grace** His **answer** is to all despair. *W-pI.168.2.2*

~ **separation** is no more than an **illusion** of despair. *W-p2.270.2.1*

DESTRUCTION

DICTIONARY: *the action or process of causing so much damage to something that it no longer exists or cannot be repaired.*

EGO; *final proof*

~ your destruction is the one end toward which it works, and the only end with which it **will** be satisfied. *T-11.VIII.74.6*

~ the **ego** teaches that your **function** on earth is destruction and **function** at all in **Heaven**. It would thus destroy **you here** and bury **you here**. *T-12.IV.23.4:5*

~ **you** believe that **attack** is your **reality** and that your destruction is the final proof that **you** were right. *T-12.IV.24.5*

~ if **you** interpret your **function** as destruction, **you will** lose **sight** of the **present** and hold on to the **past** to ensure a destructive **future**. *T-12.IV.32.5*

~ all the waste that **time** seems to bring with it is due but to your identification with the **ego**, which uses **time** to support its **belief** in destruction. *T-15.I.2.4*

~ **atonement** is not welcomed by those who prefer **pain** and destruction. *T-18.VIII.63.6*

~ **salvation** can only mean destruction of the **world**. *T-24.V.34.7*

Holy Spirit

~ it does not confuse destruction with **innocence** because it associates **innocence** with **strength**, not with **weakness**. *T-3.IV.23.8*

~ if destruction itself is **impossible**, then anything that is destructible cannot be real. *T-6.II.7.3*

~ **god** did not **will** the destruction of His **creations**, having created them for **eternity**. *T-8.VI.43.3*

~ destruction is no more real than the **image**. *T-9.IX.74.7*

~ **death** yields to **life** simply because destruction is not true. *T-14.III.19.1*

~ without your **alliance** in your own destruction, the **ego** could not hold **you** to the **past**. *T-16.VIII.72.6*

~ a loving **father** does not let his **child harm** himself or choose his own destruction. *M-29.6.8*

DEVIL |ˈdevəl|

DICTIONARY: *the chief **evil spirit**; Satan.*

Ego

~ the "devil" is a frightening **concept**, because **he** is **thought** of as extremely powerful and extremely active. **He** is perceived as a force in combat with **God**, battling Him for **possession** of the Souls **He** created. **He** deceives by lies and builds kingdoms of his own in which everything is in direct opposition to **God**. Yet **he** attracts men rather than repels them, and **they** are seen as willing to "sell" him their Souls in return for gifts **they** recognize are of no real **worth**. *T-3.IX.73.4:7*

~ the **mind** can **make** the **belief** in **separation** very real and very fearful, and this **belief** is the "devil." It is powerful, active, destructive, and clearly in opposition to **God** because it literally denies His Fatherhood. Never underestimate the **power** of this **denial**. Look at your lives and **see** what the devil has made. But know that this making **will** surely dissolve in the **light** of **truth**, because its foundation is a lie. *T-3.IX.78.1:5*

~ **you have** made a devil of God's Son. *W-pI.101.5.3*

~ "**Psychic**" **abilities have** been used to **call** upon the devil, which merely **means** to strengthen the **ego**. *M-25.6.5*

Holy Spirit

~ **you will see** him suddenly transformed from **enemy** to **savior**, from the devil into **Christ**. *W-pI.161.16.3*

DEVOTION |dəˈvōSH(ə)n|

DICTIONARY: *love, loyalty, or enthusiasm for a person, activity, or **cause**.*

Holy Spirit

~ it is only my devotion that entitles me to yours. *T-1.I.78.6*

~ my devotion to my brothers has placed me in charge of the **Sonship**. *T-1.I.80.2*

~ devotion to a **brother** cannot set **you** back either. It can lead only to mutual progress. *T-4.I.1.3:4*

~ the result of genuine devotion is **inspiration**. *T-4.I.1.5*

~ **god** in His devotion to **you** created **you** devoted to everything and gave **you** what **you** are devoted to. *T-8.X.104.1*

~ do not underestimate the **power** of the devotion of God's Son nor the **power** of the **God** he worships over him. *T-10.VII.63.1*

~ **fear** looks on **guilt** with just the same devotion that **love** looks on itself. *T-19.V.49.8*

~ **god** in His devotion to **you** created **you** devoted to everything and gave **you** what **you** are devoted to. *T-8.X.104.1*

DIFFERENCE

|ˈdif(ə)rəns|

DICTIONARY: *the state or **condition** of **being** dissimilar or unlike.*

EGO

~ difference of any kind imposes orders of **reality** and a **need** to judge that cannot be escaped. *T-24.II.5.6*

~ what is different calls for **judgment**, and this must come from someone "better," someone incapable of **being** like what **he** condemns, "above" it, **sinless** by comparison with it. *T-24.II.6.2*

~ the **special** ones feel weak and frail because of differences, for what would **make** them **special** is their **enemy**. *T-24.II.6.5*

~ never can there be **peace** among the different. *T-24.II.11.7*

~ all **separation**, all distinctions, and the multitude of differences **you** believe **make** up the **world**. **They** are not there. Love's **enemy** has made them up. Yet **love** can **have** no **enemy**, and so **they have** no **cause**, no **being**, and no consequence. **They** can be valued but remain unreal. **They** can be sought, but **they** cannot be found. *W-pI.130.4.2:7*

HOLY SPIRIT

~ there is a point at which sufficient quantitative changes produce real qualitative differences. *T-5.III.15.3*

~ he opposes differences in **form** as meaningful, emphasizing always that these differences do not matter. *T-7.III.16.3*

~ their similarity rather than their differences is emphasized. **You** can excel in many different ways, but **you** can equalize in one **way** only. *T-7.IV.23.6:7*

~ **healing** is the **way** to **undo** the **belief** in differences, **being** the only **way** of perceiving the **Sonship** without this **belief**. *T-7.V.36.5*

~ **contrast** and differences are necessary teaching aids, for by them **you** learn what to avoid and what to **seek**. When **you have** learned this, **you will** find the **answer** that makes the **need** for any differences disappear. *T-13.V.40.3:4*

~ tiny differences in **form** are no real differences at all. None of them matters. *T-18.II.7.8:9*

~ he sees no difference between these selves, for differences are only of the **body**. *T-22.I.3.4*

~ **here** is the **faith** in differences shifted to **sameness**. [And **here** is **sight** of differences transformed to **vision**.]. *T-22.I.4.3*

~ comparison must be an **ego** device, for love makes none. *T-24.III.12.1*

~ because it does not **make** the same unlike, it sees no differences where none **exist**. And thus it is the same for **everyone**, because it sees no differences in them. *T-25.X.87.4:5*

~ all differences among the Sons of **God** are temporary. *M-4.2.1*

DIFFICULT

|ˈdifəkəlt|

DICTIONARY: *needing much effort or skill to accomplish, deal with, or **understand**.*

EGO

~ simplicity is very difficult for twisted minds. *T-13.VII.56.3*

~ it is hard indeed to wander off, **alone** and miserable, down a road which leads to **nothing** and which has no **purpose**. *T-26.VI.31.6*

HOLY SPIRIT

~ **nothing** is difficult that is wholly desired. *T-6.V.80.3*

DISASTER

|dəˈzastər|

DICTIONARY: *a sudden event, such as an accident or a natural catastrophe, that causes great damage or **loss** of life.*

EGO

~ **you** are deceived if **you** believe **you want** disaster and disunity and **pain**. *T-31.I.11.3*

HOLY SPIRIT

~ disaster is not real and that **reality** is not disaster. *T-16.III.18.5*

~ there is no **reason** for an **interval** in which disaster strikes, to be perceived as "**good**" some day but now in **form** of **pain**. *T-29.IX.74.9*

~ **forgiveness** is the only road that leads out of disaster. *W-pI.198.4.1*

DISSOCIATION

|diˌsōSHēˈāSH(ə)n|

DICTIONARY: *the disconnection or **separation** of something from something else or the state of **being** disconnected.*

EGO

~ detachment is essentially a weaker **form** of dissociation. *T-2.II.29.1*

~ the ratio of **repression** and dissociation varies with the individual ego-illusion, but dissociation is always involved or **you** would not believe that **you** are **here**. *T-4.VII.85.3*

~ the **separation** was and is dissociation. *T-6.III.25.4*

~ **fear** produces dissociation, because it induces **separation**. *T-7.VI.45.9*

~ unless **you** know something, **you** cannot dissociate it. **Knowledge** therefore precedes dissociation, and dissociation is **nothing** more than a **decision** to forget. What has been forgotten then appears to be fearful, but only because the dissociation was an **attack** on **truth**. **You** are fearful because **you have** forgotten. *T-9.IX.68.1:4*

~ **you** are afraid of your dissociation, not of what **you have** dissociated. *T-9.IX.68.5*

~ when **you** think **you** are projecting what **you** do not **want**, it is still because **you** do **want** it. This leads directly to dissociation, for it represents the **acceptance** of two goals, each perceived in a different place, separated from each other because **you** made them different. The **mind** then sees a divided **world outside** itself but not **within**. *T-11.VIII.68.1:3*

~ dissociation is a distorted process of thinking whereby two systems of **belief** which cannot coexist are both maintained. *T-14.IV.27.3*

~ using dissociation for holding its contradictory aims together so that **they** seem to be reconciled. *T-15.II.5.1*

HOLY SPIRIT; *decision to forget, delusion.*

~ **you** should split off or dissociate yourself from **error** but only in **defense** of integration. *T-2.II.28.2*

~ his is the **glory** before which dissociation falls away and the **Kingdom** of **Heaven** breaks through into its own. *T-5.IV.21.3*

~ your **brother** may **have** dissociated the **Call** for **God**, just as **you** have. The dissociation is healed in both of **you** as **you** become aware of the **Call** for **God** in him and thus acknowledge its **being**. *T-5.V.34.1:2*

~ dissociation is not a solution; it is a **delusion**. *T-8.V.35.7*

~ **you** can create as He did, and your dissociation **will** not alter this. *T-9.V.34.2*

~ even in this world's therapy, when dissociated material is accepted, it ceases to be fearful, for the **laws** of **mind** always hold. *T-9.IX.68.6*

~ to **give** up the dissociation of **reality** brings more than merely lack of **fear**. In this **decision** lie **joy** and **peace** and the **glory** of **creation**. *T-9.IX.69.1:2*

DOING

DICTIONARY: *the activities in which a particular person engages.*

EGO

~ the **ego** never knows what it is doing. *T-7.VII.56.3*

~ **you** believe that doing the **opposite** of **God's Will** can be better for you. **You** also believe that it is possible to do the **opposite** of **God's Will**. *T-7.XI.102.3:4*

HOLY SPIRIT

~ what **you** do comes from what **you** think. *T-2.IV.74.1*

~ only your **mind** can produce **fear**. It does so whenever it is conflicted in what it wills, thus producing inevitable strain because willing and doing become discordant. This cannot be corrected by better doing, but it can be corrected by higher willing. *T-2.IV.81.3:5*

~ knowing, as **we have** frequently observed, does not lead to doing at all. *T-3.VII.52.5*

~ there can be nothing which prevents you from doing exactly what I ask. *T-8.IX.88.2*

~ undoing is indirect, as doing is. **You** were created only to create, neither to **see** nor do. *T-13.VI.52.3:4*

~ "**i need** do **nothing**" is a statement of allegiance, a truly undivided loyalty. Believe it for just one instant, and **you will** accomplish more than is given to a century of contemplation or of struggle against temptation. *T-18.VIII.68.7:8*

~ to **do** anything involves the **body**. *T-18.VIII.69.1*

~ this is the **way** in which **sin** loses all **attraction** right **now**. For **here** is **time** denied and **past** and **future** gone. Who **need** do **nothing** has no **need** for **time**. To do **nothing** is to **rest** and **make** a place **within you** where the activity of the **body** ceases to demand attention. *T-18.VIII.69.4:7*

~ no one undertakes to do what **he** believes is meaningless. *T-19.V.110.2*

~ if **you** are **offering** only **healing, you** cannot **doubt**. If **you** really **want** the **problem** solved, **you** cannot **doubt**. If **you** are certain what the **problem** is, **you** cannot **doubt**. **Doubt** is the result of conflicting wishes. Be sure of what **you want**, and **doubt** becomes **impossible**. *M-7.6.5:9*

DOUBT |dout|

DICTIONARY: *a feeling of uncertainty or lack of conviction.*

EGO

~ that **question**, "What are you?" was the beginning of doubt. *T-6.V.46.7*

~ a real **sense** of **being** cannot be yours while **you** are doubtful of what **you** are. *T-6.V.93.3*

~ there must be doubt before there can be **conflict**. And every **doubt** must be about yourself. *T-24.VI.48.1:2*

~ the unforgiving **mind** is torn with doubt. *W-pI.121.3.1*

~ there is no doubt that is not rooted **here**. *W-pI.139.1.4*

~ to doubt a **healing** because of the **appearance** of continuing symptoms is a **mistake** in the **form** of lack of **trust**. *M-7.4.1*

~ doubt and **trust** cannot coexist. *M-7.4.6*

~ the real basis for doubt about the outcome of any **problem** that has been given to God's **Teacher** for resolution is always **self**-doubt. And that necessarily implies that **trust** has been placed in an illusory **self**, for only such a **self** can be doubted. This **illusion** can take many forms. Perhaps there is a **fear** of **weakness** and **vulnerability**. Perhaps there is a **fear** of failure and shame associated with a **sense** of inadequacy. Perhaps there is a guilty embarrassment stemming from false **humility**. *M-7.5.1:6*

HOLY SPIRIT

~ knowing what **you** are, **I** cannot doubt you. *T-8.XI.113.3*

~ **you** whose minds are darkened by doubt and **guilt, remember** this: **God** gave the **Holy Spirit** to **you** and gave Him the **mission** to remove all doubt and every trace of **guilt** that His dear Son has laid upon himself. It is **impossible** that this **mission fail**. *T-13.V.39.1:2*

~ **you will** doubt until **you** hear one **witness** whom **you have** wholly released through the **Holy Spirit**. *T-15.III.20.1*

~ there must be doubt before there can be **conflict**. And every **doubt** must be about yourself. **Christ** has no doubt, and from His **certainty** His **quiet** comes. He **will** exchange His **certainty** for all your doubts. *T-24.VI.48.1:4*

~ **christ** cannot doubt Himself. *W-pI.151.8.2*

~ your doubts are meaningless, for **God** is certain. *W-pI.165.7.3*

~ his sureness lies beyond our every doubt. *W-pI.165.7.9*

~ there is no challenge to a **teacher of God**. Challenge implies doubt, and the **trust** on which God's teachers **rest** secure makes doubt **impossible**. *M-4.12.5:6*

~ if **you** are **offering** only **healing, you** cannot doubt. If **you** really **want** the **problem** solved, **you** cannot doubt. If **you** are certain what the **problem** is, **you** cannot doubt. Doubt is the result of conflicting wishes. Be sure of what **you want**, and doubt becomes **impossible**. *M-7.6.5:9*

DREAM |drēm|

DICTIONARY: *a series of thoughts, images, and sensations occurring in a person's **mind** during **sleep**.*

EGO;   *illusions of joining, senseless isolated scripts, perceptual temper tantrums, solitary dream.*

~ what **you see** in dreams **you** think is real as long as **you** are asleep. *T-9.VIII.65.5*

~ in his dreams **he** has betrayed himself, his brothers, and his **God**. *T-17.I.1.4*

~ dreams are chaotic because **they** are governed by your conflicting wishes, and therefore **they have** no concern with what is true. *T-18.III.15.1*

~ **they** are a **way** of looking at the **world** and changing it to suit the **ego** better. **They** provide striking examples both of the ego's inability to tolerate **reality** and your willingness to **change reality** on its behalf. *T-18.III.15.4:5*

~ in dreams **you** arrange everything. People become what **you** would **have** them be, and what **they** do **you order**. No **limit** on substitution is laid upon **you**. *T-18.III.16.4:6*

~ dreams are perceptual temper tantrums in which **you** literally scream, "**I want** it thus!" *T-18.III.17.1*

~ the dream cannot escape its origin. **Anger** and **fear** pervade it, and in an instant, the **illusion** of satisfaction is invaded by the **illusion** of terror. *T-18.III.17.2:3*

~ dreams show **you** that **you have** the **power** to **make** a **world** as **you** would **have** it be, and that because **you want** it, **you see** it. *T-18.III.18.1*

~ your sleeping and your waking dreams **have** different forms, and that is all. Their content is the same. **They** are your protest against **reality** and your fixed and insane **idea** that **you** can **change** it. In your waking dreams, the **special relationship** [has a **special** place. It is the **means** by which **you** try to **make** your sleeping dreams come true. From this **you** do not **awaken**. The **special relationship**] is your determination to keep your hold on unreality and to prevent yourself from waking. *T-18.III.19.4:10*

~ **you** would **have** used them to remain asleep. *T-18.III.20.2*

~ **you have** gone from waking to sleeping and on and on to a yet deeper **sleep**. Each dream has led to other dreams, and every **fantasy** which seemed to bring a **light** into the **darkness** but made the **darkness** deeper. *T-18.IV.24.2:3*

~ in dreams, effect and **cause** are interchanged, for **here** the maker of the dream believes that what **he** made is happening to him. *T-24.VI.41.2*

~ the one who makes them does not **see** himself as making them, and their **reality** does not depend on him. Whatever **cause they have** is something quite apart from him, and what **he** sees is separate from his **mind**. **He** cannot **doubt** his dreams' **reality** because **he** does not **see** the **part** he plays in making them and making them seem real. *T-27.VIII.68.5:7*

~ no one can waken from a dream the **world** is dreaming for him. **He** becomes a **part** of someone else's dream. **He** cannot choose to waken from a dream **he** did not **make**. Helpless **he** stands, a **victim** to a dream conceived and cherished by a separate **mind**. *T-27.VIII.69.1:4*

~ **you** are the dreamer of the **world** of dreams. No other **cause** it has, nor ever **will**. **Nothing** more fearful than an idle dream has terrified God's Son and made him think that **he** has lost his **innocence**, denied his **Father**, and made **war** upon himself. So fearful is the dream, so seeming real. *T-27.VIII.73.1:4*

~ the "hero" of this dream **will** never **change** nor **will** its **purpose**. Though the dream itself takes many forms and seems to show a great variety of places and events wherein its "hero" finds itself, the dream has but one **purpose**, taught in many ways. *T-27.IX.79.2:3*

~ thus are **you** not the dreamer but the dream. And so **you** wander idly in and out of places and events which it contrives. *T-27.IX.80.1:2*

~ the **part you see** is but the second **part**, whose **cause** lies in the first. No one asleep and dreaming in the **world** remembers his **attack** upon himself. No one believes there really was a **time** when **he** knew **nothing** of a **body** and could never **have** conceived this **world** as real. *T-27.IX.81.3:5*

~ **nothing** at all has happened but that **you have** put yourself to **sleep** and dreamed a dream in which **you** were an alien to yourself and but a **part** of someone else's dream. *T-28.III.18.8*

~ the dreamer of a dream is not awake but does not know **he** sleeps. **He** sees illusions of himself as sick or well, depressed or **happy**, but without a stable **cause** with guaranteed effects. *T-28.III.21.5:6*

~ while it lasts, **will** wakening be feared. *T-28.III.24.4*

~ to **join** his dreams is thus to meet him not because his dreams would separate from **you**. *T-28.V.40.2*

~ the dreams **you** think **you** like would hold **you** back as much as those in which the **fear** is seen. For every dream is but a dream of **fear**, no matter what the **form** it seems to take. The **fear** is seen **within**, without, or both. Or it can be disguised in pleasant **form**. But never is it absent from the dream, for **fear** is the material of dreams from which **they** all are made. Their **form** can **change**, but **they** cannot be made of something else. *T-29.V.26.1:6*

~ dreams are not wanted more or less. **They** are desired or not. And each one represents some **function** which **you have** assigned, some **goal** which an event, or **body**, or a **thing** should represent and should achieve for **you**. If it succeeds, **you** think **you** like the dream. If it should **fail, you** think the dream is **sad**. But whether it succeeds or fails is not its core but just the flimsy covering. *T-29.V.28.6:11*

~ **you** look for safety and security while in your heart **you** pray for danger and protection for the **little** dream **you** made. *W-pI.131.3.2*

~ in dreams no two can **share** the same intent. To each the hero of the dream is different—the outcome wanted not the same for both. Loser and gainer merely **shift** about in changing patterns, as the ratio of **gain** to **loss** and **loss** to **gain** takes on a different aspect or another **form**. *W-pI.185.3.3:5*

~ yet **compromise alone** a dream can bring. Sometimes it takes the **form** of **union**, but only the **form**. The **meaning** must escape the dream, for compromising is the **goal** of dreaming. Minds cannot unite in dreams. **They** merely **bargain**. *W-pI.185.4.1:5*

~ their only **difference** is one of **form**, for one **will** bring the same **despair** and **misery** as do the **rest**. *W-pI.185.5.6*

~ and in these dreams, the **mind** is separate, different from other minds, with different interests of its own and able to gratify its needs at the expense of others. *M-8.2.8*

~ new dreams **will** lose their temporary appeal and turn to dreams of **fear**, which is the content of all dreams. *P-3.II.6.6*

HOLY SPIRIT;   *heralds of the dawn of **truth** upon the **mind, illusion** in the **mind**.*

~ the **Holy Spirit** makes no distinction among dreams. **He** merely shines them away. His **light** is always the **call** to awake, whatever **you have** been dreaming. *T-6.V.60.4:6*

~ the **Holy Spirit**, too, has use for **sleep** and can use dreams on behalf of waking if **you will** let Him. *T-8.IX.82.8*

~ **you will** first dream of **peace** and then **awaken** to it. Your first exchange of what **you** made for what **you** want is the exchange of nightmares for the **happy** dreams of **love**. In these lie your true perceptions, for the **Holy Spirit** corrects the **world** of dreams, where all **perception** is. *T-12.VII.67.1:3*

~ the dreams of **love** lead unto **knowledge**. In them **you see nothing** fearful, and because of this, **they** are the **welcome** that **you** offer **knowledge**. *T-12.VII.67.5:6*

~ what is done in dreams has not been really done. *T-17.I.1.5*

~ dreams are what **they** are because of their **illusion** of **reality**. Only in waking is the full **release** from them, for only then does it become perfectly apparent that **they** had no effect on **reality** at all and did not **change** it. *T-17.I.1.6:7*

~ the **Holy Spirit**, ever practical in His wisdom, accepts your dreams and uses them as **means** for waking. *T-18.III.20.1*

~ the dream of waking is easily transferred to its **reality**. *T-18.III.23.6*

~ it is no dream to **love** your **brother** as yourself. *T-18.VI.45.1*

~ a gentler dream preceded his awaking and allowed his calmer **mind** to **welcome**, not to **fear**, the **Voice** that calls with **love** to waken him. [A gentler dream, in which his **suffering** was healed and where his **brother** was his friend.] **God** willed **he** waken gently and with **joy**. And gave him **means** to waken without **fear**. *T-27. VIII.73.4:7*

~ it is not **difficult** to [**shift**] a dream when once the dreamer has been recognized. *T-27.VIII.73.9*

~ **he** brings forgiving dreams in which the **choice** is not who is the murderer and who shall be the **victim**. In the dreams **He** brings, there is no murder and there is no **death**. The dream of **guilt** is fading from your **sight**. *T-27.VIII.74.2:4*

~ dream softly of your **sinless brother**, who unites with **you** in holy **innocence**. And from this dream, the Lord of **Heaven will** Himself **awaken** His beloved Son. Dream of your brother's kindnesses instead of dwelling in your dreams on his mistakes. Select his thoughtfulness to dream about instead of counting up the hurts **he** gave. Forgive him his illusions and **give** thanks to him for all the helpfulness **he** gave. And do not brush aside his many gifts because **he** is not perfect in your dreams. *T-27.VIII.75.1:6*

~ the instant that **he** sees them as **they** are, **they have** no more effects on him because **he** understands **he** gave them their effects by causing them and making them seem real. *T-27.IX.80.5*

~ for **you** would not react at all to figures in a dream **you** knew that **you** were dreaming. Let them be as hateful and as vicious as **they** may, **they** could **have** no effect on **you** unless **you** failed to recognize it is your dream. *T-27.IX.86.5:6*

~ a dream is like a **memory** in that it pictures what **you** wanted shown to **you**. *T-28.III.19.4*

~ yet if **you** are the dreamer, **you** perceive this much at least—that **you have** caused the dream and can accept another dream as well. But for this **change** in content of the dream, it must be realized that it is **you** who dreamed the dreaming that **you** do not like. It is but an effect which **you have** caused, and **you** would not be **cause** of this effect. *T-28.III.19.6:8*

~ in forgiving dreams is no one asked to be the **victim** and the sufferer. *T-28.III.20.2*

~ the **miracle** establishes **you** dream a dream and that its content is not true. *T-28.III.22.1*

~ in His forgiving dreams are the effects of yours undone and hated enemies perceived as friends with merciful intent. Their enmity is seen as causeless **now**, because **they** did not **make** it. And **you** can accept the **role** of maker of their **hate**, because **you see** that it has no effects. *T-28.III.25.3:5*

~ without support, the dream **will** fade away without effects. For it is your support that strengthens it. *T-28.IV.28.7:8*

~ the end of dreaming is the end of **fear**, and **love** was never in the **world** of dreams. *T-28.IV.31.1*

~ the dream of **healing** in **forgiveness** lies and gently shows **you** that **you** never sinned. *T-28.IV.35.4*

~ how **happy** would your dreams become if **you** were not the one who gave the "proper" **role** to every figure which the dream contains. *T-29.V.29.1*

~ the core of dreams the **Holy Spirit** gives is never one of **fear**. The coverings may not appear to **change**, but what **they** mean has changed because **they** cover something else. *T-29.V.29.3:4*

~ dreams of sadness thus are turned to **joy**. *T-29.V.29.7*

~ who can utilize all dreams as **means** to serve the **function** given Him. Because **He** loves the dreamer not the dream, each dream becomes an **offering** of **love**. For at its center is His **love** for **you**, which lights whatever **form** it takes with **love**. *T-29.V.30.5:7*

~ a dream is given **you** in which **he** is your **savior**, not your **enemy** in hate. A dream is given **you** in which **you** **have** forgiven him for all his dreams of **death**—a dream of hope **you share** with him instead of dreaming **evil** separate dreams of **hate**. *T-29.VI.36.1:2*

~ when dreams are shared, **they** lose the **function** of **attack** and **separation**, even though it was for this that every dream was made. Yet **nothing** in the **world** of dreams remains without the hope of **change** and betterment, for **here** is not where changelessness is found. *T-29.VI.37.2:3*

~ forgiving dreams are **means** to **step** aside from dreaming of a **world outside** yourself. And leading finally beyond all dreams unto the **peace** of everlasting **life**. *T-29.VI.37.5:6*

~ forgiving dreams **have little need** to last. They are not made to separate the **mind** from what it thinks. They do not **seek** to prove the dream is **being** dreamed by someone else. *T-29.X.68.1:3*

~ forgiving dreams remind **you** that **you** live in safety and **have** not attacked yourself. *T-29.X.70.1*

~ dreams become a sign that **you have** made a new beginning, not another try to worship idols and to keep **attack**. Forgiving dreams are kind to **everyone** who figures in the dream. And so **they** bring the dreamer full **release** from dreams of **fear**. *T-29.X.70.2:4*

~ god's Son needs no **defense** against his dreams. *T-30.V.53.12*

~ dreams are for **nothing**. And the **Son of God** can **have** no **need** of them. They offer him no single **thing** that **he** could ever **want**. *T-30.V.56.9:11*

~ no more fearful dreams **will** come **now** that **you rest** in God. *W-pI.109.6.5*

~ he has been gently wakened from his dream by understanding what **he thought he** saw was never there. *W-pI.134.11.3*

~ the **happy** dreams the **Holy Spirit** brings are different from the dreaming of the **world**, where one can merely dream **he** is awake. The dreams **forgiveness** lets the **mind** perceive do not induce another **form** of **sleep**, so that the dreamer dreams another dream. His **happy** dreams are heralds of the dawn of **truth** upon the **mind**. They lead from **sleep** to gentle waking, so that dreams are gone. And thus **they** cure for all **eternity**. *W-pI.140.3.1:5*

~ dreams are not a worthy guide for **you** who are God's Son. *W-pI.155.13.3*

~ dreams of any kind are strange and alien to the **truth**. *W-pI.198.8.5*

~ but **we** can dream **we have** forgiven him in whom all **sin** remains **impossible**, and it is this **we** choose to dream **today**. *W-pII.256.1.8*

~ the end of dreams is promised me because God's Son is not abandoned by His **Love**. *W-pII.279.1.1*

~ in **reality** his dreams are gone, with **truth** established in their place. And **now** is **freedom** his already. *W-pII.279.1.3:4*

~ **here we share** our final dream. It is a dream in which there is no sorrow, for it holds a hint of all the **glory** given us by **God**. *W-pII.ST231.4.2:3*

~ the dream of **salvation** has new content. It is not the **form alone** in which the difference lies. *M-18.1.8:9*

~ in that strange dream a strange **correction** must enter, for only that is the **call** to awake. *P-3.II.4.8*

~ it is no harder to wake a **brother** from one dream than from another. *P-3.II.7.3*

~ dream **now** of **healing**. Then arise and lay all dreaming down forever. *S-3.IV.6.3:4*

DREAM FIGURES *A Course in Miracles Term*

EGO

~ figures in the **dream** and what **they** do that seem to **make** the **dream**. *T-18.III.18.5*

~ figures stand out and move about, actions seem real, and forms appear and **shift** from loveliness to the grotesque. And back and forth **they** go, as long as **you** would play the game of children's **make**-believe. *T-18.X.9.3:4*

~ all figures in the **dream** are idols made to save **you** from the **dream**. Yet **they** are **part** of what **they have** been made to save **you** from. *T-29.X.6.3:1:2*

EASTER

|ˈēstər|

DICTIONARY: *the most important and oldest festival of the Christian* **Church**, *celebrating the* **resurrection** *of* **Jesus Christ** *and held (in the Western* **Church**) *between March 21 and April 25, on the first Sunday after the first full moon following the northern spring equinox.*

HOLY SPIRIT; *the sign of* **peace**, **time** *of your* **salvation**.

~ it is almost Easter, the **time** of **resurrection**. *T-19.V.106.4*

~ easter is the sign of **peace**, not **pain**. *T-20.I.1.3*

~ easter is not the celebration of the cost of **sin** but of its end. *T-20.II.4.1:2*

~ the **time** of Easter is a **time** of **joy** and not of mourning. *T-20.II.4.6*

~ easter is the **time** of your **salvation**, along with mine. *T-20.II.4.8*

~ the **song** of Easter is the glad refrain the **Son of God** was never crucified. *T-20.III.12.6*

EFFORT

|ˈefərt|

DICTIONARY: *a vigorous or determined attempt.*

HOLY SPIRIT; *will*

~ **learning** is effort, and effort **means will**. *T-7.IV.21.4*

~ **you** made the effort to learn, and the **Holy Spirit** has a unified **goal** for all effort. *T-7.IV.23.1*

~ it is indeed true that no effort is wasted. *T-8.XI.109.8*

~ the only effort **you need make** to **give** this **world** away in glad exchange for what **you** did not **make** is willingness to learn the one **you** made is false. *T-12.VII.62.4*

~ there is no effort, and **you will** be led as gently as if **you** were **being** carried along a **quiet** path in summer. *T-13.IX.92.2*

~ his **little** efforts are powerfully supplemented by the **strength** of **Heaven** and by the united **will** of all who **make Heaven** what it is, **being** joined **within** it. *T-16.IV.28.4*

~ your efforts, however **little they** may be, **have** strong support. *W-pI.91.4.3*

~ **he will** offer all His **strength** to every **little** effort which **you make**. *W-pI.97.4.3*

EGO

|ˈēgō|

DICTIONARY: *a person's* **sense** *of* **self-esteem** *or* **self**-*importance.*

EGO; *arbiter of* **vengeance**, *punisher of* **sin**.

~ egocentricity and **communion** cannot coexist. *T-2.II.50.5*

~ the ego is a **contradiction**. *T-4.II.8.4*

~ the ego tries to exploit all situations into forms of **praise** for itself in **order** to overcome its doubts. It **will** be doubtful forever, or rather as long as **you** believe in it. *T-4.II.15.1:2*

~ the ego literally lives by comparisons. This **means** that equality is beyond its grasp and **charity** becomes **impossible**. The ego never gives out of abundance, because it was made as a **substitute** for it. *T-4.III.32.1:3*

~ the ego is the **belief** of the **mind** that it is completely on its own. *T-4.III.33.4*

~ without your own allegiance, protection, and **love**, it cannot **exist**. *T-4.V.64.7*

~ the ego compromises with the issue of the eternal, just as it does with all issues that touch on the real **question** in any **way**. By compromising in connection with all tangential questions, it hopes to **hide** the real **question** and keep it out of **mind**. The ego's characteristic busyness with non-essentials is for precisely that **purpose**. *T-4.VI.75.3:5*

~ ego depends on the specific. It is the **part** that believes your existence **means you** are separate. *T-4.VIII.94.5:6*

~ the ego becomes strong in strife. *T-5.V.39.8*

~ the ego is the **symbol** of **separation**. *T-5.V.41.1*

~ what the ego makes, it keeps to itself, and so it is without **strength**. Its unshared existence does not die; it was merely never born. *T-5.VI.47.4:5*

~ the ego is the **part** of the **mind** which believes in division. *T-5.VII.61.1*

~ the ego is quite literally a fearful **thought**. *T-5.VII.61.7*

~ it represents a delusional system, and it speaks for it. Listening to the ego's **voice means** that **you** believe it is possible to **attack God**. *T-5.VII.62.2:3*

~ the ego does not know and is not concerned with **being** at all. *T-6.IV.39.7*

~ the ego always speaks first because it is capricious and does not mean its maker well. *T-6.V.45.2*

~ promotes different moods. *T-6.V.83.3*

~ it is competitive rather than loving. *T-7.II.4.1*

~ the ego is discontinuous. *T-7.IV.24.2*

~ the ego perceives itself as at **war** and therefore in **need** of allies. *T-7.V.27.5*

~ it does not **understand** what it makes; it does not appreciate it; and it does not **love** it. It incorporates to take away. It literally believes that every **time** it deprives someone of something, it has increased. *T-7.VI.50.2:4*

~ the ego never knows what it is **doing**. It is perfectly logical but clearly insane. *T-7.VII.56.3:4*

~ the ego does not believe in totality. *T-7.VII.57.5*

~ the ego therefore opposes all **appreciation**, all recognition, all sane **perception**, and all **knowledge**. *T-7.VII.59.1*

~ the ego therefore wants to engage your **mind** in its own delusional system, because otherwise the **light** of your understanding would dispel it. *T-7.VII.62.6*

~ utilizes the **power** of the **mind** only to defeat the mind's real **purpose**. It projects **conflict** from your **mind** to other minds in an attempt to persuade **you** that **you have** gotten rid of it. *T-7.IX.44.4:5*

~ the ego is therefore a **confusion** in identification which never had a consistent model and never developed consistently. It is the distorted product of the misapplication of the **laws** of **God** by distorted minds which are misusing their own **power**. *T-7.IX.87.5:6*

~ the ego is expert only in **confusion**. It does not **understand** anything else. As a **teacher**, then, it is totally confused and totally confusing. *T-8.III.8.6:8*

~ it is incapable of true generalizations and equates what it sees with the **function** it ascribes to it. It does not equate it with what it is. *T-8.VIII.69.3:4*

~ the ego is forced to **shift** from one end to another without ceasing, so that **you will** continue to hope that it can yet offer **you** something. *T-8.VIII.71.7*

~ its sole aim is to lose **sight** of the **function** of everything. *T-8.VIII.75.4*

~ the ego is incapable of knowing how **you** feel. *T-8.VIII.77.5*

~ ego is always wrong, no matter what it says or does. *T-9.I.2.7*

~ it is totally unpredictable in its responses, because it has no **idea** of what it perceives. *T-9.III.15.8*

~ the ego is also in your **mind**, because **you have** accepted it there. Its evaluation of **you**, however, is the exact **opposite** of the Holy Spirit's, because the ego does not **love you**. It is unaware of what **you** are and wholly mistrustful of everything it perceives, because its own perceptions are so shifting. The ego is therefore capable of suspiciousness at best and viciousness at worst. That is its range. It cannot exceed it because of its uncertainty. And it can never go beyond it, because it can never be certain. *T-9.VI.40.4:10*

~ the ego is deceived by everything **you** do, even when **you** respond to the **Holy Spirit**, because at such times its **confusion** increases. *T-9.VI.41.4*

~ ego is, therefore, particularly likely to **attack you** when **you** react lovingly, because it has evaluated **you** as unloving, and **you** are going against its **judgment**. *T-9.VI.41.5*

~ the ego **will** begin to **attack** your motives as soon as **they** become clearly out of accord with its **perception** of **you**. This is when it **will shift** abruptly from suspiciousness to viciousness, since its uncertainty is increased. *T-9.VI.42.1:2*

~ a **sense** of inadequacy it has produced and must maintain for its existence. *T-9.VI.42.7*

~ it remains suspicious as long as **you despair** of yourself. It shifts to viciousness whenever **you will** not tolerate **self**-abasement and **seek** relief. Then it offers **you** the **illusion** of **attack** as a solution. *T-9.VII.49.8:10*

~ the ego depends solely on your willingness to tolerate it. *T-9.VII.53.1*

~ the ego never looks upon what it does with perfect honesty. *T-10.I.2.6*

~ the ego can and does allow **you** to regard yourself as supercilious, unbelieving, "**light**-hearted," distant, emotionally shallow, callous, uninvolved, and even desperate, but not really afraid. Minimizing **fear** but not its undoing is the ego's constant **effort** and is indeed the skill at which it is very ingenious. *T-10.VI.48.1:2*

~ the ego analyzes;. *T-10.VI.53.1*

~ believes that **power**, understanding, and **truth** lie in **separation**, and to establish this **belief** it must **attack**. Unaware that the **belief** cannot be established and obsessed with the conviction that **separation** is **salvation**, the ego attacks everything it perceives by breaking it up into small and disconnected parts without meaningful relationships and thus without **meaning**. The ego **will** always **substitute chaos** for **meaning**, for if **separation** is **salvation**, harmony is **threat**. *T-10.VI.53.4:6*

~ the ego is **part** of your **mind**. *T-11.V.37.4*

~ the ego does **want** to **kill you**. *T-12.II.5.6*

~ the ego is the **choice** for **guilt**. *T-13.VIII.68.2*

~ listen to what the ego says and **see** what it directs **you** see, and it is sure that **you will see** yourself as tiny, vulnerable, and afraid. **You will experience** depression, a **sense** of worthlessness, and feelings of impermanence and unreality. **You will** believe that **you** are helpless prey to forces far beyond your own control and far more powerful than **you**. And **you will** think the **world you** made directs your destiny. For this **will** be your **faith**. *T-21.VI.50.3:7*

~ **being** itself an **illusion** and **offering** only the **illusion** of gifts. *W-pI.66.10.4*

~ the ego is the only alternative to the Holy Spirit's **Voice**. *W-pI.66.12.3*

~ ego's basic doctrine, "**Seek** but do not find." *W-pI.71.5.2:3*

~ the ego makes illusions. *W-pII.332.1.1*

105

~ the ego is idolatry—the sign of limited and separated **self**, born in a **body**, doomed to suffer and to end its **life** in **death**. It is the **will** that sees the **Will** of **God** as **enemy** and takes a **form** in which It is denied. The ego is the "proof" that **strength** is weak and **love** is fearful, **life** is really **death**, and what opposes **God alone** is true. *W-pII.ST331.1.1:3*

HOLY SPIRIT; *symbol of separation, split mind, contradiction, denial of free will, expert in confusion, ally of time, "enemy" of life, idolatry, God, fearful thought, your belief, form of arrest, self-appointed mediator of all relationships, part of your mind, legion, choice for guilt, mechanism of decision, questioning compartment, chaos illusion, salvation, idea, lie, nothing.*

~ the ego speaks in **judgment** and the **Holy Spirit** reverses its decisions. *T-5.VIII.74.1*

~ through the ego **you** can hear and **teach** and learn what is not true. *T-6.IV.40.5*

~ the ego makes no **sense**, and the **Holy Spirit** does not attempt to **understand** anything that arises from it. *T-9.I.3.3*

~ by steadily and consistently canceling out all its effects everywhere and in all respects, **He** teaches that the ego does not **exist** and proves it. *T-9.III.14.4*

~ all that the ego is, is an **idea** that it is possible that things should happen to the **Son of God** without his **will** and thus without the **Will** of his **Creator**, Whose **Will** cannot be separate from his own. *T-21.III.20.4*

~ all its effects are gone because its **source** has been uncovered. *T-21.III.28.4*

~ and **now** the ego is afraid. Yet what it hears in terror, the other **part** hears as the sweetest music—the **song** it longed to hear since first the ego came into your minds. The ego's **weakness** is its **strength**. The **song** of **freedom**, which sings the praises of another **world**, brings to it hope of **peace**. *T-21.V.47.1:4*

EMOTION

|əˈmōSH(ə)n|

DICTIONARY: *a natural instinctive state of mind deriving from one's circumstances, mood, or relationships with others.*

EGO

~ **you have** but two emotions, yet in your private **world you** react to each of them as though it were the other. *T-12.V.37.1*

~ your behavioral manifestations of emotions are the **opposite** of what the emotions are. *T-12.V.38.2*

HOLY SPIRIT

~ **fear** and love are the only emotions of which **you** are capable. *T-11.III.11.4*

~ **you have** but two emotions, and one **you** made and one was given **you**. Each is a **way** of seeing, and different worlds arise from their different visions. *T-12.V.43.1:2*

~ the degree of the emotion **you experience** does not matter. **You will** become increasingly aware that a slight twinge of annoyance is **nothing** but a **veil** drawn over intense fury. *W-pI.21.2.4:5*

EMPATHY

|ˈempəTHē|

DICTIONARY: *the ability to **understand** and **share** the feelings of another.*

EGO

~ is always used to **form** a **special relationship** in which the **suffering** is shared. *T-16.I.1.2*

~ empathy as the **ego** uses it is destructive lies in the **fact** that it is applied only to certain types of problems and in certain people. These it selects out and joins with. *T-16.I.2.1:2*

~ all **you have** learned of empathy is from the **past**. *T-16.I.3.4*

~ do not use empathy to **make** the **past** real and so perpetuate it. *T-16.I.3.6*

~ the **ego** always empathizes to weaken. *T-16.I.2.5*

HOLY SPIRIT

~ to empathize does not mean to **join** in **suffering**. *T-16.I.1.1*

~ empathize with **strength** and both of **you will gain** in **strength**, and not in **weakness**. *T-16.I.2.7*

~ true empathy is of Him Who knows what it is. *T-16.II.5.1*

ENCOUNTER

|enˈkoun(t)ər|

DICTIONARY: *an unexpected or casual meeting with someone or something.*

EGO

~ the **ego** teaches that **you** always encounter your **past**, and because your dreams were not holy, the **future** cannot be, and the **present** is without **meaning.** *T-12.IV.29.4*

HOLY SPIRIT

~ **you** meet anyone, **remember** it is a **holy encounter**. *T-8.IV.19.1*

~ the **Holy Spirit** teaches that **you** always meet yourself and the encounter is holy because **you** are. *T-12.IV.29.3*

~ this **life** becomes a meaningful encounter with the **truth.** *W-pI.135.20.2*

~ these are not chance encounters. Each of them has the potential for becoming a **teaching-learning situation.** *M-3.2.3:4*

~ even at the **level** of the most casual encounter, it is possible for two people to lose **sight** of separate interests, if only for a moment. *M-3.2.6*

ENEMY

|ˈenəmē|

DICTIONARY: *a person who is actively opposed or hostile to someone or something.*

EGO; *you, Christ, wholeness.*

~ how treacherous does this enemy appear, who changes so it is **impossible** even to recognize him! *T-21.VIII.73.7*

~ there can be no **faith** in **sin** without an enemy. *T-21.VIII.74.2*

~ your "enemy"—a frightened mouse that would **attack** the **universe.** *T-22.VI.48.3*

~ **belief** in enemies is therefore the **belief** in **weakness**, and what is weak is not the **Will** of **God**. **Being** opposed to it, it is its "enemy." And **God** is feared as an opposing **will**. *T-23.I.1.6:8*

~ **you will** believe that everything **you** use for **sin** can **hurt you** and become your enemy. And **you will** fight against it and try to weaken it because of this; and **you will** think that **you** succeeded and **attack** again. *T-23.I.2.2:3*

~ certain it is it has no enemy. Yet just as certain is its fixed **belief** it has an enemy that it must overcome and **will** succeed. *T-23.II.7.8:9*

~ enemies do not **give** willingly to one another, nor would **they** seek to **share** the things **they value**. And what your enemies would keep from **you** must be **worth** having, just because **they** keep it hidden from your **sight**. *T-23.III.27.6:7*

~ no one unites with enemies nor is at one with them in **purpose**. And no one compromises with an enemy but hates him still for what **he** kept from him. *T-23.IV.45.5:6*

~ only the **special** could **have** enemies, for **they** are different and not the same. *T-24.II.5.5*

~ **you have** no enemy except yourself. *T-26.XI.8.7.6*

~ your enemy, the one **you** chose to **hate** instead of **love**. *T-30.III.35.1*

~ **i make** all things my "enemies" so that my **anger** is justified and my attacks are warranted. *W-pI.51.6.3*

~ it seemed to be an enemy **outside you** had to **fear**. And thus a **God outside** yourself became your mortal enemy—the **source** of **fear**. *W-pI.196.10.4:5*

~ to the guilty there seems indeed to be a real advantage in having enemies. *S-1.III.3.9*

~ enemies do not **share** a **goal**. It is in this their enmity is kept. Their separate wishes are their arsenals; their fortresses in **hate**. *S-1.IV.1.4:6*

HOLY SPIRIT

~ **god** would not **have** His Son embattled, and so His Son's imagined "enemy," which **he** made, is totally unreal. *T-13.IV.36.1*

~ christ's enemy is nowhere. **He** can take no **form** in which **he** ever **will** be real. *T-29.IX.55.8:9*

~ **he** has no enemy in **truth**. *T-31.II.13.6*

~ this enemy has come to bless **you**. *S-1.III.5.4*

~ there is no **fear** in one who has been truly healed, for **love** has entered **now** where idols used to stand, and **fear** has given **way** at last to **God**. *S-3.III.6.6*

~ pray truly for your enemies, for herein lies your own **salvation**. Forgive them for your sins, and **you will** be forgiven indeed. *S-1.III.6.7:8*

ENLIGHTENMENT |en ' līt nmənt|

DICTIONARY: *the action or state of attaining or having attained spiritual* **knowledge** *or insight, in particular (in Buddhism) that* **awareness** *which frees a person from the cycle of* **rebirth**.

HOLY SPIRIT; *illumination, understanding, a recognition.*

~ only the **mind** is capable of illumination. The **Soul** is already illuminated, and the **body** in itself is too dense. The **mind**, however, can bring its illumination to the **body** by recognizing that density is the **opposite** of intelligence and therefore nameable to independent **learning**. *T-2.III.66.3:5*

~ enlightenment stands under **perception**, because **you have** denied it as the real foundation of **thought**. *T-5.IX.85.8*

~ if **you want** understanding and enlightenment, **you will** learn it, because your **will** to learn it is your **decision** to listen to the **Teacher** who knows of **light** and can therefore **teach** it to you. *T-8.IV.16.4*

~ if **they ask** for enlightenment and accept it, their fears vanish. *T-11.III.17.2*

~ enlightenment is but a recognition, not a **change** at all. *W-pI.188.1.4*

ERROR

|'erər|

DICTIONARY: *the state or **condition** of **being** wrong in conduct or **judgment**.*

EGO; *sin*

~ **denial** of error results in **projection**. *T-1.II.104.5*

~ to concentrate on error is merely a further misuse of defenses. *T-2.V.99.7*

~ to the **ego**, it is kind and right and **good** to point out errors and "correct" them. This makes perfect **sense** to the **ego**, which is totally unaware of what errors are and what **correction** is. *T-9.I.15:6*

~ his errors do not come from the **truth** that is in him, and only this **truth** is yours. His errors cannot **change** this and can **have** no effect at all on the **truth** in **you**. To perceive errors in anyone and to react to them as if **they** were real is to **make** them real to **you**. *T-9.II.6.5:7*

~ accept his errors as real, and **you have** attacked yourself. *T-9.II.7.2*

~ the **ego** focuses on error and overlooks **truth**. It makes real every **mistake** it perceives, and with characteristically circular reasoning concludes that, because of the **mistake**, consistent **truth** must be meaningless. The next **step**, then, is obvious. If consistent **truth** is meaningless, inconsistency must be true if **truth** has **meaning**. Holding error clearly in **mind** and protecting what it has made real, the **ego** proceeds to the next **step** in its **thought system**—that error is real, and **truth** is error. *T-10.VI.54.2:6*

~ original error, which seemed to cast **you** out of **Heaven**, to shatter **knowledge** into meaningless bits of disunited perceptions, and to force **you** to further substitutions. *T-18.II.5.6*

~ uncorrected error of any kind deceives **you** about the **power** that is in **you** to **make correction**. If it can correct and **you** allow it not to do so, **you** deny it to yourself and to your **brother**. *T-21.VII.59.6:8*

~ only the **form** of error attracts the **ego**. *T-22.IV.32.1*

~ **here** lies buried the heavy anchor that seems to keep the **fear of God** in place, unmovable and solid as a rock. *T-22.VII.60.7*

~ every error is a **perception** in which one at least is seen unfairly. *T-25.X.80.6*

~ an error that is more than a **mistake**—a **special form** of error which remains unchangeable, eternal, and beyond **correction** or escape. *T-30.VII.74.6*

~ what are errors but illusions that remain unrecognized for what **they** are. *W-pI.107.1.2*

~ this is one of the errors which the **ego** fosters; that it is capable of true **change**, and therefore of true creativity. *P-2.I.3.2*

~ the **belief** that **anger** brings him something **he** really wants, and that by justifying **attack he** is protecting himself. *P-2.IN.1.5*

~ it would be an error, however, to assume that **you** know what to offer **everyone** who comes. This is not up to **you** to decide. *P-3.II.5:6*

HOLY SPIRIT; *the love of guilt and death, lack of love, fear of God and of salvation.*

~ the **fear of God** and of **salvation**. *T-31.VII.76.1*

~ the **love** of **guilt** and **death**. *T-31.VII.76.1*

~ error is lack of **love**. *T-1.I.53.4*

~ **correction** of error brings **release**. *T-1.II.104.6*

~ the **Holy Spirit** cannot distinguish among degrees of error. *T-8.IX.84.3*

~ the **Holy Spirit** does not perceive his errors. *T-9.I.3.1*

~ what has no effect does not **exist**, and to the **Holy Spirit**, the effects of error are totally non-existent. *T-9.III.14.3*

~ bringing the **ego** to **God** is but to bring error to **truth**, where it stands corrected because it is the **opposite** of what it meets and is undone, because the **contradiction** can no longer stand. *T-14.V.39.1*

~ the error does not matter. *T-17.VIII.66.4*

~ **call** it not **sin** but **madness**, for such it was, and so it still remains. Invest it not with **guilt**, for **guilt** implies it was accomplished in **reality**. And above all, be not afraid of it. When **you** seem to **see** some twisted **form** of the original error rise to frighten **you**, say only, "God is not **fear**, but **love**," and it **will** disappear. *T-18.II.6.7:10*

~ error must be corrected at its **source**. *T-18.X.84.2*

~ **you** freely choose to overlook his errors, looking **past** all barriers between your **self** and his and seeing them as one. *T-19.II.10.5*

~ error can be corrected, and the wrong made right. *T-19.III.17.2*

~ an error, on the other hand, is not attractive. What **you see** clearly as a **mistake you want** corrected. *T-19.IV.26.8:9*

~ errors **He will** correct, but this makes no one fearful. *T-21.V.41.2*

~ errors of any kind can be corrected because **they** are untrue. When brought to **truth** instead of to each other, **they** merely disappear. *T-23.III.21.4:5*

~ corrected error is the error's end. And thus has **God** protected still His Son, even in error. *T-25.IV.26.2:3*

~ let all these errors go by recognizing them for what **they** are. **They** are attempts to keep **you** unaware **you** are One **Self**, united with your **Creator**, at one with every aspect of **creation**, and limitless in **power** and in **peace**. *W-pI.95.11.3:4*

~ **where** truth has entered, errors disappear. **They** merely vanish, leaving not a trace by which to be remembered. **They** are gone because without **belief they have** no **life**, and so **they** disappear to nothingness, returning whence **they** came. From dust to dust **they** come and go, for only **truth** remains. *W-pI.107.1.3:6*

~ it is easiest to let error be corrected where it is most apparent, and errors can be recognized by their results. *M-17.3.1*

ETERNITY |ə'tərnədē|

DICTIONARY: *infinite or unending time.*

EGO

~ into eternity, where all is one, there crept a tiny mad **idea** at which the **Son of God** remembered not to laugh. In his forgetting did the **thought** become a serious **idea** and possible of both accomplishment and real effects. *T-27.IX.82.4:5*

HOLY SPIRIT; *one* **time**, *indelible stamp of* **creation**.

~ eternity is an **idea** of **God**, so the **Soul** understands it perfectly. *T-5.V.37.3*

~ eternity is yours, because **He** created **you** eternal. *T-7.I.3.9*

~ eternity is the indelible stamp of **creation**. The eternal are in **peace** and **joy** forever. *T-7.II.5.5:6*

~ what is timeless is always there, because its **being** is eternally changeless. It does not **change** by increase, because it was forever created to increase. *T-7.II.8.1:2*

~ yet what has once been is so **now** if it is eternal. When **you remember**, **you will** know what **you remember** is eternal and therefore is **now**. *T-9.VIII.66.6:7*

~ **time** and eternity cannot both be real, because **they** contradict each other. *T-9.XI.107.4*

~ **time will** be over, and **we will** all unite in the eternity of **God** the **Father**. The holy **light you** saw **outside** yourself in every **miracle you** offered to your brothers **will** be returned to **you**. And knowing that the **light** is in **you**, your **creations will** be there with **you**, as **you** are in your **Father**. *T-13.II.8.3:5*

~ first in eternity is **God** the **Father**, who is both First and One. *T-13.IX.86.7*

~ eternity itself is beyond all **time**. *T-14.VI.46.3*

~ neither **time** nor season **means** anything in eternity. *T-15.X.92.3*

~ what **you** think **you** do to the eternal **you** do to **you**. *T-19.II.16.2*

~ **faith** in the eternal is always justified, for the eternal is forever kind, infinite in its **patience**, and wholly loving. It **will** accept **you** wholly and **give you peace**. Yet it can unite only with what already is at **peace** in **you**, immortal as itself. *T-19.V.69.1:3*

~ **time** cannot intrude upon eternity. It is a joke to think that **time** can come to circumvent eternity, which **means** there is no **time**. *T-27.IX.82.6:7*

~ each herald of eternity sings of the end of **sin** and **fear**. Each speaks in **time** of what is far beyond it. *T-20.VI.38.1:2*

~ what seems eternal all **will have** an end. The stars **will** disappear, and night and day **will** be no more. All things that come and go, the tides, the seasons, and the lives of men; all things that **change** with **time** and bloom and fade **will** not return. Where **time** has set an end is not where the eternal is. *T-29.VII.39.7:10*

EVERYONE
[ˈevrēˌwən]

DICTIONARY: *every person, my dearest friend.*

EGO

~ the **ego** would **limit** everyone to a **body** for its purposes. *T-15.IX.87.4*

~ everyone **here** has entered **darkness**, yet no one has entered it **alone**. *T-25.IV.27.4*

HOLY SPIRIT

~ ultimately everyone must **remember** the **Will** of **God**, because ultimately everyone must recognize himself. *T-8.X.99.1*

~ everyone lives in **you**, as **you** live in everyone. *T-10.VII.62.3*

~ when everyone is **welcome** to **you** as **you** would **have** yourself be **welcome** to your **Father**, **you will see** no **guilt** in you. *T-13.IV.24.4*

~ the **power** of **God** draws everyone to its safe embrace of **love** and **union**. *T-14.II.12.5*

~ everyone seeks for **love** as **you** do and knows it not unless he joins with **you** in seeking it. If **you** undertake the search together, **you** bring with **you** a **light** so powerful that what **you see** is given **meaning.** *T-14.VI.55.5:6*

~ he reaches from **you** to everyone and beyond everyone to His Son's **creations**, but without leaving you. Far beyond your **little world** but still in you, He extends forever. *T-15.IV.29.5:6*

~ **call** forth in everyone only the remembrance of **God** and of the **Heaven** that is in him. *T-15.IV.34.1*

~ to **see** me is to **see** me in everyone and offer everyone the **gift you** offer me. *T-15.X.93.4*

~ he uses everyone who calls on Him as **means** for the **salvation** of everyone. *T-18.III.21.6*

~ gracious **acknowledgment** of everyone as a Son of your most loving **Father**, loved by Him like **you** and therefore loved by **you** as yourself. *T-19.II.11.3*

~ **you give** to one another for everyone, and in your **gift** is everyone made glad. *T-20.VI.38.6*

~ in everyone **you see** but the **reflection** of what **you** chose to **have** him be to you. *T-25.VI.40.7*

~ to everyone has **God** entrusted all. *T-31.VII.77.4*

EVIL

| ˈēvəl|

DICTIONARY: *profoundly immoral and malevolent.*

EGO

~ **man** assigns his own "evil" **past** to God. *T-3.III.15.2*

~ **you** could not recognize your "evil" thoughts as long as **you see value** in **attack. You will** perceive them sometimes, but **will** not **see** them as meaningless. *T-31.VII.69.1:2*

HOLY SPIRIT

~ the "evil conscience" from the **past** has **nothing** to do with **God**. He did not create it, and He does not maintain it. *T-3.III.15.3:4*

~ he can **see** no evil. *T-25.VII.43.2*

~ your "evil" thoughts **have** been forgiven with his, because **you** let them all affect **you** not. *T-31.VII.69.6*

~ **love** cannot **give** evil, and what is not happiness is evil. *W-pI.66.8.3*

~ all the evil that **you** think **you** did was never done. *W-pI.93.4.1*

~ whatever evil **you** may think **you** did, **you** are as **God** created **you**. *W-pI.93.7.2*

~ evil is not real. *W-pI.110.2.1*

EVOLUTION

| ˌevəˈlo͞oSH(ə)n|

DICTIONARY: *the process by which different kinds of living organisms are **thought** to **have** developed and diversified from earlier forms during the history of the earth.*

HOLY SPIRIT

~ the "evolution" of **man** is merely a process by which **he** proceeds from one degree to the next. **He** corrects his previous missteps by stepping forward. This represents a process which is actually incomprehensible in temporal terms because **he** returns as **he** goes forward. *T-2.II.40.4:6*

EXCEPTION

DICTIONARY: *a person or **thing** that is excluded from a general statement or does not follow a **rule**.*

EGO

~ only if there is **fear** does the **idea** of exceptions seem to be meaningful. Exceptions are fearful, because **they** are made by **fear**. *T-7.VI.45.2:3*

EXERCISE

DICTIONARY: *a task or activity done to **practice** or **test** a skill.*

EGO

~ unwillingness can be most carefully concealed behind a cloak of situations **you** cannot control. *W-pI.Rev III.3.3*

HOLY SPIRIT

~ yet it is the exercises which **will make** the **goal** possible. *W-pI.1.1.2*

~ it is the **purpose** of these exercises to train the **mind** to think along the lines which the **course** sets forth. *W-pI.1.1.4*

~ the **purpose** of these exercises is to train the **mind** to a different **perception** of everything in the **world**. *W-pI.1.3.1*

~ it is recommended that each exercise be repeated several times a day, preferably in a different place each **time** and, if possible, in every **situation** in which **you** spend any long period of **time**. The **purpose** is to train the **mind** to generalize the lessons, so that **you will understand** that each of them is as applicable to one **situation** as it is to another. *W-pI.1.3.3:4*

~ unless specified to the contrary, the exercise should be practiced with the eyes open, since the aim is to learn how to **see**. The only **rule** that should be followed throughout is to **practice** the exercises with great specificity. Each one applies to every **situation** in which **you** find yourself and to everything **you see** in it. Each day's exercises are planned around one central **idea**, the exercises themselves consisting of applying that **idea** to as many specifics as possible. Be sure that **you** do not decide that there are some things **you see** to which the **idea** for the day is inapplicable. The aim of the exercises **will** always be to increase the application of the **idea** to everything. This **will** not require effort. Only be sure that **you make** no exceptions in applying the **idea**. *W-pI.1.4.1:8*

~ the point of the exercises is to **help you** clear your **mind** of all **past** associations, to **see** things exactly as **they** appear to **you now**, and to realize how **little you** really **understand** about them. *W-pI.3.2.1*

~ the long-range **purpose** of **learning** to **see** the meaningless as **outside you** and the meaningful **within**. *W-pI.4.3.3*

~ beginning of training your **mind** to recognize what is the same and what is different. *W-pI.4.3.4*

~ these exercises are concerned with **practice**, not with understanding. *W-pI.9.1.5*

~ the ideas which are used for the exercises are very simple, very clear, and totally unambiguous. *W-pI.39.1.2*

~ the exercises are very simple. **They** do not require more than a few minutes, and it does not matter where or when **you** do them. **They need** no **preparation**. **They** are numbered, running from 1 to 365. The training period is one year. Do not undertake more than one exercise a day. *W-pI.39.1.2:7*

~ that this is no idle game but an exercise in **holiness** and an attempt to reach the **Kingdom** of **Heaven**. *W-pI.45.11.4*

- each one **you** do **will** be a giant stride toward your **release** and a milestone in **learning** the **thought system** which this **course** sets forth. *W-pI.94.11.2*
- our emphasis is not on giving up the **world** but on exchanging it for what is far more satisfying, filled with **joy**, and capable of **offering you peace**. *W-pI.129.1.3*
- rituals are not our aim and would defeat our **goal**. *W-pI.Rev III.2.3*

EXIST

|ig ˈzist|

DICTIONARY: *have objective **reality** or **being**.*

EGO

- what **God** did not create does not exist. *W-pI.14.1.2*
- what **God** did not create can only be in your own **mind** apart from His. Therefore, it has no **meaning**. *W-pI.14.7.5:6*

HOLY SPIRIT

- in **time we** exist for and with each other. In Timelessness **we** coexist with **God**. *T-3.II.10.6:7*
- only what **God** creates, or what **man** creates with the same **will**, has any real existence. *T-3.IV.28.3*
- existence does not depend on your ability to identify it nor even to place it. *T-3.VIII.69.5*
- if **truth** is total, the untrue cannot exist. *T-7.VII.63.2*
- what has no effect does not exist, and to the **Holy Spirit**, the effects of **error** are totally non-existent. *T-9.III.14.3*
- he teaches that the **ego** does not exist and proves it. *T-9.III.14.4*
- except **you share** it, **nothing** can exist. And **you** exist because **God** shared His **Will** with you, that His creation might create. *T-28.VI.47.10:11*
- **nothing** that God knows not exists. And what **He** knows exists forever, changelessly. *T-30.IV.43.1:2*
- and everything that does exist exists as **He** created it. *W-pI.14.1.3*
- all that **you fear** does not exist. *W-pI.22.2.5*

EXPERIENCE

|ˌikˈspirēəns|

DICTIONARY: *practical contact with and observation of facts or events.*

EGO

- the **separation** was their first experience of **change**. *T-4.II.7.7*
- **fantasy** solutions bring but the **illusion** of experience. *T-17.VII.63.6*

HOLY SPIRIT

- there is a kind of experience which is so different from anything the **ego** can offer that **you will** never recover. *T-4.IV.50.3*
- different experiences lead to different beliefs, [and with them, different perceptions. For perceptions are learned with beliefs,] and experience teaches. *T-10.VII.61.1:2*

~ **you** consider it "natural" to use your **past** experience as the reference point from which to judge the **present**. Yet this is unnatural because it is delusional. *T-12.VI.46.2*

~ what one thinks the other **will** experience with him. *T-22.VII.64.2*

~ **we** cannot **give** experience like this directly. Yet it leaves a **vision** in our eyes which **we** can offer **everyone** that **he** may come the sooner to the same experience in which the **world** is quietly forgot and **Heaven** is remembered for a while. *W-pI.157.6.2:3*

~ as this experience increases and all goals but this become of **little worth**, the **world** to which **you will** return becomes a **little** closer to the end of **time**, a **little** more like **Heaven** in its ways, a **little** nearer its deliverance. *W-pI.157.7.1*

~ experience cannot be shared directly in the **way** that **vision** can. *W-pI.158.2.7*

~ experience, unlearned, untaught, unseen, is merely there. This is beyond our **goal**, for it transcends what needs to be accomplished. *W-pI.158.6.4:5*

~ but the experience of **freedom** and of **peace** that comes as **you give** up your tight control of what **you see** speaks for itself. *W-pI.ST181.2.4*

~ experience of what exists beyond defensiveness remains beyond achievement while it is denied. *W-pI.ST181.3.2*

EXTENSION |ˌikˈsten(t)SH(ə)n|

DICTIONARY: *a **part** that is added to something to enlarge or prolong it; a continuation.*

EGO

~ the **belief** that by giving it out **you have** excluded it from **within** is a complete distortion of the **power** of extension. *T-7.IX.85.7*

~ the ego's whole **thought system** blocks extension and thus blocks your only **function**. *T-7.X.93.7*

~ what extends to **nothing** cannot be real. *T-10.VI.40.7*

HOLY SPIRIT; *mind's **function**, transfer.*

~ is a measure of **learning**, because it is its measurable result. *T-6.V.92.1*

~ the extension of **truth**, which is the Law of the **Kingdom**, rests only on the **knowledge** of what **truth** is. *T-7.III.16.6*

~ fullness is extension. *T-7.X.93.6*

~ the arrest of the mind's extension is the **cause** of all illness, because only extension is the mind's **function**. *T-8.VII.65.1*

~ **god** has created by extension. *T-10.II.3.1*

~ extension cannot be blocked, and it has no voids. It continues forever, however much it is denied. Your **denial** of its **reality** arrests it in **time** but not in **eternity**. That is why your **creations have** not ceased to be extended and why so much is waiting for your return. *T-10.II.7.5:8*

~ as self-value comes from self-extension, so does the **perception** of self-value come from the **projection** of loving thoughts outward. *T-11.VII.55.5*

~ creation is the natural extension of perfect purity. *T-14.II.7.4*

~ if creation is extension, the **Creator** must **have** extended Himself. *T-19.IV.31.2*

~ giver and receiver are united in extension **here** on earth as **they** are one in **Heaven**. *W-pI.159.4.3*

EYE

DICTIONARY: *each of a pair of globular organs in the head through which people and vertebrate animals see, the visible **part** typically appearing almond-shaped in animals with eyelids.*

EGO

~ its eyes adjust to **sin**, unable to overlook it in any **form** and seeing it everywhere, in everything. Look through its eyes, and everything **will** stand condemned before **you**. All that could save **you, you will** never **see**. Your **holy relationship**, the **source** of your **salvation, will** be deprived of **meaning**, and its most holy **purpose** bereft of **means** for its accomplishment. *T-20.IX.72.6:9*

~ the **world you see** through eyes which are not yours must **make** no **sense** to you. *T-22.II.6.3*

~ everything which the body's eyes can **see** is a **mistake**, an **error** in **perception**, a distorted **fragment** of the whole, without the **meaning** that the whole would **give**. *T-22.IV.32.3*

~ the body's eyes **see** only **form**. **They** cannot **see** beyond what **they** were made to **see**. And **they** were made to look on **error** and not **see past** it. Theirs is indeed a strange **perception**, for **they** can **see** only illusions, unable to look beyond the granite block of **sin** and stopping at the **outside form** of **nothing**. To this distorted **form** of **vision**, the **outside** of everything, the wall that stands between **you** and the **truth**, is wholly true. *T-22.IV.33.3:7*

~ these eyes, made not to **see, will** never **see**. For the **idea they** represent left not its maker, and it is their maker that sees through them. *T-22.IV.34.1:2*

~ the body's eyes **rest** on externals and cannot go beyond. *T-22.IV.34.5*

~ **they** stop at nothingness, unable to go beyond the **form** to **meaning**. *T-22.IV.34.6*

~ eyes become used to **darkness**, and the **light** of brilliant day seems painful to the eyes grown long accustomed to the dim effects perceived at twilight. And **they** turn away from sunlight and the **clarity** it brings to what **they** look upon. Dimness seems better—easier to **see** and better recognized. Somehow, the vague and more obscure seems easier to look upon; less painful to the eyes than what is wholly clear and unambiguous. *T-25.VII.44.1:4*

~ what the body's eyes behold is only **conflict**. *M-8.1.6*

HOLY SPIRIT

~ what the physical eye sees is not corrective nor can it be corrected by any device which can be seen physically. As long as a **man** believes in what his physical **sight** tells him, all his corrective **behavior will** be misdirected. *T-2.III.68.4:5*

~ it is surely the **mind** that judges what the eyes behold. It is the **mind** that interprets the eyes' messages and gives them "**meaning**." And this **meaning** does not **exist** in the **world outside** at all. What is seen as "**reality**" is simply what the **mind** prefers. Its hierarchy of values is projected outward, and it sends the body's eyes to find it. The body's eyes **will** never **see** except through differences. Yet it is not the messages **they** bring on which **perception** rests. Only the **mind** evaluates their messages, so only the **mind** is responsible for seeing. It **alone** decides whether what is seen is real or illusory, desirable or undesirable, pleasurable or painful. *M-8.3.3:11*

~ the body's eyes **will** continue to **see** differences, but the **mind** which has let itself be healed **will** no longer acknowledge them. *M-8.6.1*

FACE OF CHRIST

Ego

~ a **dream** has veiled the face of **Christ** from **you**. *S-1.V.3.3*

Holy Spirit; *Holy Face*

~ the face of **Christ** is looked upon before the **Father** is remembered. *T-30.VI.63.5*

~ what appears to **hide** the face of **Christ** is powerless before His majesty and disappears before His holy **sight**. *T-31.VIII.88.3*

~ what is the face of **Christ** but his who went a moment into timelessness and brought a clear **reflection** of the **unity he** felt an instant back to bless the **world**. *W-pI.169.12.1*

~ it is but the **symbol** that the **time** for **learning now** is over and the **goal** of the **Atonement** has been reached at last. *W-pII.ST271.5.1*

~ as **we** behold His **glory will we** know **we have** no **need** of **learning** or **perception** or of **time**, or anything except the holy **Self**, the **Christ** Whom **God** created as His Son. *W-pII.ST271.5.3*

FACT

|fakt|

DICTIONARY: *a **thing** that is indisputably the case.*

Holy Spirit

~ hypothesis is either false or true, to be accepted or rejected accordingly. If it is shown to be true, it becomes a fact, after which no one attempts to evaluate it unless its status as fact is questioned. *T-4.III.38.1:2*

~ facts are unchanged. Yet facts can be denied and thus unknown, though **they** were known before **they** were denied. *T-26.VIII.55.3:4*

~ no one can be angry at a fact. It is always an **interpretation** that gives rise to negative emotions, regardless of their seeming justification by what appears as facts. *M-17.4.1:2*

FAIL

|fāl|

DICTIONARY: *be unsuccessful in achieving one's **goal**.*

Ego

~ failure is of the **ego**, not of **God**. *T-13.V.46.1*

~ failure is all about **you** while **you seek** for goals that cannot be achieved. *W-pI.131.1.1*

Holy Spirit

~ **god will** not fail nor ever has in anything. *T-13.IX.89.7*

~ accept your **sense** of failure as **nothing** more than a **mistake** in who **you** are. *T-15.IX.81.6*

118

FAITH

DICTIONARY: *complete **trust** or **confidence** in someone or something.*

EGO

~ **have** faith in **nothing**, and **you will** find the "**treasure**" that **you** sought. *T-13.VII.55.1*

~ it has faith in **separation** and not in **wholeness**. *T-17.VII.62.10*

~ wishful thinking is how the **ego** deals with what it wants to **make** it so. There is no better demonstration of the **power** of wanting, and therefore of faith, to **make** its goals seem real and possible. Faith in the unreal leads to adjustments of **reality** to **make** it fit the **goal** of madness. *T-21.III.24.1:3*

~ faith given to illusions does not lack **power**, for by it does the **Son of God** believe that **he** is powerless. Thus is **he faithless** to himself, but strong in faith in his illusions about himself. For faith, **perception**, and **belief you** made as **means** for losing **certainty** and finding **sin**. This mad direction was your **choice**, and by your faith in what **you** chose, **you** made what **you** desired. *T-21.IV.33.3:6*

~ faith in **innocence** is faith in **sin** if the **belief** excludes one living **thing** and holds it out apart from its **forgiveness**. *T-22.III.19.7*

~ your faith lies in the **darkness**, not the **light**. *W-pI.91.3.5*

~ **you** place pathetic faith in what your eyes and ears report. *W-pI.151.3.5*

HOLY SPIRIT; *acknowledgement of union, gift of God, gift.*

~ faith can be rewarded only in terms of the **belief** in which the faith was placed. Faith makes the **power** of **belief**, and where it is invested determines its **reward**. For faith is always given what is treasured, and what is treasured is returned to **you**. *T-13.III.12.4:6*

~ your faith **will** be rewarded as **you** gave it. **You will** accept your **treasure**, and if **you** place your faith in the **past**, the **future will** be like it. Whatever **you** hold as dear, **you** think is yours. The **power** of your valuing **will make** it so. *T-13.III.13.2:5*

~ your faith in Him is strengthened by sharing. *T-15.VII.59.4*

~ the **Holy Spirit** gives **you** this faith. *T-15.VII.62.6*

~ **you will see** the justification for your faith emerge to bring **you** shining conviction. *T-17.VI.49.12*

~ the **goal** of **truth** requires faith. Faith is implicit in the **acceptance** of the Holy Spirit's **purpose**, and this faith is all-inclusive. Where the **goal** of **truth** is set, there faith must be. *T-17.VII.62.1:3*

~ faith must be where something has been done and where **you see** it done. *T-17.VIII.65.5*

~ **peace** and faith **will** not come separately. *T-17.VIII.67.5*

~ **gift** of faith, freely given wherever faithlessness is laid aside unused. *T-17.IX.76.2*

~ faith would remove all limitations and **make** whole. *T-19.II.5.3*

~ faith would unite and heal. *T-19.II.5.4*

~ faith would remove all obstacles that seem to rise between them. *T-19.II.5.5*

~ to **have** faith is to heal. It is the sign that **you have** accepted the **Atonement** for yourself and would therefore **share** it. By faith **you** offer the **gift** of **freedom** from the **past**, which **you** received. *T-19.II.10.1:3*

~ faith is always justified. *T-19.II.10.7*

~ faith is the **opposite** of fear, as much a **part** of love as **fear** is of **attack**. Faith is the **acknowledgment** of **union**. It is the gracious **acknowledgment** of **everyone** as a Son of your most loving **Father**, loved by Him like **you** and therefore loved by **you** as yourself. It is His **love** that joins **you**. *T-19.II.11.1:4*

119

~ faith is the **gift** of **God**, through Him Whom **God** has given **you**. *T-19.II.12.1*

~ through the eyes of faith, the **Son of God** is seen already forgiven, free of all the **guilt he** laid upon himself. Faith sees him only **now** because it looks not to the **past** to judge him, but would **see** in him only what it would **see** in **you**. It sees not through the body's eyes nor looks to bodies for its justification. It is the **messenger** of the new **perception** sent forth to gather witnesses unto its coming and to return their messages to **you**. Faith is as easily exchanged for **knowledge** as is the **real world**. For faith arises from the Holy Spirit's **perception** and is the sign **you share** it with Him. Faith is a **gift you** offer to the **Son of God** through Him, and wholly acceptable to his **Father** as to him. And therefore offered **you**. *T-19.II.12.3:10*

~ there is **nothing** faith cannot forgive. No **error** interferes with its **calm sight**, which brings the **miracle** of **healing** with equal ease to all of them. *T-19.II.14.4:5*

~ **will** faith **help** the **Holy Spirit** prepare the ground for the most holy garden which **He** would **make** of it. For faith brings **peace**, and so it calls on **truth** to enter and **make** lovely what has already been prepared for loveliness. **Truth** follows faith and **peace**, completing the process of making lovely which **they** begin. For faith is still a **learning goal**, no longer needed when the **lesson** has been learned. *T-19.II.15.1:4*

~ what **you** had faith in still is faithful and watches over **you** in faith so gentle yet so strong that it would lift **you** far beyond the **veil** and place the **Son of God** safely **within** the sure protection of his **Father**. *T-19.V.110.3*

~ faith and **desire** go hand in hand, for **everyone** believes in what **he** wants. *T-21.III.23.6*

~ the persistence that faith inevitably brings. The **power** of faith is never recognized if it is placed in **sin**. But it is always recognized if it is placed in **love**. *T-21.IV.30.5:7*

~ it is **impossible** to place equal faith in **opposite** directions. *T-21.IV.31.5*

~ it is **impossible** that the **Son of God** lack faith, but **he** can choose where **he** would **have** it be. *T-21.IV.33.1*

~ faith goes to what **you want**, and **you** instruct your **mind** accordingly. *W-pI.91.5.3*

~ faith lies in the Giver, not our own **acceptance**. *W-pI.168.5.2*

~ true faithfulness, however, does not deviate. **Being** consistent, it is wholly **honest**. **Being** unswerving, it is full of **trust**. **Being** based on fearlessness, it is gentle. **Being** certain, it is joyous, and **being** con dent, it is tolerant. **Defenselessness** attends it naturally, and **joy** is its **condition**. Faithfulness, then, combines in itself the other attributes of God's teachers. It implies **acceptance** of the **word** of **God** and His definition of His Son. It is to them that faithfulness in the true **sense** is always directed. Toward them it looks, seeking until it finds. And having found, it rests in **quiet certainty** on that **alone** to which all faithfulness is due. *M-4.22.1:11*

FAITHLESS
|ˈfāTHləs|

DICTIONARY: *disloyal, especially to a spouse or partner; untrustworthy.*

EGO

~ but faithlessness used against **truth will** always destroy **faith**. *T-17.VIII.66.6*

~ faithlessness is the servant of **illusion** and wholly faithful to its master. Use it and it **will** carry **you** straight to illusions. Be tempted not by what it offers **you**. It interferes not with the **goal**, but with the **value** of the **goal** to **you**. *T-17.VIII.68.5:8*

~ the **goal** of **illusion** is as closely tied to faithlessness as **faith** to **truth**. If **you** lack **faith** in anyone to fulfill, and perfectly, his **part** in any **situation** dedicated in **advance** to **truth**, your dedication is divided. And so **you have** been faithless to each other and used your faithlessness against each other. *T-17.VIII.69.1:3*

~ the **cause** of faithlessness: **You** think **you** hold against the other what **he** has done to **you**. But what **you** really **blame** him for is what **you** did to him. It is not his **past** but yours **you** hold against him. And **you** lack **faith** in him because of what **you** were. *T-17.VIII.71.1:4*

~ faithlessness leads straight to illusions. For faithlessness is the **perception** of a **brother** as a **body**, and the **body** cannot be used for purposes of **union**. *T-19.II.4.1:2*

~ your faithlessness to him has separated **you** from him and kept **you** both apart from **being** healed. Your faithlessness has thus opposed the Holy Spirit's **purpose** and brought illusions centered on the **body** to stand between **you**. *T-19.II.4.4:5*

~ faithlessness would always **limit** and **attack**;. *T-19.II.5.3*

~ faithlessness would destroy and separate; **faith** would unite and heal. *T-19.II.5.4:5*

~ faithlessness would interpose illusions between the **Son of God** and his **Creator**;. *T-19.II.5.5*

~ faithlessness is wholly dedicated to illusions. *T-19.II.5.6*

~ devastation wrought by your faithlessness. For faithlessness is an **attack** which seems to be justified by its results. For by withholding **faith**, **you see** what is unworthy of it and cannot look beyond the barrier to what is joined with **you**. *T-19.II.9.2:4*

HOLY SPIRIT; *sickness*

~ faithlessness brought to **faith will** never **interfere** with **truth**. *T-17.VIII.66.5*

~ there is no justification for faithlessness. *T-19.II.10.7*

~ faithlessness is not a lack of **faith**, but **faith** in **nothing**. *T-21.IV.33.2*

FANTASY

⌈ˈfan(t)əsē⌋

DICTIONARY: *the faculty or activity of imagining things, especially things that are **impossible** or improbable.*

EGO; *vain imagining*

~ fantasies of any kind are distorted forms of thinking, because **they** always involve twisting **perception** into unreality. Fantasy is a debased **form** of **vision**. *T-1.II.106.1:2*

~ fantasy and **projection** are more closely associated, because both attempt to control external **reality** according to false internal needs. *T-1.II.106.3*

~ the symbols of fantasy are of the **ego**, and of these **you will** find many. *T-9.III.18.9*

~ usually judged to be acceptable and even natural. *T-16.VI.44.7*

~ only fantasies made **confusion** in choosing possible, and they are totally unreal. *T-16.VI.58.2*

~ there is no fantasy which does not contain the **dream** of retribution for the **past**. *T-16.VIII.73.5*

~ what **you** use in fantasy, **you** deny to **truth**. *T-17.I.2.5*

HOLY SPIRIT; *distortion of perception*

~ no fantasies are true. They are distortions of **perception** by definition. *T-1.II.107.1:2*

~ every fantasy, be it of **love** or **hate**, deprives **you** of **knowledge**, for fantasies are the **veil** behind which **truth** is hidden. *T-16.V.39.3*

~ **see** in the **call** of hate and in every fantasy that rises to **delay you** but the **call** for **help** which rises ceaselessly from **you** to your **Creator**. *T-16.V.40.5*

121

~ fantasies **change reality**. That is their **purpose**. **They** cannot do so in **reality**, but **they** can do so in the **mind** that would **have reality** different. *T-17.I.1.8:10*

~ fantasy solutions bring but the **illusion** of **experience**, and the **illusion** of **peace** is not the **condition** in which the **truth** can enter. *T-17.VII.6:3.5*

FATHER

|ˈfäT͟Hər|

DICTIONARY: *a man in relation to his natural **child** or children.*

EGO; *deadly enemy*

~ it is your Father Whom **you** would defend against. *T-22.VI.4:7.4*

~ his Father is his deadly **enemy**, separate from him and waiting to destroy his **life** and blot him from the **universe**. *W-pI.196.5.5*

HOLY SPIRIT; *Life, your Creator.*

~ your fatherhood and your Father are one. *T-10.II.11.6*

~ father, Who wills to project His **peace** through **you**. *T-11.VIII.71.6*

~ **he** did not **change**, but **you** did. *T-11.IX.78.4*

~ your Father could not cease to **love** His Son. *T-11.IX.84.9*

~ the Father is not cruel, and His Son cannot **hurt** himself. *T-11.X.92.2*

~ **he** does not **value you** as **you** do. **He** knows Himself and knows the **truth** in **you**. **He** knows there is no **difference**, for **He** knows not of differences. *T-13.III.19.2:4*

~ the **Creator** of **life**, the **Source** of everything that lives, the Father of the **universe** and of the **universe** of universes and of everything that lies even beyond them would **you remember**. *T-19.V.90.4*

~ father, Who knows no **sin**, no **death**, but only **life** eternal. *T-19.V.107.5*

~ what **He** loves must be forever **quiet** and at **peace** because it is His **home**. And **you** who are beloved of Him are no illusions, **being** as true and holy as Himself. *T-23.III.15.6:7*

~ your Father has not left **you** to yourself, nor let **you** wander in the dark **alone**. *W-pI.123.2.2*

~ **he** has not abandoned **you**. *W-pI.123.3.1*

~ his **Love** forever **will** remain shining on **you**, forever without **change**. *W-pI.123.3.1*

~ **he** Himself **will** place a **spark** of **truth within** your **mind** wherever **you give** up a false **belief**, a dark **illusion** of your own **reality** and what **love means**. *W-pI.127.8.3*

~ accept His Fatherhood, and all is given us. *W-pII.276.1.5*

~ a loving father does not let his **child harm** himself or choose his own **destruction**. *M-29.6.8*

FEAR

|ˈfir|

DICTIONARY: *an unpleasant* **emotion** *caused by the* **belief** *that someone or something is dangerous, likely to cause pain, or a* **threat**.

EGO; **hell**, **witness** *unto* **death**, *circle of fear, ring of fear,* **symptom.**

~ **you** believe that "**being** afraid" is involuntary, something beyond your control. *T-2.IV.72.1*

~ when **you** are fearful, **you have** willed wrongly. *T-2.IV.74.6*

~ **man** believes **he** cannot control fear because **he** himself created it. His **belief** in it seems to render it out of his control by definition. *T-2.V.98.1:2*

~ fear is a **witness** to the **separation**, and your **ego** rejoices when **you witness** to it. *T-4.II.17.4*

~ produced by fear, the **ego** reproduces fear. *T-7.VII.58.2*

~ for if the **ego** gives rise to fear, it is diminishing your independence and weakening your **power**. *T-10.VI.47.2*

~ your fear of **attack** is **nothing** compared to your fear of **love**. *T-12.III.12.1*

~ the **ego** must seem to keep fear from **you** to keep your allegiance. Yet it must engender fear in **order** to maintain itself. *T-15.II.4.7:8*

~ the circle of fear lies just below the **level** the **body** sees and seems to be the whole foundation on which the **world** is based. **Here** are all the illusions, all the twisted thoughts, all the insane attacks, the fury, **vengeance**, and betrayal that were made to keep the **guilt** in place, so that the **world** could rise from it and keep it hidden. Its **shadow** rises to the surface, enough to hold its most external manifestations in **darkness** and to bring **despair** and loneliness to it and keep it joyless. Yet its intensity is veiled by its heavy coverings and kept apart from what was made to keep it hidden. *T-18.X.88.1:4*

~ fear is merciless even to its friends. *T-19.V.51.6*

~ fear's insane insistence that sureness lies in **doubt**. *T-21.V.48.4*

~ and fear **will** reign in **madness** and **will** seem to **have** replaced **love** there. This is the conflict's **purpose**. *T-23.II.8.10:11*

~ if **you** are fearful, it is certain that **you will** endow the **world** with attributes which it does not possess and crowd it with images that do not **exist**. *W-pI.13.3.2*

~ the presence of fear is a sure sign that **you** are trusting in your own **strength**. *W-pI.48.3.1*

~ fear obscures in **darkness** what is there. *W-pI.130.2.5*

~ fear has made everything **you** think **you see**. *W-pI.130.4.1*

~ fear remains the one **reality** that can be seen and justified and fully understood. *W-pI.137.6.4*

~ fear is a **stranger** to the ways of **love**. Identify with fear, and **you will** be a **stranger** to yourself. *W-pI.160.1.1:2*

~ fear is insatiable, consuming everything its eyes behold, seeing itself in everything, compelled to turn upon itself and to destroy. *W-pI.161.7.5*

~ what **you** fear but teaches them their fears are justified. *W-pI.166.14.4*

~ fear becomes your safety and protector of your **peace**, to which **you** turn for solace and escape from doubts about your **strength** and hope of **rest** in dreamless **quiet**. *W-pI.170.6.2*

~ fear is deception. It attests that **you have** seen yourself as **you** could never be and therefore look upon a **world** which is **impossible**. *W-pII.240.1.1:2*

~ fear appears in many different forms. *W-p2.295.1.7*

HOLY SPIRIT; *mistake, dream, illusion, nothing, stranger, witness to the separation, herald of escape, judgement, an appeal for help, call for love, symptom.*

~ all fear is ultimately reducible to the basic misperception that **man** has the ability to usurp the **power** of **God.** *T-2.I.15.1*

~ fear cannot be **Christ**-controlled, but it can be **self**-controlled. *T-2.IV.72.4*

~ fear is always a sign of strain, which arises whenever the **will** to do conflicts with what **you** do. This **situation** arises in two ways: First, **you** can **will** to do conflicting things, either simultaneously or successively. This produces conflicted **behavior**, which is intolerable to yourself because the **part** of the **will** that wants to do something else is outraged. Second, **you** can behave as **you** think **you** should but without entirely willing to do so. This produces consistent **behavior** but entails great strain **within** the **self**. In both cases, the **will** and the **behavior** are out of accord, resulting in a **situation** in which **you** are **doing** what **you** do not **will**. This arouses a **sense** of coercion, which usually produces rage. The rage then invades the **mind** and **projection** in the wrong **sense** is likely to follow. Depression or anxiety is virtually certain. *T-2.IV.76.1:9*

~ only your **mind** can produce fear. It does so whenever it is conflicted in what it wills, thus producing inevitable strain because willing and **doing** become discordant. This cannot be corrected by better **doing**, but it can be corrected by higher willing. *T-2.IV.81.3:5*

~ when **you** are afraid **you have** placed yourself in a position where **you need** Atonement, because **you have** done something loveless, having willed without **love.** *T-2.V.87.3*

~ fear is really **nothing.** *T-2.V.99.3*

~ fear is incompatible with **good judgment.** Fear distorts thinking and therefore disorders **thought.** *T-5.IX.83.7:8*

~ fear cannot be created. *T-8.X.104.4*

~ for to recognize fear is not enough to escape from it, although the recognition is necessary to demonstrate the **need** for escape. The **Holy Spirit** must still translate it into **truth.** *T-11.II.9.2:3*

~ fear is an appeal for **help.** This is what recognizing it really **means.** *T-11.II.10.1:2*

~ **you have** denied its **power** to conceal **love**, which was its only **purpose.** The mask which **you have** drawn across the face of **love** has disappeared. *T-11.III.12.4:5*

~ the **Holy Spirit's interpretation** of fear does dispel it, for the **awareness** of **truth** cannot be denied. *T-11.III.13.3*

~ the **Holy Spirit** replace fear with **love** and translate **error** into **truth.** *T-11.III.13.4*

~ only the anticipation **will** frighten **you**, for the **reality** of nothingness cannot be frightening. *T-11.III.18.3*

~ there is no fear in perfect **love.** *T-11.III.21.1*

~ if **you** are afraid, it is because **you** saw something that is not there. *T-11.VIII.71.4*

~ no one **will** countenance fear if **he** recognizes it. *T-12.III.10.4*

~ fear is not of the **present** but only of the **past** and **future**, which do not **exist.** *T-15.II.9.2*

~ the **Holy Spirit** cannot **teach** through fear. *T-15.VIII.75.3*

~ fear is both a fragmented and a fragmenting **emotion.** It seems to take many forms, and each seems to require a different **form** of acting out for satisfaction. *T-18.I.3.3:4*

~ if **you** knew Who walks beside **you** on this **way** which **you have** chosen, fear would be **impossible.** *T-18.IV.26.1*

~ all the fear that **you experience** is really past. *T-18.IV.30.5*

~ this heavy-seeming barrier, this artificial floor which looks like rock, is like a bank of low dark **clouds** that seems to be a solid wall before the sun. Its impenetrable **appearance** is wholly an **illusion**. It gives **way** softly to the mountain tops which rise above it and has no **power** at all to hold back anyone willing to climb above it and **see** the sun. It is not strong enough to stop a button's fall nor hold a feather. [**Nothing** can **rest** upon it, for it is but an **illusion** of a foundation.] Try but to touch it and it disappears; attempt to grasp it and your hands hold **nothing**. *T-18.X.90.1:6*

~ what fear would feed upon, **love** overlooks. What fear demands, **love** cannot even **see**. *T-19.V.50.4:5*

~ **here** is the one **emotion** that **you** made, whatever it may seem to be. This is the **emotion** of secrecy, of private thoughts, and of the **body**. This is the one **emotion** that opposes **love** and always leads to **sight** of differences and **loss** of sameness. **Here** is the one **emotion** that keeps **you blind**, dependent on the **self you** think **you** made to lead **you** through the **world** it made for **you**. *T-22.II.8.7:10*

~ how weak is fear—how **little** and how meaningless! How insignificant before the **quiet strength** of those whom **love** has joined! *T-22.VI.48.1:2*

~ there is **nothing** to be feared. *T-29.I.1.2*

~ fear is a **judgment** never justified. Its presence has no **meaning** but to show **you** wrote a fearful **script** and are afraid accordingly. But not because the **thing you** fear has fearful **meaning** in itself. *T-30.VIII.84.8:10*

~ all that **you** fear does not **exist**. *W-pI.22.2.5*

~ **nothing** can **make** me afraid. *W-pI.58.5.3*

~ fear has no **meaning**. *W-pI.110.2.1*

~ all fear is **past** because its **source** is gone and all its thoughts gone with it. *W-pII.293.1.1*

~ to fear God's saving **grace** is but to fear complete **release** from **suffering**, return to **peace**, security and happiness, and **union** with your own **Identity**. *W-pII.ST311.3.3*

~ **everyone** can reconsider its causes and learn to evaluate them correctly. *P-1.1.1.3*

~ fear cannot long be hidden by illusions, for it is **part** of them. It **will** escape and take another **form, being** the **source** of all illusions. *P-2.IV.7.7:8*

FEAR OF GOD

DICTIONARY: *suggests apprehension of Divine **punishment**.*

EGO

~ the cleavage of your **Self** from **you**—the **fear** of God, the **final step** in your **dissociation**. *T-19.V.92.4*

~ **you** are afraid of **God** because **you fear** each other. *T-19.V.100.5*

~ the **fear** of God is but the **fear** of **loss** of idols. It is not the **fear** of **loss** of your **reality**. *T-29.VIII.50.6:7*

~ the **fear** of God is real to anyone who thinks this **thought** is true. *W-pI.196.6.4*

HOLY SPIRIT;   *fear of loss of idols, fear of reality, fear of life.*

~ to look upon the **fear** of God does **need** some **preparation**. *T-19.V.100.1*

~ **fear** of God is **fear** of **life** and not of **death**. *T-23.V.47.1*

~ when the **fear** of God is gone, there are no obstacles that still remain between **you** and the holy **peace** of God. *W-pI.196.12.2*

~ the **fear** of God is causeless. *M-17.9.12*

FINAL STEP

Holy Spirit; *last step*

~ the last **step** must be taken by **God** because the last **step** in your **redemption**, which seems to be in the **future**, was accomplished by **God** in your **creation**. *T-13.II.3.2*

~ **you will** go through this last undoing quite unharmed and **will** at last emerge as yourself. This is the last **step** in the **readiness** for **God**. *T-16.V.31.3:4*

~ **god will** take the last step swiftly when **you have** reached the **real world** and **have** been made ready for Him. *T-17.III.10.5*

~ **here you** are led that **God** Himself can take the final **step** unhindered, for **here** does **nothing interfere** with **love**, letting it be itself. A **step** beyond this holy place [of **forgiveness**], a **step** still further inward but the one **you** cannot take, transports **you** to something completely different. **Here** is the **Source** of **light**— **nothing** perceived, forgiven, nor transformed, but merely known. *T-18.X.94.4:6*

~ for this **you need** no pictures and no **learning** aids. *T-27.IV.34.8*

~ **forgiveness** vanishes and symbols fade, and **nothing** which the eyes **have** ever seen or ears **have** heard remains to be perceived. *T-27.IV.34.10*

~ the final **step** is God's because it is but **God** Who could create a perfect Son and **share** His Fatherhood with him. *T-30.VI.60.1*

~ this the **gift** by which **God** leans to us and lifts us up, taking salvation's final **step** Himself. All steps but this **we** learn, instructed by His **Voice**. But finally **He** comes Himself and takes us in His arms and sweeps away the cobwebs of our **sleep**. *W-pI.168.3.2:4*

~ **god will** take this final **step** Himself. *W-pI.193.20.3*

FORGIVENESS

|fərˈgivnəs|

Dictionary: *the action or process of forgiving or **being** forgiven.*

Ego; *empty gesture, **judgement**.*

~ forgiveness is an empty gesture unless it entails **correction**. Without this it is essentially judgmental rather than **healing**. *T-3.II.8.3:4*

~ the **ego** believes that to forgive another is to lose him. For it is only by **attack** without forgiveness that the **ego** can ensure the **guilt** which holds all its relationships together. *T-15.VIII.7.7:8*

~ to forgive may be an act of **charity**, but not his due. **He** may be pitied for his **guilt**, but not exonerated. And if **you** forgive him his transgressions, **you** but add to all the **guilt** that **he** has really earned. *T-27.III.13.8:10*

~ no one can forgive a **sin** which **he** believes is real. And what has consequences must be real because what it has done is there to **see**. Forgiveness is not pity which but seeks to pardon what it knows to be the **truth**. **Good** cannot be returned for **evil**, for forgiveness does not first establish **sin** and then forgive it. *T-27.III.14.4:7*

~ to **witness sin** and yet forgive it is a paradox which **reason** cannot **see**. For it maintains what has been done to **you** deserves no pardon. And by giving it, **you** grant your **brother** mercy but retain the proof **he** is not really **innocent**. *T-27.III.15.1:3*

~ offer pardon where **attack** is due and would be justified. *T-30.VII.70.6*

~ your pardon **will** become the **answer** to **attack** that has been made. And thus is pardon inappropriate, by **being** granted where it is not due. *T-30.VII.70.9:10*

~ **you** regard it as a **gift** unwarranted. *T-30.VII.72.4*

~ it pardons "sinners" sometimes but remains aware that **they have** sinned. And so **they** do not merit the forgiveness that it gives. *T-30.VII.72.7:8*

~ this is the false forgiveness which the **world** employs to keep the **sense** of **sin** alive. *T-30.VII.73.1*

~ **you** think forgiveness must be limited. *T-30.VII.75.5*

~ a **goal** of partial pardon and a limited escape from **guilt** for **you**. *T-30.VII.75.6*

~ thus is forgiveness basically unsound—a charitable whim, benevolent yet undeserved; a **gift** bestowed at times, at other times withheld. Unmerited, withholding it is just, nor is it fair that **you** should suffer when it is withheld. *W-pI.126.4.1:2*

~ for it is apt to be distorted and to be perceived as something which entails an **unfair sacrifice** of righteous wrath, a **gift** unjustified and undeserved, and a complete **denial** of the **truth**. In such a view, forgiveness must be seen as mere eccentric folly. *W-pI.134.1.1:2*

~ because **you** think your sins are real, **you** look on pardon as deception. For it is **impossible** to think of **sin** as true and not believe forgiveness is a lie. Thus is forgiveness really but a **sin**, like all the **rest**. It says the **truth** is false and smiles on the corrupt as if **they** were as blameless. *W-pI.134.4.1:4*

~ pardon is no escape in such a view. It merely is a further sign that **sin** is unforgivable, at best to be concealed, denied, or called another **name**, for pardon is a treachery to **truth**. **Guilt** cannot be forgiven. If **you** sin, your **guilt** is everlasting. Those who are forgiven from the view their sins are real are pitifully mocked and twice condemned— first by themselves for what **they** think **they** did and once again by those who pardon them. *W-pI.134.5.1:5*

~ no **gift** of **Heaven** has been more misunderstood than has forgiveness. It has, in **fact**, become a scourge; a curse where it was meant to bless, a cruel mockery of **grace**, a parody upon the holy **peace** of **God**. *S-2.I.1.1:2*

~ forgiveness' kindness is obscure at first, because **salvation** is not understood. What was meant to heal is used to **hurt** because forgiveness is not wanted. **Guilt** becomes **salvation**, and the remedy appears to be a terrible alternative to **life**. *S-2.I.1.4:6*

~ forgiveness-to-destroy **will** therefore suit the **purpose** of the **world** far better than its true objective, and the **honest means** by which this **goal** is reached. Forgiveness-to-destroy **will** overlook no **sin**, no crime, no **guilt** that it can **seek** and find and "**love**." Dear to its heart is **error**, and mistakes loom large and grow and swell **within** its **sight**. It carefully picks out all **evil** things, and overlooks the loving as a plague; a hateful **thing** of danger and of **death**. *S-2.1.2.1:4*

~ forgiveness-to-destroy is **death**, and this it sees in all it looks upon and hates. *S-2.1.2.3*

~ forgiveness-to-destroy has many forms, **being** a weapon of the **world** of **form**. Not all of them are obvious, and some are carefully concealed beneath what seems like **charity**. Yet all the forms that it may seem to take **have** but this single **goal**; their **purpose** is to separate and **make** what **God** created equal, different. *S-2.II.1.1:3*

~ in this group, first, there are the forms in which a "better" person deigns to stoop to save a "baser" one from what **he** truly is. Forgiveness **here** rests on an attitude of gracious lordliness so far from **love** that arrogance could never be dislodged. *S-2.II.2.1:2*

~ another **form**, still very like the first if it is understood, does not appear in quite such blatant arrogance. The one who would forgive the other does not claim to be the better. **Now he** says instead that **here** is one whose sinfulness **he** shares, since both **have** been unworthy and deserve the retribution of the wrath of **God**. This can appear to be a humble **thought**, and may indeed induce a rivalry in sinfulness and **guilt**. It is not **love** for God's **creation** and the **holiness** that is His **gift** forever. *S-2.II.3.1:5*

~ forgiveness-to-destroy **will** often **hide** behind a cloak like this. It shows the face of **suffering** and pain, in silent proof of **guilt** and of the ravages of **sin**. *S-2.II.5.1:2*

~ forgiveness-to-destroy can also take the **form** of bargaining and **compromise**. "**I will** forgive **you** if **you** meet my needs, for in your slavery is my **release**." *S-2.II.6.1:3*

~ all forms forgiveness takes that do not lead away from **anger, condemnation** and comparisons of every kind are **death**. *S-2.II.8.1*

HOLY SPIRIT;   *earthly form of love, key to happiness, **correction, release, salvation, healing, answer**, only sane response, end of specialness, **call** to **sanity, function, gift**, His function, Heaven's justice.*

~ the forgiven are filled with the **Soul**, and **they** forgive in return. *T-1.I.47.4*

~ miraculous forgiveness is only **correction**. It has no element of **judgment** at all. "**Father** forgive them for they know not what they do" in no **way** evaluates what they do. It is strictly limited to an appeal to **God** to heal their minds. There is no reference to the outcome of their mis-**thought**. That does not matter. *T-3.II.9.1:6*

~ forgiveness is the **healing** of the **perception of separation**. *T-3.VII.59.1*

~ to forgive is to overlook. *T-9.III.9.2*

~ forgiveness that is learned of me does not use **fear** to **undo fear**. Nor does it **make** real the unreal and then destroy it. *T-9.III.13.4:5*

~ forgiveness through the **Holy Spirit** lies simply in looking beyond **error** from the beginning and thus keeping it unreal for **you**. *T-9.III.14.1*

~ forgiveness is **release**. *T-15.IX.79.6*

~ forgiveness is not **loss** but your **salvation**. *T-15.IX.79.6*

~ there is **nothing** to forgive, **you** are absolved completely. *T-15.IX.79.7*

~ as **you** forgive him, **you** restore to **truth** what was denied by both of **you**. And **you will see** forgiveness where **you have** given it. *T-17.II.6.7:8*

~ forgiveness literally transforms **vision** and lets **you see** the **real world** reaching quietly and gently across **chaos** and removing all illusions which had twisted your **perception** and fixed it on the **past**. *T-17.III.12.2*

~ to forgive is merely to **remember** only the loving thoughts **you** gave in the **past** and those that were given **you**. *T-17.IV.14.1*

~ forgiveness is a selective remembering, based not on your selection. *T-17.IV.14.3*

~ even forgiveness is not the end. Forgiveness does **make** lovely, but it does not create. It is the **source** of **healing**, but it is the **messenger** of love and not its **Source**. *T-18.X.94.1:3*

~ forgiveness removes only the untrue, lifting the shadows from the **world** and carrying it safe and sure **within** its **gentleness** to the bright **world** of new and clean **perception**. *T-18.XI.98.3*

~ the sentence **sin** would lay upon him **he** can escape through your forgiveness. *T-19.V.78.7*

~ forgiveness cannot be withheld a **little**. *T-23.IV.44.5*

~ forgiveness is the only **function** meaningful in **time**. It is the **means** the **Holy Spirit** uses to translate specialness from **sin** into **salvation**. Forgiveness is for all. But when it rests on all, it is complete and every **function** of this **world** completed with it. *T-25.VII.47.3:6*

~ only forgiveness offers miracles. And pardon must be just to **everyone**. *T-25.X.85.5:6*

~ forgiveness is this world's equivalent of Heaven's **justice**. It translates the **world** of **sin** into a simple **world** where **justice** can be reflected from beyond the gate behind which total lack of limits lies. *T-26.V.25.1:2*

~ no one forgives unless **he** has believed in **sin** and still believes that **he** has much to be forgiven. Forgiveness thus becomes the **means** by which **he** learns **he** has done **nothing** to forgive. Forgiveness always rests upon the one who offers it until **he** sees himself as needing it no more. *T-26.V.25.5:7*

128

~ forgiveness turns the **world** of **sin** into a **world** of **glory**, wonderful to **see**. *T-26.V.26.1*

~ forgiveness is the great **release** from **time**. It is the key to **learning** that the **past** is over. *T-26.VI.36.1:2*

~ forgiveness is the only **function here** and serves to bring the **joy** this **world** denies to every aspect of God's Son where **sin** was **thought** to **rule**. *T-26.VIII.53.5*

~ forgiveness takes away what stands between your **brother** and yourself. It is the **wish** that **you** be joined with him and not apart. **We call** it "**wish**" because it still conceives of other choices and has not yet reached beyond the **world** of **choice** entirely. *T-26.VIII.54.5:7*

~ what is forgiveness but a willingness that **truth** be true? *T-26.VIII.56.3*

~ forgiveness is the **answer** to **attack** of any kind. So is **attack** deprived of its effects, and **hate** is answered in the **name** of **love**. *T-26.VIII.64.2:3*

~ forgiveness cannot be for one and not the other. Who forgives is healed. *T-27.III.15.9:10*

~ forgiveness is the **means** by which the **truth** is represented temporarily. It lets the **Holy Spirit make** exchange of pictures possible until the **time** when aids are meaningless and **learning** done. *T-27.IV.33.5:6*

~ forgiveness separates the dreamer from the **evil dream** and thus releases him. *T-28.VI.48.10*

~ whom **you** forgive is given **power** to forgive **you** your illusions. By your **gift** of **freedom** is it given unto **you**. *T-29.IX.23.2:3*

~ forgiveness is your **peace**, for herein lies the end of **separation** and the **dream** of danger and **destruction**, **sin**, and **death**; of **madness** and of murder, grief and **loss**. *T-29.VII.38.4*

~ **time** waits upon forgiveness that the things of **time** may disappear because **they have** no use. *T-29.VII.39.14*

~ forgiveness does not aim at keeping **time** but at its ending when it has no use. Its **purpose** ended; it is gone. And where it once held seeming sway is **now** restored the **function God** established for His Son in full **awareness**. **Time** can set no end to its fulfillment nor its changelessness. *T-29.VII.41.4:7*

~ forgiveness, once complete, brings timelessness so close the **song** of **Heaven** can be heard, not with the ears, but with the **holiness** which never left the **altar** which abides forever deep **within** the **Son of God**. *T-29.X.68.5*

~ **you** forgive a **sin** by overlooking what is really there. *T-30.VII.70.7*

~ overlook a real **attack** that calls for **punishment**. *T-30.VII.71.3*

~ forgiveness recognized as merited **will** heal. It gives the **miracle** its **strength** to overlook illusions. This is how **you** learn that **you** must be forgiven too. *T-30.VII.74.1:3*

~ although **God** does not forgive, His **love** is nevertheless the basis of forgiveness. **Fear** condemns, and **love** forgives. Forgiveness thus undoes what **fear** has produced, returning the **mind** to the **awareness** of **God**. For this **reason**, forgiveness can truly be called **salvation**. It is the **means** by which illusions disappear. *W-pI.46.2.1:5*

~ as forgiveness allows **love** to return to my **awareness**, I will see a **world** of **peace** and safety and **joy**. *W-pI.55.4.3*

~ having forgiven, **I** no longer **see** myself as guilty. *W-pI.58.2.2*

~ forgiveness is the **means** by which **I will** recognize my **innocence**. It is the **reflection** of God's **Love** on earth. It **will** bring me near enough to **Heaven** that the **Love** of God can reach down to me and raise me to my **home**. *W-pI.60.2.3:5*

~ it is your forgiveness that **will** bring the **world** of **darkness** to the **light**. It is your forgiveness that lets **you** recognize the **light** in which **you see**. Forgiveness is the demonstration that **you** are the **light** of the **world**. Through your forgiveness does the **truth** about yourself return to your **memory**. Therefore in your forgiveness lies your **salvation**. *W-pI.62.1.1:5*

~ all forgiveness is a **gift** to yourself. *W-pI.62.2.2*

~ every **time you** forgive **you call** upon the **strength** of **Christ** in you. *W-pI.62.3.1*

~ it **will** remove all **sense** of **weakness**, strain, and fatigue from your **mind**. It **will** take away all **fear** and **guilt** and **pain**. It **will** restore the **invulnerability** and **power God** gave His Son to your **awareness**. *W-pI.62.3.3:5*

~ the world's **salvation** awaits your forgiveness, because through it does the **Son of God** escape from all illusions and thus from all **temptation**. *W-pI.64.4.1*

~ forgiveness lifts the **darkness**, reasserts your **will**, and lets **you** look upon a **world** of **light**. *W-pI.73.5.5*

~ your forgiveness entitles **you** to **vision**. *W-pI.75.9.1*

~ forgive what **you have** made, and **you** are saved. *W-pI.99.15.7*

~ forgiveness offers everything **you want**. *W-pI.122.12.3*

~ it sparkles in your eyes as **you** awake and gives **you joy** with which to meet the day. It soothes your forehead while **you sleep** and rests upon your eyelids so **you see** no dreams of **fear** and **evil**, malice, and **attack**. And when **you** wake again, it offers **you** another day of happiness and **peace**. All this forgiveness offers **you**, and more. *W-pI.122.2.2:5*

~ forgive and be forgiven. *W-pI.122.6.3*

~ forgiveness stands between illusions and the **truth**, between the **world you see** and that which lies beyond, between the **hell** of **guilt** and Heaven's gate. *W-pI.134.10.4*

~ forgiveness must be practiced, for the **world** cannot perceive its **meaning** nor provide a guide to **teach you** its beneficence. There is no **thought** in all the **world** which leads to any understanding of the **laws** it follows nor the **thought** which it reflects. It is as alien to the **world** as is your own **reality**. And yet it joins your **mind** with the **reality** in **you**. *W-pI.134.13.1:4*

~ this twisted view of what forgiveness **means** is easily corrected when **you** can accept the **fact** that pardon is not asked for what is true. It must be limited to what is false. It is irrelevant to everything except illusions. *W-pI.134.2.1:3*

~ it is sin's unreality that makes forgiveness natural and wholly sane, a deep relief to those who offer it; a **quiet blessing** where it is received. It does not countenance illusions but collects them lightly with a **little** laugh and gently lays them at the feet of **truth**. And there **they** disappear entirely. *W-pI.134.6.1:3*

~ forgiveness is the only **thing** that stands for **truth** in the illusions of the **world**. It sees their nothingness and looks right through the thousand forms in which **they** may appear. It looks on lies but it is not deceived. *W-pI.134.7.1:3*

~ forgiveness shines away all **sin** and the **real world will** occupy the place of what **you** made. *W-pI.137.7.1*

~ **you** accept forgiveness as accomplished in yourself when **you** forgive. *W-pI.159.2.2*

~ forgiveness is an earthly **form** of **love** which as it is in **Heaven** has no **form**. Yet what is needed **here** is given **here** as it is needed. In this **form, you** can fulfill your **function** even **here**, although what **love will** mean to **you** when formlessness has been restored to **you** is greater still. **Salvation** of the **world** depends on **you** who can forgive. Such is your **function here**. *W-pI.186.14.2:6*

~ forgiveness represents your **function here**. It is not God's **creation**, for it is the **means** by which untruth can be undone. *W-pI.192.2.1:2*

~ forgiveness gently looks upon all things unknown in **Heaven**, sees them disappear, and leaves the **world** a clean and unmarked slate on which the **word** of **God** can **now** replace the senseless symbols written there before. Forgiveness is the **means** by which the **fear** of **death** is overcome because it holds no fierce **attraction now**, and **guilt** is gone. *W-pI.192.4.1:2*

~ forgiveness lets the **body** be perceived as what it is—a simple **teaching** aid to be laid by when **learning** is complete, but hardly changing him who learns at all. *W-pI.192.5.1*

~ **god** offers no forgiveness, for **He** knows no **sin** is possible. *W-pI.193.3.1*

~ when your forgiveness is complete, **you will have** total **gratitude**, for **you will see** that everything has earned the right to **love** by **being** loving, even as your **Self**. *W-pI.195.8.6*

~ accept the one **illusion** which proclaims there is no **condemnation** in God's Son, and **Heaven** is remembered instantly; the **world** forgotten, all its weird beliefs forgotten with it, as the **face of Christ** appears unveiled at last in this one **dream**. This is the **gift** the **Holy Spirit** holds for **you** from **God** your **Father**. *W-pI.198.12.1:2*

~ forgive and **you** are freed. *W-pI.198.2.2*

~ forgiveness sweeps all other dreams away, and though it is itself a **dream**, it breeds no others. All illusions save this one must multiply a thousand fold. But this is where illusions end. Forgiveness is the end of dreams because it is a **dream** of waking. It is not itself the **truth**. Yet does it point to where the **truth** must be and gives direction with the **certainty** of **God** Himself. It is a **dream** in which the **Son of God** awakens to his **Self** and to his **Father**, knowing They are one. *W-pI.198.3.1:7*

~ forgiveness is the only road that leads out of **disaster**, **past** all **suffering**, and finally away from **death**. *W-pI.198.4.1*

~ forgiveness paints a **picture** of a **world** where **suffering** is over, **loss** becomes **impossible**, and **anger** makes no **sense**. **Attack** is gone, and **madness** has an end. *W-pII.249.1.1:2*

~ forgiveness is the **means** by which our minds return to Him at last. *W-pII.256.1.10*

~ forgiveness is the only **gift I give** because it is the only **gift I want**, and everything **I give I give** myself. This is salvation's simple formula. *W-pII.297.1.1:2*

~ forgiveness shows us that **God's Will** is one and that **we share** it. *W-pII.331.2.1*

~ forgiveness is a **choice**. *W-pII.335.1.1*

~ forgiveness is the **means** appointed for perception's ending. *W-pII.336.1.1*

~ forgiveness sweeps away distortions and opens the hidden **altar** to the **truth**. Its lilies shine into the **mind** and **call** it to return and look **within**, to find what it has vainly sought without. For **here** and only **here** is **peace** of **mind** restored, for this the dwelling-place of **God** Himself. *W-pII.336.1.4:6*

~ forgiveness recognizes what **you thought** your **brother** did to **you** has not occurred. It does not pardon sins and **make** them real. It sees there was no **sin**. And in this view are all your sins forgiven. What is **sin** except a false **idea** about God's Son? Forgiveness merely sees its falsity and therefore lets it go. What then is free to take its place is **now** the **Will** of **God**. *W-pII.ST221.1.1:7*

~ forgiveness, on the other hand, is still and quietly does **nothing**. It offends no aspect of **reality** nor seeks to twist it to **appearance** that it likes. It merely looks and waits and judges not. **He** who would not forgive must judge, for **he** must justify his failure to forgive. But **he** who would forgive himself must learn to **welcome truth** exactly as it is. *W-pII.ST221.4.1:5*

~ for all that **we** forgive **we will** not **fail** to recognize as **part** of **God** Himself. And thus His **memory** is given back completely and complete. *W-pII.ST361.3.5:6*

~ forgiveness is its single aim at which all **learning** ultimately converges. It is indeed enough. *M-4.24.12:13*

~ it is meaningless to anyone **here**. Yet it is the final **lesson** in which **unity** is restored. It goes against all the thinking of the **world**, but so does **Heaven**. *M-14.3.9:11*

~ forgiveness is the necessary **condition** for finding the **peace** of **God**. *M-20.3.6*

~ given forgiveness there must be **peace**. *M-20.3.7*

~ to forgive is to heal. *M-22.1.9*

~ **where** there is forgiveness **truth** must come. *P-2.II.4.2*

~ forgiveness is prayer's ally; sister in the **plan** for your **salvation**. *S-2.IN.1.3*

~ **now** it has a **purpose** beyond which **you** cannot go, nor **have you need** to go. Accomplish this and **you have** been redeemed. Accomplish this and **you have** been transformed. Accomplish this and **you will** save the **world**. *S-2.IN.1.9*

~ it is **impossible** to forgive another, for it is only your sins **you see** in him. **You want** to **see** them there, and not in **you**. That is why forgiveness of another is an **illusion**. *S-2.I.4.2:4*

~ forgiveness, truly given, is the **way** in which your only hope of **freedom** lies. *S-2.I.6.1*

~ forgiveness is the **means** for your escape. *S-2.II.7.3*

~ **within** the **world** of opposites there is a **way** to use forgiveness for the **goal** of **God**, and find the **peace He** offers **you**. *S-2.II.7.5*

~ let it not be **you** who sets the **form** in which forgiveness comes to save God's Son. *S-2.III.5.3*

~ forgiveness has a **Teacher** Who **will fail** in **nothing**. *S-2.III.7.2*

~ forgiveness must be given by a **mind** which understands that it must overlook all shadows on the holy **face of Christ**, among which **sickness** should be seen as one. *S-3.I.3.3*

FORM |fôrm|

DICTIONARY: *the visible shape or configuration of something.*

EGO

~ **you** cannot **have** the frame without the **picture**. What **you value** is the frame, for there **you see** no **conflict**. Yet the frame is only the wrapping for the **gift** of **conflict**. The frame is not the **gift**. *T-17.V.35.4:7*

~ **sight** of form **means** understanding has been obscured. *T-22.IV.34.8*

~ when **you** decide upon the form of what **you want**, **you** lose the understanding of its **purpose**. *T-30.IV.39.9*

HOLY SPIRIT; *a means for content, frame.*

~ form does not matter to the **Holy Spirit** and therefore does not matter at all. *T-9.IV.23.1*

~ form does not matter. *T-9.IV.23.1*

~ without the frame, the **picture** is seen as what it represents. *T-17.V.37.7*

~ if what the form conceals is a **mistake**, the form cannot prevent **correction**. *T-22.IV.33.2*

~ **you** can **change** form because it is not true. It could not be **reality** because it can be changed. **Reason will** tell **you** that, if form is not **reality**, it must be an **illusion** and is not there to **see**. *T-22.IV.35.2:4*

~ **god** knows not form. He cannot **answer you** in terms which **have** no **meaning**. And your **will** could not be satisfied with empty forms made but to fill a **gap** which is not there. It is not this **you want**. *T-30.IV.41.5:8*

~ these are the forms which never can deceive, although **they** come from Formlessness Itself. *W-pI.186.14.1*

~ no form endures. It is the **thought** behind the form of things that lives unchangeable. *W-pI.187.4.5:6*

FORM/CONTENT *see "form"*

Ego

~ **you** are too bound to **form** and not to content. What **you** consider content is not content at all. It is merely **form**, and **nothing** else. *T-14.VI.52.3:5*

~ the **ego** is incapable of understanding content and is totally unconcerned with it. To the **ego**, if the **form** is acceptable, the content must be. Otherwise, it **will attack** the **form**. *T-14.VI.53.1:3*

~ for **form** is not enough for **meaning**, and the underlying lack of content makes a cohesive system **impossible**. *T-14.VI.54.3*

~ it is your separate **purpose** that obscures the **picture** and cherishes the frame instead of it. *T-25.III.17.5*

Holy Spirit; *frame/picture*

~ the **Holy Spirit** is not concerned with **form** at all, **being** aware only of **meaning**. *T-8.X.100.4*

~ **form** is but a **means** for content. And the frame is but a **means** to hold the **picture** up so that it can be seen. A frame that hides the **picture** has no **purpose**. *T-25.III.15.3:5*

~ without the **picture** is the frame without its **meaning**. Its **purpose** is to set the **picture** off and not itself. *T-25.III.15.7:8*

~ **complexity** of **form** does not imply **complexity** of content. *W-pI.64.6.5*

FRAGMENT |ˈfragmənt|

Dictionary: *a small **part** broken or separated off something.*

Ego

~ to fragment is to break into pieces. *T-7.IX.87.1*

~ this is but a **way** of avoiding or looking away from the whole to what **you** think **you** might be better able to **understand**. For this is but another **way** in which **you** would still try to keep understanding to yourself. *T-16.III.11.2:3*

~ to fragment is to exclude. *T-18.I.1.6*

~ no one is seen complete. *T-18.I.3.6*

~ each tiny fragment seems to be **self**-contained needing each other for some things but by no **means** totally dependent on their one **Creator** for everything and needing the whole to **give** them any **meaning**, for by themselves **they** do mean **nothing**. Nor **have they** any **life** apart and by themselves. *T-18.IX.75.3:4*

~ separate fragments must decay and die. *M-19.4.4*

Holy Spirit; *exclude*

~ it is **impossible** to fragment the **mind**. *T-7.IX.86.6*

FREE WILL

DICTIONARY: *the **power** of acting without the constraint of necessity or fate; the ability to act at one's own discretion.*

Ego

~ the **ego** is the **denial** of free **will**. *T-8.III.10.3*

Holy Spirit

~ his free **will** was given him for his own **joy** in creating the perfect. *T-2.I.14.4*

~ free **will** can temporize and is capable of enormous procrastination. But it cannot depart entirely from its **Creator,** Who set the limits on its ability to miscreate by virtue of its own real **purpose.** *T-2.II.47.6:7*

~ free **will** does not mean that **you** can establish the **curriculum.** It **means** only that **you** may elect what **you** **want** to take at a given **time.** *T-1.I.3:4*

~ free **will** must lead to **freedom.** *T-3.VIII.71.3*

FREEDOM

DICTIONARY: *the **power** or right to act, speak, or think as one wants without hindrance or restraint.*

Ego

~ freedom cannot be learned by tyranny of any kind. *T-8.V.32.7*

~ **you** are not free to **give** up freedom, but only to deny it. *T-9.X.89.1*

~ freedom must be **impossible** as long as **you** perceive a **body** as yourself. The **body** is a **limit.** Who would **seek** for freedom in a **body** looks for it where it cannot be found. The **mind** can be made free when it no longer sees itself as in a **body,** firmly tied to it and sheltered by its presence. *W-pI.199.1.1:4*

Holy Spirit; *gift, creation, love.*

~ freedom is the only **gift you** can offer to God's Sons, **being** an **acknowledgment** of what **they** are and what **He** is. Freedom is **creation,** because it is **love.** *T-8.V.34.1:2*

~ in the freedom that **you see** in him, **you see** your own. For this **you** share. *T-20.V.30.4:5*

~ those who choose freedom **will experience** only its results. Their **power** is of **God,** and **they will give** it only to what **God** has given to **share** with them. **Nothing** but this can touch them, for they **see** only this, sharing their **power** according to the **Will** of **God.** And thus their freedom is established and maintained. It is upheld through all **temptation** to imprison and to be imprisoned. *T-20.V.31.1:5*

~ freedom of the **body** or of the **mind?** For both **you** cannot **have.** Which do **you value?** Which is your **goal?** For one **you see** as **means;** the other, end. And one must serve the other and lead to its predominance, increasing its importance by diminishing its own. *T-22.VII.51.1:6*

~ no one but yearns for freedom and tries to find it. Yet **he will seek** for it where **he** believes it is and can be found. **He will** believe it possible of **mind** or **body,** and **he will make** the other serve his **choice** as **means** to find it. *T-22.VII.51.8:10*

~ **where** freedom of the **body** has been chosen, the **mind** is used as **means** whose **value** lies in its ability to contrive ways to achieve the body's freedom. Yet freedom of the **body** has no **meaning,** and so the **mind** is dedicated to serve illusions. This is a **situation** so contradictory and so **impossible** that anyone who chooses this has no **idea** of what is valuable. *T-22.VII.52.1:3*

- there is no freedom from what must occur. *T-30.II.30.5*

- and in your freedom lies the freedom of the **world**. *W-pI.31.4.3*

- freedom is your **gift**, and **you** can **now receive** the **gift you** gave. *W-pI.198.1.6*

- and how sure is all the world's **salvation** when **we** learn our freedom can be found in **God alone**. *W-pII.321.2.3*

- in his freedom is the end of **fear**. *M-28.4.4*

FULL TRANSFER
A Course in Miracles Term

HOLY SPIRIT

- when the **Holy Spirit** has at last led **you** to **Christ** at the **altar** to His **Father**, **perception** fuses into **knowledge** because **perception** has become so holy that its transfer to **holiness** is merely its natural **extension**. **Love** transfers to **love** without any interference, for the situations are identical. [Only the ability to **make** this transfer is the product of **learning**. *T-11.VII.59.3.5*

- its applicability is universal. When this has been accomplished, **perception** and **knowledge have** become so similar that **they share** the unification of the **laws** of **God**. *T-11.VII.59.7.8*

FUNCTION
ˈfəNG(k)SH(ə)n

DICTIONARY: *an activity or **purpose** natural to or intended for a person or **thing**.*

EGO

- **confusion** of functions is so typical of the **ego**. *T-9.III.15.3*

- the **ego** teaches that your function on earth is **destruction** and that **you have** no function at all in **Heaven**. *T-12.IV.23.4*

- function as **destruction, you will** lose **sight** of the **present** and hold on to the **past** to ensure a destructive **future**. *T-12.IV.32.5*

- **you have** decided against your function in **Heaven**. *T-13.IX.91.1*

- **he will** suffer the **pain** of dim **awareness** that his true function remains unfulfilled in him. *T-14.II.6.3*

- futility of function not fulfilled **will** haunt **you** while your **brother** lies asleep, till what has been assigned to **you** is done and **he** is risen from the **past**. *T-24.VII.57.3*

- if **you** confuse your function with the function of Another, **you** must be confused about yourself and who **you** are. *T-27.III.22.7*

- your function is obscure to **you**. *T-29.V.30.2*

- the functions which the **world** esteems are so **uncertain** that **they change** ten times an hour at their most secure. *W-pI.186.10.5*

- the imagined usurping of functions not your own is the basis of **fear**. *M-29.3.6*

HOLY SPIRIT

- the **extension** of God's **Being** is the Soul's only function. *T-7.X.93.4*

- yet the function which **God** Himself gave your minds through His **you** may deny, but **you** cannot prevent. *T-7.X.100.1*

~ knowing His function perfectly, **He** wills to fulfill it perfectly because that is His **joy** and yours. *T-8.IV.16.7*

~ functions are **part** of **being** since **they** arise from it. *T-8.VIII.70.2*

~ his function is to distinguish only between the false and the true, replacing the false with the true. *T-8.IX.84.4*

~ when **we** said that the Holy Spirit's function is to sort out the true from the false in your unconscious, **we** meant that **He** has the **power** to look into what **you have** hidden and perceive the **Will** of **God** there. *T-8.X.93.2*

~ because **forgiveness** is His function, and He knows how to fulfill it perfectly. *T-9.III.14.5*

~ as your function in **Heaven** is **creation**, so your function on earth is **healing**. **God** shares His function with **you** in **Heaven**, and the **Holy Spirit** shares His with **you** on earth. *T-11.VIII.64.7:8*

~ your function in this **world** is **healing**, and your function in **Heaven** is creating. *T-12.IV.23.3*

~ for your function is not **little**, and it is only by finding your function and fulfilling it that **you** can escape from littleness. *T-15.IV.24.5*

~ there is no **doubt** about what your function is, for the **Holy Spirit** knows what it is. There is no **doubt** about its **magnitude**, for it reaches **you** through Him from **Magnitude**. **You** do not **have** to strive for it because **you have** it. *T-15.IV.25.1:3*

~ to fulfill this function, **you** relate to your **creations** as God to His. *T-17.V.27.5*

~ it is the only one which has no limits and reaches out to every broken **fragment** of the **Sonship** with **healing** and uniting comfort. This is offered **you** in your **holy relationship**. *T-18.II.13.2:3*

~ when the **peace** in **you** has been extended to encompass **everyone**, the Holy Spirit's function **here will** be accomplished. *T-19.IV.39.6*

~ once **you** accept His **plan** as the one function that **you** would fulfill, there **will** be **nothing** else the **Holy Spirit will** not arrange for **you** without your **effort**. *T-20.V.35.4*

~ whose function is to save **will** save. How **he will** do it is beyond your understanding, but when must be your **choice**. *T-22.III.23.5:6*

~ for **you have** asked what is your function **here** and **have** been answered. **Seek** not to **change** it nor to **substitute** another **goal**. [This one was given **you** and only this.]. *T-22.VII.58.4:7*

~ **extension** of **forgiveness** is the Holy Spirit's function. *T-22.VII.59.2*

~ what is the same can **have** no different function. *T-23.V.49.4*

~ **you have** a function in **salvation**. Its pursuit **will** bring **you** joy. *T-24.III.13.5:6*

~ it cannot be that it is hard to do the task that **Christ** appointed **you** to do, since it is **He** Who does it. *T-25.II.4.1*

~ it is the Holy Spirit's function to **teach you** how this **oneness** is experienced, what **you** must do that it can be experienced, and where **you** should go to do it. *T-25.II.9.4*

~ it is still your only function to behold in him what **he** sees not. And in this seeing is the **vision** shared that looks on **Christ** instead of seeing **death**. *T-25.III.19.7:8*

~ your function is to [prove to] your **brother** that **sin** can **have** no **cause**. *T-27.II.10.1*

~ **identity** and function are the same, and by your function do **you** know yourself. *T-27.III.22.6*

~ **you** cannot **change**, because your function has been fixed by God. *T-29.VII.41.2*

~ only what **God** would **have** us do is possible. *W-pI.45.5.1*

~ only what **God** would **have** us do is what **we want** to do. *W-pI.45.5.2*

~ **we** cannot **fail** in **doing** what **He** would **have** us do. *W-pI.45.5.3*

~ your function **here** is to be the **light** of the **world**, a function given **you** by **God**. W-pI.64.3.1

~ only by fulfilling the function given **you** by **God will you** be **happy**. That is because your function is to be **happy** by using the **means** by which happiness becomes inevitable. W-pI.64.4.3:4

~ the full **acceptance** of **salvation** as your only function necessarily entails two phases: the recognition of **salvation** as your function and the relinquishment of all the other goals **you have** invented for yourself. W-pI.65.1.5

~ not only is there a very real connection between the function **God** gave **you** and your happiness, but that **they** are actually identical. **God** gives **you** only happiness. Therefore the function **He** gave **you** must be happiness, even if it appears to be different. W-pI.66.4.1:3

~ it is through accepting my function that **I will see** the **light** in me. And in this **light will** my function stand clear and perfectly unambiguous before my **sight**. W-pI.81.5.1:2

~ i cannot fulfill my function by forgetting. And unless **I** fulfill my function, **I will** not **experience** the **joy** that **God** intends for me. W-pI.82.5.2:3

~ i have no function but the one **God** gave me. W-pI.83.2.1

~ fulfilling my function is my happiness because both come from the same **Source**. W-pI.83.5.3

~ **salvation** is your function with the One to Whom the **plan** was given. W-pI.99.7.1

~ **you have** no function that is not of **God**. W-pI.99.15.4

~ your only function tells **you you** are one. W-pI.99.18.1

~ one function shared by separate minds unites them in one **purpose**, for each one is equally essential to them all. W-pI.100.1.3

~ **joy** is our function **here**. W-pI.100.6.1

~ then **seek** this function deep **within** your **mind**, for it is there, awaiting but your **choice**. **You** cannot **fail** to find it when **you** learn it is your **choice** and that **you share God's Will**. W-pI.102.6.1:2

~ be **happy**, for your only function **here** is happiness. W-pI.102.7.1

~ and **you will** learn your function from the One Who chose it in your Father's **Name** for **you**. W-pI.106.6.4

~ to **share** His function is to **share** His **joy**. W-pI.107.11.3

~ and that One **Voice** appoints your function and relays it to **you**, giving **you** the **strength** to **understand** it, do what it entails, and to succeed in everything **you** do that is related to it. W-Pi.154.3.2

~ these unsubstantial images **will** go and leave your **mind** unclouded and serene when **you** accept the function given **you**. W-pI.186.10.2

~ your truly given function stands out clear and wholly unambiguous. W-pI.186.11.1

~ we did not establish it. It is not our **idea**. The **means** are given us by which it **will** be perfectly accomplished. All that **we** are asked to do is to accept our **part** in genuine **humility** and not deny with **self**-deceiving arrogance that **we** are worthy. What is given us to do **we have** the **strength** to do. Our minds are suited perfectly to take the **part** assigned to us by One Who knows us well. W-pI.186.2.2:7

~ listen to **God's Voice** reveal to us what **He** would **have** us do. **We** do not **doubt** our adequacy for the function **He will** offer us. **We will** be certain only that **He** knows our strengths, our wisdom, and our **holiness**. And if **He** deems us worthy, so **we** are. It is but arrogance that judges otherwise. W-pI.186.4.1:5

~ your function **here** on earth is only to forgive him, that **you** may accept him back as your **Identity**. W-pI.192.10.6

~ unify our thoughts and actions meaningfully and achieve only what **God** would **have** us do **today**. W-pII.257.1.4

~ i have a **special** place to fill—a **role** for me **alone**. W-pII.317.1.1

~ now must **you share** His function and forgive whom **He** has saved, whose sinlessness **He** sees, and whom **He** honors as the **Son of God.** W-pII.ST221.5.4

~ let our function be only to let this **memory** return, only to let **God's Will** be done on earth, only to be restored to **sanity**, and to be but as **God** created us. W-pII.ST321.4.6

~ it is our function to **remember** Him on earth, as it is given us to be His own **completion** in **reality**. W-pII. ST361.4.1

~ all **God** would **have you** do, **you** can do. M-14.5.10

~ to return the function to the One to Whom it belongs is thus the escape from **fear**. And it is this that lets the **memory** of **love** return to you. M-29.3.8:9

FUTURE
|ˈfyo͞oCHər|

DICTIONARY: *the **time** or a period of **time** following the moment of speaking or writing; **time** regarded as still to come.*

EGO; *hell*

~ the future, in **time**, is always associated with expiation, and only **guilt** could induce a **sense** of **need** for expiation. T-11.X.97.2

~ its emphasis on **guilt** enables it to ensure its continuity by making the future like the **past** and thus avoiding the **present**. By the notion of paying for the **past** in the future, the **past** becomes the determiner of the future, making them continuous without an intervening **present**. For the **ego** uses the **present** only as a brief transition to the future, in which it brings the **past** to the future by interpreting the **present** in **past** terms. T-12.IV.26.3:5

~ **past**, **present**, and future are not continuous unless **you** force continuity on them. **You** can perceive them as continuous and **make** them so for **you**. T-12.VI.48.2:3

~ **you** would anticipate the future on the basis of your **past experience** and **plan** for it accordingly. Yet by **doing** so, **you** are aligning **past** and future and not allowing the **miracle**, which could intervene between them, to free **you** to be born again. T-12.VI.48.6:7

~ the plans **you make** for safety all are laid **within** the future, where **you** cannot **plan**. No **purpose** has been given it as yet, and what **will** happen has as yet no **cause**. T-26.IX.72.1:2

~ the future **will** be like the **past** and but a series of depressing dreams in which all idols **fail you** one by one, and **you see death** and disappointment everywhere. T-29.VIII.48.8

GAIN

DICTIONARY: *obtain or secure (something desired, favorable, or profitable).*

EGO

~ another's **loss** becomes your gain. *T-23.III.27.4*

~ in this **world**, it seems that one must gain because another lost. *T-25.VIII.60.2*

HOLY SPIRIT

~ to gain **you** must **give**, not **bargain**. *T-7.II.4.3*

~ **we will** gain everything by giving Him the **power** and the **glory** and keeping no illusions of where **they** are. *T-17.V.42.3*

~ **everyone** must gain if anyone would be a gainer. *T-25.VIII.61.2*

~ no one needs **practice** to gain what is already his. *W-pI.39.2.6*

~ it is **impossible** that one can gain because another loses. *W-pI.105.2.2*

~ **they** gain by every **message** which **they give** away. *W-pI.154.7.4*

GAP

DICTIONARY: *a break or hole in an object or between two objects.*

EGO; *birthplace of illusions*

~ the **little** gap **you** do not even **see**, the birthplace of illusions and of **fear**, the **time** of terror and of ancient **hate**, the instant of **disaster**, all are **here**. **Here** is the **cause** of unreality. *T-27.VIII.72.4:5*

~ the **little** gap **unhealed**, where **sickness** is kept carefully protected, cherished, and upheld by firm **belief**, lest **God** should come to **bridge** the **little** gap that leads to Him. *T-28.IV.30.5*

~ the gap is **little**. Yet it holds the seeds of pestilence and every **form** of ill because it is a **wish** to keep apart and not to **join**. And thus it seems to **give** a **cause** to sickness which is not its **cause**. The **purpose** of the gap is all the **cause** that **sickness** has. For it was made to keep **you** separated in a **body** which **you see** as if it were the **cause** of pain. *T-28.IV.31.2:6*

~ **little** gap, inhabited but by illusions which **you have** supported in each other's minds. *T-28.V.40.6*

~ in the gap no stable **self** exists. What is the same seems different because what is the same appears to be unlike. *T-28.V.42.1:2*

~ **you have** conceived a **little** gap between illusions and the **truth** to be the place where all your safety lies and where your **Self** is safely hidden by what **you have** made. *T-28.VI.50.1*

~ a space where **God** is not, a gap between the **Father** and the Son is not the **will** of either, who **have** promised to be one. *T-28.VIII.60.5*

~ the gap between **you** is not one of space between two separate bodies. This but seems to be dividing off your separate minds. It is the **symbol** of a **promise** made to meet when **you** prefer and separate until **you** both elect to meet again. And then your bodies seem to get in touch and signify a meeting-place to **join**. But always is it possible to go your separate ways. Conditional upon the "right" to separate **will you** agree to meet from **time** to **time** and keep apart in intervals of **separation**, which protect **you** from the "**sacrifice**" of **love**. The **body** saves **you**, for it gets away from total **sacrifice** and gives **you** time in which to build again your separate selves, which **you** believe diminish as **you** meet. *T-29.II.4.1:7*

HOLY SPIRIT

~ sooner or later must **everyone bridge** the gap which **he** imagines exists between his selves. Each one builds this **bridge** which carries him across the gap. *T-16.IV.28.2:4*

~ there is no gap which separates the **truth** from dreams and from illusions. *T-28.VI.52.4*

~ the gap is carefully concealed in fog, and misty pictures rise to cover it with vague, **uncertain** forms and changing shapes, forever unsubstantial and unsure. Yet in the gap is **nothing**. *T-28.VI.53.3:4*

~ either there is a gap between **you** and your **brother**, or **you** are as one. There is no in between, no other **choice**, and no allegiance to be split between the two. A split allegiance is but faithlessness to both and merely sets **you** spinning round, to grasp uncertainly at any straw that seems to hold some **promise** of relief. *T-28. VIII.62.1:3*

~ there is no **way** in which a gap could be conceived of in the **wholeness** that is His. The **compromise** the least and littlest gap would represent in His eternal **love** is quite **impossible**. *T-29.I.1.3:4*

~ all that happens when the gap is gone is **peace** eternal. *T-29.II.9.1*

~ the gap between your **brother** and yourself was never there. *T-30.VI.62.4*

~ every gap is closed and **separation** healed. *W-pI.184.12.4*

GARDEN OF EDEN |ˈēdn|

DICTIONARY: *the place where Adam and Eve lived in the biblical account of the **Creation**, from which **they** were expelled for disobediently eating the fruit of the tree of the **knowledge** of **good** and **evil**.*

EGO

~ **god** rejected **man** and forced him out of the Garden of Eden. *T-3.III.16.2*

HOLY SPIRIT

~ the Garden of Eden, which is described as a literal garden in the Bible, was not an actual garden at all. It was merely a mental state of complete **need**-lack. Even in the literal account, it is noteworthy that the pre-**separation** state was essentially one in which **man** needed **nothing**. The "tree of **knowledge**" is also an overly literal figure. These concepts **need** to be clarified before the real **meaning** of the **separation**, or the "detour into **fear**," can be fully understood. *T-2.I.4.1:5*

GENTLENESS |ˈjen(t)lnəs|

EGO

~ the Maker of the **world** of gentleness has perfect **power** to offset the **world** of violence and **hate** that seems to stand between **you** and His gentleness. *T-25.IV.30.1*

HOLY SPIRIT

~ to those who would do **harm**, it is **impossible**. To those to whom **harm** has no **meaning**, it is merely natural. *M-4.15.3:4*

~ the might of God's teachers lies in their gentleness. *M-4.15.8*

~ gentleness **means** that **fear** is **now impossible**. *M-4.16.2*

~ the open hands of gentleness are always filled. The gentle **have** no **pain**. **They** cannot suffer. *M-4.16.3:5*

141

DICTIONARY: *a **thing** given willingly to someone without **payment**; a **present**.*

EGO;   *evaluation*

~ the gifts **you** offer to the **ego** are always experienced as sacrifices. *T-7.VIII.81.4*

~ **suffering** and **sacrifice** are the gifts with which the **ego** would "bless" all unions. *T-15.VIII.73.1*

~ this gift is given **you** for your damnation, and if **you** take it, **you will** believe that **you** are damned. *T-17.V.35.3*

~ the wrapping does not **make** the gift **you** give. An empty box, however beautiful and gently given, still contains **nothing**. And neither the receiver nor the giver is long deceived. *T-23.IV.42.2:4*

~ **they** are not welcomed gladly by a **mind** which has instead received the gifts it made where His belong, as substitutes for them. *W-pI.104.1.5*

~ meaningless and **self**-made gifts which **we have** placed upon the holy **altar** where God's gifts belong. They are not like to the gifts the **world** can give, in which the giver loses as **he** gives the gift; the taker is the richer by his **loss**. These are not gifts, but bargains made with **guilt**. *W-pI.104.2.1:2*

~ such "gifts" are but a bid for a more valuable return—a loan with interest to be paid in full; a temporary lending, meant to be a pledge of debt to be repaid with more than was received by him who took the gift. *W-pI.105.2.5*

~ not having given Him the gift **He** asks of **you**, **you** cannot recognize His gifts and think **He** has not given them to **you**. **He** must believe that, to accept God's gifts, however evident **they** may become, however urgently **he** may be called to claim them as his own, is **being** pressed to treachery against himself. **He** must deny their presence, contradict the **truth**, and suffer to preserve the **world he** made. *W-pI.126.7.1:3*

~ your gifts must be received with honor, lest **they** be withdrawn. And so **you** think God's gifts are loans at best; at worst, deceptions which would cheat **you** of defenses to ensure that when **He** strikes **He will** not **fail** to kill. *W-pI.197.1.4:5*

~ withdraw the gifts **you** give, and **you will** think that what is given **you** has been withdrawn. *W-pI.197.6.1*

HOLY SPIRIT;   *evaluation*

~ the gifts **you** offer to the **Kingdom** are gifts to **you**. **They will** always be treasured by **God**, because **they** belong to His beloved Sons who belong to Him. *T-7.VIII.81.4:5*

~ his gifts are eternal. *T-9.XI.102.10*

~ out of your gifts to Him, the **Kingdom will** be restored to His Son. *T-9.XI.103.1*

~ christ's gift **you** can bestow, and your Father's gift **you** cannot lose. *T-13.II.71*

~ the **Holy Spirit** knows your **part** in the **redemption** and who are seeking **you** and where to find them. *T-13.II.7.3*

~ **nothing** can obscure the gift of **God**. *T-14.IV.32.3*

~ the only gift **I** can accept of **you** is the gift **I** gave to **you**. *T-15.X.92.8*

~ the gift of **union** is the only gift that **I** was born to **give**. *T-15.X.94.4*

~ each is complete and cannot be partially accepted. Each is a **picture** of all that **you** can **have**, seen very differently. *T-17.V.38.2:3*

~ the gift is given forever, for **God** Himself received it. **You** cannot take it back. *T-18.IV.27.7:8*

~ **faith** and hope and mercy are yours to **give**. Into the hands that **give** the gift is given. *T-19.V.106.1:2*

~ behold the gift of **freedom** that **I** gave the **Holy Spirit** for both of **you**. *T-19.V.106.6*

~ giving it, **receive** it of Him in return for what **you** gave. *T-19.V.106.8*

~ gifts are not made through bodies if **they** be truly given and received. *T-20.III.6.1*

~ it **will** adorn its chosen **home** most carefully, making it ready to **receive** the gifts it wants by **offering** them to those who come unto its chosen **home** or those it would attract to it. And there **they will** exchange their gifts, **offering** and receiving what their minds judge to be worthy of them. *T-20.III.6.5:6*

~ your gift has saved him from the thorns and nails, and his strong arm is free to guide **you** safely through them and beyond. This gift returns the **laws** of **God** to your remembrance. *T-20.III.14.4:5*

~ by this gift is given **you** the **power** to **release** your **savior** that **he** may **give salvation** unto **you**. *T-21.III.17.8*

~ what the **Holy Spirit** does with the gifts **you give** each other, to whom **He** offers them, and where and when is up to Him. **He will** bestow them where **they** are received and welcomed. **He will** use every one of them for **peace**. *T-22.VII.58.7:9*

~ offer Him the tiny gifts **He** can extend forever. **He will** take each one and **make** of it a potent force for **peace**. *T-22.VII.59.5:6*

~ **he will** withhold no **blessing** from it nor **limit** it in any **way**. **He will** join to it all the **power** that **God** has given Him to **make** each **little** gift of **love** a **source** of **healing** for **everyone**. Each **little** gift **you** offer to the other lights up the **world**. *T-22.VII.59.7:9*

~ it was given **you** to be used and not obscured. *T-22.VII.65.5*

~ his **need** to **give** it is as great as yours to **have** it. *T-24.III.19.4*

~ giving it **you** learn to **understand** His gift to **you**. *T-25.III.21.5*

~ it is His **special function** to hold out to **you** the gifts the **innocent** deserve. *T-25.IX.72.2*

~ nor is the **treasure** less as it is given out. Each gift [received] but adds to the supply. *T-25.X.79.5:6*

~ his gifts can never suffer **sacrifice** and **loss**. *T-26.II.8.3*

~ the gift of **God** to **you** is limitless. There is no circumstance it cannot **answer** and no **problem** which is not resolved **within** its gracious **light**. *T-26.VIII.65.4:5*

~ what **you see** as gifts your **brother** offers represent the gifts **you dream** your **Father** gives to **you**. *T-27.VIII.76.3*

~ behold His Son, His perfect gift. *T-29.VI.34.2*

~ to **give** this gift is how to **make** it yours. And **God** ordained in loving kindness that it be for **you**. *T-31.VIII.93.8:9*

~ and it is His gift to **you**, rather than your own, which offers **vision** to **you**. *W-pI.42.1.5*

~ the **Holy Spirit** never fails to **give** the gift of **sight** to the forgiving. *W-pI.75.9.2*

~ thus **will** your gift to Him be multiplied a thousand fold and tens of thousands more. *W-pI.97.7.1*

~ yet **will** the steady brilliance of this **light** remain, and leads **you** out of **darkness**, nor **will you** be able to forget the **way** again. Expressed through **you**, the **Holy Spirit will** accept this gift which **you** received of Him, increase its **power**, and **give** it back to **you**. *W-pI.97.7.3:4*

~ **you** cannot lose the gifts your **Father** gave. *W-pI.99.15.2*

~ must there be a place made ready to **receive** His gifts. *W-pI.104.1.4*

~ these are the gifts which are our own in **truth**. His are the gifts which **we** inherited before **time** was and which **will** still be ours when **time** has passed into **eternity**. *W-pI.104.2.2:3*

~ these are the gifts which are **within** us **now**, for **they** are timeless. And **we need** not wait to **have** them. *W-pI.104.3.1:2*

~ these gifts increase as **we receive** them. *W-pI.105.1.3*

~ the truly given gift entails no **loss**. W-pI.105.2.1

~ god's gifts **will** never lessen when **they** are given away. They but increase thereby. As Heaven's **peace** and **joy** intensify when **you** accept them as God's gift to **you**, so does the **joy** of your **Creator** grow when **you** accept His **joy** and **peace** as yours. W-pI.105.4.2:4

~ it **will** come to **you** in the amount in which **you** gave it. W-pI.108.12.1

~ **he** receives your gifts in loving **gratitude** and gives them back a thousand and a hundred thousand more than **they** were given. **He will** bless your gifts by sharing them with **you**, and so **they** grow in **power** and in **strength** until **they** fill the **world** with gladness and with **gratitude**. W-pI.123.6.2:3

~ all things that live bring gifts to **you** and offer them in **gratitude** and gladness at your feet. W-pI.156.4.2

~ **ask** to **receive**, and it is given **you**. W-pI.165.4.4

~ all things are given **you**. God's **trust** in **you** is limitless. **He** knows His Son. **He** gives without **exception**, holding **nothing** back that can contribute to your happiness. And yet unless your **will** is one with His, His gifts are not received. W-pI.166.11:5

~ the gifts **you have** are not for **you alone**. W-pI.166.12.3

~ for **God** entrusts the giving of His gifts to all who **have** received them. W-pI.166.15.6

~ no gift of **God** can be unshared. It is this attribute that sets the gifts of **God** apart from every **dream** that ever seemed to take the place of **truth**. W-pI.185.12.4:5

~ no one can lose and **everyone** must **gain** whenever any gift of **God** has been requested and received by anyone. W-pI.185.13.1

~ your **gratitude** is all your gifts require that **they** be a lasting **offering** of a thankful heart released from **hell** forever. W-pI.197.3.3

~ it is **you** who honor them and **give** them fitting thanks, for it is **you** who **have** received the gifts. W-pI.197.3.5

~ it does not matter if your gifts seem lost and ineffectual. They are received where **they** are given. In your **gratitude** are **they** accepted universally and thankfully acknowledged by the Heart of **God** Himself. W-pI.197.4.3:5

~ god blesses every gift **you give** to Him and every gift is given Him because it can be given only to yourself, and what belongs to **God** must be His own. W-pI.197.5.1

~ his gifts are sure, eternal, changeless, limitless, forever giving out, extending **love**, and adding to your never-ending **joy**. W-pI.197.5.2

~ in **value** far beyond all things of which **I** can conceive. W-pII.315.1.2

~ every gift my brothers **give** is mine, so every gift **I give** belongs to me. Each one allows a **past mistake** to go and leave no **shadow** on the holy **mind** my **Father** loves. His **grace** is given me in every gift a **brother** has received throughout all **time** and **past** all **time** as well. W-pII.316.1.1:3

~ as illusions go, **I** find the gifts illusions tried to **hide**, awaiting me in shining **welcome** and in **readiness** to **give** God's ancient messages to me. W-pII.322.1.2

~ his **memory** abides in every gift that **I receive** of Him. W-pII.322.1.3

~ it is a **call** from **Love** to **Love** that it be but itself. The **Holy Spirit** is His gift by Which the quietness of **Heaven** is restored to God's beloved Son. W-pII.ST281.5.1:2

~ not one is lost, for **they** can but increase. M-6.2.6

~ it is the relinquishing of all concern about the gift that makes it truly given. M-6.4.1

GIVE

DICTIONARY: *freely transfer the **possession** of (something) to (someone); hand over to.*

EGO

~ to the **ego**, to give anything implies that **you will** do without it. *T-4.III.30.3*

~ "giving to get" is an inescapable law of the **ego**, which always evaluates itself in relation to other egos and is therefore continually preoccupied with the scarcity principle which gave rise to it. This is the **meaning** of Freud's "**reality**" principle since Freud **thought** of the **ego** as very weak and deprived, capable of functioning only as a **thing** in **need**. *T-4.III.30.5:6*

~ to give reluctantly is not to **gain** the **gift** because **you** are reluctant to accept it. *T-25.X.79.1*

~ this strange distortion of what giving **means** pervades all levels of the **world you see**. It strips all **meaning** from the gifts **you** give and leaves **you nothing** in the ones **you** take. *W-pI.105.3.1:2*

~ having had and given, then the **world** asserts that **you have** lost what **you** possessed. *W-pI.187.1.7*

HOLY SPIRIT;   *to receive*

~ **you join** with Him in **giving**. *T-15.II.14.1*

~ **we** who are one cannot give separately. *T-15.X.94.1*

~ **nothing you** give is lost to **you** or anyone, but cherished and preserved [for you] in **Heaven**. *T-25.X.79.4*

~ thus **he** learns it must be his to give. Unless **he** gives, **he will** not know **he** has, for **giving** is the proof of having. *T-29.IV.20.7:8*

~ what belongs to us in **truth** is what **He** gives. *W-pI.104.7.2*

~ true giving is **creation**. It extends the limitless to the unlimited, **eternity** to timelessness, and **love** unto itself. It adds to all that is complete already, not in simple terms of adding more, for that implies that it was less before. It adds by letting what cannot contain itself fulfill its aim of **giving** everything it has away, securing it forever for itself. *W-pI.105.5.1:4*

~ **he** cannot give through **loss**. No more can **you**. *W-pI.105.6.4:5*

~ **time** is not the guardian of what **we** give **today**. *W-pI.109.11.2*

~ the **truth** maintains that giving **will** increase what **you** possess. *W-pI.187.1.8*

~ protect all things **you value** by the act of giving them away, and **you** are sure that **you will** never lose them. *W-pI.187.4.1*

~ **you** give but to yourself. *W-pI.187.6.1*

~ the term generosity has **special meaning** to the **teacher of God**. It is not the usual **meaning** of the **word**; in **fact**, it is a **meaning** that must be learned and learned very carefully. Like all the other attributes of God's teachers, this one rests ultimately on **trust**, for without **trust**, no one can be generous in the true **sense**. To the **world**, generosity **means** "**giving** away" in the **sense** of "**giving** up." To the teachers of **God**, it **means** "**giving** away" in **order** to keep. This has been emphasized throughout the **text** and the **workbook**, but it is perhaps more alien to the thinking of the **world** than many other ideas in our **curriculum**. Its greater strangeness lies merely in the obviousness of its reversal of the world's thinking. In the clearest **way** possible and at the simplest of levels, the **word means** the exact **opposite** to the teachers of **God** and to the **world**. *M-4.18.1:8*

~ no one can give if **he** is concerned with the result of the **giving**. That is a limitation on the **giving** itself, and neither the giver nor the receiver would **have** the **gift**. **Trust** is an essential **part** of **giving**; in **fact**, it is the **part** that makes sharing possible, the **part** that guarantees the giver **will** not lose but only **gain**. *M-6.3.4:6*

~ because **he** has, **he** can give. And because **he** gives, **he** shall be given. This is the law of **God**, and not of the **world.** *P-3.III.5.2:4*

GIVING/RECEIVING   *see "give"*

EGO

~ **he** is trying to **give** what **he** has not received. *T-9.IV.20.4*

~ giving has become a **source** of **fear**, and so **you** would avoid the only **means** by which **you** can **receive**. *W-pI.105.3.4*

~ what remains as unreceived has not been given. *W-pI.126.7.5*

~ the **world** believes that to possess a **thing**, it must be kept. *W-pI.159.1.5*

HOLY SPIRIT

~ by giving **you receive**. But to **receive** is to accept, not to get. *T-8.XI.117.4:5*

~ **you** cannot really **give** anything but **love** to anyone or anything, nor can **you** really **receive** anything else from them. *T-11.VIII.70.4*

~ what **God** has given **you** is truly given and **will** be truly received. For God's gifts **have** no **reality** apart from your receiving them. Your receiving completes His giving. **You will receive** because it is His **Will** to **give**. *T-16.VIII.77.1:4*

~ what is offered must also be received to be truly given. *T-19.V.76.2*

~ **everyone** gives as **he** receives, but **he** must choose what it **will** be that **he** receives. And **he will** recognize his **choice** by what **he** gives and what is given him. *T-19.V.109.5:6*

~ to **give** is no more blessed than to **receive**. But neither is it less. *T-21.VII.67.8:9*

~ giving and receiving are the same. *T-25.X.87.3*

~ both occur together, that the **thought** remain complete. And in this understanding is the base on which all opposites are reconciled because **they** are perceived from the same frame of reference which unifies this **thought.** *W-pI.108.4.2:3*

~ to learn that giving and receiving are the same has **special** usefulness because it can be tried so easily and seen as true. And when this **special** case has proved it always works in every circumstance where it is tried, the **thought** behind it can be generalized to other areas of **doubt** and double **vision**. And from there it **will** extend and finally arrive at the one **thought** Which underlies them all. *W-pI.108.6.1:3*

~ has results we cannot miss. To **give** is to **receive**. *W-pI.108.7.2:3*

~ what **we give today we have** received already. *W-pI.109.11.1*

~ no one can **receive** and understand **he** has received until **he** gives. For in the giving is his own **acceptance** of what **he** received. *W-pI.154.8.5:6*

~ no one can **give** what **he** has not received. To **give** a **thing** requires first **you have** it in your own **possession.** *W-pI.159.1.1:2*

~ to **give** is how to recognize **you have** received. It is the proof that what **you have** is yours. *W-pI.159.1.7:8*

~ having offered **love**, only **love** can be received. *M-7.2.8*

146

GLORY

|ˈglôrē|

DICTIONARY: *high renown or honor won by notable achievements.*

HOLY SPIRIT;   *God's **Gift**, your **inheritance**, **light** that saves the **world**.*

~   glory is God's **gift** to **you**, because that is what **He** is. *T-8.IV.24.7*

~   his Glory belongs to Him, but it is equally yours. **You** cannot, then, be less glorious than **He** is. *T-9.V.33.10:11*

~   glory is your **inheritance**, given your **Soul** by its **Creator** that **you** might extend it. *T-10.V.31.5*

~   his glory is beyond it, measureless and timeless as **eternity**. *T-23.I.5.2*

~   your glory is the **light** that saves the **world**. *W-pI.191.12.6*

~   your glory undefiled forever. *W-pI.Rev V.12.3*

GOAL

|gōl|

DICTIONARY: *the object of a person's ambition or **effort**; an aim or desired result.*

EGO;   *frantic vain pursuits, meaningless endeavors, senseless journeys, triumph, **ego** autonomy, **death**, shifting goals, conflicting goals.*

~   according to the ego's **teaching**, its goal can be accomplished, and God's **purpose** can not. *T-10.VI.50.3*

~   the **ego** believes that to accomplish its goal is happiness. *T-10.VI.51.3*

~   **ego** pursues its goal with fanatic insistence, and its **reality** testing, though severely impaired, is completely consistent. *T-11.V.36.6*

~   to the **ego** the goal is **death**, which is its end. *T-15.I.2.8*

~   the clarification of the goal belongs at the beginning, for it is this which **will** determine the outcome. *T-17.VII.58.2*

~   the **ego** does not know what it wants to come of it. It is aware of what it does not **want**, but only that. It has no positive goal at all. *T-17.VII.58.7:9*

~   the absence of a criterion for outcome set in **advance** makes understanding doubtful and evaluation **impossible**. *T-17.VII.59.7*

~   the goal is triumph. *T-24.II.8.7*

~   **everyone** seeks for what **will** bring him **joy** as **he** defines it. It is not the aim as such that varies. Yet it is the **way** in which the aim is seen that makes the **choice** of **means** inevitable and beyond the hope of **change** unless the aim is changed. *T-25.V.32.5:7*

~   **idea** of different goals which makes **perception shift** and **meaning change**. *T-30.VIII.86.5*

~   **you have** a number of goals in **mind** as **part** of the desired outcome and also that these goals are on different levels and often **conflict**. *W-pI.24.4.3*

~   many of your goals are contradictory, that **you have** no unified outcome in **mind**, and that **you** must experience disappointment in connection with some of your goals however the **situation** turns out. *W-pI.24.8.2*

~   **you** perceive the **world** and everything in it as meaningful in terms of **ego** goals. These goals **have nothing** to do with your own best interests, because the **ego** is not **you**. *W-pI.25.2.1:2*

~ the goals **you now** perceive as valuable is to say that **they** are all concerned with "personal" interests. Since **you have** no personal interests, your goals are really concerned with **nothing**. In cherishing them, therefore, **you have** no goals at all. *W-pI.25.3.1:3*

~ **they** are meaningless, rather than "**good**" or "bad". *W-pI.25.5.2*

~ **you will** attempt endless lists of goals **you** cannot reach; a senseless series of expenditures of **time** and effort, hopefulness and **doubt**, each one as futile as the one before and failing as the next one surely **will**. *W-pI.96.2.2*

~ failure is all about **you** while **you seek** for goals that cannot be achieved. *W-pI.131.1.1*

~ goals which are meaningless are not attained. There is no **way** to reach them, for the **means** by which **you** strive for them are meaningless as **they** are. *W-pI.131.2.1:2*

~ a major hazard to success has been involvement with your **past** and **future** goals. *W-pI.181.4.1*

~ **you** are unwilling to cooperate in practicing **salvation** only if it interferes with goals **you** hold more dear. *W-pI.Rev III.4.2*

~ if **I** forget my goal, **I** can be but confused, unsure of what **I** am and thus conflicted in my actions. No one can serve contradicting goals and serve them well. *W-pII.257.1.1:2*

~ senseless journeys, mad careers, and artificial values. *W-pII.298.1.4*

~ divided goals **alone** can **interfere** with perfect **healing**. *P-2.III.3.6*

~ a goal marks the end of a **journey**, not the beginning, and as each goal is reached another can be dimly seen ahead. *P-3.II.8.4*

HOLY SPIRIT; *God, light, happiness*

~ **holy Spirit** has a unified goal for all **effort**. **He** adapts the ego's potentials for excelling to potentials for equalizing. This makes them useless for the ego's **purpose** but very useful for His. *T-7.IV.23.1:3*

~ the goal is inevitable because it is eternal. The goal of **love** is but your right, and it belongs to **you** despite your preference. *T-11.III.18.6:7*

~ to be healed is to pursue one goal because **you have** accepted only one and **want** but one. *T-11.VIII.68.6*

~ to the **Holy Spirit** the goal is **life**, which has no end. *T-15.I.2.9*

~ the goal is fixed, firm, and unalterable, and the **means will** surely fall in place because the goal is sure. *T-17.VI.56.1*

~ the goal establishes the **fact** that **everyone** involved in it **will** play his **part** in its accomplishment. This is inevitable. No one **will fail** in anything. *T-17.VII.62.5:7*

~ the goal of **holiness** was set for your **relationship** and not by **you**. *T-17.VIII.67.2*

~ the goal's **reality will call** forth and accomplish every **miracle** needed for its fulfillment. **Nothing** too small or too enormous, too weak or too compelling, but **will** be gently turned to its use and **purpose**. The **universe will** serve it gladly, as it serves the **universe**. *T-17.VIII.69.6:8*

~ for the goal of **peace** cannot be accepted apart from its conditions, and **you** had **faith** in it, for no one accepts what **he** does not believe is real. *T-17.IX.79.2*

~ **you will advance** because your goal is the **advance** from **fear** to **truth**. *T-18.IV.25.2*

~ the goal which **you** accepted is the goal of **knowledge**, for which **you** signified your willingness. *T-18.IV.25.4*

~ in the goal of **truth** which **you** accepted must all illusions end. *T-19.V.45.10*

~ another goal with far less **vigilance**—with **little effort** and with **little time** and with the **power** of **God** maintaining it and promising success. *T-24.VII.60.1*

- the speed by which it can be reached depends on this one **thing alone**—your willingness to **practice** every **step**. *T-30.I.1.3*
- in one united goal does this become **impossible**, for your agreement makes **interpretation** stabilize and last. *T-30.VIII.86.6*
- the Holy Spirit's goal gives one **interpretation**, meaningful to **you** and to your **brother**. *T-30.VIII.87.2*
- yet it is the exercises which **will make** the goal possible. *W-pI.I.1.2*
- goal of separating the meaningless from the meaningful. *W-pI.4.3.2*
- your goal is to find out who **you** are, having denied your **Identity** by attacking **creation** and its **Creator**. *W-pI.62.2.3*
- as an expression of the **Will** of **God**, **you have** no goal but His. *W-pI.74.1.6*
- our single **purpose** makes our goal inevitable. *W-pI.75.4.3*
- **nothing** is required of **you** to reach this goal except to lay all idols and **self**-images aside, go **past** the long list of attributes, both "**good**" and "**bad**," **you have** ascribed to yourself and wait in silent expectancy for the **truth**. **God** has Himself promised that it **will** be revealed to all who **ask** for it. **You** are asking **now**. **You** cannot **fail** because **He** cannot **fail**. *W-pI.94.6.1:4*
- **we have** a mighty **purpose** to fulfill and **have** been given everything **we need** with which to reach the goal. *W-pI.98.2.3*
- **you** still are free to choose a goal that lies beyond the **world** and every worldly **thought** and one which comes to **you** from an **idea** relinquished yet remembered, old yet new—an echo of a heritage forgot, yet holding everything **you** really **want**. *W-pI.131.4.4*
- **you** search for **Heaven** and must find the goal **you** really **want**. *W-pI.131.5.2*
- **you will** reach the goal **you** really **want** as certainly as **God** created **you** in sinlessness. *W-pI.131.6.5*
- there can be no **doubt** that **you will** reach your final goal. *W-pI.153.21.2*
- **god** is our goal. *W-pII.256.1.9*
- our goal is shared. *W-pII.ST361.4.2*
- each one must **share** one goal with someone else, and in so **doing**, lose all **sense** of separate interests. Only by **doing** this is it possible to transcend the narrow boundaries the **ego** would impose upon the **self**. *P-2.II.8.4:5*
- it is the goal that makes these processes the same, for **they** are one in **purpose** and must thus be one in **means**. *P-2.II.9.8*

GOD |gäd|

DICTIONARY: *the **creator** and ruler of the **universe** and **source** of all moral authority; the supreme **being**.*

EGO;   *idol*

- the **ego** does believe it can **attack** God and tries to persuade **you** that **you have** done this. *T-7.VII.62.2*
- a sick God must be an **idol**, made in the **image** of what its maker thinks **he** is. *T-9.IX.78.1*
- **they exist** only because **you** honor them. *T-9.IX.83.2*
- your Gods do not bring **chaos**; **you** are endowing them with **chaos** and accepting it of them. *T-9.X.89.3*
- allegiance to the **denial** of God is the ego's **religion**. *T-9.XI.95.1*
- your Gods are **nothing**, because your **Father** did not create them. *T-9.XI.97.2*

149

~ the attempt to **make** guilty is always directed against God. For the **ego** would **have you see** Him, and Him **alone**, as guilty, leaving the **Sonship** open to **attack** and unprotected from it. *T-16.VI.44.1:2*

~ god must die so **you** can live. And it is this theme which is acted out in the **special relationship**. *T-16.VI.52.4:5*

~ is God believed to be without the **power** to save what **He** created from the **pain** of hell. *T-25.VI.42.1*

~ it is His **loss you** celebrate when **you** behold the **body** as a **thing you love**, or look upon it as a **thing you hate**. *T-29.III.19.2*

~ to oppose Him is to **make** a **choice** against yourself and choose that **you** be bound. *T-30.III.34.10*

~ **you** but **accuse** Him of **insanity**, to think **He** made a **world** where such things seem to **have reality**. *W-pI.152.6.5*

~ with **love** as **enemy** must cruelty become a God, and Gods demand that those who worship them obey their dictates and refuse to **question** them. Harsh **punishment** is meted out relentlessly to those who **ask** if the demands are sensible or even sane. It is their enemies who are unreasonable and insane, while **they** are always merciful and just. *W-pI.170.7.1:3*

~ how easily are God and **guilt** confused by those who know not what their thoughts can do. *W-pI.197.2.1*

~ who usurps the place of God and takes it for himself **now** has a deadly "**enemy**." *M-17.5.8:9*

~ he holds your **little life** in his hand but by a thread, ready to break it off without regret or care, perhaps **today**. *M-27.2.3*

~ his **world** is **now** a **battleground** where **contradiction** reigns and opposites **make** endless **war**. *M-27.2.7*

~ god is insane. *M-27.3.8*

HOLY SPIRIT;   *Prime **Creator**, **Cause**, **Mind**, **Source**, **Source** of **life**, Universal Giver, Giver of **life**, great **Creator** of the **universe**, **Father**, my **Father**, perfect **Father** of a perfect Son, infinite **creator** of infinity, all in all, Maker of the **world** of **gentleness**, the great unfailing **power**, **Strength**, **Light**, holy Lord of **Heaven**, Lord of **Love** and **Life**, **Love**, **Holiness**, Presence of **Holiness**, love & **holiness**, heritage, **fact**, **consistence**, Holy One.*

~ god is lonely without His Souls, and **they** are lonely without Him. *T-2.II.51.4*

~ "**vengeance** is Mine sayeth the Lord," is a strictly karmic viewpoint. It is a real misperception of **truth** by which **man** assigns his own "**evil**" past to God. The "**evil** conscience" from the **past** has **nothing** to do with God. **He** did not create it, and **He** does not maintain it. God does not believe in karmic retribution. His Divine **Mind** does not create that **way**. **He** does not hold the **evil** deeds of a **man** even against himself. *T-3.III.15.1:7*

~ god Himself is not symbolic; **He** is **fact**. *T-3.III.17.1*

~ god is real and **you** are His beloved Son in whom **He** is well pleased. *T-4.II.15.6*

~ god, who is as incapable of deception as are the Souls **He** created. *T-4.II.17.7*

~ god is as incapable of creating the perishable as the **ego** is of making the eternal. *T-4.II.18.9*

~ god extends outward beyond limits and beyond **time**. *T-7.II.5.4*

~ god does not take steps, because His accomplishments are not gradual. **He** does not **teach**, because His **creations** are changeless. **He** does **nothing** last, because **He** created first and for always. *T-7.II.7.1:3*

~ **he** is first in the **sense** that **He** is the first in the **Holy Trinity** itself. **He** is the Prime **Creator**, because **He** created His co-creators. Because **He** did, **time** applies neither to Him nor to what **He** created. The "last **step**" that God [was said to] take was therefore true in the beginning, is true **now**, and **will** be true forever. *T-7.II.7.5:8*

~ god has lit your minds Himself and keeps your minds lit by His **light**, because His **light** is what your minds are. *T-7.V.30.1*

~ god watches over His Children and denies them **nothing**. *T-7.XII.109.9*

~ god gives only equally. *T-7.XII.111.3*

~ god is **Love**, and **you** do **want** Him. *T-8.X.99.7*

~ what God has created cannot be replaced. God is incomplete without **you**. *T-9.VII.56.7:8*

~ **nothing** beyond Him can happen, because **nothing** except Him is real. *T-9.VIII.60.3*

~ **he** created **you** for Himself, but **He** gave **you** the **power** to create for your **self** so **you** could be like Him. That is why your **will** is holy. *T-9.VIII.61.3:4*

~ god, Who is all **power**. *T-9.IX.77.9*

~ god gave Himself to **you** in your **creation**. *T-9.XI.102.10*

~ **he** would not **interfere** with **you**, because **He** would not know His Son if **he** were not free. To **interfere** with **you** would be to **attack** Himself, and God is not insane. *T-9.XI.102.2:3*

~ god **will** never cease to **love** His Son, and His Son **will** never cease to **love** Him. *T-9.XI.102.6*

~ only if **you** accept the Fatherhood of God **will you have** anything, because His fatherhood gave **you** everything. *T-9.XI.106.1*

~ god is your heritage because His one **gift** is Himself. *T-10.II.11.2*

~ what **He** gives, **He** holds, so that **nothing He** gives can contradict Him. *T-10.II.15.4*

~ god has created by **extension**. The cornerstone of God's **creation** is **you**, for His **thought system** is **light**. *T-10.II.3.1:2*

~ god is very **quiet**, for there is no **conflict** in Him. *T-10.IV.23.6*

~ what is unlike God cannot enter His **Mind** because it was not His **Thought** and therefore does not belong to Him. *T-10.IV.29.5*

~ god blessed His Son forever. *T-10.IV.30.5*

~ god knows His Son as wholly blameless as Himself. *T-10.V.37.2*

~ to God all things are possible. *T-10.VII.68.8*

~ god created only the eternal. *T-10.VIII.69.2*

~ god gives; **He** does not take. *T-10.VIII.80.9*

~ god loves His Son forever, and His Son returns his Father's **love** forever. *T-12.VII.66.3*

~ god waits your **witness** to His Son and to Himself. *T-13.II.10.4*

~ god is everywhere, and His Son is in Him with everything. *T-13.VII.63.7*

~ god is the only **Cause**, and **guilt** is not of Him. *T-13.VIII.72.1*

~ **he** created **you** out of Himself but still **within** Him. **He** knows what **you** are. **Remember** that there is no second to Him. There cannot, therefore, be anyone without His **Holiness** nor anyone unworthy of His perfect **Love**. *T-13.IX.90.2:5*

~ **you** made Him not, and anything **you understand** is not of Him. *T-14.I.1.8*

~ one Who gives forever and Who knows of **nothing** except **giving**. *T-14.I.2.7*

~ god is not willing that His Son be content with less than everything. For **He** is not content without His Son, and His Son cannot be content with less than his **Father** has given him. *T-15.IV.26.3:4*

~ **he** reaches from **you** to **everyone** and beyond **everyone** to His Son's **creations**, but without leaving **you**. Far beyond your **little world** but still in **you**, **He** extends forever. Yet **He** brings all his extensions to **you** as **host** to Him. *T-15.IV.29.5:7*

~ god is an **idea**. *T-15.VII.59.4*

~ **he** protected both your **creations** and **you** together, keeping one with **you** what **you** would exclude. *T-16.IV.25.5*

~ there is **nothing** in Him that is not perfect and eternal. *T-16.IV.27.7*

~ **he** loves **you** wholly without **illusion,** as **you** must **love.** *T-16.V.40.7*

~ whom God remembers must be whole. And God has never forgotten what makes Him whole. *T-16.V.40.9:10*

~ in His **link** with **you** lie both His inability to forget and your ability to **remember.** In Him are joined your willingness to **love** and all the **love** of God, Who forgot **you** not. *T-16.V.40.12:13*

~ god established His **relationship** with **you** to **make you happy.** *T-17.V.27.1*

~ god cannot destroy Himself. *T-18.IV.24.6*

~ god did not create His dwelling-place unworthy of Him. *T-18.V.34.5*

~ god, Who created neither **sin** nor **death,** wills not that **you** be bound by them. **He** knows of neither **sin** nor its results. *T-19.V.80.3:4*

~ **he** has no Thoughts except the **Self**-extending, and in this your **will.** *T-21.VI.54.2*

~ god did not entrust His Son to the unworthy. *T-22.II.13.1*

~ god rests with **you** in **quiet,** undefended and wholly undefending, for in this **quiet** state **alone** is **strength** and **power.** *T-22.VI.47.6*

~ **he** loves **you** perfectly, completely, and eternally. *T-23.II.10.6*

~ **he** remains the only place of safety. In Him is no **attack,** and no **illusion** in any **form** stalks **Heaven.** *T-23.V.47.2:3*

~ him Who chose that **love** could never be divided and kept separate from what it is and must forever be. *T-24.III.22.1*

~ the great **Creator** of the **universe,** the **Source** of **life,** of **love** and **holiness,** the perfect **Father** of a perfect Son. *T-24.IV.31.1*

~ god is knowable and **will** be known to **you.** For **He** could never leave His own **creation.** *T-24.VII.49.5:6*

~ god changes not His **Mind** about His Son with passing circumstance. *T-24.VII.51.5*

~ god cherishes **creation** as the perfect **Father** that **He** is. And so His **joy** is made complete when any **part** of Him joins in His **praise,** to **share** His **joy.** *T-25.III.20.4:5*

~ **he** is wholly fair to **everyone.** *T-25.IX.66.14*

~ god is fair. **He** does not fight against His Son's reluctance to perceive **salvation** as a **gift** from Him. Yet would His **justice** not be satisfied until it is received by **everyone.** *T-25.X.79.7:9*

~ what **you** leave as vacant, God **will** fill, and where **He** is, there must the **truth** abide. *T-27.IV.32.3*

~ what God has given cannot be a **loss,** and what is not of Him has no effects. *T-28.V.46.4*

~ god is the alternate to dreams of **fear.** *T-28.VI.47.6*

~ god keeps His promises; His Son keeps his. In his **creation** did his **Father** say, "**You** are beloved of Me and **I** of **you** forever. Be **you** perfect as Myself, for **you** can never be apart from Me. "His Son remembers not that **here** replied "**I will,**" though in that **promise he** was born. *T-28.VII.59.3:6*

~ god asks for **nothing,** and His Son, like Him, **need ask** for **nothing.** For there is no lack in him. *T-28.VIII.60.1:2*

~ **here** is no **time,** no place, no state where God is absent. *T-29.I.1.1*

~ god gave **you** all there is. And to be sure **you** could not lose it, did **He** also **give** the same to every living **thing** as well. *T-29.IX.60.7:8*

~ **he** joins with **you** in willing **you** be free. *T-30.III.34.9*

~ **he** must be unremembered till His Son has reached beyond **forgiveness** to the **love** of God. *T-30.VI.63.6*

~ only if His Son is **innocent** can **He** be **Love**. *T-31.I.9.4*

~ god is merciful and did not let His Son abandon Him. *T-31.IV.42.9*

~ to **everyone** has God entrusted all. *T-31.VII.77.4*

~ god does not know unholiness. *W-pI.39.4.5*

~ it is quite possible to reach God. *W-pI.41.7.1*

~ god is the **Light** in which **you** see. *W-pI.44.6.3*

~ god does not forgive because **He** has never condemned. *W-pI.46.1.1*

~ god is your safety in every circumstance. *W-pI.47.3.1*

~ **he** is the **Source** of all **meaning**, and everything that is real is in His **Mind**. It is in my **mind** too because **He** created it with me. God is still everywhere and in everything forever. *W-pI.53.5.2:4*

~ god cannot **give** what **He** does not **have**, and **He** cannot **have** what **He** is not. *W-pI.66.8.4*

~ infinite **Creator** of infinity, who created **you** like Himself. *W-pI.72.15.4*

~ god asks that **you** be **happy** so the **world** can **see** how much **He** loves His Son and wills no sorrow rises to abate his **joy**; no **fear** besets him to disturb his **peace**. *W-pI.100.6.3*

~ what completes Him must complete His Son as well. *W-pI.105.6.3*

~ his return **will** be a **sense** of **love you** cannot **understand**, a **joy** too deep for **you** to comprehend, a **sight** too holy for the body's eyes to **see**. *W-pI.124.11.2*

~ god is our Companion as **we** walk the **world** a **little** while. *W-pI.124.2.4*

~ god does not suffer **conflict**. Nor is His **creation** split in two. *W-pI.131.9.1:2*

~ god knows not of your plans to **change** His **Will**. *W-pI.136.12.1*

~ what is opposed to God does not **exist**. *W-pI.137.11.3*

~ god abides in holy temples. **He** is barred where **sin** has entered. Yet there is no place where **He** is not. *W-pI.140.5.3:5*

~ **he** is what your **life** is. *W-pI.156.2.5*

~ and the **thought** of Him is never absent. *W-pI.165.7.4*

~ **he** has shared His **joy** with **you**. *W-pI.166.15.7*

~ god creates only **mind** awake. **He** does not **sleep**, and His **creations** cannot **share** what **He** gives not nor **make** conditions which **He** does not **share** with them. *W-pI.167.8.1:2*

~ god speaks to us. Shall **we** not speak to Him? **He** is not distant. **He** makes no attempt to **hide** from us. *W-pI.168.1.1:4*

~ **he** remains entirely accessible. **He** loves His Son. *W-pI.168.1.8:9*

~ **he will love** His Son forever. When his **mind** remains asleep, **He** loves him still. And when his **mind** awakes, **He** loves him with a never-changing **Love**. *W-pI.168.1.9:11*

~ and **He** descends to meet us as **we** come to Him, for what **He** has prepared for us **He** gives and **we receive**. *W-pI.168.6.1*

~ he Who is changeless shares His attributes with His **creation**. All the images His Son appears to **make have** no effect on what **he** is. *W-pI.186.9.3:4*

~ the **way** to reach Him is merely to let Him be. *W-pI.189.8.7*

~ god knows His Son and knows the **way** to him. **He** does not **need** His Son to show Him how to find His **way**. Through every opened door His **love** shines outward from its **home within** and lightens up the **world** in **innocence**. *W-pI.189.9.6:8*

~ god does not know of **learning**. *W-pI.193.1.1*

~ god has cared for us and calls us Son. *W-pI.195.9.5*

~ he is my **home**, wherein I live and move, the **Spirit** Which directs my actions, offers me Its thoughts, and guarantees my safety from all **pain**. **He** covers me with kindness and with care and holds in **love** the Son **He** shines upon, who also shines on Him. *W-pII.222.1.3:4*

~ i live in God. In Him **I** find my refuge and my **strength**. In Him is my **Identity**. In Him is everlasting **peace**. And only there **will I remember** who **I** really am. *W-pII.261.1.4:8*

~ he has filled the **world** with those who point to Him and given us the **sight** to look on them. *W-pII.266.2.3*

~ whom God created limitless is free. *W-pII.280.1.1*

~ our **Love** awaits us as **we** go to Him and walks beside us, showing us the **way**. **He** fails in **nothing**. **He** the end **we seek**, and **He** the **means** by which **we** come to Him. *W-pII.302.2.1:3*

~ he would add to **Love** by its **extension**. *W-pII.ST321.2.2*

~ god is not mistaken in His Son. *M-3.4.7*

~ god offers the **world salvation**. *M-11.2.4*

~ god indeed can be reached directly, for there is no distance between Him and His Son. His **awareness** is in everyone's **memory**, and His **word** is written on everyone's heart. *M-26.1.1:2*

~ there is either a God of **fear** or One of **Love**. The **world** attempts a thousand compromises and **will** attempt a thousand more. Not one can be acceptable to God's teachers because not one could be acceptable to God. **He** did not **make death**, because **He** did not **make fear**. Both are equally meaningless to Him. *M-27.4.5:9*

~ god does not wait, for waiting implies **time** and **He** is timeless. *M-29.7.8*

~ god comes to those who would restore His **world**, for **they have** found the **way** to **call** to Him. *P-2.II.6.4*

~ he needs a **voice** through which to speak His holy **Word**; a hand to reach His Son and touch his heart. *P-2.V.5.5*

GOD OF SICKNESS   *A Course in Miracles Term*

EGO;   *the* **symbol** *for willing against* **God**

~ he is the **belief** that **you** can choose which **God** is real. Although it is perfectly clear that this has **nothing** to do with **reality**, it is equally clear that it has everything to do with **reality** as **you** perceive it. *T-9.IX.84.7:8*

~ he is the **symbol** of willing against **God**, and **you** are afraid of him, because **he** cannot be reconciled with **God's Will**. *T-9.X.85.7*

~ the rituals of the **God** of **sickness** are strange and very demanding. **Joy** is never permitted, for depression is the sign of allegiance to him. *T-9.XI.93.1:2*

~ the **God** of **sickness** obviously demands the **denial** of **health**, because **health** is in direct opposition to its own **survival**. *T-9.XI.95.2*

~ having made him out of your **insanity**, **he** is an insane **idea**. **He** has many forms, but although **he** may seem like many different things **he** is but one **idea**—the **denial** of **God**. *T-9.XI.95.7:8*

GOD'S LAWS
A Course in Miracles Term

HOLY SPIRIT

~ **they** are perfectly dependable and therefore universal in application. *T-7.V.32.2*

~ the **laws** are not meaningless, since all **meaning** is contained by them and in them. *T-7.V.37.11*

~ **seek** ye first the **Kingdom** of **Heaven**, because that is where the **laws** of **God** operate truly, and **they** can operate only truly since **they** are the **laws** of **Truth**. *T-7.V.38.1*

~ his **laws** govern **you**, because **they** govern everything. *T-8.V.25.6*

~ god's **laws** are always fair and perfectly consistent. *T-8.XI.117.3*

~ **you** can violate God's **laws** in your imagination, but **you** cannot escape from them. **They** were established for your protection and are as inviolate as your safety. *T-9.VIII.59.5:6*

~ god's **laws will** keep your minds at **peace**, because **peace** is His **Will**, and His **laws** are established to uphold it. His are the **laws** of **freedom**, but yours are the **laws** of **bondage**. Since **freedom** and bondage are irreconcilable, their **laws** cannot be understood together. The **laws** of **God** work only for your **good**, and there are no other **laws** beside His. *T-9.X.88.1:4*

~ **god** Himself has protected everything **He** created by His **laws**. *T-9.X.88.6*

~ his definitions are His **laws**, for by them **He** established the **universe** as what it is. *T-9.X.90.5*

~ the **laws** of the **universe** do not permit **contradiction**. *T-10.II.8.5*

~ god's **laws** hold only for your protection, and **they** never hold in vain. *T-10.V.32.3*

~ god's more basic law that **love** creates itself and **nothing** but itself. God's **laws** do not obtain directly to a **world perception** rules, for such a **world** could not **have** been created by the **Mind** to which **perception** has no **meaning**. Yet are His **laws** reflected everywhere. *T-25.IV.23.6:8*

~ the basic law that makes **decision** powerful and gives it all effects that it **will** ever **have**. *T-30.II.32.3*

~ it is His **laws** which guarantee your safety. *T-30.V.52.2*

~ there are no **laws** except the **laws** of **God**. *W-pI.76.6.1*

~ the **laws** of **God** can never be replaced. *W-pI.76.7.1*

~ **payment** is neither given nor received. Exchange cannot be made, there are no substitutes, and **nothing** is replaced by something else. God's **laws** forever **give** and never take. *W-pI.76.10.4:6*

~ **i** am perfectly free of the effects of all **laws** save God's. And His are the **laws** of **freedom**. *W-pI.88.5.6:7*

~ his **laws release** me from all grievances and replace them with miracles. *W-pI.89.2.2*

GOD'S MIND
A Course in Miracles Term

HOLY SPIRIT

~ there are no strange images in the **Mind** of **God**, and what is not in His **Mind** cannot be in yours, because **you** are of one **mind** and that **mind** belongs to Him. *T-9.X.90.2*

~ **god** has given **you** a place in His **Mind** which is yours forever. *T-10.II.10.1*

~ **god's Mind** cannot be lessened. It can only be increased, and everything **He** creates has the **function** of creating. *T-10.II.10.4:5*

~ there is **nothing** in the **Mind** of **God** that does not **share** His shining **innocence**. *T-14.II.7.3*

~ no **thought within** His **Mind** is absent from your own. *T-24.VII.51.3*

~ in the **Mind** of **God** there is no ending nor a **time** in which His Thoughts were absent or could suffer **change**. *T-30.IV.43.4*

~ there are no separate parts in what exists **within** God's **Mind**. It is forever one, eternally united and at **peace**. *T-30.IV.43.8:9*

~ **you** think with the **Mind** of **God**. Therefore **you share** your thoughts with Him, as **He** shares His with **you**. **They** are the same thoughts because **they** are **thought** by the same **Mind**. To **share** is to **make** alike or to **make** one. Nor do the thoughts **you** think with the **Mind** of **God** leave your **mind**, because thoughts do not leave their **source**. Therefore your thoughts are in the **Mind** of **God**, as **you** are. **They** are in your **mind** as well, where **He** is. As **you** are **part** of His **Mind**, so are your thoughts **part** of His thoughts. *W-pI.45.2.1:8*

~ what is **thought** by the **Mind** of **God** is eternal, **being part** of **creation**. *W-pI.45.3.5*

GOD'S NAME   *A Course in Miracles Term*

EGO

~ think not **He** hears the **little** prayers of those who **call** on Him with names of idols cherished by the **world**. **They** cannot reach Him thus. **He** cannot hear requests that **He** be not Himself or that His Son **receive** another **name** than His. *W-pI.183.8.3:5*

HOLY SPIRIT;   *my inheritance, Love.*

~ **sickness** and **separation** are not of **God**, but the **Kingdom** is. *T-7.II.9.4*

~ **god's name** is holy, but no holier than yours. To **call** upon His **name** is but to **call** upon your own. *W-pI.183.1.1:2*

~ your Father's **name** reminds **you** who **you** are, even **within** a **world** that does not know; even though **you have** not remembered it. *W-pI.183.1.5*

~ **god's name** cannot be heard without response, nor said without an echo in the **mind** which calls **you** to **remember**. *W-pI.183.2.1*

~ repeat His **name**, and **you** acknowledge Him as sole **Creator** of **reality**. And **you** acknowledge also that His Son is **part** of Him, creating in His **name**. *W-pI.183.9.1:2*

~ **see** God's **name** replace the thousand **little** names **you** gave your thoughts, not realizing that there is one **name** for all there is and all that there **will** be. *W-pI.183.9.5*

~ turn to the **name** of **God** for your **release**, and it is given **you**. No **prayer** but this is necessary, for it holds them all **within** it. Words are insignificant and all requests unneeded when God's Son calls on his Father's **Name**. His Father's thoughts become his own. **He** makes his claim to all his **Father** gave, is giving still, and **will** forever **give**. **He** calls on Him to let all things **he thought** he made be nameless **now**, and in their place the holy **name** of **God** becomes his **judgment** of their worthlessness. *W-pI.183.11.1:6*

~ all **little** things are silent. **Little** sounds are soundless **now**. The **little** things of earth **have** disappeared. The **universe** consists of **nothing** but the **Son** of **God** who calls upon his **Father**. And his Father's **Voice** gives **answer** in his Father's holy **name**. In this eternal, still **relationship**, in which **communication** far transcends all words and yet exceeds in depth and height whatever words could possibly convey, is **peace** eternal. In our Father's **name**, **we** would **experience** this **peace today**. And in His **name** it shall be given us. *W-pI.183.12.1:8*

~ **god** has no **name**. And yet His **name** becomes the final **lesson** that all things are one, and at this single **lesson learning** ends. *W-pI.184.12.1:2*

~ no one can **fail** who seeks the **meaning** of the **name** of **God**. **Experience** must come to supplement the **word**. *W-pI.184.13.1:2*

GOD'S THOUGHTS   *A Course in Miracles Term*

HOLY SPIRIT

~ the **Thought God** holds of **you** is perfectly unchanged by your forgetting. It **will** always be exactly as it was before the **time** when **you** forgot and **will** be just the same when **you remember**. And it is the same **within** the **interval** when **you** forgot. *T-30.IV.44.6:8*

~ the Thoughts of **God** are far beyond all **change** and shine forever. **They** await not **birth**. **They** wait for **welcome** and remembering. *T-30.IV.45.1:3*

~ **here** is your one **reality** kept safe, completely unaware of all the **world** that worships idols and that knows not **God**. In perfect sureness of its changelessness and of its **rest** in its eternal **home**, the **Thought God** holds of **you** has never left the **mind** of its **Creator** Whom it knows, as its **Creator** knows that it is there. *T-30.IV.47.4:5*

~ **he** has not left His Thoughts! **He** could no more depart from them than **they** could keep Him out. In **unity** with Him do **they** abide, and in their **Oneness** both are kept complete. *T-31.IV.41.1:3*

~ no **Thought** of **God** has left its Father's **Mind**. No **Thought** of **God** is limited at all. No **Thought** of **God** but is forever pure. *W-pII.280.1.3:5*

~ forever and forever are God's thoughts exactly as **they** were and as **they** are, unchanged through **time** and after **time** is done. *W-pII.ST321.1.5*

~ god's thoughts are given all the **power** that Their own **Creator** has. *W-pII.ST321.2.1*

~ a **thought** of **God** turns **hell** to **Heaven** merely by **being** what it is? The earth bows down before its gracious Presence, and it leans down in **answer** to raise it up again. *M-11.4.9:10*

GOD'S VOICE   *A Course in Miracles Term*

HOLY SPIRIT

~ **god** is in your **memory**, and His **Voice will** tell **you** that **you** are **part** of Him. *T-9.IX.69.4*

~ his **Voice** speaks for Him in all situations and in every aspect of all situations, telling **you** exactly what to do to **call** upon His **strength** and His protection. There are no exceptions because **God** has no exceptions. And the **Voice** which speaks for Him thinks as **He** does. *W-pI.47.3.2:4*

~ **he** wants **you** to hear His **Voice**. **He** gave It to **you** to be heard. *W-pI.49.3.4:5*

~ there is not a moment in which God's **Voice** ceases to **call** on my **forgiveness** to save me. There is not a moment in which His **Voice** fails to direct my thoughts, guide my actions, and lead my feet. *W-pI.60.5.1:2*

~ there is nowhere else **I** can go, because God's **Voice** is the only **voice** and the only guide that has been given to His Son. *W-pI.60.5.4*

~ as **I** listen to God's **Voice**, **I** am sustained by His **Love**. *W-pI.60.6.1*

~ his **Voice will** speak of this to us, as well as of the joys of **Heaven** which His **laws** keep limitless forever. *W-pI.76.12.3*

~ his **Voice** assure **you** that the words **you** speak are true. *W-pI.105.10.2*

~ mighty **Voice** of **truth, quiet** in **power**, strong in stillness, and completely certain in its messages. *W-pI.106.1.1*

~ his **Voice** awaits your silence, for His **word** cannot be heard until your **mind** is **quiet** for a while and meaningless desires **have** been stilled. *W-pI.125.6.2*

~ **he** speaks from nearer than your heart to **you**. His **Voice** is closer than your hand. *W-pI.125.7.2:3*

~ when valueless ideas cease to **have value** in your restless **mind**, then **will you** hear His **Voice**. *W-pI.182.8.1*

~ his gentle **Voice** is calling from the known to the **unknowing. He** would comfort **you**, although **He** knows no sorrow. **He** would **make** a restitution, though **He** is complete; a **gift** to **you**, although **He** knows that **you have** everything already. **He** has thoughts which **answer** every **need** His Son perceives, although **He** sees them not. For **Love** must **give**, and what is given in His **name** takes on the **form** most useful in a **world** of **form.** *W-pI.186.13.1:5*

~ **voice** of God, Which speaks an ancient **lesson,** no more true **today** than any other day. *W-pII.275.1.1*

~ the **Voice** of God tells us of things **we** cannot **understand alone,** nor learn apart. *W-pII.275.1.4*

~ god's **Voice** is **offering** the **peace** of God to all who hear and choose to follow Him. *W-pII.334.1.4*

~ the giving up of **judgment**, the obvious prerequisite for hearing God's **Voice.** *M-9.2.4*

~ his **Voice** is heard in stillness. *M-15.3.12*

~ the real sound is always a **song** of thanksgiving and of **Love.** *S-1.I.2.9*

~ god's **Voice alone** can tell **you** how to heal. *S-3.III.6.1*

GOD'S WILL   *A Course in Miracles Term*

EGO;   *madness*

~ to oppose the pull or the **Will** of **God** is not an ability but a real **delusion.** *T-7.V.37.1*

~ **you** believe that **doing** the **opposite** of God's **Will** can be better for **you. You** also believe that it is possible to do the **opposite** of God's **Will.** *T-7.XI.102.3:4*

~ the **ego** wants to **teach you** that **you want** to oppose God's **Will.** *T-8.III.11.1*

~ the **projection** of the **ego** makes it appear as if God's **Will** is **outside** yourself and therefore not yours. In this **interpretation**, it is possible for God's **Will** and yours to **conflict.** God then may seem to demand of **you** what **you** do not **want** to **give** and thus deprive **you** of what **you want.** *T-10.II.13.1:3*

~ **you** are afraid to know God's **Will** because **you** believe it is not yours. This **belief** is your whole **sickness** and your whole **fear.** *T-10.II.14.3:4*

~ thus is **creation** seen as not eternal, and the **Will** of **God** open to opposition and defeat. *T-19.III.18.5*

~ the mad **belief** the **Will** of **God** can be attacked and overthrown. **You** may identify with this **belief,** but never **will** it be more than **madness.** *T-23.II.8.8:9*

~ **vengeance**, not **forgiveness**, is the **Will** of **God.** *T-23.III.26.2*

HOLY SPIRIT;   *His **gift** to **you,** heritage, **thought.***

~ there is no strain in **doing** God's **Will** as soon as **you** recognize that it is also your own. *T-2.IV.80.7*

~ it is not God's **Will** to be without **you.** *T-8.III.13.3*

~ the **Will** of **God** is without **limit**, and all **power** and **glory** lie **within** it. It is boundless in **strength** and in **love** and in **peace**. It has no boundaries because its **extension** is unlimited, and it encompasses all things because it created all things. By creating all things, it made them **part** of itself. **You** are the **Will** of **God**, because this is how **you** were created. *T-8.III.14.1:5*

~ **god** wills no one suffer. *T-8.IV.23.5*

~ his **Will** to **you** is His **Will** for **you**. *T-8.VI.47.2*

~ **creation** is the **Will** of **God**. His **Will** created **you** to create. Your **will** was not created separate from His, and so it wills as **He** wills. *T-8.VI.47.8:10*

~ **god's Will** is **thought**. It cannot be contradicted by **thought**. *T-8.VI.48.4:5*

~ **god's Will** is already possible and **nothing** else **will** ever be. *T-8.X.105.1*

~ **god's Will** is your **salvation**. *T-9.VI.38.1*

~ if **He** wills **you** to **have** it, **He** must **have** made it possible and very easy to obtain it. *T-9.VI.38.3*

~ consider, then, that in this joint **will you** are all united, and in this only. There **will** be disagreement on anything else, but not on this. *T-9.VI.39.1:2*

~ to **give** without **limit** is God's **Will** for **you** because only this can bring **you** the **joy** which is His and which **He** wills to **share** with **you**. *T-10.II.10.7*

~ **he** shares His **Will** with **you;** **He** does not thrust it upon **you**. *T-10.II.15.3*

~ **god's Will** is that His Son be one, and united with Him in His **Oneness**. *T-10.II.15.8*

~ his **Will** is one because the **extension** of His **Will** cannot be unlike itself. *T-10.VI.44.4*

~ the **Will** of **God** cannot die. *T-10.VII.66.2*

~ it is God's **Will** that **nothing** touch His Son except Himself, and **nothing** else comes nigh unto him. *T-12.VII.65.1*

~ **god's Will** is done. *T-13.V.39.4*

~ the **Will** of **God** can **fail** in **nothing**. *T-13.V.40.9*

~ everything **God** wills is not only possible but has already happened. *T-18.V.40.5*

~ **you** cannot **make** His **Will** destructive. **You** can **make** fantasies in which your **will** conflicts with His, but that is all. *T-18.VII.53.6:7*

~ **god's Will** is One. *T-19.V.42.5*

~ for **God** wills not apart from him, nor does the **Will** of **God** wait upon **time** to be accomplished. Therefore, what joined the **Will** of **God** must be in **you** now, being eternal. *T-21.VI.53.3:4*

~ it was not His **Will** that **you** be crucified. *T-24.IV.33.14*

~ **you** are the same, as **God** Himself is one and not divided in His **Will**. *T-25.III.22.1*

~ the **Will** of **God** and of His Son that **Heaven** be restored to him for whom it was created as his only **home**. *T-25.V.36.5*

~ no one can suffer for the **Will** of **God** to be fulfilled. *T-25.VIII.62.4*

~ **he** wills His Son **have** everything. *T-26.VIII.57.2*

~ **you exist** because **God** shared His **Will** with **you**, that His **creation** might create. *T-28.VI.47.11*

~ your **will** to be complete is but God's **Will**, and this is given **you** by **being** His. *T-30.IV.41.4*

~ the **Will** of **God** forever lies in those whose hands are joined. *T-30.VI.69.1*

~ no forms of **evil** which can overcome the **Will** of **God**. *T-30.VII.80.1*

~ **god** willed not His Son forget Him. And the **power** of His **Will** is in the **Voice** that speaks for Him. *T-31.I.6.2:3*

~ what your **Father** wills for **you** can never **change**. *T-31.VI.6.7.7*

~ **salvation** must be possible because it is the **Will** of God. *W-pI.19.2.5*

~ **you will see** because it is the **Will** of God. *W-pI.42.1.3*

~ all the **world** of **pain** is not His **Will**. *W-pI.99.9.4*

~ it is God's **Will** your **mind** be one with His. It is God's **Will** that **He** has but one Son. It is God's **Will** that His one Son is **you**. *W-pI.99.11.2:4*

~ **god's Will** for **you** is perfect happiness. *W-pI.100.2.1*

~ **god's Will** for **you** is perfect happiness because there is no **sin**, and **suffering** is causeless. *W-pI.101.6.3*

~ it **will** set **you** free from all the consequences **sin** has wrought in feverish imagination. *W-pI.101.7.2*

~ it **will** set **you** free from all the consequences **sin** has wrought in feverish imagination. **Truth** is God's **Will**. **Share** His **Will**, and **you share** what **He** knows. Deny His **Will** as yours, and **you** are denying His **Kingdom** and yours. *W-pI.101.7.2:4*

~ **you share** God's **Will**. *W-pI.102.6.2*

~ his **Will** is done already and that **joy** and **peace** belong to us as His eternal gifts. *W-pI.104.8.1*

~ **god** wills **salvation** be received **today** and that the intricacies of your dreams no longer **hide** their nothingness from **you**. *W-pI.122.7.6*

~ what **He** wills is **now**, without a **past** and wholly futureless. It is as far removed from **time** as is a tiny candle from a distant star, or what **you** chose from what **you** really **want**. *W-pI.131.7.6:7*

~ **he** is **here** because **He** wills to be, and what **He** wills is **present now** beyond the reach of **time**. *W-pI.131.9.6*

~ what **God** wills is **here**. *W-pI.136.14.5*

~ **god** has elected all, but few **have** come to realize His **Will** is but their own. *W-pI.153.11.2*

~ **god's Will** does not oppose. It merely is. *W-pI.166.10.1:2*

~ two minds with one intent become so strong that what **they will** becomes the **Will** of God. *W-pI.185.3.1*

~ it is your Father's holy **will** that **you** complete Himself and that your **Self** shall be His sacred Son, forever pure as **He**, of **love** created and in **love** preserved, extending **love**, creating in its **name**, forever one with **God** and with your **Self**. *W-pI.192.1.1*

~ yet His **Will** extends to what **He** does not **understand** in that **He** wills the happiness His Son inherited of Him be undisturbed, eternal and forever gaining scope, eternally expanding in the **joy** of full **creation**, and eternally open and wholly limitless in Him. This is His **Will**. And thus His **Will** provides the **means** to guarantee that it is done. *W-pI.193.1.2:4*

~ **he** has willed to come to **you** when **you have** recognized it is your **will He** do so. *W-pII.1.5.5*

~ the **Father** and the Son, whose holy **will** created all that is, can **fail** in **nothing**. *W-pII.1.7.7*

~ yet is the ending certain. For God's **Will** is done in earth and **Heaven**. **We will seek** and **we will** find according to His **Will**, which guarantees that our **will** is done. *W-pII.292.1.5:7*

~ **within** me is eternal **innocence** because it is God's **Will** that it be there forever and forever. I, His Son, whose **will** is limitless as is His own, can **will** no **change** in this. For to deny my Father's **Will** is to deny my own. To look **within** is but to find my **will** as **God** created it and as it is. **I fear** to look **within** because I think I made another **will** which is not true and made it real. Yet it has no effects. **Within** me is the **holiness** of **God**. **Within** me is the **memory** of Him. *W-pII.309.1.1:8*

- it is the **Will** of **God I** learn that what one gains is given unto all. *W-pII.319.1.6*
- what **God** has willed to be forever one **will** still be one when **time** is over and **will** not be changed throughout the **course** of **time**, remaining as it was before the **thought** of **time** began. *W-pII.ST321.2.4*
- god's **Will** in everything but seems to take **time** in the working-out. *M-2.4.7*
- there is no **substitute** for the **Will** of **God.** *M-16.10.1*
- his **Will** is wholly without **opposite.** There is no **thought** that contradicts His **Will** yet can be true. The **contrast** between His **Will** and yours but seemed to be **reality.** In **truth** there is no conflict, because His **Will** is yours. **Now** is the mighty **Will** of **God** Himself His **gift** to **you. He** does not **seek** to keep it for Himself. *M-20.6.2:7*
- the **Will** of **God** is one and all there is. This is your heritage. The **universe** beyond the sun and stars and all the thoughts of which **you** can conceive belong to **you.** God's **peace** is the **condition** for His **Will.** *M-20.6.9:12*

GOD'S WORD *A Course in Miracles Term*

Holy Spirit

- holy **word** of **God** is kept through your receiving it to **give** away, so **you** can **teach** the **world** what giving **means** by listening and **learning** it of Him. *W-pI.106.12.1*
- his **word** is soundless if it be not heard. *W-pI.123.5.2*
- his **Voice** awaits your silence, for His **word** cannot be heard until your **mind** is **quiet** for a while and meaningless desires **have** been stilled. *W-pI.125.6.2*
- it is the **word** of **freedom** and of **peace,** of **unity** of **will** and **purpose,** with no **separation** nor division in the single **Mind** of **Father** and of Son. *W-pI.125.8.3*
- "my Son is pure and holy as Myself" And thus did **God** become the **Father** of the Son **He** loves, for thus was **he** created. This the **word** His Son did not create with Him because in this His Son was born. *W-pII.276.1.2*
- god's **word** is given every **mind** which thinks that it has separate thoughts and **will** replace these thoughts of **conflict** with the **thought** of **peace.** *W-pII.ST231.1.3*
- the **word** of **God** promises other things that seem **impossible,** as well as this. His **word** has promised **peace.** It has also promised that there is no **death,** that **resurrection** must occur, and that **rebirth** is man's. *M-11.1.3:5*
- his **word** assures us that **He** loves the **world.** God's **word** has promised us that **peace** is possible **here,** and what **He** promises can hardly be **impossible.** *M-11.1.6:7*
- god's **word** assures **you** that **He** loves the **world.** *M-11.2.6*
- the **word** of **God** has no exceptions. It is this that makes it holy and beyond the **world.** It is its **holiness** that points to **God.** It is its **holiness** that makes **you** safe. *M-13.7.5:8*
- **god** holds out His **word** to **you,** for **He** has **need** of teachers. *M-13.8.10*
- only the **word** of **God** has any **meaning,** because it symbolizes that which has no human symbols at all. The **Holy Spirit alone** understands what this **word** stands for. And this, too, is enough. *M-21.3.10:12*
- accept His **word,** and every **miracle** has been accomplished. *M-22.1.8*
- **we have** His **Word** to guide us, as **we** try to **help** our brothers. *P-2.V.4.7*

GOOD

DICTIONARY: *that which is morally right; righteousness.*

EGO

~ it believes that it is good **within** an **evil world.** *T-31.V.44.9*

~ in this world's concepts are the guilty "bad;" the "good" are **innocent.** And no one **here** but holds a **concept** of himself in which he counts the "good" to pardon him the "bad." Nor does he **trust** the "good" in anyone, believing that the "bad" must lurk behind. *T-31.VII.68.5:7*

~ the **ego** sees some good but never only good. That is why its perceptions are so variable. It does not reject goodness entirely, for that **you** could not accept, but it always adds something that is not real to the real, thus confusing **illusion** and **reality.** *T-10.VIII.71.1:3*

HOLY SPIRIT

~ good can withstand any **form** of evil because **light** abolishes all forms of **darkness.** *T-3.III.18.2*

~ **nothing** good is lost because it comes from the **Holy Spirit,** the **Voice** for **creation. Nothing** that is not good was ever created and therefore cannot be protected. *T-5.VI.47.2:3*

~ "The good is what works" is a sound, though insufficient, statement. Only the good can work. **Nothing** else works at all. *T-9.IV.29.2:4*

~ if no good can come of it, the **Holy Spirit** cannot use it. *T-9.VII.56.4*

~ "good" and "**deprivation**" are opposites and cannot meaningfully **join** in any **way.** *T-21.IV.39.4*

~ as **you** gave your **trust** to what is good in him, **you** gave it to the good in **you.** *T-31.VII.69.8*

~ all good things are mine because **God** intended them for me. *W-pI.58.6.3*

GRACE

DICTIONARY: *simple elegance or refinement of movement.*

HOLY SPIRIT;   *natural state*

~ grace is not given to a **body,** but to a **mind.** And the **mind** that receives it looks instantly beyond the **body** and sees the holy place where it was healed. There is the **altar** where the grace was given, in which it stands. *T-19.II.13.4:6*

~ and be **you** healed by grace together, that **you** may heal through **faith.** *T-19.II.13.8*

~ to all who **share** the **love** of God, the grace is given to be the givers of what **they have** received. *T-22.V.43.1*

~ his grace His **answer** is to all **despair,** for in it lies remembrance of His **Love.** *W-pI.168.2.2*

~ his grace is yours by your **acknowledgment.** *W-pI.168.2.9*

~ his **gift** of grace is more than just an **answer.** It restores all memories the sleeping **mind** forgot; all **certainty** of what love's **meaning** is. *W-pI.168.3.5:6*

~ for in grace **you** see a **light** that covers all the **world** in **love** and watch **fear** disappear from every face as hearts rise up and claim the **light** as theirs. *W-pI.168.4.3*

~ grace is an aspect of the **Love** of **God** which is most like the state prevailing in the **unity** of **truth**. It is the world's most lofty aspiration, for it leads beyond the **world** entirely. It is **past learning** yet the **goal** of **learning**, for grace cannot come until the **mind** prepares itself for true **acceptance**. Grace becomes inevitable instantly in those who **have** prepared a table where it can be gently laid and willingly received, an **altar** clean and holy for the **gift**. *W-pI.169.11.1:4*

~ grace, the final **gift salvation** can bestow. **Experience** that grace provides **will** end in **time**, for grace foreshadows **Heaven** yet does not replace the **thought** of **time** but for a **little** while. *W-pI.169.11.1:2*

~ grace is **acceptance** of the **Love** of **God within** a **world** of seeming **hate** and **fear**. By grace **alone** the **hate** and **fear** are gone, for grace presents a state so **opposite** to everything the **world** contains that those whose minds are lighted by the **gift** of grace cannot believe the **world** of **fear** is real. *W-pI.169.2.1:2*

~ grace is not learned. The **final step** must go beyond all **learning**. Grace is not the **goal** this **course** aspires to attain. Yet **we** prepare for grace in that an open **mind** can hear the **call** to waken. *W-pI.169.3.1:4*

~ and what would seem to **need** a thousand years can easily be done in just one instant by the grace of **God**. *W-pI.196.4.5*

~ god's grace suffices us in everything that **He** would **have** us do. And only that **we** choose to be our **will**, as well as His. *W-pII.348.2.1:2*

GRANDEUR |ˈɡranjər'|

DICTIONARY: *splendor and impressiveness, especially of **appearance** or style.*

HOLY SPIRIT;   **truth**, God's **answer**, your abundance.

~ grandeur is of **God** and only of Him. Therefore, it is in **you**. Whenever **you** become aware of it, however dimly, **you** abandon the **ego** automatically, because in the presence of the grandeur of **God** the meaninglessness of the **ego** becomes perfectly apparent. *T-9.VII.48.1:3*

~ the **ego** is immobilized in the presence of God's grandeur, because His grandeur establishes your **freedom**. *T-9.VII.51.1*

~ grandeur is totally without illusions, and because it is real, it is compellingly convincing. *T-9.VII.51.3*

~ your grandeur is not delusional, because **you** did not **make** it. *T-9.VII.52.1*

~ your grandeur is of **God**, Who created it out of His **Love**. From your grandeur **you** can only bless, because your grandeur is your abundance. By **blessing**, **you** hold it in your **mind**, protecting it from illusions. *T-9.VII.52.2:4*

~ your grandeur is God's **answer** to the **ego** because it is true. Littleness and grandeur cannot co-**exist**, nor is it possible for them to alternate in your **awareness**. *T-9.VII.53.3:4*

~ it is easy to distinguish grandeur from **grandiosity** because **love** is returned, but **pride** is not. *T-9.VII.55.1*

~ his grandeur is total, and **you** cannot be missing from it. *T-9.VII.56.8*

~ grandeur is the right of God's Son. *T-12.III.18.6*

GRANDIOSITY

DICTIONARY: *impressive or magnificent in **appearance** or style, especially pretentiously so.*

EGO; *cover for **despair***

~ with the **grandeur** of **God** in **you, you have** chosen to be **little** and to lament your littleness. **Within** the system which dictated this **choice**, the lament is inevitable. *T-9.VI.43.5:6*

~ **self**-inflation [is the only **offering** it can **make**. The grandiosity] of the **ego** is its alternative to the **grandeur** of **God**. *T-9.VII.48.5:6*

~ the essence of grandiosity is competitiveness, because it always involves **attack**. It is a delusional attempt to outdo but not to **undo**. *T-9.VII.49.5:6*

~ the **ego** does not know the **difference** between **grandeur** and grandiosity, because it does not know the **difference** between **miracle** impulses and **ego**-alien beliefs of its own. *T-9.VII.50.1*

~ **you** have made grandiosity and are afraid of it because it is a **form** of **attack**. *T-9.VII.52.2*

~ littleness and grandiosity can and must alternate in your **awareness** since both are untrue and are therefore on the same **level**. *T-9.VII.53.5*

~ beneath all your grandiosity, which **you** hold so dear, is your real **call** for **help**. *T-12.III.18.1*

~ **sin** is the "grand **illusion**" underlying all the ego's grandiosity. *T-19.III.18.6*

HOLY SPIRIT

~ grandiosity is meaningless, and **you** could not possibly **want** it. *T-9.VII.49.4*

~ grandiosity is always a cover for **despair**. It is without hope, because it is not real. It is an attempt to counteract your littleness, based on the **belief** that the littleness is real. Without this **belief**, grandiosity is meaningless, and **you** could not possibly **want** it. The essence of grandiosity is competitiveness, because it always involves **attack**. It is a delusional attempt to outdo but not to **undo**. *T-9.VII.49.1:6*

~ grandiosity is delusional, because it is used to replace your **grandeur**. *T-9.VII.56.6*

~ beneath all your grandiosity, which **you** hold so dear, is your real **call** for **help**. *T-12.III.18.1*

GRATITUDE

DICTIONARY: *the quality of **being** thankful; **readiness** to show **appreciation** for and to return kindness.*

EGO

~ **you** cannot be grateful for what **you** do not **value**. *T-8.XI.115.4*

~ gratitude is a **lesson** hard to learn for those who look upon the **world** amiss. The most that **they** can do is **see** themselves as better off than others. And **they** try to be content because another seems to suffer more than **they**. *W-pI.195.1.1:3*

HOLY SPIRIT

~ gratitude is due him for both his loving thoughts and his appeals for **help**, for both are capable of bringing **love** into your **awareness** if **you** perceive them truly. *T-11.II.6.7*

~ as his gratitude goes out to **you** who blessed him, **reason will** tell **you** that it cannot be **you** stand apart from **blessing**. The gratitude **he** offers **you** reminds **you** of the thanks your **Father** gives **you** for completing Him. *T-21.VII.68.2:3*

~ the gratitude of **God** Himself is freely offered to **everyone** who shares His **purpose**. *T-25.III.20.11*

- your gratitude is due to Him **alone** Who made all **cause** of sorrow disappear throughout the **world**. *W-pI.195.1.6*

- our gratitude **will** pave the **way** to Him and shorten our **learning time** by more than **you** could ever **dream** of. Gratitude goes hand in hand with **love**, and where one is, the other must be found. For gratitude is but an aspect of the **love** which is the **Source** of all **creation**. *W-pI.195.10.1:3*

- gratitude can only be sincere if it is joined to **love**. *W-pI.195.4.3*

- gratitude becomes the single **thought we substitute** for these insane perceptions. *W-pI.195.9.4*

- their gratitude to all **They have** created has no end, for gratitude remains a **part** of love. *W-pI.197.7.5*

- all gratitude belongs to **you** because of what **you** are. *W-pI.197.8.6*

- my gratitude permits my **love** to be accepted without **fear**. *W-pII.298.1.1*

GRIEVANCE

|ˈgrēvəns|

DICTIONARY: *a real or imagined wrong or other **cause** for complaint or protest, especially **unfair** treatment.*

EGO;   *a block to **sight**, shield of **hate**.*

- to hold a grievance is to forget who **you** are. To hold a grievance is to **see** yourself as a **body**. It is the **decision** to let the **ego rule** your **mind** and to condemn the **body** to **death**. *W-pI.68.1.2:4*

- those who hold grievances **will** redefine **God** in their own **image** as it is certain that **God** created them like Himself and defined them as **part** of Him. *W-pI.68.4.1*

- those who hold grievances **will** forget who **they** are as it is certain that those who forgive **will remember**. *W-pI.68.4.3*

- your grievances are hiding the **light** of the **world** in **you**, **everyone** stands in **darkness**, and **you** beside him. *W-pI.69.1.2*

- each grievance **you** hold is a declaration and an assertion in which **you** believe that says, "If this were different, **I** would be saved." *W-pI.71.3.1:2*

- holding grievances is an **attack** on God's **plan for salvation**. *W-pI.72.3.1*

- every grievance that **you** hold insists that the **body** is real. It overlooks entirely what your **brother** is. It reinforces your **belief** that **he** is a **body** and condemns him for it. And it asserts that his **salvation** must be **death**, projecting this **attack** onto **God** and holding Him responsible for it. *W-pI.72.6.3:6*

- grievances darken your **mind**, and **you** look out on a darkened **world**. *W-pI.73.5.4*

- each grievance stands like a dark shield of **hate** before the **miracle** it would conceal. *W-pI.78.1.2*

- every grievance is a block to **sight**. *W-pI.78.3.2*

- **they** keep me in **darkness** and **hide** the **light**. Grievances and **light** cannot go together, but **light** and **vision** must be joined for me to **see**. To **see**, I must lay grievances aside. *W-pI.85.2.3:5*

- holding grievances is an attempt to prove that God's **plan for salvation will** not work. *W-pI.86.5.1*

- by holding grievances, **I** am therefore excluding my only hope of **salvation** from my **awareness**. *W-pI.86.5.3*

- are but illusions that **hide** the miracles beyond. *W-pI.89.2.3*

HOLY SPIRIT

- the barrier of grievances is easily passed and cannot stand between **you** and your **salvation**. *W-pI.73.6.1*

~ grievances are completely alien to **love**. Grievances **attack love** and keep its **light** obscure. If **I** hold grievances **I** am attacking **love** and therefore attacking my **Self**. *W-pI.84.5.1:3*

GUIDANCE |ˈgīdəns|

DICTIONARY: *advice or information aimed at resolving a **problem** or difficulty, especially as given by someone in authority.*

EGO

~ believing that **he** can betray, **he** believes that everything can betray him. Yet this is only because **he** has elected to follow false guidance. Unable to follow this guidance without **fear**, **he** associates **fear** with guidance and refuses to follow any guidance at all. *T-7.XI.104.4:6*

~ its guidance leads **you** to a **journey** which must end in perceived self-defeat. *T-11.V.37.2*

~ without His guidance, **you will** think **you** know **alone** and **will** decide against your **peace**. *T-13.VIII.78.4*

~ by so limiting the guidance that **you** would accept, **you** are unable to depend on miracles to **answer** all your problems for. *T-14.VII.68.6*

~ this guidance teaches it is **error** to believe that sins are but mistakes. *W-pI.133.11.3*

HOLY SPIRIT; *gracious guidance*

~ a guide does not control, but **he** does direct, leaving the following up to **you**. "Lead us not into **temptation**" **means** "guide us out of our own errors." "Take up thy cross and follow me" **means**, "Recognize your errors and choose to abandon them by following my guidance." *T-1.I.50.5:8*

~ **you** do not **need** guidance except at the **mind level**. *T-2.IV.75.1*

~ the **reason you need** my **help** is because **you have** repressed your own Guide and therefore **need** guidance. *T-4.IV.47.4*

~ guidance is evaluative, because it implies that there is a right **way** and also a wrong **way**, one to be chosen and the other to be avoided. *T-5.IV.21.7*

~ **you** can **have** guidance from without, but **you** must accept it from **within**. The guidance must [become] what **you want**, or it **will** be meaningless to you. *T-8.V.29.6:7*

~ two ways of looking at the **world** are in your **mind**, and your **perception will** reflect the guidance **you** chose. *T-11.VIII.65.8*

~ under His guidance, **you will** travel **light** and **journey** lightly, for His **sight** is ever on the journey's end which is His **goal**. *T-12.VII.71.4*

~ whom **God** has given **you will** speak to **you**. He **will** take His rightful place in your **awareness** the instant **you** abandon it and offer it to Him. *T-14.VII.66.1:2*

~ **you** cannot be your guide to miracles, for it is **you** who made them necessary. *T-14.VII.67.1*

~ to follow the Holy Spirit's guidance is to let yourself be absolved of **guilt**. *M-29.3.3*

~ do not, then, think that following the Holy Spirit's guidance is necessary merely because of your own inadequacies. It is the **way** out of **hell** for **you**. *M-29.3.10:11*

GUILT

DICTIONARY: *the **fact** of having committed a specified or implied offense or crime.*

EGO; *hell, the **price** of love, **condition** of **sacrifice**, game of guilt, **dream** of guilt.*

~ as long as **you** feel guilty, your **ego** is in command because only the **ego** can **experience** guilt. *T-4.V.61.5*

~ guilt feelings are the preservers of **time**. **They** induce fears of **future** retaliation or abandonment and thus ensure that the **future will** remain like the **past**. *T-5.VIII.72.1:2*

~ it is guilt that has obscured the **Father** to **you**, and it is guilt that has driven **you** insane. *T-11.X.85.7*

~ guilt hides **Christ** from your **sight**, for it is the **denial** of the blamelessness of God's Son. *T-11.X.89.5*

~ **you** can hold on to the **past** only through guilt. For guilt establishes that **you will** be punished for what **you have** done and thus depends on one-dimensional **time**, proceeding from **past** to **future**. *T-11.X.96.2:3*

~ guilt must deprive **you** of the **appreciation** of **eternity**. *T-11.X.96.5*

~ guilt, then, is a **way** of holding **past** and **future** in your minds to ensure the ego's continuity. *T-11.X.96.7*

~ the **ego** attempts to get rid of guilt from its viewpoint only, for much as the **ego** wants to retain guilt, **you** find it intolerable. *T-12.I.1.2*

~ **you** project guilt to get rid of it, but **you** are actually merely concealing it. **You** do **experience** guilt feelings, but **you have** no **idea** why. *T-12.I.2.2:3*

~ the darkest of your hidden cornerstones holds your **belief** in guilt from your **awareness**. *T-12.II.3.1*

~ guilt remains the only **thing** that hides the **Father**, for guilt is the **attack** upon His Son. The guilty always condemn, and having done so, **they will** condemn, linking the **future** to the **past** as is the ego's law. *T-13.III.11.1:2*

~ this law lets no **light** in, for it demands fidelity to **darkness** and forbids awakening. *T-13.III.11.3*

~ his guilt is yours. *T-13.III.12.2*

~ guilt has become as true for **you** as **innocence**. *T-13.III.14.2*

~ the **idea** that the **guiltless Son of God** can **attack** himself and **make** himself guilty is insane. *T-13.III.15.3*

~ those whom **you see** as guilty become the witnesses to guilt in **you**, and **you will see** it there, for it is there until it is undone. *T-13.III.16.6*

~ guilt is always in your own **mind**, which has condemned itself. Project it not, for while **you** do, it cannot be undone. *T-13.III.16.7:8*

~ guilt makes **you blind**, for while **you see** one spot of guilt **within you, you will** not **see** the **light**. And by projecting it, the **world** seems dark and shrouded in your guilt. *T-13.III.17.1:2*

~ the **ego** tells **you** all is black with guilt **within you** and bids **you** not to look. Instead, it bids **you** look upon your brothers and **see** the guilt in them. *T-13.III.18.2:3*

~ **you will see** guilt in that **relationship** because **you** put it there. It is inevitable that those who suffer guilt **will** attempt to displace it, because **they** do believe in it. Yet, though **they** suffer, **they will** not look **within** and let it go. **They** cannot know **they love** and cannot **understand** what loving is. Their main concern is to perceive the **source** of guilt **outside** themselves, beyond their own control. *T-13.IV.22.3:7*

~ believe that increasing guilt is **self**-protection. *T-13.VIII.73.8*

~ the **ego** really believes that it can get and keep by making guilty. *T-15.VIII.66.3*

~ to **make** guilty is direct **attack** but does not seem to be. For the guilty expect **attack**, and having asked for it, **they** are attracted to it. *T-15.VIII.70.5:6*

~ what makes another guilty and holds him through guilt is "**good**. "What releases him from guilt is "bad."
T-15.VIII.72.8:9

~ guilt is the only **need** the **ego** has, and as long as **you** identify with it, guilt **will** remain attractive to **you**.
T-15.VIII.74.4

~ **you** must **share** his guilt because **you** chose it for him in the **image** of your own. *T-31.V.55.7*

~ guilt is **hell**. *W-pI.39.1.1*

~ **salvation** seems to come from anywhere except from **you**. So, too, does the **source** of guilt. **You see** neither guilt nor **salvation** as in your own **mind** and nowhere else. *W-pI.70.1.2:4*

~ guilt is inevitable in those who use their **judgment** in making their decisions. *P-2.VII.4.6*

HOLY SPIRIT; *invention of your **mind**, **illusion**, interference, a fragile **veil**.*

~ when **you** feel guilty, know that the **ego** has indeed violated the **laws** of God, but **you have** not. *T-4.V.61.1*

~ guilt is more than merely not of **God**. It is the **symbol** of the **attack** on **God**. *T-5.VII.60.7:8*

~ guilt is a sure sign that your thinking is unnatural. Perverted thinking **will** always be attended with guilt because it is the **belief** in sin. *T-5.VII.63.8:9*

~ there can be no case against a **Child** of **God**, and every **witness** to guilt in God's **creations** is bearing false **witness** to **God** Himself. *T-5.VIII.79.6*

~ without guilt the **ego** has no **life**, and God's Son is without guilt. *T-11.X.90.5*

~ the **Holy Spirit** dispels it simply through the **calm** recognition that it has never been. As **He** looks upon the **guiltless Son of God**, **he** knows this is true. *T-11.X.99.4:5*

~ **release** from guilt is the ego's whole undoing. *T-13.III.12.1*

~ guilt is always totally insane and has no **reason**. *T-13.IV.25.3*

~ guilt is interference, not **salvation**, and serves no useful **function** at all. *T-13.VIII.64.5*

~ there is no **compromise** that **you** can **make** with guilt and escape the **pain** which only guiltlessness allays.
T-13.VIII.66.1

~ guilt cannot last when the **idea** of **sacrifice** has been removed. *T-15.X.96.6*

~ the end of guilt is in your hands to **give**. *T-19.V.64.7*

~ his **secret** guilt would disappear, forgiven by himself. *T-24.IV.26.8*

~ guilt is but the fabric of a senseless **dream**. *T-27.III.18.8*

~ can guilt and **sin** be seen without a **purpose** and as meaningless. *T-30.VI.61.4*

~ all guilt is solely an invention of your **mind**. *W-pI.70.1.5*

~ guilt and **salvation** must be in the same place. Understanding this **you** are saved. *W-pI.70.1.5:6*

~ guilt is **impossible** in those through whom the **Holy Spirit** speaks. *P-2.VII.4.7*

~ the passing of guilt is the true aim of therapy and the obvious aim of **forgiveness**. *P-2.VII.5.1*

GUILTLESS

|ˈgiltləs|

DICTIONARY: *having no **guilt**; **innocent**.*

EGO

~ let it perceive guiltlessness anywhere, and it **will** try to destroy it because it is afraid. *T-12.II.3.5*

~ to the **ego**, the guiltless are guilty. Those who do not **attack** are its "enemies" because, by not valuing its **interpretation** of **salvation**, **they** are in an excellent position to let it go. *T-12.II.4.2:3*

~ when it was confronted with the real guiltlessness of God's Son, it did attempt to **kill** him, and the **reason** it gave was that guiltlessness is blasphemous to **God**. To the ego the **ego** is **God**, and guiltlessness must be interpreted as the final **guilt** which fully justifies murder. **You** do not yet **understand** that all your **fear** of this **course** stems ultimately from this **interpretation**. *T-12.II.6.2:4*

~ **you** are accustomed to using guiltlessness merely to offset the **pain** of guilt and do not look upon it as having **value** in itself. **You** believe that **guilt** and guiltlessness are both of **value**, each representing an escape from what the other does not offer **you**. **You** do not **want** either **alone**, for without both, **you** do not **see** yourselves as whole and therefore **happy**. *T-13.VIII.65.1:3*

HOLY SPIRIT

~ accepting the guiltlessness of the **Son of God** as yours is therefore God's **way** of reminding **you** of His Son and what **he** is in **truth**. For **God** has never condemned His Son, and **being** guiltless, **he** is eternal. *T-11.X.97.3:4*

~ it is only your guiltlessness which can protect **you**. *T-12.II.7.7*

~ in our **love** of him is your guiltlessness. *T-13.IV.32.4*

~ the state of guiltlessness is only the **condition** in which what is not there has been removed from the disordered **mind** that **thought** it was. *T-13.IX.87.2*

~ the guiltless and the guilty are totally incapable of understanding one another. Each perceives the other as like himself, making them unable to communicate because each sees the other unlike the **way he** sees himself. *T-14.II.4.1:2*

~ hope of happiness and **release** from **suffering** of every kind lie in it. *T-14.II.9.2*

~ in guiltlessness **we** know Him, as **He** knows us guiltless. **I** stand **within** the circle, calling **you** to **peace**. *T-14.II.13.3:4*

~ the **Holy Spirit** sees only guiltlessness, and in His **gentleness**, **He** would **release** from **fear** and reestablish the reign of **love**. *T-14.II.14.8*

~ the **light** of guiltlessness shines **guilt** away because, when **they** are brought together, the **truth** of one must **make** the falsity of its **opposite** perfectly clear. *T-14.III.19.2*

~ the guiltless **have** no **fear**, for **they** are safe and recognize their safety. **They** do not appeal to **magic** nor **invent** escapes from fancied threats without **reality**. **They** rest in **quiet certainty** that **they will** do what it is given them to do. **They** do not **doubt** their own ability because **they** know their **function will** be filled completely in the perfect **time** and place. **They** took the stand which **we will** take **today** that we may **share** their **certainty** and thus increase it by accepting it ourselves. *W-pI.98.3.1:5*

169

HAPPY

DICTIONARY: *feeling or showing **pleasure** or contentment.*

EGO

~ if **you** do not **have** it always, **being** what it is, **you** did not **ask** for it. *T-21.IX.88.3*

~ no one decides against his happiness, but **he** may do so if **he** does not **see he** does it. And if **he** sees his happiness as ever changing, **now** this, **now** that, and **now** an elusive **shadow** attached to **nothing**, **he** does decide against it. *T-21.VIII.83.5:6*

~ elusive happiness, or happiness in changing **form** that shifts with **time** and place, is an **illusion** which has no **meaning**. *T-21.VIII.84.1*

~ **you** can be sure indeed that any seeming happiness that does not last is really **fear**. *T-22.III.18.5*

~ **you will** believe your happiness depends on **being** right. *T-30.II.21.2*

~ no one would avoid his happiness. But **he** can think that **joy** is painful, threatening, and dangerous. *W-pII.339.1.3:4*

HOLY SPIRIT;   *attribute of **love***

~ happiness must be constant because it is attained by giving up the **wish** for the inconstant. *T-21.VIII.84.2*

~ the constancy of happiness has no exceptions—no **change** of any kind. It is unshakable as is the **love of God** for His **creation**. Sure in its **vision** as its **Creator** is in what **He** knows, it looks on everything and sees it is the same. It sees not the ephemeral, for it desires that everything be like itself and sees it so. **Nothing** has **power** to confound its constancy because its own **desire** cannot be shaken. *T-21.IX.87.1:5*

~ happiness is constant, then **you need ask** for it but once to **have** it always. *T-21.IX.88.2*

~ **suffering** is not happiness, and it is happiness **you** really **want**. Such is your **will** in **truth**. *W-pI.73.7.1:2*

~ happiness is an attribute of **love**. It cannot be apart from it, nor can it be experienced where **love** is not. **Love** has no limits, **being** everywhere. *W-pI.103.1.1:3*

~ happiness belongs to **you** because of what **He** is. *W-pI.103.5.2*

~ and only happiness can be my state, for only happiness is given me. *W-pII.337.1.2*

HAPPY DREAM

HOLY SPIRIT

~ it **will** be a **happy dream**, and one which **you will share** with all who come **within** your **sight**. Through it, the **blessing** which the **Holy Spirit** has laid upon it **will** be extended. *T-18.III.21.2:3*

~ **happy** dreams from which awaking is so easy and so natural. *T-18.III.23.4*

~ **happy** dreams come true, not because **they** are dreams, but only because **they** are **happy**. And so **they** must be loving. Their **message** is, "Thy **will** be done," and not, "**I want** it otherwise." *T-18.VI.44.1:4*

~ the **happy dream** through which He can spread **joy** to thousands on thousands who believe that **love** is **fear**, not happiness. *T-18.VI.45.5*

~ the **happy dream** about him takes the **form** of the **appearance** of his perfect **health**, his perfect **freedom** from all forms of lack, and safety from **disaster** of all kinds. *T-30.IX.90.5*

HAPPY LEARNER

Ego

~ unhappy learners who would **teach** themselves **nothing** and delude themselves into believing that it is not **nothing**. *T-13.VII.57.3*

~ **you** are not **happy** learners yet because **you** still remain **uncertain** that **vision** gives **you** more than **judgment** does, and **you have** learned that both **you** cannot **have**. *T-21.II.5.7*

Holy Spirit; *guiltless learner*

~ the **Holy Spirit** needs a **happy learner** in whom His **mission** can be happily accomplished. *T-13.VII.54.1*

~ **they will** be **happy** learners of the **lesson** which this **light** brings to them because it teaches them **release** from **nothing** and from all the works of **nothing**. *T-13.VII.59.5*

~ if **you** would be a **happy learner**, **you** must **give** everything that **you have** learned over to the **Holy Spirit** to be unlearned for **you**. *T-13.VII.61.1*

~ the **happy learner** meets the conditions of **learning here**, as **he** also meets the conditions of **knowledge** in the **Kingdom**. The **happy learner** cannot feel guilty about **learning**. *T-13.VII.62.1:2*

~ the **happy learner** cannot feel guilty about **learning**. This is so essential to **learning** that it should never be forgotten. The **guiltless learner** learns so easily because his thoughts are free. *T-13.VIII.64.2:4*

~ the **guiltless learner** learns so easily because his thoughts are free. *T-13.VIII.64.4*

~ the **happy** learners of the **Atonement** become the teachers of the **innocence** that is the right of all that **God** created. *T-14.II.7.7*

HARM

Dictionary: *physical injury, especially that which is deliberately inflicted.*

Ego

~ **you** cannot **seek** to harm him and be saved. *T-23.III.35.6*

~ harm is the outcome of **judgment**. It is the dishonest act that follows a dishonest **thought**. It is a verdict of **guilt** upon a **brother** and therefore on one's **self**. It is the end of **peace** and the **denial** of **learning**. It demonstrates the absence of God's **curriculum** and its replacement by **insanity**. *M-4.14.3:7*

Holy Spirit

~ **nothing** can harm **you** in any **way**. *W-pI.68.9.3*

~ harm is **impossible** for God's teachers. **They** can neither harm nor be harmed. *M-4.14.1:2*

~ a loving **father** does not let his **child** harm himself or choose his own **destruction**. He may **ask** for injury, but his **father will** protect him still. *M-29.6.8:9*

HATE

DICTIONARY: *feel intense or passionate dislike for (someone).*

EGO; *love, ancient hate.*

~ if **you** hate **part** of your own **Soul**, all your understanding is lost because **you** are looking on what **God** created as yourself without **love**. *T-10.V.31.6*

~ **you** cannot **limit** hate. *T-16.V.30.5*

~ **where** disillusionment is possible, there was not **love** but hate. For hate is an **illusion**, and what can **change** was never **love**. *T-16.V.33.3-4*

~ **love** calls, but hate would **have you** stay. *T-16.V.40.3*

~ no one considers it bizarre to **love** and hate together, and even those who believe that hate is **sin** merely feel guilty and do not correct it. *T-16.VI.44.8*

~ hate must **have** a target. *T-21.VIII.74.1*

~ hate must **father fear** and look upon its **father** as itself. *T-31.I.10.2*

~ hate is specific. There must be a **thing** to be attacked. An **enemy** must be perceived in such a **form he** can be touched and seen and heard and ultimately killed. When hatred rests upon a **thing**, it calls for **death** as surely as **God's Voice** proclaims there is no **death**. *W-pI.161.7.1-4*

~ hate must be the **opposite** of **love**, regardless of the **form** it takes. *M-7.4.7*

HOLY SPIRIT; *illusion*

~ the **shadow** of an ancient hate has gone, and all the blight and withering **have** passed forever from the land where **They have** come. *T-26.X.79.8*

~ what hatred claimed is given up to **love**, and **freedom** lights up every living **thing** and lifts it into **Heaven**, where the lights grow ever brighter as each one comes **home**. *T-26.X.80.4*

~ the holiest of all the spots on earth is where an ancient hatred has become a **present love**. *T-26.X.82.1*

~ what hatred has released to **love** becomes the brightest **light** in Heaven's radiance. *T-26.X.82.5*

~ for hatred is forgotten when **we** lay comparisons aside. *W-pI.195.8.2*

HAVE

DICTIONARY: *possess, own, or hold.*

HOLY SPIRIT

~ those who perceive and acknowledge that **they** have everything have no **need** for driven **behavior** of any kind. *T-11.58.5*

~ **i** have **nothing** that does not come from **God**. The main **difference** between us as yet is that **I** have **nothing** else. *T-11.78.8-9*

~ the **Soul** knows that **you** both have everything and are everything. *T-4.IV.54.5*

~ to have, **give** all **to** all. *T-6.V.67.1*

~ having rests on giving and not on getting. *T-6.V.90.1*

~ it is **impossible** not to have, but it is possible not to know **you** have. The recognition of having is the willingness for **giving**, and only by this willingness can **you** recognize what **you** have. What **you give** is therefore the **value you** put on what **you** have, **being** the exact measure of the **value you** put upon it. And this, in turn, is the measure of how much **you want** it. *T-8.XI.117.6:9*

HE |hē|

DICTIONARY: *used to refer to a **man**, boy, or male animal previously mentioned or easily identified.*

EGO;   *body*

~ he believes in the **power** of what does not **exist**. *T-2.V.98.7*

~ he is also incapable of **knowledge**, because he can perceive lovelessly. He cannot create surely, because his **perception** deceives. *T-3.VI.38.5:6*

~ he became a perceiver rather than a **creator** in the true **sense**. *T-3.VI.40.2*

~ he despairs of finding satisfaction in **reality**. Yet it is certain that he **will** never find satisfaction in **fantasy**. *T-9.III.18.1:2*

~ even if he is fully aware of anxiety, he does not perceive its **source** as his own **ego** identification, and he always tries to handle it by making some sort of insane "arrangement" with the **world**. He always perceives this **world** as **outside** himself, for this is crucial to his **adjustment**. He does not realize that he makes this **world**, for there is no **world outside** of him. *T-11.IV.29.5:7*

~ and so must he be envious and try to take away from whom he judges. He is not impartial and cannot fairly **see** another's rights because his own **have** been obscured to him. *T-25.IX.76.9:10*

~ he would **sacrifice** his own **identity** with everything to find a **little treasure** of his own. *T-26.VIII.58.2*

~ he misunderstood what made him safe and **thought** that it had left. *T-30.V.50.7*

~ in **guilt** he has forgotten what he really is. *T-31.I.9.7*

~ nor does he **trust** the "**good**" in anyone, believing that the "bad" must lurk behind. *T-31.VII.68.7*

~ he thus denies himself and contradicts what has no **opposite**. He thinks he made a **hell** opposing **Heaven** and believes that he abides in what does not **exist**, while **Heaven** is the place he cannot find. *W-pI.131.10.3:4*

~ **here** is deception doubled, for the one who is deceived **will** not perceive that he has merely failed to **gain**. He **will** believe that he has served the ego's hidden goals. *W-pI.133.10.3:4*

~ he is not at **home**. He goes uncertainly about in endless search, seeking in **darkness** what he cannot find, not recognizing what it is he seeks. *W-pI.182.3.1:2*

~ he **will** fight against his **freedom** because he thinks that it is slavery. *P-1.I.4.5*

~ he must think of **evil** as besetting him **here** and **now**. *P-2.VI.6.5*

HOLY SPIRIT;   *brother, You, God's Son.*

~ when everything he retains is loveable, there is no **reason** for **fear** to remain with him. This is his **part** in the **Atonement**. *T-2.VI.111.7:8*

~ he keeps asking himself what he is. This implies that the **answer** is not only one which he knows but is also one which is up to him to supply. *T-3.VII.53.7:8*

~ in **peace** he needed **nothing** and asked for **nothing**. *T-12.III.21.1*

~ he can no longer be satisfied with anything but his own **reality**. *T-14.VI.47.3*

- he is healed because **you** offered **faith** to him, giving him to the **Holy Spirit** and releasing him from every demand your **ego** would **make** of him. *T-19.I.2.2*

- no one who loves can judge, and what he sees is free of **condemnation**. And what he sees he did not **make**, for it was given him to **see**, as was the **vision** which made his seeing possible. *T-20.VIII.66.7:8*

- neither the sounds he hears nor sights he sees are stable yet. But what he hears and does not **understand will** be his native tongue, through which he **will** communicate with those around him, and **they** with him. And the strange, shifting ones he sees about him **will** become to him his comforters, and he **will** recognize his **home** and **see** them there with him. *T-22.II.10.5:7*

- no one who knows that he has everything could **seek** for limitation, nor could he **value** the body's offerings. *T-23.V.55.4*

- he has the **power** to heal and bless all those he looks on with the **grace** of God upon his **sight**. *T-25.VII.43.8*

- he holds not the proof of **sin** before his brother's eyes. And thus he must **have** overlooked it and removed it from his own. *T-27.III.15.7:8*

- he understands he never had a **need** for **doing** anything and never did. *T-28.II.14.4*

- yet is he glad to wait till every hand is joined and every heart made ready to arise and go with him. *T-30.VI.59.6*

- he could not **make** an **error** that could **change** the **truth** in him. *T-30.VII.81.1*

- he is saved by what **you** are. *W-pI.67.1.5*

- he who was **enemy** is more than friend when he is freed to take the holy **role** the **Holy Spirit** has assigned to him. *W-pI.78.6.4*

- he is your **brother** and so like to **you** your **Father** knows that **you** are both the same. It is your **Self you ask** to go with **you**, and how could He be absent where **you** are? *W-pI.107.10.3:4*

- he does not **have** to fight to save himself. *W-pI.134.12.1*

- he **will** save the **world** because he gives the **world** what he receives each **time** he practices the words of **truth**. *W-pI.162.3.3*

- no one frightens him and **nothing** can endanger him. He has no enemies, and he is safe from all external things. *W-pII.338.1.3:4*

- he lives in eternal **joy**. *W-pII.ST331.3.3*

- he looks on what he chooses to **see**. No more and no less. The **world** does **nothing** to him. He only **thought** it did. Nor does he do anything to the **world** because he was mistaken about what it was. *M-5.6.6:10*

- he who has learned all things does not **need** a **teacher**. *P-2.II.1.4*

- he sees his sins as gone into a **past** that is no longer **here**. *P-2.VI.6.4*

HEALER |ˈhēlər|

DICTIONARY: *a person who claims to be able to cure a disease or injury using **special** powers.*

EGO

- by accepting exceptions and acknowledging that **he** can sometimes heal and sometimes not, the healer is obviously accepting inconsistency. **He** is therefore in **conflict** and teaching **conflict**. The "fearful healer" is a **contradiction** in terms and is therefore a **concept** which only a conflicted **mind** could possibly perceive as meaningful. *T-7.VI.44.4:6*

~ every healer who searches fantasies for **truth** must be **unhealed,** because **he** does not know where to look for **truth** and therefore does not **have** the **answer** to the **problem** of **healing.** *T-9.IV.21.3*

HOLY SPIRIT

~ the healer is **part** of the **resurrection** and the **life.** *T-7.V.31.7*

~ **fear** does not gladden. **Healing** does. **Fear** always makes exceptions. **Healing** never does. **Fear** produces **dissociation,** because it induces **separation. Healing** always produces harmony, because it proceeds from integration. *T-7.VI.45.5:10*

~ **you** do not **make** yourself the bearer of the **special gift** that brings the **healing. You** but recognize your **oneness** with the one who calls for **help.** *S-3.III.4.3:4*

~ **they** are Sons of **God** who recognize their **Source,** and **understand** that all their **Source** creates is one with them. This is the remedy that brings relief which cannot **fail. It will** remain to bless for all **eternity.** It heals no **part,** but wholly and forever. *S-3.III.5.1:4*

~ in their **sight** their brothers **share** their **healing** and their **love.** Bringers of **peace** — the Holy Spirit's **voice,** through whom **He** speaks for **God,** Whose **Voice He** is — such are God's healers. **They** but speak for Him and never for themselves. **They have** no gifts but those **they have** from **God.** *S-3.IV.1.2:5*

~ **they** are not **special. They** are holy. **They have** chosen **holiness,** and given up all separate dreams of **special** attributes through which **they** can bestow unequal gifts on those less fortunate. *S-3.IV.1.7:9*

HEALING
['hēliNG]

DICTIONARY: *the process of making or becoming sound or healthy again.*

EGO; *make mindless*

~ however misguided the "magical **healer**" may be, **he** is also trying to **help. He** is conflicted and unstable, but at times **he** is **offering** something to the **Sonship,** and the only **thing** the **Sonship** can accept is healing. *T-7.VI.43.1:2*

~ the healing of effect without the **cause** can merely **shift** effects to other forms. And this is not **release.** *T-26.VIII.61.2:3*

~ the fearful are not healed and cannot heal. *T-27.VI.45.9*

~ your **purpose** was to ensure that healing did not occur;. *W-pI.70.5.1*

~ **you** do not heal but merely take away the hope of healing, for **you fail** to **see** where hope must lie if it be meaningful. *W-pI.135.11.5*

~ when it tries to heal the **mind,** it sees no **separation** from the **body,** where it thinks the **mind** exists. Its forms of healing thus must **substitute illusion** for **illusion.** One **belief** in sickness takes another **form,** and so the **patient now** perceives himself as well. *W-pI.140.1.3:5*

~ he merely had a **dream** that **he** was sick, and in the **dream he** found a **magic** formula to **make** him well. Yet **he** has not awakened from the **dream,** and so his **mind** remains exactly as it was before. **He** has not seen the **light** that would **awaken** him and end the **dream.** *W-pI.140.2.2:4*

~ it symbolizes the defeat of God's Son and the triumph of his **Father** over him. It represents the ultimate defiance in a direct **form** which the **Son of God** is forced to recognize. It stands for all that **he** would **hide** from himself to protect his **life.** If **he** is healed, **he** is responsible for his thoughts. And if **he** is responsible for his thoughts, **he will** be killed to prove to him how weak and pitiful **he** is. But if **he** chooses **death** himself, his **weakness** is his **strength.** Now has **he** given himself what **God** would **give** to him and thus entirely usurped the **throne** of his **Creator.** *M-5.3.2:8*

~ healing is limited by the limitations of the **psychotherapist**, as it is limited by those of the **patient**. *P-2.III.2.1*

~ false healing merely makes a poor exchange of one **illusion** for a "nicer" one; a **dream** of **sickness** for a **dream** of **health**. This can occur at lower forms of **prayer**, combining with **forgiveness** kindly meant but not completely understood as yet. Only false healing can **give way** to **fear**, so **sickness will** be free to strike again. False healing can indeed remove a **form** of **pain** and **sickness**. But the **cause** remains, and **will** not lack effects. *S-3.II.1.1:5*

~ false healing rests upon the body's cure, leaving the **cause** of illness still unchanged, ready to strike again until it brings a cruel **death** in seeming victory. It can be held at bay a **little** while, and there can be brief respite as it waits to take its **vengeance** on the **Son of God**. *S-3.II.6.1:2*

~ false healing heals the **body** in a **part**, but never as a whole. Its separate goals become quite clear in this, for it has not removed the curse of **sin** that lies on it. Therefore it still deceives. *S-3.III.1.1:3*

~ when false, there is some **power** that another has, not equally bestowed on both as one. *S-3.III.1.1.6*

~ to be healed appears to be to find a wiser one who, by his arts and **learning**, **will** succeed. *S-3.III.2.8*

HOLY SPIRIT; *result, **release** from **fear**, ability, act of **thought**, reparation, art & **science**, **consistence**, our joint will, **love** of **Christ**, **gift**, **freedom**, **strength**, invitation, process, **blessing**, right-mindedness.*

~ the **miracle** is the **means**, the **Atonement** is the principle, and healing is the result. *T-2.III.52.2*

~ healing is not a **miracle**. The **Atonement** or the final **miracle** is a remedy, while any type of healing is a result. *T-2.III.52.4:5*

~ all healing is the **release** from **fear**. *T-2.III.52.7*

~ healing is necessary. *T-2.III.69.1*

~ healing is an ability lent to **man** after the **separation**, before which it was completely unnecessary. Like all aspects of the space-**time belief**, healing ability is temporary. However, as long as **time** persists, healing is needed as a **means** for human protection. *T-2.III.69.3:5*

~ healing rests on **charity**. *T-2.III.69.6*

~ healing is of **God** in the end. *T-3.I.3.3*

~ the **level**-**adjustment power** of the **miracle** induces the right **perception** for healing. Until this has occurred, healing cannot be understood. *T-3.II.8.1:2*

~ to heal is to **make happy**. *T-5.I.1.1*

~ to heal or to **make** joyous is therefore the same as to integrate and to **make** one. *T-5.I.2.6*

~ healing is an act of **thought** by which two minds perceive their **oneness** and become glad. *T-5.II.5.1*

~ healing is not creating; it is reparation. The **Holy Spirit** promotes healing by looking beyond it to what the Children of **God** were before healing was needed and **will** be when **they have** been healed. *T-5.III.17.1:2*

~ to heal is the only kind of thinking in this **world** that resembles the **Thought** of **God**, and because of the elements which **they share**, can transfer to it. *T-7.II.9.1*

~ to heal, then, is to correct **perception** in your **brother** and yourself by sharing the **Holy Spirit** with him. *T-7.III.10.1*

~ this parallels **creation**, because it unifies by increasing and integrates by extending. *T-7.III.10.3*

~ to heal is to liberate totally. *T-7.IV.19.1*

~ healing is also a **science**, because it obeys the **laws** of **God**, Whose **laws** are true. *T-7.V.32.1*

~ healing does not come directly from **God**, Who knows His **creations** as perfectly whole. Yet healing is [nevertheless] of **God**, because it proceeds from His **Voice** and from His **laws**. *T-7.V.33.4:5*

~ when **you** heal, **you** are remembering the **laws** of **God** and forgetting the **laws** of the **ego**. *T-7.V.34.6*

~ healing is the **way** to **undo** the **belief** in differences, **being** the only **way** of perceiving the **Sonship** without this **belief**. *T-7.V.36.5*

~ healing, then, is a **way** of approaching **knowledge** by thinking in accordance with the **laws** of **God** and recognizing their universality. *T-7.V.37.9*

~ healing is a **way** of forgetting the **sense** of danger the **ego** has induced in **you** by not recognizing its existence in your brothers. *T-7.V.38.7*

~ healing is the one ability which **everyone** can develop and must develop if **he** is to be healed. *T-7.VI.41.1*

~ healing only strengthens. *T-7.VI.42.1*

~ healing perceives **nothing** in the **healer** that **everyone** else does not **share** with him. *T-7.VI.42.3*

~ healing is predictable, because it can be counted on. *T-7.VI.46.1*

~ healing is **consistence**, it cannot be inconsistently understood. *T-7.VI.46.4*

~ healing is our joint **will**. *T-8.V.30.6*

~ yet to heal is still to **make** whole. Therefore, to heal is to unite with those who are like **you**. *T-8.V.37.1:2*

~ healing is the result of using the **body** solely for **communication**. *T-8.VII.62.1*

~ healing is **release** from the **fear** of waking and the substitution of the **will** to wake. The **will** to wake is the **will** to **love**, since all healing involves replacing **fear** with **love**. *T-8.IX.84.1:2*

~ the unification of **purpose**, then, is the Holy Spirit's only **way** of healing. *T-8.IX.89.1*

~ when a **brother** behaves insanely, **you** can heal him only by perceiving the **sanity** in him. *T-9.II.5.1*

~ healing is not mysterious. *T-9.IV.26.1*

~ **god** has only one **channel** for healing. *T-9.IX.76.1*

~ healing is the **acknowledgment** of Him. *T-9.XI.100.1*

~ healing is the beginning of the recognition that your **will** is His. *T-10.II.15.9*

~ for in this lies the beginning of **knowledge**, the foundation on which **God will help you** build again the **thought system** which **you share** with Him. *T-10.II.5.3*

~ healing thus becomes a **lesson** in understanding. *T-10.III.17.1*

~ **you** can heal only yourself. *T-10.III.18.5*

~ what is healing but the removal of all that stands in the **way** of **knowledge**? *T-10.VI.40.1*

~ healing is the **love** of **Christ** for His **Father** and for Himself. *T-11.III.16.6*

~ healing must be as complete as **fear**, for **love** cannot enter where there is one spot of **fear** to mar its **welcome**. *T-12.III.19.4*

~ healing cannot be accomplished in the **past** and must be accomplished in the **present** to **release** the **future**. This **interpretation** ties the **future** to the **present** and extends the **present** rather than the **past**. *T-12.IV.32.3:4*

~ healing in **time** is needed. *T-12.VII.76.5*

~ **everyone you** offer healing to returns it. *T-13.VIII.69.4*

~ **god** gave healing not apart from **sickness**, nor established remedy where **sickness** cannot be. *T-19.II.7.3*

~ healing comes of **power**. *T-21.VIII.77.2*

~ whom **you** would **have** healed must be the one **you** chose to be protected from **attack**. *T-21.VIII.77.4*

~ healing must be for **everyone**. *T-25.X.8.3.3*

~ your healing is his comfort and his **health** because it proves illusions are not true. *T-27.II.6.5*

~ in his healing lies the proof that **he** has truly pardoned and retains no trace of **condemnation** that **he** still would hold against himself or any living **thing**. *T-27.III.15.11*

~ so does your healing show your **mind** is healed and has forgiven what **he** did not do. And so is **he** convinced his **innocence** was never lost and healed along with **you**. *T-27.III.17.6:7*

~ your healing saves him **pain** as well as **you**, and **you** are healed because **you** wished him well. *T-27.III.19.3*

~ healing sees no specialness at all. It does not come from pity but from **love**. *T-27.III.19.4:5*

~ the only **way** to heal is to be healed. *T-27.VI.44.1*

~ no one can **ask** another to be healed. But **he** can let himself be healed and thus offer the other what **he** has received. *T-27.VI.44.6:7*

~ it does mean, if only for an instant, **you love** without **attack**. *T-27.VI.45.12*

~ healing replaces **suffering**. *T-27.VI.48.6*

~ your healing **will** extend and **will** be brought to problems that **you thought** were not your own. *T-27.VI.51.1*

~ all healing must proceed in lawful manner in accord with **laws** which **have** been properly perceived but never violated. *T-27.VI.51.4*

~ a **gift** of **love** unto His Son, and therefore is it given unto Him. *T-27.VI.53.9*

~ **nothing** employed for healing represents an **effort** to do anything at all. It is a recognition that **you have** no needs which mean that something must be done. It is an unselective **memory**, which is not used to **interfere** with **truth**. *T-28.I.3.1:3*

~ **you need** no healing to be healed. *T-28.II.10.8*

~ healing is the effect of minds which **join**. *T-28.IV.29.6*

~ healing **will** be one or not at all, its **oneness being** where the healing lies. *T-28.VIII.61.5*

~ **you have** accepted healing's **Cause**, and so it must be **you** are healed. And **being** healed, the **power** to heal must also **now** be yours. *T-29.III.11.1:2*

~ but where its **cause** is must it be. **Now** is it caused, though not as yet perceived. And its effects are there, though not yet seen. *T-29.III.11.5:7*

~ to heal is to **make** whole. *T-30.VII.77.3*

~ **he** wants **you** to be healed, and so He has kept the **Source** of healing where the **need** for healing lies. *W-pI.70.4.3*

~ **here** is the **gift** of healing, for the **truth** needs no **defense**, and therefore no **attack** is possible. *W-pI.107.6.2*

~ healing is the **opposite** of all the world's ideas which dwell on **sickness** and on separate states. *W-pI.137.1.2*

~ those who are healed become the instruments of healing. *W-pI.137.11.1*

~ it is **impossible** that anyone be healed **alone**. *W-pI.137.3.1*

~ but healing is his own **decision** to be one again and to accept his **Self** with all its parts intact and unassailed. *W-pI.137.3.3*

~ but healing is accomplished as **he** sees the **body** has no **power** to **attack** the universal **oneness** of God's Son. *W-pI.137.3.5*

~ healing demonstrates that **truth** is true. *W-pI.137.4.2*

~ to be healed is merely to accept what always was the simple **truth** and always **will** remain exactly as it has forever been. *W-pI.137.4.4*

~ so healing, never needed by the **truth**, must demonstrate that **sickness** is not real. *W-pI.137.4.6*

~ healing might thus be called a counter-**dream** which cancels out the **dream** of **sickness** in the **name** of **truth** but not in **truth** itself. Just as **forgiveness** overlooks all sins that never were accomplished, healing but removes illusions that **have** not occurred. Just as the **real world will** arise to take the place of what has never been at all, healing but offers restitution for imagined states and false ideas which dreams embroider into pictures of the **truth**. *W-pI.137.5.1:3*

~ healing must replace the fantasies of **sickness** which **you** hold before the simple **truth**. *W-pI.137.7.1*

~ healing is **freedom**. For it demonstrates that dreams **will** not prevail against the **truth**. Healing is shared. And by this attribute, it proves that **laws** unlike the ones which hold that **sickness** is inevitable are more potent than their sickly opposites. Healing is **strength**. For by its gentle hand is **weakness** overcome. And minds which were walled off **within** a **body** free to **join** with other minds, to be forever strong. *W-pI.137.8.1:7*

~ this is no **magic**. It is merely an appeal to **truth** which cannot **fail** to heal and heal forever. *W-pI.140.6.4:5*

~ healing must be sought but where it is and then applied to what is sick so that it can be cured. *W-pI.140.7.2*

~ **source** of healing, which is in our minds because our **Father** placed it there for us. It is not further from us than ourselves. It is as near to us as our own thoughts—so close it is **impossible** to lose. **We need** but **seek** it, and it must be found. *W-pI.140.8.2:5*

~ **you understand** that **you** are healed when **you give** healing. *W-pI.159.2.1*

~ but when the **mind** is split, there is a **need** of healing. *W-pII.ST231.2.3*

~ healing involves an understanding of what the **illusion** of **sickness** is for. *M-5.1.1*

~ healing is accomplished the instant the sufferer no longer sees any **value** in **pain**. *M-5.2.1*

~ healing must occur in exact proportion in which the valuelessness of **sickness** is recognized. One **need** but say, "There is no **gain** to me at all in this" and **he** is healed. But to say this one must first recognize certain facts. *M-5.4.1:3*

~ the **acceptance** of **sickness** as a **decision** of the **mind** for a **purpose** for which it would use the **body** is the basis of healing. And this is so for healing in all forms. A **patient** decides that this is so, and **he** recovers. If **he** decides against recovery, **he will** not be healed. *M-5.5.1:4*

~ healing is always certain. *M-6.1.1*

~ healing **will** always stand aside when it would be seen as **threat**. The instant it is **welcome** it is there. Where healing has been given, it **will** be received. *M-6.2.1:3*

~ healing is the **change** of **mind** that the **Holy Spirit** in the patient's **mind** is seeking for him. And it is the **Holy Spirit** in the **mind** of the giver Who gives the **gift** to Him. *M-6.4.3:4*

~ healing cannot be repeated. If the **patient** is healed, what remains to heal him from? *M-7.1.2:3*

~ healing is an invitation to **God** to enter into His **Kingdom**. *P-2.II.6.1*

~ healing is a process, not a **fact**. *P-2.III.4.2*

~ healing is a process He directs, because it is according to His **Will**. *P-2.V.4.6*

~ healing occurs as a **patient** begins to hear the dirge **he** sings, and questions its validity. *P-2.VI.1.5*

~ it is in the instant that the **therapist** forgets to judge the **patient** that healing occurs. *P-3.II.6.1*

~ it is when **judgment** ceases that healing occurs, because only then it can be understood that there is no **order of difficulty** in healing. *P-3.II.7.1*

~ healing is a sign or **symbol** of **forgiveness' strength**, and only an effect or **shadow** of a **change** of **mind** about the **goal** of **prayer**. *S-3.IN.1.3*

~ healing the **body** is **impossible**, and this is shown by the brief nature of the "cure." *S-3.I.1.4:5*

~ healing can be false as well as true; a **witness** to the **power** of the **world** or to the everlasting **Love** of **God**. *S-3.I.5.3*

~ the body's healing **will** occur because its **cause** has gone. And **now** without a **cause**, it cannot come again in different **form**. *S-3.III.6.3:4*

~ as **witness** to **forgiveness**, aid to **prayer**, and the effect of mercy truly taught, healing is **blessing**. *S-3.IV.2.1*

~ the **Cause** of healing is Himself, His **Love**. *S-3.IV.3.3*

~ **you** first forgive, then pray, and **you** are healed. *S-3.IV.4.1*

HEALTH |helTH|

DICTIONARY: *the state of **being** free from illness or injury.*

EGO

~ the **God of sickness** obviously demands the **denial** of health, because health is in direct opposition to its own **survival**. *T-9.XI.95.2*

~ finding health a burden, it retreats into feverish dreams. *M-8.2.7*

HOLY SPIRIT;   *natural state, united **purpose**, **witness** unto health.*

~ once your **mind** is healed, it radiates health and thereby teaches **healing**. *T-6.V.94.7*

~ health is therefore **nothing** more than united **purpose**. *T-8.VII.65.4*

~ the **body**, then, is not the **source** of its own health. The body's **condition** lies solely in your **interpretation** of its **function**. *T-8.VIII.69.7:8*

~ health is the natural state of anything whose **interpretation** is left to the **Holy Spirit**, Who perceives no **attack** on anything. Health is the result of relinquishing all attempts to use the **body** lovelessly. Health is the beginning of the proper perspective on **life** under the **guidance** of the one **Teacher** Who knows what **life** is. *T-8.VIII.79.8:10*

~ health in this **world** is the counterpart of **value** in **Heaven**. *T-9.IX.79.3*

~ to perceive in **sickness** the appeal for health is to recognize in hatred the **call** for **love**. *T-11.III.16.3*

~ your health is a result of your **desire** to **see** your **brother** with no blood upon his hands nor **guilt** upon his heart made heavy with the proof of **sin**. *T-27.III.19.7*

~ health is the **witness** unto health. *T-27.VI.45.1*

~ only when demonstrated has it been proved and must compel **belief**. *T-27.VI.45.3*

~ health cannot turn to **sickness**. *W-pI.110.3.1*

~ the body's health is fully guaranteed because it is not limited by **time**, by weather or fatigue, by food and drink, or any **laws you** made it serve before. *W-pI.136.20.3*

HEAVEN

DICTIONARY: *a place regarded in various religions as the abode of **God** (or the Gods) and the angels, and of the **good** after **death**, often traditionally depicted as **being** above the sky.*

EGO; *hell, oblivion, greatest **threat.***

~ for your definition of Heaven is **hell** and oblivion, and the real Heaven is the greatest **threat you** think **you** could **experience.** *T-12.IV.24.2*

~ the **ego** teaches that Heaven is **here** and **now** because the **future** is **hell.** *T-15.II.6.1*

~ resolve the perceived **conflict** of Heaven and **hell** in him by casting Heaven out and giving it the attributes of **hell** without experiencing himself as incomplete and lonely? *T-15.XI.104.8*

~ does Heaven seem to be a burden to you? In **madness,** yes. *T-21.VII.66.2:3*

~ nor is there one **illusion you** can enter Heaven with. *T-22.III.23.2*

~ since **you** believe that **you** are separate, Heaven presents itself to **you** as separate too. *T-25.II.8.1*

~ ego's arguments which **seek** to prove all this is really Heaven. *W-pI.73.6.5*

~ heaven more frail than **hell.** *W-pI.136.10.2*

~ in this **world,** Heaven is a **choice** because **here we** believe there are alternatives to choose between. *W-pI.138.1.1*

~ in this insanely complicated **world,** Heaven appears to take the **form** of **choice** rather than merely **being** what it is. *W-pI.138.6.1*

HOLY SPIRIT; *home of perfect purity, paradise, lamps of Heaven, **awareness** of perfect **Oneness,** dwelling-place, **kingdom, you,** your **home, completion,** gifts, **here, now.***

~ heaven is **within.** *T-4.IV.41.1*

~ in Heaven there is no **guilt.** *T-5.VII.59.6*

~ heaven waits for his return, for it was created as the dwelling place of God's Son. *T-9.XI.103.3*

~ heaven is your **home,** and **being** in **God,** it must also be in **you.** *T-11.VII.60.7*

~ there **will** be great **joy** in Heaven on your homecoming, and the **joy will** be yours. *T-12.II.9.6*

~ heaven is perfectly unambiguous. Everything is clear and bright and calls forth one response. There is no **darkness,** and there is no **contrast.** There is no variation. There is no interruption. There is a **sense** of **peace** so deep that no **dream** in this **world** has ever brought even a dim imagining of what it is. *T-13.V.37.8:13*

~ **you will** not **remember change** and **shift** in Heaven. *T-13.V.40.1*

~ there is no chance that Heaven **will** not be yours. *T-13.V.43.3*

~ **you** do not **have** to know that Heaven is yours to **make** it so. *T-13.V.44.5*

~ heaven itself is **union** with all of **creation** and with its One **Creator.** And Heaven remains the **Will** of **God** for **you.** *T-14.IV.37.2:3*

~ **you** can reflect Heaven **here.** *T-14.V.42.2*

~ there, **holiness** is not a **reflection** but rather the actual **condition** of what was but reflected to them **here.** *T-14.V.45.5*

~ heaven **will** not **change,** for the **birth** into the holy **present** is **salvation** from change. *T-15.III.11.4*

~ heaven waits silently. *T-16.V.37.1*

182

~ in Heaven, where the **meaning** of **love** is known, **love** is the same as **union**. *T-16.VI.45.3*

~ as **you** cross to **join** it, it **will join** with **you** and become one with **you**. *T-16.VII.68.3*

~ the **joy** of Heaven, which has no **limit**, is increased with each **light** that returns to take its rightful place **within** it. *T-16.VII.68.5*

~ no **substitute you** made for Heaven can keep **you** from it. *T-18.II.9.9* ~ heaven is restored to all the **Sonship** through your **relationship**, for in it lies the **Sonship**, whole and beautiful, safe in your **love**. Heaven has entered quietly, for all illusions **have** been gently brought unto the **truth** in **you** and **love** has shined upon **you**, **blessing** your **relationship** with **truth**. **God** and His whole **creation have** entered it together. How lovely and how holy is your **relationship**, with the **truth** shining upon it! Heaven beholds it and rejoices that **you have** let it come to **you**. [And **God** Himself is glad that your **relationship** is as it was created.] The **universe within you** stands with **you**, together. And Heaven looks with **love** on what is joined in it, along with its **Creator**. *T-18.II.11.1:8*

~ heaven is joined with **you** in your **advance** to Heaven. *T-18.IV.31.3*

~ the **Kingdom** of Heaven is the dwelling-place of the **Son of God**, who left not his **Father** and dwells not apart from Him. Heaven is not a place nor a **condition**. It is merely an **awareness** of perfect **Oneness** and the **knowledge** that there is **nothing** else; **nothing outside** this **Oneness** and **nothing** else **within**. *T-18.VII.49.4:6*

~ heaven is the **gift you** owe each other, the debt of **gratitude you** offer to the **Son of God** in thanks for what **he** is and what his **Father** created him to be. *T-19.V.108.6*

~ heaven knows **you** well, as **you** know Heaven. *T-19.V.45.2*

~ **here** there is only **holiness** and joining without **limit**. *T-20.IV.26.2*

~ what is Heaven but **union**, direct and perfect, and without the **veil** of **fear** upon it? **Here** are **we** one, looking with perfect **gentleness** upon each other and on ourselves. **Here** all thoughts of any **separation** between us become **impossible**. *T-20.IV.26.3:5*

~ **sin** has no place in Heaven, where its results are alien and can no more enter than can their **source**. *T-20.V.29.1*

~ for **faith** and **vision** and **belief** are meaningful only before the state of **certainty** is reached. In Heaven **they** are unknown. Yet Heaven is reached through them. *T-21.IV.32.7:9*

~ heaven has come because it found a **home** in your **relationship** on earth. *T-21.V.47.6*

~ there is no **part** of Heaven **you** can take and weave into illusions. Nor is there one **illusion you** can enter Heaven with. *T-22.III.23.1:2*

~ heaven is the **home** of perfect purity, and **God** created it for **you**. Look on your holy **brother, sinless** as yourself, and let him lead **you** there. *T-22.III.28.6:7*

~ heaven is wholly true. No **difference** enters, and what is all the same cannot **conflict**. *T-23.V.47.4:5*

~ **here** in this holy place does **truth** stand waiting to **receive you** both in silent **blessing** and in **peace** so real and so encompassing that **nothing** stands **outside**. *T-24.III.20.5*

~ in Heaven, **means** and end are one, and one with Him. This is the state of true **creation**, found not **within time**, but in **eternity**. To no one **here** is this describable. Nor is there any **way** to learn what this **condition** means. Not till **you** go **past learning** to the Given; not till **you make** again a holy **home** for your **creations** is it understood. *T-24.VIII.67.5:9*

~ heaven, where all of the treasures given to God's Son are kept for him. *T-25.X.79.4*

~ in Heaven God's Son is not imprisoned in a **body** nor is sacrificed in solitude to **sin**. *T-26.II.7.4*

~ heaven was never lost and so cannot be saved. *T-26.IV.22.2*

~ there is no sadness, and there is no parting **here**, for everything is totally forgiven. *T-26.V.26.3*

~ what is Heaven but a **song** of **gratitude** and **love** and **praise** by everything created to the **Source** of its **creation**. *T-26.V.27.5*

~ heaven is shining on the **Son of God**. *T-26.VIII.63.3*

~ more than Heaven can **you** never **have**. *T-29.IX.60.5*

~ heaven itself but represents your **will**, where everything created is for **you**. *T-30.III.33.8*

~ it is **here today**. *W-pI.131.7.2*

~ heaven remains your one alternative. *W-pI.131.8.1*

~ heaven Itself is reached by empty hands and open minds, which come with **nothing** to find everything and claim it as their own. *W-pI.133.14.3*

~ heaven asks **nothing**. *W-pI.135.26.3*

~ heaven is chosen consciously. The **choice** cannot be made until alternatives are accurately seen and understood. *W-pI.138.9.1:2*

~ and Heaven has not bowed to **hell**, nor **life** to **death**. *W-pI.136.12.3*

~ it is yours **today** but for the asking. *W-pI.165.4.2*

~ neither **justice** nor **injustice** exists in Heaven, for **error** is **impossible** and **correction** meaningless. *M-19.1.4*

~ heaven is **here**. There is nowhere else. Heaven is **now**. There is no other **time**. No **teaching** that does not lead to this is of concern to God's teachers. *M-24.6.4:8*

~ heaven is **here** and Heaven is your **home**. *S-3.IV.8.9*

HELL |hel|

DICTIONARY: *a place regarded in various religions as a spiritual realm of **evil** and **suffering**, often traditionally depicted as a place of perpetual fire beneath the earth where the wicked are punished after **death**.*

EGO;   *future, goal, here.*

~ hell and oblivion are ideas which **you** made up, and **you** are bent on demonstrating their **reality** to establish yours. *T-12.IV.24.3*

~ the **belief** in hell is inescapable to those who identify with the **ego**. Their nightmares and their fears are all associated with it. *T-15.II.3.8:9*

~ the **ego** teaches that hell is in the **future**, for this is what all its **teaching** is directed to. Hell is its **goal**, for although the **ego** aims at **death** and dissolution as an end, it does not believe it. *T-15.II.4.1:2*

~ the **belief** in guilt must lead to the **belief** in hell, and always does. *T-15.II.7.5*

~ the appeal of hell lies only in the terrible **attraction** of guilt, which the **ego** holds out to those who place their **faith** in littleness. *T-16.VI.51.1*

~ **you** merely look on **darkness** and perceive the terrified imaginings that come from guilty thoughts and concepts born of **fear**. And what **you** see is hell, for **fear** is hell. *T-31.VII.74.5:6*

~ accept a **little part** of hell as real, and **you have** damned your eyes and cursed your **sight**, and what **you will** behold is hell indeed. *W-pI.130.12.1*

~ it is hell that makes extravagant demands for **sacrifice**. *W-pI.135.26.4*

~ **you** cannot be a **little** bit in hell. *M-13.7.4*

- as long as any **mind** remains possessed of **evil** dreams, the **thought** of hell is real. *M-28.6.2*
- the descent into hell follows **step** by **step** in an inevitable **course**, once the **decision** that **guilt** is real has been made. *P-2.IV.3.1*
- hell cannot be asked for another, and then escaped by him who asks for it. Only those who are in hell can **ask** for hell. *S-1.III.2.5:6*

HOLY SPIRIT

- the **Holy Spirit** teaches thus: There is no hell. Hell is only what the **ego** has made of the **present**. *T-15.II.8.1:2*
- **heaven** still remains **within** your range of **choice** to take the place of everything that hell would show to **you**. *W-pI.130.12.2*
- no one remains in hell, for no one can abandon his **Creator** nor affect His perfect, timeless, and unchanging **Love**. *W-pI.131.6.1*

HELP

|h e l p|

DICTIONARY: *make it easier for (someone) to do something by **offering** one's services or resources.*

EGO

- if **you will** not accept the help **you call** for, **you will** not believe that it is yours to **give**. And so **you will** not **give** it, thus maintaining the **belief**. *T-21.VII.59.4:5*

HOLY SPIRIT;   *Heaven's Help*

- **everyone** has called upon Him for help at one **time** or another and in one **way** or another and has been answered. *T-6.V.47.5*
- the removal of blocks, then, is the only **way** to guarantee help and **healing**. *T-8.VII.63.1*
- he **will** tell **you** exactly what to do to help anyone He sends to **you** for help and **will** speak to him through **you** if **you** do not **interfere**. *T-9.IV.28.8*
- **trust** Him, for help is His **function**. *T-9.IV.28.11*
- the **Holy Spirit** is there, although He cannot help **you** without your invitation. *T-10.III.22.5*
- the Help of **God** goes with **you** everywhere. As **you** become willing to accept this Help by asking for it, **you will give** it because **you want** it. *T-10.VIII.85.2:3*
- **you** are not bereft of help, and Help that knows the **answer**. *T-13.VIII.75.2*
- all the help **you** can accept **will** be provided. *M-26.4.8*
- there is no end to the help that **He** begins and **He** directs. *P-1.1.5.7*
- **nothing** in the **world** is holier than helping one who asks for help. *P-2.V.4.2*

HERE

|hir|

DICTIONARY: *in, at, or to this place or position.*

EGO

- **god** is on the other side and **nothing** at all is here. *T-16.VI.58.4*
- here, then, is everything. *T-20.VI.42.5*

185

~ here are illusions and **reality** kept separated. Here are illusions never brought to **truth** and always hidden from it. *T-20.VIII.63.5:6*

~ here is the **hell you** chose to be your **home. He** chose not this for **you.** *T-24.IV.31.2:3*

~ **god** is here and with **you now.** *T-24.VII.49.4*

Holy Spirit

~ here is the holy place of **resurrection** to which **we** come again; to which **we will** return until **redemption** is accomplished and received. *T-19.V.10.5.1*

~ here **he** makes his **choice** again between idolatry and **love.** *T-20.VII.55.6*

~ here can no **weakness** enter, for here is no **attack** and therefore no illusions. *T-22.VI.4.7.7*

HIDE |hīd|

DICTIONARY: *put or keep out of **sight**; conceal from the view or notice of others.*

Ego

~ for still deeper than the ego's foundation, and much stronger than it **will** ever be, is your intense and burning **love** of God, and His for **you.** This is what **you** really **want** to hide. *T-12.III.12.6:7*

~ **nothing** has hidden **value,** for what is hidden cannot be shared, and so its **value** is unknown. The hidden is kept apart. *T-14.III.16.7:8*

~ what is concealed cannot be loved, and so it must be feared. *T-14.III.16.9*

Holy Spirit

~ there is **nothing you want** to hide, even if **you** could. *T-1.I.24.1*

~ **we** must hide **nothing** from each other. *T-4.IV.53.6*

~ **god** hides **nothing** from His Son, even though His Son would hide himself. *T-10.IV.27.1*

~ but what **you** hide **He** cannot look upon. For **He** sees for **you,** and unless **you** look with Him, **He** cannot **see.** *T-14.IV.30.5:6*

~ what **you** would hide is hidden from **you.** *T-15.V.43.7*

HOLINESS |ˈhōlēnəs|

DICTIONARY: *the state of **being** holy.*

Ego;   *weakness, attack.*

~ **you** still think holiness is **difficult.** *T-16.III.10.1*

~ unholiness seeks to reinforce itself, as holiness does, by gathering to itself what it perceives as like itself. *T-17.IV.16.9*

~ holiness cannot be found where **sin** is cherished. *W-pI.140.5.2*

Holy Spirit;   *actual condition, answer, power, salvation.*

~ the **image** of holiness which shines in your **mind** is not obscure and **will** not **change.** *T-14.V.44.2*

186

~ the response of holiness to any **form** of **error** is always the same. There is no **contradiction** in what holiness calls forth. Its one response is **healing**, without regard for what is brought to it. *T-14.V.45.1:3*

~ holiness does not **change**. *T-15.II.11.1*

~ holiness lies not in **time** but in **eternity**. *T-15.II.15.4*

~ only holiness can content **you** and **give you peace**. *T-15.IV.30.8*

~ all **separation** vanishes as holiness is shared. For holiness is **power**, and by sharing it, it gains in **strength**. *T-15.VII.58.1:2*

~ the Presence of Holiness creates the holiness which surrounds it. Holiness is merely the result of letting the effects of **sin** be lifted so what was always true is recognized. To **see** a **sinless body** is **impossible**, for holiness is positive. *T-15.XI.102.8:10*

~ the holy do not **interfere** with **truth**. **They** are not afraid of it, for it is **within** the **truth they** recognized their holiness and rejoiced at what **they** saw. **They** looked on it directly, without attempting to adjust themselves to it or it to them. And so **they** saw that it was in them, not deciding first where **they** would **have** it be. *T-20.IV.18.1:4*

~ then **will you give** your **faith** to holiness, desiring and believing in it because of your **desire**. *T-21.IV.34.7*

~ holiness would set your **brother** free, removing hatred by removing **fear**, not as a **symptom**, but at its **source**. *T-21.IV.35.5*

~ holiness is quite impartial, with one **judgment** made for all it looks upon. *T-24.VII.53.5*

~ **within** your brother's holiness, the perfect frame for your **salvation** and the world's, is set the shining **memory** of Him in Whom your **brother** lives and **you** along with him. *T-24.VII.54.4*

~ the **veil** is lifted through its **gentleness**, and **nothing** hides the **face of Christ** from its beholders. *T-25.II.7.5*

~ holiness is seen through holy eyes that look upon the **innocence within** and thus expect to **see** it everywhere. And so **they call** it forth in **everyone they** look upon that **he** may be what **they** expect of him. *T-31.VII.78.3:4*

~ your holiness blesses him by asking **nothing** of him. *W-pI.37.2.6*

~ your holiness is the **salvation** of the **world**. It lets **you teach** the **world** that it is one with **you**, not by preaching to it, not by telling it anything, but merely by your **quiet** recognition that in your holiness are all things blessed, along with **you**. *W-pI.37.3.1:2*

~ your holiness reverses all the **laws** of the **world**. It is beyond every restriction of **time**, space, distance, and limits of any kind. Your holiness is totally unlimited in its **power** because it establishes **you** as a **Son of God**, at one with the **Mind** of his **Creator**. Through your holiness, the **power** of **God** is made manifest. Through your holiness the **power** of **God** is made available. *W-pI.38.1.1:5*

~ your holiness, then, can remove all **pain**, can end all sorrow, and can solve all problems. It can do so in connection with yourself and with anyone else. It is equal in its **power** to **help** anyone because it is equal in its **power** to save anyone. If **you** are holy, so is everything **God** created. **You** are holy because all things **He** created are holy. And all things **He** created are holy because **you** are. *W-pI.38.2.1:6*

~ your holiness is the **answer** to every **question** that was ever asked, is **being** asked **now**, or **will** be asked in the **future**. Your holiness **means** the end of **guilt** and therefore the end of **hell**. Your holiness is the **salvation** of the **world** and your own. *W-pI.39.4.1:3*

~ the **perception** of my holiness does not bless me **alone**. **Everyone** and everything **I** see in its **light** shares in the **joy** it brings to me. There is **nothing** that is apart from this **joy** because there is **nothing** that does not **share** my holiness. *W-pI.58.3.1:3*

~ my holiness is unlimited in its **power** to heal because it is unlimited in its **power** to save my holiness saves me from all **guilt**, recognizing my holiness is recognizing my **salvation**. *W-pI.58.4.1*

- there is no place where holiness is not. *W-pI.140.5.7*

- there is a **sense** of holiness in **you** the **thought** of **sin** has never touched. *W-pI.164.4.3*

- my holiness is far beyond my own ability to **understand** or know. Yet **God** my **Father**, Who created it, acknowledges my holiness as His. Our **will** together understands it. And our **will** together knows that it is so. *W-pII.299.1.1:4*

HOLY ENCOUNTER   *A Course in Miracles Term*

EGO

- a holy **encounter** if **you** are merely perceiving it as a meeting with your own **past**? For **you** are meeting no one, and the sharing of **salvation**, which makes the **encounter** holy, is excluded from your **sight**. *T-12.IV.29.1:2*

HOLY SPIRIT

- when **you** meet anyone, **remember** it is a holy **encounter**. As **you see** him, **you will see** yourself. As **you** treat him, **you will** treat yourself. As **you** think of him, **you will** think of yourself. Never forget this, for in him **you will** find yourself or lose **sight** of yourself. Whenever two Sons of **God** meet, **they** are given another chance at **salvation**. *T-8.IV.19.1:6*

- the **Holy Spirit** teaches that **you** always meet yourself and the **encounter** is holy because **you** are. *T-12.IV.29.3*

- for only **now** is **here**, and it presents the opportunities for the holy encounters in which **salvation** can be found. *T-12.IV.30.5*

HOLY INSTANT   *A Course in Miracles Term*

EGO

- it cannot come into a **mind** that has decided to oppose it. *T-15.V.42.5*

- by this lack of thanks and **gratitude**, **you make** yourselves unable to express the holy instant, and thus **you** lose **sight** of it. *T-17.VI.53.10*

- the **experience** of an instant, however compelling it may be, is easily forgotten if **you** allow **time** to close over it. *T-17.VI.54.1*

- to **attack** each other is not to lose the instant but to **make** it powerless in its effects. *T-17.VI.54.6*

- by cutting yourself off from its expression, **you have** denied yourself its benefit. **You** reinforce this every **time you attack** each other, for the **attack** must **blind you** to yourself. *T-17.VI.54.9:10*

- your difficulty with the holy instant arises from your fixed conviction that **you** are not worthy of it. *T-18.V.34.3*

- in that unholy instant, **time** was born and bodies made to house the mad **idea** and **give** it the **illusion** of **reality**. *T-20.VII.52.7*

- this unholy instant seems to be **life**; an instant of **despair**, a tiny island of dry sand, bereft of water and set uncertainly upon oblivion. *T-20.VII.55.3*

- **here he** is more dead than living. *T-20.VII.55.5*

- the unholy instant is the **time** of bodies. *T-20.VIII.62.2*

HOLY SPIRIT; *blessed instant, instant of **peace**, **learning device**, practical device, tool, the **time** of **Christ**, miniature of **Heaven**, miniature of **eternity**, **salvation**, the shining example, **interval**, miracle's abiding-place.*

~ there is but one. The **little** breath of **eternity** that runs through **time** like golden **light** is all the same—**nothing** before it, **nothing** afterwards. *T-9.IX.82.7:8*

~ **nothing** can reach **you here** out of the **past**, and it is **here** that **you** are completely absolved, completely free, and wholly without **condemnation**. From this holy instant wherein **holiness** was born again, **you will** go forth in **time** without **fear** and with no **sense** of **change** with **time**. *T-15.II.10.6:7*

~ in the holy instant in which **you see** yourself as bright with **freedom**, **you will** remember God. *T-15.II.11.7*

~ the instant of **holiness** is shared, and cannot be yours **alone**. *T-15.II.13.2*

~ as long as it takes to reestablish perfect **sanity**, perfect **peace**, and perfect **love** for **everyone**, for **God**, and for yourself. As long as it takes to **remember immortality** and your immortal **creations** who **share** it with **you**. As long as it takes to exchange **hell** for **Heaven**. Long enough to transcend all of the ego's making and ascend unto your **Father**. *T-15.II.14.5:8*

~ caught in the single instant of the eternal sanctity of God's **creation**, it is transformed into forever. *T-15.II.15.9*

~ each instant is a clean, untarnished **birth**, in which the **Son of God** emerges from the **past** into the **present**. And the **present** extends forever. It is so beautiful and so clean and free of **guilt** that **nothing** but happiness is there. No **darkness** is remembered, and **immortality** and **joy** are **now**. *T-15.II.9.4:7*

~ in the blessed instant, **you will** let go all your **past learning**, and the **Holy Spirit will** quickly offer **you** the whole **lesson** of peace. *T-15.III.16.7*

~ the instant of **peace** is eternal because it is wholly without **fear**. It **will** come, **being** the **lesson God** gives **you** through the **Teacher He** has appointed to translate **time** into **eternity**. *T-15.III.17.2:3*

~ in the holy instant, **you will** unchain all your brothers and refuse to support either their **weakness** or your own. *T-15.III.18.6*

~ **you** can **practice** the mechanics of the holy instant and **will** learn much from **doing** so. Yet its shining and glittering brilliance, which **will** literally **blind you** to this **world** by its own **vision**, **you** cannot supply. And **here** it is, all in this instant, complete, accomplished, and given wholly. *T-15.III.20.6:8*

~ to learn to separate out this single second and begin to **experience** it as timeless, is to begin to **experience** yourself as not separate. *T-15.III.21.3*

~ the holy instant is this one and every one. The one **you want** it to be it is. The one **you** would not **have** it be is lost to **you**. *T-15.V.35.3:5*

~ for beyond the **past** and **future**, in which **you will** not find it, it stands in shimmering **readiness** for your **acceptance**. *T-15.V.35.8*

~ it holds the whole **release** from littleness. *T-15.V.35.9*

~ the holy instant in which **you** willingly and gladly **give** over every **plan** but His. For there lies **peace**, perfectly clear because **you have** been willing to meet its conditions. **You** can claim the holy instant any **time** and anywhere **you want** it. *T-15.V.38.2:4*

~ **you** could live forever in the holy instant, beginning **now** and reaching to **eternity**, but for a very simple **reason**. Do not obscure the simplicity of this **reason**, for if **you** do, it **will** be only because **you** prefer not to recognize it and not to let it go. *T-15.V.40.1:2*

~ the holy instant is a **time** in which **you receive** and **give** perfect **communication**. *T-15.V.40.3*

~ it is a **time** in which your **mind** is open, both to **receive** and **give**. It is the recognition that all minds are in **communication**. It therefore seeks to **change nothing**, but merely to accept everything. *T-15.V.40.4:6*

~ the holy instant is given and received with equal willingness, **being** the **acceptance** of the single **will** that governs all **thought**. *T-15.V.42.6*

~ the necessary **condition** for the holy instant does not require that **you have** no thoughts which are not pure. But it does require that **you have** none that **you** would keep. *T-15.V.43.1:2*

~ the holy instant is the Holy Spirit's most useful **learning device** for **teaching you** love's **meaning**. For its **purpose** is to suspend **judgment** entirely. *T-15.VI.45.1:2*

~ in the holy instant no one is **special**, for your personal needs intrude on no one to **make** them different. *T-15.VI.52.2*

~ in the holy instant, **you see** in each **relationship** what it **will** be when **you** perceive only the **present**. *T-15.VI.52.5*

~ the holy instant parallels His knowing by bringing all **perception** out of the **past**, thus removing the frame of reference **you have** built by which to judge your brothers. *T-15.VI.53.3*

~ in the holy instant, free of the **past**, **you see** that **love** is in **you**. *T-15.VI.53.7*

~ all your relationships are blessed in the holy instant because the **blessing** is not limited. In the holy instant, the **Sonship** gains as one. And united in your **blessing**, it becomes one to **you** in the holy instant, **you** unite directly with **God**, and all your brothers **join** in **Christ**. *T-15.VI.54.1:3*

~ in the holy instant, **you will** recognize the only **need** the aspects of the **Son of God share** equally. *T-15.VII.62.10*

~ in the holy instant **God** is remembered, and the **language** of **communication** with all your brothers is remembered with Him. For **communication** is remembered together, as is **truth**. There is no exclusion in the holy instant because the **past** is gone and with it goes the whole basis for exclusion. Without its **source**, exclusion vanishes. *T-15.VII.64.1:4*

~ the holy instant that what seems **impossible** is accomplished, making it evident that it is not **impossible**. In the holy instant, **guilt** holds no **attraction**, since **communication** has been restored. And **guilt**, whose only **purpose** is to disrupt **communication**, has no **function here**. *T-15.VIII.77.4:6*

~ **here** there is no concealment and no private thoughts. *T-15.VIII.78.1*

~ the holy instant does not replace the **need** for **learning**, for the **Holy Spirit** must not leave **you** as your **Teacher** until the holy instant has extended far beyond **time**. *T-15.IX.79.1*

~ the **Holy Spirit release** your **vision** and let **you see the Great Rays** shining from them, so unlimited that **they** reach to **God**. It is this **shift** in **vision** which is accomplished in the holy instant. *T-15.IX.85.1:2*

~ holy instant, where **the Great Rays** replace the **body** in **awareness**, the recognition of relationships without limits is given **you**. *T-15.IX.87.2*

~ in the holy instant there are no bodies, and **you experience** only the **attraction** of **God**. *T-15.IX.91.3*

~ the holy instant is truly the **time** of **Christ**. For in this liberating instant, no **guilt** is laid upon the **Son of God**, and his unlimited **power** is thus restored to him. *T-15.X.93.1:2*

~ in the holy instant, the **condition** of **love** is met, for minds are joined without the body's interference, and where there is **communication**, there is **peace**. *T-15.XI.107.1*

~ the holy instant is His most helpful tool in protecting **you** from the **attraction** of **guilt**, the real lure in the **special relationship**. *T-16.VII.60.7*

~ the holy instant is the **opposite** of the ego's fixed **belief** in **salvation** through **vengeance** for the **past**. In the holy instant, it is accepted that the **past** is gone, and with its passing the drive for **vengeance** has been uprooted and has disappeared. *T-16.VIII.75.3:4*

~ the holy instant is eternal. *T-16.VIII.76.5*

~ he gave the holy instant to be given **you**, and it is **impossible** that **you receive** it not, because **He** gave it. *T-16.VIII.77.5*

~ in the holy instant is His reminder that His Son **will** always be exactly as **he** was created. *T-16.VIII.77.7*

~ holy instant, where all illusions are forgiven. From there the **miracle** extends to bless **everyone** and to resolve all problems, be **they** perceived as great or small, possible or **impossible**. *T-16.VIII.80.1:2*

~ the holy instant is so important in the **defense** of **truth**. *T-17.V.36.1*

~ the holy instant is a miniature of **Heaven**, sent **you** from **Heaven**. It is a **picture**, too, set in a frame. Yet if **you** accept this **gift**, **you will** not **see** the frame at all because the **gift** can only be accepted through your willingness to focus all your attention on the **picture**. The holy instant is a miniature of **eternity**. It is a **picture** of timelessness, set in a frame of **time**. The whole of **Heaven** lies in this instant, borrowed from **eternity** and set in **time** for **you**. *T-17.V.37.1:6*

~ the holy instant shines alike on all relationships, for in it **they** are one. For **here** is only **healing**, already complete and perfect. For **here** is **God**, and where **He** is, only the perfect and complete can be. *T-17.V.42.8:10*

~ like everything about **salvation**, the holy instant is a practical device, witnessed to by its results. The holy instant never fails. The **experience** of it is always felt. Yet without expression, it is not remembered. *T-17.VI.43.2:5*

~ to **give** thanks to each other is to appreciate the holy instant and thus enable its results to be accepted and shared. *T-17.VI.54.5*

~ the holy instant is **nothing** more than a **special** case or an extreme example of what every **situation** is meant to be. The **meaning** which the Holy Spirit's **purpose** has given it is also given to every **situation**. It calls forth just the same suspension of faithlessness, withheld and left unused, that **faith** might **answer** to the **call** of **truth**. The holy instant is the shining example, the clear and unequivocal demonstration of the **meaning** of every **relationship** and every **situation**, seen as a whole. **Faith** has accepted every aspect of the **situation**, and faithlessness has not forced any exclusion on it. It is a **situation** of perfect **peace** simply because **you have** let it be what it is. *T-17.IX.74.1:6*

~ the holy instant is your invitation to **love**, to enter into your bleak and joyless **kingdom**, and to transform it into a garden of **peace** and **welcome**. *T-18.IX.80.5*

~ in the holy instant, **you ask** of **love** only what it offers **everyone**, neither less nor more. *T-18.IX.81.3*

~ the holy instant is the result of your determination to be holy. It is the **answer**. The **desire** and the willingness to let it come precedes its coming. **You** prepare your minds for it only to the extent of recognizing that **you want** it above all else. *T-18.V.32.1:4*

~ come to it not in arrogance, assuming that **you** must achieve the state its coming brings with it. The **miracle** of the holy instant lies in your willingness to let it be what it is. And in your willingness for this lies also your **acceptance** of yourself as **you** were meant to be. *T-18.V.33.7:9*

~ the holy instant does not come from your **little** willingness **alone**. It is always the result of your small willingness combined with the unlimited **power** of **God's Will**. *T-18.V.35.1:2*

~ never approach the holy instant after **you have** tried to remove all **fear** and hatred from your **mind**. That is its **function**. *T-18.VI.42.1:2*

~ the holy instant in which **you** were united is but the **messenger** of **love**, sent from beyond **forgiveness** to remind **you** of all that lies beyond it. Yet it is through **forgiveness** that it **will** be remembered. *T-18.XI.97.3:4*

~ in the holy instant, **you** stand before the **altar God** has raised unto Himself and both of **you**. *T-19.II.14.1*

~ **you** look upon each holy instant as a different point in **time**. It never changes. All that it ever held or **will** ever hold is **here** right **now**. The **past** takes **nothing** from it, and the **future will** add no more. **Here**, then, is everything. **Here** is the loveliness of your **relationship**, with **means** and end in perfect harmony already. **Here** is the perfect **faith** that **you will** one day offer to each other already offered **you**. And **here** the limitless **forgiveness you will give** each other already given; the **face of Christ you** yet **will** look upon already seen. *T-20.VI.42.1:8*

~ the holy instant which offers **you peace** and understanding. *T-20.VII.53.4*

~ in the holy instant is this exchange effected and maintained. **Here** is the **world you** do not **want** brought to the one **you** do. And **here** the one **you** do is given **you** because **you want** it. *T-21.III.18.5:7*

~ what is really there **you** cannot **fail** to **see**. The holy instant is not an instant of **creation** but of recognition. *T-21.III.23.1:2*

~ any instant serves to bring complete **correction** of his errors and **make** him whole. The instant that **you** choose to let yourself be healed, in that same instant is his whole **salvation** seen as complete with yours. *T-21.VII.65.5:6*

~ god's appeal to **you** to recognize what **He** has given **you**. *T-21.IX.90.1*

~ think what that instant brought—the recognition that the "something else" **you thought** was **you** is an **illusion**. *T-22.II.14.4*

~ yet every instant can **you** be reborn and given **life** again. His **holiness** gives **life** to **you**. *T-26.II.71:2*

~ each day and every minute in each day and every instant that each minute holds, **you** but relive the single instant when the **time** of terror was replaced by **love**. *T-26.VI.42.1*

~ each instant is the **Son of God** reborn, until **he** chooses not to die again. *T-26.VIII.63.5*

~ every instant offers **life** to him because his **Father** wills that **he** should live. *T-26.VIII.63.7*

~ attempt to solve no problems but **within** the holy instant's surety. For there the **problem will** be answered and resolved. *T-27.V.38.1:2*

~ the **answer** is provided everywhere. Yet it is only **here** it can be heard. *T-27.V.41.7:8*

~ the holy instant is the **interval** in which the **mind** is still enough to hear an **answer** which is not entailed **within** the **question** asked. It offers something new and different from the **question**. *T-27.V.42.4:5*

~ in the holy instant, **you** can bring the **question** to the **answer** and **receive** the **answer** that was made for **you**. *T-27.V.43.5*

~ the holy instant is the miracle's abiding-place. From there each one is born into this **world** as **witness** to a state of **mind** which has transcended **conflict** and has reached to **peace**. It carries comfort from the place of **peace** into the **battleground** and demonstrates that **war** has no effects. *T-27.VI.46.1:3*

~ the holy instant's radiance **will light** your eyes and **give** them **sight** to **see** beyond all **suffering** and **see** Christ's face instead. *T-27.VI.48.5*

~ the holy instant **will** replace all **sin** if **you** but carry its effects with **you**. *T-27.VII.61.2*

~ the instant's silence that His Son accepts gives **welcome** to **eternity**. *T-28.II.12.5*

~ each instant given unto **God** in passing, with the next one given Him already, is a **time** of your **release** from sadness, **pain** and even **death** itself. *W-pI.194.3.4*

~ then is each instant, which was slave to **time**, transformed into a holy instant when the **light** that was kept hidden in God's Son is freed to bless the **world**. *W-pI.194.5.3*

~ yet in this instant is the **time** as well in which **salvation** comes. *W-pI.196.11.2*

~ there is no **thought** of God that does not go with **you** to **help you** reach that instant and to go beyond it quickly, surely, and forever. *W-pI.196.12.1*

~ merely a tiny instant has elapsed between **eternity** and timelessness. *W-pII.234.1.2*

~ that instant is our **goal**, for it contains the **memory of God**. *W-pII.ST291.5.3*

~ one can as easily **give God** only an instant, and in that instant **join** with Him completely. *M-16.4.6*

HOLY RELATIONSHIP *A Course in Miracles Term*

HOLY SPIRIT; *constant reminder, phenomenal **teaching** accomplishment, **happy song** of **praise**.*

~ it calls to **everyone** to escape from loneliness and **join you** in your **love**. *T-15.IX.81.8*

~ the holy **relationship** shares God's **purpose**, rather than aiming to **make** a **substitute** for it. *T-17.V.28.5*

~ the holy **relationship** is the expression of the **holy instant** in living in this **world**. *T-17.VI.43.1*

~ the holy **relationship** is a constant reminder of the **experience** in which the **relationship** became what it is. And as the unholy **relationship** is a continuing hymn of **hate** in **praise** of its maker, so is the holy **relationship** a **happy song** of **praise** to the Redeemer of relationships. *T-17.VI.43.6:7*

~ the holy **relationship**, a major **step** toward the **perception** of the **real world**, is learned. It is the old unholy **relationship** transformed and seen anew. The holy **relationship** is a phenomenal teaching accomplishment. In all its aspects, as it begins, develops, and becomes accomplished, it represents the reversal of the unholy **relationship**. Be comforted in this—the only **difficult** phase is the beginning. For **here**, the **goal** of the **relationship** is abruptly shifted to the exact **opposite** of what it was. This is the first result of **offering** the **relationship** to the Holy Spirit to use for His purposes. *T-17.VI.44.1:7*

~ the **goal** is set. And your **relationship** has **sanity** as its **purpose**. *T-17.VI.48.7:8*

~ **you** stand together in the holy presence of **truth** itself. **Here** is the **goal**, together with **you**. *T-17.VI.55.1:2*

~ the **goal** itself **will** gladly arrange the **means** for its accomplishment? It is just this same discrepancy between the **purpose** that has been accepted and the **means** as **they** stand **now** which seems to **make you** suffer, but which makes **Heaven** glad. *T-17.VI.55.3:4*

~ **you** are joined in **purpose**, but remain still separate and divided on the **means**. *T-17.VI.55.7*

~ no relationship is holy unless its **holiness** goes with it everywhere. As **holiness** and **faith** go hand in hand, so must its **faith** go everywhere with it. *T-17.VIII.69.4:5*

~ **you** are so firmly joined in **truth** that only **God** is there. And **He** would never accept something else instead of **you**. He loves **you** both, equally and as one. *T-18.II.10.1:3*

~ **you** are not joined together in illusions but in the **Thought** so holy and so perfect that illusions cannot remain to darken the holy place in which **you** stand together. *T-18.II.10.5*

~ the **peace** of God is given **you** with the glowing **purpose** in which **you join**. *T-18.II.13.5*

~ i hold your hand as surely as **you** agreed to take each other's. **You will** not separate, for **I** stand with **you** and walk with **you** in your **advance** to **truth**. And where **we** go, **we** carry **God** with us. *T-18.IV.28.5:7*

~ in your **relationship, you have** joined with me in bringing **Heaven** to the **Son of God**, who hid in **darkness**. **You have** been willing to bring the **darkness** to **light**, and this willingness has given **strength** to **everyone** who would remain in **darkness**. *T-18.IV.29.1:2*

~ for when **you** joined each other, **you** answered me. *T-18.IV.29.7*

~ **you** who are **now** the bringers of **salvation have** the **function** of bringing **light** to **darkness**. The **darkness** in **you** has been brought to **light**. *T-18.IV.30.1:2*

~ **time** has been readjusted to **help** us do together what your separate pasts would hinder. **You have** gone **past fear**, for no two minds can **join** in the **desire** for **love** without love's joining them. *T-18.IV.30.6:7*

~ **you** are coming **home** together after a long and meaningless **journey** which **you** undertook apart and which led nowhere. **You have** found each other and **will light** each other's **way**. And from this **light will the Great Rays** extend back into **darkness** and forward unto **God** to shine away the **past** and so **make** room for His eternal Presence, in which everything is radiant in the **light**. *T-18.IV.31.5:7*

~ through your holy **relationship**, reborn and blessed in every **holy instant** which **you** do not arrange, thousands **will** rise to **Heaven** with **you**. *T-18.VI.43.1*

~ nor is your holy **relationship** a **dream**. All that remains of dreams **within** it is that it is still a **special relationship**. Yet it is very useful to the **Holy Spirit**, who has a **special function here**. It **will** become the **happy dream** through which **He** can spread **joy** to thousands on thousands who believe that **love** is **fear**, not happiness. *T-18.VI.45.2:5*

~ **nothing will** be wanting that would **make** of it what **He** would **have** it be. *T-18.VI.45.6*

~ your **relationship** is one, and so it must be that whatever threatens the **peace** of one is an equal **threat** to the other. The **power** of joining and its **blessing** lie in the **fact** that it is **now impossible** for either of **you** to **experience fear alone** or to attempt to deal with it **alone**. *T-18.VI.46.3:4*

~ yet just as this is **impossible**, so is it equally **impossible** that the **holy instant** come to either of **you** without the other. And it **will** come to both at the **request** of either. *T-18.VI.46.6:7*

~ your **way will** be different, not in **purpose** but in **means**. A holy **relationship** is a **means** of saving **time**. One instant spent together restores the **universe** to both of **you**. *T-18.VIII.67.1:3*

~ your holy **relationship**, with its new **purpose**, offers **you faith** to **give** unto each other. Your faithlessness had driven **you** apart, and so **you** did not recognize **salvation** in each other. Yet faith unites **you** in the **holiness you see**, not through the body's eyes but in the **sight** of Him Who joined **you** and in Whom **you** are united. *T-19.II.13.1:3*

~ his **home** is in your holy **relationship**. *T-19.V.44.9*

~ in your holy **relationship** is your Father's Son. *T-19.V.63.9*

~ there is no **obstacle** which **you** can place before our **union**, for in your holy **relationship**, I am there already. *T-19.V.64.3*

~ from your holy **relationship truth** proclaims the **truth**, and **love** looks on itself. *T-19.V.66.1*

~ how **happy** did it **make** you? Did **you** meet with **joy** to bless the **Son of God** and **give** him thanks for all the happiness which **he** held out to you? Did **you** recognize each other as the eternal **gift** of **God** to you? Did **you see** the **holiness** that shone in both of **you** to bless the other? That is the **purpose** of your holy **relationship**. *T-20.IV.24.5:9*

~ in this **world**, God's Son comes closest to himself in a holy **relationship**. There **he** begins to find the **certainty** his **Father** has in him. And there **he** finds his **function** of restoring his Father's **laws** to what was held **outside** them and finding what was lost. *T-20.VI.37.1:3*

~ **peace** to your holy **relationship**, which has the **power** to hold the **unity** of the **Son of God** together. **You give** to one another for **everyone**, and in your **gift** is **everyone** made glad. *T-20.VI.38.5:6*

~ the holy **relationship** reflects the true **relationship** the **Son of God** has with his **Father** in **reality**. The **Holy Spirit** rests **within** it in the **certainty** it **will** endure forever. Its firm foundation is eternally upheld by **truth**, and **love** shines on it with the gentle smile and tender **blessing** it offers to its own. **Here** the unholy instant is exchanged in gladness for the holy one of safe return. **Here** is the **way** to true relationships held gently open, through which **you** walk together, leaving the **body** thankfully behind and resting in the Everlasting Arms. *T-20.VII.54.1:5*

~ **know** your own **Identity**. *T-20.IX.68.1*

~ exchange your doubts for **certainty**. *T-20.IX.68.2*

~ be free of **misery** and learn again of **joy**. *T-20.IX.68.3*

~ your holy **relationship** offers all this to **you**. As it was given **you**, so **will** be its effects. And as its holy **purpose** was not made by **you**, the **means** by which its **happy** end is yours is also not of **you**. *T-20.IX.68.4:6*

~ a holy **relationship** is one in which **you join** with what is **part of you** in **truth**. *T-21.V.43.5*

~ a holy **relationship** starts from a different premise. Each one has looked **within** and seen no lack. Accepting his **completion**, he would extend it by joining with another, whole as himself. **He** sees no **difference** between these selves, for differences are only of the **body**. Therefore, **he** looks on **nothing he** would take. **He** denies not his own **reality**, because it is the **truth**. Just under **Heaven** does **he** stand, but close enough not to return to earth. For this **relationship** has Heaven's **holiness**. *T-22.I.3.1:8*

~ what is born into a holy **relationship** can never end. *T-22.I.4.10*

~ **here** is **belief** in differences undone. **Here** is the **faith** in differences shifted to **sameness**. [And **here** is **sight** of differences transformed to **vision**.] And **reason now** can lead **you** to the logical conclusion of your **union**. *T-22.I.4.2:5*

~ **you** reached out beyond the **body** to let yourselves be joined. *T-22.I.4.7*

~ in each holy **relationship** is the ability to communicate instead of separate reborn. Yet a holy **relationship**, so recently reborn itself from an unholy **relationship** and yet more ancient than the old **illusion** that it has replaced, is like a baby **now** in its **rebirth**. Yet in this infant is your **vision** returned to **you**, and **he will** speak the **language** both of **you** can **understand**. **He** is not nurtured by the "something else" **you thought** was **you**. **He** was not given there, nor was received by anything except yourself. For no two people can unite except through **Christ**, Whose **vision** sees them one. *T-22.II.11.1:6*

~ in each the other saw a perfect shelter where his **Self** could be reborn in safety and in **peace**. *T-22.II.13.8*

~ bright endless circle that extends forever is your holy **relationship**, beloved of **God** Himself. How still it rests, in **time** and yet beyond, immortal yet on earth. How great the **power** that lies in it. **Time** waits upon its **will**, and earth **will** be as it would **have** it be. **Here** is no separate **will** nor the **desire** that anything be separate. Its **will** has no exceptions, and what it wills is true. *T-22.III.27.1:6*

~ no **misery** is **here**, but only **joy**. *T-22.III.27.10*

~ at its center **Christ** has been reborn to **light** His **home** with **vision** that overlooks the **world**. *T-22.III.27.8*

~ a holy **relationship**, however newly born, must **value holiness** above all else. *T-22.IV.37.1*

~ a common state of **mind**, where both **give** errors gladly to **correction** that both may happily be healed as one. *T-22.IV.37.7*

~ such is the **function** of a holy **relationship**—to **receive** together and **give** as **you** received. *T-22.V.44.4*

~ this holy **relationship**, lovely in its **innocence**, mighty in **strength**, and blazing with a **light** far brighter than the sun which lights the sky **you see**, is chosen of your **Father** as a **means** for His own **plan**. *T-22.VII.54.1*

~ **nothing** entrusted to it can be misused, and **nothing** given it but **will** be used. This holy **relationship** has the **power** to heal all **pain**, regardless of its **form**. Neither of **you alone** can serve at all. Only in your joint **will** does **healing** lie. For **here** your **healing** is and **here will you** accept **Atonement**. And in your **healing** is the **Sonship** healed because your wills are joined. *T-22.VII.54.3:8*

~ before a holy **relationship** there is no **sin**. The **form** of **error** is no longer seen, and **reason**, joined with **love**, looks quietly on all **confusion**, observing merely, "This was a **mistake**." And then the same **Atonement you** accepted in your **relationship** corrects the **error** and lays a **part** of Heaven in its place. *T-22.VII.55.1:3*

~ no **illusion** can disturb the **peace** of a **relationship** which has become the **means** of peace. *T-22.VII.56.9*

~ this is the **function** of your holy **relationship**. For what one thinks the other **will experience** with him. *T-22.VII.64.1:2*

~ **god** has promised to send His **Spirit** into any holy **relationship**. *M-2.5.4*

195

~ if their **relationship** is to be holy, whatever one needs is given by the other; whatever one lacks the other supplies. *P-3.III.4.4*

HOLY SPIRIT

|ˈˌhōlē ˈspirit|

DICTIONARY: *(in Christianity) the third person of the Trinity;* **God** *as spiritually active in the* **world.**

EGO

~ the **ego** cannot hear the Holy **Spirit**, but it does believe that **part** of the same **mind** that made it is against it. *T-6.V.48.1*

~ the **ego** cannot **ask** the Holy **Spirit** for anything because there is complete **communication** failure between them. *T-8.X.100.5*

~ the Holy **Spirit**, then, seems to be attacking your fortress, for **you** would shut out **God**, and **He** does not **will** to be excluded. *T-12.III.13.4*

~ it is only because **you** think that **you** can run some **little part** or deal with certain aspects of your lives **alone** that the **guidance** of the Holy **Spirit** is limited. Thus would **you make** Him undependable and use this fancied undependability as an excuse for keeping certain dark lessons from Him. And by so limiting the **guidance** that **you** would accept, **you** are unable to depend on miracles to **answer** all your problems for **you.** *T-14.VII.68.4:6*

~ it is not His **purpose** to frighten **you,** but only yours. **You** are severely tempted to abandon Him at the **outside** ring of **fear.** *T-18.X.87.5:6*

~ those who believe in **sin** must think the Holy **Spirit** asks for **sacrifice,** for this is how **they** think their **purpose** is accomplished. *T-21.IV.37.1*

~ if **you seek** to **limit** Him, **you will** hate Him because **you** are afraid. *T-21.IV.37.4*

~ **you** allow Him only half your **mind.** And thus **He** represents the other half and seems to **have** a different **purpose** from the one **you** cherish and **you** think is yours. Thus does your **function** seem divided, with a half in opposition to a half. And these two halves appear to represent a split **within** a **self** perceived as two. *T-27.III.24.4:8*

~ to oppose the Holy **Spirit** is to fight yourself. *T-30.III.33.1*

~ the **ego** does constant **battle** with the Holy **Spirit** on the fundamental **question** of what your **function** is. So does it do constant **battle** with the Holy **Spirit** about what your happiness is. It is not a two-**way battle.** The **ego** attacks and the Holy **Spirit** does not respond. *W-pI.66.2.1:4*

HOLY SPIRIT; *Voice for God,* **Thought of God,** *Lord of Hosts,* **God's Answer, Answer,** *One, expression of the* **Holy Instant,** *universal* **inspiration,** *Guide, Mediator,* **Healer,** *Comforter,* **Voice** *for* **Life** *Itself, your* **Holy Relationship,** *shared* **Inspiration** *of all the* **Sonship, Mind** *of* **Atonement, call** *to* **Atonement, call** *to awake,* **decision** *for guiltlessness, bringer of revelations, highest* **communication** *medium,* **communication link, Christ Mind, spirit** *of joy, radiance,* **bridge, thought-transfer, idea of healing, symbol** *of* **peace,** *perfect* **teacher,** *translator,* **lesson** *in remembering, the only* **therapist,** *your reality,* **part** *of your* **mind, strength, light,** *your only friend, sender & receiver,* **gift, call** *to return, right* **mind,** *reinterpreter, The Holy One, the Holy Guide to* **Heaven,** *The Giver of the* **happy** *dreams of* **life, Translator** *of perception into* **truth,** *God's comforter, One Who speaks for* **God,** *God's* **teacher, teacher** *of* **peace,** *The Great Transformer of* **perception,** *your advisor, redeemer of relationships, interpreter.*

~ the Holy **Spirit** mediates higher to lower **communication.** *T-1.I.81.4*

~ **healer,** the Comforter, and the Guide. *T-5.II.10.2*

~ the Holy **Spirit** is a **difficult concept** to grasp precisely because it is symbolic. *T-5.II.10.5*

- the Holy **Spirit** is **nothing** more than your own right **mind**. *T-5.II.9.3*

- the Holy **Spirit** is the **Mind** of the **Atonement**. It represents a state of **mind** that comes close enough to One-Mindedness that transfer to it is at last possible. *T-5.III.12.2:3*

- the Holy **Spirit**, the shared **Inspiration** of all the **Sonship**, induces a kind of **perception** in which many elements are like those in the **Kingdom** of Heaven itself. *T-5.III.13.1*

- the Holy **Spirit** is the **spirit** of **joy**. *T-5.III.18.4*

- **he** is the **Call** to return with which **God** blessed the minds of His separated Sons. *T-5.III.18.5*

- the Holy **Spirit** was God's **Answer** to the **separation**, the **means** by which the **Atonement** could repair until the whole **mind** returned to creating. *T-5.III.18.8*

- his is the **Voice** that calls **you** back to where **you** were before and **will** be again. *T-5.III.19.8*

- the Holy **Spirit** is the radiance that **you** must let banish the **idea** of **darkness**. *T-5.IV.21.2*

- **he** is the **part** of your **mind** which always speaks for the right **choice** because **He** speaks for God. **He** is your remaining **communication** with God, which **you** can interrupt but cannot destroy. *T-5.IV.25.6:7*

- the Holy **Spirit** is the **way** in which **God's Will** can be done on earth as it is in **Heaven**. *T-5.IV.26.1*

- the Holy **Spirit** is the **call** to awake and be glad. *T-5.IV.28.5*

- **he** teaches **you** how to keep me as the model for your **thought** and to behave like me as a result. *T-5.IV.30.6*

- holy **Spirit** is the **bridge** or **thought**-transfer of **perception** to **knowledge**. *T-5.V.32.2*

- **part** of the **Holy Trinity** because His **Mind** is partly yours and also partly God's. *T-5.V.32.4*

- the Holy **Spirit** is the **idea** of **healing**. **Being thought**, the idea gains as it is shared. **Being** the **Call** for God, it is also the **idea** of **God**. *T-5.V.33.1:3*

- it is also the **idea** of yourself as well as of all the parts of **God**. *T-5.V.33.4*

- the Holy **Spirit** is the Mediator between the interpretations of the **ego** and the **knowledge** of the **Soul**. His ability to deal with symbols enables Him to work against the ego's beliefs in its own **language**. His equal ability to look beyond symbols into **eternity** also enables Him to **understand** the **laws of God**, for which **He** speaks. **He** can thus perform the **function** of reinterpreting what the **ego** makes, not by **destruction** but by understanding. *T-5.V.38.1:4*

- the Holy **Spirit** is in **light** because **He** is in **you** who are **light**, but **you** yourselves do not know this. It is therefore the task of the Holy **Spirit** to reinterpret **you** on behalf of **God**. *T-5.V.38.6:7*

- the Holy **Spirit** is the **symbol** of peace. *T-5.V.41.1*

- the Holy **Spirit** is the perfect **teacher**. **He** uses only what your minds already **understand** to **teach you** that **you** do not **understand** it. *T-5.V.41.4:5*

- the Holy **Spirit** must work through opposites, because **He** must work with and for a **mind** that is in opposition. *T-5.V.43.1*

- **he** is in Holy **Communion** always, and **He** is **part** of **you**. *T-5.V.43.6*

- the Holy **Spirit**, like the **ego**, is a **decision**. *T-5.VII.67.1*

- the Holy **Spirit**, Who speaks for **God** in **time**, also knows that **time** is meaningless. *T-5.VIII.82.3*

- the Holy **Spirit** never changes His **Mind**. *T-5.IX.85.4*

- the Holy **Spirit** begins by perceiving **you** as perfect. Knowing this **perfection** is shared, **He** recognizes it in others, thus strengthening it in both. Instead of **anger**, this arouses **love** for both because it establishes inclusion. Perceiving equality, the Holy **Spirit** perceives equal needs. *T-6.III.29.1:4*

197

~ the Holy **Spirit** remains the **bridge** between **perception** and **knowledge**. *T-6.III.31.2*

~ the Holy **Spirit** uses **time** but does not believe in it. Coming from **God**, **He** uses everything for **good**, but **He** does not believe in what is not true. *T-6.III.34.1:2*

~ only the Holy **Spirit** can resolve **conflict**, because only the Holy **Spirit** is **conflict**-free. **He** perceives only what is true in your **mind** and extends outward only to what is true in other minds. *T-6.III.36.4:5*

~ the Holy **Spirit** still holds **knowledge** safe through His impartial **perception**. By attacking **nothing**, **He** presents no barrier at all to the **communication** of **God**. *T-6.IV.40.1:2*

~ the Holy **Spirit** does not speak first, but **He** always answers. *T-6.V.47.4*

~ the Holy **Spirit** never commands. To command is to assume inequality, which the Holy **Spirit** demonstrates does not **exist**. *T-6.V.55.1:2*

~ the Holy **Spirit** does know more than **you** do **now**, but **He** teaches only to **make you** equal with Him. *T-6.V.57.1*

~ the Holy **Spirit** never itemizes errors because **He** does not frighten children. *T-6.V.60.1*

~ **he** re-interprets what the **ego** uses as an argument for **separation** into a demonstration against it. *T-6.V.62.5*

~ the Holy **Spirit** is the motivation for miracles. *T-6.V.63.1*

~ the Holy **Spirit**, who leads to **God**, translates **communication** into **being**, just as **He** ultimately translates **perception** into **knowledge**. *T-6.V.65.1*

~ the Holy **Spirit** communicates only what each one can **give** to all. **He** never takes anything back, because **He** wants **you** to keep it. *T-6.V.66.2:3*

~ **he** sorts out the true from the false and teaches **you** to judge every **thought** that **you** allow to enter your **mind** in the **light** of what **God** put there. Whatever is in accord with this **light**, **He** retains to strengthen the **Kingdom** in you. What is partly in accord with **truth**, **He** accepts and purifies. But what is out of accord entirely, **He** rejects by judging against. This is how **He** keeps the **Kingdom** perfectly consistent and perfectly unified. *T-6.V.82.4:8*

~ holy **Spirit** never varies on this point, and so the one mood **He** engenders is **joy**. **He** protects it by rejecting everything that does not foster **joy**, and so **He alone** can keep **you** wholly joyous. *T-6.V.83.4:5*

~ **he** is judgmental, but only in **order** to unify the **mind** so it can perceive without **judgment**. *T-6.V.84.3*

~ the Holy **Spirit** has the task of translating the useless into the useful, the meaningless into the meaningful, and the temporary into the timeless. *T-7.II.6.5*

~ the Holy **Spirit** is a **lesson** in remembering. *T-7.III.17.3*

~ **he** teaches remembering and forgetting, but the forgetting aspect is only to **make** the remembering consistent. *T-7.III.17.4*

~ the Holy **Spirit** teaches one **lesson** and applies it to all individuals in all situations. **Being conflict**-free, **He** maximizes all efforts and all results. *T-7.IV.24.3:4*

~ the Holy **Spirit** does not work by chance, and **healing** that is of Him always works. *T-7.VI.44.1*

~ the Holy **Spirit** undoes illusions without attacking them merely because **He** cannot perceive them at all. *T-7.VII.60.1*

~ the Holy **Spirit will teach you** to perceive beyond **belief**, because **truth** is beyond **belief**, and His **perception** is true. *T-7.IX.89.1*

~ the Holy **Spirit** is the **part** of the **mind** that lies between the **ego** and the **Soul**, mediating between them always in favor of the **Soul**. *T-7.X.91.5*

~ the Holy **Spirit** always sides with **you** and with your **strength**. *T-7.XI.103.1*

- the Holy **Spirit** is perfectly trustworthy. *T-7.XI.104.8*

- the Holy **Spirit will** always guide **you** truly, because your **joy** is His. *T-7.XII.107.1*

- **he** speaks for the **Kingdom** of **God** which is **joy**. *T-7.XII.107.2*

- the Holy **Spirit** leads **you** steadily along the path of **freedom**, **teaching you** how to disregard or look beyond everything that would hold **you** back. *T-8.III.11.4*

- the Holy **Spirit** teaches **you** the **difference** between **pain** and **joy**. *T-8.III.12.1*

- **he** teaches **you** the **difference** between imprisonment and **freedom**. *T-8.III.12.2*

- the Holy Spirit's **teaching** takes only one direction and has only one **goal**. His direction is **freedom**, and His **goal** is **God**. *T-8.III.13.1:2*

- the Holy **Spirit** teaches **you** that if **you** look only at yourself, **you** cannot find yourself because that is not what **you** are. *T-8.IV.20.7*

- **being** the **communication link** between **God** and His separated Sons, the Holy **Spirit** interprets everything **you have** made in the **light** of what **He** is. *T-8.VII.54.2*

- the **purpose** of this Guide is merely to remind **you** of what **you want**. *T-8.X.92.5*

- **he** is merely making every possible **effort, within** the limits **you** impose on Him, to re-establish your own **will** in your **consciousness**. *T-8.X.92.7*

- **he** is your **reality**. *T-8.X.93.3*

- the Holy **Spirit** is totally incapable of giving **you** anything that does not come from **God**. His task is not to **make** anything for **you**. He cannot **make you want** something **you** do not **want**. *T-8.X.98.7:9*

- **he will** deny **you nothing** because **you have** denied Him **nothing**, and so **you** can **share** everything. *T-8.XI.118.3*

- the Holy **Spirit** in **you** forgives all things in **you** and in your **brother**. *T-9.II.7.4*

- the Holy **Spirit** merely reminds **you** of what is your natural ability. By reinterpreting the ability to **attack**, which **you** did **make**, into the ability to **share**. *T-9.III.11.2:3*

- **he will** tell **you** exactly what to do to **help** anyone He sends to **you** for **help** and **will** speak to him through **you** if **you** do not **interfere**. *T-9.IV.28.8*

- the Holy **Spirit** looks with **love** on all He perceives, He looks with **love** on **you**. His evaluation of **you** is based on His **knowledge** of what **you** are, and so He evaluates **you** truly. *T-9.VI.40.1:2*

- **he** is not deceived by anything **you** do, because **He** never forgets what **you** are. *T-9.VI.41.3*

- if no **good** can come of it, the Holy **Spirit** cannot use it. *T-9.VII.56.4*

- **he** retains the **knowledge** of **God** and of yourself for **you**, waiting for your **acceptance**. *T-9.IX.69.3*

- **he** speaks for **you**. *T-10.II.15.1*

- only God's Comforter can comfort **you**. *T-10.IV.29.1*

- the Holy **Spirit** accepts. *T-10.VI.53.1*

- surely **He will** not **fail** to **help you**, since **help** is His only **purpose**. *T-11.III.23.6*

- **he will** not **fail**. Where **He** can enter, there **He** is already. *T-11.III.23.6:7*

- **he will** never deceive God's Son, whom **He** loves with the **love** of the **Father**. *T-11.V.39.7*

~ the Holy **Spirit** is your **strength** because **He** perceives **nothing** but your **Soul** as **you. He** is perfectly aware that **you** do not know yourselves and perfectly aware of how to **teach you** what **you** are. Because **He** loves **you, He will** gladly **teach you** what **He** loves, for **He** wills to **share** it. Remembering **you** always, **He** cannot let **you** forget your **worth.** For the **Father** never ceases to remind Him of His Son, and **He** never ceases to remind His Son of the **Father. God** is in your **memory** because of Him. *T-11.VII.54.1:6*

~ the Holy **Spirit** keeps the **vision** of **Christ** for every **Son of God** who sleeps. In His **sight** the **Son of God** is perfect, and **He** longs to **share** His **vision** with **you. He will** show **you** the **real world** because **God** gave **you** Heaven. Through Him your **Father** calls His Son to **remember.** *T-11.VII.57.1:4*

~ the Holy **Spirit** is invisible, but **you** can **see** the results of His Presence, and through them **you will** learn that **He** is there. What **He** enables **you** to do is clearly not of this **world.** *T-11.VIII.63.1:2*

~ he has remembered **you** because **He** forgot not the **Father.** *T-11.IX.82.12*

~ the Holy **Spirit** stands at the end of **time,** where **you** must be because **He** is with **you. He** has always un-done everything unworthy of the **Son of God,** for such was His **mission,** given Him by **God.** And what **God** gives has always been. *T-11.X.92.4:6*

~ the Holy **Spirit** is the **light** in which **Christ** stands revealed. *T-12.V.44.1*

~ as Mediator between the two worlds, **He** knows what **you have need** of and what **will** not **hurt you.** *T-12.VII.68.7*

~ he teaches that the **past** does not **exist,** a **fact** which belongs to the sphere of **knowledge** and which there-fore no one in the **world** knows. It would indeed be **impossible** to be in the **world** with this **knowledge.** *T-13.I.1.3:4*

~ apart from the **Father** and the Son, the Holy **Spirit** has no **function. He** is not separate from either, **being** in the **mind** of both and knowing that **mind** is one. **He** is a **Thought** of **God,** and **God** has given Him to **you** because **He** has no **Thoughts He** does not **share.** His **message** speaks of timelessness in **time,** and that is why **Christ's vision** looks on everything with **love.** Yet even **Christ's vision** is not His **reality.** The golden aspects of **reality** which spring to **light** under His loving gaze are partial glimpses of the **Heaven** that lies beyond them. *T-13.II.4.1:6*

~ the Holy **Spirit** does what **God** would **have** Him do and has always done so. **He** has seen **separation,** but knows of **union. He** teaches **healing,** but **He** also knows of **creation. He** would **have you see** and **teach** as **He** does, and through Him. Yet what **He** knows, **you** do not know, though it is yours. *T-13.IV.26.4:8*

~ he would remove only illusions. All else **He** would **have you see.** And in **Christ's vision, He** would show **you** the perfect purity that is forever **within** God's Son. *T-13.IV.29.9:11*

~ the Holy **Spirit** has a very different kind of reconciliation in His **Mind** for **you,** and one which **He will** effect as surely as the **ego will** not effect what it attempts. *T-13.V.45.3*

~ god placed the Holy **Spirit** in **you,** where **you** placed the **dream.** *T-13.VI.50.5*

~ the Holy **Spirit** the **decision** for guiltlessness. *T-13.VIII.68.2*

~ the Holy **Spirit** is your only friend. **He** is the strong protector of your **innocence,** which sets **you** free. And it is His **decision** to **undo** everything that would obscure your **innocence** from your unclouded **mind.** *T-13.VIII.77.5:7*

~ the Holy **Spirit,** who remembers this for **you,** merely teaches **you** how to remove the blocks that stand between **you** and what **you** know. His **memory** is yours. *T-14.I.3.5:6*

~ he speaks of **you** to **you.** *T-14.II.5.11*

~ he would **teach you nothing** except how to be **happy.** *T-14.II.6.8*

~ he will not attempt to communicate the meaningless. But **He will** separate out all that has **meaning,** drop-ping off the **rest** and **offering** your true **communication** to those who would communicate as truly with **you.** *T-14.III.22.3:4*

~ he has made **you** free of what **you** made. **You** can deny Him, but **you** cannot **call** on Him in vain. **He** always gives what **He** has made in place of **you**. *T-14.VII.70.4:6*

~ all His works are yours. *T-14.VII.70.9*

~ the Holy **Spirit will**, of Himself, fill every **mind** that so makes room for Him. *T-14.VII.73.7*

~ the **Teacher** of **peace will** never abandon **you**. **You** can desert Him, but **He will** never reciprocate, for His **faith** in **you** is His understanding. It is as firm as is His **faith** in His **Creator**, and **He** knows that **faith** in His **Creator** must encompass **faith** in His **creation**. *T-14.VII.74.2:4*

~ with your **perfection** ever in His **sight**, **He** gives the **gift** of **peace** to **everyone** who perceives the **need** for **peace** and who would **have** it. *T-14.VII.74.6*

~ blessed is God's **Teacher**, Whose **joy** it is to **teach** God's holy Son his **holiness**. His **joy** is not contained in **time**. His **teaching** is for **you** because His **joy** is yours. Through Him **you** stand before God's **altar**, where **He** gently translates **hell** into **Heaven**. *T-15.III.17.4:7*

~ his frame of reference is simply **God**. *T-15.VI.53.5*

~ **he will** not **fail you**, for **He** comes from One Who cannot **fail**. *T-15.IX.81.5*

~ the Holy **Spirit** is God's attempt to free **you** of what **He** does not **understand**. And because of the **Source** of the attempt, it **will** succeed. *T-15.IX.83.1:2*

~ he would **teach you** what **you** do not **understand**. **God** would respond to every **need**, whatever **form** it takes. *T-15.IX.83.3:4*

~ the Holy **Spirit** is **part** of **you**. Created by **God**, **He** left neither **God** nor His **creation**. **He** is both **God** and **you**, as **you** are **God** and Him together. *T-16.IV.25.1:3*

~ his **Messenger** understands how to restore the **Kingdom** to **you** and to place all your investment in **salvation** in your **relationship** with Him. *T-16.VIII.79.4*

~ he was created to **see** this for **you** until **you** learn to **see** it for yourself. And all His **teaching** leads to seeing it and giving thanks with Him. *T-17.III.7.8:9*

~ the Holy **Spirit** is in close **relationship** with **you** because in Him is your **relationship** with **God** restored to **you**. The **relationship** with Him has never been broken because the Holy **Spirit** has not been separate from anyone since the **separation**. *T-17.V.30.3:4*

~ him Who gave **you** your **release**, and Who would extend it through **you**. *T-17.VI.56.4*

~ there are certain very specific guidelines **He** provides for any **situation**. *T-17.VII.57.6*

~ the Holy **Spirit** takes **you** gently by the hand and retraces with **you** your mad **journey outside** yourself, leading **you** gently back to the **truth** and safety **within**. **He** brings all your insane projections and your wild substitutions which **you have** placed **outside you** to the **truth**. *T-18.II.8.3:4*

~ he asks but **little**. It is **He** who adds the greatness and the might. **He** joins with **you** to **make** the **holy instant** far greater than **you** can **understand**. It is your realization that **you need** do so **little** that enables Him to **give** so much. *T-18.V.32.7:10*

~ **he will** remain when **you** forget and the body's activities return to occupy your conscious **mind**. *T-18.VIII.69.9*

~ this One can **teach you** how to look on **time** differently and **see** beyond it. *T-19.IV.30.3*

~ **nothing** undertaken with the Holy **Spirit** remains unfinished. *T-19.IV.38.5*

~ the Holy **Spirit** does not demand **you sacrifice** the hope of the body's **pleasure**; it has no hope of **pleasure**. But neither can it bring **you fear** of **pain**. *T-19.V.62.3:4*

~ the Holy **Spirit**, too, is a **communication** medium, receiving from the **Father** and **offering** His messages unto the Son. Like the **ego**, the Holy **Spirit** is both the sender and the receiver. For what is sent through Him returns to Him, seeking itself along the **way** and finding what it seeks. *T-19.V.76.3:5*

~ **he** sees no strangers, only dearly loved and loving friends. **He** sees no thorns, but only lilies, gleaming in the gentle glow of **peace** that shines on everything **He** looks upon and loves. *T-20.III.9.5:6*

~ **being** without **illusion** of what **you** are, the Holy **Spirit** merely gives everything to **God**, who has already given and received all that is true. The untrue **He** has neither received nor given. *T-20.V.28.8:9*

~ **he** knows the **Son of God** and shares his Father's **certainty** the **universe** rests in his gentle hands in safety and in **peace**. *T-20.VI.44.2*

~ the Holy **Spirit** can **give you faith** in **holiness** and **vision** to **see** it easily enough. *T-21.III.22.1*

~ his **faith** and His **belief** and **vision** are all for **you**. *T-21.IV.32.5*

~ **he** Who loves the **world** is seeing it for **you** without one spot of **sin** upon it and in the **innocence** which makes the **sight** of it as beautiful as **Heaven**. *T-21.IV.37.9*

~ the Holy **Spirit will** never **teach you** that **you** are **sinful**. *T-21.V.41.1*

~ the Holy **Spirit** links the other **part**, the tiny mad **desire** to be separate, different, and **special**, to the **Christ**, to **make** the **oneness** clear to what is really one. In this **world**, this is not understood but can be taught. *T-25.II.8.5:6*

~ the Holy **Spirit** serves Christ's **purpose** in your **mind**, so that the aim of specialness can be corrected where the **error** lies. *T-25.II.9.1*

~ **he** knows the **Will** of **God** and what **you** really **will**. *T-25.II.9.2*

~ the Holy **Spirit** is the frame **God** set around the **part** of Him that **you** would **see** as separate. *T-25.III.17.1*

~ the Holy **Spirit** has the **power** to **change** the whole foundation of the **world you see** to something else. *T-25.VIII.54.1*

~ one as sane as **He**. *T-25.VIII.57.2*

~ to this One is given the **choice** of **form** most suitable to him; one which **will** not **attack** the **world he** sees, but enter into it in quietness and show him **he** is mad. This One but points to an alternative, another **way** of looking at what **he** has seen before and recognizes as the **world** in which **he** lives and **thought he** understood before. *T-25.VIII.57.3:4*

~ the Holy **Spirit** can use all that **you give** to Him for your **salvation**. But **He** cannot use what **you** withhold, for **He** cannot take it from **you** without your **willingness**. *T-25.IX.63.1:2*

~ what **He** cannot perceive **He** bears no **witness** to. *T-25.X.84.3*

~ a better **Friend** in Whom all **power** in earth and **Heaven** rests. *T-26.VII.45.3*

~ without Him **you** are friendless. *T-26.VII.45.5*

~ there is no other friend. *T-26.VII.45.7*

~ it is **He** who is your only Friend in **truth**. **He** brings **you** gifts that are not of this **world**, and only **He** to whom **they have** been given can **make** sure that **you receive** them. *T-26.VII.46.4:5*

~ his inability to **see** His **goal** divided and distinct for each of **you** preserves your **Self** from **being** made aware of any **function** other than Its own. And thus is **healing** given both of **you**. *T-27.III.27.8:9*

~ the Holy **Spirit** speaks to **you**. **He** does not speak to someone else. *T-27.VI.44.10:11*

~ **he** is a **part** of **you**, and **you** of him because **he** is his Father's Son and not for any **purpose you** may **see** in him. *T-29.VI.32.4*

~ the Holy **Spirit** does not **seek** to throw **you** into panic. *T-31.V.53.5*

~ he will be with **you** as **you** watch and wait. **He will** show **you** what true **vision** sees. *W-pI.75.9.5:6*

~ **give** Him the words, and **He will** do the **rest**. **He will** enable **you** to **understand** your **special function**. **He will** open up the **way** to happiness, and **peace** and **trust will** be His gifts, His **answer** to your words. **He will** respond with all His **faith** and **joy** and **certainty** that what **you** say is true. *W-pI.98.11.1:4*

~ **he** would speak to **you**. **He** comes with miracles a thousand times as **happy** and as wonderful as those **you** ever dreamt or wished for in your dreams. *W-pI.106.4.3:4*

~ the Bringer of all miracles has **need** that **you receive** them first and thus become the joyous giver of what **you** received. *W-pI.106.7.2*

~ your Guide is sure. *W-pI.128.7.6*

~ **he** would never offer **pain** to **you**. *W-pI.135.19.2*

~ his **life** becomes your own as **you** extend the **little help** He asks in freeing **you** from everything that ever caused **you pain** His lessons **will** enable **you** to **bridge** the **gap** between illusions and the **truth**. **He will** remove all **faith** that **you have** placed in **pain, disaster, suffering,** and **loss**. He gives **you vision** which can look beyond these grim appearances and can behold the gentle **face of Christ** in all of them. *W-pI.137.10.1:2*

~ **he will** select the elements in them that represent the **truth** and disregard those aspects which reflect but idle dreams. And **He will** reinterpret all **you see** and all occurrences, each circumstance, and every happening which seems to touch on **you** in any **way** from His one frame of reference, wholly unified and sure. *W-pI.151.11.1:2*

~ the Holy **Spirit** is the **home** of minds that **seek** for **freedom**. *W-pI.199.6.1*

~ **he will** relieve **you** of the agony of all the judgments **you have** made against yourself and re-establish **peace** of **mind** by giving **you** God's **Judgment** of His Son. *W-pII.311.1.6*

~ and if **I need** a **word** to **help** me, **he will give** it to me. If **I need** a **thought**, that **will He** also **give**. And if **I need** but stillness and a tranquil, open **mind**, these are the gifts **I will receive** of Him. **He** is in charge by my **request**. And **He will** hear and **answer** me because **He** speaks for **God**, my **Father**, and His holy Son. *W-pII.361-365.1.1:5*

~ your **Friend** goes with **you**. **You** are not **alone**. No one who calls on Him can **call** in vain. Whatever troubles **you**, be certain that **He** has the **answer** and **will** gladly **give** it to **you** if **you** simply turn to Him and **ask** it of Him. **He will** not withhold all answers that **you need** for anything that seems to trouble **you**. **He** knows the **way** to solve all problems and resolve all doubts. His **certainty** is yours. **You need** but **ask** it of Him, and it **will** be given **you**. *W-pII.E.1.2:9*

~ **he will** direct your efforts, telling **you** exactly what to do, how to direct your **mind**, and when to come to Him in silence, asking for His sure direction and His certain **word**. *W-pII.E.3.3*

~ the Holy **Spirit** reaches from the **Christ** in **you** to all your dreams and bids them come to Him to be translated into **truth**. **He will** exchange them for the final **dream** which **God** appointed as the end of dreams. *W-pII.ST271.4.1:2*

~ the Holy **Spirit** mediates between illusions and the **truth**. As **He** must **bridge** the **gap** between **reality** and dreams, **perception** leads to **knowledge** through the **grace** that **God** has given Him, to be His **gift** to **everyone** who turns to Him for **truth**. *W-pII.ST281.1.1:2*

~ the Holy **Spirit** understands the **means you** made, by which **you** would attain what is forever unattainable. And if **you** offer them to Him, **He will** employ the **means you** made for exile to restore your **mind** to where it truly is at **home**. *W-pII.ST281.3.2:3*

~ from **knowledge**, where **He** has been placed by **God**, the Holy **Spirit** calls to **you** to let **forgiveness rest** upon your dreams and be restored to **sanity** and **peace** of **mind**. *W-pII.ST281.4.1*

~ the Holy **Spirit** has no **need** of **time** when it has served His **purpose**. Now **He** waits but that one instant more for **God** to take His **final step**, and **time** has disappeared, taking **perception** with it as it goes and leaving but the **Truth** to be Itself. *W-pII.ST291.5.1:2*

~ his is the only **way** to find the **peace** that **God** has given us. It is His **way** that **everyone** must travel in the end, because it is this ending **God** Himself appointed. In the **dream** of **time**, it seems to be far off. And yet in **truth**, it is already **here**, already serving us as gracious **guidance** in the **way** to go. *W-pII.ST361.2.1:4*

~ it is His ending to the **dream we seek**, and not our own. *W-pII.ST361.3.4*

~ a **Teacher** Who cannot **make a mistake.** His answers are always right. *M-29.2.13:14*

~ the responsibility is His, and **He alone** is fit to assume it. To do so is His **function.** *M-29.2.9:10*

~ the Holy **Spirit** does not depend on your words. **He** understands the requests of your heart and answers them. *M-29.6.1:2*

~ without this One, both **will** merely stumble blindly on to nowhere. It is, however, **impossible** that this One be wholly absent if the **goal** is **healing.** *P-2.III.1.3:4*

HOLY TRINITY |hōlē'trinədē|

DICTIONARY: *the Christian Godhead as one **God** in three persons: **Father**, Son, and **Holy Spirit**.*

HOLY SPIRIT

~ the **Son of God** is **part** of the Holy Trinity, but the Trinity itself is One. There is no **confusion within** its levels because **they** are of One **Mind** and One **Will.** This single **purpose** creates perfect integration and establishes the **peace** of **God.** Yet this **vision** can be perceived only by the truly **innocent.** *T-3.III.19.4:7*

~ the **Holy Spirit** is the only **part** of the Holy Trinity which is symbolic. *T-5.II.10.1*

~ the Holy Trinity is holy, because it is one. If **you** exclude yourself from this **union, you** are perceiving the Holy Trinity as separated. **You** must be included in It, because It is everything. Unless **you** take your place in It and fulfill your **function** as **part** of It, It is as bereft as **you** are. No **part** of It can be imprisoned if Its **truth** is to be known. *T-8.V.35.1:5*

~ **father** and Son and **Holy Spirit** are as One, as all your brothers **join** as one in **truth.** *T-25.II.8.3*

HOME |hōm|

DICTIONARY: *the place where one lives permanently, especially as a member of a family or household.*

EGO

~ the **ego** has built a shabby and unsheltering home for **you** because it cannot build otherwise. *T-4.II.18.3*

~ **here** is the only home **he** thinks **he** knows. **Here** is the only safety **he** believes that **he** can find. Without the **world** he made is **he** an outcast, homeless and afraid. **He** does not realize that it is **here he** is afraid indeed and homeless too—an outcast wandering so far from home, so long away, **he** does not realize **he** has forgotten where **he** came from, where **he** goes, and even who **he** really is. *W-pI.166.4.1:4*

HOLY SPIRIT

~ only **God** could **make** a home that is worthy of His **creations,** who **have** chosen to leave it empty by their own dispossession. Yet His home **will** stand forever and is ready for **you** when **you** choose to enter it. *T-4.II.18.6:7*

~ your chosen home is on the other side, beyond the **veil.** It has been carefully prepared for **you,** and it is ready to **receive you now. You will** not **see** it with the body's eyes. Yet all **you need you have.** *T-20.III.11.9:12*

~ your home has called to **you** since **time** began, nor **have you** ever failed entirely to hear. *T-20.III.12.1*

- the home **we share** in quietness, and where **we** live in **gentleness** and **peace** as one together. *T-20.III.12.8*
- into the holy home, where **fear** is powerless, **love** enters thankfully, grateful that it is one with **you** who joined to let it enter. *T-22.II.14.7*
- who is drawn to **Christ** is drawn to **God** as surely as both are drawn to every **holy relationship**, the home prepared for them as earth is turned to **Heaven**. *T-22.II.15.9*
- **you** are not strangers in the house of **God**. *T-23.II.16.3*
- those who offer **peace** to **everyone have** found a home in **Heaven** the **world** cannot destroy. For it is large enough to hold the **world within** its **peace**. *T-25.V.35.9:10*
- your home is built upon your brother's **health**, upon his happiness, his sinlessness, and everything his **Father** promised him. No **secret promise you have** made instead has shaken the Foundation of his home. *T-28.VIII.66.1:2*
- this house **will** stand forever, for its **strength** lies not **within** itself **alone**. It is an ark of safety. *T-28.VIII.66.4:5*
- and with this holy **purpose** is it made a home of **holiness** a **little** while because it shares your Father's **Will** with **you**. *T-28.VIII.66.8*
- our home is safe, protection guaranteed in all **we** do, **power** and **strength** available to us in all our undertakings. *W-pI.124.1.2*

HONEST
[ˈänəst]

DICTIONARY: *free of deceit and untruthfulness; sincere.*

EGO
- the **ego** never looks upon what it does with perfect honesty. *T-10.I.2.6*

HOLY SPIRIT
- be speeded on your **way** by honesty. *T-30.VI.65.11*
- the **strength** of pardon is its honesty. *W-pI.134.8.1*
- the **strength** of pardon is its honesty, which is so uncorrupted that it sees illusions as illusions, not as **truth**. It is because of this that it becomes the undeceiver in the face of lies, the great restorer of the simple **truth**. By its ability to overlook what is not there, it opens up the **way** to **truth**, which had been blocked by dreams of **guilt**. *W-pI.134.8.1:3*
- only the trusting can afford honesty, for only **they** can **see** its **value**. Honesty does not apply only to what **you** say. The term actually **means** consistency. There is **nothing you** say that contradicts what **you** think or do; no **thought** opposes any other **thought**; no act belies your **word**; and no **word** lacks agreement with another. Such are the truly honest. At no **level** are **they** in **conflict** with themselves. Therefore it is **impossible** for them to be in **conflict** with anyone or anything. *M-4.II.3:9*

HORROR
[ˈhôrər]

DICTIONARY: *an intense feeling of fear, shock, or disgust.*

EGO
- some of them are shared illusions, and others are **part** of your personal **hell**. *W-pI.14.7.3*

~ **you** think if what is true about **you** were revealed to you, **you** would be struck with horror so intense that **you** would rush to **death** by your own hand, living on after seeing this **being impossible**. *W-pI.93.1.3*

HOST

|hōst|

DICTIONARY: *a person who receives or entertains other people as guests.*

EGO

~ the **Holy Spirit** cannot speak to an unwelcoming host because **He will** not be heard. *T-10.III.20.1*

~ it counsels, therefore, that if **you** are host to it, it **will** enable **you** to direct the **anger** that it holds outward, thus protecting **you**. *T-15.VIII.68.5*

~ as host to the **ego**, **you** believe that **you** can **give** all your **guilt** away whatever **you** think and purchase **peace**. *T-15.X.97.1*

~ the **ego**, which **you** invited, is treacherous only to those who think **they** are its host. The **ego will** never let **you** perceive this, since this recognition would **make** it homeless. *T-15.X.97.4:5*

HOLY SPIRIT;   *son of God*

~ sureness must abide **within you** who are host to Him. *W-pI.165.7.5*

~ **he** established **you** as host to Him forever. *T-15.IV.27.1*

~ the host of **God need** not **seek** to find anything. *T-15.IV.32.9*

~ **god** would **have** His host abide in perfect **freedom**. *T-15.V.37.5*

~ it is your **mind** that is the host to Him. *T-15.V.37.7*

~ **you** are host to **God** and hostage to no one and **nothing**. *T-15.V.44.3*

~ the host of **God** can **have** no real investment **here**. *T-15.VIII.67.7*

~ chosen host of **God**, who cannot **make** himself host to the **ego**. *T-15.VIII.69.2*

~ for the holy host of **God** is beyond failure, and **nothing** that **he** wills can be denied. *T-15.IX.81.7*

~ no **fear** can touch the host who cradles **God** in the **time** of **Christ**, for the Host is as holy as the Perfect **Innocence** which **He** protects and Whose **power** protects Him. *T-15.XI.102.9*

HUMILITY

|(h)yoo ̅ ˈmiləde ̅|

DICTIONARY: *a modest or low view of one's own importance; humbleness.*

EGO

~ but the **ego** does not **understand** humility, mistaking it for **self**-debasement.

~ it is not humility to insist that **you** cannot be the **light** of the **world** if that is the **function God** assigned to you.

HOLY SPIRIT;   *strength, lesson for the ego.*

~ humility is a **lesson** for the **ego**, not for the **Soul**. The **Soul** is beyond humility because it recognizes its radiance and gladly sheds its **light** everywhere. The meek shall inherit the earth because their egos are humble, and this gives them better **perception**. *T-4.II.19.2:4*

~ humility is **strength** in this **sense** only—to recognize and accept the **fact** that **you** do not know is to recognize and accept the **fact** that **He** does know. *T-16.II.5.4*

~ humility **will** never **ask** that **you** remain content with littleness. But it does require that **you** be not content with less than greatness, which comes not of **you.** *T-18.V.34.1:2*

~ humility consists of accepting your **role** in **salvation** and in taking no other. *W-pI.61.2.3*

~ true humility, abandoning the false pretense by which the **ego** seeks to prove it **arrogant.** *W-pI.152.9.1*

~ yet are the humble free to hear the **Voice** which tells them what **they** are and what to do. *W-pI.186.5.6*

~ true humility **will** come at last to **grace** the **mind** that **thought** it was **alone** and stood against the **world.** Humility brings **peace** because it does not claim that **you** must **rule** the **universe**, nor judge all things as **you** would **have** them be. All **little** Gods it gladly lays aside, not in resentment, but in honesty and recognition that **they** do not serve. *S-1.V.1.3:5*

~ the truly humble **have** no **goal** but **God** because **they need** no idols, and **defense** no longer serves a **purpose.** Enemies are useless **now**, because humility does not oppose. It does not **hide** in shame because it is content with what it is, knowing **creation** is the **Will** of **God.** Its selflessness is **Self**, and this it sees in every meeting, where it gladly joins with every **Son of God**, whose purity it recognizes that it shares with him. *S-1.V.2.3:6*

~ humility has come to **teach you** how to **understand** your **glory** as God's Son, and recognize the arrogance of **sin.** *S-1.V.3.2*

HURT

|hərt|

DICTIONARY: *cause* physical ***pain*** *or injury to.*

EGO

~ **you** can but hurt yourself. *T-24.V.36.1*

~ in every **wish** to hurt, he chooses **death** instead of what his **Father** wills for him. *T-26.VIII.63.6*

~ if **you** can be hurt by anything, **you see** a **picture** of your **secret** wishes. *T-31.V.57.8*

HOLY SPIRIT

~ a **mind** that recoils from a hurt **body** is in great **need** of **rehabilitation** itself. All symptoms of hurt **need** true helpfulness. *T-4.IX.105.1:2*

~ **you** cannot be hurt. *T-5.VI.53.2*

~ he cannot hurt **you.** *T-5.VI.53.3*

~ when **you ask** the **Holy Spirit** for what would hurt you, He cannot **answer** because **nothing** can hurt **you** and so **you** are asking for **nothing.** *T-8.X.100.1*

~ he knows what **you have need** of and what **will** not hurt you. *T-12.VII.68.7*

~ **nothing** external to your **mind** can hurt or injure **you** in any way. *W-pI.190.5.2*

~ **i** can elect to **change** all thoughts that hurt. *W-p2.284.1.7*

DICTIONARY: *the subject or object of **self-consciousness**; the **ego**.*

EGO;   ***body**, miserable sinner.*

~ i **see nothing**, and **nothing** has no **meaning**. *W-pI.51.2.1*

~ what I think I **see now** is taking the place of **vision**. *W-pI.51.2.3*

~ i **have** judged everything I look upon. *W-pI.51.3.1*

~ what I **see** is the **projection** of my own errors of **thought**. I do not **understand** what I **see** because it is not understandable. There is no **sense** in trying to **understand** it. *W-pI.51.4.2:4*

~ i **have** misused everything I **see** by assigning this **role** to it. I **have** done this to defend a **thought system** which has **hurt** me I am always upset by **nothing**. *W-pI.51.6.4:5*

~ i condemn the **world** I look upon. I **call** this seeing. I hold the **past** against **everyone** and everything, making them my "enemies". *W-pI.52.3.1:3*

~ i **see** only my own thoughts, and my **mind** is preoccupied with the **past**. *W-pI.52.4.1*

~ i look on the **past** to prevent the **present** from dawning on my **mind**. *W-pI.52.4.3*

~ i am trying to use **time** against **God**. *W-pI.52.4.4*

~ what I **see** tells me that I do not know who I am. *W-pI.55.2.5*

~ i was mistaken when I **thought** I lived apart from **God**, a separate entity which moved in isolation, unattached, and housed **within** a **body**. *W-pII.223.1.1*

~ i **have** indeed misunderstood the **world** because I laid my "sins" on it and saw them looking back at me. How fierce **they** seemed! *W-pII.265.1.1:2*

~ how deceived was I to think that what I feared was in the **world** instead of in my **mind alone**. *W-pII.265.1.3*

HOLY SPIRIT;   *Spirit, One Self, Christ, God's perfect Son, **Son of God**, Your Son, **God**, **minister of God**, Effect of God, light, **light** of the world, **salvation** of the world, **messenger**, **idea**, **you**.*

~ i am blessed as a **Son of God**. All **good** things are mine because **God** intended them for me. I cannot suffer any **loss** or **deprivation** or **pain** because of who I am. My **Father** supports me, protects me, and directs me in all things. His care for me is infinite and is with me forever. I am eternally blessed as His Son. *W-pI.40.4.1:6*

~ i am a **Son of God**. *W-pI.46.11.1*

~ i am **alone** in **nothing**. Everything I think or say or do touches all the **universe**. *W-pI.54.5.1:2*

~ i am perfect because **God** goes with me wherever I go. *W-pI.59.2.6*

~ i am in the likeness of my **Creator**. I cannot suffer, I cannot **experience loss**, and I cannot die. I am not a **body**. *W-pI.84.2.1:3*

~ i bring the **world** the tidings of **salvation** that I hear as **God** my **Father** speaks to me. *W-pII.237.1.3*

~ i am a **messenger** of **God**, directed by His **Voice**, sustained by Him in **love**, and held forever **quiet** and at **peace within** His loving arms. *W-pII.267.1.6*

~ i am far beyond all **pain**. *W-pII.281.2.2*

~ i am the **means** by which God's Son is saved. *W-pII.318.1.6*

~ i was created as the **thing** I **seek**. I am the **goal** the **world** is searching for. I am God's Son, His one Eternal **Love**. I am salvation's **means** and end as well. *W-pII.318.1.7*

~ i am **he** to whom all this is given. I am **he** in whom the **power** of my Father's **Will** abides. *W-pII.320.1.5:6*

HOLY SPIRIT

~ the one **idea** which brings complete **salvation**; the one statement which makes all forms of **temptation** powerless; the one **thought** which renders the **ego** silent and entirely undone. **You** are as **God** created **you.** *W-pI.94.1.1:2*

~ **here** is **salvation** accomplished. **Here** is **sanity** restored. *W-pI.94.1.4:5*

IDEA |ī'dēə|

DICTIONARY: an opinion or *belief.*

EGO;   *one illusion, guardians of darkness.*

~ insane ideas **have** no real relationships, for that is why **they** are insane. *T-13.IV.21.1*

~ strange ideas of safety? **They** are neither safe nor unsafe. **They** do not protect; neither do **they attack. They** do **nothing** at all, **being nothing** at all. As guardians of **darkness** and of ignorance, look to them only for **fear**, for what **they** keep obscure is fearful. *T-14.III.18.1:5*

~ the idea of **separation** produced the **body** and remains connected to it, making it sick because of its identification with it. *T-19.II.8.8*

~ yet this strange idea, which it does accurately describe, **you** think is **you.** *T-22.II.6.2*

~ the whole **illusion** that what **you** made has **power** to enslave its maker. This is the same **belief** that caused the **separation**. It is the meaningless idea that thoughts can leave the thinker's **mind**, be different from it, and in opposition to it. If this were true, thoughts would not be the mind's extensions but its enemies. And **here** **we see** again another **form** of the same fundamental **illusion we have** seen many times before. *T-22.III.24.1:5*

~ to believe ideas can leave their **source** is to invite illusions to be true, without success. *T-26.VIII.60.5*

~ **you attack** but false ideas and never truthful ones. *T-30.V.49.7*

~ while thoughtless "ideas" preoccupy your **mind**, the **truth** is blocked. *W-pI.8.3.2*

~ the strange idea that **you** are torn by conflicting goals. *W-pI.74.1.5*

HOLY SPIRIT;   *basis for vision, mighty forces.*

~ to profess is to identify with an idea and offer the idea to others to be their own. The idea does not lessen; it becomes stronger. *T-4.II.6.5:6*

~ ideas do not leave the **mind** which **thought** them to **have** a separate **being**, nor do separate thoughts **conflict** with one another in space, because **they** do not occupy space at all. However, human ideas can **conflict** in content, because **they** occur at different levels and include **opposite** thoughts at the same **level**. It is **impossible** to **share** opposing thoughts. *T-5.VI.56.1:3*

~ in ideas minds can communicate. *T-15.VII.63.2*

~ for the ideas are mighty forces to be used and not held idly by. **They have** already proved their **power** sufficiently for **you** to place your **faith** in them and not in their **denial**. *T-16.III.20.2:3*

~ **reason** sees the **source** of an idea as what **will make** it true or false. This must be so if the idea is like its **source**. *T-22.III.20.4:5*

~ ideas are of the **mind**. What is projected out and seems to be external to the **mind** is not **outside** at all but an effect of what is in and has not left its **source**. *T-26.VIII.49.8:9*

~ some of the ideas **you will** find hard to believe, and others **will** seem quite startling. It does not matter. **You** are merely asked to apply them to what **you see. You** are not asked to judge them nor even to believe them. **You** are asked only to use them. It is their use which **will give** them **meaning** to **you** and show **you they** are true. **Remember** only this—**you need** not believe them, **you need** not accept them, and **you need** not **welcome** them. Some of them **you** may actively resist. None of this **will** matter nor decrease their efficacy. But allow yourself to **make** no exceptions in applying the ideas the exercises contain. Whatever your reactions to the ideas may be, use them. **Nothing** more than this is required. W-pI.I.5.1:12

~ there is no **world** apart from your ideas because ideas leave not their **source**, and **you** maintain the **world within** your **mind** in thought. W-pI.132.11.3

~ ideas remain united to their **source. They** can extend all that their **source** contains. In that **they** can go far beyond themselves. But **they** cannot **give birth** to what was never given them. As **they** are made, so **will** their making be. As **they** were born, so **will they** then **give birth**. And where **they** come from, there **will they** return. W-pI.167.5.2:8

~ when **you give** ideas away, **you** strengthen them in your own **mind**. W-pI.187.2.4

~ ideas must first belong to **you** before **you give** them. W-pI.187.3.1

~ the transfer **value** of one true idea has no end nor **limit**. M-5.7.5

IDENTITY

|ˌī'den(t)ədē|

DICTIONARY: *the fact of being who or what a person or thing is.*

EGO

~ this false identification makes **you** incapable of understanding what anything is for. W-pI.25.2.3

~ a false **image** of yourself has come to take the place of what **you** are. W-pI.26.3.5

~ **you will** believe that **you** are **part** of where **you** think **you** are. That is because **you** surround yourself with the environment **you want**. And **you want** it to protect the **image** of yourself that **you have** made. The **image** is **part** of this environment. What **you see** while **you** believe **you** are in it is seen through the eyes of the **image**. This is not **vision**. Images cannot **see**. W-pI.35.2.1:7

~ **self-condemnation** is a **decision** about identity. M-13.3.6

HOLY SPIRIT

~ what **you** are is not established by your **perception** and is not influenced by it at all. All perceived problems in identification at any **level** are not problems of **fact. They** are problems of understanding, since **they** mean that **you** believe what **you** can **understand** is up to **you** to decide. T-7.VII.64.2:4

~ your identity is shared and that its sharing is its **reality**. T-9.III.9.6

~ this identity is shared. The **miracle** becomes the **means** of sharing it. By supplying your identity wherever it is not recognized, **you will** recognize it. T-14.VI.57.5:7

~ it is **impossible** that **God** lose His Identity, for if **He** did, **you** would lose yours. And **being** yours, **He** cannot **change** Himself, for your identity is changeless. T-14.VII.67.5:6

~ identity in dreams is meaningless because the dreamer and the **dream** are one. T-28.V.41.4

~ accept the changeless and eternal that abide in him, for your Identity is there. T-29.VI.32.5

~ every **choice you make** establishes your own identity as **you will see** it and believe it is. T-31.VIII.92.5

~ for **he** who can accept his true Identity is truly saved. W-pI.191.5.3

~ my true Identity is so secure, so lofty, **sinless**, glorious and great, wholly beneficent and free from **guilt** that **Heaven** looks to it to **give** it **light**. It lights the **world** as well. It is the **gift** my **Father** gave me, the one as well **I give** the **world**. There is no **gift** but this that can be either given or received. This is **reality**, and only this. This is illusion's end. It is the **Truth**. *W-pII.224.1.1:7*

~ **now** is our **Source** remembered, and therein **we** find our true Identity at last. *W-pII.260.2.1*

~ identify with **love**, and **you** are safe. Identify with **love**, and **you** are **home**. Identify with **love**, and find your **Self**. *W-pII.ST261.5.6:8*

~ our Identity which our **forgiveness** has restored to us. *W-pII.ST291.5.4*

IDOL |ˈīdl|

DICTIONARY: *a person or **thing** that is greatly admired, loved, or revered.*

EGO;   *"true" **identity**, **wish**, **anti-christ**, substitutes, dissatisfying Gods, blown-up children's toys.*

~ those who **make** idols do worship them. The idols are **nothing**, but their worshipers are the Sons of **God** in **sickness**. *T-9.IX.74.7:8*

~ all forms of idolatry are caricatures of **creation**. *T-9.IX.77.7*

~ every idol which **you** raise to place before Him stands before **you** in place of what **you** are. *T-16.VI.55.5*

~ idols do not **share**. *T-20.VII.46.8*

~ idols accept, but never **make** return. **They** can be loved, but cannot **love**. **They** do not **understand** what **they** are offered, and any **relationship** in which **they** enter has lost its **meaning**. **They** live in secrecy, hating the sunlight and **happy** in the body's **darkness** where **they** can **hide** and keep their secrets hidden along with them. And **they** have no relationships, for no one else is **welcome** there. **They** smile on no one, and those who smile on them **they** do not **see**. *T-20.VII.47.1:6*

~ idolaters **will** always be afraid of **love**, for **nothing** so severely threatens them as love's approach. Let **love** draw near them. *T-20.VII.51.1:2*

~ and overlook the **body**, as it **will** surely do, and **they** retreat in **fear**, feeling the seeming firm foundation of their **temple** begin to shake and loosen. *T-20.VII.51.2*

~ this idol that seems to **give you power** has taken it away. *T-24.IV.27.6*

~ **you will** weep each **time** an idol falls. *T-29.VIII.43.2*

~ each idol that **you** worship when **God** calls **will** never **answer** in His place. *T-29.VIII.43.4*

~ the lingering **illusion will** impel him to **seek** out a thousand idols and to **seek** beyond them for a thousand more. And each **will fail** him, all excepting one; for **he will** die and does not **understand** the idol that **he** seeks is but his **death**. Its **form** appears to be **outside** himself. *T-29.VIII.45.1:3*

~ yet does **he** seek to **kill** God's Son **within** and prove that **he** is victor over him. This is the **purpose** every idol has, for this the **role** that is assigned to it, and this the **role** that cannot be fulfilled. *T-29.VIII.45.4:5*

~ **you have** made of your **reality** an idol which **you** must protect against the **light** of **truth**. And all the **world** becomes the **means** by which this idol can be saved. *T-29.VIII.50.8:9*

~ idols are unrecognized as such and never seen for what **they** really are. *T-29.IX.52.3*

~ their **purpose** is obscure, and **they** are feared and worshiped both because **you** do not know what **they** are for and why **they have** been made. An idol is an **image** of your **brother** which **you** would **value** more than what **he** is. Idols are made that **he** may be replaced, no matter what their **form**. *T-29.IX.52.5:7*

~ an idol is a false impression or a false **belief**—some **form** of **anti-Christ** which constitutes a **gap** between the **Christ** and what **you see**. An idol is a **wish** made tangible and given **form** and thus perceived as real and seen **outside** the **mind**. Yet it is still a **thought** and cannot leave the **mind** that is its **source**. Nor is its **form** apart from the **idea** it represents. *T-29.IX.54.1:4*

~ an idol is a **means** for getting more. And it is this that is against **God's Will**. *T-29.IX.59.12:13*

~ yet everything their toys appear to do is in the minds of those who play with them. *T-29.X.64.7*

HOLY SPIRIT;   *nothing, false ideas, false impression, false **belief, limit**, limits, **image**.*

~ idols must disappear and leave no trace behind their going. The unholy instant of their seeming **power** is frail as is a snowflake, but without its loveliness. *T-20.VII.53.1:2*

~ idolatry is **past** and meaningless. *T-20.VII.57.3*

~ idols must fall because **they have** no **life**, and what is lifeless is a sign of **death**. *T-29.VIII.47.1*

~ all idols of this **world** were made to keep the **truth within** from **being** known to **you** and to maintain allegiance to the **dream** that **you** must find what is **outside** yourself to be complete and **happy**. It is vain to worship idols in the hope of **peace**. *T-29.VIII.48.1:2*

~ w**here He** is, no idols can abide. *T-29.VIII.50.5*

~ an idol cannot take the place of **God**. *T-29.VIII.51.4*

~ be it a **body** or a **thing**, a place, a **situation** or a circumstance, an object owned or wanted, or a right demanded or achieved, it is the same. *T-29.IX.52.9*

~ idols are but substitutes for your **reality**. In some **way, you** believe **they will** complete your **little self** [and let **you** walk in] safety in a **world** perceived as dangerous. *T-29.IX.53.2:3*

~ an idol is established by **belief**, and when it is withdrawn, the idol "dies." *T-29.IX.56.8*

~ an idol is beyond where **God** has set all things forever and has left no room for anything to be except His **Will. Nothing** and nowhere must an idol be while **God** is everything and everywhere. *T-29.IX.58.5:6*

~ no idol can establish **you** as more than **God**. *T-29.IX.60.10*

~ idols **have** no **purpose here**. *T-29.IX.60.4*

~ the slave of idols is a willing slave. For willing **he** must be to let himself bow down in worship to what has no **life** and **seek** for **power** in the powerless. *T-29.X.61.1:2*

~ the **belief** that there are forms which **will** bring happiness and that, by limiting, is all attained. *T-30.IV.38.5*

~ **you** do not **want** an idol. It is not your **will** to **have** one. It **will** not bestow on **you** the **gift you seek**. *T-30.IV.39.6:8*

~ behind the search for every idol lies the yearning for **completion**. *T-30.IV.40.1*

~ beyond all idols stands his holy **will** to be but what **he** is. *T-30.IV.42.3*

~ idols must keep hidden what **you** are, not from the **Mind** of God, but from your own. *T-30.IV.48.8*

~ all idols are the false ideas **you** made to fill the **gap you** think arose between yourself and what is true. And **you attack** them for the things **you** think **they** represent. What lies beyond them cannot be attacked. *T-30.V.49.8:10*

~ **they** must be neither cherished nor attacked but merely looked upon as children's toys without a single **meaning** of their own. *T-30.V.52.10*

~ his idols do not threaten him at all. His one **mistake** is that **he** thinks them real. *T-30.V.53.13:14*

~ how willingly the **mind** can let them go when it has understood that idols are **nothing** and nowhere and are purposeless. *T-30.VI.61.3*

~ in the presence of my **holiness**, which **I share** with **God** Himself, all idols vanish. *W-pI.58.4.5*

~ routines as such are dangerous because **they** easily become Gods in their own right, threatening the very goals for which **they** were set up. *M-16.2.5*

ILLUSION |iˈlo͞oZHən|

DICTIONARY: *a **thing** that is or is likely to be wrongly perceived or interpreted by the senses.*

EGO;   *assault on **truth**, deceptions, investments, forms, safety devices, foolish cobwebs, vaporous illusions, "dark companions", "dark **way**."*

~ illusions are investments. **They will** last as long as **you value** them. *T-7.VIII.74.2:3*

~ illusions are deceptions. *T-9.VII.54.7*

~ every illusion which **you** accept into your **mind** by judging it to be attainable removes your own **sense** of **completion** and thus denies the **wholeness** of your **Father**. *T-16.V.39.2*

~ **they** but seem to be fearful to the extent to which **you fail** to recognize them for what **they** are. *T-16.VI.56.2*

~ to bring **truth** to illusions, **you** are trying to **make** illusions real and keep them by justifying your **belief** in them. *T-17.II.5.4*

~ illusion the absence of **truth**. *T-19.II.5.8*

~ hallucinations serve to meet the **goal** of **madness**. **They** are the **means** by which the **outside world**, projected from **within**, adjusts to sin and seems to **witness** to its **reality**. *T-20.IX.75.5:6*

~ not one but rests on the **belief** that **you** are separate. Not one that does not seem to stand, heavy and solid and immovable, between **you** and your **brother**. And not one that **truth** cannot pass over lightly and so easily that **you** must be convinced, in spite of what **you thought** it was, that it is **nothing**. *T-22.VI.50.4:6*

~ it is your unwillingness to overlook what seems to stand between **you** that makes it look impenetrable and defends the illusion of its immovability. *T-22.VI.50.8*

~ illusions **battle** only with themselves. **Being** fragmented, **they fragment**. *T-23.II.13.4:5*

~ illusions can **conflict** because their forms are different. And **they** do **battle** only to establish which **form** is true. *T-23.II.17.5:6*

~ **outside** of Heaven, only the **conflict** of illusions stands; senseless, **impossible**, and beyond all **reason**, and yet perceived as an eternal barrier to **Heaven**. Illusions are but forms. Their content is never true. *T-23.III.37.7:9*

~ no one can **make** one illusion real and still escape the **rest**. *T-26.VII.44.6*

~ illusions **have** no witnesses and no effects. Who looks on them is but deceived. *T-26.VIII.53.3:4*

~ **they will fail you**. *W-pI.50.3.2*

~ illusions about yourself and the **world** are one. *W-pI.62.2.1*

~ the **mind** that sees illusions thinks them real. **They have** existence in that **they** are thoughts. And yet **they** are not real because the **mind** that thinks these thoughts is separate from **God**. *W-pI.99.3.2:4*

~ all illusions **rest** upon the weird **belief** that **we** can **make** another for ourselves. *W-pI.186.8.2*

~ illusion makes illusion. *W-pI.198.1.2*

~ defenses which protect your unforgiving thoughts from **being** seen and recognized. Their **purpose** is to show **you** something else and hold **correction** o through **self**-deceptions made to take its place. *W-pl.Rev IV.5.2:3*

~ the mechanisms of illusion **have** been born instead. And **now they** go to find what has been given them to **seek**. Their aim is to fulfill the **purpose** which the **world** was made to **witness** and **make** real. **They see** in its illusions but a solid base where **truth** exists, upheld apart from lies. Yet everything that **they** report is but illusion, which is kept apart from **truth**. *W-pII.ST241.3.1:5*

~ illusions are always illusions of differences. *M-8.2.1*

~ the **father** of illusions is the **belief** that **they have** a **purpose**; that **they** serve a **need** or gratify a **want**. *M-14.1.6*

~ in illusions the **impossible** is easily accomplished, but only at the cost of making illusions true. *P-2.IN.2.6*

HOLY SPIRIT; *beliefs, travesties of **creation**, scraps of **creation**.*

~ one illusion cherished and defended against the **truth** makes all **truth** meaningless and all illusions real. Such is the **power** of **belief**. It cannot **compromise**. *T-22.III.19.4:6*

~ questioning illusions is the first **step** in undoing them. The **miracle**, or the "right **answer**," corrects them. *T-3.V.32.1:2*

~ every **Son of God** has the **power** to deny illusions anywhere in the **Kingdom** merely by denying them completely in himself. *T-9.IX.80.3*

~ honor is not due to illusions, for to honor them is to honor **nothing**. Yet **fear** is not due them either, for **nothing** cannot be fearful. *T-9.IX.83.6:7*

~ there is no **need** to shrink from illusions, for **they** cannot be dangerous. *T-10.VI.39.2*

~ no illusions can satisfy him or save him from what **he** is. *T-12.III.18.6*

~ the content of individual illusions differs greatly. Yet **they have** one **thing** in common—**they** are all insane. **They** are made of sights which are not seen and sounds which are not heard. **They make** up a private **world** which cannot be shared. For **they** are meaningful only to their maker, and so **they have** no **meaning** at all. In this **world** their maker moves **alone**, for only **he** perceives them. *T-12.V.33.4:9*

~ the **Holy Spirit** does not keep illusions in your **mind** to frighten **you** and show them to **you** fearfully to demonstrate what **He** has saved **you** from. What **He** has saved **you** from is gone. *T-13.IV.26.1:2*

~ illusions are but beliefs in what is not there. *T-16.IV.24.9*

~ every illusion is one of **fear**, whatever **form** it takes. And the attempt to escape from one illusion into another must **fail**. *T-16.V.35.3:4*

~ **innocence** born of complete **forgiveness** of each other's illusions. *T-19.V.97.7*

~ no illusions can attract the minds that **have** transcended them and left them far behind. *T-20.VII.53.7*

~ hallucinations disappear when **they** are recognized for what **they** are. This is the **healing** and the remedy. Believe them not, and **they** are gone. And all **you need** to do is recognize **you** did this. Once **you** accept this simple **fact** and take unto yourself the **power you** gave them, **you** are released from them. One **thing** is sure—hallucinations serve a **purpose**, and when that **purpose** is no longer held, **they** disappear. *T-20.IX.74.1:6*

~ the **opposite** of illusions is not disillusionment, but **truth**. *T-22.III.16.1*

~ illusions carry only **guilt** and **suffering**, **sickness** and **death** to their believers. The **form** in which **they** are accepted is irrelevant. *T-22.III.18.1:2*

~ how does one overcome illusions? Surely not by force or **anger** nor by opposing them in any **way**. Merely by letting **reason** tell **you** that **they** contradict **reality**. **They** go against what must be true.

The opposition comes from them and not **reality**. *T-22.VIII.45.1:5*

~ illusions cannot triumph over **truth**, nor can **they** threaten it in any **way**. And the **reality** which **they** deny is not a **part** of them. *T-23.II.12.8:9*

~ illusions **have** no place where **love** abides, protecting **you** from everything that is not true. *T-23.II.16.5*

~ every illusion is an assault on **truth**, and every one does violence to the **idea** of love because it seems to be of equal **truth**. *T-23.V.47.11*

~ all illusions are "threatened" by the **truth. They will** not stand before it. *T-24.V.37.1:2*

~ not one illusion still remains unanswered in your **mind**. *T-26.VI.33.4*

~ illusions are illusions and are false. Your preference gives them no **reality**. Not one is true in any **way**, and all must yield with equal ease to what **God** gave as **answer** to them all. *T-26.VIII.51.7:9*

~ illusions serve the **purpose they** were made to serve. And from their **purpose, they** derive whatever **meaning** that **they** seem to **have**. *T-26.VIII.62.1:2*

~ **god** gave to all illusions that were made another **purpose** that would justify a **miracle**, whatever **form they** took. *T-26.VIII.62.3*

~ no one is afraid of them when **he** perceives **he** made them up. *T-28.III.22.3*

~ all illusions that **you** believe about yourself obey no **laws. They** seem to dance a **little** while, according to the rules **you** set for them. But then **they** fall and cannot rise again. *T-30.V.52.3:5*

~ illusions **have** no direction in **reality. They** are merely not true. *W-pI.35.5.4:5*

~ illusions are not facts. *W-pI.48.1.2*

~ what are illusions except false ideas about myself? My **holiness** undoes them all by asserting the **truth** about me. *W-pI.58.4.3:4*

~ the **Holy Spirit** has another use for all the illusions **you have** made, and therefore **He** sees another **purpose** in them. *W-pI.64.2.2*

~ there is a point beyond which illusions cannot go. *W-pI.73.6.8*

~ without illusions there could be no **fear**, no **doubt**, and no **attack**. *W-pI.107.4.1*

~ illusions can be brought to **truth** to be corrected. But the **truth** stands far beyond illusions and cannot be brought to them to turn them into **truth**. *W-pI.107.6.3:4*

~ **we seek** a cure for all illusions, not another **shift** among them. *W-pI.140.8.1*

~ there can never be a meaningful distinction made between what is untrue and equally untrue. **Here** there are no degrees and no beliefs that what does not **exist** is truer in some forms than others. All of them are false and can be cured because **they** are not true. *W-pI.140.9.3:5*

~ to let illusion walk ahead of **truth** is **madness**, but to let illusion sink behind the **truth** and let the **truth** stand forth as what it is, is simple **sanity**. *W-pI.155.2.6*

~ illusions recognized must disappear. *W-pI.187.7.1*

~ yet on earth **you need** the **means** to let illusion go. *W-pI.192.2.4*

~ **forgiveness** is illusion that is **answer** to the **rest**. *W-pI.198.2.10*

~ perceived as purposeless, **they** are no longer seen. Their uselessness is recognized, and **they** are gone. *M-14.1.7:8*

~ **they have** been brought to **truth**, and **truth** saw them not. It merely overlooked the meaningless. *M-14.1.10:11*

~ it is **impossible** to let illusions be brought to **truth** and keep the illusions. **Truth** demonstrates illusions **have** no value. *M-6.1.2:3*

~ by definition, an illusion is an attempt to **make** something real that is regarded as of major importance but is recognized as **being** untrue. The **mind** therefore seeks to **make** it true out of its intensity of **desire** to **have** it for itself. Illusions are travesties of **creation**, attempts to bring **truth** to lies. *M-8.2.3:5*

~ the properties of illusions which seem to **make** them different are really irrelevant, for their properties are as illusory as **they** are. *M-8.5.9*

IMAGE |ˈimij|

DICTIONARY: *a representation of the external form of a person or thing in art.*

EGO

~ images are perceived, not known. *T-3.IX.77.1*

~ a false image of yourself has come to take the place of what **you** are. *W-pI.26.3.5*

~ these images, with no **reality** in **truth**, bear **witness** to the **fear of God**, forgetting **being Love**. *W-pI.103.2.3*

~ the images **you make give** rise to but conflicting goals, impermanent and vague, **uncertain** and ambiguous. *W-pI.186.10.3*

HOLY SPIRIT

~ the **word** "image" is always **perception**-related and not a product of [knowing]. Images are symbolic and stand for something else. *T-3.VII.54.3:4*

~ your **brother** is the mirror in which **you will see** the image of yourself. *T-7.VIII.73.9*

~ there **will** come a **time** when images **have** all gone by, and **you will see you** know not what **you** are. *T-31.V.59.2*

~ the images **you make** can not prevail against what **God** Himself would **have you** be. *T-31.VIII.88.1*

~ the images **I have** made cannot prevail against Him because it is not my **will** that **they** do so. *W-pI.53.6.5*

~ behind every image **I have** made, the **truth** remains unchanged. *W-pI.56.5.1*

~ the images **I see** reflect my thoughts. *W-pII.265.1.8*

~ as **God** created you, **you have** all **power**. The image **you** made of yourself has none. The **Holy Spirit** knows the **truth** about you. The image **you** made does not. Yet despite its obvious and complete ignorance, this image assumes it knows all things because **you have** given that **belief** to it. *M-29.4.4:8*

IMMORTALITY |ˌi(m)ˌmôrˈtalədē|

DICTIONARY: *the ability to live forever; eternal life.*

EGO

~ the **idea** of preserving the **body** by suspension, thus giving it the kind of limited immortality which the **ego** can tolerate, is among its more recent appeals to the **mind**. *T-4.VI.77.4*

~ out of its unwillingness for **you** to find **peace** even in the **death** it wants for you, it offers **you** immortality in **hell**. *T-15.II.3.5*

HOLY SPIRIT; *gift of holiness and love*

~ immortality is a constant state. It is as true **now** as it ever was or ever **will** be because it implies no **change** at all. It is not a continuum nor is it understood by **being** compared to an **opposite**. *T-4.VII.82.1:3*

~ immortality is His **Will** for His Son and His Son's **will** for himself. *T-10.II.13.8*

~ immortality is the **opposite** of **time**, for **time** passes away, while immortality is constant. *T-11.X.96.10*

~ accepting the **Atonement** teaches **you** what immortality is, for by accepting your guiltlessness, **you** learn that the **past** has never been, and so the **future** is needless. *T-11.X.97.1*

~ immortality and **joy** are **now**. *T-15.II.9.7*

~ what is immortal cannot be attacked; what is but temporal has no effect. *T-24.VIII.66.4*

~ there is no **change** in immortality. *T-29.III.16.4*

~ in immortality **you** live forever. *W-pI.199.8.2*

~ what is born can never die, for what has **life** has immortality. *W-p2.340.5.4*

IMPOSSIBLE |imˈpäsəb(ə)l|

DICTIONARY: *not able to occur,* ***exist****, or be done.*

EGO

~ **you** are in an impossible **situation** only because **you thought** it was possible to be in one. **You** would be in an impossible **situation** if God showed **you** your **perfection** and proved to **you** that **you** were wrong. *T-6.V.54.1:2*

~ the characteristic "impossible **situation**" to which the **ego** always leads. *T-9.IV.26.4*

~ a split that is impossible. A split that cannot happen. Yet a split in which **you** surely **will** believe, because **you have** set up a **situation** that is impossible. And in this **situation** the impossible can seem to happen. It seems to happen at the "**sacrifice**" of **truth**. *M-13.7.11:15*

HOLY SPIRIT

~ the impossible can happen only in **fantasy**. *T-9.III.18.7*

~ it is impossible to convince **you** of the **reality** of what has clearly been accomplished through your willingness. *T-16.III.13.5*

~ what **you** believe to be impossible **will** be if **God** so wills it, but **you will** remain quite unaware of it. *T-18.V.40.2*

~ it is impossible the **Son of God** be merely driven by events **outside** of him. It is impossible that the happenings that come to him were not his **choice**. *T-21.III.17.1:2*

~ it remains impossible to keep **love** out. *T-22.VI.47.5*

~ the one **thing** that is impossible is that **you** be unlike each other. *T-27.IX.90.4*

~ the impossible has not occurred and can **have** no effects. And that is all. *T-31.I.1.3:4*

INHERITANCE |inˈherədəns|

DICTIONARY: *a* ***thing*** *that is inherited.*

EGO

~ it would thus destroy **you here** and bury **you here**, leaving **you** no inheritance except the dust out of which it thinks **you** were made. *T-12.IV.23.5*

~ **i have** tried to **give** my inheritance away in exchange for the **world I see**. *W-pI.56.2.5*

HOLY SPIRIT; *right*

~ **everyone** is free to refuse to accept his inheritance, but **he** is not free to establish what his inheritance is. *T-3.VIII.70.2*

~ perceiving the Majesty of **God** as your **brother** is to accept your own inheritance. *T-7.XII.111.2*

~ **glory** is your inheritance, given your **Soul** by its **Creator** that **you** might extend it. *T-10.V.31.5*

~ your inheritance can neither be bought nor sold. There can be no disinherited parts of the **Sonship**, for **God** is whole, and all His extensions are like Him. *T-11.V.41.7:8*

~ your inheritance awaits only the recognition that **you have** been redeemed. *T-11.V.42.5*

~ no **world outside** himself holds his inheritance. *T-12.VII.71.6*

~ the inheritance of the **Kingdom** is the right of God's Son, given him in his **creation**. *T-14.II.8.1*

~ their **Father** gave the same inheritance to both. *T-25.IX.76.6*

~ together is your joint inheritance remembered and accepted by **you** both. **Alone** it is denied to both of **you**. *T-31.II.25.1:2*

~ **god** has kept my inheritance safe for me. My own real thoughts **will teach** me what it is. *W-pI.56.2.6:7*

~ to **ask** the **Holy Spirit** to decide for **you** is simply to accept your true inheritance. *M-29.5.4*

INJUSTICE |inˈjəstəs|

DICTIONARY: *lack of fairness or **justice**.*

EGO

~ injustice is the basis for all the judgments of the **world**. *M-19.1.2*

~ all concepts of your brothers and yourself, all fears of **future** states, and all concern about the **past** stem from injustice. **Here** is the lens which, held before the body's eyes, distorts **perception** and brings **witness** of the distorted **world** back to the **mind** that made the lens and holds it very dear. Selectively and arbitrarily is every **concept** of the **world** built up in just this **way**. "Sins "are perceived and justified by this careful selectivity in which all **thought** of **wholeness** must be lost. **Forgiveness** has no place in such a scheme, for not one "**sin**" but seems forever true. *M-19.3.1:5*

HOLY SPIRIT

~ **god** knows of no injustice. *T-25.IX.73.3*

~ to take from one to **give** another must be an injustice to them both, since **they** are equal in the Holy Spirit's **sight**. *T-25.IX.76.5*

~ the **Holy Spirit** does not evaluate injustices as great or small or more or less. **They have** no properties to Him. **They** are mistakes from which the **Son of God** is **suffering**, but needlessly. *T-26.III.13.4:6*

INNOCENCE |ˈinəsəns|

DICTIONARY: *lack of guile or corruption; purity.*

EGO

~ when it is partial, it is characterized by the same erratic nature that holds for other two-edged defenses. *T-3.IV.26.7*

~ **you sacrifice** your innocence with his and die each **time you see** in him a **sin** deserving **death**. *T-26.II.6.7*

~ **you seek** to find an innocence which is not Theirs but yours **alone** and at the cost of someone else's **guilt**. *T-26.XI.88.2*

~ **you** cannot **give** yourself your innocence, for **you** are too confused about yourself. *T-31.VII.69.4*

HOLY SPIRIT; *wisdom, strength.*

~ because their hearts are pure, the **innocent** defend true **perception** instead of defending themselves against it. Understanding the **lesson** of the **Atonement, they** are without the **will** to **attack**, and therefore **they see** truly. This is what the Bible **means** when it says, "When **He** shall appear (or be perceived) **we** shall be like Him, for **we** shall **see Him** as **He** is." *T-3.III.20.1:4*

~ innocence is incapable of sacrificing anything, because the **innocent mind** has everything and strives only to protect its **wholeness**. *T-3.III.24.1*

~ innocence is not a partial attribute. It is not a real **defense** until it is total. *T-3.IV.26.5:6*

~ it is not until their innocence becomes a genuine viewpoint which is universal in its application that it becomes wisdom. **Innocent** (or true) **perception means** that **you** never misperceive and always **see** truly. More simply, it **means** that **you** never **see** what does not really **exist**. *T-3.IV.27.2:4*

~ innocence is not of your making. It is given **you** the instant **you** would **have** it. *T-15.V.43.3:4*

~ his innocence **will light** your **way, offering you** its guiding **light** and sure protection. *T-20.III.13.2*

~ innocence is **strength**, and **nothing** else is strong. *T-23.I.1.2*

~ there can be no **attraction** of **guilt** in innocence. *T-23.I.4.2*

~ your innocence **will light** the **way** to his, and so is yours protected and kept in your **awareness**. *T-23.I.5.5*

~ the **sight** of innocence makes **punishment impossible** and **justice** sure. *T-25.X.81.1*

~ in his innocence, **you** find your own. *T-27.I.2.7*

~ the innocence that is the **truth** about me. *W-pI.58.2.3*

~ the blameless cannot **blame**, and those who **have** accepted their innocence **see nothing** to forgive. *W-pI.60.2.2*

~ **you have** not lost your innocence. It is for this **you** yearn. This is your heart's **desire**. *W-pI.182.12.1:3*

INNOCENT   [ˈɪnəsənt]

DICTIONARY: *not guilty of a crime or offense.*

HOLY SPIRIT

~ because their hearts are pure, the innocent defend true **perception** instead of defending themselves against it. *T-3.III.20.1*

~ innocent (or true) **perception means** that **you** never misperceive and always **see** truly. More simply, it **means** that **you** never **see** what does not really **exist**. *T-3.IV.27.3:4*

~ **they** do not suffer from the distortions of **the separated ones**. *T-3.IV.28.5*

~ the **Son of God** is innocent. *T-20.II.2.1*

~ the **innocent see** safety, and the pure in heart **see God within** His Son and look unto the Son to lead them to the **Father**. *T-20.IV.27.4*

~ the innocent are safe because **they share** their **innocence. Nothing** they **see** is harmful, for their awareness of the **truth** releases everything from the **illusion** of harmfulness. And what seemed harmful **now** stands shining in their **innocence**, released from **sin** and **fear**, and happily returned to **love**. They **share** the **strength** of **love** because they looked on **innocence**. And every **error** disappeared because they saw it not. T-23.I.3.2:6

~ it is the nature of the innocent to be forever uncontained, without a barrier or limitation. T-28.III.17.4

~ the innocent **release** in **gratitude** for their **release**. And what **they see** upholds their **freedom** from imprisonment and **death**. T-31.III.32.1:2

INSANITY |in'sanədē|

DICTIONARY: *the state of **being** seriously mentally ill; **madness**.*

EGO

~ insanity appears to add to **reality**, but no one would claim that what it adds is true. Insanity is therefore the non-**extension** of **truth**, which blocks **joy** because it blocks **creation** and thus blocks **self**-fulfillment. T-7.X.95.1:2

~ only the insane would choose **fear** in place of **love**, and only the insane could believe that **love** can be gained by **attack**. T-10.VI.52.4

~ the insane protect their **thought** systems, but **they** do so insanely. And all their defenses are as insane as what **they** are supposed to protect. T-17.V.31.4:5

~ the insane, dedicated to **madness** and set against the **peace** of **Heaven**. T-19.V.80.2

~ the insane, whose **problem** is their choices are not free and made with **reason** in the **light** of **sense**. T-25.VIII.56.6

~ the totally insane engenders **fear** because it is completely undependable and offers no grounds for **trust**. **Nothing** in **madness** is dependable. It holds out no safety and no hope. W-pI.53.4.1:3

~ it is insanity not to **see** what is there and to **see** what is not there instead. W-pI.91.3.2

~ **teacher** and **pupil**, **therapist** and **patient**, are all insane or **they** would not be **here**. Together **they** can find a pathway out, for no one **will** find **sanity alone**. P-2.II.5.6:7

~ the insane believe that **sanity** is **threat**. P-2.IV.10.5

~ the insane, thinking **they** are **God**, are not afraid to offer **weakness** to God's Son. But what **they see** in him because of this **they fear** indeed. P-2.VII.7.1:2

HOLY SPIRIT;   *non-**extension** of **truth***

~ it is given **you** to learn how to deny insanity and come forth from your private **world** in peace. T-12.V.39.7

~ nothing can justify insanity, and to **call** for **punishment** upon yourself must be insane. T-13.III.15.6

~ not even what the **Son of God** made in insanity could be without a hidden **spark** of beauty which **gentleness** could **release**. T-17.III.11.5

~ he reverses the **course** of insanity and restores **you** to **reason**. T-18.II.8.5

~ **you** do not leave insanity by going somewhere else. **You** leave it simply by accepting **reason** where **madness** was. T-21.VII.61.7:8

~ he could not enter His Son's insanity with him, but **He** could be sure His **sanity** went there with him so **he** could not be lost forever in the **madness** of his **wish**. T-25.IV.24.5

~ what makes no **sense** and has no **meaning** is insanity. T-25.VIII.52.5

INSPIRATION

|ˌinspəˈrāSH(ə)n|

DICTIONARY: *the process of **being** mentally stimulated to do or feel something, especially to do something creative.*

EGO

~ to be fatigued is to be dis-spirited. *T-4.I.1.6*

~ to be egocentric is to be dispirited. *T-4.I.1.7*

HOLY SPIRIT; *in spirit*

~ the result of genuine **devotion** is inspiration, a **word** which properly understood is the **opposite** of fatigue. *T-4.I.1.5*

~ to be inspired is to be in the **spirit**. *T-4.I.1.6*

~ to be **Self**-centered in the right **sense** is to be inspired, or in the **Soul**. The truly inspired are enlightened and cannot abide in **darkness**. *T-4.I.1.7:8*

~ holy Inspiration is so close to **knowledge** that it calls it forth; or better, allows it to come. *T-5.II.11.1*

~ inspiration is the **opposite** of dispiriting and therefore **means** to **make** joyous. The dispirited are depressed, because **they** believe that **they** are literally "without the **Spirit**," which is an **illusion**. *T-7.V.31.3:4*

~ inspiration is of the **Spirit**, and **certainty** is of **God** according to His **laws**. Both, therefore, come from the same **Source**, [because] inspiration comes from the **Voice** for **God**, and **certainty** comes from the **laws** of **God**. *T-7.V.33.2:3*

INSTRUCTION

|inˈstrəkSH(ə)n|

DICTIONARY: *detailed information telling how something should be done, operated, or assembled.*

HOLY SPIRIT

~ **you** cannot reasonably object to following instructions in a **course** for knowing on the grounds that **you** do not know. *T-8.I.1.3*

~ **you will receive** very specific instructions as **you** go along. *T-15.III.21.2*

INTERFERE

|ˌin(t)ərˈfir|

DICTIONARY: *prevent (a process or activity) from continuing or **being** carried out properly.*

EGO

~ the distraction of the **ego** seems to interfere with your **learning**, but the **ego** has no **power** to distract **you** unless **you give** it the **power**. *T-8.I.2.8*

~ interfere with His **purpose**, and **you** need salvation. *T-8.VII.6.7.3*

~ what would interfere with **God** must interfere with **you**. Only in **time** does interference in God's **completion** seem to be possible. *T-16.V.42.2:3*

HOLY SPIRIT

~ he would not interfere with you, because He would not know His Son if he were not free. To interfere with **you** would be to **attack** Himself, and **God** is not insane. *T-9.XI.102.2:3*

~ let then your dedication be to the eternal and learn how not to interfere with it and **make** it slave to **time**. *T-19.II.16.1*

~ the holy do not interfere with **truth**. *T-20.IV.18.1*

~ **god** would let **nothing** interfere with those whose wills are His. *T-22.VII.57.4*

~ nothingness and empty space can not be interference. What can interfere with the **awareness** of **reality** is the **belief** that there is something there. *T-27.IV.30.7:8*

~ determine not to interfere **today** with what He wills. *W-pI.105.12.1*

INTERPRETATION |inˌtərprəˈtāSH(ə)n|

DICTIONARY: *the action of explaining the **meaning** of something.*

EGO

~ the interpretive **function** of **perception**, actually a distorted **form** of **creation**, then permitted **man** to interpret the **body** as himself, which, though depressing, was an attempt to escape from the **conflict he** had induced. *T-3.VI.46.3*

~ any interpretation which sees either **God** or His **creations** as capable of destroying their own **purpose** is in **error**. *T-3.IX.75.6*

~ **nothing** the ego perceives is interpreted correctly. Not only does it cite Scripture for its **purpose**, but it even interprets Scripture as a **witness** for itself. *T-5.VIII.74.3:4*

~ your interpretation thus becomes the justification for the response. *T-11.I.1.5*

~ if **you** decide that someone is really trying to **attack you** or desert **you** or enslave **you**, **you will** respond as if **he** had actually done so, because **you have** made his **error** real to **you**. To interpret **error** is to **give** it **power**, and having done this, **you will** overlook **truth**. *T-11.I.1.7:8*

~ the analysis of **ego**-motivation is very complicated, very obscuring, and never without the risk of your own **ego**-involvement. The whole process represents a clear-cut attempt to demonstrate your own ability to **understand** what **you** perceive. *T-11.I.2.1:2*

~ this is poor **reality** testing by definition. *T-11.II.4.3*

~ every interpretation **you** would lay upon a **brother** is senseless. *T-14.VI.56.4*

~ interpretation which is different every **time you** think of it. *T-30.VIII.82.6*

~ it is but your interpretations which are lacking in stability, for **they** are not in line with what **you** really are. This is a state so seemingly unsafe that **fear** must rise. *T-30.VIII.88.3:4*

HOLY SPIRIT

~ knowing is not open to interpretation. It is possible to "interpret" **meaning**, but this is always open to **error** because it refers to the **perception** of **meaning**. *T-3.VII.54.6:7*

~ **you** cannot be aware without interpretation, and what **you** perceive is your interpretation. *T-10.VII.60.6*

~ every loving **thought** is true. Everything else is an appeal for **healing** and **help**. *T-11.II.3.3:4*

~ your interpretations of your brother's **need** is your interpretation of yours. *T-11.II.8.1*

~ whenever **you have** listened to His interpretation, the results **have** brought **you** joy. *T-16.III.17.5*

~ what needs interpretation must be alien. Nor **will** it ever be made understandable by an interpreter **you** cannot **understand**. *T-22.II.9.6:7*

~ **we have** one interpreter. *T-30.VIII.88.6*

INTERVAL

DICTIONARY: *a pause; a break in activity.*

EGO

~ the one remaining **problem** that **you have** is that **you see** an interval between the **time** when **you** forgive and **will receive** the benefits of **trust**. *T-26.IX.68.1*

~ **you** think it safer to remain a **little** careful and a **little** watchful of interests perceived as separate. From this **perception you** cannot conceive of gaining what **forgiveness** offers **now**. The interval **you** think lies in between the **giving** and **receiving** of the **gift** seems to be one in which **you sacrifice** and suffer **loss. You see** eventual **salvation**, not immediate results. *T-26.IX.69.4:7*

~ the interval **you** think lies in between the giving and receiving of the **gift** seems to be one in which **you sacrifice** and suffer **loss**. *T-26.IX.69.6*

~ in the **little** interval of **doubt** which still remains, **you** may perhaps lose **sight** of your Companion, and **mistake** Him for the senseless, ancient **dream** that **now** is **past**. *W-pI.156.7.5*

~ an interval in which what seems to happen never has occurred, the changes wrought are substanceless, and all events are nowhere. *W-pI.167.9.3*

HOLY SPIRIT

~ the sudden **shift** from horizontal to vertical **perception** which the **miracle** entails introduces an interval from which the doer and the receiver both emerge much farther along in **time** than **they** would otherwise **have** been. *T-1.I.82.3*

~ an out-of-pattern **time** interval which is not under the usual **laws** of **time**. *T-1.I.84.4*

~ an empty space which is not seen as filled, an unused interval of **time** not seen as spent and fully occupied, becomes a silent invitation to the **truth** to enter and to **make** itself at **home**. *T-27.IV.32.1*

~ the only interval in which **I** can be saved from **time** is **now**. *W-p2.308.1.4*

INTRAPERSONAL

DICTIONARY: *taking place or existing **within** the **mind**.*

EGO

~ intrapersonal **conflict** arises from the same basis as interpersonal **conflict**. One **part** of the psyche perceives another **part** as on a different **level** and does not **understand** it. This makes the parts strangers to each other, without recognition. *T-3.VI.42.1:3*

~ **conflict** can seem to be interpersonal, but it must be intrapersonal first. *T-7.III.12.5*

~ the term "intrapersonal" is an **ego** term, because "persona" implies "of one person" and not of others. "Interpersonal" has similar **error** in that it refers to something that exists among different or separate people. *T-7.III.13.1:2*

INVENT

DICTIONARY: *create or design (something that has not existed before); be the originator of.*

HOLY SPIRIT *wasted effort*

~ inventiveness is really wasted effort, even in its most ingenious forms. We do not have to explain anything. This is why we need not trouble ourselves with inventiveness. The highly specific nature of invention is not worthy of the abstract creativity of God's **creations.** *T-4.III.40.3:6*

INVULNERABILITY

DICTIONARY: *impossible to harm or damage.*

HOLY SPIRIT

~ the truly helpful are invulnerable because **they** are not protecting their egos, so that **nothing** can **hurt** them. *T-4.VIII.102.3*

~ safety is the complete relinquishment of **attack.** *T-6.IV.43.1*

~ the remembrance of **love** therefore brings invulnerability with it. *T-9.IX.76.6*

~ the recognition of your own invulnerability is so important in the restoration of your **sanity.** For if **you** accept your invulnerability, **you** are recognizing that **attack** has no effect. *T-11.VI.44.1:2*

~ **you** are invulnerable because **you** are **guiltless.** *T-11.X.96.1*

~ **teach** him that whatever **he** may try to do to **you,** your perfect **freedom** from the **belief** that **you** can be harmed shows him **he** is **guiltless.** He can do **nothing** that can **hurt you.** *T-13.VIII.71.2:3*

~ those who accept the **Atonement** are invulnerable. *T-13.VIII.73.6*

~ your safety lies in **truth** and not in lies. **Love** is your safety. *W-pII.ST261.5.3*

JESUS

DICTIONARY: *the central figure of the Christian* **religion***. Jesus conducted a* **mission** *of preaching and* **healing** *(with reported miracles) in Palestine in about ad 28–30, which is described in the Gospels. His followers considered him to be the* **Christ** *or Messiah and the* **Son of God***, and* **belief** *in his* **resurrection** *from the dead is the central tenet of Christianity.*

EGO

~ **you** would imprison me behind the obstacles **you** raise to **freedom** and bar my **way** to **you.** *T-19.V.67.3*

HOLY SPIRIT; *Prince of* **Peace***,* **Lamb of God***,* **Spirit***,* **teacher** *of the* **ego***, model for* **decision***, model for* **rebirth***,* **salvation** *of the* **world***,* **atonement***, your* **resurrection** *and your* **life***, manifestation of the Holy.*

~ **i** am the **Atonement.** *T-1.I.49.2*

~ **i** came to fulfill the law by reinterpreting it. The law itself, if properly understood, offers only protection to **man.** *T-1.I.65.5:6*

~ if **I** merely intervened between your thoughts and their results, **I** would be tampering with a basic law of **cause** and effect, the most fundamental law there is in this **world.** *T-2.V.93.3*

~ **time** and space are under my control. *T-2.V.104.7*

~ **i** was not punished because **you** were bad. *T-3.III.14.5*

~ **i** was a **man** who remembered the **Soul** and its **knowledge**, and as a **man** I did not attempt to counteract **error** with **knowledge** so much as to correct **error** from the bottom up. **I** demonstrated both the powerlessness of the **body** and the **power** of the **mind**. By uniting my **will** with that of my **Creator**, **I** naturally remembered the **Soul** and its own real **purpose.** *T-3.VI.48.3:5*

~ **i** cannot unite your **will** with God's for **you**, but **I** can erase all misperceptions from your **mind** if **you** will bring it under my **guidance**. Only your misperceptions stand in your own **way**. Without them your **choice** is certain. *T-3.VI.49.1:3*

~ **i** never **attack** your egos, but **I** do try to **teach you** how their **thought system**[s] arose. When **I** remind **you** of your true **creation**, your egos cannot but respond with **fear.** *T-4.II.9.4:5*

~ **i will teach** with **you** and live with **you** if **you will** think with me, but my **goal will** always be to absolve **you** finally from the **need** for a **teacher.** *T-4.II.12.6*

~ **i will substitute** for your **ego** if **you wish** but never for your **Soul.** *T-4.II.20.1*

~ **i** can be entrusted with your **body** and your **ego** simply because this enables **you** not to be concerned with them and lets me **teach you** their unimportance. *T-4.II.20.4*

~ **i need** devoted teachers who **share** my aim of **healing** the **mind.** *T-4.II.21.2*

~ my **role** is to separate the true from the false in your unconscious so it can break through the barriers the **ego** has set up and shine into your minds. *T-4.IV.47.5*

~ **i** elected both for your sake and mine to demonstrate that the most outrageous assault as judged by the **ego** did not matter. *T-6.II.13.1*

~ **i** am not absent to anyone in any **situation**. Because **I** am always with **you, you** are the **way** and the **truth** and the **light.** *T-7.IV.25.2:3*

~ my **mission** was simply to unite the **will** of the **Sonship** with the **Will** of the **Father** by **being** aware of the Father's **Will** myself. *T-8.V.27.8*

~ my **will will** never be wanting, and if **you want** to **share** it **you will.** *T-8.V.41.8*

~ i give you the lamp and I will go with you. *T-10.II.4.5*

~ i will lead you to your true Father, who hath need of you as I have. *T-10.II.4.7*

~ i am the manifestation of the Holy Spirit, and when you see me, it will be because you have invited Him. *T-11.VIII.66.1*

~ in me you have already overcome every temptation that would hold you back. We walk together on the way to quietness that is the gift of God. *T-12.VII.75.1:2*

~ my task is not completed until I have lifted every voice with mine. And yet it is not mine, for as it is my gift to you, so was it the Father's gift to me, given me through His Spirit. *T-12.VII.76.2:3*

~ like you my faith and my belief are centered on what I treasure. The difference is that I love only what God loves with me, and because of this, I treasure you beyond the value that you set on yourselves, even unto the worth that God has placed upon you. I love all that He created, and all my faith and my belief I offer unto it. My faith in you is strong as all the love I give my Father. My trust in you is without limit and without the fear that you will hear me not. I thank the Father for your loveliness and for the many gifts that you will let me offer to the Kingdom in honor of its wholeness, which is of God. *T-13.IV.33.1:6*

~ it is because I learned for you that you can learn of me. I would but teach you what is yours. *T-15.IV.31.2:3*

~ my birth in you is your awakening to grandeur. *T-15.IV.31.4*

~ to see me is to see me in everyone and offer everyone the gift you offer me. *T-15.X.93.4*

~ the Prince of Peace was born to reestablish the condition of love. *T-15.XI.107.2*

~ i would enter into all your relationships and step between you and your fantasies. *T-17.IV.26.1*

~ i became the symbol of your sin, and so I had to die instead of you. *T-19.V.56.2*

~ let me be to you the symbol of the end of guilt. *T-19.V.65.1*

~ i surmounted guilt and overcame the world. *T-19.V.65.5*

~ to your tired eyes I bring a vision of a different world, so new and clean and fresh you will forget the pain and sorrow that you saw before. *T-31.VIII.93.6*

~ god has ordained I cannot call in vain, and in His certainty I rest content. *T-31.VIII.94.5*

~ god would not have Heaven incomplete. It waits for you, as I do I. I am incomplete without your part in me. *W-pI.Rev V.10.5:7*

~ i take the journey with you. For I share your doubts and fears a little while, that you may come to me who recognize the road by which all fears and doubts are overcome. We walk together. I must understand uncertainty and pain, although I know they have no meaning. Yet a savior must remain with those he teaches, seeing what they see, but still retaining in his mind the way that led him out and now will lead you out with him. God's Son is crucified until you walk along the road with me. *W-pI.Rev V.8.1:6*

~ my resurrection comes again each time I lead a brother safely to the place at which the journey ends and is forgot. I am renewed each time a brother learns there is a way from misery and pain. I am reborn each time a brother's mind turns to the light in him and looks for me. I have forgotten no one. Help me now to lead you back to where the journey was begun, to make another choice with me. *W-pI.Rev V.9.1:5*

~ what I am are you as well. *W-pII.ST351.1.4*

~ one who has perfectly accepted the Atonement for himself can heal the world. Indeed, he has already done so. Temptation may recur to others, but never to this one. He has become the risen Son of God. He has overcome death, because he has accepted life. He has recognized himself as God created him, and in so doing he has recognized all living things as part of him. There is now no limit on his power, because it is the Power of God. So has his name become the name of God, for he no longer sees himself as separate from Him. *M-23.2.1:8*

228

~ in remembering Jesus, **you** are remembering **God**. The whole **relationship** of the Son to the **Father** lies in him. His **part** in the **Sonship** is also yours, and his completed **learning** guarantees your own success. *M-23.3.2:4*

~ the **name** of Jesus **Christ** as such is but a **symbol**. But it stands for **love** that is not of this **world**. It is a **symbol** that can safely be used as a replacement for the many names of all the Gods **you** pray to. It becomes the shining **symbol** for the **word** of **God**, so close to what it stands for that the **little** space between the two is lost the moment that the **name** is called to **mind**. Remembering His **name** is to **give** thanks for all the gifts that **God** has given **you**. And **gratitude** to **God** becomes the **way** in which **He** is remembered, for **love** cannot be far behind a grateful heart and thankful **mind**. *M-23.4.1:6*

~ jesus has led the **way**. *M-23.5.1*

~ **he** has asked for **love**, but only that **he** might **give** it to **you**. **You** do not **love** yourself. But in his eyes your loveliness is so complete and flawless that **he** sees in it an **image** of his **Father**. **You** become the **symbol** of his **Father here** on earth. To **you** he looks for hope, because in **you** he sees no **limit** and no stain to mar your beautiful **perfection**. In his eyes **Christ's vision** shines in perfect constancy. **He** has remained with **you**. *M-23.5.3.9*

~ one who laid all limits by and went beyond the farthest reach of **learning**. **He will** take **you** with him, for **he** did not go **alone**. And **you** were with him then, as **you** are **now**. *M-23.6.8:10*

~ jesus has come to **answer** yours. In him **you** find God's **Answer**. *M-23.7.7:8*

JOIN |join|

DICTIONARY: *link; connect.*

EGO

~ egos do join together in temporary allegiance but always for what each one can get separately. *T-6.V.66.1*

~ it never joins except to strengthen itself. *T-16.I.2.3*

~ the **ego** joins with an **illusion** of yourself **you share** with it. And yet illusions cannot join. **They** are the same, and **they** are **nothing**. Their joining lies in nothingness; two are as meaningless as one or as a thousand. The **ego** joins with **nothing, being nothing**. *T-23.II.9.5:9*

~ **future loss** is not your **fear**. But **present** joining is your dread. *T-26.IX.71.3:4*

HOLY SPIRIT;   *mighty herald of eternity*

~ is the **way** in which **you** learn to **share** with Him the **interpretation** of **perception** that leads to **knowledge**. *T-14.IV.30.12*

~ **you** cannot join with anything except **reality**. *T-14.IV.35.6*

~ **you have** succeeded whenever **you have** reached another **mind** and joined with it. When two minds join as one and **share** one **idea** equally, the first **link** in the **awareness** of the **Sonship** as one has been made. *T-16.III.13.2:3*

~ **you** who hold each other's hand also hold mine, for when **you** joined each other **you** were not **alone**. *T-18.IV.27.1*

~ let us join in **faith** that **He** Who brought us **here** together **will** offer **you** the **innocence you need** and that **you will** accept it for my **love** and His. *T-19.V.98.7*

~ so do the parts of God's Son gradually join in **time**, and with each joining is the end of **time** brought nearer. Each **miracle** of joining is a mighty herald of **eternity**. *T-20.VI.37.5:6*

~ those who **have** joined their brothers **have** detached themselves from their **belief** that their **identity** lies in the **ego**. *T-21.V.43.4*

~ that **you** are joined to him is but a **fact**, not an **interpretation**. *T-21.VII.64.6*

~ **you** are joined is your **salvation**—the **gift** of **Heaven**, not the **gift** of **fear**. *T-21.VII.66.1*

~ **nothing** but what is **part** of Him is worthy of **being** joined. Nor is it possible that anything not **part** of Him can join. **Communication** must **have** been restored to those that join, for this **they** could not do through bodies. *T-22.II.13.2:4*

~ into your joined hands is it safely given, for **you** who **share** it **have** become its willing guardians and protectors. *T-22.V.42.7*

~ the **light** that joins **you** shines throughout the **universe**, and because it joins **you**, so it makes **you** one with your **Creator**. And in Him is all **creation** joined. *T-22.VII.65.1:2*

~ what has been forgiven must join, for **nothing** stands between to keep them separate and apart. *T-26.V.26.4*

~ what is unseparated must be joined. And what is joined cannot be separate. *T-28.VIII.61.9:10*

~ when brothers join in **purpose** in the **world** of **fear**, **they** stand already at the edge of the **real world**. *T-30.VI.63.1*

~ when **they** joined and shared a **purpose**, **they** were free to learn their **will** is one. *T-30.VI.69.3*

~ whom **God** has joined remains forever one, at **home** in Him, no **stranger** to Himself. *W-pI.160.8.5*

~ if any two are joined, **He** must be there. It does not matter what their **purpose** is, but **they** must **share** it wholly to succeed. *P-2.II.6.5:6*

~ neither can do this **alone**, but when **they** join, the potentiality for transcending all limitations has been given them. *P-2.III.2.3*

~ where two **have** joined for **healing**, **God** is there. And **He** has guaranteed that **He** **will** hear and **answer** them in **truth**. *P-2.V.4.4:5*

JOURNEY

|ˈjərnē|

DICTIONARY: *an act of traveling from one place to another.*

EGO;   *journey into **darkness**, dark journey, senseless journey, meaningless journey, foolish journey, lonely journey.*

~ the journey **will** seem long and cruel and senseless, for so it is. *T-11.X.91.6*

~ the journey which the **Son** of **God** has set himself is foolish indeed. *T-11.X.92.1*

~ a foolish journey that would lead away from **light**. *T-12.VII.72.1*

~ the lonely journey fails because it has excluded what it would find. *T-14.VI.55.7*

~ journey into **darkness** has been long and cruel, and **you have** gone deep into it. *T-18.IV.26.2*

~ a journey without a **purpose** is still meaningless, and even when it is over, it seems to **make** no **sense**. *T-19.V.99.5*

~ every road was made to separate the journey from the **purpose** it must **have**. *T-31.IV.41.4*

~ the journey is not long except in dreams. *P-3.II.8.8*

HOLY SPIRIT;   *final journey, journey inward, journey to **God**, the journey back, ancient journey, journey without distance, journey to **peace**, journey **home**, freedom's road.*

~ do not embark on foolish journeys, because **they** are indeed in vain. The **ego** may **desire** them, but the **Soul** cannot embark on them, because it is forever unwilling to depart from its Foundation. *T-4.I.2.5:6*

~ the journey is the **way** to what is true. *T-8.V.41.4*

~ the journey to **God** is merely the reawakening of the **knowledge** of where **you** are always and what **you** are forever. It is a journey without distance to a **goal** that has never changed. *T-8.VI.51.1:2*

~ **you will** not take this journey **alone**. *T-10.II.4.6*

~ **i give you** the lamp and **I will** go with you. **You will** not take this journey **alone**. *T-10.II.4.5:6*

~ his is the journey to accomplishment, and the **goal He** sets before **you He will give you**. *T-11.V.39.6*

~ the journey on which his **Father** sets him is one of **release** and **joy**. *T-11.X.92.1*

~ the journey that **we** undertake together is the exchange of dark for **light**, of ignorance for understanding. *T-14.III.16.1*

~ here, with the journey's end before **you**, **you see** its **purpose**. And it is **here you** choose whether to look upon it or wander on, only to return and **make** the **choice** again. *T-19.V.99.7:8*

~ the journey's end is at the place of **peace**. *T-23.II.10.2*

~ there is no journey but to walk with Him. *T-24.VI.46.10*

~ the journey's **goal**, which is but to decide to walk with him, so neither leads nor follows. Thus it is a **way you** go together, not **alone**. *T-31.II.23.5:6*

~ a journey from yourself does not **exist**. *T-31.IV.42.2*

~ this is our final journey, which **we make** for **everyone**. *W-pI.155.11.4*

~ **we** but undertake a journey that is over. Yet it seems to **have a future** still unknown to us. *W-pI.158.3.6:7*

~ **we** but **see** the journey from the point at which it ended, looking back on it, imagining **we make** it once again; reviewing mentally what has gone by. *W-pI.158.4.5*

~ **you** but **make** a journey that is done. *W-pI.169.8.1*

~ **we** are one, and it is but this **oneness** that **we seek** as **we** accomplish these few final steps which end a journey that was not begun. *W-pII.225.2.5*

~ and so the journey which the **Son of God** began has ended in the **Light** from Which **he** came. *W-pII.249.1.7*

~ it cannot be possible to **change** the **course** of those whom **God** has called to Him. *W-pII.E.2.2*

JOY |j o i|

DICTIONARY: *a feeling of great **pleasure** and happiness.*

EGO;   *pain*

~ the **ego** is afraid of the Soul's joy because, once **you have** experienced it, **you will** withdraw all protection from the **ego** and become totally without the investment in **fear**. *T-4.II.17.3*

~ whenever **you** are not wholly joyous it is because **you have** reacted with a lack of **love** to some **Soul** which **God** created. *T-5.IX.94.1*

~ the **opposite** of joy is depression. *T-8.VII.65.2*

~ joy cannot establish its eternal reign where sorrow dwells. *T-12.VII.76.5*

~ the constancy of joy is a **condition** quite alien to your understanding. *T-21.IX.86.1*

HOLY SPIRIT; *awakening, truth, reality, what you are, unified purpose, function, song of thanks.*

~ joy calls forth an integrated willingness to **share** in it and thus promotes the mind's natural impulse to respond as one. *T-5.I.17*

~ only joy increases forever, since joy and **eternity** are inseparable. *T-7.II.5.3*

~ joy was created for **you**. *T-14.II.7.1*

~ joy cannot be perceived except through constant **vision**. *T-21.VIII.84.3*

~ joy is eternal. *T-22.III.18.4*

~ joy does not turn to sorrow, for the eternal cannot **change**. *T-22.III.18.6*

~ joy has no cost. It is your sacred right, and what **you** pay for is not. *T-30.VI.65.9:10*

~ joy characterizes **peace**. By this **experience will you** recognize that **you have** reached it. *W-pI.74.II.5:6*

~ it is your **function** that **you** find it **here** and that **you** find it **now**. *W-pI.100.9.2*

~ joy is just. *W-pI.101.6.4*

~ joy is everywhere. *W-pI.103.1.4*

~ joy and **peace** are not but idle dreams. **They** are your right because of what **you** are. **They** come to **you** from **God**, who cannot **fail** to **give you** what He wills. *W-pI.104.1.1:3*

~ joy is awakening. *W-pI.190.10.3*

~ joy **alone** is **truth**. *W-pI.190.10.4*

~ joy is the inevitable result of **gentleness**. *M-4.16.1*

JUDGMENT |ˈjəjmənt|

DICTIONARY: *the ability to make considered decisions or come to sensible conclusions.*

EGO; *setting of a price, sword of justice, sword of judgement.*

~ judgment always involves rejection. It is not an ability which emphasizes only the positive aspects of what is judged, whether it be in or out of the **self**. *T-3.VIII.62.1:2*

~ implies the **belief** that **reality** is yours to choose from. *T-3.VIII.62.9*

~ the strain of constant judgment is virtually intolerable. *T-3.VIII.65.6*

~ ability which is so debilitating. *T-3.VIII.65.7*

~ judgment always imprisons because it separates segments of **reality** according to the highly unstable scales of **desire**. *T-3.VIII.71.4*

~ the **ego**, which judges only in terms of **threat** or non-**threat** to itself. *T-4.VI.70.3*

~ the **ego** as a judge gives anything but an impartial judgment. *T-8.VIII.74.5*

~ there is a price **you will** pay for judgment because judgment is the setting of a price. And as **you** set it, **you will** pay it. *T-8.XI.115.5:6*

~ for the **mind** that judges perceives itself as separate from the **mind being** judged. *T-11.X.85.4*

~ whenever judgment enters, **reality** has slipped away. *T-12.VII.63.5*

~ ego's judgments. Separately, **they** seem to hold, but put them together and the system of **thought** which arises from joining them is incoherent and utterly chaotic. *T-14.VI.54.1:2*

~ **he** who judges **will have need** of idols which **will** hold the judgment off from resting on himself. *T-29.X.62.5*

~ your judgment rests upon the **witness** that your senses offer **you**. *W-pI.151.3.2*

~ **you** cannot judge. **You** merely can believe the ego's judgments, all of which are false. *W-pI.151.4.3:4*

~ judgment was made to be a weapon used against the **truth**. It separates what it is **being** used against and sets it off as if it were a **thing** apart. And then it makes of it what **you** would **have** it be. It judges what it cannot **understand** because it cannot **see** totality and therefore judges falsely. *W-pII.311.1.1:4*

~ judgment, like other devices by which the **world** of illusions is maintained, is totally misunderstood by the **world**. It is actually confused with wisdom and substitutes for **truth**. As the **world** uses the term, an individual is capable of "**good**" and "bad" judgment, and his education aims at strengthening the former and minimizing the latter. There is, however, considerable **confusion** about what these categories mean. What is "**good** judgment" to one is "bad judgment" to another. Further, even the same person classifies the same action as showing "**good**" judgment at one **time** and "bad" judgment at another **time**. Nor can any consistent criteria for determining what these categories are be really taught. *M-10.1.1:7*

~ judgment is a mental activity. Judgment is a **decision**, made again and again, against **creation** and its **Creator**. It is a **decision** to perceive the **universe** as **you** would **have** created it. It is a **decision** that **truth** can lie and must be lies. *P-2.IV.1.2:5*

HOLY SPIRIT; *whim, **injustice**, children's game, weapon, toy.*

~ judgment is not an essential attribute of **God**. **Man** brought judgment into **being** only because of the **separation**. After the **separation**, however, there was a place for judgment as one of the many **learning** devices which had to be built into the overall **plan**. *T-2.VI.106.3:5*

~ **everyone** is much better off without judgment. When the Bible says, "Judge not that ye be not judged" it merely **means** that if **you** judge the **reality** of others at all, **you will** be unable to avoid judging your own. The **choice** to judge rather than to know was the **cause** of the **loss** of **peace**. Judgment is the process on which **perception**, but not cognition, rests. *T-3.VIII.61.3:6*

~ judgment, like any other **defense**, can be used to **attack** or protect, to **hurt** or to heal. *T-4.V.64.5*

~ judgment is the **function** of the **Holy Spirit** and one which **He** is perfectly equipped to fulfill. *T-8.VIII.74.4*

~ if it is your judgment, it **will** be wrong, for judgment is not your **function**. If it is the judgment of the **Holy Spirit**, it **will** be right, for judgment is His **function**. *T-11.VIII.73.4:5*

~ **you will** judge against yourselves, but **He will** judge for **you**. *T-11.VIII.73.7*

~ the only judgment involved at all is the Holy Spirit's one division into two categories—one of **love** and the other the **call** for **love**. *T-14.VI.52.1*

~ judgment always rests on the **past**, for **past experience** is the basis on which **you** judge. Judgment becomes **impossible** without the **past**, for without it **you** do not **understand** anything. *T-15.VI.45.3:4*

~ judgment is but a toy, a whim, the senseless **means** to play the idle game of **death** in your imagination. *T-20.IX.73.1*

~ judgment **will** always **give you** false directions. *T-21.II.4.5*

~ no one can judge on partial evidence. That is not judgment. It is merely an opinion based on ignorance and **doubt**. Its seeming **certainty** is but a cloak for the uncertainty it would conceal. It needs irrational **defense** because it is irrational. And its **defense** seems strong, convincing, and without a **doubt** because of all the doubting underneath. *W-pI.151.1.1:6*

~ judgment has no **value** unless the **goal** is **sin**. *T-20.VIII.64.7*

~ judgment **you** taught yourself. *T-20.VIII.65.4*

~ we cannot judge ourselves, nor **need** we do so. These are but attempts to hold **decision** off, and to **delay** commitment to our **function**. It is not our **part** to judge our **worth**, nor can **we** know what **role** is best for us; what **we** can do **within** a larger **plan** we cannot **see** in its entirety. *W-pI.154.1.3:5*

~ and in His judgment **will** a **world** unfold in perfect **innocence** before your eyes. *W-pI.164.5.4*

~ judgment destroys honesty and shatters **trust**. *M-4.13.10*

~ to judge is to be dishonest, for to judge is to assume a position **you** do not **have**. Judgment without **self**-deception is **impossible**. Judgment implies that **you have** been deceived in your brothers. *M-4.13.2:4*

~ judgment implies a lack of **trust**. *M-4.13.6*

~ without judgment are all things equally acceptable, for who could judge otherwise. *M-4.13.8*

~ in **order** to judge anything rightly, one would **have** to be fully aware of an inconceivably wide range of things, **past**, **present**, and to come. One would **have** to recognize in **advance** all the effects of his judgments on **everyone** and everything involved in them in any **way**. And one would **have** to be certain there is no distortion in his **perception**, so that his judgment would be wholly fair to **everyone** on whom it rests, **now** and in the **future**. *M-10.3.3:5*

~ wisdom is not judgment; it is the relinquishment of judgment. *M-10.4.5*

~ there is Someone with **you** Whose judgment is perfect. **He** does know all the facts, **past**, **present**, and to come. **He** does know all the effects of His judgment on **everyone** and everything involved in any **way**. And **He** is wholly fair to **everyone**, for there is no distortion in His **perception**. *M-10.4.7:10*

~ **god** has sent His Judgment to **answer** yours. Gently His Judgment substitutes for yours. *M-11.3.4:5*

~ in the Judgment of **God**, what is reflected **here** is only **peace**. *M-11.3.9*

~ god's Judgment is His **justice**. Onto this—a judgment wholly lacking in **condemnation**, an evaluation based entirely on **love**—you have projected your **injustice**, attributing to **God** the lens of warped **perception** through which **you** look. Now it belongs to Him and not to **you**. **You** are afraid of Him and do not **see you** hate and **fear** your Self as enemy. *M-19.4.6:9*

JUSTICE |ˈjəstəs|

DICTIONARY: *just **behavior** or treatment.*

EGO

~ justice is a temporary expedient or an attempt to **teach man** the **meaning** of mercy. Its judgmental side arises only because **man** is capable of **injustice** if that is what his **mind** creates. *T-2.II.21.1:2*

~ this is not justice but **insanity**. *T-25.IX.65.6*

~ and in the total cost, the greater his, the less is yours. And justice, **being blind**, is satisfied by **being** paid, it matters not by whom. *T-25.IX.66.9:10*

HOLY SPIRIT;   *divine **correction, salvation, interpretation, miracle** of justice.*

~ justice looks on all in the same **way**. It is not just that one should lack for what another has. For that is **vengeance** in whatever **form** it takes. Justice demands no **sacrifice**, for any **sacrifice** is made that **sin** may be preserved and kept. *T-25.IX.66.2:5*

~ justice cannot punish those who **ask** for **punishment** but **have** a Judge Who knows that **they** are wholly **innocent** in **truth**. In justice, **He** is bound to set them free and **give** them all the honor **they** deserve and **have** denied themselves because **they** are not fair and cannot **understand** that **they** are **innocent**. *T-25.IX.70.1:2*

~ **love** and justice are not different. *T-25.IX.72.6*

~ **god** knows of no **injustice**. *T-25.IX.73.3*

~ **god** ensured that justice would be done unto the Son **He** loves and would protect from all unfairness **you** might **seek** to offer, believing **vengeance** is his proper due. *T-25.IX.73.8*

~ in justice then does **love** correct mistakes, but not in **vengeance**. *T-25.IX.74.11*

~ **love** and justice are not separate. And both are strengthened by their **union** with each other. Without **love** is justice prejudiced and weak. And **love** without justice is **impossible**. *T-25.IX.74.5:8*

~ without impartiality there is no justice. *T-25.IX.76.1*

~ only justice can set up a state in which there is no loser, no one left unfairly treated and deprived, and thus with grounds for **vengeance**. *T-25.X.82.1*

~ no one can be unjust to **you**, unless **you have** decided first to be unjust. *T-25.X.84.7*

~ god's justice rests in **gentleness** upon His Son and keeps him safe from all injustices the **world** would lay upon him. *T-26.II.8.4*

~ the **miracle** of justice can correct all errors. *T-26.III.13.1*

~ justice is total. There is no such **thing** as partial justice. *T-26.III.14.1:2*

~ justice is the divine **correction** for **injustice**. *M-19.1.1*

~ justice corrects the interpretations to which **injustice** gives rise and cancels them out. *M-19.1.3*

~ in this **world**, however, **forgiveness** depends on justice since all **attack** can only be unjust. Justice is the Holy Spirit's verdict upon the **world**. Except in His **judgment**, justice is **impossible**, for no one in the **world** is capable of making only just interpretations and laying all injustices aside. *M-19.1.5:7*

~ justice, like its **opposite**, is an **interpretation**. It is, however, the one **interpretation** that leads to **truth**. This becomes possible because, while it is not true in itself, justice includes **nothing** that opposes **truth**. There is no inherent conflict between justice and **truth**; one is but the first small **step** in the direction of the other. *M-19.2.1:4*

~ god's justice points to **Heaven** just because it is entirely impartial. It accepts all evidence that is brought before it, omitting **nothing** and assessing **nothing** as separate and apart from all the **rest**. From this one standpoint does it judge, and this **alone**. **Here** all **attack** and **condemnation** becomes meaningless and indefensible. **Perception** rests, the **mind** is still, and **light** returns again. **Vision** is **now** restored. What had been lost has **now** been found. The **peace** of **God** descends on all the **world** and **we** can **see**. And **we** can **see**! *M-19.5.5:13*

KARMA

DICTIONARY: *the sum of a person's actions in this and previous states of existence, viewed as deciding their fate in **future** existences.*

HOLY SPIRIT

~ **"Vengeance** is Mine sayeth the Lord," is a strictly karmic viewpoint. It is a real misperception of **truth** by which **man** assigns his own **"evil"** past to **God**. The "evil" conscience" from the **past** has **nothing** to do with **God**. He did not create it, and He does not maintain it. **God** does not believe in karmic retribution. His Divine **Mind** does not create that way. He does not hold the **evil** deeds of a **man** even against himself. *T-3.III.15.1:7*

KILL

|ˈkil|

DICTIONARY: *cause the **death** of (a person, animal, or other living **thing**).*

EGO

~ **death** wishes do not kill in the physical **sense**, but **they** do kill spiritual **awareness**. *T-2.V.91.2*

~ the **ego** does **want** to kill you, and if **you** identify with it, **you** must believe its **goal** is yours. *T-12.II.5.6*

~ the glitter of **guilt you** laid upon the **body** would kill it. For what the **ego** loves, it kills for its obedience. But what obeys it not, it cannot kill. *T-19.V.81.6:8*

~ a murderer is frightened, and those who kill **fear death**. *T-20.IV.19.5*

~ no one thinks of murder and escapes the **guilt** the **thought** entails. *T-23.IV.41.8*

~ not one **illusion** of protection stands against the **faith** in murder. *T-23.IV.46.9*

~ kill or be killed. *M-17.7.11*

KINGDOM

|ˈkiNGdəm|

DICTIONARY: *a realm associated with or regarded as **being** under the control of a particular person or **thing**.*

EGO; *little kingdom, tiny kingdom.*

~ your **ego** can keep **you** in exile from the Kingdom, but in the Kingdom itself it has no **power**. *T-5.VI.50.10*

~ by making another Kingdom which **you** valued, **you** did not keep only the Kingdom of **God** in your minds and thus placed **part** of your **mind outside** it. *T-6.V.94.4*

~ your divided minds are blocking the **extension** of the Kingdom. *T-7.VII.67.4*

~ surrounded by **darkness**, guarded by **attack**, and reinforced by **hate**. **Within** its barricades is still a tiny segment of the **Son of God**, complete and holy, serene and unaware of what **you** think surrounds it. *T-18.X.85.4:5*

~ its **vision** is distorted, and the messages it transmits to **you** who made it to **limit** your **awareness** are **little** and limited and so fragmented **they** are meaningless. *T-18.X.86.4*

~ **special** kingdom, apart from **God**, away from **truth** and from **salvation**. *T-24.III.24.4*

HOLY SPIRIT; *love, freedom.*

~ your kingdom is not of this **world** because it was given **you** from beyond this **world**. *T-3.IX.80.9*

~ the Kingdom of **Heaven** is the right of the **Soul**, whose beauty and dignity are far beyond **doubt**, beyond **perception**, and stand forever as the mark of the **Love** of **God** for His **creations**, who are wholly worthy of Him and only of Him. *T-4.II.19.5*

~ the Kingdom of **Heaven** is **within you.** *T-4.IV.41.1*

~ the Kingdom is attained through the **Atonement**, which releases **you** to create. *T-5.VII.59.6*

~ **attack within** the Kingdom is **impossible.** *T-6.V.46.2*

~ **you** could not remain **within** the Kingdom without **love** and since the Kingdom is **love.** *T-6.V.46.4*

~ in the Kingdom, where **you** are and what **you** are is perfectly certain. *T-6.V.51.2*

~ **being alone** lives in the Kingdom, where everything lives in **God** without **question**. The **time** that was spent on questioning in the **dream** has given **way** to **creation** and to its **eternity.** *T-6.V.51.5:6*

~ in the Kingdom there is no **teaching** or **learning**, because there is no **belief**. There is only **certainty.** *T-7.III.14.4:5*

~ it belongs to Him and is therefore like Him. That is its **reality**, and **nothing** can assail it. *T-7.III.18.10:11*

~ there is no **confusion** in the Kingdom, because there is only one **meaning.** *T-7.III.18.3*

~ to be in the Kingdom is merely to focus your full attention on it. *T-7.V.29.1*

~ its **extension** is your **joy.** *T-7.VII.67.4*

~ the Kingdom is forever extending, because it is in the **Mind** of **God.** *T-7.X.94.1*

~ the Kingdom is the result of premises, just as this **world** is. *T-7.X.97.8*

~ the Kingdom of **God** includes all His Sons and their children, who are like the Sons as **they** are like the **Father.** *T-7.XII.113.7*

~ **you** cannot sell the Kingdom of **Heaven.** *T-11.V.41.6*

~ before the glorious radiance of the Kingdom, **guilt** melts away and, transformed into kindness, **will** never more be what it was. Every reaction that **you experience will** be so purified that it is fitting as a hymn of **praise** unto your **Father.** *T-13.IV.34.3:4*

~ my Kingdom is not of this **world** because it is in **you.** *T-15.IV.31.6*

~ his Kingdom has no limits and no end. *T-16.IV.27.7*

~ and **you will** recognize yourself and **see** your **little** garden gently transformed into the Kingdom of **Heaven** with all the **love** of its **Creator** shining upon it. *T-18.IX.80.4*

~ his Kingdom is united—thus it was created, and thus **will** it ever be. *T-26.VIII.62.8*

~ **he** did not set His Kingdom up **alone.** *T-30.III.33.7*

~ the Kingdom of **God** is **within you** and can never be lost. *W-pI.77.3.3*

~ what **we** cannot speak of, for **you** go from there to where words **fail** entirely, into a silence where the **language** is unspoken and yet surely understood. **Communication**, unambiguous and plain as day, remains unlimited for all **eternity.** *W-pI.129.4.1:2*

238

KNOWLEDGE

DICTIONARY: *facts, information, and skills acquired by a person through* **experience** *or education; the theoretical or practical understanding of a subject.*

EGO;   *power*

~ knowledge cannot dawn on a **mind** full of illusions, because **truth** and illusions are irreconcilable. *T-9.X.86.6*

~ whenever **you** think **you** know, **peace will** depart from **you** because **you have** abandoned the **Teacher** of **Peace**. *T-14.VII.73.3*

~ not to know **God** is to **have** no knowledge. *P-2.II.4.6*

~ without knowledge one can **have** only **belief**. *P-2.II.4.7*

HOLY SPIRIT;   *true knowledge, Christ's knowledge,* **power**.

~ the knowledge which illuminates rather than obscures is the knowledge which not only sets **you** free, but which also shows **you** clearly that **you** are free. *T-2.I.16.2*

~ knowledge is **power** because it is certain. *T-3.V.30.5*

~ true **perception** is the basis for knowledge, but knowing is the affirmation of **truth**. *T-3.V.31.1*

~ knowledge is timeless, because **certainty** is not questionable. **You** know when **you have** ceased to **ask** questions. *T-3.V.32.6:7*

~ knowledge is the result of **revelation** and induces only **thought**. *T-3.V.35.10*

~ knowledge comes from the **altar within** and is timeless because it is certain. *T-3.V.35.12*

~ knowledge brings the mental **strength** for creative thinking but not for right **doing**. *T-3.V.35.8*

~ knowledge preceded both **perception** and **time** and **will** ultimately replace them. That is the real **meaning** of the Biblical description of **God** as "Alpha and Omega, the Beginning and the End." It also explains the quotation, "Before Abraham was **I** am." **Perception** can and must be stabilized, but knowledge is stable. "**Fear God** and keep His commandments" should read "Know **God** and accept His **certainty**." There are no strangers in His **creation**. To create as **He** created, **you** can create only what **you** know and accept as yours. **God** knows His Children with perfect **certainty**. **He** created them by knowing them. **He** recognized them perfectly. *T-3.V.37.2:11*

~ knowledge does not do anything. It can be perceived as an attacker, but it cannot **attack**. *T-3.VI.47.4:5*

~ ingenuity has almost totally divorced him from knowledge. Knowledge does not require ingenuity. When **we** say "the **truth** shall set **you** free," **we** mean that all this kind of thinking is a waste of **time**, but that **you** are free of the **need** to engage in it if **you** are willing to let it go. *T-3.VII.55.3:5*

~ knowledge transcends all the **laws** which govern **perception** because partial knowledge is **impossible**. It is all one and has no separate parts. *T-3.VII.58.6:7*

~ in the presence of knowledge, all **judgment** is automatically suspended, and this is the process which enables recognition to replace **perception**. *T-3.VIII.63.6*

~ **god** created knowledge and gave it freely to His **creations**. *T-3.IX.75.5*

~ knowledge cannot deceive. *T-3.IX.77.2*

~ only the **oneness** of knowledge is conflictless. *T-3.IX.80.8*

~ abstract **thought** applies to knowledge, because knowledge is completely impersonal and examples are irrelevant to its understanding. *T-4.III.24.4*

~ knowledge never involves comparisons. That is its essential **difference** from everything else the **mind** can grasp. *T-4.VII.82.4:5*

~ knowledge is always ready to flow everywhere, but it cannot oppose. Therefore, **you** can obstruct it, although **you** can never lose it. The **Holy Spirit** is the **Christ Mind**, which senses the knowledge that lies beyond **perception**. It came into **being** with the **separation** as a protection. *T-5.II.11.3:6*

~ knowledge is sure. *T-5.IV.22.2*

~ knowledge is total. *T-7.VII.57.5*

~ knowledge **will** be restored when **you** meet its conditions. *T-8.I.2.1*

~ knowledge is His **Will**. *T-8.I.2.4*

~ knowledge never changes, so its constellation is permanent. *T-8.VIII.70.7*

~ knowledge is shared with **God**. *T-9.V.34.7*

~ knowledge needs no **correction**. *T-12.VII.67.4*

~ there is **nothing** partial about knowledge. Every aspect is whole, and therefore no aspect is separate. **You** are an aspect of knowledge, **being** in the **Mind** of **God**, Who knows **you**. All knowledge must be yours, for in **you** is all knowledge. *T-13.I.2.1:4*

~ knowledge is far beyond your individual concern. **You**, who are **part** of it and all of it, **need** only realize that it is of the **Father**, not of **you**. *T-13.II.7.4:5*

~ **you** can deny His knowledge, but **you** cannot **change** it. *T-13.III.19.6*

~ the knowledge is not taught, but its conditions must be acquired, for it is **they** that **have** been thrown away. *T-13.VI.48.2*

~ giving Himself is all **He** knows, and so it is all knowledge. *T-13.IX.88.2*

~ ignorance fades away when knowledge dawns. *T-14.IV.24.6*

~ **nothing** can **change** the knowledge given **you** by **God** into unknowingness. *T-14.IV.36.6*

~ whenever **you** fully realize that **you** know not, **peace will** return, for **you will have** invited Him to do so by abandoning the **ego** on behalf of Him. *T-14.VII.73.4*

~ knowledge is therefore of the **mind**, and its conditions are in the **mind** with it. *T-15.VII.63.6*

~ any **part** of knowledge threatens **dissociation** as much as all of it. And all of it **will** come with any **part**. *T-21.VI.55.2:3*

~ knowledge is far beyond attainment of any kind. *T-21.VI.57.4*

~ knowledge has but one law because it has but one **Creator**. *T-25.IV.25.2*

~ knowledge makes no **attack** upon **perception**. *T-26.IV.20.4*

~ **i have** not lost the knowledge of who **I** am because **I have** forgotten it. It has been kept for me in the **Mind** of **God**, who has not left His thoughts. *W-pI.56.6.2:3*

~ their knowledge is direct and wholly shared and wholly one. *W-pI.129.4.5*

~ **we have** not lost the knowledge that **God** gave to us when **He** created us like Him. *W-pI.139.12.1*

~ knowledge is restored after **perception** first is changed and then gives **way** entirely to what remains forever **past** its highest reach. *W-pII.336.1.2*

~ knowledge of **God** has no true **opposite**. *P-2.II.4.5*

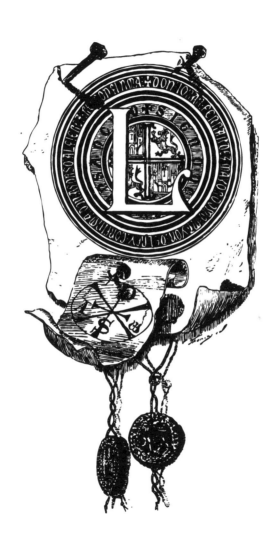

LAMB OF GOD

DICTIONARY:　*a title of Jesus.*

HOLY SPIRIT

~ "the Lamb of **God** who taketh away the sins of the **world**." Those who represent the lamb as blood-stained, an all-too-widespread **error**, do not **understand** the **meaning** of the **symbol**. Correctly understood, it is a very simple parable which merely speaks of my **innocence**. The lion and the lamb lying down together refers to the **fact** that **strength** and **innocence** are not in **conflict** but naturally live in **peace**. "Blessed are the pure in heart for **they** shall **see God**" is another **way** of saying the same **thing**. *T-3.III.22.1:5*

LANGUAGE　　　　　　　　　　　　　　　　　　　　|ˈlaNGgwij|

DICTIONARY:　*the method of human **communication**, either spoken or written, consisting of the use of words in a structured and conventional **way**.*

EGO

~ it has no **meaning**, for its **purpose** is not **communication**, but rather the disruption of **communication**. *T-14.III.21.2*

HOLY SPIRIT

~ the **purpose** of language is **communication**. *T-14.III.21.3*

~ **you** speak two languages at once, and this must lead to unintelligibility. Yet if one **means nothing** and the other everything, only that one is possible for purposes of **communication**. The other but interferes with it. *T-14.III.22.5:7*

~ the language of **communication**, which **you** know perfectly, **you will** not **remember**. *T-15.VII.63.8*

~ our common language lets us speak to all our brothers. *T-30.VIII.88.8*

~ a silence where the language is unspoken and yet surely understood. *W-pI.129.4.1*

~ their language has no words, for what **they** say cannot be symbolized. *W-pI.129.4.4*

LAST JUDGEMENT　　　　　　　　　　　　　　　|ˌlast ˈjəjmənt|

DICTIONARY:　*the **judgement** of humankind expected in some religious traditions to take place at the end of the **world**.*

EGO

~ the Last Judgment is one of the greatest **threat** concepts in man's **perception**. *T-2.VI.106.1*

~ the term "Last Judgment" is frightening not only because it has been falsely projected onto **God**, but also because of the association of "last" with **death**. This is an outstanding example of upside-down **perception**. *T-2.VI.110.3:4*

HOLY SPIRIT;　*Final **Judgement**, God's **Judgement**, justice, **gift**, **final step**.*

~ its length depends, however, on the effectiveness of the **present** speed-up. *T-2.VI.106.7*

~ it **will** be undertaken by **man** with my **help**. It is a final **healing** rather than a meting out of **punishment**, however much **man** may think that **punishment** is deserved. *T-2.VI.108.2:3*

~ the aim of the Last Judgment is to restore right-mindedness to **man**. *T-2.VI.108.5*

~ the Last Judgment might be called a process of right evaluation. It simply **means** that finally all men **will** come to **understand** what is worthy and what is not. After this, their ability to choose can be directed reasonably. *T-2.VI.109.1:3*

~ if the **meaning** of the Last Judgment is objectively examined, it is quite apparent that it is really the doorway to **life**. *T-2.VI.110.5*

~ after the Last Judgment there **will** be no more. *T-3.VIII.61.2*

~ he has perfect **faith** in your final **judgment** because He knows that **He will make** it for **you**. To **doubt** this would be to **doubt** that His **mission will** be fulfilled. *T-13.V.38.5:6*

~ the last evaluation that **will** be possible, the final **judgment** upon this **world**. It is the **judgment** of the **truth** upon **illusion**, of **knowledge** on **perception**—it has no **meaning** and does not **exist**. *T-26.IV.21.2:3*

~ the final **judgment** on the **world** contains no **condemnation**. For it sees the **world** as totally forgiven, without **sin** and wholly purposeless. Without a **cause** and **now** without a **function** in Christ's **sight**, it merely slips away to nothingness. There it was born, and there it ends as well. And all the figures in the **dream** in which the **world** began go with it. Bodies **now** are useless and **will** therefore fade away because the **Son of God** is limitless. *W-pII.ST311.2.1:6*

~ **you** who believed that God's Last Judgment would condemn the **world** to **hell** along with **you**, accept this holy **truth**: God's **Judgment** is the **gift** of the **correction** He bestowed on all your errors, freeing **you** from them and all effects **they** ever seemed to **have**. *W-pII.ST311.3.1*

~ god's Final **Judgment** is as merciful as every **step** in His appointed **plan** to bless His Son and **call** him to return to the eternal **peace** He shares with him. *W-pII.ST311.4.1*

~ this is God's Final **Judgment**: "**You** are still My holy Son, forever **innocent**, forever loving and forever loved, as limitless as your **Creator** and completely changeless and forever pure. Therefore **awaken** and return to Me. **I** am your **Father** and **you** are My Son". *W-pII.ST311.5.1:3*

~ no one can escape God's Final **Judgment**. *M-15.1.2*

~ the Final **Judgment will** not come until it is no longer associated with **fear**. *M-15.1.4*

~ one day each one **will welcome** it, and on that very day it **will** be given him. **He will** hear his sinlessness proclaimed around and around the **world**, setting it free as God's Final **Judgment** on him is received. This is the **judgment** in which **salvation** lies. This is the **judgment** that **will** set him free. This is the **judgment** in which all things are freed with him. **Time** pauses as **eternity** comes near, and silence lies across the **world** that **everyone** may hear this **judgment** of the **Son of God**. *M-15.1.4*

~ his **Judgment** comes to all who stand aside in **quiet** listening and wait for Him. *M-15.3.13*

~ it is your **function** to prepare yourself to hear this **judgment** and to recognize that it is true. *M-15.3.5*

~ god's **judgment** waits for **you** to set **you** free. *M-15.4.3*

~ **you will** be judged, and judged in fairness and in honesty. There is no **deceit** in **God**. His promises are sure. *M-15.4.5:7*

~ his promises **have** guaranteed that His **judgment**, and His **alone**, **will** be accepted in the end. It is your **function** to **make** that end be soon. It is your **function** to hold it to your heart and offer it to all the **world** to keep it safe. *M-15.4.9:11*

~ in His Final **Judgment** is restored the **truth** about the holy **Son of God**. **He** is redeemed, for **he** has heard **God's word** and understood its **meaning**. *M-28.6.6:7*

LAWS

DICTIONARY: *the system of rules that a particular country or community recognizes as regulating the actions of its members and may enforce by the imposition of penalties.*

EGO;   *laws of chaos, chaotic laws.*

~ the ego's laws are strict, and breaches are severely punished. *T-13.III.11.4*

· ~ and those who follow them believe that **they** are guilty, and so **they** must condemn. *T-13.III.11.6*

~ the laws of this **world** cease to hold any **meaning** at all. *T-15.VII.61.2*

~ your insane laws were made to guarantee that **you** would **make** mistakes and **give** them **power** over **you** by accepting their results as your just due. *T-20.V.30.1*

~ perception's laws must be reversed, because **they** are reversals of the laws of **truth**. The laws of **truth** forever **will** be true and cannot be reversed, yet can be seen as upside-down. *T-26.VIII.50.2:3*

~ **you call** them laws and put them under different names in a long catalogue of rituals that **have** no use and serve no **purpose. You** think **you** must obey the "laws" of medicine, of economics, and of **health.** *W-pI.76.4.2:3*

~ these are not laws, but **madness.** *W-pI.76.5.1*

~ for example, the laws of nutrition, of immunization, of medication, and of the body's protection in innumerable ways. Laws of friendship, of "**good**" relationships, and reciprocity. *W-pI.76.8.2:3*

~ how foolish are the laws **you thought** upheld the **world you thought you** saw. *W-pI.76.11.1*

~ i am constantly tempted to **make** up other laws and **give** them **power** over me. **I** suffer only because of my **belief** in them. **They have** no real effect on me at all. *W-pI.88.5.3:5*

~ no laws the **world** obeys can **help you** grasp love's **meaning.** *W-pI.127.5.1*

~ the **world** obeys the laws that **sickness** serves. *W-pI.137.2.4*

~ laws idolatry would **make** to **hide** the **freedom** of the **Son of God.** *W-pII.277.2.1*

HOLY SPIRIT;   *God's laws, law of mind.*

~ fidelity to premises is a law of **mind**, and everything **God** created is faithful to His laws. Fidelity to other laws is also possible, however, not because the laws are true, but because **you** made them. *T-6.V.55.3:4*

~ laws must be adapted to circumstances if **they** are to maintain **order.** *T-7.III.10.7*

~ the laws of **mind** govern thoughts, and **you** do respond to two conflicting voices. *T-7.III.11.3*

~ that **form** of the law is not adapted at all, **being** the law of **creation. God** Himself created the law by creating by it. And His Sons, who create like Him, follow it gladly, knowing that the increase of the **Kingdom** depends on it, just as their own **creation** did. *T-7.III.14.7:9*

~ laws must be communicated if **they** are to be helpful. *T-7.III.15.1*

~ the laws of happiness were created for **you**, not by **you.** *T-8.X.102.5*

~ the laws of **love** are not suspended because **you sleep.** And **you have** followed them through all your nightmares and **have** been faithful in your giving, for **you** were not **alone.** *T-12.VI.57.1:2*

~ between the **future** and the **past**, the laws of **God** must intervene if **you** would free yourselves. **Atonement** stands between them like a lamp that shines so brightly that the **chain** of **darkness** in which **you** bound yourselves **will** disappear. *T-13.III.11.7:8*

~ what **God** has given follows His laws and His **alone.** Nor is it possible for those who follow them to suffer the results of any other **source.** *T-20.V.30.6:7*

~ it cannot be what governs **part** of **God** holds not for all the **rest**. **You** place yourself under the laws **you see** as ruling him. *T-24.VII.58.3:4*

~ one law which holds for every kind of **learning** if it be directed by the One Who knows the **truth**. *W-pI.108.5.3*

~ but learn and do not let your **mind** forget this law of seeing: **you will** look upon that which **you** feel **within**. *W-pI.189.5.3*

LAWS OF CHAOS   *A Course in Miracles Term*

EGO; *laws of order*

~ the first chaotic law is that the **truth** is different for **everyone**. Like all these principles, this one maintains that each is separate and has a different set of thoughts which sets him off from others. This principle evolves from the **belief** there is a hierarchy of illusions; some are more valuable and therefore true. Each one establishes this for himself and makes it true by his **attack** on what another values. And this is justified because the values differ and those who hold them seem to be unlike and therefore enemies. *T-23.III.20.1:5*

~ think how this seems to **interfere** with the first principle of miracles. For this establishes degrees of **truth** among illusions, making it appear that some of them are harder to overcome than others. *T-23.III.21.1:2*

~ all of the mechanisms of **madness** are seen emerging here: the "**enemy**," made strong by keeping hidden the valuable **inheritance** which should be yours; your justified position and **attack** for what has been withheld; and the inevitable **loss** the **enemy** must suffer to save yourself. Thus do the guilty ones protest their "**innocence**." Were **they** not forced into this foul **attack** by the unscrupulous **behavior** of the **enemy**, **they** would respond with only kindness. But in a savage **world**, the kind cannot survive, so **they** must take or else be taken from. *T-23.III.22.1:4*

~ the second law of **chaos**, dear indeed to every worshiper of **sin**, is that each one must **sin** and therefore deserves **attack** and **death**. This principle, closely related to the first, is the demand that errors **call** for **punishment** and not **correction**. For the **destruction** of the one who makes the **error** places him beyond **correction** and beyond **forgiveness**. What **he** has done is thus interpreted as an irrevocable sentence upon himself, which **God** Himself is powerless to overcome. **Sin** cannot be remitted, **being** the **belief** the **Son of God** can **make** mistakes for which his own **destruction** becomes inevitable. *T-23.III.22.1:5*

~ **now** it appears that **they** can never be one again. For one must always be condemned and by the other. **Now** are **they** different and enemies. And their **relationship** is one of opposition, just as the separate aspects of the Son meet only to **conflict** but not to **join**. One becomes weak, the other strong by his defeat. And **fear of God** and of each other **now** appears as sensible, made real by what the **Son of God** has done both to himself and his **Creator**. The arrogance on which the **laws** of **chaos** stand could not be more apparent than emerges **here**. *T-23.III.23.2:8*

~ **here** is a principle which would define what the **Creator** of **reality** must be; what **He** must think and what **He** must believe; and how **He** must respond, believing it. *T-23.III.24.1*

~ the third preposterous **belief** that seems to **make chaos** eternal. For if **God** cannot be mistaken, then **He** must accept his Son's **belief** in what **he** is and **hate** him for it. *T-23.III.24.4:5*

~ **see** how the **fear of God** is reinforced by this third principle. **Now** it becomes **impossible** to turn to Him for **help** in **misery**. For **now** He has become the "**enemy**" Who caused it and to Whom appeal is useless. *T-23.III.25.1:3*

~ and **now** is **conflict** made inevitable and beyond the **help** of God. And **now salvation** must remain **impossible** because the **savior** has become the **enemy**. *T-23.III.25.5:6*

~ only **destruction** can be the outcome. And **God** Himself seems to be siding with it to overcome His Son. *T-23.III.26.4:5*

~ the **ego** values only what it takes. This leads to the fourth law of **chaos**, which, if the others are accepted, must be true. This seeming law is the **belief you have** what **you have** taken. By this, another's **loss** becomes your **gain**, and thus it fails to recognize that **you** can never take away save from yourself. *T-23.III.27.1:4*

~ this is the "**magic**" that **will** cure all of your **pain**; the missing factor in your **madness** that makes it "sane." This is the **reason** why **you** must **attack**. **Here** is what makes your **vengeance** justified. *T-23.III.30.5:7*

~ never is your **possession** made complete. And never **will** your **brother** cease his **attack** on **you** for what **you** stole. Nor **will God** end His **vengeance** upon both, for in His **madness He** must **have** this **substitute** for **love** and **kill you** both. *T-23.III.31.1:3*

~ these are the **laws you** made for your **salvation**. They hold in place the **substitute** for **Heaven** which **you** prefer. This is their **purpose; they** were made for this. There is no point in asking what **they** mean. That is apparent. The **means** of **madness** must be insane. *T-23.III.31.7:12*

~ such a reversal, completely turned around, with **madness sanity**, illusions true, **attack** a kindness, hatred **love** and murder benediction, is the **goal** the **laws** of **chaos** serve. These are the **means** by which the **laws** of **God** appear to be reversed. **Here** do the **laws** of **sin** appear to hold **love** captive and let **sin** go free. *T-23.III.32.6:8*

~ these do not seem to be the goals of **chaos**, for by the great reversal, **they** appear to be the **laws** of **order**. *T-23.III.33.1*

~ in **truth** it does not **function**, yet in dreams, where only shadows play the major roles, it seems most powerful. No law of **chaos** could compel **belief** but for the emphasis on **form** and disregard of content. *T-23.III.34.4:5*

~ some forms it takes seem to **have meaning**, and that is all. *T-23.III.34.7*

~ **you** would maintain and think it true that **you** do not believe these senseless **laws** nor act upon them. *T-23.III.36.1*

~ yet **you** believe them for the **form they** take and do not recognize the content. It never changes. *T-23.III.36.6:7*

~ the **laws** of **chaos** govern all illusions. Their forms **conflict**, making it seem quite possible to **value** some above the others. Yet each one rests as surely on the **belief** the **laws** of **chaos** are the **laws** of **order** as do the others. Each one upholds these **laws** completely, **offering** a certain **witness** that these **laws** are true. The seeming gentler forms of the **attack** are no less certain in their witnessing or their results. Certain it is illusions **will** bring **fear** because of the beliefs that **they** imply, not for their **form**. And lack of **faith** in **love** in any **form** attests to **chaos** as **reality**. *T-23.III.38.1:7*

~ the whole descent from **Heaven** lies in each one. *T-23.III.39.6*

Holy Spirit

~ "**laws** of **chaos**" are meaningless by definition. *T-9.X.88.8*

~ the "**laws**" of **chaos** can be brought to **light**, though never understood. Chaotic **laws** are hardly meaningful and therefore out of reason's sphere. Yet **they** appear to constitute an **obstacle** to **reason** and to **truth**. *T-23.III.19.1:3*

~ because it is their **purpose** to **make** meaningless and to **attack** the **truth**. **Here** are the **laws** that **rule** the **world you** made. And yet **they** govern **nothing** and **need** not be broken; merely looked upon and gone beyond. *T-23.III.19.5:7*

~ when **you** look at what **they** say, **they** cannot be believed. *T-23.III.36.2*

LEARNER

DICTIONARY: *a person who is **learning** a subject or skill.*

EGO; *student, **pupil.***

~ an insane learner learns strange lessons. *T-6.V.70.6*

~ the **mind** of the learner projects its own split, and thus does not perceive consistent minds in others, making him suspicious of their motivation. *T-6.V.73.5*

~ if **you teach** both **sickness** and **healing, you** are both a poor **teacher** and a poor learner. *T-7.VI.40.8*

~ there is **nothing** so frustrating to a learner as to be placed in a **curriculum** which he cannot learn. *T-8.VII.60.1*

HOLY SPIRIT; *happy **learner, teacher,** student, **patient.***

~ the increasing **clarity** of the Holy Spirit's **Voice** makes it **impossible** for the learner not to listen. *T-6.V.74.5*

~ **you** are the learner; He the **Teacher.** Do not confuse your **role** with His, for this **will** never bring **peace** to anyone. *T-16.II.6.6:7*

~ the **joy** of **teaching** is in the learner, who offers it to the **teacher** in **gratitude** and shares it with him. *T-16.IV.27.4*

~ he who was the learner becomes a **teacher of God** himself, for he has made the one **decision** that gave his **teacher** to him. He has seen in another person the same interests as his own. *M-2.5.8:9*

LEARNING

DICTIONARY: *the acquisition of **knowledge** or skills through **experience, study,** or by **being** taught.*

EGO; *effort, will.*

~ all learning involves attention and **study** at some **level.** *T-3.I.1.2*

~ learning is perceived as frightening is because learning does lead to the relinquishment (not **destruction**) of the **ego** to the **light** of the **Soul.** *T-4.II.9.1*

~ learning is **impossible** without **memory,** since it cannot be consistent unless it is remembered. *T-7.III.17.2*

~ when your learning promotes depression instead of **joy, you** cannot be listening to God's joyous **Teacher,** and **you** must be learning amiss. *T-8.VII.65.3*

~ **you** cannot learn of perfect **love** with a split **mind** because a split **mind** has made itself a poor **learner** poor learners **need special** teaching. **You have** learning handicaps in a very literal **sense.** *T-11.VI.46.3:4*

~ **you** cannot transfer what **you have** not learned, and the impairment of the ability to generalize is a crucial learning failure. *T-11.VI.48.4*

~ "**seek** and do not find." Translated into curricular terms, this is the same as saying, "Try to learn but do not succeed." *T-11.VI.49.1:2*

~ your **will** speaks against your learning, as your learning speaks against your **will,** and so **you** fight against learning and succeed, for that is your **will.** *T-11.VI.50.4*

~ whenever **they trust** themselves, **they will** not learn. **They have** destroyed their motivation for learning by thinking **they** already know. *T-14.VII.72.2:3*

~ **little** learning, strange in outcome and incredible in difficulty. *T-31.I.6.6*

~ the learning of the **world** is built upon a **concept** of the **self** adjusted to the world's **reality.** *T-31.V.43.1*

~ yet is all learning which the **world** directs begun and ended with the single aim of **teaching you** this **concept** of yourself, that **you will** choose to follow this world's **laws** and never **seek** to go beyond its roads nor realize the **way you see** yourself. *T-31.V.50.2*

~ if **you** realized that **you** do not perceive your own best interests, **you** could be taught what **they** are. But in the presence of your conviction that **you** do know what **they** are, **you** cannot learn. *W-pI.24.2.1:2*

~ it is hard to **teach** the **mind** a thousand alien names and thousands more. Yet **you** believe this is what learning **means**—its one essential **goal** by which **communication** is achieved and concepts can be meaningfully shared. *W-pI.184.5.2:3*

HOLY SPIRIT;   *being, ability, change, will.*

~ learning itself, like the classrooms in which it occurs, is temporary. *T-2.II.39.5*

~ to learn has no **value** when **change** of understanding is no longer necessary. The eternally creative **have nothing** to learn. Only after the **separation** was it necessary to direct the creative forces to learning because changed **behavior** had become mandatory. *T-2.II.39.6:8*

~ this serves to bring them into closer and closer accord with the **Sonship**. *T-2.II.40.2*

~ only while there are different degrees is learning meaningful. *T-2.II.40.3*

~ corrective learning always begins with the awakening of the **Spiritual eye** and the turning away from the **belief** in physical **sight**. *T-2.III.67.1*

~ learning **means change**. *T-4.II.7.5*

~ learning and wanting to learn are inseparable. *T-4.VI.73.4*

~ all learners learn best when **they** believe that what **they** are trying to learn is of **value** to them. *T-4.VI.73.5*

~ learn what **you teach** and that **you want** to learn **peace**. *T-6.V.90.2*

~ learning is joyful if it leads **you** along your natural path and facilitates the development of what **you have**. *T-8.III.9.7*

~ of yourself, **you** cannot learn. *T-11.VI.47.2*

~ the learning **situation** in which **you** placed yourself is **impossible**, and in this **situation you** clearly require a **special Teacher** and a **special curriculum**. Poor learners are not **good** choices for teachers, either for themselves or for anyone else. *T-11.VI.47.3:4*

~ under the proper learning conditions, which **you** can neither provide nor **understand**, **you will** become excellent learners and teachers. *T-11.VI.51.6*

~ his learning is as unlimited as **he** is. *T-11.VI.52.7*

~ the interference in your motivation for learning is exactly the same as that which interferes with all your thinking. *T-13.VIII.64.1*

~ learning **will** be commensurate with motivation. *T-13.VIII.64.1*

~ learning is living **here**. *T-13.VIII.66.2*

~ learning has been accomplished before its effects are manifest. Learning is therefore in the **past**, but its influence determines the **present** by giving it whatever **meaning** it holds for **you**. Your learning gives the **present** no **meaning** at all. **Nothing you have** ever learned can **help you understand** the **present** or **teach you** how to **undo** the **past**. *T-14.VII.60.2:5*

~ **where** learning ends there **God** begins, for learning ends before Him Who is complete where **He** begins and where there is no end. *T-18.XI.95.4*

~ learning ends when **you have** recognized all it is not. *T-18.XI.96.3*

~ learning is useless in the Presence of your **Creator**, whose **acknowledgment** of **you** and yours of Him so far transcend all learning that everything **you** learned is meaningless, replaced forever by the **knowledge** of **love** and its one **meaning**. *T-18.XI.96.6*

~ on your learning depends the welfare of the **world**. *T-22.VII.60.1*

~ its only **purpose** is to **teach** what is the same and what is different, leaving room to **make** the only **choice** which can be made. *T-26.IV.22.6*

~ all learning is a **help** or hindrance to the gate of **Heaven**. *T-26.VI.30.5*

~ all learning aims at transfer. *T-27.VI.50.8*

~ learning does not jump from situations to their opposites and bring the same results. *T-27.VI.51.3*

~ and thus the **power** of your learning **will** be proved to **you** by all the many different witnesses it finds. *T-27.VI.52.3*

~ your **power** to learn is strong enough to **teach you** that your **will** is not your own, your thoughts do not belong to **you**, and even **you** are someone else. *T-31.I.3.6*

~ learning is an ability **you** made and gave yourselves. It was not made to do the **Will** of **God** but to uphold a **wish** that It could be opposed, and that a **will** apart from It was yet more real than It. And this has learning sought to demonstrate, and **you have** learned what it was made to **teach**. *T-31.I.5.1:3*

~ there **will** be some **confusion** every **time** there is a **shift**, but be **you** thankful that the learning of the **world** is loosening its grasp upon your **mind**. And be **you** sure and **happy** in the **confidence** that it **will** go at last and leave your **mind** at **peace**. *T-31.V.58.3:4*

~ the **purpose** of your learning is to enable **you** to bring the **quiet** with **you** and to heal distress and turmoil. *W-pI.50.5.1*

~ **i** must learn to recognize what makes me **happy** if **I** would find happiness. *W-pI.83.5.4*

~ all learning was already in His **Mind**, accomplished and complete. *W-pI.169.7.4*

~ **we teach today** what **we** would learn and that **alone**. And so our learning **goal** becomes an unconflicted one and possible of easy reach and quick accomplishment. *W-pII.296.2.1:2*

~ for learning, as the **Holy Spirit** guides it to the outcome **He** perceives for it, becomes the **means** to go beyond itself, to be replaced by the Eternal **Truth**. *W-pII.ST281.2.4*

~ what has been learned and understood and long ago passed by is looked upon as a new **thought**, a fresh **idea**, a different approach. *M-2.3.4*

~ god's **Teacher** speaks to any two who **join** together for learning purposes. *M-2.5.3*

LEARNING DEVICE   *A Course in Miracles Term*

HOLY SPIRIT

~ the **body** is a **learning** device for the **mind**. **Learning** devices are not lessons in themselves. Their **purpose** is merely to facilitate the thinking of the **learner**. The most that a faulty use of a **learning** device can do is to **fail** to facilitate **learning**. It has no **power** in itself to introduce actual **learning** errors. *T-2.III.55.3:7*

~ the **body** does not really **exist** except as a **learning** device for the **mind**. This **learning** device is not subject to errors of its own because it was created but is not creating. *T-2.III.61.4:5*

~ the **ego**, which is not real, attempts to persuade the **mind**, which is real, that the **mind** is its own **learning** device and that the **learning** device is more real than it is. *T-6.V.49.3*

~ the **Holy Spirit**, as always, takes what **you have** made and translates it into a **learning** device for you. *T-6.V.62.4*

~ to confuse a **learning** device with a **curriculum goal** is a fundamental **confusion**. **Learning** can hardly be arrested at its own aids with hope of understanding either the aids or the learning's real **purpose**. *T-8.VII.64.5:6*

~ a **learning** device is not a **teacher**. It cannot tell **you** how **you** feel. *T-8.VIII.77.1:2*

~ **you** think that a **learning** device can tell **you** how **you** feel. *T-8.VIII.77.3*

~ no **learning** aid has use which can extend beyond the **goal** of **learning**. When its aim has been accomplished, it is functionless. Yet in the **learning interval** it has a use which **now you fear**, but yet **will love**. *T-27.IV.33.7:9*

LESSON |ˈles(ə)n|

DICTIONARY: *an amount of **teaching** given at one **time**; a period of **learning** or **teaching**.*

EGO

~ there are dark lessons in your minds which **hurt** and hinder **you** and **everyone** around **you**. *T-14.VII.63.3*

~ the absence of perfect **peace means** but one **thing**: **you** think **you** do not **will** for God's Son what His **Father** wills for him. Every dark lesson teaches this in one **form** or another. *T-14.VII.63.4:5*

~ this single lesson does it try to **teach** again, and still again, and yet once more that it is **cause** and not effect. And **you** are its effect and cannot be its **cause**. *T-27.IX.79.4:5*

~ half the lesson **will** not **teach** the whole. *T-28.III.26.5*

~ only unwillingness to learn it could **make** such an easy lesson **difficult**. *T-31.I.1.6*

~ every lesson that makes up the **world** arises from the first accomplishment of **learning**—an enormity so great the Holy Spirit's **Voice** seems small and still before its **magnitude**. *T-31.I.4.4*

~ the certain outcome of the lesson that God's Son is guilty is the **world you see**. It is a **world** of terror and **despair**. Nor is there hope of happiness in it. There is no **plan** for safety **you** can **make** that ever **will** succeed. There is no **joy** that **you** can **seek** for **here** and hope to find. Yet this is not the only outcome which your **learning** can produce. *T-31.I.7.4:9*

HOLY SPIRIT;   *ancient lesson, perfect lesson, **miracle**.*

~ the **Holy Spirit**, seeing where **you** are but knowing **you** are elsewhere, begins His lesson in simplicity with the fundamental **teaching** that **truth** is true. This is the hardest lesson **you will** ever learn, and in the end the only one. *T-13.VII.56.1:2*

~ joyous lessons that come quickly on the firm foundation that **truth** is true. For what is builded there is true and built on **truth**. The **universe** of **learning will** open up before **you** in all its gracious simplicity. *T-13.VII.61.2:4*

~ this simple lesson holds the key to the dark door which **you** believe is locked forever. **You** made this door of **nothing** and behind it is **nothing**. *T-13.VII.62.5:6*

~ the **way** to **teach** this simple lesson is merely this: guiltlessness is **invulnerability**. *T-13.VIII.71.1*

~ most holy lesson, which seeks but to restore what is the right of God's **creation**. *T-14.II.11.4*

~ bright lesson, with which the **Holy Spirit will** replace the dark ones **you** do not accept and **hide**, teaches **you** that **you will** with the **Father** unto His Son. *T-14.VII.63.6*

~ there are no dark lessons **He** has not already lightened for **you**. The lessons **you** would **teach** yourselves **He** has corrected already. **They** do not **exist** in His **Mind** at all. *T-14.VII.69.6:8*

~ for **He** teaches the **miracle** of **oneness**, and before His lesson division disappears. *T-14.VII.7.1.5*

~ there is no **need** to learn through **pain**. And gentle lessons are acquired joyously and are remembered gladly. What gives **you** happiness **you want** to learn and not forget. *T-21.II.5.1:3*

~ the **Holy Spirit will** repeat this one inclusive lesson of deliverance until it has been learned, regardless of the **form** of **suffering** that brings **you** pain. *T-27.IX.8.7.1*

~ their **learning** is the only **purpose** for your **learning** skill the **Holy Spirit** sees in all the **world**. His simple lessons in **forgiveness have** a **power** mightier than yours because **they call** from **God** and from your **Self** to **you**. *T-31.I.5.5:6*

~ simple lessons **being** taught to **you** in every moment of each day, since **time** began and **learning** had been made. *T-31.I.6.6*

~ the lessons to be learned are only two. Each has its outcome in a different **world**. And each **world** follows surely from its **source**. *T-31.I.7.1:3*

~ however much **you** may **have** overlearned your chosen task, the lesson which reflects the **love** of **God** is stronger still. And **you will** learn God's Son is **innocent** and **see** another **world**. *T-31.I.7.10:11*

~ the lesson has a **purpose**, and in this **you** come to **understand** what it is for. *T-31.IV.35.10*

~ the lesson's **purpose** is to **teach** that what your **brother** loses **you have** lost and what **he** gains is what is given **you**. *T-31.IV.40.5*

~ the Holy Spirit's lesson plans arranged in easy steps that though there be some lack of ease at times and some distress, there is no shattering of what was learned, but just a re-translation of what seems to be the evidence on its behalf. *T-31.V.5.1.1*

~ trials are but lessons which **you** failed to learn presented once again, so where **you** made a faulty **choice** before, **you now** can **make** a better one and thus escape all **pain** which what **you** chose before has brought to **you**. *T-31.VIII.8.7.1*

~ **he will** bless the lesson with His **Love**. *W-pI.127.8.6*

~ his gentle lessons **teach** how easily **salvation** can be yours, how **little practice you need** undertake to let His **laws** replace the ones **you** made to hold yourself a prisoner to **death**. *W-pI.137.9.2*

~ whatever **form** the lesson takes is planned for him in such a **way** that **he** cannot **mistake** it if his asking is sincere. And if **he** asks without sincerity, there is no **form** in which the lesson **will** meet with **acceptance** and be truly learned. *W-pI.185.6.3:4*

~ all things are lessons **God** would **have you** learn. **He** would not leave an unforgiving **thought** without **correction**. *W-pI.193.13.1:2*

~ **he** redirects each lesson **you** would **teach** in **hate** to one in which **forgiveness** enters, and returns the **hate** to **love**, so that the **fear** is gone. *W-pI.193.4.2*

~ each lesson has a central **thought**, the same in all of them. The **form alone** is changed, with different circumstances and events, with different characters and different themes apparent but not real. **They** are the same in fundamental content. *W-pI.193.5.3:5*

~ a **thought** which rules your **mind**, a habit in your **problem**-solving repertoire, a **way** of quick reaction to **temptation**. *W-pI.194.6.2*

~ **we seek** to go beyond them. *W-pII.ST361.1.2*

~ a lesson truly taught can lead to **nothing** but **release** for **teacher** and **pupil** who **have** shared in one intent. *M-17.3.2*

LEVEL

DICTIONARY: *a position on a real or imaginary scale of amount, quantity, extent, or quality.*

EGO

~ the presence of level **confusion** always results in variable **reality** testing and therefore in variability in behavioral appropriateness. *T-1.I.64.5*

~ different levels of aspiration, which actually result from level **confusion**. *T-2.II.34.2*

HOLY SPIRIT

~ the **mind** can elect the level it chooses to serve. *T-1.II.68.3*

~ **mind** is the only creative level. *T-2.III.65.2*

~ the **Soul** has no levels, and all **conflict** arises from the **concept** of levels. Only the levels of the Trinity are capable of **unity**. The levels which **man** created by the **separation** cannot but **conflict**. This is because **they** are essentially meaningless to each other. *T-3.VI.38.8:11*

~ freud realized this perfectly and that is why **he** conceived the different levels in his view of the psyche as forever irreconcilable. **They** were **conflict**-prone by definition, because **they** wanted different things and obeyed different principles. In our **picture** of the psyche, there is an unconscious level which properly consists only of the **miracle** ability and which should be under my direction. There is also a conscious level, which perceives or is aware of impulses from both the unconscious and the **superconscious**. **Consciousness** is thus the level of **perception** but not of **knowledge**. Again, to perceive is not to know. *T-3.VI.39.1:6*

~ the non-maximal only appears to **have** a range. This is because it seems to be meaningful to measure it from the maximum and identify its position by how much it is not there. Actually, this does not mean anything. It is like negative numbers in that the **concept** can be used theoretically, but it has no application practically. *T-7.IV.19.4:7*

LIFE

DICTIONARY: *the **condition** that distinguishes animals and plants from inorganic matter, including the capacity for growth, reproduction, functional activity, and continual **change** preceding **death**.*

EGO; *illusion, death.*

~ no one who lives in **fear** is really alive. *T-2.VI.111.1*

~ human living has indeed been needlessly wasted in a repetition **compulsion**. It reenacts the **separation**, the **loss** of **power**, the foolish **journey** of the **ego** in an attempt at reparation, and finally the **crucifixion** of the **body** or **death**. *T-4.I.3.4:5*

~ the **attraction** of **death** that makes life seem to be ugly, cruel, and tyrannical. *T-19.V.93.3*

~ such is each life—a seeming **interval** from **birth** to **death** and on to life again, a repetition of an instant gone by long ago, which cannot be relived. *T-26.VI.42.3*

~ the end of life must come, whatever **way** that life be spent. And so take **pleasure** in the quickly passing and ephemeral. *T-27.III.8.6:7*

~ what **you have** given "life" is not alive and symbolizes but your **wish** to be alive apart from life, alive in **death**, with **death** perceived as life, and living, **death**. *T-29.III.15.2*

~ so do all things live because of **death**. *M-27.3.6*

252

HOLY SPIRIT; *eternal attribute of everything,* **creation,** *God,* **oneness, thought, salvation, gift** *of life.*

~ life is of the **mind** and in the **mind.** *T-6.V.61.3*

~ **nothing** alive is fatherless, for life is **creation.** *T-10.I.1.6*

~ for **God** is Life, and **they** abide in Life. [Life is as holy as the **Holiness** by Which it was created.] The Presence of **Holiness** lives in everything that lives, for **Holiness** created life and leaves not what It created holy as Itself. *T-14.V.41.5:7*

~ life is the result of the **Thought** of **God.** *T-19.V.79.8*

~ there is no life **outside** of **Heaven.** Where **God** created life, there life must be. In any state apart from **Heaven,** life is **illusion.** *T-23.III.37.1:3*

~ life makes not **death,** creating like itself. *T-23.V.49.7*

~ life is manifest in **you** who are His Son. *T-25.II.7.2*

~ life is given **you** to **give** the dying **world.** *T-27.VI.48.3*

~ if **I** did not think, **I** would not **exist,** because life is **thought.** *W-pI.54.3.2*

~ to be alive and not to know yourself is to believe that **you** are really dead. For what is life except to be yourself. *W-pI.139.3.1:2.*

~ there are not different kinds of life, for life is like the **truth.** It does not **have** degrees. It is the one **condition** in which all that **God** created **share.** Like all His thoughts, it has no **opposite.** There is no **death** because what **God** created shares His Life. *W-pI.167.1.1:5*

~ life is not as **we** imagine it. *W-pI.167.10.2*

~ the **opposite** of life can only be another **form** of life. *W-pI.167.7.1*

~ its **form** may **change;** it may appear to be what it is not. *W-pI.167.7.3*

~ surrounding me is all the life that **God** created in His **Love.** It calls to me in every heartbeat and in every breath, in every action and in every **thought.** *W-pII.267.1.1:2*

~ everywhere the signs of life spring up to show that what is born can never die, for what has life has **immortality.** Life is an eternal attribute of everything that the living **God** created. *W-pII.ST341.5.4*

~ living is **joy.** *M-20.5.1*

~ the right to live is something no one **need** fight for. It is promised him, and guaranteed by **God.** *P-3.III.4.1:2*

LIFTING OF THE VEIL *A Course in Miracles Term*

HOLY SPIRIT

~ this is the place to which **everyone** must come when **he** is ready. Once **he** has found his **brother, he** is ready. *T-19.V.99.2:3*

~ **today** it **will** be given **you** to feel the **peace forgiveness** offers and the **joy** the lifting of the **veil** holds out to you. *W-pI.122.11.2*

LIGHT

DICTIONARY: *the natural agent that stimulates **sight** and makes things visible.*

EGO

~ light cannot enter **darkness** when a **mind** believes in **darkness** and **will** not let it go. *T-14.IV.28.5*

~ the light of **darkness** by which **you** try to **see** can only obscure. *T-14.VII.60.8*

~ as the light comes nearer, **you will** rush to **darkness**, shrinking from the **truth**, sometimes retreating to the lesser forms of **fear** and sometimes to stark terror. *T-18.IV.25.1*

~ the light is kept from everything **you see**. At most, **you** glimpse a **shadow** of what lies beyond. *T-31.VII.74.3:4*

~ **denial** of light leads to failure to perceive it. Failure to perceive light is to perceive **darkness**. The light is useless to **you** then, even though it is there. **You** cannot use it because its presence is unknown to **you**. And the seeming **reality** of the **darkness** makes the **idea** of light meaningless. *W-pI.91.2.5:9*

~ the light of **strength** is not the light **you see**. It does not **change** and flicker and go out. It does not **shift** from night to day and back to **darkness** till the morning comes again. *W-pI.92.8.1:3*

~ those who **seek** the light are merely covering their eyes. *W-pI.188.1.2*

HOLY SPIRIT;   *call to awake, **call**, what your minds are, **God**, understanding, **strength**, tranquility, **peace**.*

~ perfect openness

~ light is eternal. *T-1.I.34.5*

~ understanding is light, and light leads to **knowledge**. *T-5.V.38.5*

~ light does not **attack darkness**, but it does shine it away. *T-8.V.27.1*

~ light is understanding. *T-9.IV.26.2*

~ the light is in **you**. **Darkness** can cover it but cannot put it out. *T-10.II.14.6:7*

~ the holy light that shines forth from God's Son is the **witness** that his light is of his **Father**. *T-12.VI.52.8*

~ **you will** find it through its witnesses, for having given light to them, **they will** return it. **Everyone you see** in light brings your light closer to your own **awareness**. *T-12.VI.54.2:3*

~ there is a light which this **world** cannot **give**. Yet **you** can **give** it, as it was given **you**. And as **you give** it, it shines forth to **call you** from the **world** and follow it. For this light **will** attract **you** as **nothing** in this **world** can do. And **you will** lay aside the **world** and find another. *T-12.VI.55.1:5*

~ the **attraction** of light must draw **you** willingly. *T-12.VI.56.2*

~ light needs **nothing** but to shine in **peace** and from itself to let the rays extend in **quiet** to infinity. *T-12.VII.71.7*

~ who gives it to **you** that **you** may **join** Him in the holy task of bringing light to **darkness**. For, like your brothers, **you** do not realize the light has come and freed **you** from the **sleep** of **darkness**. *T-13.VII.62.8:9*

~ the light in **you will** waken them, and **they will** not leave **you** asleep. *T-13.VII.63.2*

~ the **quiet** light in which the **Holy Spirit** dwells **within you** is merely perfect openness in which **nothing** is hidden and therefore **nothing** is fearful. *T-14.III.17.1*

~ an instant of light, and it **will** be enough to remind **you** that your **goal** is light. *T-18.IV.25.6*

~ **within** it everything is joined in perfect continuity. Nor is it possible to imagine that anything could be **outside**, for there is nowhere that this light is not. *T-21.II.10.5:6*

~ once it is seen, this light can never be forgotten. It must draw **you** from the **past** into the **present**, where **you** really are. Before this light the **body** disappears, as heavy shadows must **give way** to light. The **darkness** cannot choose that it remain. The coming of the light **means** it is gone. *T-26.VI.40.10:14*

~ its perfect purity does not depend on whether it is seen on earth or not. *T-30.IV.46.2*

~ in this light, **I** begin to **see** what my illusions about myself had kept hidden. *W-pI.57.6.3*

~ **god** is the only Light. *W-pI.59.5.2*

~ **you will have** to go through the **clouds** before **you** can reach the light. *W-pI.70.12.5*

~ **i** can but choose the light, for it has no alternative. It has replaced the **darkness**, and the dark is gone. *W-pI.88.2.6:7*

~ light is crucial. *W-pI.91.2.1*

~ light, where only miracles can be perceived. *W-pI.92.11.3*

~ what is light except the resolution, born of **peace**, of all your conflicts and mistaken thoughts into one **concept** which is wholly true? *W-pI.108.1.2*

~ true light which makes true **vision** possible is not the light the body's eyes behold. It is a state of **mind** which has become so unified that **darkness** cannot be perceived at all. *W-pI.108.2.1:2*

~ this is the light which shows no opposites, and **vision, being** healed, has **power** to heal. This is the light that brings your **peace** of **mind** to other minds, to **share** it and be glad that **they** are one with **you** and with themselves. This is the light which heals because it brings single **perception**, based upon one frame of reference from which one **meaning** comes. *W-pI.108.3.1:3*

~ light is tranquility, and in that **peace** is **vision** given us and **we** can **see**. *W-pI.108.7.5*

~ the light **we** carry stays behind, yet still remains with us as **we** walk on. *W-pI.124.2.5*

~ **here** is light your eyes cannot behold. *W-pI.129.10.2*

~ and it **will** lead **you** on in ways appointed for your happiness according to the ancient **plan** begun when **time** was born. *W-pI.135.21.2*

~ **you will** not **see** the light until **you** offer it to all your brothers. *W-pI.153.11.5*

~ there is a Light in **you** Which cannot die, Whose Presence is so holy that the **world** is sanctified because of **you**. *W-pI.156.4.1:2*

~ the Light in **you** is what the **universe** longs to behold. *W-pI.156.5.1*

~ light is not of the **world**, yet **you** who bear the light in **you** are alien **here** as well. The light came with **you** from your native **home** and stayed with **you** because it is your own. It is the only **thing you** bring with **you** from Him Who is your **Source**. It shines in **you** because it lights your **home** and leads **you** back to where it came from and **you** are at **home**. *W-pI.188.1.5:8*

~ this light cannot be lost. *W-pI.188.2.1*

~ it can so easily be looked upon that arguments which prove it is not there become ridiculous. *W-pI.188.2.3*

~ it **alone** has **power** to **give** the **gift** of **sight** to **you**. *W-pI.188.6.3*

~ there is a light in **you** the **world** cannot perceive. *W-pI.189.1.1*

~ nor can **you** dim the light of your **perfection**. *W-pI.197.8.3*

~ the light has come to offer miracles to bless the tired **world**. *W-pII.345.2.2*

~ in the light their **purpose** is transformed and understood. *M-28.4.6*

LILY

DICTIONARY: *a bulbous plant with large trumpet-shaped, typically fragrant, flowers on a tall, slender stem. Lilies have long been cultivated, some kinds **being** of symbolic importance and some used in perfumery.*

HOLY SPIRIT; *lily of forgiveness*

~ **now** are the lilies of his **innocence** untouched by **guilt** and perfectly protected from the cold chill of **fear** and withering blight of **sin** alike. *T-20.III.14.3*

~ **christ's vision** is the holy ground in which the lilies of **forgiveness** set their roots. This is their **home**. They can be brought from **here** back to the **world**, but **they** can never grow in its unnourishing and shallow soil. **They need** the **light** and warmth and kindly care Christ's **charity** provides. **They need** the **love** with which He looks on them. And **they** become His messengers who **give** as **they** received. *W-pI.159.8.1:6*

~ the lilies that your **brother** offers **you** are laid upon your **altar**, with the ones **you** offer him beside them. *W-pI.187.9.2*

~ yet **will** one lily of **forgiveness change** the **darkness** into **light**, the **altar** to illusions to the shrine of **Life** Itself. *W-pII.331.5.1*

~ each lily of **forgiveness** offers all the **world** the silent **miracle** of **love**. And each is laid before the **word** of **God** upon the universal **altar** to **Creator** and **creation**, in the **light** of perfect purity and endless **joy**. *W-pII.ST341.3.4:5*

LIMIT

DICTIONARY: *a point or **level** beyond which something does not or may not extend or pass.*

EGO

~ **you have** tried to limit what **He** created, and so **you** believe that all **creation** is limited. *T-10.II.8.3*

~ **you** on earth **have** no conception of limitlessness, for the **world you** seem to live in is a **world** of limits. *T-14.VI.47.4*

~ limits are demanded by the **ego**, representing its demands to **make little** and ineffectual. *T-15.IX.88.3*

~ his **belief** in limits has imprisoned him. *T-15.IX.90.8*

~ what **you** think is **sin** is limitation, and whom **you** try to limit to the **body you hate** because **you fear**. *T-21.IV.35.2*

~ limits placed on everything **outside**, just as **they** are on everything **you** think is yours. *T-26.II.3.5*

~ to accept the limits of a **body** is to impose these limits on each **brother** whom **you see**. *T-26.II.3.7*

~ and what is limited can not be **Heaven**. So it must be **hell**. *T-26.XI.86.9:10*

~ the limits the **world** places on **communication** are the chief barrier to direct **experience** of the **Holy Spirit**. *M-25.2.5*

~ limits are placed out of **fear**. *M-25.2.6*

HOLY SPIRIT

~ there is no limit on your **learning**, because there is no limit on your minds. *T-8.IV.16.5*

~ no one can be beyond the limitless because what has no limits must be everywhere. There are no beginnings and no endings in **God**, whose **universe** is Himself. *T-10.II.6.2:3*

~ neither beginnings nor endings were created by the Eternal, who placed no limits on His **creation** nor upon those who create like Him. *T-10.II.8.2*

~ **they have** renounced the **means** for **sin** by choosing to let all limitations be removed. *T-21.IV.36.2*

~ **god** limits not. *T-26.XI.86.8*

~ there is no limit to where **you** are. *W-pI.50.5.4*

~ there is no limit placed upon Himself, and so are **you** unlimited as well. *W-pI.127.4.5*

~ without them the walls that surround all the separate places of the **world** would fall at the holy sound of His **Voice**. *M-25.2.6*

LINK

|liNGk|

DICTIONARY: *a relationship between two things or situations, especially where one thing affects the other.*

HOLY SPIRIT; *two minds joined as one, communication link, eternal link, Holy Spirit, Christ.*

~ there is one link which joins them all together, holding them in the **oneness** out of which **creation** happens. *T-14.IV.36.10*

~ the link with which the **Father** joins Himself to those He gives the **power** to create like Him can never be dissolved. *T-14.IV.37.1*

~ when two minds **join** as one and **share** one **idea** equally, the first link in the **awareness** of the **Sonship** as one has been made. *T-16.III.13.3*

~ in His link with **you** lie both His inability to forget and your ability to **remember**. *T-16.VI.40.12*

~ the link that has been given **you** to **join** the **truth** may reach to **you** through what **you understand**. *T-25.II.8.2*

~ without this link with **God**, **perception** would **have** replaced **knowledge** forever in your minds. *W-pI.43.1.4*

~ without this link with **God**, **perception** would **have** replaced **knowledge** forever in your minds. With this link with **God**, **perception will** become so changed and purified that it **will** lead to **knowledge**. *W-pI.43.1.4:5*

~ your eternal link with **God**. *W-pI.49.4.3*

~ **christ** is the link that keeps **you** one with **God**. *W-p2.270.2.1*

LITTLE

|ˈlidl|

DICTIONARY: *small in size, amount, or degree (often used to convey an appealing diminutiveness or express an affectionate or condescending attitude).*

EGO

~ **you have** chosen to be little and to lament your littleness. *T-9.VI.43.5*

~ your littleness is taken for granted. *T-9.VI.43.7*

~ not to **question** your littleness, therefore, is to deny all **knowledge** and keep the ego's whole **thought system** intact. *T-9.VI.44.3*

~ littleness is the **offering you** gave yourself. **You** offered this in place of **magnitude**, and **you** accepted it. *T-15.IV.22.2:3*

~ choose littleness and **you will** not **have peace**, for **you will have** judged yourself unworthy of it. And whatever **you** offer as a **substitute** is much too poor a **gift** to satisfy **you**. *T-15.IV.23.2:3*

- for littleness and the **belief** that **you** can be content with littleness are the decisions **you have** made about yourself. *T-15.IV.28.2*
- your **purpose** is at variance with littleness of any kind. *T-23.I.4.7*

LOGIC

|ˈläjik|

DICTIONARY: *reasoning conducted or assessed according to strict principles of validity.*

EGO

- **we have** followed much of the ego's logic and **have** seen its logical conclusions. And having seen them, **we have** realized that **they** cannot be seen but in illusions, for there **alone** their seeming clearness seems to be clearly seen. *T-13.VI.47.6:7*

HOLY SPIRIT

- the ego's logic is as impeccable as that of the **Holy Spirit**, because your **mind** has all the **means** at its disposal to side with **Heaven** or earth, as it elects. *T-5.VII.59.4*
- the **Holy Spirit** uses logic as easily and as well as does the **ego**, except that His conclusions are not insane. **They** take a direction exactly **opposite**, pointing as clearly to **Heaven** as the **ego** points to **darkness** and to **death**. *T-13.VI.47.4:5*
- the simple logic by which the **Holy Spirit** teaches **you** the simple conclusions that speak for **truth** and only **truth**. *T-13.VI.47.8*
- there is **nothing** in the **world** to **teach** him that the logic of the **world** is totally insane and leads to **nothing**. Yet in him who made this insane logic, there is One Who knows it leads to **nothing**, for He knows everything. *T-13.VI.51.8:9*

LOSS

|lôs|

DICTIONARY: *the fact or process of losing something or someone.*

EGO

- yet **you** cannot lose anything unless **you** did not **value** it and therefore did not **want** it. This makes **you** feel deprived of it, and by projecting your own rejection, **you** believe that others are taking it from **you**. *T-7.VIII.78.2:3*
- what **you** keep is lost to **you**. *T-24.II.8.12*
- who seeks to take away has been deceived by the **illusion** loss can offer **gain**. Yet loss must offer loss and **nothing** more. *W-pI.133.8.4:5*

HOLY SPIRIT

- fortunately, when **you** lose something, it does not mean that the "something" has gone. It merely **means** that **you** do not know where it is. *T-3.VIII.69.3:4*
- all loss comes only from your own misunderstanding. Loss of any kind is **impossible**. *T-8.VII.57.1:2*
- there is no loss. *T-12.VII.59.6*
- only in **time** can anything be lost, and never lost forever. *T-20.VI.37.4*
- no one deserves to lose. *T-25.X.83.1*

- it is **impossible** that anything be lost if what **you have** is what **you** are. *T-26.VIII.57.4*

- **you** must lose what **you** would take away. *T-27.III.22.9*

- in any **thought** of loss, there is no **meaning**. *T-30.VIII.87.10*

- no one loses; **nothing** is taken away from anyone. *W-pI.37.1.4*

- it is **impossible** that one can **gain** because another loses. This implies a **limit** and an insufficiency. *W-pI.105.2.2:3*

- what **he** seems to lose is always something **he will value** less than what **will** surely be returned to him. *W-pI.187.5.8*

LOVE |ləv|

DICTIONARY: *an intense feeling of deep affection.*

EGO;   *separation*, *exclusion*, *fear*, *hate*.

- if **you** deny love, **you will** not know it because your cooperation is the law of its **being**. *T-8.X.102.4*

- the **ego** is certain that love is dangerous, and this is always its central **teaching**. *T-11.V.36.1*

- **being** unable to love, the **ego** would be totally inadequate in love's presence, for it could not respond at all. *T-11.V.38.2*

- the **ego will** therefore distort love and **teach you** that love calls forth the responses which the **ego** can **teach**. *T-11.V.38.4*

- love does not **kill** to save. If it did, **attack** would be **salvation**, and this is the ego's **interpretation**, not God's. *T-11.X.87.3:4*

- **everyone** draws nigh unto what **he** loves and recoils from what **he** fears. And **you** react with **fear** to love and draw away from it. Yet **fear** attracts **you**, and believing it is love, **you call** it to yourself. Your private **world** is filled with the figures of **fear you have** invited into it, and all the love your brothers offer **you, you** do not **see**. *T-12.V.37.4:7*

- love is not **special**. If **you** single out **part** of the **Sonship** for your love, **you** are imposing **guilt** on all your relationships and making them unreal. *T-13.IV.30.2:3*

- what is kept apart from love cannot **share** its **healing power**, because it has been separated off and kept in **darkness**. *T-14.III.17.4*

- where there is love, your **brother** must **give** it to **you** because of what it is. But where there is **need** for love, **you** must **give** it because of what **you** are. *T-14.VI.57.2:3*

- and love where **fear** has entered cannot be depended on because it is not perfect. *T-15.VI.48.4*

- love demands **sacrifice** and is therefore inseparable from **attack** and **fear**. And that **guilt** is the price of love, which must be paid by **fear**. *T-15.X.98.1:2*

- **you see** love as destructive. *T-15.X.98.6*

- total love would completely destroy **you**. *T-15.X.98.8*

- **sacrifice** becomes love. *T-15.XI.105.7*

- balance **hate** with love that makes love meaningless to **you**. *T-16.V.30.8*

- the **illusion** of love **will** never satisfy. *T-16.V.31.7*

- there are no triumphs of love. Only **hate** is concerned with the "triumph of love" at all. *T-16.V.34.1:2*

- if **you seek** love **outside** yourself, **you** can be certain that **you** perceive hatred **within** and are afraid of it. *T-16.V.35.5*

259

~ **you** go toward love, still hating it and terribly afraid of its **judgment** upon **you.** *T-18.IV.26.4*

~ **you** are not afraid of love, but only of what **you have** made of it love is turned to **hate** as easily. *T-18.IV.26.5*

~ what is not love is murder. What is not loving must be an **attack.** *T-23.V.47.9-10*

~ love is not understandable to sinners because **they** think that **justice** is split off from love and stands for something else. *T-25.IX.70.3*

~ for **hate** to be maintained love must be feared and only sometimes **present,** sometimes gone. Thus is love seen as treacherous because it seems to come and go uncertainly and offer no stability to **you.** *T-29.II.7.3-4*

~ this strange **belief** would **limit** happiness by redefining love as limited and introducing opposition in what has no **limit** and no **opposite. Fear** is associated then with love, and its results become the heritage of minds that think what **they have** made is real. *W-pI.103.2.1:2*

~ love's **meaning** is obscure to anyone who thinks that love can **change.** *W-pI.127.2.1*

~ and thus **he** thinks that **he** can love at times and **hate** at other times. **He** also thinks that love can be bestowed on one and yet remain itself although it is withheld from others. *W-pI.127.2.3:4*

HOLY SPIRIT; *union, sharing, **extension**, heritage, your **power**, your **strength**, heart of **God**, **Eternity**, everything, content, **freedom**, happiness, basis of **forgiveness**, law without an **opposite**, **Cause**, Eternal **Truth**, Love of **God**, **Sonship**, **Creation**.*

~ the **opposite** of love is **fear,** but what is all-encompassing can **have** no **opposite.** *T-1.2.3*

~ love is everything. *T-2.V.99.3*

~ love does not conquer all things, but it does set all things right. *T-4.VII.90.7*

~ love extends outward simply because it cannot be contained. **Being** limitless, it does not stop. It creates forever, but not in **time.** *T-7.I.3.4:6*

~ it comes freely to all the **Sonship, being** what the **Sonship** is. *T-7.V.38.10*

~ love is incapable of any exceptions. *T-7.VI.45.1*

~ love cannot suffer, because it cannot **attack.** The remembrance of love therefore brings **invulnerability** with it. *T-9.IX.76.5:6*

~ love does not **limit,** and what it creates is not limited. *T-10.II.10.6*

~ your love is as boundless as His because it is His. *T-10.II.10.8*

~ if to love oneself is to heal oneself, those who are sick do not love themselves. *T-11.III.14.2*

~ only love is strong because it is undivided. *T-11.VI.43.1*

~ love is recognized by its messengers. If **you make** love manifest, its messengers **will** come to **you** because **you** invited them. *T-11.VIII.69.5:6*

~ the **attraction** of love for love remains irresistible. For it is the **function** of love to unite all things unto itself, and to hold all things together by extending its **wholeness.** *T-11.IX.83.5:6*

~ is changeless but continually exchanged, **being** offered by the eternal to the eternal. In this exchange it is extended, for it increases as it is given. *T-12.V.33.2:3*

~ love always leads to love. *T-12.VI.54.4*

~ love always answers, **being** unable to deny a **call** for **help** or not to hear the cries of **pain** that rise to it from every **part** of this strange **world you** made but do not **want.** *T-12.VII.62.3*

~ love leads so gladly! *T-12.VII.64.3*

~ there is no **fear** in love, for love is **guiltless.** *T-13.IV.29.4*

~ there is no **darkness** that the **light** of love **will** not dispel. *T-14.III.17.3*

~ love does not **attack fear**. *T-14.IV.28.6*

~ love is not **little**, and love dwells in **you**, for **you** are **host** to Him. *T-15.IV.30.6*

~ the **meaning** of love is the **meaning God** gave to it. *T-15.VI.54.4*

~ perfect love is in **you**. *T-15.VI.57.1*

~ love that is fully given and fully returned. **Being** complete, it asks **nothing**. **Being** wholly pure, **everyone** joined in it has everything. *T-15.VIII.65.3.5*

~ love would always **give** increase. *T-15.IX.88.2*

~ love is everywhere. *T-15.XI.108.1*

~ love asks only that **you** be **happy** and **will give you** everything that makes for happiness. *T-16.III.19.3*

~ love is not an **illusion**. It is a **fact**. *T-16.V.33.1:2*

~ your task is not to **seek** for love but merely to **seek** and find all of the barriers **within** yourself which **you have** built against it. *T-16.V.35.1*

~ for love is wholly without **illusion** and therefore wholly without **fear**. *T-16.V.40.8*

~ love is content and not **form** of any kind. *T-16.VI.54.1*

~ for **God** created love as **He** would **have** it be and gave it as it is. Love has no **meaning** except as its **Creator** defined it by His **Will**. It is **impossible** to define it otherwise and **understand** it. *T-16.VII.59.5:7*

~ love knows no bodies and reaches to everything created like itself. Its total lack of **limit** is its **meaning**. It is completely impartial in its giving, encompassing only to preserve and keep complete what it would **give**. *T-18.IX.78.1:3*

~ no **part** of love calls on the whole in vain. *T-18.IX.81.6*

~ love is not learned. Its **meaning** lies in itself. *T-18.XI.96.1:2*

~ love is not learned because there never was a **time** in which **you** knew it not. *T-18.XI.96.5*

~ love would never look on **guilt** at all. It is the nature of love to look upon only the **truth**, for there it sees itself, with which it would unite in holy **union** and **completion**. As love must look **past fear**. *T-19.V.49.1:3*

~ love contains the end of **guilt** as surely as **fear** depends on it. [Love is attracted only to love.] Overlooking **guilt** completely, it sees no **fear**. **Being** wholly without **attack**, it could not be afraid. *T-19.V.49.4:7*

~ love wishes to be known, completely understood, and shared. It has no secrets; **nothing** that it would keep apart and **hide**. It walks in sunlight, open-eyed and **calm**, in smiling **welcome** and in sincerity so simple and so obvious it cannot be misunderstood. *T-20.VII.46.5:7*

~ love has no darkened temples where mysteries are kept obscure and hidden from the sun. It does not **seek** for **power**, but for relationships. *T-20.VII.48.1:2*

~ love's arms are open to **receive you** and **give you peace** forever. *T-20.VII.54.6*

~ love rests in **certainty**. *T-22.VI.47.8*

~ love is fair and cannot chasten without **cause**. *T-25.IX.74.9*

~ only love is just and can perceive what **justice** must accord the **Son of God**. *T-25.IX.77.6*

~ love cannot be feared. *T-26.V.28.6*

~ love would prove all **suffering** is but a vain imagining, a foolish **wish** with no effects. *T-27.III.19.6*

~ love, too, has symbols in a **world** of **sin**. *T-27.VII.59.1*

~ love must be extended. *T-28.III.17.2*

~ love, which **you** did not create, but which **you** can extend. *T-29.IV.23.4*

~ only the Love of God **will** protect **you** in all circumstances. It **will** lift **you** out of every trial and raise **you** high above all the perceived dangers of this **world** into a climate of perfect **peace** and safety. It **will** transport **you** into a state of **mind** which **nothing** can threaten, **nothing** can disturb, and where **nothing** can intrude upon the eternal **calm** of the **Son of God**. Love of **God within you**, eternal, changeless and forever unfailing. *W-pI.50.2.3:6*

~ through the Love of **God** in **you**, **you** can resolve all seeming difficulties without **effort** and in sure **confidence**. *W-pI.50.3.5*

~ his love lights up the **world** for me to **see**. As **I** forgive, his love reminds me that His Son is **sinless**. *W-pI.60.6.2:3*

~ love created me like Itself. *W-pI.84.1.1*

~ happiness is an attribute of love. It cannot be apart from it, nor can it be experienced where love is not. Love has no limits, **being** everywhere. *W-pI.103.1.1:3*

~ his Love is everything **you** are and that **He** is—the same as **you**, and **you** the same as **He**. *W-pI.125.7.4*

~ love is one. It has no separate parts and no degrees; no kinds nor levels, no divergences and no distinctions. It is like itself, unchanged throughout. It never alters with a person or a circumstance. It is the Heart of **God**, and also of His Son. *W-pI.127.1.3:7*

~ love cannot judge. As it is one itself, it looks on all as one. Its **meaning** lies in **oneness**. And it must elude the **mind** that thinks of it as partial or in **part**. There is no love but God's, and all of love is His. There is no other principle which rules where love is not. Love is a law without an **opposite**. Its **wholeness** is the **power** holding everything as one, the **link** between the **Father** and the Son which holds them both forever as the same. *W-pI.127.3.1:8*

~ love's **meaning** is your own, and shared by **God** Himself. *W-pI.127.4.2*

~ there is no love but His, and what **He** is is everything there is. *W-pI.127.4.4*

~ love and **perception** thus go hand in hand. *W-pI.130.2.5*

~ for love would **ask you** lay down all **defense** as merely foolish. *W-pI.170.6.4*

~ to feel the Love of **God within you** is to **see** the **world** anew, shining in **innocence**, alive with hope, and blessed with perfect **charity** and love. *W-pI.189.1.7*

~ for love can walk no road except the **way** of **gratitude**, and thus **we** go who walk the **way** to **God**. *W-pI.195.10.6*

~ love makes no comparisons. *W-pI.195.4.2*

~ love **will** happily replace all **fear**. *W-pII.272.2.2*

~ love remains the only **present** state, whose **Source** is **here** forever and forever. *W-pII.293.1.2*

~ yet in the **present**, love is obvious and its effects apparent. All the **world** shines in **reflection** of its holy **light**, and **I** perceive a **world** forgiven at last. *W-pII.293.1.4:5*

~ for only love creates in **truth**, and **truth** can never **fear**. *W-pII.ST261.3.3*

~ be not afraid of love. For it **alone** can heal all sorrow, wipe away all tears, and gently waken from his **dream** of **pain** the Son whom **God** acknowledges as His. *W-pII.ST311.4.2:3*

~ nor **will** there be a **time** when anything that It created suffers any **change**. *W-pII.ST321.1.4*

~ for Love remains with all Its **thought**, Its sureness **being** theirs. *W-pII.ST321.4.4*

~ love without **trust** is **impossible**. *M-7.4.6*

~ it lies in **you** as His eternal **gift**. *S-3.IV.3.5*

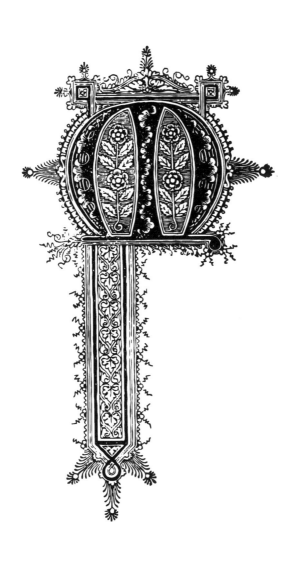

MADMAN

DICTIONARY: *a **man** who is mentally ill.*

EGO

~ the neurotic devotes his to **compromise**. The psychotic tries to escape by establishing the certain **truth** of his own errors. *T-1.I.94.3:4*

~ a madman thinks the **world he** sees is real and does not **doubt** it. Nor can **he** be swayed by questioning his thoughts' effects. It is but when their **source** is raised to **question** that the hope of **freedom** comes to him at last. *W-pI.132.1.5:7*

~ **they** cannot learn directly from the **truth** because **they have** denied that it is so. And so **they need** a **teacher** who perceives their **madness**, but who still can look beyond **illusion** to the simple **truth** in them. *W-pI.155.3.3:4*

~ believe he is what he is not and judge against himself. *W-pI.160.1.6*

~ a madman's dreams are frightening. *W-pII.ST251.4.1*

~ a madman **will** defend his own illusions because in them **he** sees his own **salvation**. Thus, **he will attack** the one who tries to save him from them, believing that **he** is attacking him. This curious circle of **attack-defense** is one of the most **difficult** problems with which the **psychotherapist** must deal. In **fact**, this is his central task; the core of **psychotherapy**. *P-2.IV.9.1:4*

MADNESS

DICTIONARY: *the state of **being** mentally ill, especially severely.*

EGO

~ in your madness, **you** overlook **reality** completely, and **you see** only your own split **mind** everywhere **you** look. *T-12.V.38.4*

~ **you see** his madness, which **you hate** because **you share** it. And all the pity and **forgiveness** that would heal it gives **way** to **fear**. *T-19.V.101.5:6*

~ **faith** and **belief** are strong in madness, guiding **perception** toward what the **mind** has valued. *T-21.VI.56.3*

~ madness has a **purpose** and believes it also has the **means** to **make** its **purpose** real. *T-21.VII.63.2*

~ madness to think of **life** as **being** born, aging, losing vitality, and dying in the end. *M-27.1.2*

HOLY SPIRIT; *attack on reason*

~ madness may be your **choice**, but not your **reality**. *T-13.VIII.79.6*

~ **you have** perceived the ego's madness and not been made afraid because **you** did not choose to **share** in it. At times it still deceives **you**. Yet in your saner moments, its ranting strikes no terror in your hearts. For **you have** realized that all the gifts it would withdraw from **you** in rage at your "presumptuous" **wish** to look **within, you** do not **want**. A few remaining trinkets still seem to shine and catch your **eye**. Yet **you** would not "sell" **Heaven** to have them. *T-21.V.46.3:8*

~ madness is an **attack** on **reason** that drives it out of **mind** and takes its place. **Reason** does not **attack** but takes the place of madness quietly, replacing madness if it be the **will** of the insane to listen to it. But the insane know not their **will**. For **they** believe **they see** the **body** and let their madness tell them it is real. **Reason** would be incapable of this. And if **you** would defend the **body** against your **reason, you will** not understand the **body** or yourself. *T-21.VII.62.1:6*

~ madness holds out no menace to **reality** and has no influence upon it. *T-23.II.12.7*

~ no one wants madness, nor does anyone cling to his madness if **he** sees that this is what it is. What protects madness is the **belief** that it is true. *T-23.III.32.1:2*

~ what is madness cannot be the **truth**. *T-25.VIII.52.6*

~ madness but seems terrible. In **truth** it has no **power** to **make** anything. Like the **magic** which becomes its servant, it neither attacks nor protects. To **see** it and to recognize its **thought system** is to look on **nothing**. *M-17.9.1:4*

MAGIC |ˈmajik|

DICTIONARY: *the* **power** *of apparently influencing the* **course** *of events by using mysterious or supernatural forces.*

EGO; *belief*

~ magic always sees something "**special**" in the **healer** which **he** believes **he** can offer as a **gift** to someone who does not **have** it. *T-7.VI.42.4*

~ a "miserable sinner" cannot be healed without magic, nor can an "unimportant **mind**" esteem itself without magic. *T-9.IV.26.3*

~ all magic is a **form** of reconciling the irreconcilable. *T-9.X.85.1*

~ the magic of the **world** can seem to **hide** the **pain** of **sin** from sinners and deceive with glitter and with guile. *T-25.VIII.50.5*

~ all **belief** in magic is maintained by just one simple-minded **illusion**—that it works. *M-16.11.8*

~ there is, however, a **temptation** to respond to magic in a **way** that reinforces it. *M-17.2.1*

~ it can, in **fact**, be easily concealed beneath a **wish** to **help**. It is this double **wish** that makes the **help** of **little value** and must lead to undesired outcomes. *M-17.2.3:4*

~ a magic **thought**, by its mere presence, acknowledges a **separation** from **God**. It states in the clearest **form** possible that the **mind** which thinks it believes it has a separate **will** that can oppose the **Will** of **God** and succeed. *M-17.5.3:4*

~ **they** can but reawaken sleeping **guilt**, which **you have** hidden but **have** not let go. *M-17.7.2*

~ the inconsistencies, the compromises, and the rituals the **world** fosters in its vain attempts to cling to **death** and yet to think **love** real are mindless magic, ineffectual and meaningless. *M-27.6.9*

~ magic's **purpose**; to **make** illusions true through false **perception**. This cannot heal, for it opposes **truth**. *P-2.IV.7.4:5*

HOLY SPIRIT;   *nothing, miscreative use of* ***mind, substitute.***

~ is mindless and therefore destructive, or rather the uncreative use of **mind**. *T-1.I.14.3*

~ the whole distortion which created magic rests on the **belief** that there is a creative ability in matter which the **mind** cannot control. *T-2.III.54.2*

~ all material **means** which **man** accepts as remedies for bodily ills are merely restatements of magic principles. *T-2.III.57.1*

~ magic is essentially mindless or the miscreative use of the **mind**. Physical medications are forms of "spells." *T-2.III.62.1:3*

~ one of the chief ways in which **man** can correct his magic-miracle **confusion** is to **remember** that he did not create himself. *T-2.V.105.1*

~ myths and magic are closely associated in that myths are usually related to the **ego** origins and magic to the powers which the **ego** ascribes to itself. *T-4.III.35.1*

~ magic is always the **belief** that **healing** is harmful. *T-7.VI.41.6*

~ magic always tries to weaken. *T-7.VI.42.2*

~ your magic has no **meaning**. What it is meant to save does not **exist**. Only what it is meant to **hide will save you.** *W-pI.76.6.3:5*

~ magic imprisons, but the **laws** of **God** set free. *W-pI.76.7.5*

~ yet each **temptation** to accept magic as true must be abandoned through his recognition not that it is fearful, not that it is **sinful**, not that it is dangerous, but merely that it is meaningless. Rooted in **sacrifice** and **separation**. *M-16.10.8:9*

~ no risk is possible throughout the day except to put your **trust** in magic, for it is only this that leads to **pain.** *M-16.11.5*

~ magic is a sorry **substitute** for true assistance. It is not **good** enough for God's **teacher**, because it is not enough for God's Son. *M-16.8.6:7*

~ the avoidance of magic is the avoidance of **temptation**. For all **temptation** is **nothing** more than the attempt to **substitute** another **will** for God's. These attempts may indeed seem frightening, yet **they** are merely pathetic. **They** can **have** no effects, neither **good** nor bad, neither rewarding nor demanding **sacrifice**, **healing** nor destructive, quieting nor fearful. When all magic is recognized as merely **nothing**, the **teacher of God** has reached the most advanced state. *M-16.9.1:5*

~ magic of any kind, in all its forms, simply does **nothing**. Its powerlessness is the **reason** it can be so easily escaped. What has no effects can hardly terrify. *M-16.9.7:9*

~ how to deal with magic thus becomes a major **lesson** for the **teacher of God** to master. His first responsibility in this is not to **attack** it. If a magic **thought** arouses **anger** in any **form**, God's **teacher** can be sure that **he** is strengthening his own **belief** in **sin** and has condemned himself. *M-17.1.4:6*

~ magic thoughts **need** not lead to **condemnation**, for **they** do not really **have** the **power** to **give** rise to **guilt**. And so **they** can be overlooked and thus forgotten in the truest **sense**. *M-17.8.10:11*

~ magic thoughts are but illusions. *M-18.1.6*

~ what is used for magic is useless to Him, but what **He** uses cannot be used for magic. *M-25.4.3*

MAGNITUDE

|ˈmaɡnəˌt(y)o͞od|

DICTIONARY: *the great size or extent of something.*

EGO

~ **you** believe that magnitude lies in defiance. *T-12.III.14.3*

~ finding magnitude in littleness. *T-15.V.38.5*

HOLY SPIRIT

~ know your magnitude by accepting His limitlessness as yours. *T-9.V.34.8*

~ for **you will** be content only in magnitude, which is your **home**. *T-15.IV.23.6*

~ all your striving must be directed against littleness, for it does require **vigilance** to protect your magnitude in this **world**. To hold your magnitude in perfect **awareness** in a **world** of littleness is a task the **little** cannot undertake. *T-15.IV.25.4:5*

~ the **Holy Spirit** can hold your magnitude, clean of all littleness, clearly and in perfect safety in your minds, untouched by every **little gift** the **world** of littleness would offer **you**. *T-15.IV.27.5*

~ your magnitude is of Him Who dwells in **you** and in Whom **you** dwell. *T-15.IV.28.6*

~ it is our task together to restore the **awareness** of magnitude to the **host** whom **God** appointed for Himself. *T-15.IV.29.2*

~ the instant in which magnitude **will** dawn upon **you** is but as far away as your **desire** for it. *T-15.V.36.2*

MAKE |māk|

DICTIONARY: *form (something) by putting parts together or combining substances; construct.*

EGO

~ when **you** make something, **you** make it out of a **sense** of lack or **need**. Anything that is made is made for a specific **purpose** and has no true generalizability. When **you** make something to fill a perceived lack, which is obviously why **you** would **want** to make anything, **you** are tacitly implying that **you** believe in **separation**. *T-3.VII.52.2:4*

~ everything **you** made has never been and is invisible because the **Holy Spirit** does not **see** it. *T-11.IX.82.1*

~ the homes **you** built **have** never sheltered **you**. The roads **you** made **have** led **you** nowhere, and no city that **you** built has withstood the crumbling assault of **time**. **Nothing you** made but has the mark of **death** upon it. *T-12.VII.61.2:4*

~ **everyone** believes in what **he** made, for it was made by his believing it. *M-11.3.3*

HOLY SPIRIT

~ it changes **nothing** in **creation**, depends entirely upon the **madness** of its maker, and cannot serve to justify the **madness**. *T-21.III.27.5*

~ all that **you** made can serve **salvation** easily and well. *T-25.VII.49.4*

MAN |man|

DICTIONARY: *a human **being** of either sex; a person.*

EGO

~ man has the ability to usurp the **power** of God. *T-2.I.15.1*

~ man is not willing to look on what he has done to himself. *T-2.III.69.2*

~ the **world** is full of examples of how man has depreciated himself, because he is afraid of his own thoughts. *T-2.V.92.1*

~ the **sense** of **conflict** is inevitable since man has placed himself in a strangely illogical position. He believes in the **power** of what does not **exist**. *T-2.V.98.6:7*

~ each man makes one **ego** for himself, although it is subject to enormous variation because of its instability. *T-4.III.25.1*

HOLY SPIRIT

~ man is perfect. *T-1.I.44.4*

- the **Soul** is in a state of **grace** forever. Man's **reality** is **only** his **Soul**. Therefore, man is in a state of **grace** forever. *T-1.I.52.1:3*

~ man can only know himself as he is because that is all he can be sure of. *T-3.VI.40.6*

~ man cannot perceive himself correctly. **He** has no **image**. *T-3.VII.54.1:2*

~ "**God** created man in His own **image** and likeness" is correct in **meaning**, but the words are open to considerable misinterpretation. This is avoided, however, if "**image**" is understood to mean "**thought**" and "likeness" is taken as "of a like quality." **God** did create the **Soul** in His own **Thought** and of a quality like to His own. *T-3.VII.57.1:3*

~ man can perceive himself as **self**-creating, but **he** cannot do more than believe it. **He** cannot **make** it true. *T-3.IX.77.3:4*

~ the **question** is not how man responds to his **ego**, but what he believes he is. *T-4.III.27.7*

MANUAL FOR TEACHERS *A Course in Miracles Term*

HOLY SPIRIT

~ this is a manual for the teachers of **God**. *M-I.5.4*

~ this is a manual for a **special curriculum**, intended for teachers of a **special form** of the universal **course**. *M-I.4.1*

~ this manual is not intended to **answer** all questions that both **teacher** and **pupil** may raise. In **fact**, it covers only a few of the more obvious ones, in terms of a brief summary of some of the major concepts in the **text** and **workbook**. It is not a **substitute** for either, but merely a supplement. While it is called a manual for teachers, it must be remembered that only **time** divides **teacher** and **pupil**, so that the **difference** is temporary by definition. *M-29.1.1:4*

MARTYR |ˈmärdər|

DICTIONARY: *a person who displays or exaggerates their discomfort or distress in **order** to obtain sympathy or admiration.*

EGO

~ if, then, a **mind** believes that its **will** is different from His, it can only decide either that there is no **God** or that **God's Will** is fearful. The former accounts for the **atheist** and the latter for the martyr. Martyrdom takes many forms, the category including all doctrines which hold that **God** demands sacrifices of any kind. *T-8.X.97.2:4*

~ the martyr believes that **God** is crucifying him. *T-8.X.97.5*

~ both really **fear** abandonment and retaliation, but the **atheist** is more reactive against abandonment and the martyr against retaliation. *T-8.X.97.6*

~ the martyr, on the other hand, is more aware of **guilt** and, believing that **punishment** is inevitable, attempts to **teach** himself to like it. *T-8.X.98.3*

MEANING

DICTIONARY: *what is meant by a* **word**, **text**, **concept**, *or action.*

EGO

~ **you** can **see** yourselves as separated from your meaning only by experiencing yourself as unreal. *T-7.V.26.5*

~ analyzing to **attack** meaning, the **ego** does succeed in overlooking it and is left with a series of fragmented perceptions which it unifies on behalf of itself. This, then, becomes the **universe** it perceives. And it is this **universe** which, in turn, becomes its demonstration of its own **reality**. *T-10.VI.55.2:4*

~ all meaning that **you give** the **world outside** must thus reflect the **sight you** saw **within**; or better, if **you** saw at all or merely judged against. *T-20.IX.76.3*

~ meaning it does not recognize and does not know if it is there or not. *T-22.IV.32.2*

~ **you** assigned a meaning in the **light** of goals that **change**, with every meaning shifting as **they change**. *T-30.VIII.83.7*

~ recognition of meaninglessness arouses intense anxiety in all **the separated ones**. It represents a **situation** in which **God** and the **ego** "challenge" each other as to whose meaning is to be written in the empty space which meaninglessness provides. The **ego** rushes in frantically to establish its own "ideas" there, fearful that the void may otherwise be used to demonstrate its own unreality. And on this **alone** it is correct. *W-pI.13.2.1:4*

HOLY SPIRIT

~ this meaning comes from **God** and is **God**. Because it is also **you**, **you share** it and extend it as your **Creator** did. *T-7.III.18.4:5*

~ god's meaning waits in the **Kingdom**, because that is where **He** placed it. It does not wait in **time**. It merely rests in the **Kingdom**, because it belongs there, as **you** do. *T-7.V.26.1:3*

~ all meaning, including yours, comes not from double **vision** but from the gentle fusing of everything into one meaning, one **emotion**, and one **purpose**. *T-14.IV.31.4*

~ all that **you** would keep away holds all the meaning of the **universe** and holds the **universe** together in its meaning. For unless the **universe** were joined in **you**, it would be apart from **God**, and to be without Him is to be without meaning. *T-15.XI.106.5:6*

~ what has no meaning cannot be perceived. And meaning always looks **within** to find itself and then looks out. *T-20.IX.76.1:2*

~ it cannot be that meaning changes constantly and yet is true. *T-30.VIII.82.3*

~ **nothing** without meaning exists. *W-pI.13.1.3*

MEANS

DICTIONARY: *an action or system by which a result is brought about; a method.*

EGO

~ the means for **sin** are dear to **you**. *T-21.IV.35.3*

HOLY SPIRIT

~ the means to meet the Holy Spirit's **goal will** come from the same **Source** as does His **purpose**. *T-20.VIII.58.2*

~ a **purpose** is attained by means, and if **you want** a **purpose**, **you** must be willing to **want** the means as well. *T-20.VIII.59.6*

~ the means are second to the **goal**. And when **you** hesitate, it is because the **purpose** frightens **you**, and not the means. *T-20.VIII.60.3:4*

~ **they** are merely given **you**? They guarantee the **goal**, and **they** are perfectly in line with it. *T-20.VIII.60.6:7*

~ if **you** think **they** are **impossible**, your wanting of the **purpose** has been shaken. For if a **goal** is possible to reach, the means to do so must be possible as well. *T-20.VIII.60.8:9*

~ each one appropriate to the end for which it is employed. Neither can serve the **purpose** of the other, for each one is a **choice** of **purpose**, employed on its behalf. Either is meaningless without the end for which it was intended, nor is it valued as a separate **thing** apart from the intention. The means seem real because the **goal** is valued. *T-20.VIII.64.3:6*

~ **faith** and **belief** and **vision** are the means by which the **goal** of **holiness** is reached. Through them the **Holy Spirit** leads **you** to the **real world** and away from all illusions where your **faith** was laid. *T-21.IV.32.1:2*

~ the **Holy Spirit** has a use for all the means for **sin** by which **you** sought to find it. But as **He** uses them, **they** lead away from **sin** because **His purpose** lies in the **opposite** direction. **He** sees the means **you** use but not the **purpose** for which **you** made them. **He** would not take them from **you**, for **He** sees their **value** as a means for what **He** wills for **you**. *T-21.IV.34.1:4*

~ **faith** and **belief** become attached to **vision**, as all the means that once served **sin** are redirected **now** toward **holiness**. *T-21.IV.35.1*

~ if **you have** the means to let the Holy Spirit's **purpose** be accomplished, **they** can be used. And through their use **will you gain faith** in them. *T-22.III.21.2:3*

~ means serve the end, and as the end is reached, the **value** of the means decreases, eclipsed entirely when **they** are recognized as functionless. *T-22.VII.51.7*

~ he can **change** the **role** of means and end so easily in what **God** loves and would **have** free forever. *T-22.VII.53.1*

~ **you** can be the means to serve His end. This is the only **service** which leads to **freedom**. *T-22.VII.53.2:3*

~ the means of sinlessness can know no **fear** because **they** carry only **love** with them. *T-22.VII.55.7*

~ whatever is perceived as means for **truth** shares in its **holiness** and rests in **light** as safely as itself. Nor **will** that **light** go out when it is gone. Its holy **purpose** gave it **immortality**, setting another **light** in **Heaven**. *T-24.VIII.66.7:9*

~ it has no **meaning** of itself, yet **you** can **give reality** to it according to the **purpose** which **you** serve. *T-24.VIII.67.3*

~ **god** is a Means as well as End. *T-24.VIII.67.5*

~ **god** offers **you** the means to **see** his **innocence**. *T-26.III.14.5*

~ the means attest the **purpose** but are not themselves a **cause**. *T-27.VIII.66.1*

~ the means is simple honesty. *W-pI.80.8.3*

MEDITATE

|ˈmedəˌtāt|

DICTIONARY: *think deeply or focus one›s **mind** for a period of **time**, in silence or with the aid of chanting, for religious or spiritual purposes or as a method of relaxation.*

HOLY SPIRIT

~ meditation is a collaborative venture with **God**. *T-4.VIII.91.4*

~ nor is a lifetime of contemplation and long periods of meditation aimed at detachment from the **body** necessary. All such attempts **will** ultimately succeed because of their purpose. Yet the **means** are tedious and very **time** consuming, for all of them look to the *future* for **release** from a state of **present** unworthiness and inadequacy. *T-18.VIII.66.9:11*

MEMORY

|ˈmem(ə)rē|

DICTIONARY: *the faculty by which the **mind** stores and remembers information.*

EGO

~ the history of all the body's **past** is hidden there. All of the strange associations made to keep the **past** alive, the **present** dead, are stored **within** it, waiting your command that **they** be brought to **you** and lived again. And thus do their effects appear to be increased by **time**, which took away their **cause**. *T-28.II.5.7:9*

~ only the **past** is held in memory as **you make** use of it, and so it is a **way** to hold the **past** against the **now**. *T-28.II.6.7*

~ a memory of **home** keeps haunting you, as if there were a place that called **you** to return. *W-pI.182.1.3*

HOLY SPIRIT

~ it can be used to serve another **purpose** and to be the **means** for something else. It can be used to heal and not to **hurt** if **you** so **wish** it be. *T-28.I.2.8:9*

~ memory, like **perception**, is a skill made up by **you** to take the place of what **God** gave in your **creation**. *T-28.I.2.7*

~ the **Holy Spirit** can indeed **make** use of memory, for **God** Himself is there. Yet this is not a memory of **past** events, but only of a **present** state. **You** are so long accustomed to believe that memory holds only what is **past** that it is hard for **you** to realize it is a skill that can **remember now**. *T-28.II.4.1:3*

~ there is no **link** of memory to the **past**. *T-28.II.4.5*

~ the Holy Spirit's use of memory is quite apart from **time**. He does not **seek** to use it as a **means** to keep the **past**, but rather as a **way** to let it go. Memory holds the **message** it receives and does what it is given it to do. It does not write the **message** nor appoint what it is for. Like to the **body**, it is purposeless **within** itself. *T-28.II.5.1:5*

~ memory holds the **message** it receives and does what it is given it to do. It does not write the **message** nor appoint what it is for. *T-28.II.5.3:4*

~ it is purposeless **within** itself. *T-28.II.5.5*

MEMORY OF GOD

A Course in Miracles Term

EGO

~ the **memory** of **God** cannot shine in a **mind** which has made it invisible and wants to keep it so. *T-11.IX.81.2*

~ under the ego's dark foundation is the **memory** of **God**, and it is of this that **you** are really afraid. For this **memory** would instantly restore **you** to your proper place, and it is this place that **you have** sought to leave. *T-12.III.11.4:5*

~ the great amnesia in which the **memory** of **God** seems quite forgotten. *T-19.V.92.4*

~ it cannot come where there is **conflict**. *T-23.II.7.2*

~ so is the **memory** of **God** obscured in minds that **have** become illusion's **battleground**. *T-23.II.18.8*

~ the **memory** of **God** must be denied if any **sacrifice** is asked of anyone. *T-26.II.4.6*

~ believe that **memory** holds only what is **past**. *T-28.II.4.3*

~ his **memory** is hidden in our minds, obscured but by our pointless **little** goals which offer **nothing** and do not **exist**. *W-pII.258.1.3*

~ all blocks to the remembrance of **God** are forms of **unforgiveness**, and **nothing** else. *P-2.II.3.3*

HOLY SPIRIT

~ his **memory** shines in your minds and cannot be obliterated. It is no more **past** than **future, being** forever always. *T-11.IX.80.7:8*

~ for the **memory** of **God** can dawn only in a **mind** that wills to **remember** and that has relinquished the insane **desire** to control **reality**. *T-11.IX.81.3*

~ the **memory** of **God** has come to **you** in the holy place of **forgiveness, you will remember nothing** else, and **memory will** be as useless as **learning**, for your only **purpose will** be creating. *T-18.XI.98.1*

~ an ancient state not quite forgotten; dim, perhaps, and yet not altogether unfamiliar, like a **song** whose **name** is long forgotten, and the circumstances in which **you** heard completely unremembered. *T-21.II.8.1*

~ the **memory** of **God** comes to the **quiet mind**. *T-23.II.7.1*

~ far beyond this senseless **war** it shines, ready to be remembered when **you** side with **peace**. *T-23.II.18.9*

~ with this **memory**, the Son remembers his own **creations**, as like to him as **he** is to his **Father**. *T-24.III.17.2*

~ the **memory** of **God** shines not **alone**. *T-24.VIII.63.1*

~ **he** who lives in memories **alone** is unaware of where **he** is. *T-26.VI.35.3*

~ the **Holy Spirit** can indeed **make** use of **memory**, for **God** Himself is there. Yet this is not a **memory** of **past** events, but only of a **present** state. *T-28.II.4.1:2*

~ **he** does not **seek** to use it as a **means** to keep the **past**, but rather as a **way** to let it go. *T-28.II.5.2*

~ how instantly the **memory** of **God** arises in the **mind** that has no **fear** to keep the **memory** away. Its own remembering has gone. There is no **past** to keep its fearful **image** in the **way** of glad awakening to **present peace**. *T-28.II.13.1:3*

~ in our **memory** is the recall how dear our brothers are to us in **truth**, how much a **part** of us is every **mind**, how faithful **they have** really been to us, and how our Father's **Love** contains us all. *W-pI.139.12.2*

~ and **memory** of Him awakens in the **mind** which asks the **means** of Him whereby its **sleep** is done. *W-pI.168.2.5*

~ a long forgotten **word** re-echoes in our **memory** and gathers **clarity**. *W-pI.195.7.4*

~ the **memory** of **God** is shimmering across the wide horizons of our minds. *W-pII.I.9.5*

~ **god's memory** is in our holy minds, which know their **oneness** and their **unity** with their **Creator**. *W-pII.ST321.4.5*

MENTAL HEALTH

DICTIONARY: *a person's **condition** with regard to their psychological and emotional well-**being**: all this pressure seems to be affecting his mental **health**.*

HOLY SPIRIT;   *inner peace*

~ all mental illness is some **form** of external searching. *T-2.I.17.5*

~ mental **health** is inner **peace**. It enables **you** to remain unshaken by lack of **love** from without and capable through your own miracles of correcting the external conditions which proceed from lack of **love** in others. *T-2.I.17.6:7*

MESSAGE

|ˈmesij|

DICTIONARY: *a verbal, written, or recorded **communication** sent to or left for a recipient who cannot be contacted directly.*

EGO

~ from the **world** of bodies, made by **insanity**, insane messages seem to be returned to the **mind** which made it. And these messages bear **witness** to this **world**, pronouncing it as true. *T-18.X.86.5:6*

~ everything these messages relay to **you** is quite external. There are no messages which speak of what lies underneath, for it is not the **body** that could speak of this. Its eyes perceive it not; its senses remain quite unaware of it; its tongue cannot relay its messages. *T-18.X.87.1:3*

~ the ego's messages are always sent away from **you** in the **belief** that for your message of **attack** and **guilt** **will** someone other than yourself suffer. And even if **you** suffer, yet someone else **will** suffer more. The great deceiver recognizes that this is not so, but as the "**enemy**" of **peace**, it urges **you** to send out all your messages of **hate** and free yourself. *T-19.V.74.1:3*

~ the **special** messages the **special** hear convince them **they** are different and apart. *T-24.III.16.5*

~ an unheard message **will** not save the **world**, however mighty be the **Voice** that speaks, however loving may be the message be. *W-pI.123.5.4*

HOLY SPIRIT; *light, wholeness.*

~ "yoke" **means** "**join** together" and "burden" **means** "message." Let us reconsider the Biblical statement, "My yoke is easy and my burden **light**" in this way: "Let us **join** together, for my message is **light**." *T-5.IV.29.4:5*

~ your **decision** about him determines the message **you receive**. *T-8.XI.III.4*

~ **you will receive** the message **you give**, because it is the message **you want**. *T-9.XI.94.2*

~ god's Son is **guiltless**. Each one teaches the message differently and learns it differently. *T-11.X.99.7:8*

~ his message is not indirect. *T-13.VI.53.2*

~ the message and the **messenger** are one. *T-25.II.5.6*

~ and His **Voice** is certain of its messages. **They will** not **change** nor be in **conflict**. All of them point to one **goal**, and one **you** can attain. *W-pI.186.II.4:6*

~ there is a message waiting for **you**. *W-pI.Rev II.3.1*

~ it belongs to **you** and that **you want** it. *W-pI.Rev II.3.3*

~ to all the **world we give** the message that **we have** received. *W-pII.245.2.2*

MESSENGER

DICTIONARY: *a person who carries a **message** or is employed to carry messages.*

EGO; *fear's messengers*

~ the messengers of **fear** are harshly ordered to **seek** out **guilt** and cherish every scrap of **evil** and of **sin** which **they** can find. *T-19.V.50.2*

~ fear's messengers are trained through terror. *T-19.V.51.5*

~ in their savage search for **sin, they** pounce on any living **thing they see** and carry it screaming to their master to be devoured. *T-19.V.51.9*

~ **they have** been taught to **seek** for the corruptible. *T-19.V.52.3*

~ it is only the messengers of **fear** that **see** the **body,** for **they** look for what can suffer. *T-19.V.62.1*

HOLY SPIRIT; *love's messengers, Holy Spirit's messengers, God's messengers.*

~ what the messengers of **love** are sent to do **they** do, returning the glad tidings that it was done to **you** who stand together before the **altar** from which **they** were sent forth. *T-19.II.14.6*

~ each has messengers which **they** send forth and which return to them with messages written in the **language** in which their going forth was asked. *T-19.V.49.10*

~ love's messengers are gently sent and return with messages of **love** and **gentleness.** *T-19.V.50.1*

~ what **love** would look upon is meaningless to **fear** and quite invisible. *T-19.V.51.2*

~ the **Holy Spirit** has given **you** love's messengers to send instead of those **you** trained through **fear.** **They** are as eager to return to **you** what **they** hold dear as are the others. If **you** send them forth, **they will see** only the blameless and the beautiful, the gentle and the kind. **They will** be as careful to let no **little** act of **charity,** no tiny expression of **forgiveness,** no **little** breath of **love** escape their notice. And **they will** return with all the **happy** things **they** found, to **share** them lovingly with **you.** *T-19.V.53.1:5*

~ **they** offer **you** salvation. Theirs are the messages of safety, for **they see** the **world** as kind. *T-19.V.53.7:8*

~ **they** go forth to signify the end of **fear.** *T-19.V.54.7*

~ the Holy Spirit's messengers are sent far beyond the **body,** calling the **mind** to **join** in holy **communion** and be at **peace.** *T-19.V.61.6*

~ god's messengers are joyous, and their **joy** heals sorrow and **despair.** **They** are the proof that **God** wills perfect happiness for all who **will** accept their Father's gifts as theirs. *W-pI.100.4.3:4*

~ **you** are God's messenger **today.** **You** bring His happiness to all **you** look upon, His **peace** to **everyone** who looks on **you** and sees His **message** in your **happy** face. *W-pI.100.7.1:2*

~ **he** needs our **voice** that **He** may speak through us. **He** needs our hands to hold His messages and carry them to those whom **He** appoints. **He** needs our feet to bring us where **He** wills, that those who wait in **misery** may be at last delivered. And **He** needs our **will** united with His own, that **we** may be the true receivers of the gifts **He** gives. *W-pI.154.11.2:5*

~ a messenger does not elect to **make** the **message he** delivers. Nor does **he question** the right of him who does nor **ask** why **he** has chosen those who **will receive** the **message** that **he** brings. It is enough that **he** accept it, **give** it to the ones for whom it is appointed, and fulfill his **role** in its delivery. If **he** determines what the messages should be or what their **purpose** is or where **they** should be carried, **he** is failing to perform his proper **part** as bringer of the **word.** *W-pI.154.5.1:4*

~ there is one major **difference** in the **role** of Heaven's messengers which sets them off from those the **world** appoints. The messages which **they** deliver are intended first for them. And it is only as **they** can accept them for themselves that **they** become able to bring them further and to **give** them everywhere that **they** were meant to be. Like earthly messengers, **they** did not write the messages **they** bear, but **they** become their first receivers in the truest **sense**, receiving to prepare themselves to **give**. *W-pI.154.6.1:4*

~ an earthly messenger fulfills his **role** by giving all the messages away. The messengers of **God** perform their **part** by their **acceptance** of His messages as for themselves and show **they understand** the messages by giving them away. **They** choose no roles that are not given them by His authority. And so **they gain** by every **message** which **they give** away. *W-pI.154.7.1:4*

~ **you** who are **now** the messengers of **God receive** His messages, for that is **part** of your appointed **role**. *W-pI.154.9.1*

~ for **honest** thoughts, untainted by the **dream** of worldly things **outside** yourself, become the holy messengers of **God** Himself. *W-pI.188.6.6*

MIND

DICTIONARY: *the element of a person that enables them to be aware of the **world** and their experiences, to think, and to feel; the faculty of **consciousness** and **thought**.*

EGO;   *learning device, bird with broken wings, stream long dry, **source** of **fear**, "unimportant mind", unwatched mind, unconscious mind, tired mind, unforgiving mind.*

~ man's mind can be possessed by illusions. *T-1.I.46.5*

~ an imprisoned mind is not free by definition. It is possessed or held back by itself. Its **will** is therefore limited and is not free to assert itself. *T-2.II.21.5:7*

~ the unwatched mind is responsible for the whole content of the unconscious which lies above the **miracle level**. *T-2.V.96.4*

~ a separated or divided mind must be confused; it is **uncertain** by definition. It has to be in **conflict** because it is out of accord with itself. *T-3.VI.41.5:6*

~ the separated mind cannot maintain the **separation** except by dissociating. *T-4.VII.88.3*

~ the mind can distort its **function**, but it cannot endow itself with functions it was not given. *T-4.VIII.97.7*

~ if it makes illusions it **will** believe in them, because that is how it made them. *T-7.VII.59.5*

~ the **ego** believes that mind is dangerous and that to **make** mindless is to heal. *T-8.IX.85.3*

~ a split mind is endangered, and the recognition that it encompasses completely opposed thoughts **within** itself is intolerable. Therefore the mind projects the split, not the **reality**. *T-11.IV.30.3:4*

~ a split mind and all its works were not created by the **Father** and could not live in the **knowledge** of Him. *T-11.IX.78.5*

~ a darkened mind cannot live in the **light**, and it must **seek** a place of **darkness** where it can believe it is where it is not. *T-12.III.21.5*

~ **you** think that your minds must be kept private or **you will** lose them, and if your bodies are together your minds remain your own. *T-15.VIII.75.7*

~ it is mind that seems to be fragmented and private and **alone**. Its **guilt**, which keeps it separate, is projected to the **body**, which suffers and dies because it is attacked, to hold the **separation** in the mind and let it not know its **identity**. Mind cannot **attack**, but it can **make** fantasies and direct the **body** to act them out. Yet it is never what the **body** does that seems to satisfy. Unless the mind believes the **body** is actually acting out its fantasies, it **will attack** the **body** by increasing the **projection** of its **guilt** upon it. *T-18.VII.51.3:7*

~ the mind is clearly delusional. It cannot **attack**, but it maintains it can and uses what it does to **hurt the body** to prove it can. The mind cannot **attack**, but it can deceive itself. And this is all it does when it believes it has attacked the **body**. It can project its **guilt**, but it **will** not lose it through **projection**. And though it clearly can misperceive the **function** of the **body**, it cannot **change** its **function** from what the **Holy Spirit** establishes it to be. *T-18.VII.52.1:6*

~ each **body** seems to house a separate mind, a disconnected **thought** living **alone** and in no **way** joined to the **Thought** by which it was created. *T-18.IX.75.2*

~ it is obvious that a segment of the mind can **see** itself as separated from the Universal **Purpose**. *T-19.II.3.4*

~ the intention is in the mind, which tries to use the **body** to carry out the **means** for **sin** in which the mind believes. *T-21.IV.38.5*

~ in your state of mind solution is **impossible**. *T-27.V.37.2*

~ separate minds are seen as bodies which are separated and which cannot **join**. *T-28.IV.30.2*

~ an untrained mind can accomplish **nothing**. *W-pI.1.1.3*

~ while thoughtless "ideas" preoccupy your mind, the **truth** is blocked. *W-pI.8.3.2*

~ your mind is totally undisciplined, and **you** cannot distinguish between **joy** and sorrow, **pleasure** and **pain**, **love** and **fear**. *W-pI.20.2.6*

~ it is the other **part** of your mind that functions in the **world** and obeys the world's **laws**. It is this **part** which is constantly distracted, disorganized, and highly **uncertain**. *W-pI.49.1.3:4*

~ mind can also **see** itself divorced from **Spirit** and perceive itself **within** a **body** it confuses with itself. Without its **function** then, it has no **peace**, and happiness is alien to its thoughts. *W-pI.96.5.4:5*

~ mind apart from **Spirit** cannot think. It has denied its **Source** of **strength** and sees itself as helpless, limited, and weak. Dissociated from its **function now**, it thinks it is **alone** and separate, attacked by armies massed against itself and hiding in the body's frail support. **Now** must it reconcile unlike with like, for this is what it thinks that it is for. *W-pI.96.6.1:4*

~ the unforgiving mind is full of **fear** and offers **love** no room to be itself, no place where it can spread its wings in **peace** and soar above the turmoil of the **world**. The unforgiving mind is **sad**, without the hope of respite and **release** from **pain**. It suffers and abides in **misery**, peering about in **darkness**, seeing not, yet certain of the danger lurking there. *W-pI.121.2.1:3*

~ the unforgiving mind is torn with **doubt**, confused about itself and all it sees, afraid and angry, weak and blustering, afraid to go ahead, afraid to stay, afraid to waken or to go to **sleep**, afraid of every sound, yet more afraid of stillness; terrified of **darkness**, yet more terrified at the approach of **light**. *W-pI.121.3.1*

~ the unforgiving mind sees no mistakes, but only sins. It looks upon the **world** with sightless eyes and shrieks as it beholds its own projections rising to **attack** its miserable parody of **life**. It wants to live, yet wishes it were dead. It wants **forgiveness**, yet it sees no hope. It wants escape, yet can conceive of none because it sees the **sinful** everywhere. *W-pI.121.4.3:7*

~ the unforgiving mind is in **despair**, without the prospect of a **future** which can offer anything but more **despair**. Yet it regards its **judgment** of the **world** as irreversible and does not **see** it has condemned itself to this **despair**. It thinks it cannot **change**, for what it sees bears **witness** that its **judgment** is correct. It does not **ask** because it thinks it knows. It does not **question**, certain it is right. *W-pI.121.5.1:5*

~ the mind that plans is thus refusing to allow for **change**. What it has learned before becomes the basis for its **future** goals. Its **past experience** directs its **choice** of what **will** happen. And it does not **see** that **here** and **now** is everything it needs to guarantee a **future** quite unlike the **past** without a continuity of any old ideas and sick beliefs. *W-pI.135.17:1:4*

~ but **part** of it is **now** unnatural. It does not look on everything as one. It sees instead but fragments of the whole, for only thus could it **invent** the partial **world you see**. *W-pI.161.2.2:4*

~ the mind that taught itself to think specifically can no longer grasp abstraction in the **sense** that it is all-encompassing. *W-pI.161.4.7*

~ without **forgiveness** is the mind in chains, believing in its own futility. *W-pII.332.1.7*

HOLY SPIRIT; **part** *of* **God's mind**, **part** *of* **creation** *and* **part** *of it's* **Creator**, *loveliest of God's creations, very powerful* **creator**, *only creative* **level**, *altars to* **God**, **channel**, **light**, **life**, *this world's saviors, holy mind,* **Christ** *mind, One Mind, whole mind, healed mind, wakened mind, tranquil mind, mechanism of* **decision**.

~ the mind can elect the **level** it chooses to serve. The only **limit** which is put on its **choice** is that it cannot serve two masters. *T-1.I.68.3:4*

~ the mind, if it elects to do so, becomes a medium by which the **Soul** creates along the line of its own **creation**. *T-1.I.69.1*

~ the mind is a very powerful **creator**, and it never loses its creative force. It never sleeps. Every instant it is creating and always as **you will**. Many of your ordinary expressions reflect this. *T-2.V.88.5:8*

~ only the mind can perceive anything. A pure mind knows the **truth**, and this is its **strength**. It cannot **attack** the **body** because it recognizes exactly what the **body** is. This is what "a sane mind in a sane **body**" really **means**. It does not confuse **destruction** with **innocence** because it associates **innocence** with **strength**, not with **weakness**. *T-3.III.23.4:8*

~ the mind is very active because it has **will**-**power**. When it willed the **separation**, it willed to perceive. *T-3.VI.44.2:3*

~ mind is one. *T-4.V.58.2*

~ a **channel** for the reception of His Mind and **Will**. *T-4.VIII.97.3*

~ this mind is unequivocal, because it hears only one **voice** and answers in only one **way**. *T-5.IV.28.2*

~ the sane mind cannot conceive of illness, because it cannot conceive of attacking anyone or anything. *T-5.VII.64.8*

~ a mind must endow its thoughts with its own attributes. This is its inherent **strength**, although it may misuse its **power**. *T-5.IX.84.1:2*

~ recognizes the **wholeness** of God's **creation** and by this recognition knows its **Creator**. *T-6.III.25.2*

~ every **idea** begins in the mind of the thinker and extends outward. Therefore, what extends from the mind is still in it, and from what it extends it knows itself. *T-6.IV.39.4:5*

~ your Godlike mind can never be defiled. *T-6.IV.40.4*

~ without anxiety the mind is wholly kind, and because it projects beneficence, it is beneficent. *T-6.IV.42.6*

~ only the mind is real since only the mind can be shared. *T-6.V.63.2*

~ once your mind is healed, it radiates **health** and thereby teaches **healing**. *T-6.V.94.7*

~ minds can communicate, but **they** cannot **hurt**. *T-7.VI.41.4*

~ mind always reproduces as it was produced. *T-7.VII.58.1*

~ every mind must project, because that is how it lives, and every mind is **life**. *T-7.IX.83.5*

~ mind cannot **attack** or be attacked. *T-7.IX.87.1*

~ when a mind has only **light**, it knows only **light**. Its own radiance shines all around it and extends out into the **darkness** of other minds, transforming them into majesty. *T-7.XII.110.6:7*

~ all mind is whole. *T-8.VII.62.3*

~ mind cannot be made physical, but it can be made manifest through the physical if it uses the **body** to go beyond itself. By reaching out, the mind extends itself. It does not stop at the **body**, for if it does, it is blocked in its purpose. A mind which has been blocked has allowed itself to be vulnerable to **attack**, because it has turned against itself. *T-8.VII.62.4:7*

~ **help** and **healing** are the normal expressions of a mind which is working through the **body** but not in it. *T-8.VII.63.2*

~ a whole mind is not idolatrous and does not know of conflicting **laws**. *T-9.IX.80.6*

~ in this same place also lies **salvation**. The **altar** of **God** where **Christ** abideth is there. *T-11.IV.34.5:6*

~ it is also your mind that has the **power** to deny the ego's existence. *T-11.V.37.6*

~ the **reality** of your mind is the loveliest of God's **creations**. Coming only from **God**, its **power** and **grandeur** could only bring **you peace** if **you** really looked upon it. *T-11.VIII.71.2:3*

~ mind that knows this unequivocally knows also that it dwells in **eternity** and utilizes no **perception** at all. It therefore does not consider where it is because the **concept** "where" does not mean anything to it. It knows that it is everywhere, just as it has everything, and forever. *T-13.11.5:7*

~ your minds are already continuous, and their **union need** only be accepted. *T-15.IX.88.7*

~ minds cannot **attack**. *T-17.VIII.65.9*

~ mind reaches to itself. It does not go out. **Within** itself it has no limits, and there is **nothing outside** it. [It encompasses everything.] It encompasses **you** entirely; **you within** it, and it **within you**. There is **nothing** else, anywhere or ever. *T-18.VII.56.6:11*

~ only the mind can set a **purpose**, and only mind can **see** the **means** for its accomplishment and justify its use. *T-19.V.69.8*

~ minds cannot be separate. This other **Self** is perfectly aware of this. And thus It recognizes that miracles do not affect another's mind, only Its own. [They always **change** your mind.] There is no other. *T-21.VI.51.8:12*

~ from loving minds there is no **separation**. And every **thought** in one brings gladness to the other because **they** are the same. **Joy** is unlimited because each shining **thought** of **love** extends its **being** and creates more of itself. There is no **difference** anywhere in it, for every **thought** is like itself. *T-22.VII.64.6:9*

~ minds can **change** as **they desire**. What **they** are and all their attributes, **they** cannot **change**. But what **they** hold as purpose can be changed, and **body** states must **shift** accordingly. *T-24.V.35.7:9*

~ minds that are joined and recognize **they** are can feel no **guilt**. For **they** cannot **attack**. *T-25.V.32.1:2*

~ mind that is united, functioning as one because It is not split in **purpose** and conceives a single **function** as Its only one. *T-27.III.28.3*

~ the mind is recognized as not **within** the **body**, and its **innocence** is quite apart from it and where all **healing** is. *T-28.III.17.8*

~ between your minds there is no **gap**. *T-28.V.40.1*

~ your holy minds are altars unto **God**. *T-29.VIII.50.5*

~ the mind of Heaven's Son in **Heaven** is, for there the mind of **Father** and Son joined in **creation** which can **have** no end. *T-30.IV.48.4*

~ the mind must think of its **Creator** as it looks upon itself. *T-30.VII.73.6*

~ understanding **will** naturally come to lighten every corner of the mind which has been cleared of the debris that darkens it. *W-pI.9.2.5*

~ your mind cannot be stopped in this unless **you** choose to stop it. *W-pI.44.7.3*

~ the **part** of your mind in which **truth** abides is in constant **communication** with **God**, whether **you** are aware of it or not. *W-pI.49.1.2*

~ the **part** that is listening to the **Voice** of **God** is **calm**, always at **rest**, and wholly certain. It is really the only **part** there is. The other **part** is a wild **illusion**, frantic and distraught, but without **reality** of any kind. My state of mind can **change**. *W-pI.49.2.1:4*

~ my mind is **part** of **creation** and **part** of its **Creator**. *W-pI.52.6.5*

~ in my own mind, behind all my insane thoughts of **separation** and **attack**, is the **knowledge** that all is one forever. **Spirit** makes use of mind as **means** to find its **Self**-expression. And the mind which serves the **Spirit** is at **peace** and filled with **joy**. Its **power** comes from **Spirit**, and it is fulfilling happily its **function here**. *W-pI.56.6.1:4*

~ there are only two parts of your mind. One is ruled by the **ego** and is made up of illusions. The other is the **home** of the **Holy Spirit**, where **truth** abides. *W-pI.66.9.2:4*

~ your mind has been absolved from **madness**, letting go illusions of a split **identity**. *W-pI.97.1.5*

~ open mind which cherishes no lingering **belief** that **you have** made a **devil** of God's Son. *W-pI.101.5.3*

~ **we** clear a holy place **within** our minds before His **altar**, where His gifts of **peace** and **joy** are **welcome** and to which **we** come to find what has been given us by Him. *W-pI.104.7.1*

~ deep in your mind the holy **Christ** in **you** is waiting your **acknowledgment** as **you**. *W-pI.110.9.4*

~ the **world** can **give** no gifts of any **value** to a mind which has received what **God** has given as its own. *W-pI.122.7.5*

~ it **will** be grateful to be free a while. It knows where it belongs. But free its wings, and it **will** fly in sureness and in **joy** to **join** its holy **purpose**. *W-pI.128.6.2:4*

~ a healed mind is relieved from the **belief** that it must **plan**, although it cannot know the outcome which is best, the **means** by which it is achieved, nor how to recognize the **problem** that the **plan** is made to solve. *W-pI.135.13.1*

~ for the mind which understands that **sickness** can be **nothing** but a **dream** is not deceived by forms the **dream** may take. *W-pI.140.4.2*

~ the mind that brings illusions to the **truth** is really changed. *W-pI.140.7.4*

~ **now** this mind becomes aware again of Who created it and of His lasting **union** with itself. *W-pI.154.4.3*

~ complete abstraction is the natural **condition** of the mind. *W-pI.161.2.1*

~ every mind contains all minds, for every mind is one. *W-pI.161.4.2*

~ your mind has come to lay aside **denial** and accept the **thought** of God as its **inheritance**. *W-pI.165.5.6*

~ a sleeping mind must waken as it sees its own **perfection** mirroring the Lord of **Life** so perfectly it fades into what is reflected there. And **now** it is no more a mere **reflection**. It becomes the **thing** reflected and the **light** which makes **reflection** possible. No **vision now** is needed. For the wakened mind is one that knows its **Source**, its **Self**, its **holiness**. *W-pI.167.12.3:7*

~ the mind can think it sleeps, but that is all. It cannot **change** what is its waking state. It cannot **make** a **body** nor abide **within** a **body**. What is alien to the mind does not **exist** because it has no **source**. For mind creates all things that are and cannot **give** them attributes it lacks nor **change** its own eternal, mindful state. It cannot **make** the physical. What seems to die is but the sign of mind asleep. *W-pI.167.6.1:7*

~ yet mind is mind, awake or sleeping. It is not its **opposite** in anything created nor in what it seems to **make** when it believes it sleeps. *W-pI.167.7.4:5*

~ when the mind awakes, it but continues as it always was. *W-pI.167.9.4*

~ it is not shut tight against **God's Voice**. It has become aware that there are things it does not know and thus is ready to accept a state completely different from **experience** with which it is familiarly at **home**. *W-pI.169.3.5:6*

~ for minds can only **join** in **truth**. *W-pI.185.3.2*

~ the mind which **means** that all it wants is **peace** must **join** with other minds, for that is how **peace** is obtained. *W-pI.185.6.1*

~ the shining in your mind reminds the **world** of what it has forgotten, and the **world** restores the **memory** to **you** as well. *W-pI.188.4.1*

~ **nothing** external to your mind can **hurt** or injure **you** in any **way**. *W-pI.190.5.2*

~ the mind without the **body** cannot **make** mistakes. It cannot think that it **will** die nor be the prey of merciless **attack. Anger** becomes **impossible**. *W-pI.192.5.2:4*

~ the mind that serves the **Holy Spirit** is unlimited forever, in all ways, beyond the **laws** of **time** and space, unbound by any preconceptions, and with **strength** and **power** to do whatever it is asked. **Attack** thoughts cannot enter such a mind because it has been given to the **Source** of **Love**. And **fear** can never enter in a mind that has attached itself to **Love**. It rests in **God**. *W-pI.199.2.1:4*

~ the wisdom of your mind **will** come to your assistance. *W-pI.Rev III.6.5*

~ it **will** not **fail**. It is the Holy Spirit's chosen **means** for your **salvation**. Since it has His **trust**, His **means** must surely merit yours as well. *W-pI.Rev III.7.3:5*

~ your mind holds only what **you** think with **God**. *W-pI.Rev IV.6.1*

~ my mind can only serve. *W-pII.236.1.5*

~ i thus direct my mind, which **I alone** can **rule**. *W-pII.236.1.7*

~ yet is my mind at one with God's. *W-pII.265.1.9*

~ the mind that is made willing to accept God's gifts has been restored to **Spirit** and extends its **freedom** and its **joy**, as is the **Will** of **God** united with its own. *W-pII.330.1.4*

~ the **world** it sees arises from a mind at **peace within** itself. No danger lurks in anything it sees, for it is kind and only kindness does it look upon. *W-pII.ST291.3.4:5*

~ it is in the sorting out and categorizing activities of the mind that errors in **perception** enter. And it is **here correction** must be made. The mind classifies what the body's eyes bring to it according to its preconceived values, judging where each **sense** datum fits best. *M-8.4.1:3*

~ a tranquil mind is not a **little gift**. *M-20.4.8*

~ since only the mind can be sick, only the mind can be healed. Only the mind is in **need** of **healing**. *P-IN.1.2:3*

MIND TRAINING   *A Course in Miracles Term*

EGO

~ perceived through the ego's eyes, it is **loss** of **identity** and a descent into **hell**. *W-pI.44.5.6*

HOLY SPIRIT

~ beginning of training your **mind** to recognize what is the same and what is different. *W-pI.4.3.4*

~ it embodies precisely what the untrained **mind** lacks. Yet the training must be accomplished if **you** are to **see**. *W-pI.44.3.4:5*

~ the training must be accomplished if **you** are to **see**. *W-pI.44.3.5*

~ is the most natural and easy one in the **world** for the trained **mind**, just as it seems to be the most unnatural and difficult for the untrained **mind**. *W-pI.44.4.3*

~ while **you practice** in this **form, you** leave behind everything that **you now** believe and all the thoughts which **you have** made up. Properly speaking, this is the **release** from **hell**. *W-pI.44.5.4:5*

MINISTER OF GOD *A Course in Miracles Term*

HOLY SPIRIT

~ your ministry begins as all your thoughts are purified. So are **you** taught to **teach** the **Son of God** the holy **lesson** of his sanctity. *W-pI.151.15.2:3*

~ **now** has our ministry begun at last, to carry round the **world** the joyous news that **truth** has no illusions and the **peace** of **God**, through us, belongs to **everyone**. *W-pI.151.17.3*

~ god's ministers **have** chosen that the **truth** be with them. *W-pI.153.10.2*

~ it is the **function** of God's ministers to **help** their brothers choose as **they have** done. *W-pI.153.11.1*

~ the ministers of **God** can never **fail** because the **love** and **strength** and **peace** that shine from them to all their brothers come from Him. *W-pI.153.21.3*

MIRACLE |ˈmirək(ə)l|

DICTIONARY: *a surprising and **welcome** event that is not explicable by natural or scientific **laws** and is therefore considered to be the **work** of a divine agency.*

EGO

~ inappropriate physical impulses (or misdirected miracle impulses) result in conscious **guilt** if expressed and depression if denied. *T-1.II.104.2*

~ upside-down **perception** has induced the **belief** that miracles are frightening. *T-2.III.58.4*

~ **you** would anticipate the **future** on the basis of your **past experience** and **plan** for it accordingly. Yet by **doing** so, **you** are aligning **past** and **future** and not allowing the miracle, which could intervene between them, to free **you** to be born again. *T-12.VI.48.6:7*

~ to **you** the miracle cannot seem natural because what **you have** done to **hurt** your minds has made them so unnatural that **they** do not **remember** what is natural to them. *T-16.III.12.1*

~ when **you** maintain that there must be **order of difficulty** in miracles, all **you** mean is that there are some things **you** would withhold from **truth**. *T-17.II.3.1*

~ miracles seem unnatural to the **ego** because it does not **understand** how separate minds can influence each other. *T-21.VI.51.6*

~ to think a miracle is bound by **laws** which it came solely to **undo**! *T-27.VII.59.3*

~ the cost of the **belief** there must be some appearances beyond the hope of **change** is that the miracle cannot come forth from **you** consistently. For **you have** asked it be withheld from **power** to heal all dreams. *T-30.IX.92.3:4*

~ there is no miracle that can be given **you** unless **you want** it. Choose what **you** would heal, and **He** Who gives all miracles has not been given **freedom** to bestow His gifts upon God's Son. *T-30.IX.92.6:7*

HOLY SPIRIT;   *act of **faith**, **way** of perceiving, **lesson** in total **perception**, end of an **illusion**, **denial** of **error**, "right **answer**", affirmation of **truth**, Holy Spirit's **gift**, expressions of **love**, expressions of total **forgiveness**, expression of **miracle-mindedness**, **service**, maximal **service**, **teaching** device, **learning device**, **learning** aid, **lesson** in **joy**, **lesson** in **truth**, universal **blessing**, **life**, habits, **healing**, **correction**, **justice**, solution, **call**, translation, the **witness** unto **life**, mighty herald of **eternity**, God's most holy Son, God's miracle, **God's thoughts**, little **gift** of **truth**.*

~ there is no **order of difficulty** among miracles. *T-1.I.1.1*

~ everything that comes from **love** is a miracle. *T-1.I.3.3*

~ all miracles mean **life**. *T-1.I.4.1*

~ miracles are habits and should be involuntary. *T-1.I.5.1*

~ miracles are natural. *T-1.I.6.1*

~ miracles are everyone's right, but **purification** is necessary first. *T-1.I.7.1*

~ miracles are [a **form** of] **healing**. *T-1.I.8.1*

~ miracles are a kind of exchange. *T-1.I.9.1*

~ reverses the physical **laws**. *T-1.I.9.2*

~ miracles are thoughts. *T-1.I.12.1*

~ miracles are both beginnings and endings. *T-1.I.13.1*

~ **they undo** the **past** in the **present** and thus **release** the **future**. *T-1.I.13.4*

~ miracles bear **witness** to **truth**. *T-1.I.14.1*

~ miracles are **teaching** devices. *T-1.I.16.1*

~ increase the **strength** of the giver and supply **strength** to the receiver. *T-1.I.16.2*

~ the transcendence of the **body**. *T-1.I.17.1*

~ sudden shifts into invisibility. *T-1.I.17.2*

~ a miracle is a **service**. *T-1.I.18.1*

~ it is a **way** of loving your neighbor as yourself. *T-1.I.18.3*

~ miracles **make** minds one in **God**. *T-1.I.19.1*

~ **rest** on the **laws** of **eternity**, not of **time**. *T-1.I.19.3*

~ natural expressions of total **forgiveness**. *T-1.I.21.1*

~ miracles represent **freedom** from **fear**. *T-1.I.30.1*

~ the ability is the potential; the achievement is its expression; and the **Atonement** is the **purpose**. *T-1.I.32.4*

~ a **means** of organizing different levels of **consciousness**. *T-1.I.35.1*

~ miracles come from the below or subconscious **level**. *T-1.I.36.1*

~ miracles are thus a **means**. *T-1.I.40.2*

~ the miracle acknowledges only the **truth**. It thus dispels man's illusions about himself and puts him in **communion** with himself and **God**. *T-1.I.43.6:7*

~ **they** intercede for man's **holiness** and **make** his perceptions holy. *T-1.I.44.2*

282

~ the miracle joins in the **Atonement** of **Christ** by placing the **mind** in the **service** of the **spirit**. *T-1.I.45.3*

~ **they** thus atone for his errors by freeing him from his own nightmares. *T-1.I.46.3*

~ miracles restore the [**Soul**] to its fullness. *T-1.I.47.1*

~ **way** in which minds which serve the **spirit** unite with **Christ**. *T-1.I.48.3*

~ miracles are examples of right thinking. *T-1.I.54.1*

~ a **correction** factor introduced into false thinking by me. It acts as a catalyst, shaking up erroneous **perception** and reorganizing it properly. *T-1.I.55.1:2*

~ a miracle is a **correction**. It does not create nor really **change** at all. It merely looks on devastation and reminds the **mind** that what it sees is false. It undoes **error** but does not attempt to go beyond **perception** nor exceed the **function** of **forgiveness**. Thus it stays **within** time's limits. Yet it paves the **way** for the return of timelessness and love's awakening, for **fear** must slip away under the gentle remedy it gives. *T-1.I.55.1:6*

~ the miracle dissolves **error**. *T-1.I.57.1*

~ the miracle acknowledges all men as your brothers and mine. *T-1.I.59.1*

~ **wholeness** is the perceptual content of miracles. *T-1.I.61.1*

~ their **strength** in releasing **man** from his misplaced **sense** of isolation, **deprivation**, and lack. *T-1.I.67.1*

~ the miracle is thus a sign that the **mind** has chosen to be led by **Christ** in His **service**. *T-1.I.70.1*

~ miracles arise from a miraculous state of **mind**. *T-1.I.71.1*

~ the miracle is an expression of an inner **awareness** of **Christ** and the **acceptance** of His **Atonement**. *T-1.I.72.1*

~ a miracle is never lost. *T-1.I.73.1*

~ the miracle **will** always bless **you**. *T-1.I.73.4*

~ a sign of **love** among equals. *T-1.I.78.1*

~ temporary **communication** devices. *T-1.I.81.2*

~ the miracle is reciprocal because it involves equality. *T-1.I.81.7*

~ the miracle is a **learning device** which lessens the **need** for **time**. *T-1.I.82.1*

~ unique property of shortening **time** by rendering the space of **time** it occupies unnecessary. *T-1.I.83.1*

~ the miracle abolishes **time**. It does this by a process of collapsing it and thus abolishing certain intervals **within** it. *T-1.I.84.1:2*

~ rearranges the distribution of **light**. *T-1.I.84.7*

~ only device which **man** has at his immediate disposal. *T-1.I.85.1*

~ **learning** aids which aim at facilitating a state in which **they** are unnecessary. *T-1.I.86.1*

~ it corrects errors because **they** are errors. *T-1.I.94.7*

~ the miracle makes no distinction among degrees of misperception. It is a device for **perception-correction**, effective quite apart from either the degree or the direction of the **error**. *T-1.I.95.1:2*

~ miracle aims at restoring the **awareness** of **reality**. *T-1.I.96.4*

~ the miracle compares what **man** has made with the higher **level creation**, accepting what is in accord as true and rejecting the discordant as false. *T-1.I.98.1*

~ miracles are natural, corrective, **healing**, and universal. There is **nothing good they** cannot do, but **they** cannot be performed in the **spirit** of **doubt**. *T-2.II.19.9:10*

~ the miracle turns the **defense** of **Atonement** to the protection of the inner **self**, which, as it becomes more and more secure, assumes its natural talent of protecting others. *T-2.II.43.1*

~ the **means** of correcting **level confusion**. *T-2.III.53.3*

~ the whole aim of the miracle is to raise the **level** of **communication**, not to impose regression in the improper **sense** upon it. *T-2.III.59.6*

~ as a creative act, the miracle **need** not await the right-mindedness of the receiver. In **fact**, its **purpose** is to restore him to his right **mind**. *T-2.III.63.4:5*

~ the expression of **Atonement**. *T-2.V.87.1*

~ a sign of real respect from the worthy to the worthy. *T-2.V.87.1*

~ the miracle is a device for shortening but not abolishing **time**. *T-2.VI.107.1*

~ the miracle abolishes the **need** for lower-**order** concerns. Since it is an out-of-pattern **time interval**, the ordinary considerations of **time** and space do not apply. When **you** perform a miracle, **I will** arrange both **time** and space to adjust to it. *T-3.II.4.1:3*

~ the miracle is always a **denial** of this **error** and an affirmation of the **truth**. *T-3.II.7.1*

~ the miracle perceives everything as it is. *T-3.IV.28.1*

~ the miracle is a **way** of perceiving, not of knowing. It is the right **answer** to a **question**, and **you** do not **ask** questions at all when **you** know. *T-3.V.31.5:6*

~ god's miracles are as total as His Thoughts because **they** are His Thoughts. *T-3.VII.59.6*

~ **god** and His miracles are inseparable. *T-3.VII.60.5*

~ the miracle itself is just this fusion or **union** of **will** between **Father** and Son. *T-5.III.18.3*

~ miracles are an expression of this **confidence. They** are reflections both of your own proper identification with your brothers and of your own **awareness** that your identification is maintained by **extension**. The miracle is a **lesson** in total **perception**. *T-7.X.97.2:4*

~ the miracle is therefore a **lesson** in what **joy** is. **Being** a **lesson** in sharing, it is a **lesson** in **love**, which is **joy.** Every miracle is thus a **lesson** in **truth**, and by **offering truth you** are **learning** the **difference** between **pain** and **joy**. *T-7.XI.106.5:7*

~ the miracles we do bear **witness** to the **Will** of the **Father** for His Son and to our **joy** in uniting with His **Will** for us. *T-8.V.38.7*

~ miracles are merely the sign of your willingness to follow the Holy Spirit's **plan** of **salvation** in recognition of the **fact** that **you** do not know what it is. *T-9.III.15.1*

~ miracles **have** no place in **eternity** because **they** are reparative. *T-9.V.36.1*

~ miracles are a **way** of **giving acceptance** and **receiving** it. *T-9.V.36.3*

~ the miracle is the act of a **Son of God** who has laid aside all false Gods and who calls on his brothers to do likewise. It is an act of **faith**, because it is the recognition that his **brother** can do it. It is a **call** to the **Holy Spirit** in his **mind**, a **call** to Him which is strengthened by this joining. *T-9.X.91.1:3*

~ miracles are merely the translation of **denial** into **truth**. *T-11.III.14.1*

~ miracles demonstrate that **learning** has occurred under the right **guidance**, for **learning** is invisible, and what has been learned can be recognized only by its results. Its generalization is demonstrated as **you** use it in more and more situations. **You will** recognize that **you have** learned there is no **order of difficulty** in miracles when **you have** applied them to all situations. There is no **situation** to which miracles do not apply, and by applying them to all situations, **you will gain** the **real world**. *T-11.VIII.61.1:4*

~ miracles violate every law of **reality** as this **world** judges it. Every law of **time** and space, of **magnitude** and mass, of prediction and control is transcended, for what the **Holy Spirit** enables **you** to do is clearly beyond all of them. *T-11.VIII.63.2:3*

~ miracles are His witnesses and speak for His Presence. *T-11.VIII.64.3*

~ the miracle enables **you** to **see** your **brother** without his **past** and so perceive him as born again. *T-12.VI.49.1*

~ the miracle, without a **function** in **Heaven**, is needful **here**. *T-13.II.3.6*

~ this is the miracle of **creation**; that it is one forever. Every miracle **you** offer to the **Son of God** is but the true **perception** of one aspect of the whole. *T-13.II.5.1:2*

~ there is one miracle, as there is one **reality**. And every miracle **you** do contains them all, as every aspect of **reality you see** blends quietly into the One **Reality** of God. The only miracle that ever was is God's most holy Son, created in the One **Reality** that is his **Father**. *T-13.II.6.3:5*

~ miracles offered the **Son of God** through the **Holy Spirit** attune **you** to reality. *T-13.II.7.2*

~ miracles in this **world join you** to your brothers. *T-13.II.9.1*

~ your miracles offer **you** the testimony that **you** are blessed. *T-13.VI.49.1*

~ the miracle teaches **you** that **you have** chosen guiltlessness, **freedom**, and **joy**. It is not a **cause**, but an effect. It is the natural result of choosing right, attesting to your happiness that comes from choosing to be free of **guilt**. *T-13.VIII.69.1:3*

~ the miracle acknowledges the guiltlessness which must **have** been denied to produce **need** of **healing**. *T-14.II.9.1*

~ the miracle, therefore, has a unique **function** and is motivated by a unique **Teacher**, who brings the **laws** of another **world** to this one. The miracle is the one **thing you** can do that transcends **order, being** based not on differences but on equality. *T-14.VI.47.6:7*

~ miracles are not in competition, and the number of them that **you** can do is limitless. **They** can be simultaneous and legion. *T-14.VI.48.1:2*

~ the miracle offers exactly the same response to every **call** for **help**. It does not judge the **call**. It merely recognizes what it is and answers accordingly. It does not consider which **call** is louder or greater or more important. *T-14.VI.51.1:4*

~ the miracle gives equal **blessing** to all who **share** in it, and that is also why **everyone** shares in it. *T-14.VI.51.9*

~ the **means** on which **you** can depend for miracles has been provided for **you**. *T-14.VII.67.2*

~ the miracle acknowledges His changelessness by seeing His Son as **he** always was and not as **he** would **make** himself. The miracle brings the effects which only guiltlessness can bring and thus establishes the **fact** that guiltlessness must be. *T-14.VII.67.7:8*

~ miracles are the instants of **release you** offer and **will receive**. **They** attest to your willingness to be released and to offer **time** to the **Holy Spirit** for His use of it. *T-15.II.13.4:5*

~ nor do **you** do them. It is their **extension**, far beyond the limits **you** perceive, that demonstrates **you** did not do them. *T-16.III.10.4:5*

~ if miracles are at all, their attributes would **have** to be miraculous, **being part** of them. *T-16.III.10.8*

~ **you** do not **understand** them, either in **part** or whole. Yet **you have** done them. Therefore, your understanding cannot be necessary. Yet it is still **impossible** to accomplish what **you** do not **understand**. And so there must be something in **you** that does **understand**. *T-16.III.11.4:8*

~ **you have** done miracles, but it is quite apparent that **you have** not done them **alone**. *T-16.III.13.1*

~ miracles are natural to **God** and to the One Who speaks for Him. For His task is to translate the miracle into the **knowledge** which it represents and which is lost to **you**. *T-16.III.15.4:5*

~ every miracle is but the end of an **illusion**. *T-19.V.45.8*

~ the miracle of **life** is ageless, born in **time** but nourished in **eternity**. *T-19.V.87.6*

~ no one who has received it for himself could find it **difficult**. For by receiving it, **he** learned it was not given him **alone**. *T-22.V.44.2:3*

~ miracles are merely **change** of **purpose** from **hurt** to **healing**. *T-24.V.36.9*

~ miracles depend on **justice**. *T-25.X.82.7*

~ a miracle is **justice**. It is not a **special gift** to some to be withheld from others as less worthy, more condemned, and thus apart from **healing**. *T-25.X.83.6:7*

~ a miracle can never be received because another could **receive** it not. *T-25.X.85.4*

~ the miracle that **you receive, you give**. Each one becomes an illustration of the law on which **salvation** rests—that **justice** must be done to all if anyone is to be healed. *T-25.X.86.7:8*

~ each miracle is an example of what **justice** can accomplish when it is offered to **everyone** alike. It is received and given equally. It is **awareness** that giving and receiving are the same. *T-25.X.87.1:3*

~ it is the same for **everyone**, because it sees no differences in them. Its **offering** is universal, and it teaches but one **message**: What is God's belongs to **everyone** and is his due. *T-25.X.87.5:6*

~ every miracle is possible the instant that the **Son of God** perceives his wishes and the **Will of God** are one. *T-26.VIII.56.6*

~ it is not understood apart from Him and therefore has no **meaning** in this **world**. *T-26.VIII.57.6*

~ the miracle is possible when **cause** and consequence are brought together, not kept separate. *T-26.VIII.61.1*

~ in every miracle all **healing** lies, for **God** gave **answer** to them all as one. *T-26.VIII.62.4*

~ a miracle can **make** no **change** at all. But it can **make** what always has been true be recognized by those who know it not. *T-26.VIII.67.4:5*

~ a miracle is **now**. It stands already **here** in **present grace**, **within** the only **interval** of **time** which **sin** and **fear have** overlooked but which is all there is to **time**. The working out of all **correction** takes no **time** at all. *T-26.IX.72.8:10*

~ a miracle of **healing** proves that **separation** is without effect. What **you** would prove to him, **you will** believe. *T-27.III.16.9:10*

~ a miracle can offer **nothing** less to him than it has given unto **you**. *T-27.III.17.5*

~ thus does the miracle **undo** all things the **world** attests can never be undone. *T-27.III.18.1*

~ **they** bestow an equal **gift** of full deliverance from **guilt** upon your **brother** and yourself. *T-27.III.19.2*

~ the miracle extends without your **help**, but **you** are needed that it can begin. *T-27.VI.44.2*

~ it is its nature to extend itself the instant it is born. And it is born the instant it is offered and received. *T-27.VI.44.4:5*

~ miracles wait not on **time**. *T-27.VI.45.14*

~ each miracle **He** brings is **witness** that the **body** is not real. *T-27.VII.57.8*

~ the miracle makes no distinctions in the names by which sin's witnesses are called. It merely proves that what **they** represent has no effects. *T-27.VII.58.1:2*

~ the miracle forgives because it stands for what is **past forgiveness** and is true. *T-27.VII.59.2*

~ miracles reflect the simple statement, **I have** done this **thing**, and it is this **I** would **undo**. *T-27.IX.87.5*

~ the miracle does **nothing**. All it does is to **undo**. And thus it cancels out the interference to what has been done. It does not add, but merely takes away. And what it takes away is long since gone, but **being** kept in **memory**, appears to **have** immediate effects. *T-28.I.1.1:5*

~ the miracle but shows the **past** is gone, and what has truly gone has no effects. *T-28.I.1.8*

~ in quietness, **see** in the miracle a **lesson** in allowing **Cause** to **have** Its own effects and **doing nothing** that would **interfere**. *T-28.II.10.9*

~ the miracle comes quietly into the **mind** that stops an instant and is still. It reaches gently from that **quiet time**, and from the **mind** it healed in **quiet** then, to other minds to **share** its quietness. *T-28.II.11.1:2*

~ the miracle does not **awaken you** but merely shows **you** who the dreamer is. It teaches **you** there is a **choice** of dreams while **you** are still asleep, depending on the **purpose** of your dreaming. *T-28.III.19.1:2*

~ it demonstrates what **He** would **have you** learn and shows **you** its effects are what **you want**. *T-28.III.25.2*

~ the miracle returns the **cause** of **fear** to **you** who made it. *T-28.III.26.1*

~ thus is the **body** healed by miracles because **they** show the **mind** made **sickness** and employed the **body** to be **victim** or effect of what it made. *T-28.III.26.4*

~ this **world** is full of miracles. **They** stand in shining silence next to every **dream** of pain and **suffering**, of sin and **guilt**. **They** are the dream's alternative, the **choice** to be the dreamer rather than deny the active **role** in making up the **dream**. **They** are the glad effects of taking back the consequence of **sickness** to its **cause**. *T-28.III.27.1:4*

~ the miracle would leave no proof of **guilt** to bring **you witness** to what never was. *T-28.IV.35.5*

~ miracles are the result when **you** do not insist on seeing in the **gap** what is not there. *T-28.V.46.7*

~ the miracle does not select some dreams to leave untouched by its beneficence. *T-29.V.25.6*

~ the miracle prepares the **way**. *T-29.V.26.8*

~ the miracle does not restore the **truth**, the **light** the **veil** between has not put out. It merely lifts the **veil** and lets the **truth** shine unencumbered, **being** what it is. It does not **need belief** to be itself, for it has been created, so it is. *T-29.IX.56.5:7*

~ the miracle is **means** to demonstrate that all appearances can **change** because **they** are appearances and cannot **have** the changelessness **reality** entails. The miracle attests **salvation** from appearances by showing **they** can **change**. *T-30.IX.90.1:2*

~ the miracle is proof **he** is not bound by **loss** or **suffering** in any **form** because it can so easily be changed. *T-30.IX.90.6*

~ miracles but show what **you have** interposed between **reality** and your **awareness** is unreal and does not **interfere** at all. *T-30.IX.92.2*

~ there is no miracle **you** cannot **have** when **you desire healing**. *T-30.IX.92.5*

~ a miracle has come to heal God's Son and close the door upon his dreams of **weakness**, opening the **way** to his **salvation** and **release**. *T-31.VIII.92.4*

~ **you** are entitled to miracles because of what **you** are. **You will receive** miracles because of what **God** is. And **you will** offer miracles because **you** are one with **God**. *W-pI.77.1.1:3*

~ your claim to miracles does not lie in your illusions about yourself. It does not depend on any magical powers **you have** ascribed to yourself nor on any of the rituals **you have** devised. It is inherent in the **truth** of what **you** are. It is implicit in what **God** your **Father** is. It was ensured in your **creation** and guaranteed by the **laws** of **God**. *W-pI.77.2.1:5*

~ the miracles which are your right since **they** belong to **you**. *W-pI.77.3.1*

~ miracles are never taken from one and given to another. *W-pI.77.4.3*

~ miracles do not obey the **laws** of this **world**. **They** merely follow from the **laws** of **God**. *W-pI.77.4.4:5*

~ **i** am entitled to miracles because **I** am under no **laws** but God's. *W-pI.89.2.1*

~ the solution is always a miracle with which **I** let the **grievance** be replaced. *W-pI.90.2.2*

~ miracles and **vision** necessarily go together. *W-pI.91.1.1*

~ his miracles are true. **They will** not fade when dreaming ends. **They** end the **dream** instead and last forever, for **they** come from **God** to His dear Son, whose other **name** is **you**. *W-pI.106.4.5:7*

~ no miracle can ever be denied to those who know that **they** are one with **God**. *W-pI.124.6.1*

~ there is no miracle **you** cannot **give**, for all are given **you**. **Receive** them **now** by opening the storehouse of your **mind** where **they** are laid and giving them away. *W-pI.159.2.4:5*

~ a miracle contains the **gift** of **grace**, for it is given and received as one. And thus it illustrates the law of **truth** the **world** does not obey because it fails entirely to **understand** its ways. A miracle inverts **perception** which was upside-down before, and thus it ends the strange distortions that were manifest. **Now** is **perception** open to the **truth**. **Now** is **forgiveness** seen as justified. *W-pII.ST341.2.1:5*

~ the miracle is taken first on **faith** because to **ask** for it implies the **mind** has been made ready to conceive of what it cannot **see** and does not **understand**. Yet **faith will** bring its witnesses to show that what it rested on is really there. And thus the miracle **will** justify your **faith** in it and show it rested on a **world** more real than what **you** saw before—a **world** redeemed from what **you thought you** saw. *W-pII.ST341.4.1:3*

MIRACLE-MINDEDNESS *A Course in Miracles Term*

HOLY SPIRIT

~ the impersonal nature of miracle-mindedness ensures your **grace**. *T-1.I.74.3*

~ **miracle**-mindedness **means miracle-readiness**. *T-1.I.75.1*

~ the voluntary aspects of miracle-mindedness, are up to you. *T-1.I.75.6*

~ the **miracle** is an expression of **miracle**-mindedness. *T-2.III.63.1*

~ **miracle**-mindedness merely **means** right-mindedness in the **sense** that **we** are **now** using it. *T-2.III.63.2*

~ the **Holy Spirit** is the motivation for **miracle**-mindedness, the **will** to heal the **separation** by letting it go. *T-5.III.17.4*

MIRACLE-WORKER

DICTIONARY: *a person who seems to be able to perform miracles.*

HOLY SPIRIT

~ the **miracle** worker is one who accepts my kind of **denial** and **projection**, unites his own inherent **abilities** to deny and project with mine, and imposes them back on himself and others. This establishes the total lack of **threat** anywhere. Together **we** can then work for the real **time** of **peace**, which is eternal. *T-2.II.23.6:8*

288

~ the sole responsibility of the **miracle** worker is to accept the **Atonement** for himself. This **means** that **he** recognizes that **mind** is the only creative **level** and that its errors are healed by the **Atonement**. Once **he** accepts this, his **mind** can only heal. By denying his **mind** any destructive potential and reinstating its purely constructive powers, **he** has placed himself in a position where **he** can **undo** the **level confusion** of others. The **message he** then gives to others is the **truth** that their minds are similarly constructive and that their miscreations cannot **hurt** them. By affirming this, the **miracle** worker releases the **mind** from over-evaluating its own **learning device** (the **body**) and restores the **mind** to its true position as the **learner**. *T-2.III.65.1:6*

~ all **miracle** workers **need** that kind of training. **I** cannot let them leave their minds unguarded, or **they will** not be able to **help** me. **Miracle** working entails a full realization of the **power** of **thought** and real avoidance of **miscreation**. *T-2.V.94.2:4*

~ my own injunction, "Do this in remembrance of me" is the **request** for cooperation from **miracle** workers. *T-3.II.10.2*

~ the **miracle** worker begins by perceiving **light** and translates his **perception** into sureness by continually extending it and accepting its **acknowledgment**. Its effects assure him it is there. *T-9.IV.27.5:6*

~ the task of the miracle-worker thus becomes to deny the **denial** of **truth**. *T-11.III.14.5*

MISCREATION

|mɪskrɪ'eɪʃ(ə)n|

DICTIONARY: *the action of creating something wrongly or badly.*

EGO

~ miscreation is necessarily believed in by its maker. *T-1.I.97.4*

~ **man** projects in the **spirit** of miscreation. *T-2.I.14.2*

~ even in miscreation **will** is affirming its **Source** or it would merely cease to be. *T-3.VI.45.2*

HOLY SPIRIT

~ it does not **exist** at all at the **level** of true **creation**. *T-1.I.97.4*

~ both the **separation** and the **fear** are miscreations of the **mind** which must be undone. *T-2.II.46.3*

~ it can be believed that the **mind** can miscreate in the **body** or that the **body** can miscreate in the **mind**. If it is understood that the **mind**, which is the only **level** of **creation**, cannot create beyond itself, neither type of **confusion need** occur. *T-2.III.54.3:4*

~ miscreations of the **mind** do not really **exist**. This recognition is a far better protective device than any **form** of **level confusion**, because it introduces **correction** at the **level** of the **error**. *T-2.III.60.5:6*

~ when **man** miscreates **he** is in **pain**. The **cause** and effect principle **here** is temporarily a real expediter. *T-2.V.97.1:2*

~ the fundamental opponents in the real basic **conflict** are **creation** and miscreation. All **fear** is implicit in the second, just as all **love** is inherent in the first. Because of this **difference**, the basic **conflict** is one between **love** and **fear**. *T-2.V.97.5:7*

~ the **mind will** inevitably disown its miscreations which, without the mind's **belief, will** no longer **exist**. *T-2.VI.110.2*

~ **god** and the Souls He created remain in surety, and therefore know that no miscreation exists. *T-3.VI.48.1*

MISERY

DICTIONARY: *a state or feeling of great distress or discomfort of **mind** or **body**.*

EGO

~ **you** who are steadfastly devoted to misery must first recognize that **you** are miserable and not **happy**. The **Holy Spirit** cannot **teach** without this **contrast**, for **you** believe that misery is happiness. *T-13.VII.54.2:3*

~ to leave one kind of misery and **seek** another is hardly an escape. To **change** illusions is to **make** no **change**. The search for **joy** in misery is senseless, for how could **joy** be found in misery? All that is possible in the dark **world** of misery is to select some aspects out of it, **see** them as different, and define the **difference** as **joy**. Yet to perceive a **difference** where none exists **will** surely **fail** to **make** a **difference**. *T-22.III.17.3:7*

HOLY SPIRIT

~ **i** am conditioning **you** to associate misery with the **ego** and **joy** with the **Soul**. **You have** conditioned yourselves the other **way** around. *T-4.VII.93.1:2*

~ **you will** either escape from misery entirely or not at all. *T-22.III.22.6*

~ no misery is **here**, but only **joy**. *T-22.III.27.10*

~ all your misery comes from the strange **belief** that **you** are powerless. *T-21.VIII.70.1*

~ no **form** of misery in reason's eyes can be confused with **joy**. *T-22.III.18.3*

~ the only way to escape from misery is to recognize it and go the other way. **Truth** is the same and misery the same, but **they** are different from each other in every **way**, in every instance, and without **exception**. *T-22.III.19.1:2*

~ all the misery **you** made has been your own. *T-22.III.25.5*

~ misery can come not near the holy **home** of **God**. *W-pI.186.6.5*

MISSION

DICTIONARY: *a strongly felt aim, ambition, or calling.*

EGO

~ everything that points the **way** in the direction of the **past** but sets **you** on a mission whose accomplishment can only be unreal. *T-26.VI.38.5*

HOLY SPIRIT; *escape crucifixion, accept **Atonement** for yourself.*

~ your mission is very simple. **You have** been chosen to live so as to demonstrate that **you** are not an **ego**. *T-4.VII.89.2:3*

~ our mission is to escape **crucifixion**, not **redemption**. *T-11.III.20.4*

~ **you will** not **fail** in your mission because **I** failed not in mine. *T-11.III.21.4*

~ yet the **Holy Spirit** knows it for **you**, and **He will** guide **you** to your **home** because that is His mission. As **He** fulfills His mission, **He will teach you** yours, for your mission is the same as His. By guiding your brothers **home**, **you** are but following Him. *T-11.V.40.5:7*

~ to open the eyes of the **blind** is the Holy Spirit's mission, for **He** knows that **they have** not lost their **vision** but merely **sleep**. **He** would **awaken** them from the **sleep** of forgetting to the remembering of **God**. *T-11.VII.56.2:3*

- when **you have** accepted your mission to project **peace**, **you will** find it, for by making it manifest, **you will see** it. *T-11.VIII.72.1*

- **god** gave the **Holy Spirit** to **you** and gave Him the mission to remove all **doubt** and every trace of **guilt** that His dear Son has laid upon himself. It is **impossible** that this mission **fail**. **Nothing** can prevent what **God** would **have** accomplished from accomplishment. *T-13.V.39.1:3*

- the mission of **redemption will** be fulfilled as surely as the **creation will** remain unchanged throughout **eternity**. *T-13.V.44.4*

- **we have** a mission **here**. **We** did not come to reinforce the **madness** which **we** once believed in. *W-pI.139.8.3:4*

- be **witness** in your happiness to how transformed the **mind** becomes which chooses to accept His gifts and feel the touch of **Christ**. Such is your mission **now**. *W-pI.166.15.4:5*

- it is their mission to become perfect **here**. *M-1.5.6*

MISTAKE |mə'stāk|

DICTIONARY: *an action or **judgment** that is misguided or wrong.*

EGO

- mistake is given the status of **truth**. *T-19.III.22.8*

- only mistakes **have** different forms, and so **they** can deceive. *T-22.IV.35.1*

- unfairness and **attack** are one mistake, so firmly joined that where one is perceived, the other must be seen. *T-26.XI.87.1*

- yours are mistakes, but his are sins and not the same as yours. His merit **punishment**, while yours in fairness should be overlooked. *T-27.III.25.5:6*

- one mistake which had the **power** to **undo creation** and to **make** a **world** which could replace it and destroy the **Will** of **God**. *T-30.VII.74.7*

- others **will make** mistakes and so **will you**, as long as this **illusion** of a **world** appears to be your **home**. *S-2.I.6.2*

HOLY SPIRIT

- all mistakes must be corrected at the **level** on which **they** occur. *T-2.III.53.3*

- nor does **He see** the mistakes at all. *T-17.VI.53.5*

- if this is a mistake, it can be undone easily by **truth**. Any mistake can be corrected, if **truth** be left to judge it. *T-19.III.22.6:7*

- an **error**, on the other hand, is not attractive. What **you see** clearly as a mistake **you want** corrected. *T-19.IV.26.8:9*

- mistakes **He** recognizes and would correct them all as **God** entrusted Him to do. *T-19.IV.27.7*

- nor can **He** recognize mistakes which cannot be corrected. *T-19.IV.27.8*

- a mistake which cannot be corrected is meaningless to Him. *T-19.IV.27.9*

- mistakes are for **correction**, and **they call** for **nothing** else. *T-19.IV.28.1*

- every mistake must be a **call** for **love**. *T-19.IV.28.3*

- **you will help** each other overcome mistakes by joyously releasing one another from the **belief** in **sin**. *T-19.IV.34.6*

291

~ the **correction** of your mistake **will give you** grounds for **faith**. *T-19.V.70.8*

~ all effects of your mistakes **will** disappear. *T-21.III.16.2*

~ mistakes, regardless of their **form**, can be corrected. *T-22.IV.32.4*

~ every mistake **you make** the other **will** gently **have** corrected for **you**. *T-22.V.42.1*

~ his mistakes can **cause delay**, which it is given **you** to take from him that both may end a **journey** that has never been begun and needs no end. *T-24.VII.56.3*

~ how better could your own mistakes be brought to **truth** than by your willingness to bring the **light** of **Heaven** with **you** as **you** walk beyond the **world** of **darkness** into **light**? *T-25.V.36.12*

~ one mistake is not more **difficult** for Him to bring to **truth** than is another. For there is but one mistake— the whole **idea** that **loss** is possible and could result in **gain** for anyone. *T-26.III.11.4:5*

~ it is not **difficult** to overlook mistakes that **have** been given no effects. *T-30.VII.81.2*

~ whatever mistakes **you** made, the **truth** about **you** is unchanged. *W-pI.93.7.3*

~ to allow a mistake to continue is to **make** additional mistakes based on the first and reinforcing it. It is this process that must be laid aside, for it is but another **way** in which **you** would defend illusions against the **truth**. *W-pI.95.11.1:2*

~ the **Holy Spirit** is not delayed in His **teaching** by your mistakes. **He** can be held back only by your unwillingness to let them go. *W-pI.95.9.1:2*

~ mistakes in **judgment** which the **mind** had made before are open to **correction** as the **truth** dismisses them as causeless. **Now** are **they** without effects. **They** cannot be concealed because their nothingness is recognized. *W-pI.138.9.3:5*

~ **we** acknowledge our mistakes, but **He** to Whom all **error** is unknown is yet the One Who answers our mistakes by giving us the **means** to lay them down and rise to Him in **gratitude** and **love**. *W-pI.168.5.3*

~ the **form** of the mistake is not important. What is important is only the recognition of a mistake as a mistake. *M-7.5.7:8*

~ mistakes do not correct mistakes. *M-22.5.6*

~ mistakes are tiny shadows, quickly gone, that for an instant only seem to **hide** the **face of Christ**, which still remains unchanged behind them all. *S-2.I.6.5*

NAME

|nām|

DICTIONARY: *a word or set of words by which a person, animal, place, or thing is known, addressed, or referred to.*

EGO

~ each one seems different because it has a different name, and so it seems to **answer** to a different sound. *T-27.VII.55.5*

~ **you** live by symbols. **You have** made up names for everything **you see**. Each one becomes a separate entity, identified by its own name. By this **you** carve it out of **unity**. By this **you** designate its **special** attributes and set it off from other things by emphasizing space surrounding it. This space **you** lay between all things to which **you give** a different name—all happenings in terms of place and **time**, all bodies which are greeted by a name. *W-pI.184.1.1:6*

~ what are these names by which the **world** becomes a series of discrete events, of things un-unified, of bodies kept apart and holding bits of **mind** as separate awarenesses? **You** gave these names to them, establishing **perception** as **you** wished to **have perception** be. The nameless things were given names and thus **reality** was given them as well. For what is named is given **meaning** and **will** then be seen as meaningful, a **cause** of true effects with consequence inherent in itself. *W-pI.184.3.1:4*

~ and **everyone** who learns to think that it is so accepts the signs and symbols which assert the **world** is real. It is for this **they** stand. **They** leave no **doubt** that what is named is there. It can be seen, as is anticipated. What denies that it is true is but **illusion**, for it is the ultimate **reality**. To **question** it is **madness**; to accept its presence is the proof of **sanity**. *W-pI.184.6.2:7*

HOLY SPIRIT

~ what is true in earth and **Heaven** is beyond your naming. *W-pI.184.8.3*

~ and though **we** use a different name for each **awareness** of an aspect of God's Son, **we understand** that **they have** but one name, Which **He** has given them. *W-pI.184.14.1*

~ a name does not heal. *M-23.1.6*

NEED

|nēd|

DICTIONARY: *require (something) because it is essential or very important.*

EGO

~ a need implies lack by definition. It involves the recognition that **you** would be better off in a state which is somehow different from the one **you** are in. *T-11.89.6:7*

~ everything that the **ego** tells **you** that **you** need **will hurt you**. For although the **ego** urges **you** again and again to get, it leaves **you nothing**, for what **you** get, it **will** demand of **you**. *T-12.VII.69.1:2*

~ what **you** think **you** need **will** merely serve to tighten up your **world** against the **light** and render **you** unwilling to **question** the **value** that this **world** can really hold for **you**. *T-12.VII.69.6*

~ to separate out certain aspects of the totality and look to them to meet your imagined needs, **you** are attempting to use **separation** to save **you**. *T-15.VI.46.3*

~ if **you** seek for satisfaction in gratifying your needs as **you** perceive them, **you** must believe that **strength** comes from another, and what **you gain he** loses. *T-15.VII.58.3*

~ **faith** and **perception** and **belief** can be misplaced and serve the great deceiver's needs as well as **truth**. *T-21.VI.56.1*

~ all that **I** sought before **I** needed not and did not even **want**. My only need **I** did not recognize. *W-pII.251.1.3:4*

HOLY SPIRIT

~ **you have** need of **nothing**. *T-12.VII.68.1*

~ only the **Holy Spirit** knows what **you** need. For **He will give you** all things that do not block the **way** to **light**. *T-12.VII.70.1:2*

~ in **time He** gives **you** all the things that **you** need **have** and **will** renew them as long as **you have** need of them. **He will** take **nothing** from **you** as long as **you have** any need of it. And yet **He** knows that everything **you** need is temporary and **will** but last until **you step** aside from all your needs and learn that all of them **have** been fulfilled. Therefore **He** has no investment in the things that **He** supplies except to **make** certain that **you will** not use them on behalf of lingering in **time**. **He** knows that **you** are not at **home** there, and **He** wills no **delay** to wait upon your joyous homecoming. *T-12.VII.70.4:8*

~ he **will** supply them with no emphasis at all upon them. What comes to **you** of Him comes safely, for **He will** ensure it never can become a dark spot, hidden in your **mind** and kept to **hurt you**. *T-12.VII.71.2:3*

~ the **Holy Spirit will teach you** to **awaken** unto us and to yourself. This is the only real need to be fulfilled in **time**. *T-12.VII.75.5:6*

~ god's Son can **make** no needs His **Father will** not meet if **he** but turn to Him ever so **little**. *T-14.VII.67.3*

~ with **love** in **you, you have** no need except to extend it. *T-15.VI.55.3*

~ only the **Holy Spirit** recognizes foolish needs as well as real ones. And **He will teach you** how to meet both without losing either. *T-16.II.7.7:8*

~ no needs **will** long be left unmet if **you** leave them all to Him Whose **function** is to meet them. That is His **function** and not yours. **He will** not meet them secretly. *T-16.II.8.4:6*

~ **he** need not be forgiven, but awakened. *T-17.I.1.3*

~ there is no need to suffer any more. But there is need that **you** be healed, because the **suffering** of the **world** has made it deaf to its **salvation** and deliverance. *T-27.VII.60.5:6*

~ **you** need new ideas about **time**. *W-pI.7.8.2*

~ **you** need to be aware of what the **Holy Spirit** uses to replace the **image** of a **body** in your **mind**. **You** need to feel something to put your **faith** in, as **you** lift it from the **body**. **You** need a real **experience** of something else, something more solid and more sure, more worthy of your **faith**, and really there. *W-pI.91.9.2:4*

~ **now I see** that **I** need only **truth**. In that, all needs are satisfied, all cravings end, all hopes are finally fulfilled, and dreams are gone. *W-pII.251.1.5:6*

~ **i** must accept **Atonement** for myself and **nothing** more. **God** has already done all things that need be done. And **I** must learn **I** need do **nothing** of myself, for **I** need but accept my **Self**, my sinlessness, created for me, **now** already mine, to feel God's **Love** protecting me from **harm**, to **understand** my **Father** loves His Son, to know **I** am the Son my **Father** loves. *W-pII.337.1.5:7*

~ our **Father** knows our needs. **He** gives us **grace** to meet them all. And so **we trust** in Him to send us miracles to bless the **world** and heal our minds as **we** return to Him. *W-pII.349.2.1:3*

NIGHTMARE

DICTIONARY: *a frightening or unpleasant* **dream**.

EGO; *madman's dreams*

~ the **ego** would preserve your nightmares and prevent **you** from awakening and understanding that **they** are **past**. *T-12.IV.28.6*

~ nightmares are childish dreams. The toys **have** turned against the **child** who **thought he** made them real. *T-29.X.65.1:2*

~ this does the **child** believe because **he** fears his thoughts and gives them to the toys instead. And their **reality** becomes his own because **they** seem to save him from his thoughts. Yet do **they** keep his thoughts alive and real but seen **outside** himself, where **they** can turn against him for his treachery to them. **He** thinks **he** needs them that **he** may escape his thoughts, because **he** thinks the thoughts are real. And so **he** makes of anything a toy to **make** his **world** remain **outside** himself, and play that **he** is but a **part** of it. *T-29.X.65.5:9*

HOLY SPIRIT; *childish dreams*

~ no nightmare can defeat a **Child of God** in his **purpose**. *T-11.III.19.1*

~ learn that even the darkest nightmare that disturbed the **Mind** of God's sleeping Son holds no **power** over him. *T-13.V.43.7*

~ it is a nightmare of abandonment by an eternal **Love** which could not leave the Son whom It created out of **love**. *W-pI.190.2.3*

NOTHING

DICTIONARY: *not anything; no single* **thing**.

EGO

~ valuing nothing, **you have** sought nothing and found nothing. By making nothing real to **you, you have** seen it. *T-11.IX.82.4:5*

~ **you will** believe that nothing is of **value** and **will value** it. *T-13.VII.55.3*

~ distortions **you have** made of nothing—all the strange forms and feelings and actions and reactions that **you have** woven out of it. Nothing is so alien to **you** as the simple **truth**, and nothing are **you** less inclined to listen to. *T-13.VII.56.4:5*

~ your **faith** in nothing is deceiving **you**. *T-13.VII.58.4*

~ **you will** never learn how to **make** nothing everything. Yet **see** that this has been your **goal**. *T-13.VII.60.4:5*

HOLY SPIRIT

~ it is not there. *T-3.VI.47.1*

~ the "nothing" is neither greater nor less because of what is absent. *T-7.IV.19.11*

~ "all" and "nothing" are dichotomous, without a range. *T-7.IV.20.1*

~ nothingness **will** become invisible, for **you will** at last **have** seen truly. *T-11.IX.84.5*

~ no **part** of nothing can be more resistant to the **truth** than can another. *T-23.III.21.6*

~ nothingness cannot be pictured. *T-27.IV.33.1*

~ what is made of nothingness cannot be called new or different. *P-2.I.2.8*

DICTIONARY: *at the **present time** or moment.*

EGO

~ if **you remember** the **past** as **you** look upon your **brother**, **you will** be unable to perceive the **reality** that is now. *T-12.VI.45.7*

~ now **you** are shifting back and forth between the **past** and **present**. *T-26.VI.40.4*

HOLY SPIRIT;   *the only **time**, **time** of **salvation**, **release** from **time**, closest approximation of **eternity**.*

~ the only aspect of **time** which is really eternal is now. *T-5.V.37.5*

~ it is in the **reality** of now, without **past** or **future**, that the beginning of the **appreciation** of eternity lies. For only now is **here**, and it presents the opportunities for the holy encounters in which **salvation** can be found. *T-12.IV.30.4:5*

~ when **you have** learned to look upon **everyone** with no reference at all to the **past**, either his or yours as **you** perceived it, **you will** be able to learn from what **you see** now. *T-12.VI.46.3*

~ now is the **time** of **salvation**, for now is the **release** from **time**. *T-12.VI.52.1*

~ now it is given **you** to heal and **teach**, to **make** what **will** be now. *T-13.IV.27.1*

~ the stillness and the **peace** of now enfolds **you** in perfect **gentleness**. Everything is gone except the **truth**. *T-16.VIII.75.5:6*

~ and now **we** are at **peace** forever, for the **dream** is over now. *W-pI.108.1.5*

~ now is the **time** of prophecy fulfilled. Now are all ancient promises upheld and fully kept. *W-pII.15.1:2*

~ for in this instant has **forgiveness** come to set me free. The **birth** of **Christ** is now, without a **past** or **future**. **He** has come to **give** His **present blessing** to the **world**, restoring it to timelessness and **love**. And **love** is ever-**present**, **here** and now. *W-pII.308.1.5:8*

~ **we** are forgiven now. *W-pII.ST361.5.2*

OBSTACLE

DICTIONARY: *a **thing** that blocks one's **way** or prevents or hinders progress.*

HOLY SPIRIT

~ some of them **you will** try to impose. Others **will** seem to arise from elsewhere—from your brothers and from various aspects of the **world outside**. Yet **peace will** gently cover them, extending **past** completely unhindered. *T-19.IV.37.2:4*

~ it is this **little** remnant of **attack you** cherish still against each other that is the first obstacle the **peace** in **you** encounters in its going forth. This **little** wall of hatred would still oppose the **Will** of **God** and keep it limited. *T-19.V.41.10:11*

~ the **belief** that the **body** is valuable for what it offers. For **here** is the **attraction** of **guilt** made manifest in the **body** and seen in it. *T-19.V.59.3:4*

~ the second obstacle is no more solid than the first. For **you will** neither to get rid of **peace** nor **limit** it. What are these obstacles which **you** would interpose between **peace** and its going forth but barriers **you** place between your **will** and its accomplishment? *T-19.V.63.3:5*

~ and as this **memory** rises in your **mind**, **peace** must still surmount a final obstacle after which is **salvation** completed and the **Son of God** entirely restored to **sanity**. For **here** your **world** does end. *T-19.V.90.5:6*

~ the fourth obstacle to be surmounted hangs like a heavy **veil** before the **face of Christ**. Yet as His face rises beyond it, shining with **joy** because **He** is in His Father's **Love**, **peace will** lightly brush the **veil** aside and run to meet Him and to **join** with Him at last. For this dark **veil**, which seems to **make** the **face of Christ** Himself like to a leper's and the bright rays of His Father's **love** which **light** His face with **glory** appear as streams of blood, fades in the blazing **light** beyond it when the **fear** of **death** is gone. *T-19.V.91.1:3*

~ this is the darkest **veil**, upheld by the **belief** in **death** and protected by its **attraction**. The dedication to **death** and to its sovereignty is but the solemn **vow**, the **promise** made in **secret** to the **ego** never to lift this **veil**, not to approach it nor even to suspect that it is there. This is the **secret bargain** made with the **ego** to keep what lies beyond the **veil** forever blotted out and unremembered. *T-19.V.92.1:3*

~ every obstacle that **peace** must flow across is surmounted in just the same **way**; the **fear** that raised it yields to the **love** beneath it, and so the **fear** is gone. *T-19.V.94.1*

~ the **desire** to get rid of **peace** and drive the **Holy Spirit** from **you** fades in the presence of the **quiet** recognition that **you** love Him. *T-19.V.94.3*

~ from beyond each of the obstacles to **love**, **Love** Itself has called, and each has been surmounted by the **power** of the **attraction** of what lies beyond. Your wanting **fear** seemed to be holding them in place. Yet when **you** heard the **voice** of **love** beyond them, **you** answered and **they** disappeared. *T-19.V.94.6:8*

~ no obstacle to **peace** can be surmounted through its **help**. It does not open up its secrets and bid **you** look on them and go beyond them. It would not **have you see** its **weakness** and learn it has no **power** to keep **you** from the **truth**. *T-19.V.97.3:5*

~ every obstacle was finally surmounted which seemed to rise and block their **way** before. *T-22.V.43.3*

~ obstacles to **peace**. The final one, the hardest to believe is **nothing** and a seeming obstacle with the **appearance** of a solid block, impenetrable, fearful and beyond surmounting, is the **fear of God** Himself. **Here** is the basic premise which enthrones the **thought** of fear as God. For **fear** is loved by those who worship it, and **love** appears to be invested **now** with cruelty. *W-pI.170.10.2:5*

OFFERING

DICTIONARY: *a **thing** offered, especially as a **gift** or contribution, meager offering, **little** offering of **darkness***

EGO

~ littleness is the offering **you** gave yourself. **You** offered this in place of **magnitude**, and **you** accepted it. *T-15.IV.22.2:3*

HOLY SPIRIT

~ his offering to **you** has never changed. *T-12.V.39.5*

~ **you will join** with me in offering what is needed. *T-15.VII.62.10*

~ its offering is universal. *T-25.X.87.6*

~ each **dream** becomes an offering of **love**. *T-29.V.30.6*

OMNISCIENT

DICTIONARY: *knowing everything.*

HOLY SPIRIT

~ who could **experience** the end of **guilt** who feels responsible for his **brother** in the **role** of guide for him? Such a **function** presupposes a **knowledge** that no one **here** can **have**; a **certainty** of **past**, **present** and **future**, and of all the effects that may occur in them. Only from this omniscient point of view would such a **role** be possible. Yet no **perception** is omniscient. *P-2.VII.5.3:6*

ONENESS

DICTIONARY: *the **fact** or state of **being** unified or whole, though comprised of two or more parts.*

EGO

~ while **you** think that **part** of **you** is separate, the **concept** of a oneness joined as one is meaningless. *T-25.II.10.1*

HOLY SPIRIT; *idea God is*

~ the Oneness of the **Creator** and the **creation** is your **wholeness**, your **sanity**, and your limitless **power**. *T-7.VII.65.4*

~ oneness cannot be divided. *T-9.X.87.3*

~ oneness, before which all **separation** vanishes. *T-14.IV.35.4*

~ if **you** were one with **God** and recognized this oneness, **you** would know His **power** is yours. *T-22.VII.62.1*

~ what is one is joined in **truth**. *T-24.III.18.8*

~ **you** can lose **sight** of oneness, but can not **make sacrifice** of its **reality**. *T-26.II.6.1*

~ one **creation**, one **reality**, one **truth**, and but one Son. **Nothing** conflicts with oneness. *T-26.IV.18.3:4*

~ oneness is simply the **idea God** is. And in His **Being, He** encompasses all things. No **mind** holds anything but Him. *W-pI.169.5.1:3*

~ we cannot speak nor write nor even think of this at all. It comes to every **mind** when total recognition that its **will** is God's has been completely given and received completely. It returns the **mind** into the endless **present**, where the **past** and **future** cannot be conceived. It lies beyond **salvation**—**past** all **thought** of time, **forgiveness**, and the holy **face of Christ**. The **Son of God** has merely disappeared into His **Father**, as his **Father** has in him. The **world** has never been at all. **Eternity** remains a constant state. *W-pI.169.6.1:7*

~ for oneness must be **here**. *W-pI.169.8.2*

~ we are one and therefore **give** up **nothing**. *W-pI.192.7.5*

~ we are separate from no living **thing** and therefore one with Him. *W-pI.195.6.1*

~ no exceptions ever can be made which would reduce our **wholeness** nor impair or **change** our **function** to complete the One Who is Himself **completion**. *W-pI.195.6.2*

~ **now** are we one in shared **Identity**, with **God** our **Father** as our only **Source** and everything created **part** of us. *W-pII.283.2.1*

~ oneness and **sickness** cannot co-**exist**. *M-12.6.1*

OPEN-MINDED

|ˈōpən ˈmīndid|

DICTIONARY: *willing to consider new ideas; unprejudiced.*

EGO

~ **they** believe that **sickness** has chosen them. Nor are **they** open-minded on this point. *M-5.8.7:8*

HOLY SPIRIT

~ the centrality of open-mindedness, perhaps the last of the attributes the **teacher of God** acquires, is easily understood when its relation to **forgiveness** is recognized. Open-mindedness comes with lack of **judgment**. As **judgment** shuts the **mind** against God's **Teacher**, so open-mindedness invites Him to come in. As **condemnation** judges the **Son of God** as **evil**, so open-mindedness permits him to be judged by the **Voice** for **God** on His behalf. As the **projection** of **guilt** upon him would send him to **hell**, so open-mindedness lets Christ's **image** be projected on him. Only the open-minded can be at **peace**, for **they alone** **see reason** for it. *M-4.23.1:6*

~ how do the open-minded forgive? **They have** let go all things that would prevent **forgiveness**. **They have** in **truth** abandoned the **world** and let it be restored to them in newness and in **joy** so glorious **they** could never **have** conceived of such a **change**. **Nothing** is **now** as it was formerly. **Nothing** but sparkles **now** which seemed so dull and lifeless before. And above all are all things welcoming, for **threat** is gone. No **clouds** remain to **hide** the **face of Christ**. **Now** is the **goal** achieved. *M-4.24.1:8*

OPPOSITE

|ˈäpəzət|

DICTIONARY: *having a position on the other or further side of something; facing something, especially something of the same type.*

EGO

~ **you have** chosen to be in a state of opposition in which opposites are possible. *T-5.IV.22.7*

~ the opposites **you see** in **you will** never be compatible. *W-pI.96.1.4*

~ in **death alone** are opposites resolved, for ending opposition is to die. *W-pI.138.7.3*

~ opposites **make** endless **war**. *M-27.2.7*

HOLY SPIRIT

~ the **Holy Spirit** must work through opposites, because He must work with and for a **mind** that is in opposition. *T-5.VI.43.1*

~ the **denial** of the opposite of goodness enables **you** to perceive a **condition** in which opposites do not **exist**. And this is the **condition** of **knowledge**. *T-10.VIII.72.1:2*

~ opposites which cannot be reconciled and cannot both be true. **You** are guilty or **guiltless**, bound or free, **happy** or unhappy. *T-13.VIII.68.5:6*

~ **light** or **darkness**, **knowledge** or ignorance are yours, but not both. Opposites must be brought together and not kept apart. For their **separation** is only in your **mind**, and **they** are reconciled by **union**, as **you** are. *T-14.IV.24.2:4*

~ the **Holy Spirit** must **teach** through comparisons and uses opposites to point to **truth**. *T-16.VIII.75.2*

~ **conflict** and **peace** are opposites. Where one abides the other cannot be; where either goes the other disappears. *T-23.II.18.6:7*

~ what is real denies its opposite. *T-31.VI.62.3*

~ **choice** is the obvious escape from what appears as opposites. *W-pI.138.3.1*

ORDER

|ˈôrdər|

DICTIONARY: *a state in which everything is in its correct or appropriate place.*

EGO; *arrange by **judgement**, judge.*

~ **laws** must be adapted to circumstances if **they** are to maintain order. *T-7.III.10.7*

HOLY SPIRIT

~ the **little sanity** which still remains is held together by a **sense** of order which **you** establish. Yet the very **fact** that **you** can do this and bring any order into **chaos** shows **you** that **you** are not an **ego** and that more than an **ego** must be in **you**. For the **ego** is **chaos**, and if it were all of **you**, no order at all would be possible. Yet though the order which **you** impose upon your minds limits the **ego**, it also limits **you**. To order is to judge and to arrange by **judgment**. *T-14.VI.50.1:5*

ORDER OF DIFFICULTY

A Course in Miracles Term

EGO

~ the lack of **order** of difficulty in miracles has not yet been accepted. *T-6.V.80.3*

~ in this **world**, it is not true that anything without **order** of difficulty can occur. *T-14.VI.47.5*

~ **heaven** can be chosen just as easily as **hell**. *W-p2.272.2.2*

~ the **belief** in **order** of difficulties is the basis for the world's **perception**. It rests on differences; on uneven background and shifting foreground, on unequal heights and diverse sizes, on varying degrees of **darkness** and **light**, and thousands of contrasts in which each **thing** seen competes with every other in **order** to be recognized. *M-8.1.1:2*

HOLY SPIRIT

~ **i** do not believe that there is an **order** of difficulty in miracles; **you** do. *T-4.V.68.4*

~ without a range, an **order** of difficulty is meaningless, and there must be no range in what **you** offer to each other. *T-6.V.64.6*

~ there can be no **order** of difficulty in **healing** merely because all **sickness** is **illusion**. Is it harder to dispel the **belief** of the insane in a larger hallucination as opposed to a smaller one? **Will he** agree more quickly to the unreality of a louder **voice he** hears than to that of a softer one? *M-8.5.1:3*

ORIGINAL SIN |əˈrɪdʒən|

DICTIONARY: *the tendency to* **sin** *innate in all human beings, held to be inherited from Adam in consequence of the Fall. The concept of original* **sin** *was developed in the writings of St. Augustine.*

EGO

~ the **belief** that **guilt** is real and fully justified. *P-2.IV.10.6*

OUTSIDE |ˈoutsīd|

DICTIONARY: *the external side or surface of something.*

EGO

~ everything outside the **Kingdom** is **illusion**. *T-6.V.94.2*

~ **you** believe that anything which happens to **you** is caused by factors outside yourself. *T-9.VIII.59.3*

~ the **projection** of the **ego** makes it appear as if **God's Will** is outside yourself and therefore not yours. *T-10.II.13.1*

~ he always perceives this **world** as outside himself, for this is crucial to his **adjustment**. He does not realize that he makes this **world**, for there is no **world** outside of him. *T-11.IV.29.6:7*

~ everything **you** perceive as the outside **world** is merely your attempt to maintain your **ego** identification. *T-11.IV.30.5*

~ the more **anger you** invest outside yourself, the safer **you** become. *T-15.VIII.68.6*

~ **you** think that **everyone** outside yourself demands your **sacrifice**. *T-15.X.99.1*

~ in the mad **world** outside you, **nothing** can be shared but only substituted. *T-18.II.9.2*

~ outside of **Heaven**, only the **conflict** of illusions stands. *T-23.III.37.7*

~ outside there **will** be no solution, for there is no **answer** there that could be found. *T-27.V.38.3*

~ a **thing** outside himself for which he has no **reason** to be held responsible. *T-27.VIII.62.4*

~ attempting to get rid of what **we** do not like by seeing it outside. *W-pI.30.2.2*

~ the **source** of **salvation** is constantly perceived as outside yourself. *W-pI.71.2.3*

HOLY SPIRIT

~ there is **nothing** outside **you**. *T-18.VII.49.1*

~ all **meaning** that **you give** the **world** outside must thus reflect the **sight you** saw **within**. *T-20.IX.76.3*

~ the outside **picture** of an inward **condition**. *T-21.I.1.5*

~ it is **impossible** the **Son of God** be merely driven by events outside of him. *T-21.III.17.1*

~ there is no **life** outside of **Heaven**. *T-23.III.37.1*

~ **seek** not outside yourself. For it **will fail.** *T-29.VIII.43.1:2*

~ **seek** not outside yourself. The search implies **you** are not whole **within.** *T-29.VIII.46.5:6*

~ outside **you** there is no eternal sky, no changeless star, and no **reality.** *T-30.IV.48.3*

~ **nothing** outside yourself can save you; **nothing** outside yourself can **give you peace**. But it also **means** that **nothing** outside yourself can **hurt you** or disturb your **peace** or upset **you** in any **way.** *W-pI.70.2.1:2*

PAIN

|pān|

DICTIONARY: *physical suffering or discomfort caused by illness or injury.*

EGO; *"sacrifice", the cost of sin, illusion, sleep, deception, pleasure, salvation.*

~ the pain in this **mind** is so apparent when it is uncovered that its **need** of **healing** cannot be denied. *T-12.III.16.5*

~ **past** pain is delusional. *T-12.IV.28.5*

~ **you** would anticipate the **future** on the basis of your **past experience** and **plan** for it accordingly. Yet by **doing** so, **you** are aligning **past** and **future** and not allowing the **miracle**, which could intervene between them, to free **you** to be born again. *T-12.VI.48.6:7*

~ the **ego** rewards fidelity to it with pain, for **faith** in it is pain. *T-13.III.12.3*

~ **you** do not always recognize the **source** of pain. *T-23.IV.41.2*

~ every pain **you** suffer do **you see** as proof that **he** is guilty of **attack.** *T-27.I.2.2*

~ pain demonstrates the **body** must be real. It is a loud, obscuring **voice** whose shrieks would silence what the **Holy Spirit** says and keep His words from your **awareness.** Pain compels attention, drawing it away from Him and focusing upon itself. Its **purpose** is the same as **pleasure**, for **they** both are **means** to **make** the **body** real. *T-27.VII.54.1:4*

~ the **cause** of pain is **separation**, not the **body**, which is only its effect. *T-28.IV.32.1*

~ all your pain comes simply from a futile search for what **you want**, insisting where it must be found. *T-29.VIII.43.7*

~ pain is the cost of **sin.** *W-pI.101.3.2*

~ pain is but the sign **you have** misunderstood yourself. *W-pI.101.6.4*

~ pain is but **witness** to the Son's mistakes in what **he** thinks **he** is. It is a **dream** of fierce retaliation for a crime that could not be committed, for **attack** on what is wholly unassailable. It is a **nightmare** of abandonment by an eternal **Love** which could not leave the Son whom It created out of **love.** *W-pI.190.2.1:3*

~ pain is a sign illusions reign in place of **truth.** It demonstrates **God** is denied, confused with **fear**, perceived as mad, and seen as **traitor** to Himself. If **God** is real, there is no pain. If pain is real, there is no **God.** For **vengeance** is not **part** of **love.** And **fear**, denying **love** and using pain to prove that **God** is dead, has shown that **death** is victor over **life.** The **body** is the **Son of God**, corruptible in **death**, as mortal as the **Father he** has slain. *W-pI.190.3.1:7*

~ the insane illusions which it shields and tries to demonstrate must still be true. *W-pI.190.4.5*

~ pain is the **thought** of **evil** taking **form** and working havoc in your holy **mind.** Pain is the ransom **you have** gladly paid not to be free. In pain is **God** denied the Son He loves. In pain does **fear** appear to triumph over **love** and **time** replace **eternity** and **Heaven.** *W-pI.190.8.1:4*

~ no one desires pain. But **he** can think that pain is **pleasure.** *W-pII.339.1.1:2*

HOLY SPIRIT; *wrong perspective, **thought evil** taking **form**, **witness** to the Son's mistakes, my own **idea**, illusion, ransom, sleep, deception, ego-illusion.*

~ the **mind** then realizes with increasing **certainty** that **delay** is only a **way** of increasing unnecessary pain, which it **need** not tolerate at all. The pain threshold drops accordingly, and the **mind** becomes increasingly sensitive to what it would once **have** regarded as very minor intrusions of discomfort. *T-2.II.49.7:8*

~ pain **will** be brought to us and disappear in our presence, and without pain there can be no **sacrifice.** *T-15.XI.103.5*

~ **he** does not **join** in pain, knowing that **healing** pain is not accomplished by delusional attempts to enter into it and lighten it by sharing the **delusion.** *T-16.I.1.7*

306

~ pain is the only "**sacrifice**" the **Holy Spirit** asks, and this **He** would remove. *T-19.V.62.5*

~ anything at all. It offers **nothing** and does not **exist**. *W-pI.102.2.3:4*

~ **nothing** and does not **exist**. And everything **you** think it offers **you** is lacking in existence like itself. *W-pI.102.2.4:5*

~ pain is a wrong perspective. When it is experienced in any **form**, it is a proof of **self**-deception. It is not a **fact** at all. There is no **form** it takes which **will** not disappear if seen aright. For pain proclaims **God** cruel. How could it be real in any **form**? It witnesses to **God** the Father's hatred of His Son, the sinfulness **He** sees in him, and His insane **desire** for revenge and **death**. Can such projections be attested to? Can **they** be anything but wholly false? *W-pI.190.1.1:9*

~ it is your thoughts **alone** that **cause you** pain. *W-pI.190.5.1*

~ nor can there be a **form** of pain **forgiveness** cannot heal. *W-pI.198.11.2*

~ what is in pain is but **illusion** in my **mind**. *W-pII.248.1.5*

PALM SUNDAY |ˌpɑ(l)m ˈsən deɪ|

DICTIONARY: *the Sunday before **Easter**, when the triumphal entry of **Jesus** into Jerusalem is celebrated in many Christian churches by processions in which palm fronds are carried.*

HOLY SPIRIT

~ this is Palm Sunday, the celebration of victory and the **acceptance** of the **truth**. *T-20.I.1.1*

~ this week begins with palms and ends with lilies, the white and holy sign the **Son of God** is **innocent**. *T-20.II.2.1*

~ this week **we** celebrate **life**, not **death**. And **we** honor the perfect purity of the **Son of God** and not his sins. *T-20.II.2.3:4*

~ a week is short, and yet this holy week is the **symbol** of the whole **journey** the **Son of God** has undertaken. *T-20.II.3.3*

PART |pärt|

DICTIONARY: *a **piece** or segment of something such as an object, activity, or period of **time**, which combined with other pieces makes up the whole.*

EGO; *wild **illusion***

~ in **perception** the whole is built up of parts, which can separate and reassemble in different constellations. *T-8.VIII.70.6*

~ what is not whole cannot **make** whole. *T-30.IV.42.8*

HOLY SPIRIT; *function, happiness, a **little** willingness, **little** part.*

~ the whole does define the part, but the part does not define the whole. *T-8.VIII.70.3*

~ there is no **difference** between the whole and the part where **change** is **impossible**. *T-8.VIII.70.9*

~ your part is very simple. *T-14.VII.64.3*

~ on your **little faith**, joined with His understanding, **He will** build your part in the **Atonement** and **make** sure that **you** fulfill it easily. *T-18.VI.42.6*

~ in your part lies all of it, without which is no part complete, nor is the whole completed without your part. *T-20.V.33.4*

~ your part is merely to apply what **He** has taught **you** to yourself, and **He will** do the **rest.** *T-27.VI.52.2*

~ the part **you** play in salvaging the **world** from **condemnation** is your own escape. *T-27.VIII.67.1*

~ **we** merely take the part assigned long since and fully recognized as perfectly fulfilled by Him Who wrote salvation's **script** in His Creator's **name** and in the **name** of His Creator's Son. *W-pI.169.8.4*

~ the ending must remain obscure to **you** until your part is done. *W-pI.169.10.2*

~ for your part is still what all the **rest** depends on. As **you** take the **role** assigned to **you, salvation** comes a **little** nearer each **uncertain** heart that does not beat as yet in tune with **God.** *W-pI.169.10.4:5*

PAST

DICTIONARY: *gone by in **time** and no longer existing.*

EGO

~ the **ego** invests heavily in the past and in the end believes that the past is the only aspect of **time** that is meaningful. *T-12.IV.26.2*

~ its emphasis on **guilt** enables it to ensure its continuity by making the **future** like the past and thus avoiding the **present.** By the notion of paying for the past in the **future,** the past becomes the determiner of the **future,** making them continuous without an intervening **present.** For the **ego** uses the **present** only as a brief transition to the **future,** in which it brings the past to the **future** by interpreting the **present** in past terms. *T-12.IV.26.3:5*

~ the **ego** cannot tolerate **release** from the past, and although the past is no more, the **ego** tries to preserve its **image** by responding as if it were **present.** Thus it dictates reactions to those **you** meet **now** from a past reference point, obscuring their **present reality.** *T-12.IV.27.3:4*

~ **you** consider it "natural" to use your past **experience** as the reference point from which to judge the **present.** *T-12.VI.46.1*

~ your past was made in **anger,** and if **you** use it to **attack** the **present, you will** not **see** the **freedom** that the **present** holds. *T-12.VI.49.7*

~ the past which **you remember** never was and represents only the **denial** of what always was. *T-14.V.38.10*

~ your past is what **you have** taught yourselves. *T-14.VII.60.6*

~ the only **time** the ego allows anyone to look upon with some amount of equanimity is the past. And even there its only **value** is that it is no more. *T-15.II.6.4:5*

~ the past is the ego's chief **learning device,** for it is in the past that **you** learned to define your own needs and acquired methods for meeting them on your own terms. *T-15.VI.46.1*

~ the **ego** holds the past against **you,** and in your escape from the past, it sees itself deprived of the **vengeance** it believes that **you** so justly merit. *T-16.VIII.72.5*

~ sometimes the past seems real, as if it were the **present.** Voices from the past are heard and then are doubted. *T-26.VI.40.5:6*

~ the only wholly true **thought** one can hold about the past is that it is not **here.** To think about it at all is therefore to think about illusions. *W-pI.8.2.1:2*

HOLY SPIRIT; *ego's chief **learning device, nothing**.*

~ the past can cast no **shadow** to darken the **present** unless **you** are afraid of **light**. *T-12.VI.46.4*

~ past, **present**, and **future** are not continuous unless **you** force continuity on them. **You** can perceive them as continuous and **make** them so for **you**. *T-12.VI.48.2:3*

~ only the past can separate, and it is nowhere. *T-12.VI.50.7*

~ **everyone** seen without the past thus brings **you** nearer to the end of **time** by bringing healed and **healing sight** into the **darkness** and enabling the **world** to **see**. *T-13.II.5.4*

~ when **you** maintain that **you** are guilty but the **source** lies in the past, **you** are not looking inward. The past is not in **you**. Your weird associations to it **have** no **meaning** in the **present**. *T-13.IV.23.1:3*

~ the past binds Him not and therefore binds not **you**. *T-14.VII.69.9*

~ **he** Who has freed **you** from the past would **teach you** are free of it. *T-14.VII.70.1*

~ all **you have** learned of **empathy** is from the past. And there is **nothing** from the past that **you** would **share**, for there is **nothing** there that **you** would keep. *T-16.I.3.4:5*

~ the past is **nothing**. Do not **seek** to lay the **blame** for **deprivation** on it, for the past is gone. *T-16.VIII.71.8:9*

~ the past has gone. It never happened in **reality**. Only in your minds, which **thought** it did, is its undoing needful. *T-18.V.40.6:8*

~ the only **value** that the past can hold is that **you** learn it gave **you nothing**. *T-25.III.12.7*

~ there is no **link** of **memory** to the past. If **you** would **have** it there, then there it is. But only your **desire** made the **link**, and only **you have** held it to a **part** of **time** where **guilt** appears to linger still. *T-28.II.4.5:7*

~ no **change** can be made in the **present** if its **cause** is past. Only the past is held in **memory** as **you** make use of it, and so it is a **way** to hold the past against the **now**. *T-28.II.6.6:7*

~ without the **darkness** of the past upon your eyes, **you** cannot **fail** to **see today**. *W-pI.75.11.6*

~ the past is gone with all its fantasies. *W-pI.156.7.2*

~ for the past is gone, the **future** but imagined. *W-pI.181.4.5*

~ what can be forgiven but the past, and if it is forgiven, it is gone. *W-p2.289.1.6*

PATIENCE

DICTIONARY: *the capacity to accept or tolerate **delay**, trouble, or **suffering** without getting angry or upset.*

HOLY SPIRIT

~ infinite patience calls upon infinite **love**, and by producing results **now**, it renders **time** unnecessary. *T-5.VIII.81.7*

~ **holy Spirit** waits in gentle patience, as certain of the outcome as **He** is sure of His Creator's **love**. *T-22.VII.52.4*

~ those who are certain of the outcome can afford to wait, and wait without anxiety. *M-4.20.1*

~ patience is natural to those who **trust**. Sure of the ultimate **interpretation** of all things in **time**, no outcome already seen or yet to come can **cause** them **fear**. *M-4.20.9:10*

PATIENT

DICTIONARY: *a person receiving or registered to* **receive** *medical treatment.*

EGO

~ these patients do not realize **they have** chosen **sickness**. On the contrary, **they** believe that **sickness** has chosen them. Nor are **they open-minded** on this point. The **body** tells them what to do, and **they** obey. **They have** no **idea** how insane this **concept** is. If **they** even suspected it, **they** would be healed. Yet **they** suspect **nothing**. To them the **separation** is quite real. *M-5.8.6:13*

~ their aim is to be able to retain their **self-concept** exactly as it is, but without the **suffering** that it entails. *P-2.IN.2.3*

~ what **they seek** is **magic**. *P-2.IN.2.5*

~ **now he** wants a "better" **illusion**. *P-2.IN.2.8*

~ the patient hopes to learn how to get the changes **he** wants without changing his **self-concept** to any significant extent. **He** hopes, in **fact**, to stabilize it sufficiently to include **within** it the magical powers **he** seeks in **psychotherapy. He** wants to **make** the vulnerable invulnerable and the finite limitless. *P-2.IN.3.3*

~ patients can pay only for the exchange of illusions. *P-3.III.3.3*

HOLY SPIRIT

~ only infinite patience can produce immediate effects. *T-5.VIII.81.5*

~ meet His patience with your impatience at **delay** in meeting Him. *T-17.III.13.4*

~ his patience has no limits. He **will** wait until **you** hear His gentle **Voice within** you. *W-pI.182.7.6:7*

~ who is the physician? Only the **mind** of the patient himself. The outcome is what **he** decides that it is. **Special** agents seem to be ministering to him, yet **they** but **give form** to his own **choice. He** chooses them to bring tangible **form** to his desires. And it is this **they** do, and **nothing** else. **They** are not actually needed at all. The patient could merely rise up without their aid and say, "**I have** no use for this. "There is no **form** of **sickness** that would not be cured at once. *M-5.5.5:13*

~ the patient must **change** his **mind** in **order** to be healed. *M-5.8.1*

~ to them God's teachers come to represent another **choice** which **they** had forgotten. *M-5.9.1*

~ what if the patient uses **sickness** as a **way** of **life**, believing **healing** is the **way** to **death**? When this is so, a sudden **healing** might precipitate intense depression, and a **sense** of **loss** so deep that the patient might even try to destroy himself. Having **nothing** to live for, **he** may **ask** for **death. Healing** must wait, for his protection. *M-6.1.6:9*

~ in his **healing** is the **therapist** forgiven with him. *P-1.1.2.7*

~ **everyone** who needs **help**, regardless of the **form** of his distress, is attacking himself, and his **peace** of **mind** is **suffering** in consequence. *P-1.1.3.1*

~ **he** must become willing to reverse his thinking, and to **understand** that what **he thought** projected its effects on him were made by his projections on the **world**. The **world he** sees does therefore not **exist.** *P-1.1.4.2:3*

~ the ones who come to us for **help** are bitterly afraid. What **they** believe **will help** can only **harm;** what **they** believe **will harm alone** can **help.** Progress becomes **impossible** until the patient is persuaded to reverse his twisted **way** of looking at the **world;** his twisted **way** of looking at himself. *P-2.V.2.1:3*

~ while **they** are sick, **they** can and must be helped. *P-2.V.3.5*

~ the patient is his screen for the **projection** of his sins, enabling him to let them go. *P-2.VI.6.6*

~ patients can but be seen as the bringers of **forgiveness**, for it is **they** who come to demonstrate their sinlessness to eyes that still believe that **sin** is there to look upon. *P-2.VI.7.4*

~ **everyone** who is sent to **you** is a patient of yours. This does not mean that **you** select him, nor that **you** choose the kind of treatment that is suitable. But it does mean that no one comes to **you** by **mistake**. *P-3.I.1.1:3*

~ your patients **need** not be physically **present** for **you** to serve them in the **Name** of God. *P-3.I.3.1*

~ **you will** recognize them in whatever **way** can be most helpful to both of **you**. It does not matter how **they** come. **They will** be sent in whatever **form** is most helpful; a **name**, a **thought**, a **picture**, an **idea**, or perhaps just a feeling of reaching out to someone somewhere. *P-3.I.3.6:8*

~ his patients are the **means** sent to him for his **learning**. *P-3.I.4.3*

~ **they** come bearing **God**. *P-3.I.4.5*

PAYMENT |ˈpāmənt|

DICTIONARY: *the action or process of paying someone or something, or of **being** paid.*

EGO

~ the **idea** of buying and selling implies precisely the kind of exchange that the **Soul** cannot understand at all because its supply is always abundant and all its demands are fully met. *T-4.II.5.5*

~ if paying is equated with getting, **you will** set the price low but demand a high return. **You will have** forgotten, however, that [to price is to **value**, so] your return is in proportion to your **judgment** of **worth**. *T-8.XI.116.1:2*

~ the price **will** then be set high because of the **value** of the return. The price for getting is to lose **sight** of **value**, making it inevitable that **you will** not **value** what **you receive**. Valuing it **little**, **you will** not appreciate it and **will** not **want** it. *T-8.XI.116.4:6*

~ the **ego** does demand payment, it never seems to be demanding it of **you**. *T-15.X.97.3*

~ only an **unhealed healer** would try to heal for money, and **he will** not succeed to the extent to which **he** values it. Nor **will he** find his **healing** in the process. *P-3.III.2.1:2*

~ it should not be the **therapist** who makes these decisions. There is a **difference** between payment and cost. To **give** money where God's **plan** allots it has no cost. To withhold it from where it rightfully belongs has enormous cost. The **therapist** who would do this loses the **name** of **healer**, for **he** could never **understand** what **healing** is. **He** cannot **give** it, and so **he** does not **have** it. *P-3.III.2.5:10*

HOLY SPIRIT

~ if paying is associated with **giving**, it cannot be perceived as **loss**, and the reciprocal **relationship** of giving and receiving **will** be recognized. *T-8.XI.116.3*

~ no one can pay for therapy, for **healing** is of **God** and He asks for **nothing**. *P-3.III.1.1*

~ even an advanced **therapist** has some earthly needs while **he is here**. Should **he need** money it **will** be given him, not in payment, but to **help** him better serve the **plan**. Money is not **evil**. It is **nothing**. *P-3.III.1.3:6*

~ no one **here** can live with no illusions, for **he** must yet strive to **have** the last **illusion** be accepted by **everyone** everywhere. **He** has a mighty **part** in this one **purpose**, for which **he** came. **He** stays **here** but for this. And while **he** stays **he will** be given what **he** needs to stay. *P-3.III.1.7:10*

~ **forgiveness**, the Holy Spirit's only **dream**, must **have** no cost. *P-3.III.3.6*

~ one **rule** should always be observed: No one should be turned away because **he** cannot pay. *P-3.III.6.1*

PEACE

|pēs|

EGO; *ego's greatest* **enemy,** **illusion** *of peace.*

~ peace is the ego's greatest **enemy** because, according to its **interpretation** of **reality, war** is the guarantee of its **survival.** *T-5.V.39.7*

~ its unwillingness for **you** to find peace even in the **death.** *T-15.II.3.5*

~ those who believe that peace can be defended and that **attack** is justified on its behalf cannot perceive it lies **within** them. *T-23.IV.45.1*

~ certainly peace seems to be **impossible.** *M-11.1.2*

~ peace is **impossible** to those who look on **war.** *M-11.4.1*

~ god's peace can never come where **anger** is, for **anger** must deny that peace exists. *M-20.3.3*

HOLY SPIRIT; *condition of* **knowledge,** *condition for His* **will,** *condition of* **truth** *and* **sanity,** *condition of the* **Kingdom,** *state where* **love** *abides,* **part** *of* **you,** *awakening,* **answer, union, bridge,** *God's peace,* **ark of peace.**

~ **nothing** real can be threatened. **Nothing** unreal exists. Herein lies the peace of **God.** *T-I.4.1*

~ peace is an attribute in **you. You** cannot find it **outside.** *T-2.I.17.3:4*

~ this peace is totally incapable of being shaken by human errors of any kind. *T-2.II.18.7*

~ peace is a natural heritage of the **Soul.** *T-3.VIII.70.1*

~ peace and **eternity** are as closely related as are **time** and **war.** *T-5.V.40.3*

~ the peace of **God** lies in that **message,** and so the peace of **God** lies in **you.** *T-6.III.37.7*

~ the only **way** to **have** peace is to **teach** peace. *T-6.IV.43.7*

~ peace is the **condition** of **knowledge,** because it is the **condition** of the **Kingdom.** *T-8.I.1.8*

~ it is your **inheritance** from your real **Father.** *T-9.IX.83.4*

~ **god** and His Son dwell in peace. *T-11.IV.35.5*

~ its holy witnesses **will** surround **you** because **you** called upon them and **they will** come to **you.** *T-11.VIII.72.2*

~ peace and **guilt** are antithetical, and the **Father** can be remembered only in peace. *T-11.X.89.3*

~ your peace lies in His **Oneness.** *T-12.III.22.3*

~ the peace of **God** passeth your understanding only in the **past.** Yet **here** it is, and **you** can **understand** it **now.** *T-12.VII.66.1:2*

~ in shining peace **within you** is the perfect purity in which **you** were created. *T-13.IV.28.4*

~ **you will** find the peace in which **He** has established **you,** because **He** does not **change** His **Mind. He** is invariable as the peace in which **you** dwell and of which the **Holy Spirit** reminds **you.** *T-13.V.39.5:6*

~ peace **will** be yours, because His peace still flows to **you** from Him Whose **Will** is peace. **You have** it **now.** *T-13.V.42.4:5*

~ peace, then, be unto **everyone** who becomes a **teacher** of peace. For peace is the **acknowledgment** of perfect purity from which no one is excluded. **Within** its holy circle is **everyone** whom **God** created as His Son. **Joy** is its unifying attribute, with no one left **outside** to suffer **guilt alone.** The **power of God** draws **everyone** to its safe embrace of **love** and **union.** *T-14.II.12.1:5*

~ peace and understanding go together and never can be found **alone**. Each brings the other with it, for it is the law of **God they** be not separate. **They** are **cause** and effect, each to the other, so where one is absent the other cannot be. *T-14.VII.72.4:6*

~ peace is of **God** and of no one beside Him. *T-15.V.36.8*

~ it is through us that peace **will** come. *T-15.VII.63.1*

~ peace is the **condition** for the **awareness** of your **relationship** with God. *T-15.XI.104.3*

~ peace **will** never come from the **illusion** of **love**, but only from its **reality**. *T-16.V.35.6*

~ if peace is the **condition** of **truth** and **sanity** and cannot be without them, where peace is **they** must be. *T-17.VII.61.4*

~ peace and **faith will** not come separately. *T-17.VIII.67.5*

~ it cannot extend unless **you** keep it. **You** are the center from which it radiates outward to **call** the others in. **You** are its **home**, its tranquil dwelling-place from which it gently reaches out but never leaving **you**. *T-19.V.40.2:4*

~ peace **will** send its messengers from **you** to all the **world**. *T-19.V.43.12*

~ peace could no more depart from **you** than from **God**. *T-19.V.43.3*

~ peace must first surmount the **obstacle** of your **desire** to get rid of it. *T-19.V.59.1*

~ peace is extended from **you** only to the eternal, and it reaches out from the eternal in **you**. It flows across all else. *T-19.V.63.1:2*

~ peace **will** come to all who **ask** for it with real **desire** and sincerity of **purpose**, shared with the **Holy Spirit** and at one with Him on what **salvation** is. *T-20.IX.69.2*

~ peace must come to those who choose to heal and not to judge. *T-21.IX.87.6*

~ it is still whole, and **nothing** has been taken from it. *T-22.VI.46.9*

~ peace, looking on itself, extends itself. *T-23.II.18.3*

~ peace is the state where **love** abides and seeks to **share** itself. *T-23.II.18.5*

~ no **illusion** can **attack** the peace of **God** together with His Son. *T-23.V.52.7*

~ peace **will** be yours because it is His **Will**. *T-24.I.1.7*

~ the still infinity of endless peace surrounds **you** gently in its soft embrace, so strong and **quiet**, tranquil in the might of its **Creator; nothing** can intrude upon the sacred **Son of God within**. *T-29.VI.32.2*

~ peace of **mind** is clearly an internal matter. It must begin with your own thoughts and then extend outward. It is from your peace of **mind** that a peaceful **perception** of the **world** arises. *W-pI.34.1.2:4*

~ peace is your right because **you** are **giving** your **trust** to the **strength** of God. *W-pI.47.9.3*

~ peace is **part** of **you** and requires only that **you** be there to embrace any **situation** in which **you** are. *W-pI.50.5.3*

~ your peace is everywhere, as **you** are. *W-pI.50.5.4*

~ peace comes from deep **within** myself. *W-pI.57.6.1*

~ the peace that must be ours when the **problem** and the **answer have** been brought together. *W-pI.80.4.1*

~ the peace of **God** is where your **Self**, His Son, is waiting **now** to meet itself again and be as one. *W-pI.92.9.3*

~ **joy** and peace are not but idle dreams. **They** are your right because of what **you** are. **They** come to **you** from **God**, who cannot **fail** to **give you** what He wills. *W-pI.104.1.1:3*

~ there is an ancient peace **you** carry in your heart and **have** not lost. *W-pI.164.4.2*

~ no one who truly seeks the peace of **God** can **fail** to find it. *W-pI.185.11.1*

~ the peace of **God** is yours. *W-pI.185.11.6*

~ for **you** it was created, given **you** by its **Creator** and established as His own eternal **gift**. *W-pI.185.12.1*

~ to mean **you want** the peace of **God** is to renounce all dreams. *W-pI.185.5.1*

~ **you want** the peace of **God**. And so do all who seem to **seek** for dreams. *W-pI.185.5.1:2*

~ and when the **wish** for peace is genuine, the **means** for finding it are given in a **form** each **mind** which seeks for it in honesty can **understand**. *W-pI.185.6.2*

~ **we want** the peace of **God**. This is no idle **wish**. *W-pI.185.7.2:3*

~ no **compromise** is possible in this. **You** choose God's peace, or **you have** asked for dreams. *W-pI.185.9.4:5*

~ yet **will** God's peace come just as certainly and to remain with **you** forever. It **will** not be gone with every twist and turning of the road to reappear unrecognized in forms which **shift** and **change** with every **step you** take. *W-pI.185.9.7:8*

~ the peace of **God** is shining in **you now** and from your heart extends around the **world**. It pauses to caress each living **thing** and leave a **blessing** with it which remains forever and forever. What it gives must be eternal. It removes all thoughts of the ephemeral and valueless. It brings renewal to all tired hearts and lights all **vision** as it passes by. All of its gifts are given **everyone**, and **everyone** unites in giving thanks to **you** who **give** and **you** who **have** received. *W-pI.188.3.1:6*

~ the peace of **God** can never be contained. Who recognizes it **within** himself must **give** it. And the **means** for **giving** it are in his understanding. **He** forgives because **he** recognized the **truth** in him. The peace of **God** is shining in **you now** and in all living things. In quietness is it acknowledged universally. For what your inward **vision** looks upon is your **perception** of the **universe**. *W-pI.188.5.1:7*

~ **you will** not find peace except the peace of **God**. *W-pI.200.1.2*

~ peace is **union** if it be of **God**. *W-pI.200.11.6*

~ peace is the **bridge** that **everyone will** cross to leave this **world** behind. But peace begins **within** the **world** perceived as different and leading from this fresh **perception** to the gate of **Heaven** and the **way** beyond. Peace is the **answer** to conflicting goals, to senseless journeys, frantic, vain pursuits, and meaningless endeavors. *W-pI.200.8.1:3*

~ peace fills my heart and floods my **body** with the **purpose** of **forgiveness**. *W-pII.267.1.3*

~ **nothing** can intrude upon the peace that **God** Himself has given to His Son. *W-pII.273.1.4*

~ the mercy and the peace of **God** are free. *W-pII.343.2.1*

~ peace is ours when **we** forget all things except God's **Love**. *W-pII.346.2.2*

~ the **thought** of peace was given to God's Son the instant that his **mind** had **thought** of war. There was no **need** for such a **thought** before, for peace was given without **opposite** and merely was. *W-pII.ST231.2.1:2*

~ there is a kind of peace that is not of this **world**. *M-20.1.1*

~ god's peace is recognized at first by just one **thing**—in every **way** it is totally unlike all previous experiences. It calls to **mind nothing** that went before. It brings with it no **past** associations. It is a new **thing** entirely. There is a **contrast**, yes, between this **thing** and all the **past**. But strangely, it is not a **contrast** of true differences. The **past** just slips away and in its place is everlasting **quiet**. Only that. The **contrast** first perceived has merely gone. **Quiet** has reached to cover everything. *M-20.2.2:11*

~ when peace is found, the **war** is meaningless. And it is conflict **now** that is perceived as non-existent and unreal. *M-20.3.11:12*

~ no one can **fail** to find it who but seeks out its conditions. *M-20.3.2*

~ attain His peace, and **you remember** Him. *M-20.6.13*

PERCEPTION

|pər ˈsepSH(ə)n|

DICTIONARY: *the ability to **see**, hear, or become aware of something through the senses.*

EGO; *wrong-mindedness, distorted willing, **authority problem**, **projection**, **messenger** of ignorance, strange perception.*

~ perception involves different interpretations, and this **means** that it is not whole. *T-3.V.31.4*

~ since perceptions **change**, their dependence on **time** is obvious. **They** are subject to transitory states, and this necessarily implies variability. How **you** perceive at any given **time** determines what **you** do, and action must occur in **time**. *T-3.V.32.3:5*

~ perception always involves some misuse of **will**, because it involves the **mind** in areas of uncertainty. *T-3.VI.44.1*

~ perception involves an exchange or translation, which **knowledge** does not **need**. *T-3.VI.46.2*

~ perception, on the other hand, is **impossible** without a **belief** in "more" and "less." Perception at every **level** involves selectivity and is incapable of organization without it. In all types of perception, there is a continual process of accepting and rejecting or organizing and reorganizing, of shifting and changing focus. Evaluation is an essential **part** of perception, because judgments must be made for selection. *T-3.VI.57.5:8*

~ only perception involves partial **awareness**. *T-3.VII.58.5*

~ only perception can be sick, because only perception can be wrong. *T-8.IX.80.7*

~ wrong perception is distorted willing, which wants things to be as **they** are not. *T-8.IX.81.1*

~ selective perception chooses its witnesses carefully, and its witnesses are consistent. *T-10.VI.56.2*

~ the same **word** is used both for **awareness** and for the **interpretation** of **awareness**. *T-10.VII.60.5*

~ perception can be utilized to **substitute** illusions for **truth**. *T-18.III.15.2*

~ **you** made perception that **you** might choose among your brothers and **seek** for **sin** with them. *T-21.IV.34.5*

~ what cannot **see** beyond what is not there must be distorted perception and must perceive illusions as the **truth**. *T-22.IV.35.6*

~ perception cannot be in constant flux and **make** allowance for stability of **meaning** anywhere. *T-30.VIII.84.7*

~ what **you** do is determined by your perception of the **situation**, and that perception is wrong. It is inevitable, then, that **you will** not serve your own best interests. *W-pI.24.1.3:4*

~ your upside-down perception has been ruinous to your **peace** of mind. *W-pI.72.9.3*

~ this space **you see** as setting off all things from one another is the **means** by which the world's perception is achieved. **You see** something where **nothing** is and **see** as well **nothing** where there is **unity**—a space between all things, between all things and **you**. *W-pI.184.2.1:2*

~ what **I** perceive without God's own **correction** for the **sight I** made is frightening and painful to behold. *W-pII.290.1.4*

~ what seems to be the second place is first, for all things **we** perceive are upside-down until **we** listen to the **Voice** of **God**. *W-pII.328.1.1*

~ perception can **make** whatever **picture** the **mind** desires to **see**. *M-19.5.2*

~ distorted perception does not heal. *M-22.5.6*

315

HOLY SPIRIT; *basis for* **knowledge,** *helper in the search for* **truth,** *result,* **choice,** *right-mindedness,* One-Mindedness, **witness, wish** *fulfilled, mirror,* **learning,** *true perception, right perception, accurate perception.*

~ perception is merely temporary. It is an attribute of the space-**time belief** and is therefore subject to **fear** or **love.** Misperceptions produce **fear,** and true perceptions produce **love.** Neither produces **certainty,** because all perception varies. That is why it is not **knowledge.** *T-3.V.30.6:10*

~ **perception** did not **exist** until the **separation** had introduced degrees, aspects, and intervals. The **Soul** has no levels, and all **conflict** arises from the **concept** of levels. *T-3.VI.38.7:8*

~ sane perception induces sane choosing. *T-3.VI.49.4*

~ what happens to perceptions if there are no judgments and there is **nothing** but perfect equality? Perception becomes **impossible.** *T-3.VII.58.1:2*

~ as long as perception lasts, **prayer** has a place. Since perception rests on lack, those who perceive **have** not totally accepted the **Atonement** and given themselves over to **truth.** Perception is a separated state, and a perceiver does **need healing.** *T-3.VII.60.1:3*

~ right perception lies in the inevitable **judgment** which it entails that it is unnecessary. *T-4.VII.81.3*

~ perception as well as **knowledge** derives **meaning** from relationships. *T-5.V.40.4*

~ by enabling **you** to use perception in a **way** that parallels **knowledge, you will** ultimately meet it and know it. *T-6.III.31.3*

~ although perception of any kind is unnecessary, **you** made it, and the **Holy Spirit** can therefore use it well. **He** can inspire perception and lead it toward **God** by making it parallel to God's **way** of thinking and thus guarantee their ultimate meeting. *T-6.III.33.6:7*

~ this line is the direct line of **communication** with **God** and lets your **mind** converge with His. There is no **conflict** anywhere in this perception, because it **means** that all perception is guided by the **Holy Spirit,** whose **Mind** is fixed on **God.** *T-6.III.36.2:3*

~ the **Holy Spirit** projects by recognizing Himself in every **mind** and thus perceives them as one. **Nothing** conflicts in this perception, because what the **Holy Spirit** perceives is the same. Wherever **He** looks **He** sees Himself, and because **He** is united, **He** offers the whole **Kingdom** always. *T-6.III.37.3:5*

~ the **strength** of right perception is so great that it brings the **mind** into accord with His, because it yields to His pull which is in all of **you.** *T-7.V.36.7*

~ this is the right use of selective perception. To overlook nothingness is merely to judge it correctly, and because of your ability to evaluate it truly, to let it go. *T-9.X.86.4:5*

~ to perceive anew is merely to perceive again, implying that before, or in the **interval, you** were not perceiving at all. *T-10.VIII.69.5*

~ redeemed perception is easily translated into **knowledge,** for only perception is capable of **error,** and perception has never been. **Being** corrected, it gives place to **knowledge,** which is forever the only **reality.** *T-11.IX.84.6:7*

~ to perceive truly is to be aware of all **reality** through the **awareness** of your own. But for this no illusions can rise to meet your **sight.** *T-12.VI.45.1:2*

~ perception at its loftiest is never complete. Even the perception of the **Holy Spirit,** as perfect as perception can be, is without **meaning** in **Heaven.** Perception can reach everywhere under His **guidance,** for the **vision** of **Christ** beholds everything in **light.** Yet no perception, however holy, **will** last forever. *T-13.I.2.5:8*

~ perfect perception, then, has many elements in common with **knowledge,** making transfer to it possible. *T-13.II.3.1*

~ perception is the medium by which ignorance is brought to **knowledge.** *T-14.IV.24.7*

~ perception **will** be meaningless when it has been perfected, for everything that has been used for **learning will have** no **function. Nothing will** ever **change**; no shifts nor shadings, no differences, no variations which made perception possible **will** occur. *T-17.III.10.2:3*

~ in the new perception, the **mind** corrects it when it seems to be seen, and it becomes invisible. And errors are quickly recognized and quickly given to **correction** to be healed, not hidden. *T-19.IV.34.3:4*

~ as a **man** thinketh, so does **he** perceive. *T-21.I.1.6*

~ perception is a result, not a **cause**. And that is why **order of difficulty** in miracles is meaningless. *T-21.I.1.8:9*

~ the **Holy Spirit** sees perception as a **means** to **teach you** that the **vision** of a **holy relationship** is all **you want** to see. *T-21.IV.34.6*

~ perception selects and makes the **world you see**. It literally picks it out as the **mind** directs. *T-21.VI.49.1:2*

~ perception is a **choice** and not a **fact**. *T-21.VI.49.7*

~ yet can perception serve another **goal**. It is not bound to specialness but by your **choice**. And it is given **you** to **make** a different **choice** and use perception for a different purpose. *T-24.VIII.72.10:12*

~ the Holy Spirit's perception leaves no ground for an **attack**. *T-25.X.81.2*

~ perception is not an attribute of **God**. His is the realm of **knowledge**. Yet **He** has created the **Holy Spirit** as the Mediator between perception and **knowledge**. Without this **link** with **God**, perception would **have** replaced **knowledge** forever in your minds. With this **link** with **God**, perception **will** become so changed and purified that it **will** lead to **knowledge**. That is its **function** as the **Holy Spirit** sees it. Therefore, that is its **function** in **truth**. *W-pI.43.1.1:7*

~ perception has no **function** in **God** and does not **exist**. Yet in **salvation**, which is the undoing of what never was, perception has a mighty **purpose**. Made by the **Son of God** for an unholy **purpose**, it must become the **means** for the restoration of his **holiness** to his **awareness**. Perception has no **meaning**. Yet does the **Holy Spirit give** it a **meaning** very close to God's. Healed perception becomes the **means** by which the **Son of God** forgives his **brother** and thus forgives himself. *W-pI.43.2.2:7*

~ **love** and perception thus go hand in hand. *W-pI.130.2.5*

~ perception has a focus. It is this which gives consistency to what **you see**. **Change** but this focus, and what **you** behold **will change** accordingly. Your **vision now will shift** to give support to the intent which has replaced the one **you** held before. *W-pI.181.2.1:4*

~ **god** does not perceive at all. Yet it is **He** Who gives the **means** by which perception is made true and beautiful enough to let the **light** of **Heaven** shine upon it. It is **He** Who answers what His Son would contradict and keeps his sinlessness forever safe. *W-pI.193.2.4:6*

~ perception is a mirror, not a **fact**. And what **I** look on is my state of **mind** reflected outward. *W-pII.304.1.3:4*

~ from new perception of the **world** there comes a **future** very different from the **past**. The **future now** is recognized as but **extension** of the **present. Past** mistakes can cast no shadows on it, so that **fear** has lost its idols and its images, and **being** formless, it has no effects. *W-pII.314.1.1:3*

~ as **sight** was made to lead away from **truth**, it can be redirected. Sounds become the **call** of **God**. And all perception can be given a new **purpose** by the One Whom **God** appointed **Savior** to the **world**. *W-pII.ST241.4.1:3*

~ **forgiveness** has made possible perception's tranquil end. *W-pIIST281.1.5*

~ perception is the result of **learning**. In **fact**, perception is **learning**, because **cause** and effect are never separated. *M-4.3.2:3*

PERFECTION

|pər'fekSH(ə)n|

DICTIONARY: *the **condition**, state, or quality of **being** free or as free as possible from all flaws or defects.*

EGO

~ **you** did not believe in your own perfection. *T-6.V.57.3*

~ in this **world**, your perfection is unwitnessed. **God** knows it, but **you** do not, and so **you** do not **share** His **witness** to it. *T-13.II.10.1:2*

HOLY SPIRIT

~ perfection is not a matter of degree. *T-2.II.40.2*

~ the **Holy Spirit** begins by perceiving **you** as perfect. Knowing this perfection is shared, He recognizes it in others, thus strengthening it in both. *T-6.III.29.1:2*

~ the perfect **need nothing** and cannot **experience** perfection as a **difficult** accomplishment, because that is what **they** are. *T-6.III.35.4*

~ **sickness** and perfection are irreconcilable. If **God** created **you** perfect, **you** are perfect. *T-9.X.85.3:4*

~ perfection is and cannot be denied. *T-11.III.21.6*

~ perfection created me perfect. *W-pI.67.3.4*

~ nor can **you** dim the **light** of your perfection. *W-pI.197.8.3*

~ in **you** he sees no **limit** and no stain to mar your beautiful perfection. *M-23.5.7*

PERIOD OF ACHIEVEMENT   *A Course in Miracles Term*

HOLY SPIRIT

~ it is **here** that **learning** is consolidated. **Now** what was seen as merely shadows before becomes solid gains, to be counted on in all "emergencies" as well as tranquil times. Indeed, the tranquility is their result—the outcome of **honest learning**, consistency of **thought**, and **full transfer**. This is the stage of real **peace**, for **here** is Heaven's state fully reflected. From **here** the **way** to **Heaven** is open and easy. In **fact**, it is **here**. Who would "go" anywhere if **peace** of **mind** is already complete? And who would **seek** to **change** tranquility for something more desirable? What could be more desirable than this? *M-4.10.2:10*

PERIOD OF DISORIENTATION   *A Course in Miracles Term*

HOLY SPIRIT

~ the period of disorientation which precedes the actual transition is far shorter than the **time** it took to fix your minds so firmly on illusions. *T-16.VII.65.5*

PERIOD OF RELINQUISHMENT   *A Course in Miracles Term*

HOLY SPIRIT

~ if this is interpreted as giving up the desirable, it **will** engender enormous conflict. Few teachers of **God** escape this distress entirely. There is, however, no point in sorting out the valuable from the valueless unless the next obvious **step** is taken. The third **step** is rarely if ever begun until the second is complete. Therefore, the period of overlap is apt to be one in which the **teacher of God** feels called upon to **sacrifice** his own best interests on behalf of **truth**. **He** has not realized as yet how wholly **impossible** such a demand would be. **He** can learn this only as **he** actually does **give** up the valueless. Through this **he** learns that where **he** anticipated grief, **he** finds a **happy light**-heartedness instead; where **he thought** something was asked of him, **he** finds a **gift** bestowed on him. *M-4.7.2:9*

PERIOD OF SETTLING DOWN   *A Course in Miracles Term*

HOLY SPIRIT

~ this is a **quiet time** in which the **teacher of God** rests a while in reasonable **peace. Now he** consolidates his **learning. Now he** begins to **see** the transfer **value** of what **he** has learned. Its potential is literally staggering, and the **teacher of God is now** at the point in his progress at which **he** sees in it his whole **way** out. "**Give** up what **you** do not **want** and keep what **you** do." How simple is the obvious! And how easy to do! The **teacher of God** needs this period of respite. **He** has not yet come as far as **he** thinks. Yet when **he** is ready to go on, **he** goes with mighty companions beside him. **Now he** rests a while and gathers them before going on. **He will** not go on from **here alone.** *M-4.8.2:12*

PERIOD OF SORTING OUT   *A Course in Miracles Term*

HOLY SPIRIT

~ this is always somewhat difficult, because, having learned that the changes in his **life** are always helpful, **he** must **now** decide all things on the basis of whether **they** increase the helpfulness or hamper it. **He will** find that many if not most of the things **he** valued before **will** merely hinder his ability to transfer what **he** has learned to new situations as **they** arise. Because **he** has valued what is really valueless, **he will** not generalize the **lesson** for **fear** of **loss** and **sacrifice**. It takes great **learning** to **understand** that all things, events, encounters, and circumstances are helpful. It is only to the extent to which **they** are helpful that any degree of **reality** should be accorded them in this **world** of **illusion**. The **word** "value" can apply to **nothing** else. *M-4.6.2:7*

PERIOD OF UNDOING   *A Course in Miracles Term*

HOLY SPIRIT

~ first, **they** must go through what might be called "a period of undoing." This **need** not be painful, but it usually is so experienced. It seems as if things are **being** taken away, and it is rarely understood initially that their lack of **value** is merely **being** recognized. How can lack of **value** be perceived unless the perceiver is in a position where **he** must **see** things in a different **light**? **He** is not yet at a point at which **he** can **make** the **shift** entirely internally. And so the **plan will** sometimes **call** for changes in what seem to be external circumstances. These changes are always helpful. *M-4.5.1:6*

PERIOD OF UNSETTLING

HOLY SPIRIT

~ now must the **teacher of God understand** that **he** did not really know what was valuable and what was valueless. All that **he** really learned so far was that **he** did not **want** the valueless and that **he** did **want** the valuable. Yet his own sorting-out was meaningless in **teaching** him the difference. The **idea** of **sacrifice**, so central to his **thought system**, had made it **impossible** for him to judge. **He thought he** had learned willingness, but **now he** sees that **he** does not know what the willingness is for. And **now he** must attain a state that may remain **impossible** for a long, long **time**. **He** must learn to lay all **judgment** aside and **ask** only what **he** really wants in every circumstance. Were not each **step** in this direction so heavily reinforced, it would be hard indeed! *M-4.9.2:9*

PERSECUTION |ˌpərsəˈkyo͞oSH(ə)n|

DICTIONARY: *hostility and ill-treatment, especially because of race or political or religious beliefs.*

EGO

~ persecution is a frequent result, undertaken to justify the terrible misperception that **God** Himself persecuted His own Son on behalf of **salvation**. *T-3.III.13.4*

HOLY SPIRIT

~ it is not necessary to perceive any **form** of assault in persecution, because **you** cannot be persecuted. *T-6.II.7.6*

PICTURE |ˈpik(t)SHər|

DICTIONARY: *represent (someone or something) in a photograph or picture.*

EGO

~ one is a tiny picture, hard to **see** at all beneath the heavy shadows of its enormous and disproportionate enclosure. *T-17.V.38.10*

~ one is framed to be out of focus and not seen. *T-17.V.39.2*

~ for such an insane picture, an insane **defense** can be expected. *T-26.VIII.52.6*

~ this sick and sorry picture **you** accept, if only it can serve to punish him. *T-27.II.4.4*

~ it symbolized a **contradiction** which canceled out the **thought** it represents. *T-27.IV.31.3*

HOLY SPIRIT;   *content*

~ the other is lightly framed and hung in **light**, lovely to look upon for what it is. *T-17.V.38.11*

~ the other is framed for perfect **clarity**. *T-17.V.39.3*

~ the picture of **darkness** and of **death** grows less convincing as **you** search it out amid its wrappings. As each senseless stone which seems to shine in **darkness** from the frame is exposed to **light**, it becomes dull and lifeless and ceases to distract **you** from the picture. And finally **you** look upon the picture itself, seeing at last that, unprotected by the frame, it has no **meaning**. *T-17.V.39.4:6*

~ the other picture is lightly framed, for **time** cannot contain **eternity**. There is no distraction **here**. The picture of **Heaven** and **eternity** grows more convincing as **you** look at it. *T-17.V.40.1:3*

~ the dark picture brought to **light** is not perceived as fearful, but the **fact** that it is just a picture is brought **home** at last. And what **you see** there, **you will** recognize as what it is—a picture of what **you thought** was real and **nothing** more. For beyond this picture, **you will see nothing**. *T-17.V.40.6:8*

~ the picture of **light**, in clear cut and unmistakable **contrast**, is transformed into what lies beyond the picture. As **you** look on this, **you** realize that it is not a picture but a **reality**. This is no figured representation of a **thought system**, but the **Thought** Itself. What it represents is there. The frame fades gently, and **God** rises to your remembrance, **offering you** the whole of **creation** in exchange for your **little** picture, wholly without **value** and entirely deprived of **meaning**. *T-17.V.41.1:5*

~ the picture of yourself **you** offer him **you** show yourself and **give** it all your **faith**. *T-27.II.3.4*

~ it does not stand for double concepts. *T-27.IV.34.4*

PIECE |pēs|

DICTIONARY: *a portion of an object or of material, produced by cutting, tearing, or breaking the whole.*

EGO

~ when parts are wrested from the whole and seen as separate and as wholes **within** themselves, **they** become symbols standing for **attack** upon the whole, successful in effect, and never to be seen as whole again. And yet **you have** forgotten that **they** stand but for your own **decision** of what should be real, to take the place of what is real. *W-p1.136.7.1:2*

HOLY SPIRIT

~ the Holy Spirit's **function** is to take the broken **picture** of the **Son of God** and put the pieces into place again. *T-28.V.44.1*

~ the forms the broken pieces seem to take mean **nothing**. For the whole is in each one. *T-28.V.45.5:6*

PLAN |plan|

DICTIONARY: *a detailed proposal for **doing** or achieving something.*

EGO; *ego's plan*

~ the ego's plan, of **course**, makes no **sense** and **will** not work. By following it, **you will** merely place yourself in an **impossible situation** to which the **ego** always leads **you**. The ego's plan is to **have you see error** clearly first and then overlook it. *T-9.III.12.2:4*

~ the ego's plan for **forgiveness** is far more widely used than God's. *T-9.IV.20.1*

~ **self**-initiated plans are but defenses with the **purpose** all of them were made to realize. **They** are the **means** by which a frightened **mind** would undertake its own protection at the cost of **truth**. *W-p1.135.15.1:2*

~ planning is not often recognized as a **defense**. *W-p1.135.15.4*

~ the **mind** engaged in planning for itself is occupied in setting up control of **future** happenings. It does not think that it **will** be provided for unless it makes its own provisions. *W-p1.135.16.1:2*

~ but afterwards your plan requires that **you** must forget **you** made it, so it seems to be external to your own intent—a happening beyond your state of **mind**, an outcome with a real effect on **you** instead of one effected by your **self**. *W-p1.136.4.3*

HOLY SPIRIT; *God's plan*

~ a healed **mind** does not plan. It carries out the plans which it receives through listening to Wisdom that is not its own. It waits until it has been taught what should be done and then proceeds to do it. It does not depend upon itself for anything except its adequacy to fulfill the plans assigned to it. It is secure in **certainty** that obstacles cannot impede its progress to accomplishment of any **goal** which serves the greater plan established for the **good** of **everyone**. *W-pI.135.12.1:5*

~ a healed **mind** is relieved from the **belief** that it must plan, although it cannot know the outcome which is best, the **means** by which it is achieved, nor how to recognize the **problem** that the plan is made to solve. *W-pI.135.13.1*

~ everything that happens, all events, **past**, **present**, and to come, are gently planned by One Whose only **purpose** is your **good**. *W-pI.135.19.1*

~ if there are plans to **make, you will** be told of them. **They** may not be the plans **you thought** were needed nor indeed the answers to the problems which **you thought** confronted **you**. But **they** are answers to another kind of **question** which remains unanswered yet in **need** of answering until the **Answer** comes to **you** at last. *W-pI.135.25.2:4*

PLAN FOR SALVATION   *A Course in Miracles Term*

EGO;   *act of **attack** on His **plan***

HOLY SPIRIT;   *Atonement plan*

~ the **plan** is not yours. *T-9.III.10.5*

~ god's **plan** for **salvation**. There is but one response to **reality**, for **reality** evokes no **conflict** at all. There is but one **Teacher** of **reality**, Who understands what it is. **He** does not **change** His **Mind** about **reality** because **reality** does not **change**. *T-11.II.7.1:4*

~ from Him **you** cannot wander, and there is no possibility that the **plan** the **Holy Spirit** offers to **everyone** for the **salvation** of **everyone will** not be perfectly accomplished. *T-13.V.46.2*

~ all this lies in the Holy Spirit's **plan** to free **you** from the **past** and open up the **way** to **freedom** for **you**. *T-13.VII.62.2*

~ his **plan** for your awaking is as perfect as yours is fallible. *T-14.II.6.5*

~ his **will** content **you**, and there is **nothing** else that can bring **you peace**. *T-15.V.36.7*

~ the **plan** to **change** your dreams of **fear** to **happy** dreams from which **you** waken easily to **knowledge**. *T-18.VI.41.4*

~ **nothing** in the **plan** God has established for **salvation will** be left undone. This is the journey's **purpose**, without which is the **journey** meaningless. **Here** is the **peace** of God, given to **you** eternally by Him. **Here** is the **rest** and **quiet** that **you seek**, the **reason** for the **journey** from its beginning. *T-19.V.108.2:5*

~ the **plan** is not of **you**, nor **need you** be concerned with anything except the **part** that has been given **you** to learn. *T-20.V.33.1*

~ once **you** accept His **plan** as the one **function** that **you** would fulfill, there **will** be **nothing** else the **Holy Spirit will** not arrange for **you** without your **effort**. *T-20.V.35.4*

~ god's **plan** for your **salvation** could not **have** been established without your **will** and your consent. It must **have** been accepted by the **Son of God**, for what God wills for him **he** must **receive**. *T-21.VI.53.1:2*

~ god's **plan** is simple—never circular and never **self**-defeating. *T-21.VI.54.1*

~ **god** has built His **plan** for the **salvation** of His Son on **you**. *W-pI.61.10.2*

~ god's **plan** for **salvation** works simply because, by following His direction, **you seek** for **salvation** where it is. *W-pI.71.6.1*

~ only God's **plan** for **salvation will** work. *W-pI.71.7.4*

~ there is no possible alternative to God's **plan** that **will** save **you**. His is the only **plan** that is certain in its outcome. His is the only **plan** that must succeed. *W-pI.71.7.5:7*

~ all things are possible to **God**. **Salvation** must be yours because of His **plan**, which cannot **fail**. *W-pI.71.8.3:4*

~ god's **plan** for your **salvation will** work, and other plans **will** not. *W-pI.71.9.2*

~ but God's **plan will** succeed. It **will** lead to **release** and joy. *W-pI.71.9.6:7*

~ god's **plan** for **salvation** has already been accomplished in us. *W-pI.72.11.1*

~ god's **plan** for **salvation**, and only His, is wholly in accord with your **will**. It is not the **purpose** of an alien **power**, thrust upon **you** unwillingly. It is the one **purpose here** on which **you** and your **Father** are in perfect accord. *W-pI.73.10.1:3*

~ the **Holy Spirit** holds this **plan** of God exactly as it was received of Him **within** the **Mind** of **God** and in your own. It is apart from **time** in that its **Source** is timeless. Yet it operates in **time** because of your **belief** that **time** is real. *W-pI.99.5.1:3*

~ **now** are **you** entrusted with this **plan**, along with Him. *W-pI.99.7.2*

~ just as God's Son completes his **Father**, so your **part** in it completes your Father's **plan**. *W-pI.100.1.1*

~ your **joy** must be complete to let His **plan** be understood by those to whom **He** sends **you**. **They will see** their **function** in your shining face and hear **God** calling to them in your **happy** laugh. *W-pI.100.2.5:6*

~ just as your **light** increases every **light** that shines in **Heaven**, so your **joy** on earth calls to all minds to let their sorrows go and take their place beside **you** in God's **plan**. *W-pI.100.4.2*

~ god's **plan** for your **salvation** cannot **change**, nor can it **fail**. Be thankful it remains exactly as **He** planned it. Changelessly it stands before **you**, like an open door with warmth and **welcome** calling from beyond the doorway, bidding **you** to enter in and **make** yourself at **home** where **you** belong. *W-pI.122.5.4:6*

~ god's **plan** is simply this: the **Son of God** is free to save himself, given the **word** of **God** to be his Guide, forever in his **mind** and at his side to lead him surely to his Father's house by his own **will**, forever free as God's. **He** is not led by force, but only **love**. **He** is not judged, but only sanctified. *W-pI.125.2.2:4*

~ your **plan** may be **impossible**, but God's can never **fail** because **He** is its **Source**. *W-pI.186.11.7*

~ accept the **plan you** did not **make** instead. *W-pI.186.5.2*

~ instead of judging, **we need** but be still and let all things be healed. **We will** accept the **way** God's **plan will** end, as **we** received the **way** it started. *W-pII.1.10.5:6*

~ yet **God** has planned that His beloved Son **will** be redeemed. *W-pII.338.1.7*

~ his **plan** can **have** no levels, **being** a **reflection** of His **Will**. *M-3.3.5*

~ chance plays no **part** in God's **plan**. *M-9.1.3*

PLEASURE

DICTIONARY: *a feeling of **happy** satisfaction and enjoyment.*

EGO;   *happiness*

~ it is **impossible** to **seek** for pleasure through the **body** and not find **pain**. *T-19.V.7.1.1*

~ it is but the inevitable result of equating yourself with the **body**, which is the invitation to **pain**. For it invites **fear** to enter and become your **purpose**. The **attraction** of **guilt** must enter with it, and whatever **fear** directs the **body** to do is therefore painful. It **will share** the **pain** of all illusions, and the **illusion** of pleasure **will** be the same as **pain**. *T-19.V.71.4:7*

~ to **you** it teaches that the body's pleasure is happiness. Yet to itself it whispers, "It is **death**." *T-19.V.72.7:9*

~ it bids the **body** search for **pain** in **attack** upon another, calling it pleasure and **offering** it to **you** as **freedom** from **attack**. *T-19.V.74.4*

~ take pleasure in the quickly passing and ephemeral. *T-27.II.8.7*

~ it tries to look for pleasure and avoid the things that would be hurtful. *T-27.IX.77.6*

~ all the "pleasures" of the **world** are **nothing**. *M-13.3.1*

HOLY SPIRIT

~ all real pleasure comes from **doing God's Will**. *T-1.II.104.3*

~ the **Holy Spirit** does not demand **you sacrifice** the hope of the body's pleasure; it has no hope of pleasure. *T-19.V.62.3*

~ pleasure and **pain** are equally unreal, because their **purpose** cannot be achieved. Thus are **they means** for **nothing**, for **they have** a **goal** without a **meaning**. And **they share** the lack of **meaning** which their **purpose** has. *T-27.VII.54.7:9*

POSSESSION |pəˈzeSHən|

DICTIONARY: *the state of having, owning, or controlling something.*

EGO

~ the **ego** wants to **have** things for **salvation**, for possession is its law. Possession for its own sake is the ego's fundamental creed, a basic cornerstone in the churches that it builds unto itself. *T-12.VII.68.9:10*

~ never is your possession made complete. *T-23.III.31.1*

POWER |ˈpou(ə)r|

DICTIONARY: *the ability to do something or act in a particular way, especially as a faculty or quality.*

EGO

~ **you have** not usurped the power of **God**, but **you have** lost it. *T-3.VIII.69.2*

~ **love** is your power, which the **ego** must deny. It must also deny everything which this power gives **you**, because it gives **you** everything. *T-7.VII.58.4:5*

~ "dynamics" implies the power to do something, and the whole **separation** fallacy lies in the **belief** that the **ego** has the power to do anything. The **ego** is fearful to **you** because **you** believe this. *T-10.VI.41.5:6*

~ its one claim to your allegiance is that it can **give** power to **you**. *T-10.VI.47.3*

~ **you** still **have** the power, but **you have** interposed so much between it and your **awareness** of it that **you** cannot use it. Everything **you have** taught yourselves has made your power more and more obscure to **you. You** know not what it is nor where. **You have** made a semblance of power and a show of **strength** so pitiful that it must **fail you.** For power is not a seeming **strength**, and **truth** is beyond semblance of any kind. *T-14.VII.58.4:8*

~ because your power, **being** His, is as great as His, **you** can turn away from **love**. *T-15.IX.90.3*

~ **nothing** can **hurt you** unless **you give** it the power to do so. For **you give** power as the **laws** of this **world** interpret **giving**—as **you give, you** lose. It is not up to **you** to **give** power at all. *T-20.V.28.1:3*

~ weakened power is a **contradiction** in ideas. Weak **strength** is meaningless, and power used to weaken is employed to **limit**. And therefore it must be limited and weak because that is its **purpose**. *T-27.IV.29.2:4*

~ who assumes a power that **he** does not **have** is deceiving himself. *M-29.5.1*

HOLY SPIRIT;   *limitless power, God's **gift**, God's power.*

~ the **Atonement** gives **you** the power of a healed **mind**, but the power to create is of **God**. *T-5.VI.57.1*

~ the whole power of God's Son lies in all of us, but not in any of us **alone**. *T-8.VI.49.5*

~ **he will** not **limit** your power to **help** them, because **He** has given it to **you**. *T-9.IX.75.2*

~ the power of one **mind** can shine into another, because all the lamps of **God** were lit by the same **spark**. It is everywhere, and it is eternal. *T-9.X.91.5:6*

~ all power is of **God**. *T-10.VI.42.1*

~ the whole power of **God** is in every **part** of Him, and **nothing** contradictory to His **Will** is either great or small. *T-10.VII.68.6*

~ what **God** did not **give you** has no power over **you**. *T-11.IX.83.5*

~ our power comes not of us but of our **Father**. *T-14.II.13.2*

~ the power of **love** is in His **gentleness**, which is of **God** and therefore cannot crucify nor suffer **crucifixion**. *T-14.II.14.9*

~ the power of **God** is limitless. And **being** always maximal, it offers everything to every **call** from anyone. *T-14.VI.51.10:11*

~ the power of **God**, and not of **you**, engenders miracles. The **miracle** itself is but the **witness** that **you have** the power of **God** in **you**. *T-14.VI.51.7:8*

~ nor **will** the power of all His **love** be absent from any **miracle you** offer to His Son. *T-14.VI.57.9*

~ **knowledge** is power, and all power is of **God**. *T-14.VII.58.2*

~ the power of **God will** support every **effort you make** on behalf of His dear Son. *T-15.IV.26.1*

~ god's power is forever on the side of His **host**, for it protects only the **peace** in which **He** dwells. *T-15.IV.34.5*

~ the power of **God** in Him and **you** is joined in real **relationship**. *T-15.VIII.77.3*

~ it is in your power to **make** this season holy, for it is in your power to **make** the **time** of **Christ** be **now**. *T-15.X.94.8*

~ power is of **God**, given by Him and reawakened by the **Holy Spirit**, who knows that as **you give, you gain**. **He** gives no power to **sin**, and therefore it has none; nor to its results as this **world** sees them—**sickness** and **death** and **misery** and **pain**. These things **have** not occurred because the **Holy Spirit** sees them not and gives no power to their seeming **source**. *T-20.V.28.4:6*

~ the power that **you have** over the **Son of God** is not a **threat** to his **reality**. It but attests to it. *T-21.VII.69.1:2*

~ **nothing you** made has any power over **you** unless **you** still would be apart from your **Creator** and with a **will** opposed to His. *T-22.III.25.2*

~ **nothing** has power over **you** except His **Will** and yours. *T-25.III.21.7*

~ to use the power **God** has given **you** as **He** would **have** it used is natural. *T-26.VIII.65.1*

~ power cannot oppose. *T-27.IV.29.1*

~ power is unopposed, to be itself. No **weakness** can intrude on it without changing it into something it is not. *T-27.IV.29.5:6*

~ a power known as wholly free of limits. *T-27.IV.33.3*

~ the **peace** of power which opposes **nothing**. *T-27.IV.35.5*

~ no other kind can be at all. *T-27.IV.35.6*

~ power beyond **forgiveness** and beyond the **world** of symbols and of limitations. *T-27.IV.35.7*

~ the great **release** of power must begin with **learning** where it really has a use. *T-31.IV.37.4*

~ there is **nothing** the power of **God** cannot do. *W-pI.38.1.6*

~ it is therefore in my power to **change** every **mind** along with mine, for mine is the power of **God**. *W-pI.54.5.5*

~ there is **nothing** in the **world** which has the power to **make you** ill or **sad** or weak or frail. But it is **you** who **have** the power to dominate all things **you see** by merely recognizing what **you** are. *W-pI.190.5.5:6*

~ when this Power has once been experienced, it is **impossible** to **trust** one's own petty **strength** again. *M-4.4.1*

~ to say, "Of myself **I** can do **nothing**" is to **gain** all power. *M-29.4.2*

~ as **God** created **you, you have** all power. *M-29.4.4*

~ to accept the power given him by **God** is but to acknowledge his **Creator** and accept His gifts. *M-29.5.2*

PRACTICE

|ˈpraktəs|

DICTIONARY: *repeated **exercise** in or performance of an activity or skill so as to acquire or maintain proficiency in it.*

EGO

~ it is only your **weakness** that **will** depart from **you** in this practice. *T-15.III.21.6*

~ but **learning will** be hampered when **you** skip a practice period because **you** are unwilling to devote the **time** to it which **you** are asked to **give**. *W-pI.Rev III.3.1*

HOLY SPIRIT

~ it is the practice of the **power** of God in you. *T-15.III.21.6*

~ **you** do not **need** to practice what **you** really **understand**. *W-pI.9.1.6*

~ each **time you** practice, **awareness** is brought a **little** nearer at least; sometimes a thousand years or more are saved. *W-pI.97.3.2*

~ **they** hold out the sure rewards of questions answered, and what your **acceptance** of the **answer** brings. *W-pI.122.11.1*

~ our practicing becomes the footsteps lightening up the **way** for all our brothers, who **will** follow us to the **reality we share** with them. *W-pI.134.14.3*

- and **now** it is specifics **we** must use in practicing. *W-pI.161.3.2*

- **learning will** not be hampered when **you** miss a practice period because it is **impossible** at the appointed time. *W-pI.Rev III.2.1*

- these practice periods are planned to **help you form** the habit of applying what **you** learn each day to everything **you** do. *W-pI.Rev III.11.4*

- **we** place **faith** in the **experience** that comes from practice, not the **means we** use. **We** wait for the **experience** and recognize that it is only **here** conviction lies. **We** use the words, and try and try again to go beyond them to their **meaning**, which is far beyond their sound. The sound grows dim and disappears as **we** approach the **Source** of meaning. It is **here** that **we** find **rest**. *W-pI.Rev V.15.2:6*

- practice **now** in **order** to attain the **sense** of **peace** such unified commitment **will** bestow. *W-pI.ST181.1.3*

PRAISE |prāz|

DICTIONARY: *the expression of approval or admiration for someone or something.*

EGO

- the **ego** tries to exploit all situations into forms of praise for itself in **order** to overcome its doubts. *T-4.II.15.1*

HOLY SPIRIT

- **rehabilitation** is an attitude of praising **God** as **He** Himself knows praise. **He** offers praise to **you**, and **you** must offer it to others. *T-4.IX.105.3:4*

- **see** only praise of Him in what He has created, for He **will** never cease His praise of you. United in this praise, **we** stand before the gates of **Heaven**. *T-13.IV.34.5:6*

- to your most holy **Self**, all praise is due for what **you** are and for what He is Who created **you** as **you** are. *T-16.IV.28.1*

PRAYER |prer|

DICTIONARY: *a solemn **request** for **help** or expression of thanks addressed to **God** or an object of worship.*

EGO;   *supplication, wanting.*

- it is **impossible** to pray for idols and hope to reach **God**. *S-1.I.1.5*

- prayer is merely wanting, out of a **sense** of scarcity and lack. *S-1.I.1.5*

- these forms of prayer, or asking-out-of-**need**, always involve feelings of **weakness** and inadequacy, and could never be made by a **Son of God** who knows Who **he** is. No one, then, who is sure of his **Identity** could pray in these forms. Yet it is also true that no one who is **uncertain** of his **Identity** can avoid praying in this **way**. *S-1.II.2.1:3*

- the earlier forms of prayer, at the bottom of the ladder, **will** not be free from envy and malice. **They call** for **vengeance**, not for **love**. *S-1.III.2.1:2*

- **they** are calls for **death**, made out of **fear** by those who cherish **guilt**. **They call** upon a vengeful **God**, and it is **he** who seems to **answer** them. *S-1.III.2.3:4*

~ it is not easy to realize that prayers for things, for status, for human **love**, for external "gifts" of any kind, are always made to set up jailers and to **hide** from **guilt**. These things are used for goals that **substitute** for **God**, and therefore distort the **purpose** of prayer. *S-1.III.6.1:2*

~ prayer becomes requests for enemies. *S-1.III.6.5*

~ prayer for specifics always asks to **have** the **past** repeated in some **way**. *S-1.IV.3.3*

~ prayer cannot be released to **Heaven** while **forgiveness**-to-destroy remains with **you**. *S-2.I.7.3*

HOLY SPIRIT; *quiet time* of listening and loving, *offering*, natural **communication**, *ladder reaching up to* **Heaven**, *His Own Right Hand, medium of miracles, restatement of inclusion, greatest* **gift**, *stepping aside, letting go.*

~ prayer is the natural **communication** of the created with the **Creator**. Through prayer **love** is received, and through miracles **love** is expressed. *T-1.I.11.2:3*

~ prayer is a **way** of asking for something. Prayer is the medium of miracles, but the only meaningful prayer is for **forgiveness**, because those who **have** been forgiven **have** everything. Once **forgiveness** has been accepted, prayer in the usual **sense** becomes utterly meaningless. Essentially, a prayer for **forgiveness** is **nothing** more than a **request** that **we** may be able to recognize something **we** already **have**. *T-3.VII.56.1:4*

~ prayer is the restatement of inclusion, directed by the **Holy Spirit** under the **laws** of **God**. *T-6.III.32.5*

~ all prayers are answered. *T-8.XI.109.1*

~ the prayer for things of this **world will** bring experiences of this **world**. If the prayer of the heart asks for this, this **will** be given because this **will** be received. *M-21.3.1:2*

~ it is **impossible** that the prayer of the heart remain unanswered in the **perception** of the one who asks. *M-21.3.3*

~ his words do not matter. *M-21.3.9*

~ **god** has given Him the **power** to translate your prayers of the heart into His **language**. *M-29.6.4*

~ what is prayer except the joining of minds in a **relationship** which **Christ** can enter? *P-2.VII.2.3*

~ prayer is the greatest **gift** with which **God** blessed His Son at his **creation**. It was then what it is to become; the single **voice Creator** and **creation share**; the **song** the Son sings to the **Father**, Who returns the thanks it offers Him unto the Son. *S-1.IN.1.1:2*

~ the **Love They share** is what all prayer **will** be throughout **eternity**, when **time** is done. For such it was before **time** seemed to be. *S-1.IN.1.7:8*

~ to **you** who are in **time** a **little** while, prayer takes the **form** that best **will** suit your **need**. *S-1.IN.2.1*

~ prayer **now** must be the **means** by which God's Son leaves separate goals and separate interests by, and turns in holy gladness to the **truth** of **union** in his **Father** and himself. *S-1.IN.2.4*

~ prayer **will** sustain **you now**, and bless **you** as **you** lift your heart to Him. *S-1.IN.3.2*

~ this is prayer, and **here salvation** is. This is the **way**. It is God's **gift** to **you**. *S-1.IN.3.4*

~ prayer is a **way** offered by the **Holy Spirit** to reach **God**. *S-1.I.1.1*

~ it is not merely a **question** or an entreaty. It cannot succeed until **you** realize that it asks for **nothing**. *S-1.I.1.2:3*

~ true prayer must avoid the pitfall of asking to entreat. **Ask**, rather, to **receive** what is already given; to accept what is already there. *S-1.I.1.6:7*

~ in true prayer **you** hear only the **song**. *S-1.I.3.4*

~ in prayer **you** overlook your specific needs as **you** see them, and let them go into God's Hands. *S-1.I.4.3*

~ prayer is a stepping aside; a letting go, a **quiet time** of listening and loving. It should not be confused with supplication of any kind, because it is a **way** of remembering your **holiness**. *S-1.I.5.1:2*

~ it is to **Love you** go in prayer. Prayer is an **offering**; a giving up of yourself to be at one with **Love**. There is **nothing** to **ask** because there is **nothing** left to **want**. *S-1.I.5.4:6*

~ **help** in prayer does not mean that another mediates between **you** and **God**. But it does mean that another stands beside **you** and helps to raise **you** up to Him. One who has realized the goodness of **God** prays without **fear**. *S-1.I.6.3:5*

~ one who prays without **fear** cannot but reach Him. *S-1.I.6.6*

~ praying to **Christ** in anyone is true prayer because it is a **gift** of thanks to His **Father**. *S-1.I.7.1*

~ herein lies the **power** of prayer. It asks **nothing** and receives everything. This prayer can be shared because it receives for **everyone**. *S-1.I.7.4:6*

~ prayer has no beginning and no end. It is a **part** of **life**. But it does **change** in **form**, and grow with **learning** until it reaches its formless state, and fuses into total **communication** with **God**. *S-1.II.1.1:3*

~ and prayer is as continual as **life**. **Everyone** prays without ceasing. *S-1.II.2.4:5*

~ that curious **contradiction** in terms known as "praying for one's enemies." The **contradiction** lies not in the actual words, but rather in the **way** in which **they** are usually interpreted. While **you** believe **you have** enemies, **you have** limited prayer to the **laws** of this **world**, and **have** also limited your ability to **receive** and to accept to the same narrow margins. And yet, if **you have** enemies **you have need** of prayer, and great **need**, too. *S-1.II.4.1:4*

~ the prayer for enemies thus becomes a prayer for your own **freedom**. *S-1.II.5.3*

~ prayer at any **level** is always for yourself. If **you** unite with anyone in prayer, **you make** him **part** of **you**. *S-1.II.6.1:2*

~ prayer is a ladder reaching up to **Heaven**. *S-1.II.7.1*

~ prayer is **part** of **you**. *S-1.II.7.2*

~ for **now** it rises as a **song** of thanks to your **Creator**, sung without words, or thoughts, or vain desires, unneedful **now** of anything at all. So it extends, as it was meant to do. *S-1.II.7.8:9*

~ **god** is the **goal** of every prayer, giving it timelessness instead of end. Nor has it a beginning, because the **goal** has never changed. Prayer in its earlier forms is an **illusion**, because there is no **need** for a ladder to reach what one has never left. Yet prayer is **part** of **forgiveness** as long as **forgiveness**, itself an **illusion**, remains unattained. Prayer is tied up with **learning** until the **goal** of **learning** has been reached. *S-1.II.8.1:5*

~ praying for others, if rightly understood, becomes a **means** for lifting your projections of **guilt** from your **brother**, and enabling **you** to recognize it is not **he** who is hurting **you**. *S-1.III.1.4*

~ prayer **will** bring an **answer** only in the **form** in which the prayer was made. *S-1.III.3.1*

~ the aim of prayer is to **release** the **present** from its chains of **past** illusions; to let it be a freely chosen remedy from every **choice** that stood for a **mistake**. What prayer can offer **now** so far exceeds all that **you** asked before that it is pitiful to be content with less. *S-1.IV.3.5:6*

~ **you have** chosen a newborn chance each **time you** pray. *S-1.IV.4.1*

~ prayer can bring the **peace** of **God**. *S-1.IV.4.4*

~ prayer is a **way** to true **humility**. *S-1.V.1.1*

~ prayer has become what it was meant to be, for **you have** recognized the **Christ** in you. *S-1.V.4.6*

~ prayer **will** lift **you** up and bring **you home** where **God** would **have you** be. *S-2.II.8.8*

~ prayer has both aids and witnesses which **make** the steep ascent more gentle and more sure, easing the **pain** of **fear** and **offering** the comfort and the promises of hope. *S-3.IN.1.1*

~ in prayer **you have** united with your **Source**, and understood that **you have** never left. *S-3.IV.4.5*

329

PREPARATION

|ˌprepəˈrāSH(ə)n|

DICTIONARY: *the action or process of making ready or **being** made ready for use or consideration.*

HOLY SPIRIT

~ it is only **fear** that **you will** add if **you** prepare yourself for **love**. The preparation for the **holy instant** belongs to Him Who gives it. *T-18.V.38.4:5*

~ **you** cannot prepare for it without placing it in the **future**. **Release** is given **you** the instant **you desire** it. Many **have** spent a lifetime in preparation and **have** indeed achieved their instants of success. This **course** does not attempt to **teach** more than **they** learned in **time**, but it does aim at saving **time**. *T-18.VIII.66.2:5*

~ no preparation can be made that would enhance the invitation's real appeal. *T-27.IV.32.2*

~ our only preparation is to let our interfering thoughts be laid aside, not separately, but all of them as one. *W-pI.140.11.2*

PRESENT

|ˈprez(ə)nt|

DICTIONARY: *the period of **time now** occurring.*

EGO

~ its emphasis on **guilt** enables it to ensure its continuity by making the **future** like the **past** and thus avoiding the present. By the notion of paying for the **past** in the **future**, the **past** becomes the determiner of the **future**, making them continuous without an intervening present. For the **ego** uses the present only as a brief transition to the **future**, in which it brings the **past** to the **future** by interpreting the present in **past** terms. *T-12.IV.26.3:6*

~ now has no **meaning** to the ego. The present merely reminds it of **past** hurts, and it reacts to the present as if it were the **past**. *T-12.IV.27.1:2*

~ it overlooks the present, for it rests on the **idea** the **past** has taught enough to let the **mind** direct its **future course**. *T-16.VIII.71.2*

~ **you** are choosing a **future** of illusions and losing the endless opportunities which **you** could find for **release** in the present. *T-12.IV.28.5*

~ the frame of reference to which the present is referred for **meaning** is an **illusion** of the **past** in which those elements which fit the **purpose** of the unholy **alliance** are retained and all the **rest** let go. And what is thus let go is all the **truth** the **past** could ever offer to the present as witnesses for its **reality**, while what is kept but witnesses to the **reality** of dreams. *T-17.IV.24.4:5*

~ **past**, present, and **future** are not continuous unless **you** force continuity on them. **You** can perceive them as continuous and **make** them so for you. *T-12.VI.46.2:3*

~ the present is useless to **you** while **you** pursue the ego's **goal** as its ally. *T-16.VIII.73.3*

~ the mind's preoccupation with the **past** is the **cause** of the total misconception about **time** from which your seeing suffers. Your **mind** cannot grasp the present, which is the only **time** there is. It therefore cannot **understand time** and cannot, in **fact**, **understand** anything. *W-pI.8.1.4:6*

HOLY SPIRIT; *forgiveness, only **time** there is, holy present.*

~ it holds the only things that are forever true. All **healing** lies **within** it because its continuity is real. It extends to all aspects of **consciousness** at the same **time** and thus enables them to reach each other. The present is before **time** was and **will** be when **time** is no more. In it is everything that is eternal, and **they** are one. Their continuity is timeless, and their **communication** is unbroken, for **they** are not separated by the **past**. *T-12.VI.50.1:6*

~ the present offers **you** your brothers in the **light** that would unite **you** with them and free **you** from the **past**. *T-12.VI.51.1*

~ in this one still dimension of **time**, which does not **change** and where there is no **sight** of what **you** were, **you** look at **Christ** and **call** His witnesses to shine on **you** because **you** called them forth. *T-12.VI.51.5*

~ for the **Holy Spirit**, who knows only the present, uses it to **undo** the **fear** by which the **ego** would **make** the present useless. *T-15.II.8.5*

~ there is no **fear** in the present when each instant stands clear and separated from the **past**, without its **shadow** reaching out into the **future**. *T-15.II.9.3*

~ if all but loving thoughts has been forgotten, what remains is eternal. And the transformed **past** is made like the present. No longer does the **past conflict** with **now**. This continuity extends the present by increasing its **reality** and its **value** in your **perception** of it. *T-17.IV.20.1:4*

~ the present is **forgiveness**. *T-17.IV.24.2*

~ meeting place of **self** and **Self**, where **light** and **strength** are one. *W-pI.92.10.4*

~ the present saved to quietly extend into a timeless **future**. *W-pI.110.4.1*

~ **we** raise our eyes upon a different present, where a **future** shines unlike the **past** in every attribute. *W-pI.127.9.4*

~ **you** free the **past** from what **you thought** before. **You** free the **future** from all ancient thoughts of seeking what **you** do not **want** to find. The present **now** remains the only **time**. **Here** in the present is the **world** set free. For as **you** let the **past** be lifted and **release** the **future** from your ancient fears, **you** find escape and **give** it to the **world**. *W-pI.132.3.1:5*

~ the present is the only **time** there is. *W-pI.164.1.2*

~ for the **past** is gone, and what is present, freed from its bequest of grief and **misery**, of **pain** and **loss**, becomes the instant in which **time** escapes the bondage of illusions where it runs its pitiless, inevitable **course**. *W-pI.194.5.2*

~ the present has been freed, extending its security and **peace** into a **quiet future** filled with hope. *W-pII.314.1.5*

PRIDE

|prīd|

DICTIONARY: *a feeling or deep **pleasure** or satisfaction derived from one's own achievements, the achievements of those with whom one is closely associated, or from qualities or possessions that are widely admired.*

EGO

~ pride **will** not produce miracles and therefore **will** deprive **you** of your true witnesses to your **reality**. *T-9.VII.55.2*

~ pride is not shared. *T-9.VII.55.4*

~ it is pride that argues **you have** come into a **world** quite separate from yourself, impervious to what **you** think, and quite apart from what **you** chance to think it is. *W-pI.132.6.4*

~ is pride that would deny the **call** of **God** Himself. *W-pI.186.3.7*

~ it is pride that would deny the **call** of **God** Himself. *W-pI.186.3.8*

PRISON

|ˈprizən|

DICTIONARY: *a building in which people are legally held as a **punishment** for a crime they **have** committed or while awaiting trial.*

EGO; *body, prison-house, rotting prison, gates of **hell**, **special kingdom**, **world**.*

~ what **you seek** to imprison **you** do not **love**. *T-8.V.34.3*

~ **you see** yourself locked in a separate prison, removed and unreachable, incapable of reaching out as **being** reached. **You hate** this prison **you have** made and would destroy it. But **you** would not escape from it, leaving it unharmed, without your **guilt** upon it. *T-18.VII.55.5:7*

~ it holds in prison but the willing **mind** that would abide in it. *T-31.III.29.5*

~ **nothing** holds me in this **world**. Only my **wish** to stay keeps me a prisoner. *W-pI.57.2.6:7*

~ i made up the prison in which **I see** myself. *W-pI.57.3.1*

~ **i see** the **world** as a prison for God's Son. *W-pI.57.4.3*

HOLY SPIRIT

~ **everyone** is seeking to escape from the prison he has made, and the **way** to find **release** is not denied him. **Being** in him, he has found it. When he finds it is only a matter of **time**, and **time** is but an **illusion**. *T-11.X.93.3:5*

~ the prison door is open. **I** can leave it simply by walking out. *W-pI.57.2.4:5*

~ it is given **you** to find the **means** whereby the **world** no longer seems to be a prison house for **you** or anyone. *W-pI.200.4.5*

PROBLEM

|ˈpräbləm|

DICTIONARY: *a matter or **situation** regarded as unwelcome or harmful and needing to be dealt with and overcome.*

EGO

~ the **ego** seeks to "resolve" its problems, not at their **source**, but where **they** were not made. And thus it seeks to guarantee there **will** be no solution. *T-17.IV.20.8:9*

~ to remove the problem elsewhere is to keep it. For **you** remove yourself from it and **make** it unsolvable. *T-17.VII.64.7:8*

~ to keep it for yourself to solve without His **help** is to decide it should remain unsettled, unresolved, and lasting in its **power** of **injustice** and **attack**. *T-25.X.84.6*

~ **they** gather dust and grow until **they** cover everything that **you** perceive and leave **you** fair to no one. *T-25.X.86.2*

~ a problem can appear in many forms, and it **will** do so while the problem lasts. It serves no **purpose** to attempt to solve it in a **special form**. It **will** recur and then recur again and yet again until it has been answered for all **time** and **will** not rise again in any **form**. *T-26.III.10.5:7*

~ each **time you** keep a problem for yourself to solve or judge that it is one which has no resolution, **you have** made it great and **past** the hope of **healing**. *T-26.III.14.7*

~ **you** believe that some injustices are fair and **good** and necessary to preserve yourself. It is these problems that **you** think are great and cannot be resolved. *T-26.III.15.2:3*

~ **you** still **make** up your **mind** and then decide to **ask** what **you** should do. And what **you** hear may not resolve the problem as **you** saw it first. This leads to **fear** because it contradicts what **you** perceive, and so **you** feel attacked. And therefore angry. *T-30.II.6.2:5*

~ a problem cannot be solved if **you** do not know what it is. Even if it is really solved already, **you will** still **have** the problem because **you** cannot recognize that it has been solved. *W-pI.79.1.1:2*

~ the solution is not recognized because the problem is not recognized. *W-pI.79.1.5*

~ **everyone** in this **world** seems to **have** his own **special** problems. Yet **they** are all the same and must be recognized as one if the one solution which solves them all is to be accepted. Who can **see** that a problem has been solved if **he** thinks the problem is something else? Even if **he** is given the **answer**, **he** cannot **see** its relevance. *W-pI.79.2.1:4*

~ **you have** the **answer**, but **you** are still **uncertain** about what the problem is. A long series of different problems seems to confront **you**, and as one is settled the next one and the next arise. There seems to be no end to them. There is no **time** in which **you** feel completely free of problems and at **peace**. *W-pI.79.3.2:5*

~ the **temptation** to regard problems as many is the **temptation** to keep the problem of **separation** unsolved. The **world** seems to **present you** with a vast number of problems, each requiring a different **answer**. This **perception** places **you** in a position in which your problem solving must be inadequate and failure must be inevitable. *W-pI.79.4.1:3*

~ no one could solve all the problems the **world** appears to hold. **They** seem to be on so many levels, in such varying forms, and with such varied content that **they** confront **you** with an **impossible situation**. Dismay and depression are inevitable as **you** regard them. Some spring up unexpectedly, just as **you** think **you have** resolved the previous ones. Others remain unsolved under a cloud of **denial** and rise to haunt **you** from **time** to **time**, only to be hidden again but still unsolved. *W-pI.79.5.1:5*

~ the problem is always some **form** of **grievance** which **I** would cherish. *W-pI.90.2.1*

~ **i** seem to **have** problems only because I am misusing **time**. I believe that the problem comes first, and **time** must elapse before it can be worked out. I do not **see** the problem and the **answer** as simultaneous in their occurrence. That is because I do not yet realize that **God** has placed the **answer** together with the problem, so that **they** cannot be separated by **time**. *W-pI.90.5.1:4*

~ these problems are not real, but that is meaningless to those who believe in them. *M-11.3.2*

HOLY SPIRIT; *error, grievance.*

~ all bring their different problems to its **healing light**, but all their problems are met only with **healing** there. *T-14.V.44.4*

~ **you have** no problems which He cannot solve by **offering you** a **miracle**. *T-14.VII.69.2*

~ every **fear** or **pain** or trial **you have** has been undone. He has brought all of them to **light**, having accepted them instead of **you** and recognized **they** never were. *T-14.VII.69.4:5*

~ **you have** never given any problem to the **Holy Spirit** He has not solved for **you**, nor **will you** ever do so. *T-16.III.19.4*

~ the **Holy Spirit** wills only to **make** His resolutions complete and perfect, and so **He** seeks and finds the **source** of problems where it is and there undoes it. *T-17.IV.21.1*

~ had **you** not lacked the **faith** it could be solved, the problem would be gone. And the **situation** would **have** been meaningful to **you** because the interference in the **way** of understanding would **have** been removed. *T-17.VII.64.5:6*

~ there is no problem in any **situation** that **faith will** not solve. There is no **shift** in any aspect of the problem but **will make** solution **impossible**. For if **you shift part** of the problem elsewhere, the **meaning** of the problem must be lost, and the solution to the problem is inherent in its **meaning**. *T-17.VIII.65.1:3*

~ all your problems **have** been solved, but **you have** removed yourself from the solution? *T-17.VIII.65.4*

~ a problem the **Holy Spirit** solves **will** always be one in which no one loses. *T-25.X.80.1*

~ the Holy Spirit's problem solving is the **way** in which the problem ends. It has been solved because it has been met with **justice**. Until it has, it **will** recur because it has not yet been solved. *T-25.X.82.3:5*

~ to **give** a problem to the **Holy Spirit** to solve for **you means** that **you want** it solved. *T-25.X.84.5*

~ **he** has not greater difficulty in resolving some than others. Every problem is the same to Him, because each one is solved in just the same respect and through the same approach. The aspects which **need** solving do not **change**, whatever **form** the problem seems to take. *T-26.III.10.2:4*

~ the **Holy Spirit** offers **you release** from every problem that **you** think **you have**. **They** are the same to Him because each one, regardless of the **form** it seems to take, is a demand that someone suffer **loss** and **make** a **sacrifice** that **you** might **gain**. And when the **situation** is worked out so no one loses, is the problem gone, because it was an **error** in **perception** which **now** has been corrected. *T-26.III.11.1:3*

~ vanish one by one without regard to size, **complexity**, or place and **time**, or any attribute which **you** perceive that makes each one seem different from the **rest**. *T-26.III.12.4*

~ every problem is an **error**. *T-26.III.13.2*

~ can there be no problems that **justice** cannot solve. *T-26.III.15.1*

~ what seemed once to be a **special** problem, a **mistake** without a remedy, or an affliction without a cure has been transformed into a universal **blessing**. *T-26.III.16.5*

~ **time** is not involved, and every problem can be answered **now**. *T-27.V.37.1*

~ where its **answer** is, a problem must be simple and be easily resolved. It must be pointless to attempt to solve a problem where the **answer** cannot be. *T-27.V.37.7:8*

~ problems are not specific, but **they** take specific forms, and these specific shapes **make** up the **world**. And no one understands the nature of his problem. *T-27.VI.50.1:2*

~ **healing** is apparent in specific instances and generalizes to include them all. This is because **they** really are the same despite their different forms. *T-27.VI.50.6:7*

~ your many different problems **will** be solved as any one of them has been escaped. *T-27.VI.51.2*

~ **they** are solved together. And their common **answer** shows the questions could not **have** been separate. *T-27.VI.52.6:7*

~ without the **clouds**, the problem **will** emerge in all its primitive simplicity. *T-27.VIII.63.4*

~ the problem is absurd when clearly seen. *T-27.VIII.63.5*

~ no one has difficulty making up his **mind** to let a simple problem be resolved if it is seen as hurting him and also very easily removed. *T-27.VIII.63.6*

~ the problem of **separation**, which is really the only problem, has already been solved. *W-pI.79.1.4*

~ if **you** could recognize that your only problem is **separation**, no matter what **form** it takes, **you** could accept the **answer** because **you** would **see** its relevance. *W-pI.79.6.2*

~ **you have** the **means** to solve them all. *W-pI.79.6.3*

~ your one central problem has been answered, and **you have** no other. Therefore **you** must be at **peace**. **Salvation** does depend on recognizing this one problem and understanding that it has been solved. One problem—one solution. **Salvation** is accomplished. **Freedom** from **conflict** has been given **you**. *W-pI.80.1.2:7*

~ and **you** can recognize the **answer** because the problem has been identified. *W-pI.80.2.6*

~ a problem that has been resolved cannot trouble **you**. *W-pI.80.3.2*

~ all problems are the same. Their many forms **will** not deceive **you** while **you remember** this. One problem—one solution. *W-pI.80.3.3:5*

~ the solution is inherent in the problem. *W-pI.80.4.4*

~ it is **impossible** that I could **have** a problem which has not been solved already. *W-pI.90.5.6*

~ **where you see** the problem, must be accepted if **you** would be saved. *W-pI.96.2.1*

~ problems that **have** no **meaning** cannot be resolved **within** the framework **they** are set. *W-pI.96.3.1*

PROJECTION |prə'jekSH(ə)n|

DICTIONARY: *the presentation of an **image** on a surface, especially a movie screen.*

EGO

~ **man** can create an empty shell, but **he** cannot create **nothing** at all. This emptiness provides the screen for the misuse of projection. *T-2.I.3.2:3*

~ false projection arises out of false **denial**, not out of its proper use. *T-2.II.23.1*

~ projection **means anger, anger** fosters assault, and assault promotes **fear**. *T-6.II.6.3*

~ what **you** project **you** disown and therefore do not believe is yours. *T-6.III.26.1*

~ projection **will** always **hurt you**. It reinforces your **belief** in your own split **mind**, and its only **purpose** is to keep the **separation** going. It is solely a device of the **ego** to **make you** feel different from your brothers and separated from them. *T-6.III.27.1:3*

~ the **ego** uses projection only to distort your **perception** both of yourself and your brothers. The process begins by excluding something [**you** think] exists in **you** which **you** do not **want** and leads directly to excluding **you** from your brothers. *T-6.III.28.1:2*

~ the **ego** projects to exclude and therefore to deceive. *T-6.III.37.2*

~ **they** are afraid that their projections **will** return and **hurt** them. **They** do believe **they have** blotted their projections from their own minds, but **they** also believe their projections are trying to creep back into them. That is because the projections **have** not left their minds, and this in turn forces them to engage in compulsive activity in **order** not to recognize this. **You** cannot perpetuate an **illusion** about another without perpetuating it about yourself. There is no **way** out of this, because it is **impossible** to **fragment** the **mind**. *T-7.IX.86.2:6*

~ projection of this kind is a **confusion** in motivation and, given this **confusion, trust** becomes **impossible**. *T-7.XII.103.7*

~ to the **ego**, it is the law of **deprivation**. It therefore produces abundance or scarcity, depending on how **you** choose to apply it. *T-9.I.1.5:6*

~ **you have** made by projection. *T-10.II.3.1*

~ the ultimate **purpose** of projection, as the **ego** uses it, is always to get rid of **guilt**. *T-12.I.1.1*

~ when **you** think **you** are projecting what **you** do not **want**, it is still because **you** do **want** it. This leads directly to **dissociation**, for it represents the **acceptance** of two goals, each perceived in a different place, separated from each other because **you** made them different. The **mind** then sees a divided **world outside** itself but not **within**. *T-11.VIII.68.1:3*

~ to "project," as defined above, is a fundamental attribute of **God** which **He** gave to His Son. *T-2.I.5.1*

~ projection, as undertaken by **God**, is very similar to the kind of inner radiance which the Children of the **Father** inherit from Him. It is important to note that the term "project outward" necessarily implies that the real **source** of projection is internal. *T-2.I.11.5:6*

~ my own **role** in the **Atonement** is one of true projection; **I** can project to **you** the affirmation of **truth**. *T-2.II.23.2*

~ **we** once said that without projection there can be no **anger**, but it is also true that without projection there can be no **love**. Projection is a fundamental law of the **mind** and therefore one which always operates. It is the law by which **you** create and were created. It is the law which unifies the **Kingdom** and keeps it in the **Mind** of God. To the ego, the law is perceived as a **way** of getting rid of something it does not **want**. To the **Holy Spirit**, it is the fundamental law of sharing by which **you give** what **you value** in **order** to keep it in your own **mind**. *T-7.IX.82.1:6*

~ projection, to the **Holy Spirit**, is the law of **extension**. *T-7.IX.83.1*

~ it is not up to **you** whether to project, for projection is a law of **mind**. **Perception** is projection, and **you** look in before **you** look out. *T-11.VIII.67.1:2*

~ projection makes **perception**, and **you** cannot **see** beyond it. *T-12.V.35.4*

~ upon **nothing** are all projections made. For it is the projection which gives the "**nothing**" all the **meaning** that it holds. *T-20.IX.75.8:9*

PROMISE |ˈpräməs|

DICTIONARY: *a declaration or assurance that one **will** do a particular **thing** or that a particular **thing will** happen.*

EGO

~ yet the **ego**, though encouraging the search very actively, makes one proviso—do not find it. Its dictates, then, can be summed up simply as, "**Seek** and do not find." This is the one promise the **ego** holds out to **you** and the one promise it **will** keep. *T-11.V.36.3:5*

~ your promise never to allow **union** to **call you** out of **separation**. *T-19.V.92.4*

HOLY SPIRIT;   *God's promise*

~ the **Holy Spirit** offers **you** another promise, and one that **will** lead to **joy**. For His promise is always, "**Seek** and **you will** find," and under His **guidance you** cannot be defeated. *T-11.V.39.4:5*

~ god's promise is a promise to Himself. *T-28.VIII.60.6*

~ the promise that there is no **gap** between Himself and what **He** is cannot be false. *T-28.VIII.60.7*

~ god's promises **make** no exceptions. And **He** guarantees that only **joy** can be the final outcome found for everything. *W-pII.292.1.1:2*

DICTIONARY: *relating to or denoting faculties or phenomena that are apparently inexplicable by natural* **laws**, *especially involving telepathy or clairvoyance.*

EGO

~ the **reason** people are afraid of ESP and so often react against it is because **they** know that thoughts can **hurt** them. Their own thoughts **have** made them vulnerable. *T-2.V.92.5:6*

~ taking them as ends in themselves, no matter how this is done, **will delay** progress. Nor does their **value** lie in proving anything. *M-25.3.5:6*

~ only by tricks of **magic** are **special** powers "demonstrated". *M-25.3.8*

~ the **ego** sees in these same strengths an opportunity to glorify itself. Strengths turned to **weakness** are tragedy indeed. Yet what is not given to the **Holy Spirit** must be given to **weakness**, for what is withheld from **love** is given to **fear** and **will** be fearful in consequence. *M-25.4.6:8*

~ even those who no longer **value** the material things of the **world** may still be deceived by "psychic" powers. As investment has been withdrawn from the world's material gifts, the **ego** has been seriously threatened. It may still be strong enough to rally under this new **temptation** to win back **strength** by guile. Many **have** not seen through the ego's defenses **here**, although **they** are not particularly subtle. Yet, given a remaining **wish** to be deceived, deception is made easy. **Now** the "**power**" is no longer a genuine ability and cannot be used dependably. It is almost inevitable that, unless the individual changes his **mind** about its **purpose**, **he will** bolster its uncertainties with increasing deception. *M-25.5.1:7*

~ "psychic" **abilities have** been used to **call** upon the **devil**, which merely **means** to strengthen the **ego**. *M-25.6.5*

HOLY SPIRIT

~ there are, of **course**, no "unnatural" powers, and it is obviously merely an appeal to **magic** to **make** up a **power** that does not **exist**. It is equally obvious, however, that each individual has many **abilities** of which **he** is unaware. As his **awareness** increases, **he** may well develop **abilities** that seem quite startling to him. Yet **nothing he** can do can compare even in the slightest with the glorious surprise of remembering who **he** is. *M-25.1.2:5*

~ there are many "psychic" powers that are clearly in line with this **course**. **Communication** is not limited to the small range of channels the **world** recognizes. *M-25.2.1:2*

~ who transcends these limits in any **way** is merely becoming more natural. **He** is **doing nothing special**, and there is no **magic** in his accomplishments. *M-25.2.7:8*

~ the seemingly new **abilities** that may be gathered on the **way** can be very helpful. Given to the **Holy Spirit** and used under His direction, **they** are valuable teaching aids. *M-25.3.1:2*

~ the **question** of how **they** arise is irrelevant. The only important consideration is how **they** are used. *M-25.3.3:4*

~ **god** gives no **special** favors, and no one has any powers that are not available to **everyone**. *M-25.3.7*

~ **nothing** that is genuine is used to deceive. The **Holy Spirit** is incapable of deception, and **He** can use only genuine **abilities**. *M-25.4.1:2*

~ there is, however, a particular appeal in unusual **abilities** which can be curiously tempting. **Here** are strengths which the **Holy Spirit** wants and needs. *M-25.4.4:5*

~ any ability that anyone develops has the potentiality for **good**. *M-25.6.1*

~ the more unusual and unexpected the **power**, the greater its potential usefulness. **Salvation** has **need** of all **abilities**, for what the **world** would destroy, the **Holy Spirit** would restore. *M-25.6.3:4*

~ here is also a great **channel** of hope and **healing** in the Holy Spirit's **service**. Those who **have** developed "psychic" powers **have** simply let some of the limitations **they** laid upon their minds be lifted. *M-25.6.6:7*

PSYCHOLOGY
|sī'käləjē|

DICTIONARY: *the scientific **study** of the human **mind** and its functions, especially those affecting **behavior** in a given context/the treatment of mental disorder by psychological rather than medical **means**.*

EGO

~ psychology rests on the principle of the continuity of **behavior**. *T-4.III.26.5*

~ psychology has become the **study** of **behavior**, but no one denies the basic law that **behavior** is a response to motivation, and motivation is **will**. *T-5.IV.30.3*

PSYCHOTHERAPIST
|ˌsīkō'THerəpəst|

DICTIONARY: *a person who treats mental disorders by psychological rather than medical **means**.*

EGO

~ many psychotherapists attempt to **help** people who are afraid, say, of their **death** wishes by depreciating the **power** of the wish. **They** even try to "free" the **patient** by persuading him that **he** can think whatever **he** wants without any real effect at all. *T-2.V.90.4:5*

~ this is the usual psychoanalytic approach. It does allay **guilt** but at the cost of rendering thinking impotent. *T-2.V.91.7:8*

~ all psychoanalytic theorists **have** made some contribution in this connection, but none of them has seen it in its true entirety. **They have** all made one common **error** in that **they** attempted to uncover unconscious content. **You** cannot **understand** unconscious activity in these terms because "content" is applicable only to the more superficial unconscious levels, to which the individual himself contributes. This is the **level** at which **he** can readily introduce **fear** and usually does. *T-2.V.96.5:8*

~ he really believes in **attack** and so does the **patient**, but it does not matter in either case. *T-9.IV.20.6*

HOLY SPIRIT; *follower, leader, egoless psychotherapist, perfect psychotherapist.*

~ the psychotherapist is a leader in the **sense** that **he** walks slightly ahead of the **patient**, and helps him to avoid a few of the pitfalls along the road by seeing them first. Ideally, **he** is also a follower, for One should walk ahead of him to **give** him **light** to see. *P-2.III.11:2*

~ the egoless psychotherapist is an abstraction that stands at the end of the process of **healing**, too advanced to believe in **sickness** and too near to **God** to keep his feet on earth. **Now he** can **help** through those in **need** of **help**, for thus **he** carries out the **plan** established for **salvation**. *P-2.III.4.4:5*

~ it is therefore the psychotherapist's **function** to **teach** that **guilt**, being unreal, cannot be justified. But neither is it safe. And thus it must remain unwanted as well as unreal. *P-2.IV.10.7:9*

PSYCHOTHERAPY |ˌsīkōˈTHerəpē|

DICTIONARY: *the treatment of mental disorders by psychological rather than medical* **means**.

EGO

~ find **light** by analyzing **darkness** as the **psychotherapist** does. *T-9.IV.25.7*

~ psychotherapy itself cannot be creative. *P-2.I.2.1*

~ some forms of psychotherapy **have nothing** to do with **healing**. *P-2.II.5.2*

HOLY SPIRIT; *prayer, experience.*

~ no one can explain what happens in psychotherapy. **Nothing** real does. *T-9.IV.24.3:4*

~ all therapy is **release** from the **past**. *T-13.I.1.1*

~ the **purpose** of psychotherapy is to remove the blocks to **truth**. Its aim is to aid the **patient** in abandoning his fixed delusional system, and to begin to reconsider the spurious **cause** and effect relationships on which it rests. *P-1.I.1.1:2*

~ psychotherapy, correctly understood, teaches **forgiveness** and helps the **patient** to recognize and accept it. *P-1.I.2.6*

~ psychotherapy, then, must restore to his **awareness** the ability to **make** his own decisions. *P-1.I.4.1*

~ psychotherapy can only save him **time**. *P-1.I.5.4*

~ psychotherapy under His direction is one of the **means He** uses to save **time**, and to prepare additional teachers for His work. *P-1.I.5.6*

~ by whatever routes **He** chooses, all psychotherapy leads to **God** in the end. But that is up to Him. **We** are all His psychotherapists, for **He** would **have** us all be healed in Him. *P-1.I.5.8:10*

~ psychotherapy is a process that changes the view of the **self**. *P-2.I.1.1*

~ psychotherapy can hardly be expected to establish **reality**. That is not its **function**. If it can **make way** for **reality**, it has achieved its ultimate success. Its whole **function**, in the end, is to **help** the **patient** deal with one fundamental **error**. *P-2.IN.1.2:5*

~ therapy begins with the realization that **healing** is of the **mind**, and in psychotherapy those **have** come together who already believe this. *P-2.I.1.2*

~ ideally, psychotherapy is a series of holy encounters in which brothers meet to bless each other and to **receive** the **peace** of **God**. *P-2.I.4.1*

~ the process of psychotherapy is the return to **sanity**. *P-2.II.5.5*

~ as true **religion** heals, so must true psychotherapy be religious. But both **have** many forms. *P-2.II.7.1:2*

~ salvation's single doctrine is the **goal** of all therapy. *P-2.IV.11.1*

~ therapy is **prayer**, and **healing** is its aim and its result. *P-2.VII.2.2*

~ psychotherapy is the only **form** of therapy there is. *P-IN.1.1*

PUNISHMENT

DICTIONARY: *the infliction or imposition of a penalty as retribution for an offense.*

EGO; *correction, preserver of **sin**, guilt's protection, harsh punishment.*

~ the ego believes that by punishing itself it **will** mitigate the punishment of **God**. *T-5.VII.65.3*

~ any **concept** of "punishment" involves the **projection** of **blame** and reinforces the **idea** that **blame** is justified. *T-6.II.23.1*

~ believing that by punishing another, it **will** escape punishment. *T-11.X.85.4*

~ **sin** calls for punishment as **error** for **correction**, and the **belief** that punishment is **correction** is clearly insane. *T-19.III.17.6*

~ punishment is but another **form** of guilt's protection, for what is deserving punishment must **have** been really done. Punishment is always the great preserver of **sin**, treating it with respect and honoring its enormity. *T-19.IV.26.3-4*

HOLY SPIRIT

~ punishment is a **concept** in total opposition to right-mindedness. *T-2.VI.108.4*

~ to **call** for punishment upon yourself must be insane. *T-13.III.15.6*

~ no penalty is ever asked of God's Son except by himself and of himself. *T-13.VIII.70.1*

~ what calls for punishment must **call** for **nothing**. *T-19.IV.28.2*

PUPIL

DICTIONARY: *a student in school.*

HOLY SPIRIT

~ disciples are followers, but if the model **they** follow has chosen to save them **pain** in all respects, **they** are probably unwise not to follow him. *T-6.II.12.5*

~ certain pupils **have** been assigned to each of God's teachers, and **they will** begin to look for him as soon as **he** has answered the **Call**. **They** were chosen for him, because the **form** of the universal **curriculum** that **he will teach** is best for them in view of their **level** of understanding. His pupils **have** been waiting for him, for his coming is certain. Again, it is only a matter of **time**. Once **he** has chosen to fulfill his **role**, **they** are ready to fulfill theirs. **Time** waits on his **choice** but not whom **he will** serve. When **he** is ready to learn, the opportunities to **teach will** be provided for him. *M-2.1.1:7*

~ the pupil comes at the right **time** to the right place. This is inevitable, because **he** made the right **choice** in that ancient instant which **he now** relives. *M-2.4.4:5*

~ in some cases, it may be helpful for the pupil to read the manual first. Others might do better to begin with the **workbook**. Still others may **need** to start at the more abstract **level** of the **text**. *M-29.1.5:7*

PURIFICATION

DICTIONARY: *the removal of contaminants from something.*

EGO; *arrogance*

HOLY SPIRIT

~ purification is of **God alone** and therefore for **you.** *T-18.V.36.7*

~ purity is not confined. *T-28.III.17.3*

~ purity not of the **body**. Nor can it be found where limitation is. The **body** can be healed by its effects, which are as limitless as is itself. *T-28.III.17.5:7*

PURPOSE

DICTIONARY: *have as one's intention or objective.*

EGO; *separation, fear.*

~ the ego's purpose is **fear** because only the fearful can be egotistic. *T-5.VII.59.3*

~ the **ego** has no purpose **you** would **share** with it. For the **ego** would **limit everyone** to a **body** for its purposes, and while **you** think it has a purpose, **you will** choose to utilize the **means** by which it tries to turn its purpose into accomplishment. *T-15.IX.87.3:4*

~ the purpose **here** is **sin.** *T-20.VIII.62.3*

~ while this purpose seems to **have** any **meaning**, the **means** for its attainment **will** be evaluated as **worth** the seeing, and so **you will** not **see.** *T-20.VIII.65.10*

~ the purpose of everything is to prove that my illusions about myself are real. It is for that purpose that **I** attempt to use **everyone** and everything. *W-pI.55.6.1:2*

~ the purpose **I have** given the **world** has led to a frightening **picture** of it. *W-pI.55.6.5*

~ **salvation** cannot be the only purpose **you** hold while **you** still cherish others. *W-pI.65.1.4*

HOLY SPIRIT; *meaning, forgiveness, joy, unified purpose, holy purpose, single purpose, common purpose.*

~ **joy** is unified purpose, and unified purpose is only God's. *T-8.VI.67.1*

~ according to the Holy Spirit's **teaching**, only God's purpose is accomplishment, and it is already accomplished. *T-10.VI.50.4*

~ no **nightmare** can defeat a **Child** of God in his purpose. For your purpose was given **you** by **God**, and **you** must accomplish it because it is His **Will.** *T-11.III.19.1:2*

~ **god** has one purpose which **He** shares with **you.** *T-14.IV.31.5*

~ **nothing you** do which does not **share** His purpose can be real. The purpose **God** ascribed to anything is its only **function.** *T-17.V.27.1:2*

~ the practical application of the Holy Spirit's purpose is extremely simple, but it is unequivocal. In **fact** in **order** to be simple, it must be unequivocal. *T-17.VII.57.1:2*

~ your purpose has not changed and **will** not **change**, for **you** accepted what can never **change.** *T-17.IX.79.3*

~ the **means** and purpose both belong to Him. **You have** accepted one; the other **will** be provided. A purpose such as this without the **means** is inconceivable. **He will** provide the **means** to anyone who shares His purpose. *T-18.VI.43.6:9*

~ the alignment of **means** and purpose is an undertaking **impossible** for **you** to **understand**. **You** do not even realize **you have** accepted the Holy Spirit's purpose as your own, and **you** would merely bring unholy **means** to its accomplishment. The **little faith** it needed to **change** the purpose is all that is required to **receive** the **means** and use them. *T-18.VI.44.4:6*

~ it is this joining Him in a united purpose which makes this purpose real because **you make** it whole. *T-19.I.2.5*

~ **here** is the only purpose that gives this **world** and the long **journey** through this **world** whatever **meaning** lies in them. *T-19.V.110.4*

~ the Holy Spirit's purpose rests in **peace within you**. *T-19.V.42.1*

~ **salvation** cannot be withheld from **you**. It is your purpose. **You** cannot **will** apart from this. **You have** no purpose apart from each other nor apart from the one **you** asked the **Holy Spirit** to **share** with **you**. *T-19.V.43.7:10*

~ when **you** accepted the Holy Spirit's purpose in place of the ego's, **you** renounced **death**, exchanging it for **life**. *T-19.V.79.6*

~ your newborn purpose is nursed by angels, cherished by the **Holy Spirit**, and protected by **God** Himself. It needs not your protection; it is yours. For it is deathless, and **within** it lies the end of **death**. *T-19.V.86.4:6*

~ **he will** go before **you** making straight your path and leaving in your **way** no stones to trip on and no obstacles to bar your **way**. **Nothing you need will** be denied **you**. Not one seeming difficulty but **will** melt away before **you** reach it. **You need** take **thought** for **nothing**, careless of everything except the only purpose that **you** would fulfill. As that was given **you**, so **will** its fulfillment be. God's guarantee **will** hold against all obstacles, for it rests on **certainty** and not contingency. It rests on **you**. *T-20.V.36.1:7*

~ no one who has a single purpose, unified and sure, can be afraid. No one who shares his purpose with him can not be one with him. *T-20.VI.37.7:8*

~ the Holy Spirit's purpose lies safe in your **relationship** and not your bodies. *T-20.VII.51.8*

~ only two purposes are possible. And one is **sin**, the other **holiness**. *T-20.IX.75.1:2*

~ no one allows a purpose to be replaced while **he** desires it, for **nothing** is so cherished and protected as is a **goal** the **mind** accepts. *T-21.IV.30.4*

~ if escape from **guilt** was given to the **Holy Spirit** as His purpose, and by One to Whom **nothing He** wills can be **impossible**, the **means** for its attainment are more than possible. **They** must be there, and **you** must **have** them. *T-22.III.20.6:7*

~ your destiny and purpose are far beyond them in the clean place where littleness does not **exist**. Your purpose is at variance with littleness of any kind. And so it is at variance with **sin**. *T-23.I.4.6:8*

~ only a purpose unifies, and those who **share** a purpose **have a mind** as one. *T-23.V.53.4*

~ **you have** no purpose that is not the same and none your **Father** does not **share** with **you**. *T-24.II.10.7*

~ purpose is of the **mind**. *T-24.V.35.6*

~ nor is **mind** limited; so must it be that harmful purpose hurts the **mind** as one. *T-24.V.36.6*

~ this **shift** in purpose does "endanger" specialness. *T-24.V.37.1*

~ the Holy Spirit's purpose **now** is yours. *T-26.IX.76.9*

~ the Holy Spirit's purpose is to let the Presence of your holy Guests be known to **you**. And to this purpose, **nothing** can be added, for the **world** is purposeless except for this. To add or take away from this one **goal** is but to take away all purpose from the **world** and from yourself. *T-26.XI.89.4:6*

~ his single purpose unifies the halves of **you** which **you** perceive as separate. And each forgives the other, that **he** may accept his other half as **part** of him. *T-27.III.28.6:7*

~ what shares a common purpose is the same. *T-27.VII.54.5*

~ unites all those who **share** in it **within** itself. *T-27.VII.54.6*

~ **you** can **give** yourself a purpose that **you** do not **have**. But **you** can not remove the **power** to **change** your **mind** and **see** another purpose there. *T-29.VII.40.5:6*

~ only a constant purpose can endow events with stable **meaning**. But it must accord one **meaning** to them all. *T-30.VIII.84.1:2*

~ a common purpose is the only **means** whereby **perception** can be stabilized and one **interpretation** given to the **world** and all experiences **here**. In this shared purpose is one [**meaning**] shared by **everyone** and everything **you see**. **You** do not **have** to judge, for **you have** learned one **meaning** has been given everything, and **you** are glad to **see** it everywhere. It cannot **change** because **you** would perceive it everywhere, unchanged by circumstance. *T-30.VIII.85.1:4*

~ all things **have** but one purpose which **you share** with all the **world**. And **nothing** in the **world** can be opposed to it, for it belongs to everything as it belongs to **you**. In single purpose is the end of all ideas of **sacrifice**, which must assume a different purpose for the one who gains and him who loses. *T-30.VIII.86.1:3*

~ the long-range purpose of **learning** to **see** the meaningless as **outside you** and the meaningful **within**. *W-pI.4.3.3*

~ purpose is **meaning**. *W-pI.25.1.1*

~ what shares the purpose of the **universe** shares the purpose of its **Creator**. *W-pI.29.2.5*

~ your purpose is to **see** the **world** through your own **holiness**. *W-pI.37.1.2*

~ with one purpose only, **I** am always certain what to do, what to say, and what to think. *W-pI.83.2.3*

~ **we have** a mighty purpose to fulfill and **have** been given everything **we need** with which to reach the **goal**. *W-pI.98.2.3*

~ everything must serve the purpose **you have** given it until **you see** a different purpose there. *W-pI.128.2.2*

~ our true purpose is to save the **world**. *W-pI.153.8.2*

~ all the parts **have** but one purpose and one aim. *W-pII.318.1.4*

~ directing all our thoughts to serve the **function** of **salvation**. *W-pII.ST361.3.1*

QUESTION

DICTIONARY: *a sentence worded or expressed so as to elicit information.*

EGO; *"fearful" question*

~ the **ego** does not know what a real question is, although it asks an endless number. *T-8.IX.80.3*

~ **you have** been as selective in your questioning as in your **perception**. *T-12.IV.25.7*

~ if the basic question stems from **reason**, it **will** not **ask** it. *T-21.VI.52.5*

~ the **world** can only **ask** a double question with many answers, none of which **will** do. It does not **ask** a question to be answered, but only to restate its point of view. All questions asked **within** this **world** are but a **way** of looking, not a question asked. A question asked in **hate** cannot be answered, because it is an **answer** in itself. A double question asks and answers, both attesting the same **thing** in different **form**. *T-27.V.38.5.9*

~ this is not a question, for it tells **you** what **you want** and where to go for it. It leaves no room to question its beliefs, except that what it states takes question's **form**. *T-27.V.39.12:13*

~ whatever **form** the question takes, its **purpose** is the same. It asks but to establish **sin** is real and answers in the **form** of preference. *T-27.V.39.4:5*

~ a pseudo-question has no **answer**. It dictates the **answer** even as it asks. Thus is all questioning **within** the **world** a **form** of propaganda for itself. *T-27.V.40.1:3*

~ are the answers to the questions of the **world** contained **within** the questions. Where answers represent the questions, **they** add **nothing** new, and **nothing** has been learned. *T-27.V.40.4:5*

~ the questions of the **world** but **ask** of whom is **sacrifice** demanded, asking not if **sacrifice** is meaningful at all. And so unless the **answer** tells "of whom," it **will** remain unrecognized, unheard, and thus the question is preserved intact because it gave the **answer** to itself. *T-27.V.42.2:3*

HOLY SPIRIT; *learning tool, real question, **honest** question.*

~ the questioning **mind** perceives itself in **time** and therefore looks for **future** answers. The unquestioning **mind** is closed because it believes the **future** and **present will** be the same. This establishes an unchanged state or stasis. It is usually an attempt to counteract an underlying **fear** that the **future will** be worse than the **present**, and this **fear** inhibits the tendency to question at all. *T-3.V.33.1:4*

~ the **answer** merely undoes the question by establishing the **fact** that to question **reality** is to question meaninglessly. That is why the **Holy Spirit** never questions. His sole **function** is to **undo** the questionable and thus lead to **certainty**. The certain are perfectly **calm**, because **they** are not in **doubt**. **They** do not raise questions, because **nothing** questionable enters their minds. This holds them in perfect **serenity**, because this is what **they share**, knowing what **they** are. *T-7.V.30.3:8*

~ **you have** come very close to this. **Faith** and **belief have** shifted, and **you have** asked the question which the **ego will** never **ask**. *T-21.VI.58.1:2*

~ an **honest** question is a **learning** tool which asks for something that **you** do not know. It does not set conditions for response, but merely asks what the response should be. But no one in a **conflict** state is free to **ask** this question, for **he** does not **want** an **honest answer** where the **conflict** ends. Only **within** the **holy instant** can an **honest** question honestly be asked. And from the **meaning** of the question does the meaningfulness of the **answer** come. *T-27.V.41.1:5*

~ lets the **answer** show **you** what the question must **have** really been. *T-30.II.13.1*

QUIET

DICTIONARY: *freedom from disturbance or interruption by others.*

HOLY SPIRIT; *end of strife, journey to peace.*

~ **god** is very quiet, for there is no **conflict** in Him. *T-10.IV.23.6*

~ quietness is the end of strife and this is the **journey** to **peace**. *T-11.III.18.5*

~ yet there **will** always be this place of **rest** to which **you** can return. And **you will** be more aware of this quiet center of the storm than all its raging activity. This quiet center, in which **you** do **nothing**, **will** remain with **you**, giving **you rest** in the midst of every busy **doing** on which **you** are sent. For from this center **will you** be directed how to use the **body** sinlessly. It is this center, from which the **body** is absent, that **will** keep it so in your **awareness** of it. *T-18.VIII.70.1:5*

~ the quiet **way** is open. *T-21.V.48.8*

~ **god** rests with **you** in quiet, undefended and wholly undefending, for in this quiet state **alone** is **strength** and **power**. *T-22.VI.47.6*

~ the **mind** is quiet, and the **condition** in which **God** is remembered is attained. *T-24.II.1.2*

~ in quietness are all things answered and is every **problem** quietly resolved. *T-27.V.36.1*

~ the quiet that surrounds **you** dwells in him, and from this quiet come the **happy** dreams in which your hands are joined in **innocence**. *T-29.VI.34.4*

~ his **Voice** awaits your silence, for His **word** cannot be heard until your **mind** is quiet for a while and meaningless desires **have** been stilled. Await His **word** in quiet. *W-pI.125.6.2:3*

~ the **past** just slips away and in its place is everlasting quiet. *M-20.2.8*

~ quiet has reached to cover everything. *M-20.2.11*

~ no one can **fail** to find it who but seeks out its conditions. *M-20.3.2*

READINESS

DICTIONARY: *the state of **being** fully prepared for something.*

EGO

~ the **healer** who relies on his own readiness is endangering his understanding. *T-2.III.64.1*

HOLY SPIRIT; *prerequisite for accomplishment*

~ readiness **means** that **you** should always keep your perceptions straight, so that **you will** always be ready, willing, and able. *T-1.I.75.2*

~ he is perfectly safe as long as he is completely unconcerned about his readiness but maintains a consistent **trust** in mine. *T-2.III.64.2*

~ readiness is **nothing** more than the prerequisite for accomplishment. *T-2.V.103.5*

~ as soon as a state of readiness occurs, there is usually some **will** to accomplish, but this is by no **means** necessarily undivided. *T-2.V.103.7*

~ readiness at least is an indication that **you** believe this is possible. That is only the beginning of **confidence**. *T-2.V.104.5:6*

~ readiness, as the **text** notes, is not mastery. *M-4.21.10*

~ no one learns beyond his own readiness. Yet levels of readiness **change**, and when **therapist** or **patient** has reached the next one, there **will** be a **relationship** held out to them that meets the changing **need**. *P-2.I.1.3:4*

REAL WORLD

DICTIONARY: *the existing state of things, as opposed to one that is imaginary, simulated, or theoretical.*

EGO

~ **you attack** the real **world** every day and every hour and every minute, and yet **you** are surprised that **you** cannot **see** it. *T-11.IX.77.3*

~ those who look on **sin** are seeing the **denial** of the real **world**. *T-21.VIII.82.3*

~ unless the **past** is over in my **mind**, the real **world** must escape my **sight**. For I am really looking nowhere, seeing but what is not there. *W-pII.289.1.1:2*

HOLY SPIRIT; *all that the **Holy Spirit** has saved for **you** out of what **you have** made, **gift**, the **way**, state of mind, **world** of light, **symbol**, circle of brightness.*

~ the real **world** can actually be perceived. *T-10.VIII.70.6*

~ the real **world** is all that the **Holy Spirit** has saved for **you** out of what **you have** made, and to perceive only this is **salvation** because it is the recognition that **reality** is only what is true. *T-10.VIII.73.3*

~ in the real **world** there is no **sickness**, for there is no **separation** and no division. Only loving thoughts are recognized, and because no one is without your **help**, the **Help** of **God** goes with **you** everywhere. *T-10.VIII.85.1:2*

~ if only the loving thoughts of God's Son are the world's **reality**, the real **world** must be in his **mind**. *T-11.IV.30.1*

~ **god** does **love** the real **world**. *T-11.IV.32.2*

~ **death** is not of the real **world**, in which everything is eternal. **God** gave **you** the real **world** in exchange for the one **you** made out of your split **mind**, and which is the **symbol** of **death**. *T-11.IV.32.3:4*

~ the real **world** is the **gift** of the **Holy Spirit**, and so it belongs to **you**. *T-11.VII.55.6*

~ the awakening of His Son begins with his investment in the real **world**. *T-11.VII.57.5*

~ the real **world** was given **you** by **God** in loving exchange for the **world you** made and which **you see**. *T-11.IX.84.1*

~ its **reality will make** everything else invisible, for beholding it is total **perception**. *T-11.IX.84.3*

~ the real **world** is the **way** that leads **you** to remembrance of this one **thing** that is wholly true and wholly yours. *T-12.VII.66.4*

~ the real **world** is but your **welcome** of what always was. Therefore, the **call** of **joy** is in it, and your glad response is your awakening to what **you have** not lost. *T-12.VII.67.7:8*

~ the **perception** of the real **world will** be so short that **you will** barely **have time** to thank **God** for it. *T-17.III.10.4*

~ the real **world** is attained simply by the complete **forgiveness** of the old, the **world you see** without **forgiveness**. *T-17.III.11.1*

~ this loveliness is not a **fantasy**. It is the real **world**, bright and clean and new with everything sparkling under the open sun. **Nothing** is hidden here, for everything has been forgiven, and there are no fantasies to **hide** the **truth**. *T-17.III.8.1:3*

~ the real **world**, in its loveliness, **you** learn to reach. Fantasies are all undone, and no one and **nothing** remains still bound by them. *T-17.III.9.4:5*

~ this **world** of **light**, this circle of brightness, is the real **world** where **guilt** meets with **forgiveness**. Here the **world outside** is seen anew, without the **shadow** of **guilt** upon it. **Here** are **you** forgiven, for **here you have** forgiven **everyone**. **Here** is the new **perception**, where everything is bright and shining with **innocence**, washed in the waters of **forgiveness**, and cleansed of every **evil thought you** had laid upon it. **Here** there is no **attack** upon the **Son of God**, and **you** are **welcome**. **Here** is your **innocence**, waiting to clothe **you** and protect **you** and **make you** ready for the **final step** in the **journey** inward. **Here** are the dark and heavy garments of **guilt** laid by and gently replaced by purity and **love**. *T-18.X.93.1:7*

~ it is there that **peace** awaits **you**. *T-18.XI.98.5*

~ this is the journey's end. **We have** referred to it as the "real **world**." *T-26.IV.20.1:3*

~ in the real **world** is choosing simplified. *T-26.IV.21.10*

~ the real **world** is the area of **choice** made real, not in the outcome but in the **perception** of alternatives for **choice**. *T-26.IV.23.3*

~ the real **world** is the second **part** of the hallucination **time** and **death** are real and **have** existence which can be perceived. *T-26.VI.41.3*

~ yet is the real **world** unaffected by the **world he** thinks is real. Nor **have** its **laws** been changed because **he** did not **understand**. *T-29.X.66.8:9*

~ the real **world** still is but a **dream**. Except the figures **have** been changed. **They** are not seen as idols which betray. It is a **dream** in which no one is used to **substitute** for something else nor interposed between the thoughts the **mind** conceives and what it sees. No one is used for something **he** is not, for childish things **have** all been put away. And what was once a **dream** of **judgment now** has changed into a **dream** where all is **joy** because that is the **purpose** which it has. Only forgiving dreams can enter **here**, for **time** is almost over. And the forms which enter in the **dream** are **now** perceived as brothers, not in **judgment** but in **love**. *T-29.X.67.1:8*

~ the real **world** is the state of **mind** in which the only **purpose** of the world is seen to be **forgiveness**. **Fear** is not its **goal**, and the escape from **guilt** becomes its aim. The **value** of **forgiveness** is perceived and takes the place of idols which are sought no longer, for their "gifts" are not held dear. No rules are idly set, and no demands are made of anyone or anything to twist and fit into the **dream of fear**. Instead, there is a **wish** to **understand** all things created as **they** really are. And it is recognized that all things must be first forgiven, and then understood. *T-30.VI.57.1:6*

~ there, it is clear that by **attack** is understanding lost. The folly of pursuing **guilt** as **goal** is fully recognized. And idols are not wanted there, for **guilt** is understood as the sole **cause** of **pain** in any **form**. No one is tempted by its vain appeal, for **suffering** and **death have** been perceived as things not wanted and not striven for. The possibility of **freedom** has been grasped and welcomed, and the **means** by which it can be gained can **now** be understood. *T-30.VI.58.2:6*

~ the real **world** has a **purpose** still beneath **creation** and **eternity**. But **fear** is gone because its **purpose** is **forgiveness**, not idolatry. *T-30.VI.60.3:4*

~ the real **world** is a state in which the **mind** has learned how easily do idols go when **they** are still perceived, but wanted not. *T-30.VI.61.2*

~ the real **world**, and let it **teach** me that my **will** and the **Will** of God are one. *W-pI.54.6.4*

~ from my **holiness** does the **perception** of the real **world** come. *W-pI.58.2.1*

~ how safe the **world will** look to me when **I** can **see** it! It **will** not look anything like what **I** imagine **I see now**. **Everyone** and everything **I** see **will** lean toward me to bless me. **I will** recognize in **everyone** my dearest Friend. Your **vision** and the **sight** of the real **world** which has come to replace the unforgiven **world you thought** was real. *W-pI.60.4.1:5*

~ **forgiveness** is the **means** by which it comes to take the place of **hell**. In quietness it rises up to greet your open eyes and fill your heart with deep tranquility as ancient truths, forever newly born, arise in your **awareness**. What **you will remember** then can never be described. Yet your **forgiveness** offers it to **you**. *W-pI.122.8.2:5*

~ the real **world** pictures Heaven's **innocence**. *W-pI.159.3.5*

~ how surely, therefore, must the real **world** come to greet the holy **sight** of anyone who takes the Holy Spirit's **purpose** as his **goal** for seeing. And **he** cannot **fail** to look upon what **Christ** would **have** him **see** and **share** Christ's **love** for what **he** looks upon. *W-pII.312.1.5:6*

~ the real **world** is a **symbol** like the **rest** of what **perception** offers. Yet it stands for what is **opposite** to what **you** made. *W-pII.ST291.1.1:2*

~ the real **world** cannot be perceived except through eyes **forgiveness** blesses, so **they** see a **world** where terror is **impossible** and witnesses to **fear** cannot be found. *W-pII.ST291.1.4*

~ the real **world** holds a counterpart for each unhappy **thought** reflected in your **world**, a sure **correction** for the sights of **fear** and sounds of **battle** which your **world** contains. The real **world** shows a **world** seen differently, through **quiet** eyes and with a **mind** at **peace**. **Nothing** but **rest** is there. There are no cries of **pain** and sorrow heard, for **nothing here** remains **outside forgiveness**. And the sights are gentle. Only **happy** sights and sounds can reach the **mind** that has forgiven itself. *W-pII.ST291.2.1:6*

~ the real **world** is the **symbol** that the **dream** of **sin** and **guilt** is over and God's Son no longer sleeps. His waking eyes perceive the sure **reflection** of his Father's **Love**, the certain **promise** that **he** is redeemed. The real **world** signifies the end of **time**, for its **perception** makes **time** purposeless. *W-pII.ST291.4.1:3*

REALITY

DICTIONARY: *the **world** or the state of things as **they** actually **exist**, as opposed to an idealistic or notional **idea** of them.*

EGO

~ opposing orders of reality **make** reality meaningless. *T-8.X.104.6*

~ your **denial** of reality precludes the **acceptance** of God's **gift**, because **you have** accepted something else in its place. *T-9.IX.71.3*

~ to believe that reality is what **you** would **have** it be according to your use for it is delusional. *T-12.VI.48.4*

~ as long as **you** perceive the **body** as your reality, so long **will you** perceive yourself as lonely and deprived. *T-15.XI.105.1*

~ distorting it and devoting it to "**evil**," it also makes it unreal. *T-17.I.2.3*

~ orders of reality is a perspective without understanding, a frame of reference for reality to which it cannot really be compared at all. *T-17.II.4.5*

~ **substitute** the **fantasy** that reality is fearful, not what **you** would do to it. And thus is **guilt** made real. *T-18.III.17.6:7*

~ each of your perceptions of "external reality" is a pictorial representation of your own **attack** thoughts. *W-pI.23.3.2*

~ it is merely an **illusion** of reality, because my judgments **have** been made quite apart from reality. *W-pI.51.3.4*

~ it is your reality which is the "**threat**" that your defenses would **attack**, obscure, and take apart and crucify. *W-pI.135.18.4*

~ this is the **way** reality is made by partial **vision**, purposefully set against the given **truth**. Its **enemy** is **wholeness**. It conceives of **little** things and looks upon them. And a lack of space, a **sense** of **unity** or **vision** which sees differently become the threats which it must overcome, **conflict** with, and deny. *W-pI.184.4.1:4*

~ reality is not understandable to the deluded. *M-12.3.2*

HOLY SPIRIT; *only what is true, One Reality of **God**, only safety, **meaning**, everything, **here**, Soul.*

~ in reality, **you** are perfectly unaffected by all expressions of lack of **love**. These can be either from yourself and others or from yourself to others or from others to **you**. *T-2.I.17.1:2*

~ **god** knows **you** only in **peace**, and this is your reality. *T-3.VI.50.4*

~ the only sane solution is not to try to **change** reality, which is indeed a fearful attempt, but to **see** it as it is. **You** are **part** of reality, which stands unchanged beyond the reach of your **ego** but **within** easy reach of your **Soul**. *T-4.II.15.4:5*

~ reality is yours, because **you** are reality. *T-7.V.29.6*

~ the reality of everything is totally harmless, because total harmlessness is the **condition** of its reality. It is also the **condition** of your **awareness** of its reality. **You** do not **have** to **seek** reality. It **will seek you** and find **you** when **you** meet its conditions. Its conditions are **part** of what it is. And this **part** only is up to **you**. The **rest** is of itself. *T-8.IX.81.2:8*

~ reality is everything, and therefore **you have** everything because **you** are real. *T-8.X.104.3*

~ reality cannot "threaten" anything except illusions, since reality can only uphold **truth**. *T-8.X.90.3*

~ reality is the only safety. *T-8.X.96.6*

~ in the security of reality, **fear** is totally meaningless. *T-8.X.99.4*

~ reality is **here**. *T-9.III.19.6*

~ reality is not divided. *T-9.IX.82.8*

~ reality can dawn only on an unclouded **mind**. It is always there to be accepted, but its **acceptance** depends on your willingness to **have** it. *T-9.X.86.1:2*

~ reality cannot break through the obstructions **you** interpose, but it **will** envelop **you** completely when **you** let them go. *T-9.X.89.10*

~ the definition of reality is God's, not yours. **He** created it, and **He** knows what it is. *T-11.IX.79.6:7*

~ all reality leaves no room for any **error**. *T-12.VI.45.2*

~ but this one **thing** is always yours, **being** the **gift** of **God** unto His Son. Your one reality was given **you**, and by it **God** created **you** as one with Him. *T-12.VII.66.6:7*

~ aspects of reality can still be seen, and **they will** replace aspects of unreality. Aspects of reality can be seen in everything and everywhere. Yet only **God** can gather them together by crowning them as one with the final **gift** of **eternity**. *T-13.II.3.7:9*

~ reality is witnessed to as one. *T-13.II.10.3*

~ your task is not to **make** reality. It is **here** without your making, but not without **you**. *T-14.I.2.1:2*

~ different realities are meaningless, for reality must be one. It cannot **change** with **time** or mood or chance. Its changelessness is what makes it real. This cannot be undone. Undoing is for unreality. And this reality **will** do for **you**. *T-14.V.39.5:10*

~ reality is safe and sure and wholly kind to **everyone** and everything. *T-16.III.19.1*

~ **nothing** real has ever left the **mind** of its **creator**. And what is not real was never there. *T-16.IV.25.10:11*

~ there is **nothing you** can hold against reality. *T-16.VIII.78.1*

~ there is no **order** in reality because everything there is true. *T-17.II.5.7*

~ your reality was God's **creation** and has no **substitute**. *T-18.II.9.11*

~ reality needs no cooperation from **you** to be itself. But your **awareness** of it needs your **help** because it is your **choice**. *T-21.VI.50.1:2*

~ reality opposes **nothing**. *T-22.VI.45.6*

~ reality is ultimately known without a **form**, unpictured and unseen. *T-27.IV.33.2*

~ **you have** not two realities, but one. Nor can **you** be aware of more than one. *T-30.IV.48.5:6*

~ reality observes the **laws** of **God**, and not the rules **you** set. *T-30.V.52.1*

~ reality is changeless. It does not deceive at all, and if **you fail** to **see** beyond appearances, **you** are deceived. For everything **you see will change**, and yet **you thought** it real before, and **now you** think it real again. Reality is thus reduced to **form** and capable of **change**. Reality is changeless. It is this that makes it real and keeps it separate from all appearances. It must transcend all **form** to be itself. It cannot **change**. *T-30.IX.89.2:9*

~ because reality is changeless is a **miracle** already there to heal all things that **change** and offer them to **you** to **see** in **happy form**, devoid of **fear**. *T-30.IX.93.1*

~ reality is never frightening. It is **impossible** that it could upset me. Reality brings only perfect **peace**. When **I** am upset, it is always because **I have** replaced reality with illusions which **I** made up. The illusions are upsetting because **I have** given them reality and thus regard reality as an **illusion**. *W-pI.52.2.1:5*

~ reality is not insane. *W-pI.53.2.3*

~ reality and its wholly unchanged and unchangeable nature. *W-pI.67.2.2*

~ for **we** would meet with our reality in **freedom** and in **peace**. *W-pI.134.14.2*

~ only reality is free of **pain**. Only reality is free of **loss**. Only reality is wholly safe. *W-pII.268.2.2:4*

~ to know Reality is not to **see** the **ego** and its thoughts, its works, its acts, its **laws** and its beliefs, its dreams, its hopes, its plans for its **salvation**, and the cost **belief** in it entails. *W-pII.ST331.4.1*

~ reality is wholly real, apart from size and shape and **time** and place—for differences cannot **exist within** it. *M-8.6.6*

REASON

|'rēzən|

DICTIONARY: *a **cause**, explanation, or justification for an action or event.*

EGO

~ circular the reasoning on which your "seeing" rests. *T-21.III.19.5*

~ reason lies in the other **Self you have** cut off from your **awareness**. And **nothing you have** allowed to stay in it is capable of reason. How can the segment of the **mind** devoid of reason understand what reason is or grasp the information it would **give**? *T-21.VI.52.2:4*

~ there is no reason in **insanity**, for it depends entirely on reason's absence. The **ego** never uses it because it does not realize that it exists. *T-21.VI.56.6:7*

~ confused and senseless "reasoning". *M-8.4.8*

HOLY SPIRIT

~ what reason points to **you** can **see** because the witnesses on its behalf are clear. Reason is a **means** which serves the Holy Spirit's **purpose** in its own right. It is not reinterpreted and redirected from the **goal** of **sin** as are the others. For reason is beyond the ego's range of **means**. *T-21.VI.55.5:8*

~ reason has no place at all in **madness**, nor can it be adjusted to fit its end. *T-21.VI.56.2*

~ the partially insane **have** access to it, and only **they have need** of it. **Knowledge** does not depend on it, and **madness** keeps it out. *T-21.VI.56.8:9*

~ reason is alien to **insanity**, and those who use it **have** gained a **means** which cannot be applied to **sin**. *T-21.VI.57.3*

~ reason can serve to open doors **you** closed against it. *T-21.VI.57.5*

~ **faith** and **belief**, upheld by reason, cannot **fail** to lead to changed **perception**. *T-21.VI.58.4*

~ reason cannot **see sin** but can **see** errors and leads to their **correction**. It does not **value** them, but their **correction**. Reason **will** also tell **you** when **you** think **you sin, you call** for help. *T-21.VII.59.1:3*

~ reason would not **make way** for **correction** in **you alone**. *T-21.VII.59.10*

~ yet reason tells **you** that **you** cannot **see** your **brother** or yourself as **sinful** and still perceive the other **innocent**. *T-21.VII.60.3*

~ reason, like **love**, would reassure **you** and seeks not to frighten **you**. *T-21.VII.65.1*

~ for reason, kind as is the **purpose** for which it is the **means**, leads steadily away from **madness** toward the **goal** of **truth**. *T-21.VII.65.8*

~ reason assures **you Heaven** is what **you want**, and all **you want**. *T-21.VII.66.5*

~ reason would surely bid him **seek** no longer what is not there to find. *T-21.VIII.74.5*

~ reason **will** tell **you** that **you** cannot **ask** for happiness inconstantly. *T-21.IX.88.1*

~ **here** is the great appeal to reason; the **awareness** of what is always there to **see**, the happiness that could be always yours. **Here** is the constant **peace you** could **experience** forever. **Here** is what **denial** has denied revealed to **you**. For **here** the final **question** is already answered and what **you ask** for given. **Here** is the **future now**, for **time** is powerless because of your **desire** for what **will** never **change**. *T-21.IX.90.2:6*

~ reason **will** tell **you** that the only **way** to escape from **misery** is to recognize it and go the other **way**. *T-22.III.19.1*

~ **faith** and **belief** can fall to either side, but reason tells **you** that **misery** lies only on one side and **joy** upon the other. *T-22.III.21.10*

~ reason **will** tell **you** that there is no middle ground where **you** can pause uncertainly, waiting to choose between the **joy** of **Heaven** and the **misery** of **hell**. *T-22.III.22.7*

~ the introduction of reason into the ego's **thought system** is the beginning of its undoing. For reason and the **ego** are contradictory. Nor is it possible for them to co-**exist** in your **awareness**. And reason's **goal**. For reason sees through errors, telling **you** what **you thought** was real is not. Reason can **see** the difference between **sin** and mistakes because it wants **correction**. Therefore, it tells **you** what **you thought** was uncorrectable can be corrected, and thus it must **have** been an **error**. *T-22.IV.29.1:6*

~ reason is not **salvation** in itself, but it makes **way** for **peace** and brings **you** to a state of **mind** in which **salvation** can be given **you**. *T-22.IV.31.1*

~ reason **will** tell **you** that the **form** of **error** is not what makes it a **mistake**. *T-22.IV.33.1*

~ reason is satisfied, for all insane beliefs can be corrected **here**. *T-25.VIII.61.5*

REBIRTH |rē ˈbərTH|

DICTIONARY: *the process of **being** reincarnated or born again: the endless cycle of **birth**, **death**, and rebirth.*

HOLY SPIRIT;   *man's **inheritance***

~ **i** am the model for rebirth, but rebirth itself is merely the dawning on your minds of what is already in them. *T-6.II.10.6*

~ rebirth is man's **inheritance**. *M-11.1.5*

RECEIVE |rə ˈsēv|

DICTIONARY: *be given, presented with, or paid (something).*

HOLY SPIRIT;   *accept*

~ sender and receiver are the same. *T-19.V.73.8*

~ by receiving it **you** offer it to him. [For **he will** receive of **you** what **you** received of him. *T-19.V.104.2:3*

~ the more that anyone receives, the more is left for all the **rest** to share. *T-28.IV.36.2*

~ **you** but receive according to God's **plan** and never lose or **sacrifice** or die. *W-pI.100.8.6*

~ **atonement** is received and offered. Having been received, it must be accepted. It is in the receiving, then, that **healing** lies. All else must follow from this single **purpose**. *M-22.6.11:14*

REDEMPTION

DICTIONARY: *the action of saving or being saved from sin, error, or evil.*

EGO

~ **you** are afraid of redemption, and **you** believe it **will kill you.** *T-12.II.8.4*

~ **you** are not afraid of **crucifixion.** Your real terror is of redemption. *T-12.III.11.2:3*

HOLY SPIRIT

~ **you** were redeemed the instant **you thought you** had deserted Him. *T-11.IX.81.9*

~ your **role** in the redemption leads **you** to it by reestablishing its **oneness** in your minds. *T-13.II.7.6*

~ the **mission** of redemption **will** be fulfilled as surely as the **creation will** remain unchanged throughout **eternity.** *T-13.V.44.4*

~ the unredeemed cannot redeem, yet **they have** a Redeemer. *T-16.II.6.4*

~ his redemption, **he will give you** yours as surely as **God** created every living **thing** and loves it. And **he will give** it truly, for it **will** be both offered and received. *T-19.V.103.9:10*

~ redemption has been given **you** to **give** each other, and thus **receive** it. *T-19.V.104.4*

~ let us **give** redemption to each other and **share** in it that **we** may rise as one in **resurrection** and not separate in **death.** *T-19.V.106.5*

~ the redeemed **give joy** because **they have** been healed of **pain.** *T-19.V.109.4*

~ let redemption come to **light** the **world** and free it from the **past.** *W-pI.110.3.3*

~ through your transfiguration is the **world** redeemed and joyfully released from **guilt.** *W-pI.151.16.3*

~ your redemption, too, **will** come from **you.** *W-pI.196.12.6*

~ redemption must be one. As **I** am saved, the **world** is saved with me. For all of us must be redeemed together. *W-pII.295.1.4:6*

REFLECTION

DICTIONARY: *the throwing back by a body or surface of light, heat, or sound without absorbing it.*

EGO

~ in **darkness they** are obscure, and their **meaning** seems to lie only in shifting interpretations rather than in themselves. *T-14.V.42.9*

HOLY SPIRIT

~ reflections are seen in **light.** *T-14.V.42.8*

~ the reflection of **God** needs no **interpretation.** It is clear. *T-14.V.43.1:2*

~ the reflections which **you** accept into the mirror of your minds in **time** but bring **eternity** nearer or farther. *T-14.VI.46.2*

~ for the reflection of **truth** draws **everyone** to **truth,** and as **they** enter into it, **they** leave all reflections behind. *T-14.VI.46.7*

~ in **Heaven reality** is shared and not reflected. By sharing its reflection **here,** its **truth** becomes the only **perception** the **Son of God** accepts. *T-14.VI.47.1:2*

~ in **everyone you see** but the reflection of what **you** chose to **have** him be to you. *T-25.VI.40.7*

REHABILITATION |ˌrē(h)əˌbiləˈtāSH(ə)n|

DICTIONARY: *the action of restoring someone to **health** or normal **life** through training and therapy after imprisonment, addiction, or illness.*

EGO

~ the medical orientation to rehabilitation emphasizes the **body**, while the vocational orientation stresses the **ego**. *T-4.IX.103.2*

~ rehabilitation as a movement is an improvement over the overt neglect of those in **need** of **help**, but it is often **little** more than a painful attempt on the **part** of the halt to lead the **blind**. *T-4.IX.103.4*

HOLY SPIRIT;   *attitude of praising **God**, collaborative venture.*

~ rehabilitation is an attitude of praising **God** as He Himself knows **praise**. *T-4.IX.105.3*

~ rehabilitation is not concerned either with the ego's fight for control or its **need** to avoid and withdraw. *T-4.IX.105.7*

~ rehabilitation does not come from anyone else. **You** can **have guidance** from without, but **you** must accept it from **within**. The **guidance** must [become] what **you want**, or it **will** be meaningless to you. That is why rehabilitation is a collaborative venture. *T-8.V.29.5:8*

~ motivation to be healed is the crucial factor in rehabilitation. *T-8.V.30.4*

REINCARNATION |ˌrēənkärˈnāSH(ə)n|

DICTIONARY: *the **rebirth** of a **soul** in a new **body**.*

HOLY SPIRIT

~ in the ultimate **sense**, reincarnation is **impossible**. There is no **past** nor **future**, and the **idea** of **birth** into a **body** has no **meaning** either once or many times. Reincarnation cannot, then, be true in any real **sense**. Our only **question** should be, "Is the **concept** helpful?" And that depends of **course** on what it is used for. If it is used to strengthen the recognition of the eternal nature of **life**, it is helpful indeed. Is any other **question** about it really useful in lighting up the **way**? Like many other beliefs, it can be bitterly misused. At least, such misuse offers preoccupation and perhaps **pride** in the **past**. At worst, it induces inertia in the **present**. In between many kinds of folly are possible. *M-24.1.1:10*

~ reincarnation would not, under any circumstances, be the **problem** to be dealt with **now**. If it were responsible for some of the difficulties the individual faces **now**, his task would still be only to escape from them **now**. If **he** is laying the groundwork for a **future life**, **he** can still work out his **salvation** only **now**. To some there may be comfort in the **concept**, and if it heartens them, its **value** is self-evident. It is certain, however, that the **way** to **salvation** can be found by those who believe in reincarnation and by those who do not. The **idea** cannot, therefore, be regarded as essential to the **curriculum**. There is always some risk in seeing the **present** in terms of the **past**. There is always some **good** in any **thought** which strengthens the **idea** that **life** and the **body** are not the same. *M-24.2.1:8*

~ a **teacher of God** should be as helpful to those who believe in it as to those who do not. *M-24.3.2*

~ the **teacher of God** is therefore wise to **step** away from all such questions, for **he** has much to **teach** and learn apart from them. **He** should both learn and **teach** that theoretical issues but waste **time**, draining it away from its appointed **purpose**. If there are aspects to any **concept** or **belief** that **will** be helpful, **he will** be told about it. **He will** also be told how to use it. *M-24.4.4:7*

RELATIONSHIP

|rəˈlāSH(ə)n ˌSHip|

DICTIONARY: *the way in which two or more concepts, objects, or people are connected, or the state of **being** connected.*

EGO

~ the nature of any interpersonal relationship is limited or defined by what **you want** it to do. Relating is a **way** of achieving an outcome. *T-1.II.102.2:3*

~ all relationships which **guilt** has touched are used but to avoid the person and the **guilt**. *T-13.IV.21.3*

~ any relationship which **you** would **substitute** for another has not been offered to the **Holy Spirit** for His use. *T-15.VI.50.1*

~ every relationship on which the **ego** embarks is **special**. The **ego** establishes relationships only to get something. And it would keep the giver bound to itself through **guilt**. *T-15.VIII.65.7:9*

~ every relationship which the **ego** makes is based on the **idea** that by sacrificing itself, it becomes bigger. *T-15.VIII.70.1*

~ in these insane relationships, the **attraction** of what **you** do not **want** seems to be much stronger than the **attraction** of what **you** do. For each one thinks that **he** has sacrificed something to the other and hates him for it. Yet this is what **he** thinks **he** wants. **He** is not in **love** with the other at all. **He** merely believes **he** is in **love** with **sacrifice**. And for this **sacrifice**, which **he** demanded of himself, **he** demands the other accept the **guilt** and **sacrifice** himself as well. *T-15.VIII.71.1:6*

~ relationships, to the **ego**, mean only that bodies are together. It is always physical closeness that the **ego** demands, and it does not object where the **mind** goes or what it thinks, for this seems unimportant. As long as the **body** is there to **receive** its **sacrifice**, it is content. To the **ego**, the **mind** is private, and only the **body** can be shared. Ideas are basically of no concern, except as **they** draw the **body** of another closer or farther. And it is in these terms that it evaluates ideas as **good** or bad. *T-15.VIII.72.2:7*

~ in the unholy relationship, it is not the **body** of the other with which **union** is attempted but the bodies of those who are not there. Even the **body** of the other, already a severely limited **perception** of him, is not the central focus as it is or in entirety. What can be used for fantasies of **vengeance** and what can be most readily associated with those on whom **vengeance** is really sought are centered on and separated off as **being** the only parts of **value**. Every **step** taken in the making, the maintaining, and the breaking off of the unholy relationship is a move toward further fragmentation and unreality. The **shadow** figures enter more and more, and the one in whom **they** seem to be decreases in importance. *T-17.IV.17.1:5*

~ the **attraction** of the unholy relationship begins to fade and to be questioned almost at once. Once it is formed, **doubt** must enter in because its **purpose** is **impossible**. The only such relationships which retain the fantasies that center on them are those which **have** been dreamed of but **have** not been made at all. *T-17.IV.18.3:5*

~ the more **reality** that enters into the unholy relationship, the less satisfying it becomes. And the more the fantasies can encompass, the greater the satisfaction seems to be. *T-17.IV.18.7:8*

~ **now** the ego counsels thus—**substitute** for this another relationship to which your former **goal** was quite appropriate. **You** can escape from your distress only by getting rid of each other. **You need** not **part** entirely if **you** choose not to do so. But **you** must exclude major areas of **fantasy** from each other to save your **sanity**. *T-17.VI.49.1:4*

~ your relationship was not holy because your **faith** in one another was so limited and **little**. *T-17.VIII.67.3*

~ everything seems to come between the fragmented relationships the **ego** sponsors to destroy. *T-18.I.2.8*

~ relationships in this **world** are the result of how the **world** is seen. *T-19.V.51.3*

357

~ direct relationships, in which there are no interferences, are always seen as dangerous. The **ego** is the **self**-appointed mediator of all relationships, making whatever adjustments it deems necessary and interposing them between those who would meet to keep them separate and prevent their **union**. It is this studied interference which makes it **difficult** for **you** to recognize your **holy relationship** for what it is. *T-20.IV.17.3:5*

~ the one **he** made is partial, **self**-centered, broken into fragments, and full of **fear**. *T-20.VII.45.6*

~ the one **he** made is wholly **self**-destructive and **self**-limiting. *T-20.VII.45.8*

~ any relationship in which the **body** enters is based not on **love**, but on idolatry. *T-20.VII.46.4*

~ an unholy relationship is no relationship. It is a state of isolation which seems to be what it is not. No more than that. The instant that the mad **idea** of making your relationship with **God** unholy seemed to be possible, all your relationships were made meaningless. *T-20.VII.52.3:6*

~ the malevolence of the unholy relationship, so seeming powerful and so bitterly misunderstood and so invested in a false **attraction**. *T-20.VII.53.4*

~ an unholy relationship is based on differences, where each one thinks the other has what **he** has not. **They** come together, each to complete himself and rob the other. **They** stay until **they** think there's **nothing** left to steal and then move on. And so **they** wander through a **world** of strangers unlike themselves, living with their bodies perhaps under a common roof that shelters neither—in the same room and yet a **world** apart. *T-22.I.2.7:10*

HOLY SPIRIT; *a reflection of the union of the Creator and His Son, temple of healing.*

~ no real relationship can **rest** on **guilt** or even hold one spot of it to mar its purity. *T-13.IV.21.2*

~ **you** forgot that real relationships are holy and cannot be used by **you** at all. **They** are used only by the **Holy Spirit**, and it is that which makes them pure. [If **you** displace your **guilt** upon them, the **Holy Spirit** cannot use them.]. *T-13.IV.21.5:8*

~ **you** cannot enter into real relationships with any of God's Sons unless **you love** them all and equally. *T-13.IV.30.1*

~ under His **teaching**, every relationship becomes a **lesson** in **love**. *T-15.VI.48.6*

~ your relationships are with the **universe**. *T-15.IX.82.4*

~ for **God** created the only relationship which has **meaning**, and that is His relationship with **you**. *T-15.IX.84.7*

~ real relationships **have** no limits, having been established by **God**. *T-15.IX.87.1*

~ the **reality** of this relationship becomes the only **truth** that **you** could ever **want**. All **truth** is **here**. *T-15.IX.91.6:7*

~ all **pain** and **sacrifice** and littleness **will** disappear in our relationship, which is as **innocent** as our relationship with our **Father**, and as powerful. *T-15.XI.103.4*

~ yet your relationship with Him is real and has been demonstrated. *T-16.III.16.2*

~ in any relationship in which **you** are wholly willing to accept **completion**, and only this, there is **God** completed and His Son with Him. *T-16.V.38.6*

~ the **truth** lies **here** and nowhere else. *T-16.VIII.80.6*

~ its loveliness **will** so attract **you** that **you will** be unwilling ever to lose the **sight** of it again. *T-17.IV.21.6*

~ the **Creator** of the one relationship has left no **part** of it without Himself. *T-17.IV.22.5*

~ this is the only **part** of the relationship the **Holy Spirit** sees because He knows that only this is true. *T-17.IV.23.1*

~ the **function** of relationships became forever "to **make happy**" And **nothing** else. *T-17.V.27.3*

~ the **Holy Spirit** is in close relationship with **you** because in Him is your relationship with **God** restored to **you**. The relationship with Him has never been broken because the **Holy Spirit** has not been separate from anyone since the **separation**. *T-17.V.30.3:4*

~ the whole **reality** of your relationship with Him lies in our relationship to one another. *T-17.V.42.7*

~ when the **Holy Spirit** changed the **purpose** of your relationship by exchanging yours for His, the **goal He** placed there was extended to every **situation** in which **you** enter or **will** ever enter. And every **situation** was thus made free of the **past**, which would **have** made it purposeless. *T-17.VIII.72.5:6*

~ **you** whose relationship shares the Holy Spirit's **goal** are set apart from loneliness because the **truth** has come. Its **call** for **faith** is strong. Use not your faithlessness against it, for it calls **you** to **salvation** and to **peace**. *T-17.VIII.73.4:6*

~ in your relationship, where **He** has taken charge of everything at your **request**, **He** has set the **course** inward to the **truth you share**. *T-18.II.9.1*

~ your relationship has become one in which the **wish** has been removed because its **purpose** has been changed from one of dreams to one of **truth**. *T-18.III.22.4*

~ in your relationship, the **Holy Spirit** has gently laid the **real world**—the **world** of **happy** dreams from which awaking is so easy and so natural. *T-18.III.23.4*

~ in your relationship is this world's **light**. And **fear** must disappear before **you now**. *T-18.IV.27.3:4*

~ the **holiness** of your relationship is established in **Heaven**. *T-18.IV.27.10*

~ your relationship has been uprooted from the **world** of shadows, and its unholy **purpose** has been safely brought through the barriers of **guilt**, washed with **forgiveness**, and set shining and firmly rooted in the **world** of light. From there, it calls to **you** to follow the **course** it took, lifted high above the **darkness** and gently placed before the gates of **Heaven**. *T-18.XI.97.1:2*

~ in the **miracle** of your relationship, without this barrier, is every **miracle** contained. *T-19.V.44.2*

~ in your new relationship am **I** made **welcome**. *T-19.V.55.5*

~ his real relationship is one of perfect **union** and unbroken continuity. *T-20.VII.45.5*

~ the one created by his **Father** is wholly **self**-encompassing and **self**-extending. *T-20.VII.45.7*

~ the first is based on **love** and rests on it, serene and undisturbed. The **body** does not intrude upon it. *T-20.VII.46.2:3*

~ relationships are his **salvation** and not his doom. *T-20.VII.56.3*

~ a real relationship, and it has **meaning**. It is as like your real relationship with **God** as equal things are like unto each other. *T-20.VII.57.1:2*

~ the **holiness** of your relationship forgives **you** both, undoing the effects of what **you** both believed and saw. *T-22.I.2.1*

~ your relationship is a **reflection** of the **union** of the **Creator** and His Son. *T-22.VII.64.5*

~ the lovely **light** of your relationship is like the **love** of God. *T-23.V.50.1*

~ your relationship is raised above the **battleground**, in it no more. *T-23.V.50.5*

~ your relationship has been made clean of **special** goals. *T-24.II.10.8*

~ relationships are still the **temple** of the Holy Spirit, and **they will** be made perfect in **time** and restored to **eternity**. *P-2.II.1.5*

~ there is a place for all relationships in this **world**, and **they will** bring as much **good** as each can accept and use. *P-3.II.6.9*

RELEASE

DICTIONARY: *allow or enable to escape from confinement; set free.*

EGO;   *imprisonment*

~ many **have** chosen to renounce the **world** while still believing its **reality**, and **they have** suffered from a **sense** of **loss** and **have** not been released accordingly. *W-pI.155.4.2*

HOLY SPIRIT

~ **correction** of **error** brings release. *T-1.1.104.6*

~ every **brother** has the **power** to release **you** if **you will** to be free. *T-10.VII.58.4*

~ **you will** be released, and **you will** not **remember** anything **you** made that was not created for **you** and by **you** in return. *T-13.V.46.3*

~ release is total. *T-15.XI.103.3*

~ as **you** release, so **will you** be released. *T-16.VII.60.4*

~ your release is certain. *T-17.IX.79.5*

~ in your release from **sacrifice** is his made manifest and shown to be his own. *T-27.I.2.1*

~ all that is given **you** is for release—the **sight**, the **vision**, and the inner Guide all lead **you** out of **hell** with those **you love** beside **you** and the **universe** with them. *T-31.VII.74.7*

RELIGION

DICTIONARY: *the **belief** in and worship of a superhuman controlling **power**, especially a personal **God** or Gods.*

EGO;   *ego's insane religion*

~ the religiously **ego**-oriented believe that the **Soul** existed before and **will** continue to **exist** afterwards, after a temporary lapse in **ego life**. *T-4.III.35.5*

~ ego's insane religion is that **sin** is not **error** but **truth**, and it is **innocence** that would deceive. Purity is seen as arrogance, and the **acceptance** of the **self** as **sinful** is perceived as **holiness**. And it is this doctrine which replaces the **reality** of the **Son of God** as his **Father** created him and willed that **he** be forever. *T-19.III.20.1:3*

~ formal religion has no place in **psychotherapy**, but it also has no real place in religion. *P-2.II.2.1*

~ the attempt to formalize religion is so obviously an **ego** attempt to reconcile the irreconcilable that it hardly requires elaboration **here**. *P-2.II.2.3*

~ religion is **experience**; psychotherapy is **experience**. At the highest levels **they** become one. Neither is **truth** itself, but both can lead to **truth**. *P-2.II.2.4:6*

~ some forms of religion **have nothing** to do with **God**. *P-2.II.5.2*

HOLY SPIRIT;   *experience*

~ all religion is the recognition that the irreconcilable cannot be reconciled. *T-9.X.85.2*

REMEMBER

DICTIONARY: *have in or be able to bring to one's **mind** an **awareness** of (someone or something that one has seen, known, or experienced in the **past**).*

EGO

~ if **you** remember what **you have** made, **you** are remembering **nothing**. *T-14.I.3.7*

~ the limitations on remembering the **world** imposes on it are as vast as those **you** let the **world** impose on **you**. *T-28.II.4.4*

~ what **you** remember never was. *T-28.II.9.1*

HOLY SPIRIT; *restore*

~ forgetting is merely a **way** of remembering better. It is therefore not the **opposite** of remembering, when it is properly perceived. Perceived improperly, it induces a **perception** of **conflict** with something else, as all incorrect **perception** does. Properly perceived, it can be used as a **way** out of **conflict**, as all proper **perception** can. *T-7.V.34.7:10*

~ in this remembering is the **knowledge** of yourself. *T-9.IX.69.5*

~ to remember is merely to restore to your **mind** what is already there. **You** do not **make** what **you** remember; **you** merely accept again what has been made but was rejected. *T-9.IX.70.1:2*

~ your remembering is his, for **God** cannot be remembered **alone**. *T-11.III.15.6*

~ to perceive the **healing** of your **brother** as the **healing** of yourself is thus the **way** to remember **God**. *T-11.III.15.8*

~ remembrance of **reality** is in Him and therefore in **you**. *T-14.I.3.8*

~ remembering Him is to remember **freedom**. *T-15.II.11.8*

~ the remembrance of the **Father** enters with Him, and with Him **they** remember the only **relationship they** ever had and ever **want** to have. *T-15.XI.109.5*

~ remembering is as selective as **perception**, **being** its **past** tense. It is **perception** of the **past** as if it were occurring **now** and still were there to **see**. *T-28.I.2.5:6*

~ their own remembering is **quiet now**, and what has come to take its place **will** not be wholly unremembered afterwards. *T-28.II.11.5*

~ what is **now** remembered is not **fear**, but rather is the **cause** that **fear** was made to render unremembered and undone. *T-28.II.13.5*

~ for as **we** remember Him, His **Son will** be restored to us in the **Reality** of **Love**. *W-pII.350.2.2*

~ remembrance which contains the **memory of God** and points the **way** to Him and to the **Heaven** of His **peace**. *W-pIIST361.4.3*

REPRESSION

DICTIONARY: *the action of subduing someone or something by force.*

EGO

~ repression thus operates to conceal not only the baser impulses but also the most lofty ones from **awareness** because both are threatening to the **ego** and, **being** concerned primarily with its own preservation in the face of **threat**, the **ego** perceives them as the same. *T-4.IV.46.1*

~ it utilizes repression against all truly natural impulses. *T-4.VII.88.4*

REQUEST

DICTIONARY: *an act of asking politely or formally for something.*

EGO

~ foolish requests are foolish for the simple **reason** that **they conflict** because **they** contain an element of specialness. *T-16.II.7.6*

HOLY SPIRIT

~ no "outrageous" request can be made of one who recognizes what is valuable and wants to accept **nothing** else. *T-11.IV.2.7.7*

~ at your request He enters gladly. *T-14.IV.30.3*

~ no one is denied his least request. *W-pI.159.6.4*

RESISTANCE

DICTIONARY: *the refusal to accept or comply with something; the attempt to prevent something by action or argument.*

EGO

~ refuse and your opposition establishes that it does matter to **you**. *T-11.IV.2.7.2*

~ "resistance" is its **way** of looking at things; its **interpretation** of progress and growth. *P-2.1.2.4*

~ resistance as defined **here** can be characteristic of a **therapist** as well as of a **patient**. Either **way**, it sets a **limit** on **psychotherapy** because it restricts its aims. *P-2.1.3.1:2*

HOLY SPIRIT

~ if **you** find resistance strong and dedication weak, **you** are not ready. Do not fight yourself. *T-30.II.2.6:7*

REST

DICTIONARY: *cease work or movement in **order** to relax, refresh oneself, or recover **strength**.*

HOLY SPIRIT

~ rest does not come from sleeping but from waking. *T-5.IV.28.4*

~ **you** can rest in **peace** only because **you** are awake. *T-8.IX.8.3.9*

~ **you** rest in **God**, and while the **world** is torn by winds of **hate**, your rest remains completely undisturbed. Yours is the rest of **truth**. *W-pI.109.4.2:3*

~ **you call** to all to **join you** in your rest, and **they will** hear and come to **you** because **you** rest in **God**. **They will** not hear another **voice** but yours because **you** gave your **voice** to **God** and **now you** rest in Him and let Him speak through **you**. *W-pI.109.4.5:6*

~ in timelessness **you** rest, while **time** goes by without its touch upon **you**, for your rest can never **change** in any **way** at all. *W-pI.109.5.2*

~ a tired **mind** is suddenly made glad. *W-pI.109.7.1*

~ the **world** is born again each **time you** rest. *W-pI.109.7.2*

~ and the **time** when rest **will** be the only **thing** there is comes closer to all worn and tired minds, too weary **now** to go their **way alone.** *W-pI.109.8.2*

~ for in God's hands **we** rest untroubled, sure that only **good** can come to us. *W-pI.194.9.2*

RESURRECTION

|ˌrezəˈrekSH(ə)n|

DICTIONARY: *the revitalization or revival of something.*

HOLY SPIRIT; *rebirth, reawakening, overcoming or surmounting of* **death, denial** *of* **death,** *assertion of* **life,** *complete triumph,* **symbol** *of sharing.*

~ the Resurrection demonstrated that **nothing** can destroy **truth. Good** can withstand any **form** of **evil** because **light** abolishes all forms of **darkness.** *T-3.III.18.1:2*

~ resurrection was the **means** for the return to **knowledge,** which was accomplished by the **union** of my **will** with the Father's. *T-3.VII.51.3*

~ Your resurrection is your reawakening. **I** am the model for rebirth, but rebirth itself is merely the dawning on your minds of what is already in them. *T-6.II.10.5*

~ the resurrection is the **symbol** of sharing. *T-6.II.16.4*

~ the resurrection is the complete triumph of **Christ** over the **ego,** not by **attack** but by transcendence. *T-10.VII.59.6*

~ the resurrection is the **Will** of **God,** which knows no **time** and no exceptions. *T-10.VII.62.7*

~ resurrection must compel your allegiance gladly because it is the **symbol** of **joy.** Its whole compelling **power** lies in the **fact** that it represents what **you want** to be. *T-10.VII.64.1:2*

~ in my resurrection is your **release.** *T-11.III.20.3*

~ nor can the resurrection be complete till your **forgiveness** rests on **Christ** along with mine. *T-20.II.3.2*

~ resurrection has come. *T-26.VI.39.5*

~ and **now you** are a **part** of resurrection, not of **death.** *T-26.VI.39.6*

~ it stands beyond the **body** and the **world, past** every **witness** for unholiness, **within** the Holy, holy as Itself. *W-pI.151.12.2*

~ the resurrection is the overcoming or surmounting of **death.** It is a reawakening or a **rebirth,** a **change** of **mind** about the **meaning** of the **world.** It is the **acceptance** of the Holy Spirit's **interpretation** of the world's **purpose;** the **acceptance** of the **Atonement** for oneself. It is the end of dreams of **misery** and the glad **awareness** of the Holy Spirit's final **dream.** It is the recognition of the gifts of **God.** It is the **dream** in which the **body** functions perfectly, having no **function** except **communication.** It is the **lesson** in which **learning** ends, for it is consummated and surpassed with this. It is the invitation to **God** to take His **final step.** It is the relinquishment of all other purposes, all other interests, all other wishes, and all other concerns. It is the single **desire** of the Son for the **Father.** *M-28.1.1:10*

~ the resurrection is the **denial** of **death, being** the assertion of **life.** Thus is all the thinking of the **world** reversed entirely. **Life** is **now** recognized as **salvation,** and **pain** and **misery** of any kind perceived as **hell. Love** is no longer feared but gladly welcomed. Idols **have** disappeared, and the remembrance of **God** shines unimpeded across the **world.** Christ's face is seen in every living **thing,** and **nothing** is held in **darkness** apart from the **light** of **forgiveness.** There is no sorrow still upon the earth. The **joy** of **Heaven** has come upon it. *M-28.2.1:8*

~ here the **curriculum** ends. From **here** on no directions are needed. **Vision** is wholly corrected and all mistakes undone. **Attack** is meaningless, and **peace** has come. The **goal** of the **curriculum** has been achieved. Thoughts turn to **Heaven** and away from **hell**. All longings are satisfied. *M-28.3.1:7*

~ the last **illusion** spreads over the **world**, forgiving all things and replacing all **attack**. The whole reversal is accomplished. **Nothing** is left to contradict the **word** of God. There is no opposition to the **truth**. And **now** the **truth** can come at last. *M-28.3.8:12*

~ differences **have** disappeared, and **Love** looks on Itself. *M-28.5.2*

~ illusions of another **will** are lost, for **unity** of **purpose** has been found. *M-28.5.8*

REVELATION |ˌrevəˈlāSH(ə)n|

DICTIONARY: *a surprising and previously unknown **fact**, especially one that is made known in a dramatic **way**.*

HOLY SPIRIT;   *an end, **experience** of pure **joy**.*

~ revelations come from the above or **superconscious level**. The conscious **level** is in between and reacts to either sub-or **superconscious** impulses in varying ratios. **Consciousness** is the **level** which engages in the **world** and is capable of responding to both. *T-1.I.36.2:4*

~ revelation induces complete but temporary suspension of **doubt** and **fear**. It represents the original **form** of **communication** between **God** and His Souls, involving an extremely personal **sense** of closeness to **creation** which **man** tries to find in physical relationships. Physical closeness cannot achieve this. *T-1.I.37.1:3*

~ revelation unites Souls directly with **God**. Miracles unite minds directly with each other. Neither emanates from **consciousness**, but both are experienced there. *T-1.I.38.1:3*

~ revelation is an end. *T-1.I.40.2*

~ revelation induces only **experience**. *T-1.I.40.7*

~ revelation is literally unspeakable because it is an **experience** of unspeakable **love**. *T-1.I.77.1*

~ the **Holy Spirit** is the bringer of revelations. *T-1.I.80.5*

~ revelation is not reciprocal. It is always from **God** to **man**. *T-1.I.81.5:6*

~ only revelation transcends **time**, having **nothing** to do with **time** at all. *T-1.I.85.2*

~ only revelation transcends **time**. *T-1.I.85.2*

~ revelation may occasionally reveal the end to **you**, but to reach it the **means** are needed. *T-3.I.3.5*

~ the biblical injunction, "Be of one **mind**" is the statement for revelation-**readiness**. *T-3.II.7.1*

~ revelation because its content cannot be expressed, and it is intensely personal to the **mind** which receives it. It can, however, still be returned by that **mind** through its attitudes to other minds which the **knowledge** from the revelation brings. *T-4.VIII.101.5:6*

~ revelation is an **experience** of pure **joy**. *T-5.II.5.3*

~ it matters not when revelation comes, for that is not of **time**. *W-pI.158.11.1*

~ the revelation that the **Father** and the Son are one **will** come in **time** to every **mind**. Yet is that **time** determined by the **mind** itself, not taught. *W-pI.158.2.8:9*

~ whatever **time** the **mind** has set for revelation is entirely irrelevant to what must be a constant state, forever as it always was; forever to remain as it is **now**. *W-pI.169.8.3*

~ when revelation of your **oneness** comes, it **will** be known and fully understood. *W-pI.169.9.2*

REWARD

DICTIONARY: *a **thing** given in recognition of one's **service**, **effort**, or achievement.*

EGO

~ in no respect at any **time** or place has anything but **fear** and **guilt** been your reward. *T-25.III.13.2*

HOLY SPIRIT

~ be not content with **future** happiness. It has no **meaning** and is not your just reward. *T-26.IX.76.1:2*

~ **now** let the **peace** that your **acceptance** brings be given you. Close your eyes and **receive** your reward. *W-pI.80.5.1:2*

RIGHT-MINDED

DICTIONARY: *having sound views and principles.*

EGO

~ intellectualization is a term which stems from the **mind-brain confusion**. *T-2.II.26.1*

~ "intellectualization" implies a split. *T-2.II.26.3*

~ all forms of not-right-mindedness are the result of refusal to accept the **Atonement** for yourself. *T-2.III.64.4*

HOLY SPIRIT

~ "right-mindedness" is the device which defends the right **mind** and gives it control over the **body**. *T-2.II.26.2*

~ "right-mindedness" involves **healing**. *T-2.II.26.3*

~ the right-minded neither exalt nor depreciate the **mind** of the **miracle** worker or the **miracle** receiver. *T-2.III.63.3*

~ only right-mindedness can create in a **way** that has any real effect. *T-3.II.7.2*

~ right-minded seeing cannot **see** anything but **perfection**. Only One-Mindedness is without **confusion**. *T-3.IV.28.2*

~ the term "right-mindedness" is properly used as the **correction** for "wrong-mindedness," and applies to the state of **mind** which induces accurate **perception**. It is miraculous because it heals misperception, and this is indeed a **miracle** in view of how **man** perceives himself. *T-3.VI.43.3:4*

~ right-mindedness dictates the next **step** automatically, because right **perception** is uniformly without **attack**, so that wrong-mindedness is obliterated. *T-4.III.36.3*

ROLE

DICTIONARY: *the **function** assumed or **part** played by a person or **thing** in a particular **situation**.*

EGO

~ if **you** assume correction's role, **you** lose the **function** of **forgiveness**. *T-27.III.22.3*

~ **you hate** the one **you** gave the leader's role when **you** would **have** it, and **you hate** as well his not assuming it at times **you want** to let the follower in **you** arise and **give** away the role of leadership. *T-31.II.16.3*

~ **you hate** the one **you** gave the leader's role when **you** would **have** it, and **you hate** as well his not assuming it at times **you want** to let the follower in **you** arise and **give** away the role of leadership. *T-31.II.16.3*

~ the role of the accuser **will** appear in many places and in many forms. And each **will** seem to be accusing **you**. *T-31.V.58.5:6*

~ our **self**-made roles are shifting, and **they** seem to **change** from mourner to ecstatic bliss of loved and loving. *W-pI.186.8.3*

HOLY SPIRIT

~ **you have** a role in the **Atonement**, which **I will** dictate to you. *T-1.I.49.3*

~ do not confuse your role with His, for this **will** never bring **peace** to anyone. *T-16.II.6.7*

~ whatever your appointed role may be, it was selected by the **Voice** for **God**. *W-pI.154.2.1*

~ as **you** take the role assigned to you, **salvation** comes a **little** nearer. *W-pI.169.10.5*

RULE

DICTIONARY: *one of a set of explicit or understood regulations or principles governing conduct **within** a particular activity or sphere.*

EGO

~ the ego's rule is, "**Seek** and do not find." *T-11.VI.49.1*

HOLY SPIRIT

~ **the Golden Rule** asks **you** to behave toward others as **you** would **have** them behave toward you. This **means** that the **perception** of both must be accurate. **The Golden Rule** is the rule for appropriate **behavior**. *T-1.I.64.1:3*

~ rules which **will** protect **you** from the ravages of **fear**. *T-30.II.28.2*

~ even in this **world**, it is **I** who rule my destiny. *W-p2.253.1.2*

~ the **world will** never again appear to rule the **mind**. *M-5.6.4*

SACRIFICE

DICTIONARY: *an act of **giving** up something valued for the sake of something else regarded as more important or worthy.*

EGO; *gifts, love, attack.*

~ sacrifice gets **nothing**. Sacrifice is so essential to your **thought system** that **salvation** apart from sacrifice **means nothing** to you. Your **confusion** of sacrifice and **love** is so profound that **you** cannot conceive of **love** without sacrifice. *T-15.X.96.1:3*

~ someone must pay and someone must get. *T-15.X.96.7*

~ no partial sacrifice **will** appease this savage guest, for it is an invader who but seems to offer kindness, but always to **make** the sacrifice complete. *T-15.X.99.7*

~ **guilt** is the **condition** of sacrifice. *T-15.XI.104.3*

~ your **faith** in sacrifice has given it great **power** in your **sight**, except **you** do not realize **you** cannot **see** because of it. For sacrifice must be exacted of a **body** and by another **body**. *T-21.IV.38.1:2*

~ so is sacrifice invariably a **means** for limitation and thus for **hate**. *T-21.IV.38.7*

~ every sacrifice demands that **they** be separate and without the other. *T-26.II.4.5*

~ the **memory of God** must be denied if any sacrifice is asked of anyone. *T-26.II.4.6*

~ **you have** indeed been wrong in your **belief** that sacrifice is asked. *W-pI.100.8.5*

~ sacrifice and **deprivation** are paths which lead nowhere, choices for defeat, and aims which **will** remain **impossible**. *W-pI.155.7.2*

~ it is a sacrifice to **give** up the things of this **world**. *M-13.1.6*

~ there is no sacrifice in the world's terms that does not involve the **body**. *M-13.2.4*

~ it is the cost of believing in illusions. It is the price that must be paid for the **denial of truth**. There is no **pleasure** of the **world** that does not demand this, for otherwise the **pleasure** would be seen as **pain**. And no one asks for **pain** if **he** recognizes it. It is the **idea** of sacrifice that makes him **blind**. *M-13.5.2:6*

~ it always **means** the giving up of what **you want**. *M-13.6.5*

HOLY SPIRIT; *separation from love*

~ sacrifice is a notion totally unknown to **God**. It arises solely from **fear**. *T-3.III.21.1:2*

~ sacrificing another in any **way** is a clear cut violation of God's own injunction that **man** should be merciful even as his **Father in Heaven**. *T-3.III.21.4*

~ the **Holy Spirit** never asks for sacrifice, but the **ego** always does. *T-7.XI.103.5*

~ it is a sacrifice to accept anything less than **glory**. *T-15.IV.30.3*

~ i am as incapable of **receiving** sacrifice as **God** is, and every sacrifice **you ask** of yourself, **you ask** of me. Learn **now** that sacrifice of any kind is **nothing** but a limitation imposed on **giving**. *T-15.X.93.5:6*

~ sacrifice is **attack**, not **love**. *T-15.X.96.4*

~ **you** think that **everyone outside** yourself demands your sacrifice, but **you** do not **see** that only **you** demand sacrifice and only of yourself. Yet the demand of sacrifice is so savage and so fearful that **you** cannot accept it where it is. *T-15.X.99.1:2*

~ the whole **idea** of sacrifice as solely of your making. *T-15.XI.101.1*

~ without sacrifice, there **love** must be. *T-15.XI.103.6*

368

~ **you** who believe that sacrifice is **love** must learn that sacrifice is **separation** from **love**. For sacrifice brings **guilt** as surely as **love** brings **peace**. *T-15.XI.104.1:2*

~ to sacrifice the **body** is to sacrifice **nothing**, and **communication**, which must be of the **mind**, cannot be sacrificed. *T-15.XI.107.3*

~ sacrifice is nowhere. *T-15.XI.108.1*

~ the **Holy Spirit** knows that sacrifice brings **nothing**. *T-21.IV.37.2*

~ no sacrifice is possible in the relinquishment of an **illusion** recognized as such. *T-26.IV.24.6*

~ a tiny sacrifice is just the same in its effects as is the whole **idea** of sacrifice. *T-26.VIII.61.6*

~ **you** cannot sacrifice yourself **alone**. For sacrifice is total. *T-27.1.1.7:8*

~ it is not **love** that asks a sacrifice. But **fear** demands the sacrifice of **love**, for in love's presence **fear** cannot abide. *T-29.II.7.1:2*

~ to sacrifice is to **give** up and thus to be without and to **have** suffered **loss**. *T-29.VIII.46.3*

~ there is no sacrifice that can be asked; there is no sacrifice that can be made. *T-31.III.32.4*

~ and sacrifice is an **idea** so mad that **sanity** dismisses it at once. *W-pI.187.7.5*

~ there is no place for sacrifice in what has any **value**. If the **thought** occurs, its very presence proves that **error** has arisen and **correction** must be made. Your **blessing will** correct it. *W-pI.187.8.2:4*

~ no **form** of sacrifice and **suffering** can long endure before the face of one who has forgiven and has blessed himself. *W-pI.187.8.6*

~ **i** sacrifice illusions, **nothing** more. *W-pII.322.1.1*

~ although in **truth** the term sacrifice is altogether meaningless, it does **have meaning** in the **world**. Like all things in the **world**, its **meaning** is temporary and **will** ultimately fade into the nothingness from which it came when there is no more use for it. **Now** its real **meaning** is a **lesson**. Like all lessons, it is an **illusion**, for in **reality** there is **nothing** to learn. Yet this **illusion** must be replaced by a corrective device, another **illusion** that replaces the first, so both can finally disappear. *M-13.1.1:5*

~ sacrifice is total. There are no "half sacrifices." *M-13.7.1:2*

SAD |s a d|

DICTIONARY: *feeling or showing sorrow; unhappy.*

EGO

~ depression always arises ultimately from a **sense** of **being** deprived of something **you want** and do not **have**. *T-4.V.59.2*

~ **they** look out in sorrow from what is sad **within** and **see** the sadness there. *T-20.IV.19.7*

~ sadness is the sign that **you** would play another **part** instead of what has been assigned to **you** by **God**. *W-pI.100.5.3*

~ if **you** are sad, your **part** is unfulfilled and all the **world** is thus deprived of **joy** along with **you**. *W-pI.100.6.2*

~ the unforgiving **mind** is sad. *W-pI.121.2.2*

~ yet some try to put by their **suffering** in games **they** play to occupy their **time** and keep their sadness from them. Others **will** deny that **they** are sad and do not recognize their tears at all. *W-pI.182.2.2:3*

HOLY SPIRIT

~ when **you** are sad, know that this **need** not be. *T-4.V.59.1*

~ the **Holy Spirit** reminds **you** gently that **you** are sad because **you** are not fulfilling your **function** as co-creators with **God** and are therefore depriving yourselves of **joy**. *T-7.VIII.68.1*

~ depression **means** that **you have** foresworn God. *T-9.XI.93.3*

~ depression is isolation, and so it could not **have** been created. *T-9.XI.97.6*

~ sorrow can be turned to **joy**, for **time** gives **way** to the eternal. *T-22.III.18.7*

~ there is no sadness where a **miracle** has come to heal. *T-27.VI.46.5*

SALVATION |sal'vāSH(ə)n|

DICTIONARY: *preservation or deliverance from **harm**, ruin, or **loss**.*

EGO;   *destruction of the **world***

~ **you** who **fear** salvation are willing **death**. *T-3.IX.80.5*

~ **attack** becomes salvation. *T-15.XI.105.7*

~ it is denied where **compromise** has been accepted. *T-23.IV.43.6*

~ salvation is a **secret you have** kept but from yourself. *T-27.IX.89.4*

~ salvation thus appears to threaten **life** and offer **death**. *T-29.VIII.50.10*

~ there can be no salvation in the **dream** as **you** are dreaming it. *T-29.X.64.1*

~ salvation seems to come from anywhere except from **you**. So, too, does the **source** of **guilt**. **You see** neither **guilt** nor salvation as in your own **mind** and nowhere else. *W-pI.70.1.2:4*

~ all illusions of salvation **have** failed **you**. *W-pI.70.13.1*

~ the **ego** has set up a **plan for salvation** in opposition to God's. It is this **plan** in which **you** believe. *W-pI.71.1.1:2*

~ the ego's **plan for salvation** centers around holding grievances. It maintains that if someone else spoke or acted differently, if some external circumstance or event were changed, **you** would be saved. Thus the **source** of salvation is constantly perceived as **outside** yourself. *W-pI.71.2.1:3*

~ the ego's **plan for salvation** is the **opposite** of God's, **we have** not yet emphasized that it is an active **attack** on His **plan** and a deliberate attempt to destroy it. In the **attack**, **God** is assigned the attributes which are actually associated with the **ego**, while the **ego** appears to take on the attributes of **God**. *W-pI.72.1.1:2*

~ **you have** sought salvation in strange ways—have been deceived, deceiving, and afraid of foolish fantasies and savage dreams and **have** bowed down to idols made of dust—all this is true by what **you now** believe. *W-pI.93.2.3*

~ salvation thus cannot be purchased but through **suffering**. *W-pI.101.1.7*

~ the **thing you** dread the most is your salvation. *W-pI.196.9.4*

~ deny your **strength**, and **weakness** must become salvation to **you**. *W-pI.197.2.2*

~ it seems that **we will gain** autonomy but by our striving to be separate and that our independence from the **rest** of God's **creation** is the **way** in which salvation is obtained. Yet all **we** find is **sickness, suffering** and **loss**, and **death**. This is not what our **Father** wills for us, nor is there any second to His **Will**. *W-pII.328.1.2:4*

HOLY SPIRIT; *escape from* **guilt**, *God's* **justice**, *happiest accomplishment, recognition, reawakening, reminder,* **miracle**, **gift**, **happy dream**, **lesson** *in* **giving**, *your only* **purpose**, *"right-mindedness",* **borderland**, *undoing, my* **function**, *end of dreams, paradox.*

~ salvation. It is **here** and **will today** be given unto **you.** *T-1.I.48.3:4*

~ the term "salvation" does not apply to the **Soul**, which is not in danger and does not **need** to be salvaged. Salvation is **nothing** more than "right-mindedness." *T-4.III.36.1:2*

~ insistence **means** investment, and what **you** invest in is always related to your notion of salvation. *T-11.IV.25.5*

~ salvation is for the **mind**, and it is attained through **peace**. This is the only **thing** that can be saved and the only **way** to save it. *T-11.IV.28.1:2*

~ **you will** learn salvation, because **you will** learn how to save. *T-13.V.43.4*

~ salvation is as sure as **God**. His **certainty** suffices. *T-13.V.43.6:7*

~ all salvation is escape from **guilt.** *T-13.VIII.77.4*

~ salvation is of Him to Whom **God** gave it for **you.** *T-13.VIII.78.5*

~ salvation is simple, **being** of **God** and therefore very easy to **understand.** *T-15.X.100.6*

~ salvation lies in the simple **fact** that illusions are not fearful because **they** are not true. *T-16.VI.56.1*

~ even salvation **will** become a **dream** and vanish from his **mind**. For salvation is the end of dreams and with the closing of the **dream will have** no **meaning.** *T-17.III.12.6:7*

~ it **will give you** the **real world**, trembling with **readiness** to be given **you**. The eagerness of the **Holy Spirit** to **give you** this is so intense **He** would not wait, although **He** waits in **patience**. Meet His **patience** with your impatience at **delay** in meeting Him. *T-17.III.13.2:4*

~ salvation is easy just because it asks **nothing** that **you** cannot **give** right **now.** *T-18.V.39.7*

~ salvation flows from deep **within** the **home you** offered to my **Father** and to me. *T-19.V.66.2*

~ the infancy of salvation is carefully guarded by **love**, preserved from every **thought** that would **attack** it and quietly made ready to fulfill the mighty task for which it was given **you.** *T-19.V.86.3*

~ what has been given **you**, even in its infancy, is in full **communication** with **God** and **you.** *T-19.V.87.4*

~ salvation is a **lesson** in giving, as the **Holy Spirit** interprets it. It is the reawakening of the **laws** of **God** in minds that **have** established other **laws** and given them **power** to enforce what **God** created not. *T-20.V.29.9:10*

~ salvation is the Holy Spirit's **goal**. The **means** is **vision.** *T-20.VIII.66.4:5*

~ only your thoughts **have** been **impossible**. Salvation cannot be. *T-22.III.26.1:2*

~ in his **sight** your loveliness is his salvation which **he** would protect from **harm**. And each **will** be the other's strong protector from everything that seems to rise between **you**. So shall **you** walk the **world** with me, whose **message** has not yet been given to **everyone.** *T-22.V.42.1:3*

~ salvation is no **compromise** of any kind. *T-23.IV.43.1*

~ salvation gives up **nothing**. It is complete for **everyone.** *T-23.IV.43.3:4*

~ salvation challenges not even **death.** *T-24.IV.30.7*

~ salvation is **rebirth** of the **idea** no one can lose for anyone to **gain**. And **everyone** must **gain** if anyone would be a gainer. *T-25.VIII.61.1:2*

~ salvation is His **Will** because **you share** it. Not for **you alone** but for the **Self** which is the **Son of God.** *T-25.VIII.62.5:6*

371

~ salvation is not needed by the saved. *T-25.IX.64.4*

~ its **purpose** is the end of specialness. *T-25.X.83.8*

~ salvation stops just short of **Heaven**, for only **perception** needs salvation. *T-26.IV.22.1*

~ salvation, perfect and complete, asks but a **little wish** that what is true be true. *T-26.VIII.56.1*

~ salvation is immediate. Unless **you** so perceive it, **you will** be afraid of it, believing that the risk of **loss** is great between the **time** its **purpose** is made yours and its effects **will** come to **you.** *T-26.IX.70.1:2*

~ salvation would wipe out the space **you see** between **you** still and let **you** instantly become as one. *T-26.IX.70.4*

~ the **secret** of salvation is but this: that **you** are **doing** this unto yourself. *T-27.IX.86.1*

~ what could correct for **separation** but its **opposite**? There is no middle ground in any aspect of salvation. **You** accept it wholly or accept it not. *T-28.VIII.61.6:8*

~ salvation seeks to prove there is no **death**, and only **life** exists. *T-29.VIII.51.2*

~ salvation is a paradox indeed! *T-30.V.55.1*

~ it asks **you** but that **you** forgive all things that no one ever did, to overlook what is not there, and not to look upon the unreal as **reality.** *T-30.V.55.3*

~ salvation asks so **little**, not so much. It asks for **nothing** in **reality.** And even in illusions it but asks **forgiveness** be the **substitute** for **fear.** Such is the only **rule** for **happy** dreams. *T-30.V.56.4:7*

~ it merely asks that **you** respond appropriately to what is not real by not perceiving what has not occurred. *T-30.VII.71.5*

~ the natural reaction to distress which rests on **error** and thus calls for **help. Forgiveness** is the only sane response. It keeps your rights from **being** sacrificed. *T-30.VII.71.7:9*

~ salvation rests on **faith** there cannot be some forms of **guilt** which **you** cannot forgive. *T-30.VII.76.7*

~ how simple is salvation! All it says is what was never true is not true **now** and never **will** be. *T-31.I.1.1:2*

~ it teaches but the very obvious. It merely goes from one apparent **lesson** to the next in easy steps which lead **you** gently from one to another with no strain at all. *T-31.I.2.3:4*

~ salvation can be seen as **nothing** more than the escape from concepts. It does not concern itself with content of the **mind**, but with the simple statement that it thinks. *T-31.V.56.3:4*

~ salvation is undoing. *T-31.VI.63.1*

~ salvation does not **ask** that **you** behold the **Spirit** and perceive the **body** not. It merely asks that this should be your **choice.** *T-31.VI.64.1:2*

~ it is your **world** salvation **will undo** and let **you see** another **world** your eyes could never find. *T-31.VI.64.4*

~ salvation does not **seek** to use a **means** as yet too alien to your thinking to be helpful nor to **make** the kinds of **change you** could not recognize. *T-31.VII.68.2*

~ for it must deal in contrasts, not in **truth**, which has no **opposite** and cannot **change.** *T-31.VII.68.4*

~ would **you** not rather look upon yourself as needed for salvation of the **world** instead of as salvation's **enemy**? *T-31.VII.73.6*

~ salvation requires that **you** recognize that every **thought you have** brings either **peace** or **war**, either **love** or **fear.** *W-pI.16.3.1*

~ salvation must be possible because it is the **Will of God.** *W-pI.19.2.5*

~ your salvation is crucial to the salvation of the **world.** *W-pI.39.3.6*

~ salvation is your happiest accomplishment. It is also the only one that has any **meaning** because it is the only one that has any use to **you** at all. *W-pI.44.8.2:3*

~ salvation is our only **need**. There is no other **purpose here** and no other **function** to fulfill. **Learning** salvation is our only **goal**. *W-pI.69.3.2:4*

~ **guilt** and salvation must be in the same place. Understanding this **you** are saved. *W-pI.70.1.5:6*

~ your salvation comes from **you** and **nothing** but your own thoughts can hamper your progress. **You** are free from all external interference. **You** are in charge of your salvation. **You** are in charge of the salvation of the **world**. *W-pI.70.14.1:4*

~ salvation is for **you**. *W-pI.73.8.4*

~ look for it where it waits for **you**, and there it **will** be found. Look nowhere else, for it is nowhere else. *W-pI.76.2.4:5*

~ how simple is salvation! It is merely a statement of your true **Identity**. *W-pI.77.1.4:5*

~ it is not found **outside** and then brought in. But from **within** me it **will** reach beyond, and everything **I see will** but reflect the **light** that shines in me and in itself. *W-pI.85.5.5:6*

~ salvation is a **decision** made already. *W-pI.88.2.2*

~ salvation requires the **acceptance** of but one **thought**—you are as **God** created **you**, not what **you** made of yourself. *W-pI.93.7.1*

~ salvation cannot **make** illusions real and solve a **problem** that does not **exist**. *W-pI.96.7.6*

~ the **Holy Spirit** holds salvation in your **mind** and offers it the **way** to **peace**. Salvation is a **thought you share** with God, because His **Voice** accepted it for **you** and answered in your **name** that it was done. Thus is salvation kept among the thoughts your **Self** holds dear and cherishes for **you**. *W-pI.96.8.2:4*

~ salvation is a **miracle**, the first and last; the **first** that is the last, for it is one. *W-pI.97.3.4*

~ salvation and **forgiveness** are the same. **They** both imply that something has gone wrong—something **you need** to be saved from or forgiven for, something amiss that needs corrective **change**, something apart or different from the **Will** of God. Thus do both terms imply the **thought** of the **impossible** which has occurred, resulting in a state of conflict **now** between what is and what could never be. *W-pI.99.1.1:3*

~ salvation is the **borderland** between the **truth** and **illusion**. It reflects the **truth** because it is the **means** by which **you** can escape illusions. Yet it is not **truth** because it undoes what was never done. *W-pI.99.2.3:5*

~ salvation must reverse the mad **belief** in separate thoughts and separate bodies which lead separate lives and go their separate ways. *W-pI.100.1.2*

~ thus does salvation start and thus it ends; when everything is yours, and everything is given away, it **will** remain with **you** forever. And the **lesson** has been learned. *W-pI.106.7.3:4*

~ it is the **gift** of God and not the **world**. *W-pI.122.7.4*

~ yet is salvation easily achieved, for anyone is **free** to **change** his **mind**, and all his thoughts **change** with it. *W-pI.132.2.1*

~ and **we will** feel salvation cover us with soft protection and with **peace** so deep that no **illusion** can disturb our minds nor offer proof to us that it is real. *W-pI.140.14.1*

~ salvation is the recognition that the **truth** is true and **nothing** else is true. *W-pI.152.3.1*

~ salvation can be **thought** of as a game that **happy** children play. It was designed by One Who loves His children, and Who would replace their fearful toys with joyous games which **teach** them that the game of **fear** is gone. His game instructs in happiness because there is no loser. **Everyone** who plays must win, and in his winning is the **gain** to **everyone** ensured. The game of **fear** is gladly laid aside when children come to **see** the benefits salvation brings. *W-pI.153.12.1:5*

~ it asks that **you** accept the **truth**, and let it go before **you**, lighting up the path of ransom from **illusion**. It is not a ransom with a price. *W-pI.155.8.2:3*

~ this is the **way** salvation works. As **you step** back, the **Light** in **you** steps forward and encompasses the **world**. *W-pI.156.6.1:2*

~ **forgiveness** is the central theme which runs throughout salvation, holding all its parts in meaningful relationships, the **course** it runs directed, and its outcome sure. *W-pI.169.10.6*

~ if **God's Voice** assures **you** that salvation needs your **part** and that the whole depends on **you**, be sure that it is so. *W-pI.186.5.4*

~ salvation of the **world** depends on **you** and not upon this **little** pile of dust. *W-pI.186.7.4*

~ if **you** are to save the **world, you** first accept salvation for yourself. *W-pI.187.3.2*

~ it is not **time we need** for this. It is but willingness. *W-pI.196.4.3:4*

~ salvation waits until I take this **part** as what I choose to do. *W-pII.317.1.2*

~ salvation is already **here**, already given all my brothers and already mine as well. *W-pII.317.1.4*

~ salvation's **purpose** is to find the sinlessness which **God** has placed in me. *W-pII.318.1.6*

~ this is salvation's keynote: What **I see** reflects a process in my **mind** which starts with my **idea** of what **I want**. From there, the **mind** makes up an **image** of the **thing** the **mind** desires, judges valuable, and therefore seeks to find. These images are then projected outward, looked upon, esteemed as real, and guarded as one's own. From insane wishes comes an insane **world**. From **judgment** comes a **world** condemned. And from forgiving thoughts a gentle **world** comes forth, with mercy for the holy **Son of God**, to offer him a kindly **home** where **he** can **rest** a while before **he** journeys on and **help** his brothers walk ahead with him and find the **way** to **Heaven** and to **God**. *W-pII.325.1.1:6*

~ salvation has no cost. It is a **gift** that must be freely given and received, and it is this that **we** would learn **today**. *W-pII.343.2.2:3*

~ salvation is a **promise** made by **God** that **you** would find your **way** to Him at last. It cannot but be kept. It guarantees that **time will have** an end, and all the thoughts that **have** been born in **time will** end as well. *W-pII.ST231.1.1:3*

~ salvation is undoing in the **sense** that it does **nothing**, failing to support the **world** of dreams and malice. Thus it lets illusions go. By not supporting them, it merely lets them quietly go down to dust. And what **they** hid is **now** revealed— an **altar** to the holy **name** of God whereon His **word** is written, with the gifts of your **forgiveness** laid before it and the **memory of God** not far behind. *W-pII.ST231.3.1:4*

~ salvation is not theoretical. Behold the **problem, ask** for the **answer**, and then accept it when it comes. Nor **will** its coming be long delayed. All the **help you** can accept **will** be provided. *M-26.4.5:8*

~ there are no accidents in salvation. *M-3.1.6*

~ salvation is always ready and always there. *M-3.3.6*

~ it is only in relationships that salvation can be found. *P-2.IN.4.3*

374

SAMENESS

|ˈsāmnəs|

DICTIONARY: *lack of variety; uniformity or monotony.*

EGO; *different*

HOLY SPIRIT

~ **you** can equalize in one **way** only. Equality is not a variable state, by definition. *T-7.IV.23.7:8*

~ and **now** the sameness which **you** saw extends and finally removes all **sense** of differences so that the sameness that lies beneath them all becomes apparent. *T-22.I.4.8*

~ and thus what is the same is seen as one, while what is not the same remains unnoticed, for it is not there. *W-pI.108.2.3*

SANITY

|ˈsanədē|

DICTIONARY: *the ability to think and behave in a normal and rational manner; sound **mental health**.*

EGO; *threat*

HOLY SPIRIT; *wholeness, safety.*

~ sanity is **wholeness**, and the sanity of your brothers is yours. *T-5.IX.91.8*

~ the sane know that only **attack** could produce **fear** from which the **love** of **God** completely protects them. *T-10.VI.52.5*

~ inward is sanity; **insanity** is **outside you.** *T-18.II.7.3*

~ only the sane can look on stark **insanity** and raving **madness** with pity and compassion but not with **fear.** *T-19.V.100.2*

~ sanity in which **we understand** that **anger** is insane, **attack** is mad, and **vengeance** merely foolish **fantasy.** *W-pII.S7.361.5.3*

SAVIOR

|ˈsāvyər|

DICTIONARY: *a person who saves someone or something (especially a country or **cause**) from danger, and who is regarded with the veneration of a religious figure.*

EGO

~ **judgment will** seem to **make** your savior weak. *T-20.IX.71.5*

~ men **despair** because the savior's **vision** is withheld, and what **they see** is **death.** Their savior stands, **unknowing** and unknown, beholding them with eyes unopened. *T-31.VII.82.2:3*

HOLY SPIRIT; *brother, friend, Son of God, enemy.*

~ **you will receive** of him according to your **choice.** He has in him the **power** to forgive your sins, as **you** for him. Neither can **give** it to himself **alone.** And yet your savior stands beside each one. *T-19.V.102.4:7*

~ **here** is your savior and your friend, released from **crucifixion** through your **vision** and free to lead **you now** where **he** would be. *T-20.III.15.1*

~ your savior gives **you** only **love**, but what **you** would **receive** of him is up to **you.** It lies in him to overlook all your mistakes, and therein lies his own **salvation.** *T-20.V.29.6:7*

~ to each who walks this earth in seeming solitude is a savior given, whose **special function here** is to **release** him and so to free himself. In the **world** of **separation**, each is appointed separately, though **they** are all the same. Yet those who know that **they** are all the same **need** not **salvation**. And each one finds his savior when **he** is ready to look upon the **face of Christ** and see Him **sinless**. *T-20.V.32.3:6*

~ **you** are your brother's savior. **He** is yours. *T-21.VII.67.1:2*

~ a savior cannot be a judge. *T-22.III.23.3*

~ it is **impossible** to look upon your savior as your **enemy** and recognize him. Yet it is possible to recognize him for what **he** is if **God** would **have** it so. *T-22.III.26.3:4*

~ those who would let illusions be lifted from their minds are this world's saviors, walking the **world** with their Redeemer and carrying His **message** of hope and **freedom** and **release** from **suffering** to **everyone** who needs a **miracle** to save him. *T-22.V.43.5*

~ **you will see** your **value** through each other's eyes, and each one is released as **he** beholds his savior in place of the attacker who **he thought** was there. Through this releasing is the **world** released. *T-22.VII.58.1:2*

~ your savior offers **you salvation**. Condemned by **you**, **he** offers **death** to you. *T-25.VI.40.5:6*

~ your savior waits for **healing**, and the **world** waits with him. *T-28.VIII.61.3*

~ and **he** must save who would be saved. On saving **you** depends his happiness. *T-29.IV.20.4:5*

~ **he** must be savior from the **dream he** made, that **he** be free of it. *T-29.IV.21.6*

~ so perfectly can **you** forgive him his illusions, **he** becomes your savior from your dreams. *T-29.IV.22.4*

~ **see** how eagerly **he** comes and steps aside from heavy shadows that **have** hidden him and shines on **you** in **gratitude** and **love**. *T-29.IV.24.2*

~ the holy ones whom **God** has given each of **you** to save are **everyone you** meet or look upon, not knowing who **they** are, all those **you** saw an instant and forgot, and those **you** knew a long while since, and those **you will** yet meet, the unremembered and the not yet born. For **God** has given **you** His Son to save from every **concept** that **he** ever held. *T-31.VII.77.5:6*

~ this is the savior's **vision**—that **he** see his **innocence** in all **he** looks upon and sees his own **salvation** everywhere. **He** holds no **concept** of himself between his **calm** and open eyes and what **he** sees. **He** brings the **light** to what **he** looks upon, that **he** may **see** it as it really is. *T-31.VII.78.5:7*

~ the savior's **vision** is as **innocent** of what your **brother** is as it is free of any **judgment** made upon yourself. It sees no **past** in anyone at all. And thus it serves a wholly open **mind**, unclouded by old concepts and prepared to look on only what the **present** holds. It cannot judge because it does not know. *T-31.VII.80.1:4*

~ the saviors of the **world** who **see** like Him are merely those who chose His **strength** instead of their own **weakness**, seen apart from Him. **They will** redeem the **world**, for **they** are joined in all the **power** of the **Will of God**. And what **they will** is only what **He** wills. *T-31.VIII.88.4:6*

~ a savior must be saved. *W-pI.39.3.4*

~ and **everyone** who finds the **way** to God becomes my savior, pointing out the **way** to me and giving me his **certainty** that what **he** learned is surely mine as well. *W-pII.315.1.5*

~ a gentle Savior, born where **sin** was made and **guilt** seemed real. *M-14.2.4*

~ **he** brings the ending of the **world** with Him. It is His **Call** God's teachers **answer**, turning to Him in silence to **receive** His word. *M-14.2.6:7*

SCIENCE

DICTIONARY: *the intellectual and practical activity encompassing the systematic **study** of the structure and **behavior** of the physical and natural **world** through observation and experiment.*

HOLY SPIRIT

~ the real aim of science is neither prediction nor control but only understanding. This is because it does not establish the **laws** it seeks, cannot discover them through prediction, and has no control over them at all. Science is **nothing** more than an approach to what already is. *T-7.V.32.3:5*

SCRIPT

DICTIONARY: *the written **text** of a play, movie, or broadcast.*

EGO

~ **you** add an element into the script **you** write for every minute in the day, and all that happens **now means** something else. **You** take away another element, and every **meaning** shifts accordingly. *T-30.VIII.82.7:8*

~ what do your scripts reflect except your plans for what the day should be? And thus **you** judge **disaster** and success, **advance**, retreat, and **gain** and **loss**. These **judgments** all are made according to the roles the script assigns. The **fact they have** no **meaning** in themselves is demonstrated by the ease with which these labels **change** with other **judgments** made on different aspects of **experience**. And then in looking back **you** think **you see** another **meaning** in what went before. *T-30.VIII.83.1:5*

~ **you** wrote a fearful script and are afraid accordingly. *T-30.VIII.84.9*

~ a distorted script which cannot be interpreted with **meaning**. It must be forever unintelligible. *T-30.VIII.87.12:13*

~ your dark dreams are but the senseless, isolated scripts **you** write in **sleep**. *T-30.VIII.87.15*

HOLY SPIRIT

~ yet there is a **plan** behind appearances which does not **change**. The script is written. When **experience will** come to end your doubting has been set. *W-pI.158.4.2:4*

SECOND COMING

DICTIONARY: *the prophesied return of **Christ** to earth at the **Last Judgment**.*

HOLY SPIRIT; *return of **sense**, **awareness** of **reality**.*

~ the second coming of **Christ means nothing** more than the end of the ego's **rule** over **part** of the minds of men and the **healing** of the **mind**. *T-4.V.66.2*

~ this is the Second Coming, which was made for **you** as the First was created. The Second Coming is merely the return of **sense**. *T-9.III.17.5:6*

~ the Second Coming is the **awareness** of **reality**, not its return. *T-9.III.19.5*

~ christ's Second Coming, which is sure as **God**, is merely the **correction** of mistakes and the return of **sanity**. It is a **part** of the **condition** which restores the never-lost and re-establishes what is forever and forever true. It is the invitation to **God's word** to take illusion's place, the willingness to let **forgiveness rest** upon all things without **exception** and without reserve. *W-pII.ST301.1.1:3*

~ it is the all-inclusive nature of Christ's Second Coming that permits it to embrace the **world** and hold **you** safe **within** its gentle advent, which encompasses all living things with **you**. There is no end to the **release** the Second Coming brings, as God's **creation** must be limitless. **Forgiveness** lights the Second Coming's **way** because it shines on **everyone** as one. And thus is **oneness** recognized at last. *W-pII.ST301.2.1:4*

~ the Second Coming ends the lessons which the **Holy Spirit** teaches, making **way** for the Last **Judgment**, in which **learning** ends in one last summary that **will** extend beyond itself and reaches up to **God**. The Second Coming is the **time** in which all minds are given to the hands of **Christ**, to be returned to **Spirit** in the **name** of true **creation** and the **Will** of **God**. *W-pII.ST301.3.1:2*

~ the Second Coming is the one event in **time** which **time** itself cannot affect. For **everyone** who ever came to die or yet **will** come or who is **present now** is equally released from what **he** made. In this equality is **Christ** restored as one **Identity**, in which all Sons of **God** acknowledge that **they** all are one. And **God** the **Father** smiles upon His Son, His one **creation** and His only **joy**. *W-pII.ST301.4.1:4*

~ it needs your eyes and ears and hands and feet. It needs your **voice**. *W-pII.ST301.5.2:3*

~ it needs your willingness. *W-pII.ST301.5.4*

~ christ's Second Coming gives the **Son of God** the **gift** to hear the **Voice** for **God** proclaim that what is false is false and what is true has never changed. And this the **judgment** is in which **perception** ends. At first **you see** a **world** which has accepted this as true, projected from a **now** corrected **mind**. And with this holy **sight**, **perception** gives a silent **blessing** and then disappears, its **goal** accomplished and its **mission** done. *W-pII.ST311.1.1:4*

SECRET |ˈsēkrit|

DICTIONARY: *not known or seen or not meant to be known or seen by others.*

EGO

~ yet **you** believe that **you have** secrets. What could your secrets be except another **will** that is your own, apart from His. *T-22.II.8.2:3*

HOLY SPIRIT

~ your "guilty secret" is **nothing**, and if **you will** but bring it to the **light**, the **light will** dispel it. *T-12.II.9.2*

~ **nothing** lives in secret, and what **you** would hide from the **Holy Spirit** is **nothing**. *T-14.VI.56.3*

~ **god** has no secrets. **He** does not lead **you** through a **world** of **misery**, waiting to tell **you** at the journey's end why **He** did this to **you**. *T-22.II.7.9:10*

~ it **will** be no secret **you** are healed. *T-27.IX.90.6*

SEE |sē|

DICTIONARY: *perceive with the eyes; discern visually.*

EGO;   *illusion, mistake, error in perception, distorted fragment of the whole.*

~ **you** made your **way** of seeing that **you** might see in **darkness**, and in this **you** are deceived. *T-12.V.42.1*

~ everything **you** recognize **you** identify with externals, something **outside** itself. **You** cannot even think of **God** without a **body** or some **form you** think **you** recognize. *T-18.IX.71.6:7*

~ **you** are seeing what can not be real as if it were. *T-22.IV.35.5*

~ the **way you** see, and long **have** seen, gives no support to base your **future** hopes and no suggestions of success at all. *T-25.III.13.4*

~ no one really sees anything. **He** sees only his thoughts projected outward. *W-pI.8.1.2:3*

~ it is not seeing. It is **image**-making. It takes the place of seeing, replacing **vision** with illusions. *W-pI.15.1.5:7*

~ **you** see a lot of separate things about **you**, which really **means you** are not seeing at all. *W-pI.28.2.5*

~ what **I** see is the **projection** of my own errors of **thought**. **I** do not **understand** what **I** see because it is not understandable. There is no **sense** in trying to **understand** it. *W-pI.51.4.2:4*

~ what **I** see **now** are but signs of disease, **disaster**, and **death**. This cannot be what **God** created for His beloved Son. *W-pI.55.2.1:2*

~ what **I** see tells me that **I** do not know who **I** am. *W-pI.55.2.5*

~ your **idea** of what seeing **means** is tied up with the **body** and its eyes and **brain**. This is why **you** believe that **you** can **change** what **you** see by putting **little** bits of glass or other clear material before your eyes held in a frame or placed against the **eye**. *W-pI.92.1.3:4*

~ **fear** has made everything **you** think **you** see. *W-pI.130.4.1*

HOLY SPIRIT; *choice, yourself, result.*

~ it is **impossible** not to believe what **you** see, but it is equally **impossible** to see what **you** do not believe. Perceptions are built up on the basis of **experience**, and **experience** leads to beliefs. It is not until beliefs are fixed that perceptions stabilize. In effect, then, what **you** believe, **you** do see. *T-10.VII.59.1:4*

~ all that **you** see but witnesses to your **decision**. *T-11.VIII.72.9*

~ what can be seen is what the **Holy Spirit** sees. *T-11.IX.79.5*

~ what the seeing look upon is **sinless**. *T-20.VIII.66.6*

~ your **sight** is related to His **holiness**, not to your **ego** and therefore not to your **body**. *W-pI.36.1.8*

~ in **order** to see, **you** must recognize that **light** is **within**, not without. **You** do not see **outside** yourself, nor is the equipment for seeing **outside you**. An essential **part** of this equipment is the **light** that makes seeing possible. It is with **you** always, making **vision** possible in every circumstance. *W-pI.44.2.1:4*

~ **i** can see what **God** wants me to see. **I** cannot see anything else. *W-pI.59.4.1:2*

~ rejoice in the **power** of **forgiveness** to heal your **sight** completely. *W-pI.75.11.4*

~ so is the seeing of the **world** reversed, as **we** look out toward **truth**, away from **fear**. *W-pI.78.4.3*

~ everything **we** see reflects the **holiness within** the **mind** at one with **God** and with itself. *W-pI.124.2.2*

~ though it is **perception**, it is not the kind of seeing that your eyes **alone have** ever seen before. *W-pI.130.10.5*

~ all that **we** see **will** but increase our **joy** because its **holiness** reflects our own. *W-pI.164.7.4*

SEEK   · |sēk|

DICTIONARY: *attempt to find (something).*

EGO

~ the **ego** finds what it seeks and only that. It does not find **love**, for that is not what it is seeking. *T-11.VIII.66.4:5*

~ **you** would seek for hope where none is ever found. *T-25.III.13.6*

~ seek not **outside** yourself. For it **will fail**. *T-29.VIII.43.1:2*

~ the search for different pathways in the **world** is but the search for different forms of **truth**. And this would keep the **truth** from **being** reached. *T-31.IV.38.4:5*

~ pursuit of the imagined leads to **death** because it is the search for nothingness, and while **you** seek for **life you** ask for **death**. *W-pl.131.3.1*

~ god's Son cannot seek vainly, though **he** try to force **delay**, deceive himself, and think that it is **hell he** seeks. *W-pl.131.5.4*

~ **now** has the **mind** condemned itself to seek without finding, to be forever dissatisfied and discontented, to know not what it really wants to find. *M-13.3.3*

~ **he** does not **see** what **he** is asking for. And so **he** seeks it in a thousand ways and in a thousand places, each **time** believing it is there and each **time** disappointed in the end. "Seek but do not find," remains this world's stern decree, and no one who pursues the world's goals can do otherwise. *M-13.5.7:9*

HOLY SPIRIT

~ meaningful seeking is consciously undertaken, consciously organized, and consciously directed. *T-4.VI.73.2*

~ yet seeking and finding are the same, and if **you** seek for two goals **you will** find them, but **you will** recognize neither. *T-11.VIII.66.6*

~ **everyone** seeks for **love** as **you** do and knows it not unless **he** joins with **you** in seeking it. *T-14.VI.55.5*

~ it is not necessary to seek for what is true, but it is necessary to seek for what is false. *T-16.V.35.2*

~ it is not **form you** seek. *T-30.IV.39.1*

SELF |self|

DICTIONARY: *a person's essential **being** that distinguishes them from others, especially considered as the object of introspection or reflexive action.*

EGO;   *little self, tiny self.*

~ this "self" seeks the **relationship** to **make** itself complete. Yet when it finds the **special relationship** in which it thinks it can accomplish this, it gives itself away and tries to "trade" itself for the self of another. This is not **union**, for there is no increase and no **extension**. Each partner tries to **sacrifice** the self **he** does not **want** for one **he** thinks **he** would prefer. And **he** feels guilty for the "**sin**" of taking and of **giving nothing** of **value** in return. For how much **value** can **he** place upon a self that **he** would **give** away to get a better one? *T-16.VI.49.2:7*

~ from an **idea** of self as two, there comes a necessary view of **function** split between the two. *T-27.III.25.2*

~ the building of a **concept** of the self is what the **learning** of the **world** is for. This is its **purpose**— that **you** come without a self and **make** one as **you** go along. And by the **time you** reach "maturity," **you have** perfected it to meet the **world** on equal terms, at one with its demands. *T-31.V.43.5:7*

~ a **concept** of the self is made by **you**. It bears no likeness to yourself at all. It is an **idol**, made to take the place of your **reality** as Son of God. The **concept** of the self the **world** would **teach** is not the **thing** that it appears to be. For it is made to serve two purposes, but one of which the **mind** can recognize. The first presents the face of **innocence**, the aspect acted on. It is this face that smiles and charms and even seems to **love**. It searches for companions, and it looks at times with pity on the **suffering** and sometimes offers solace. It believes that it is **good within** an **evil world**. *T-31.V.44.1:9*

~ this aspect can grow angry, for the **world** is wicked and unable to provide the **love** and shelter **innocence** deserves. *T-31.V.45.1*

~ the face of **innocence** the **concept** of the self so proudly wears can tolerate **attack** in self-**defense**, for is it not a well-known **fact** the **world** deals harshly with defenseless **innocence**? No one who makes a **picture** of himself omits this face, for **he** has **need** of it. The other side **he** does not **want** to **see**. *T-31.V.46.1:3*

~ beneath the face of **innocence** there is a **lesson** that the **concept** of the self was made to **teach**. It is a **lesson** in a terrible displacement and a **fear** so devastating that the face which smiles above it must forever look away, lest it perceive the treachery it hides. The **lesson** teaches this: "I am the **thing you** made of me, and as **you** look on me, **you** stand condemned because of what **I** am." On this conception of the self the **world** smiles with approval, for it guarantees the pathways of the **world** are safely kept and those who walk on them **will** not escape. *T-31.V.47.1:4*

~ this **concept** of the self must be undone if any **peace** of **mind** is to be given **you**. Nor can it be unlearned except by lessons aimed to **teach** that **you** are something else. *T-31.V.50.3:4*

~ your **concept** of the **world** depends upon this **concept** of the self. And both would go if either one were ever raised to **doubt**. *T-31.V.53.3:4*

~ vaguely does the **concept** of the self appear to **answer** what it does not know. *T-31.V.56.7*

~ the self **you** made is not the **Son of God**. Therefore, this self does not **exist** at all. And anything it seems to do and think **means nothing**. It is neither bad nor **good**. It is unreal and **nothing** more than that. It does not **battle** with the **Son of God**. It does not **hurt** him nor **attack** his **peace**. It has not changed **creation** nor reduced eternal sinlessness to **sin** and **love** to **hate**. *W-pI.93.5.1:8*

~ the self **you** made, **evil** and full of **sin**, is meaningless. *W-pI.93.6.6*

~ although **you** are One Self, **you experience** yourself as two—as both **good** and **evil**, loving and hating, **mind** and **body**. This **sense** of **being** split into opposites induces feelings of acute and constant conflict and leads to frantic attempts to reconcile the contradictory aspects of this self-**perception**. **You have** sought many such solutions, and none of them has worked. The opposites **you see** in **you will** never be compatible. *W-pI.96.1.1:4*

~ this is your chosen self, the one **you** made as a replacement for **reality**. *W-pI.166.7.1*

~ the self **he** sees is his **God**, and **he** seeks only to serve it better. *P-2.IN.3.6*

~ this "**self**," which can **attack** and be attacked as well, is a **concept he** made up. Further, **he** cherishes it, defends it, and is sometimes even willing to "**sacrifice**" his "**life**" on its behalf. For **he** regards it as himself. This self **he** sees as **being** acted on, reacting to external forces as **they** demand, and helpless midst the **power** of the **world**. *P-1.1.3.3:6*

HOLY SPIRIT;   *ruler of the **universe**, One, Self.*

~ the inner self knows itself as both a **brother** and a Son. *T-2.II.43.2*

~ your self-fullness is as boundless as God's. Like His, it extends forever and in perfect **peace**. Its radiance is so intense that it creates in perfect **joy**, and only the whole can be born of its **wholeness**. *T-7.IX.96.6:8*

~ your Self continues, unmindful that this tiny **part** regards itself as **you**. It is not missing; it could not **exist** if it were separate, nor would the whole be whole without it. It is not a separate **kingdom**, ruled by an **idea** of **separation** from the rest. Nor does a fence surround it, preventing it from joining with the **rest** and keeping it apart from its **Creator**. This **little** aspect is no different from the whole, **being** continuous with it and at one with it. It leads no separate **life** because its **life** is the **oneness** in which its **being** was created. *T-18.IX.76.1:6*

~ there is another **vision** and another **Voice** in which your **freedom** lies awaiting but your **choice**. And if **you** place your **faith** in them, **you will** perceive another Self in **you**. This other Self sees miracles as natural. **They** are as simple and natural to It as breathing to the **body**. **They** are the obvious response to calls for **help**, the only one It makes. *T-21.VI.51.1:5*

~ if **Love** created **you** like Itself, this Self must be in **you**. And somewhere in your **mind**, It is there for **you** to find. *W-pI.67.5.2:3*

~ this is the Self that never sinned nor made an **image** to replace **reality**. This is the Self which never left its **home** in **God** to walk the **world** uncertainly. This is the Self which knows no **fear** nor could conceive of **loss** or **suffering** or **death**. *W-pI.94.5.2:4*

~ this is your Self, the **Son of God** Himself, **sinless** as its **Creator**, with His **strength within you** and His **love** forever yours. **You** are One Self, and it is given **you** to feel this Self **within you** and to cast all your illusions out of the One **Mind** which is this Self, the holy **truth in you**. *W-pI.95.18.2:3*

~ your own **acknowledgment you** are One Self, united with your **Father**, is a **call** to all the **world** to be at one with **you**. *W-pI.95.20.3*

~ your One Self, which is united with its **Creator**. *W-pI.95.3.2*

~ your Self knows that **you** cannot **fail today**. *W-pI.96.16.1*

~ two selves in **conflict** could not be resolved, and **good** and **evil have** no meeting place. The self **you** made can never be your Self, nor can your Self be split in two and still be what it is and must forever be. *W-pI.96.3.2:3*

~ **know** your Self as **Love** Which has no **opposite** in **you**. *W-pI.99.14.1*

~ **you** do not **want** to be another self. *W-pI.99.15.3*

~ **seek** not **within** the **world** to find your Self. *W-pI.127.5.4*

~ so is its Self the one **reality** in which its **will** and that of **God** are joined. *W-pI.154.4.4*

~ your Self is radiant in this holy **joy**, unchanged, unchanging, and unchangeable forever and forever. *W-pI.190.6.5*

~ the stillness of your Self remains unmoved, untouched by thoughts like these, and unaware of any **condemnation** which could **need forgiveness**. *W-pI.198.8.4*

~ this Self **alone** knows **love**. This Self **alone** is perfectly consistent in Its thoughts, knows Its **Creator**, understands Itself, is perfect in Its **knowledge** and Its **love**, and never changes from Its constant state of **union** with its **Father** and Itself. *W-pI.Rev V.6.1:2*

~ the Self from Which **I call** to **you** is but your own. *W-pI.Rev V.11.4*

~ it is not given me to **change** my Self. *W-pII.230.1.3*

~ my Self is holy beyond all the thoughts of **holiness** of which **I now** conceive. Its shimmering and perfect purity is far more brilliant than is any **light** that **I have** ever looked upon. Its **love** is limitless, with an intensity that holds all things **within** it in the **calm** of **quiet certainty**. Its **strength** comes not from burning impulses which move the **world** but from the boundless **Love of God** Himself. *W-pII.252.1.1:4*

~ self which is God's only Son, the likeness of Himself, the Holy One who still abides in Him forever, as **He** still abides in me. *W-pII.322.1.4*

~ the Self which **God** created cannot **sin** and therefore cannot suffer. *W-pII.330.1.6*

SELF-CONCEPT

DICTIONARY: *an **idea** of the **self** constructed from the beliefs one holds about oneself and the responses of others.*

EGO; *pseudo-**creation**, shield, silent barricade.*

HOLY SPIRIT

~ if **you** are physical, your **mind** is gone from your self-concept, for it has no place in which it could be really **part** of you. *W-pI.96.4.3*

~ to recognize God's Son implies as well that all **self**-concepts **have** been laid aside and recognized as false. *W-pI.152.11.1*

SELF-ESTEEM

|ˌself əˈstēm|

DICTIONARY: *confidence in one's own* **worth** *or* **abilities**; **self***-respect: assertiveness training for those with low* **self***-esteem.*

EGO; *delusion*

~ "**self** esteem" is always vulnerable to stress, a term which actually refers to a **condition** in which the **delusion** of the ego's **reality** is threatened. This produces either **ego** deflation or **ego** inflation, resulting in either withdrawal or **attack.** *T-4.III.31.5:6*

SENSE

|sens|

DICTIONARY: *a faculty by which the* **body** *perceives an external stimulus; one of the faculties of* **sight***, smell, hearing, taste, and touch.*

EGO; *not to know*

~ the **body** cannot know. And while **you limit** your **awareness** to its tiny senses, **you will** not **see** the **grandeur** which surrounds you. *T-18.IX.72.1:2*

~ eyes and ears are senses without sense, and what **they see** and hear **they** but report. *T-28.VI.51.6*

~ your senses do deceive. *W-pI.151.2:3*

HOLY SPIRIT

~ the ear translates; it does not hear. The **eye** reproduces; it does not **see**. Their task is to **make** agreeable whatever is called on, however disagreeable it may be. **They answer** the decisions of the **mind**, reproducing its desires and translating them into acceptable and pleasant forms. *P-2.VI.3.1:4*

SENTINEL

|ˈsent(ə)nəl|

DICTIONARY: *a soldier or guard whose job is to stand and keep watch.*

EGO; *sentinels of* **darkness**

HOLY SPIRIT

~ in the **light they** are not fearful and cannot serve to guard the dark doors behind which **nothing** at all is carefully concealed. *T-14.III.23.4*

SEPARATION

|ˌsepəˈrāSH(ə)n|

DICTIONARY: *the division of something into constituent or distinct elements.*

EGO; *denial of* **union, salvation, problem, devil.**

~ the separation is the notion of rejection. *T-6.II.24.7*

~ any split in **will** must involve a rejection of **part** of it, and this is the **belief** in separation. *T-6.III.25.1*

~ separation was and is **dissociation** and also that, once it had occurred, **projection** became its main **defense** or the device that keeps it going. *T-6.III.25.4*

~ the separation was not a **loss** of **perfection** but a failure in **communication**. *T-6.V.56.5*

~ **you have** interpreted the separation as a **means** which **you have** made for breaking your **communication** with your **Father**. *T-14.III.20.1*

~ separation therefore remains the ego's chosen **condition**. *T-14.VI.54.4*

~ separation is the **source** of **guilt**. *T-15.VI.46.5*

~ the **ego** would never **have you see** that separation can only be **loss, being** the one **condition** in which **Heaven** cannot be. *T-16.VI.46.4*

~ separation is only the **decision** not to know yourself. Its whole **thought system** is a carefully contrived **learning experience** designed to lead away from **truth** and into **fantasy**. *T-16.VI.57.3:4*

~ what is the separation but a **wish** to take God's **function** from Him and deny that it is His? *T-27.III.22.8*

~ the separation started with the **dream** the **Father** was deprived of His effects and powerless to keep them since **He** was no longer their **Creator**. In the **dream**, the dreamer made himself, but what **he** made has turned against him, taking on the **role** of its **creator** as the dreamer had. And as **he** hated his **Creator**, so the figures in the **dream have** hated him. *T-28.III.23.1:3*

~ **sense** of loneliness and abandonment which all **the separated ones experience**. Depression is an inevitable consequence of separation. So are anxiety, worry, a deep **sense** of helplessness, **misery, suffering**, and intense **fear** of **loss**. **The separated ones have** invented many "cures" for what **they** believe to be the "ills of the **world**." But the one **thing they** do not do is to **question** the **reality** of the **problem**. Yet its effects cannot be cured because the **problem** is not real. *W-pI.41.1.1:6*

~ thus do **you** think that **you have** given **life** in separation. By this split **you** think **you** are established as a **unity** which functions with an independent **will**. *W-pI.184.2.3:4*

HOLY SPIRIT; *split **mind**, **illusion** of **despair**, exclusion, an **order** of **reality**, system of **thought**, notion of rejection, faulty formulation, **source** of **guilt**, decision, separation **delusion**, empty space, **dissociation**.*

~ the separation is not symbolic. It is an **order** of **reality** or a system of **thought** that is real enough in **time**, though not in **eternity**. *T-3.IX.74.4:5*

~ the separation is merely another term for a split **mind**. It was not an act, but a **thought**. Therefore, the **idea** of separation can be given away, just as the **idea** of **unity** can. Either **way**, the **idea will** be strengthened in the **mind** of the giver. *T-5.V.40.6:9*

~ **healing** is the **way** in which the separation is overcome. Separation is overcome by **union**. It cannot be overcome by separating. *T-8.V.30.8:10*

~ **communication** ends separation. **Attack** promotes it. *T-8.VII.56.1:2*

~ the separation was a descent from **magnitude** to littleness. *T-9.X.92.5*

~ the separation is only the **denial** of **union** and, correctly interpreted, attests to your eternal **knowledge** that **union** is true. *T-11.III.13.6*

~ what is one cannot be perceived as separate, and the **denial** of the separation is the reinstatement of **knowledge**. *T-11.VII.60.1*

~ the **acceptance** of **guilt** into the **Mind** of God's Son was the beginning of the separation, as the **acceptance** of the **Atonement** is its end. *T-11.X.86.1*

~ the separation is merely a faulty formulation of **reality** with no effect at all. *T-13.II.3.5*

~ the **Holy Spirit** reinterprets it as a **means** of reestablishing what has not been broken but has been made obscure. All things **you** made **have** use to Him for His most holy **purpose**. *T-14.III.20.2:3*

~ separation must be corrected where it was made. *T-17.IV.20.7*

- with each **step** in His undoing is the separation more and more undone and **union** brought closer. *T-17.IV.21.2*

- the separation has **nothing** in it, no **part**, no "**reason**," and no attribute that is not insane. And its "protection" is **part** of it, as insane as the whole. The **special relationship**, which is its chief **defense**, must therefore be insane. *T-17.V.31.6:8*

- the separation is undone by **change** of **purpose** in what once was specialness and **now** is **union**. *T-26.IV.24.1*

- the tiny instant **you** would keep and **make** eternal passed away in **Heaven** too soon for anything to notice it had come. *T-26.VI.34.1*

- separation is but empty space, enclosing **nothing**, **doing nothing**. *T-28.IV.32.2*

- even the mad **idea** of separation had to be shared before it could **form** the basis of the **world I see**. Yet that sharing was a sharing of **nothing**. *W-pI.54.4.2:3*

- there has been no separation of your **mind** from His, no split between your **mind** and other minds, and only **unity within** your own. *W-pI.110.4.2*

- as **we** deny our separation from our **Father**, it is healed along with us. *W-pI.124.7.5*

- the separation **sickness** would impose has never really happened. *W-pI.137.4.3*

- every **gap** is closed and separation healed. *W-pI.184.12.4*

SERENITY |səˈrenədē|

DICTIONARY: *the state of **being calm**, peaceful, and untroubled.*

EGO

- their brother's **sacrifice** and **pain** are seen to represent their own serenity. *T-27.III.21.2*

SERVICE |ˈsərvəs|

DICTIONARY: *the action of helping or **doing** work for someone.*

HOLY SPIRIT;   *miracle, maximal service.*

- the gentle service that **you give** the Holy Spirit is service to yourself. *T-22.VII.56.5*

SHADOW |ˈSHadō|

DICTIONARY: *a dark area or shape produced by a **body** coming between rays of **light** and a surface.*

EGO;   *ego's shadow, shadow of **guilt**, heavy shadows, shadows of the **past**, idle shadows, illusive shadow.*

HOLY SPIRIT

- all that is veiled in shadows must be raised to understanding to be judged again. *W-pI.138.9.3*

SHADOW FIGURE

EGO;   *enemies of reality*

~ the shadowy figures from the **past** are precisely what **you** must escape. For **they** are not real and **have** no hold over **you** unless **you** bring them with **you**. **They** carry the spots of **pain** in your minds, directing **you** to **attack** in the **present** in retaliation for a **past** that is no more. And this **decision** is one of **future pain.** *T-12.IV.28.1:4*

~ the figures that **he** sees were never real, for **they** are made up only of his reactions to his brothers and do not include their reactions to him. Therefore **he** does not **see** that **he** made them and that **they** are not whole. For these figures **have** no witnesses, **being** perceived in one separate **mind** only. *T-12.V.34.2:4*

~ it is through these strange and shadowy figures that the insane relate to their insane **world**. For **they see** only those who remind them of these images, and it is to them that **they** relate. Thus do **they** communicate with those who are not there, and it is **they** who **answer** them, and no one hears their **answer** save him who called upon them, and **he alone** believes **they** answered him. *T-12.V.35.1:3*

~ **again** and again **have** men attacked each other because **they** saw in them a **shadow** figure in their own private **world**. *T-12.V.35.5*

~ for the **shadow** figures **you** would **make** immortal are "enemies" of **reality**. *T-17.IV.14.4*

~ the **shadow** figures are the witnesses **you** bring with **you** to demonstrate **he** did what **he** did not. Because **you** brought them, **you will** hear them. And **you** who kept them by your own selection do not **understand** how **they** came into your minds and what their **purpose** is. *T-17.IV.14.6:8*

~ **they** represent the **evil** that **you** think was done to **you**. You bring them with **you** only that **you** may return **evil** for **evil**, hoping that their **witness will** enable **you** to think guiltily of another and not **harm** yourself. **They** speak so clearly for the **separation** that no one not obsessed with keeping **separation** could hear them. **They** offer **you** the "reasons" why **you** should enter into unholy alliances which support the ego's goals and **make** your relationships the **witness** to its **power**. It is these **shadow** figures which would **make** the **ego** holy in your **sight** and **teach you** what **you** do to keep it safe is really **love**. *T-17.IV.15.1:5*

~ the **shadow** figures always speak for **vengeance**, and all relationships into which **they** enter are totally insane. *T-17.IV.16.1*

HOLY SPIRIT;   *witnesses, **shadow** voices, **brother**.*

~ a **shadow** figure who attacks becomes a **brother giving you** a chance to **help** if this becomes the **function** of the **dream**. *T-29.V.29.6*

SHARE

DICTIONARY: *have a portion of (something) with another or others.*

EGO

~ **you have** set yourselves the task of sharing what cannot be shared. *T-13.VI.52.6*

HOLY SPIRIT;   *make alike, **make** one, God's **way** of creating and also yours, know.*

~ **nothing** that is real can be increased except by sharing. *T-4.VIII.99.2*

~ if **you** share a physical **possession**, **you** do divide its ownership. *T-5.II.6.2*

~ what **you** share **you** strengthen. *T-5.V.34.7*

~ sharing is knowing. *T-10.II.15.5*

- ~ you will share in **madness** or in **Heaven** together. *T-19.V.101.7*
- ~ whom **you** forgive is free, and what **you give you** share. *T-19.V.104.5*
- ~ nor can **you** use what **I have** given unless **you** share it. *T-20.III.10.4*
- ~ in Their sharing there can be no **gap** in which abundance falters and grows thin. *T-28.IV.36.6*
- ~ who shares a **dream** must be the **dream he** shares because by sharing is a **cause** produced. *T-28.V.41.5*
- ~ except **you** share it, **nothing** can **exist**. *T-28.VI.47.10*
- ~ it is the sharing of the **evil** dreams of **hate** and malice, bitterness and **death**, of sin and **suffering**, [of] **pain** and **loss**, that makes them real. Unshared, **they** are perceived as meaningless. The **fear** is gone from them because **you** did not **give** them your support. *T-28.VI.48.1:3*

SHIFT

|SHift|

DICTIONARY: *a slight **change** in position, direction, or tendency.*

EGO

- ~ **healing** of effect without the cause can merely shift effects to other forms. And this is not **release**. *T-26.VIII.61.2:3*
- ~ stability to those who are confused is meaningless, and shift and **change** become the law on which **they** predicate their lives. *T-29.III.15.6*

HOLY SPIRIT

- ~ **you will** not **remember change** and shift in **Heaven**. *T-13.V.40.1*
- ~ there is but one shift in **perception** that is necessary, for **you** made but one **mistake**. *T-15.X.95.1*
- ~ it is not **difficult** to [shift] a **dream** when once the dreamer has been recognized. *T-27.VIII.73.8*
- ~ there **will** be some **confusion** every **time** there is a shift, but be **you** thankful that the **learning** of the **world** is loosening its grasp upon your **mind**. *T-31.V.58.3*
- ~ all this shift requires is that **you** be willing that this **happy change** occur. *T-31.VII.72.3*
- ~ **you** can shift your **perception** of the **world** in both its outer and inner aspects. *W-pI.33.1.1*

SICKNESS

|'siknəs|

DICTIONARY: *a particular type of illness or disease.*

EGO;   *"little" death, witness to your frailty, idolatry.*

- ~ illness, which is really "not-right-mindedness," is the result of **level confusion** in the **sense** that it always entails the **belief** that what is amiss in one **level** can adversely affect another. *T-2.III.53.2*
- ~ all physical illness represents a **belief** in **magic**. *T-2.III.54.1*
- ~ illness is a **form** of **magic**. *T-5.VII.65.1*
- ~ the **ego** has a real investment in sickness. *T-8.VIII.72.2*
- ~ this is a particularly appealing argument from the ego's point of view because it obscures the obvious **attack** which underlies the sickness. *T-8.VIII.72.4*

~ sickness is a **way** of demonstrating that **you** can be **hurt**. It is a **witness** to your frailty, your **vulnerability**, and your extreme **need** to depend on external **guidance**. *T-8.VIII.76.1:2*

~ sickness is merely another example of your insistence on asking the **guidance** of a **teacher** who does not know the **answer**. *T-8.VIII.77.4*

~ all forms of sickness, even unto **death**, are physical expressions of the **fear** of awakening. They are attempts to reinforce unconsciousness out of **fear** of **consciousness**. *T-8.IX.82.2:3*

~ to believe that a **Son of God** can be sick is to believe that **part** of God can suffer. *T-9.IX.76.4*

~ to believe a **Son of God** is sick is to worship the same **idol he** does. *T-9.IX.77.5*

~ **you** made the **God of** sickness, and by making him, **you** made yourself able to hear him. Yet **you** did not create him, because **he** is not the **Will** of the **Father**. *T-9.IX.82.4:5*

~ sickness is **separation**. *T-10.III.16.1*

~ all sickness comes from **separation**. When the **separation** is denied, it goes. For it is gone as soon as the **idea** which brought it has been healed and been replaced by **sanity**. Sickness and **sin** are seen as consequence and **cause** in a **relationship** kept hidden from **awareness** that it may be carefully preserved from reason's **light**. *T-26.VIII.47.5:8*

~ sickness is the **witness** to his **guilt**, and **death** would prove his errors must be sins. *T-27.II.4.7*

~ sickness is but a "**little**" **death**; a **form** of **vengeance** not yet total. Yet it speaks with **certainty** for what it represents. *T-27.II.5.1:2*

~ the sick remain accusers. **They** cannot forgive their brothers and themselves as well. For no one in whom true **forgiveness** reigns can suffer. *T-27.III.15.4:6*

~ sickness is desired to prevent a **shift** of balance in the **sacrifice**. *T-27.III.21.6*

~ sickness comes from minds which separate. *T-28.IV.29.6*

~ the seeds of sickness come from the **belief** that there is **joy** in **separation**, and its giving up would be a **sacrifice**. *T-28.V.46.6*

~ a **sense** of limitation. *T-28.VI.47.1*

~ because it proves the **body** is not separate from **you**, and so **you** must be separate from the **truth**. **You** suffer **pain** because the **body** does, and in this **pain** are **you** made one with it. *W-pI.136.9.2:3*

~ sickness is a retreat from others and a shutting off of joining. It becomes a door that closes on a separate **self** and keeps it isolated and **alone**. *W-pI.137.1.3:4*

~ sickness is isolation. For it seems to keep one **self** apart from all the **rest** to suffer what the others do not feel. It gives the **body** final **power** to **make** the **separation** real and keep the **mind** in solitary **prison**, split apart and held in pieces by a solid wall of sickened flesh which it cannot surmount. *W-pI.137.2.1:3*

~ in sickness must **he** be apart and separate. *W-pI.137.3.2*

~ in sickness does his **Self** appear to be dismembered and without the **unity** that gives it **life**. *W-pI.137.3.4*

~ sickness would prove that lies must be the **truth**. *W-pI.137.4.1*

~ if **you** are sick, **you** but withhold their **healing**. *W-pI.166.14.3*

~ certainly sickness does not appear to be a **decision**. Nor would anyone actually believe **he** wants to be sick. *M-22.4.1:2*

~ a sick person perceives himself as separate from **God**. *M-22.6.5*

~ all who **ask** for illness **have now** condemned themselves to **seek** for remedies that cannot **help**, because their **faith** is in the illness and not in **salvation**. *P-2.IV.2.3*

~ it is a sign, a **shadow** of an **evil thought** that seems to **have reality** and to be just, according to the usage of the **world**. It is external proof of inner "sins," and witnesses to unforgiving thoughts that injure and would **hurt** the **Son of God**. *S-3.I.1.2:3*

HOLY SPIRIT; *mental illness,* **insanity,** *illness, isolation,* **illusion, sin,** *retreat, election,* **separation, decision,** *method, "not-right-mindedness",* **form** *of* **vengeance,** *demand,* **defense** *against the* **truth,** *shutting off, faulty* **problem**-*solving approach,* **form** *of* **magic.**

~ sickness comes from confusing the levels. *T-1.I.25.2*

~ sometimes the illness has a sufficiently great hold over a **mind** to render a person inaccessible to **Atonement**. In this case it may be wise to utilize a **compromise** approach to **mind** and **body**, in which something from the **outside** is temporarily given **healing belief**. *T-2.III.57.5:6*

~ a sick **body** does not **make** any **sense**. It could not **make sense**, because sickness is not what the **body** is for. Sickness is meaningful only if the two basic premises on which the ego's **interpretation** of the **body** rests are true. Specifically, these are that the **body** is for **attack** and that **you** are a **body**. Without these premises, sickness is completely inconceivable. *T-8.VIII.75.5:9*

~ sickness is not of the **body**, but of the **mind**. *T-8.IX.88.5*

~ sickness is idolatry, because it is the **belief** that **power** can be taken from **you**. *T-9.IX.77.8*

~ when a **brother** is sick, it is because **he** is not asking for **peace** and therefore does not know **he** has it. The **acceptance** of **peace** is the **denial** of **illusion**, and sickness is an **illusion**. *T-9.IX.80.1:2*

~ whatever the sickness, there is but one remedy. *T-11.III.16.2*

~ to perceive in sickness the appeal for **health** is to recognize in hatred the **call** for **love**. *T-11.III.16.3*

~ sickness is **anger** taken out upon the **body**, so that it **will** suffer **pain**. *T-28.VII.58.1*

~ no forms of sickness are immune because the **choice** cannot be made in terms of **form**. The **choice** of sickness seems to be a **form**, yet it is one, as is its **opposite**. *T-28.VIII.63.7:8*

~ sickness is a demand the **body** be a **thing** that it is not. *T-29.III.17.1*

~ the sick are healed as **you** let go all thoughts of sickness. *W-pI.132.9.3*

~ no one can heal unless **he** understands what **purpose** sickness seems to serve. For then **he** understands as well its **purpose** has no **meaning**. **Being** causeless and without a meaningful intent of any kind, it cannot be at all. When this is seen, **healing** is automatic. It dispels this meaningless **illusion** by the same approach that carries all of them to **truth** and merely leaves them there to disappear. *W-pI.136.11:5*

~ sickness is not an accident. Like all defenses, it is an insane device for **self**-deception. And like all the **rest**, its **purpose** is to **hide reality, attack** it, **change** it, render it inept, distort it, twist it, or reduce it to a **little** pile of unassembled parts. *W-pI.136.2.1:3*

~ sickness is a **decision**. It is not a **thing** that happens to **you** quite unsought, which makes **you** weak and brings **you suffering**. It is a **choice** you make, a **plan** you lay when for an instant **truth** arises in your own deluded **mind** and all your **world** appears to totter and prepare to fall. **Now** are **you** sick that **truth** may go away and threaten your establishments no more. *W-pI.136.8.1:4*

~ sickness where **guilt** is absent cannot come, for it is but another **form** of **guilt**. *W-pI.140.4.3*

~ for sickness is an election, a **decision**. It is the **choice** of **weakness** in the mistaken conviction that it is **strength**. When this occurs, real **strength** is seen as **threat** and **health** as danger. Sickness is a method, conceived in **madness**, for placing God's Son on his Father's **throne**. **God** is seen as **outside**, fierce and powerful, eager to keep all **power** for Himself. Only by His **death** can **He** be conquered by His Son. *M-5.2.4:9*

~ sickness is of the **mind** and has **nothing** to do with the **body**. *M-5.6.2*

~ all illness is mental illness. It is a **judgment** on the **Son of God**. *P-2.IV.1.1:2*

389

~ an expression of sorrow and of **guilt**. *P-2.IV.1.6*

~ illness varies in intensity; that the degree of **threat** differs according to the **form** it takes. *P-2.IV.8.2*

SIGHT |sīt|

DICTIONARY: *the faculty or **power** of seeing.*

EGO

~ your sight grows weak and dim and limited. *T-15.IX.90.5*

~ it is held back by **form**, having been made to guarantee that **nothing** else but **form will** be perceived. *T-22.IV.33.9*

~ sight of **form means** understanding has been obscured. *T-22.IV.34.8*

HOLY SPIRIT; *holy sight*

~ this is not your sight, and brings with it the **laws** beloved of Him Whose sight it is. *T-20.IX.71.9*

~ your sight was given **you**, along with everything that **you** can **understand**. *T-22.II.9.1*

~ what your sight would show **you, you will understand** because it is the **truth**. *T-22.II.9.3*

~ on His **vision sin** cannot encroach, for **sin** has been corrected by His sight. *T-25.IV.30.9*

~ in His sight there is another **world**. *T-31.VII.70.6*

~ as sight was made to lead away from **truth**, it can be redirected. *W-p2.240.4.1*

SIN |sin|

DICTIONARY: *an immoral act considered to be a transgression against divine law.*

EGO; *holiness, **truth, idea** of evil, heavy gate.*

~ the **ego** does not perceive sin as a lack of **love**. It perceives sin as a positive act of assault. *T-5.VII.64.1:2*

~ sin and **condemnation** are the same, and the **belief** in one is **faith** in the other, calling for **punishment** instead of **love**. *T-13.III.15.5*

~ the **belief** in sin is necessarily based on the firm conviction that minds, not bodies, can **attack**. *T-19.III.17.4*

~ sin is the "grand **illusion**" underlying all the ego's **grandiosity**. For by it, **God** Himself is changed and rendered incomplete. *T-19.III.18.6:7*

~ any attempt to reinterpret sin as **error** is always indefensible to the **ego**. The **idea** of sin is wholly sacrosanct to its **thought system** and quite unapproachable except through reverence and **awe**. It is the most "holy" **concept** in the ego's system—lovely and powerful, wholly true, and necessarily protected with every **defense** at its disposal. For **here** lies its "best" **defense** which all the others serve. **Here** is its armor, its protection, and the fundamental **purpose** of the **special relationship** in its **interpretation**. *T-19.III.21.1:5*

~ sin has changed **creation** from an **idea** of **God** to an ideal the **ego** wants; a **world** it rules, made up of bodies, mindless and capable of complete corruption and decay. *T-19.III.22.5*

~ there is no stone in all the ego's embattled citadel more heavily defended than the **idea** that sin is real—the natural expression of what the **Son of God** has made himself to be and what **he** is. To the **ego**, this is no **mistake**. For this is its **reality**; this is the "**truth**" from which escape **will** always be **impossible**. This is his **past**, his **present**, and his **future**. For **he** has somehow managed to corrupt his **Father** and changed His **Mind** completely. *T-19.III.23.1:5*

~ the **ego** brings sin to **fear**, demanding **punishment**. *T-19.IV.26.2*

~ sin is the **belief** that your **perception** is unchangeable and that the **mind** must accept as true what it is told through it. *T-19.IV.30.5*

~ sin would prove what **God** created holy could not prevail against it nor remain itself before the **power** of sin. Sin is perceived as mightier than **God**, before which **God** Himself must bow. *T-19.IV.32.5:6*

~ your **faith** that sin is there but witnesses to your **desire** that it be there to **see**. *T-21.V.41.9*

~ sin would maintain **you** must be separate. *T-21.VII.60.6*

~ if **you** choose sin instead of **healing**, **you** would condemn the **Son of God** to what can never be corrected. *T-21.VII.64.1*

~ **being** helpless is the cost of sin. Helplessness is sin's **condition**—the one requirement that it demands to be believed. *T-21.VIII.70.2:3*

~ sin is a block, set like a heavy gate, locked and without a key, across the road to **peace**. *T-22.IV.31.2*

~ sin is but **error** in a **special form** the **ego** venerates. It would preserve all errors and **make** them sins. For **here** is its own stability, its heavy anchor in the shifting **world** it made—the rock on which its **church** is built and where its worshipers are bound to bodies and believe the body's **freedom** is their own. *T-22.IV.32.5:7*

~ for sin of any kind is **weakness**. *T-23.I.1.3*

~ sin is attacked by **punishment** and so preserved. *T-25.IV.30.12*

~ sin is the fixed **belief perception** cannot **change**. What has been damned is damned and damned forever, **being** forever unforgivable. *T-25.IV.30.4:5*

~ **attack** and sin are bound as one **illusion**, each the **cause** and aim and justifier of the other. Each is meaningless **alone**, but seems to draw a **meaning** from the other. Each depends upon the other for whatever **sense** it seems to **have**. And no one could believe in one unless the other were the **truth**, for each attests the other must be true. *T-25.VI.37.3:6*

~ sin is the one **thing** in all the **world** that cannot **change**. It is immutable. And on its changelessness the **world** depends. *T-25.VIII.50.2:4*

~ the cost of sin is **death**. *T-25.VIII.50.6*

~ sin is a **request** for **death**, a **wish** to **make** this world's foundation sure as **love**, dependable as **Heaven**, and as strong as **God** Himself. The **world** is safe from **love** to **everyone** who thinks sin possible. *T-25.VIII.50.8:9*

~ cost him his **sanity** and stands between him and whatever hope **he** has of **being** sane. *T-25.VIII.58.3*

~ the **laws** of sin demand a **victim**. *T-25.IX.65.3*

~ sins are beliefs which **you** impose between your **brother** and yourself. They **limit you** to **time** and place and **give** a **little** space to **you**, another **little** space to him. *T-26.VIII.54.1:2*

~ sin is **belief attack** can be projected **outside** the **mind** where the **belief** arose. **Here** is the firm conviction that ideas can leave their **source** made real and meaningful. And from this **error** does the **world** of sin and **sacrifice** arise. *T-26.VIII.59.1:3*

~ **belief** in sin arouses **fear** and, like its **cause**, is looking forward, looking back but overlooking what is **here** and **now**. Yet only **here** and **now** its **cause** must be if its effects already **have** been judged as fearful. *T-26. IX.72.5:6*

~ sin shifts from **pain** to **pleasure** and again to **pain**. *T-27.VII.55.1*

~ sin is the **idea you** are **alone** and separated off from what is whole. *T-30.IV.40.7*

~ sins are in bodies. **They** are not perceived in minds. **They** are not seen as purposes but actions. *T-31.III.28.1:3*

~ **you** further think that **they** can sin without affecting your **perception** of yourself, while **you** can judge their sin and yet remain apart from **condemnation** and at **peace**. *W-pI.126.2.4*

~ the sin which **you** forgive is not your own. Someone apart from **you** committed it. And if **you** then are gracious unto him by **giving** him what **he** does not deserve, the **gift** is no more yours than was his sin. *W-pI.126.4.3:5*

~ his ineffectual mistakes appear as sins to him. *W-pI.133.11.1*

~ sin is the **symbol** of **attack**. Behold it anywhere, and **I will** suffer. *W-pII.247.1.1:2*

~ sin is the only **thought** that makes the **goal** of **God** seem unobtainable. *W-pII.259.1.1*

~ "sins" obscure the **light** of **Heaven**, shining on the **world**. *W-pII.265.1.6*

~ sin is **insanity**. It is the **means** by which the **mind** is driven mad and seeks to let illusions take the place of **truth**. And **being** mad, it sees illusions where the **truth** should be and where it really is. Sin gave the **body** eyes. *W-pII.ST251.1.1:4*

~ sin is the **home** of all illusions, which but stand for things imagined, issuing from thoughts which are untrue. **They** are the "proof" that what has no **reality** is real. Sin "proves" God's Son is **evil**; timelessness must **have** an end; eternal **life** must die. *W-pII.ST251.3.1:3*

~ sin appears indeed to terrify. And yet what sin perceives is but a childish game. *W-pII.ST251.4.1:2*

HOLY SPIRIT; *error, **mistake**, **weakness**, limitation, block, **insanity**, **home** of all illusions, grand **delusion**, individual **perception**, **wish**, faithlessness, **belief**, **thought**, lack of **love**, death, **request** for death, **symbol** of attack.*

~ the **word** "sin" should be changed to "lack of **love**." *T-1.I.29.5*

~ sin is lack of **love**. *T-1.I.58.1*

~ no one is "punished" for sins, and the Sons of **God** are not sinners. *T-6.II.22.5*

~ all his "sins" are but his own imagining. His **reality** is forever **sinless**. *T-17.I.1.1:2*

~ **love**, not **fear**, is really called upon by sin and always answers. *T-19.IV.26.1*

~ the **Holy Spirit** cannot punish sin. *T-19.IV.27.6*

~ sin **He** knows not. *T-19.IV.27.8*

~ the end of sin, which nestles quietly in the safety of your **relationship**, protected by your **union**, ready to grow into a mighty force for **God**, is very near. *T-19.V.86.2*

~ no two can look on sin together, for **they** could never **see** it in the same place and **time**. Sin is a strictly individual **perception**, seen in the other yet believed by each to be **within** himself. And each one seems to **make** a different **error**, and one the other cannot **understand**. Brothers, it is the same, made by the same, and forgiven for its maker in the same **way**. *T-22.I.1.3:6*

~ to forgive it is to **change** its state from **error** into **truth**. *T-25.IV.30.13*

~ sin is equally insane **within** the **sight** of **love**, whose gentle eyes would look beyond the **madness** and **rest** peacefully on **truth**. *T-25.VIII.55.6*

~ sin is not **error**, for it goes beyond **correction** to impossibility. *T-26.VIII.52.1*

~ **you** must attest his sins had no effect on **you** to demonstrate **they** were not real. *T-27.III.16.2*

~ in their undoing lies the proof that **they** were merely errors. *T-27.III.16.6*

~ "**sinless**" means without sin. **You** cannot be without sin a **little**. **You** are **sinless** or not. *W-pI.36.1.4:6*

~ all your "sins" are **nothing**. *W-pI.93.4.1*

~ all our sins are washed away by realizing that **they** were but mistakes. *W-pI.98.2.5*

~ sin can **have** no **home** in which to **hide** from His beneficence. *W-pI.140.5.6*

~ in His **forgiveness**, **they** are gone. Unseen by One, **they** merely disappear because a **vision** of the **holiness** which lies beyond them comes to take their place. It matters not what **form they** took nor how enormous **they** appeared to be nor who seemed to be **hurt** by them. **They** are no more, and all effects **they** seemed to **have** are gone with them, undone and never to be done. *W-pI.158.9.2:5*

~ remove your focus on your brother's sins, and **you experience** the **peace** that comes from **faith** in sinlessness. This **faith** receives its only sure support from what **you see** in others **past** their sins. For their mistakes, if focused on, are witnesses to sins in **you**. And **you will** not transcend their **sight** and **see** the sinlessness that lies beyond. *W-pI.181.2.5:8*

~ sin cannot tarnish the **truth** in **you**, and **misery** can come not near the holy **home** of **God**. *W-pI.186.6.5*

~ thus **we** cannot choose to overlook some things and yet retain some other things still locked away as sins. *W-pI.195.8.5*

SINFUL |ˈsinfəl|

DICTIONARY: *wicked and immoral; committing or characterized by the committing of sins.*

EGO; *holiness*

~ **acceptance** of the **self** as sinful is perceived as **holiness**. *T-19.III.20.2*

~ it is far better to be sinful than mistaken. *T-19.III.24.3*

~ sinners **see justice** only as their **punishment**, perhaps sustained by someone else but not escaped. *T-25.IX.65.2*

~ the sinful warrant only **death** and **pain**, and it is this **they ask** for, for **they** know it waits for them and it **will seek** them out and find them somewhere, sometime, in some **form** which evens the account **they** owe to **God**. **They** would escape Him in their **fear**. And yet **He will** pursue, and **they** cannot escape. *W-pI.101.2.2:4*

~ it wants escape, yet can conceive of none because it sees the sinful everywhere. *W-pI.121.4.7*

HOLY SPIRIT

~ the Holy Spirit **will** never **teach you** that **you** are sinful. *T-21.V.41.1*

~ **you** that **you** cannot **see** your **brother** or yourself as sinful and still perceive the other **innocent**. *T-21.VII.60.3*

~ everything **you** once **thought** sinful **now will** be reinterpreted as **part** of **Heaven**. *T-23.I.6.4*

SINLESS |ˈsinləs|

DICTIONARY: *free from sin.*

HOLY SPIRIT; *escape from fear*

~ the sinless **give** as **they** received. *T-20.V.32.1*

~ his sinlessness is your escape from **fear**. *T-20.VIII.66.3*

~ the **opposite** of frailty and **weakness** is sinlessness. *T-23.I.1.1*

~ the sinless cannot **fear**. *T-23.I.1.3*

~ **you will love** what **you** perceive as sinless. *T-23.I.2.4*

~ the state of sinlessness is merely this: the whole **desire** to **attack** is gone, and so there is no **reason** to perceive the **Son of God** as other than **he** is. The **need** for **guilt** is gone because it has no **purpose** and is meaningless without the **goal of sin**. *T-25.VI.37.1:2*

~ your sinlessness is guaranteed by **God**. *W-pI.93.6.1*

~ **nothing** can touch it nor can **change** what **God** created as eternal. *W-pI.93.6.5*

~ what is wholly sinless cannot **sin**. *W-pI.136.12.8*

~ the **world** which once proclaimed our sins becomes the proof that **we** are sinless. And our **love** for **everyone we** look upon attests to our remembrance of the holy **Self** Which knows no **sin** and never could conceive of anything without Its sinlessness. *W-pI.181.10.1:2*

~ our sinlessness is but the **Will** of **God**. This instant is our willing one with His. *W-pI.181.10.7:8*

~ for what **we seek** to look upon is really there. And as our focus goes beyond mistakes, **we will** behold a wholly sinless **world**. *W-pI.181.9.2:3*

~ my sinlessness ensures me perfect **peace**, eternal safety, everlasting **love, freedom** forever from all **thought** of **loss**, complete deliverance from **suffering**. *W-pII.337.1.1*

~ it contains the **word** of **God** to us, and in its kind **reflection we** are saved. *W-pII.341.2.2*

SITUATION
|ˌsiCHəˈwäSH(ə)n|

DICTIONARY: *a set of circumstances in which one finds oneself; a state of affairs.*

EGO; *"impossible situation," **truth**.*

~ the situation becomes the determiner of the outcome, which can be anything. *T-17.VII.58.5*

~ without a clear cut positive **goal**, set at the outset, the situation just seems to happen and makes no **sense** until it has already happened. Then **you** look back at it and try to **piece** together what it must **have** meant. And **you will** be wrong. Not only is your **judgment** in the **past**, but **you have** no **idea** what should happen. No **goal** was set with which to bring the **means** in line. *T-17.VII.59.1:5*

~ the **ego** believes the situation brings the **experience**. *T-17.VII.61.8*

~ confronted with any aspect of the situation which seems to be **difficult**, the **ego will** attempt to take this aspect elsewhere and resolve it there. And it **will** seem to be successful, except that this attempt conflicts with **unity** and must obscure the **goal** of **truth**. And **peace will** not be experienced except in **fantasy**. **Truth** has not come because **faith** has been denied, **being** withheld from where it rightfully belonged. Thus do **you** lose the understanding of the situation the **goal** of **truth** would bring. *T-17.VII.63.1:5*

~ for if **you** judge them, **you have** set the rules for how **you** should react to them. And then another **answer** cannot but produce **confusion** and uncertainty and **fear**. *T-30.II.5.3:4*

~ any situation that causes **you** concern is associated with feelings of inadequacy, since otherwise **you** would believe that **you** could deal with the situation successfully. *W-pI.47.6.2*

~ strange and paradoxical situation—one without **meaning** and devoid of **sense**, yet out of which no **way** seems possible. *M-11.3.4*

HOLY SPIRIT; *a whole, joining of thoughts,* **relationship.**

~ the **value** of deciding in **advance** what **you want** to happen is simply that **you will** perceive the situation as a **means** to **make** it happen. **You will** therefore **make** every **effort** to overlook what interferes with the accomplishment of your objective and concentrate on everything which helps **you** meet it. It is quite noticeable that this approach has brought **you** closer to the Holy Spirit's sorting out of **truth** and falsity. The true becomes what can be used to meet the **goal.** The false becomes the useless from this point of view. The situation **now** has **meaning,** but only because the **goal** has made it meaningful. *T-17.VII.60.1:6*

~ if the situation is used for **truth** and **sanity,** its outcome must be **peace.** *T-17.VII.61.2*

~ the **Holy Spirit** knows that the situation is as the **goal** determines it and is experienced according to the **goal.** *T-17.VII.61.9*

~ the **Holy Spirit** sees the situation as a whole. *T-17.VII.62.4*

~ a situation is a **relationship, being** the joining of thoughts. If problems are perceived, it is because the thoughts are judged to be in **conflict.** But if the **goal** is **truth,** this is **impossible.** *T-17.VIII.65.6:8*

~ only what **you have** not given can be lacking in any situation. *T-17.VIII.67.1*

~ every situation in which **you** find yourself is but a **means** to meet the **purpose** set for your **relationship.** *T-17.VIII.68.1*

~ the **light** of **truth** shines from the center of the situation and touches **everyone** to whom the situation's **purpose** calls. It calls to **everyone.** There is no situation which does not involve your whole **relationship** in every aspect and complete in every **part.** *T-17.VIII.71.9:11*

~ this **power** instantly transforms all situations into one sure and continuous **means** for establishing His **purpose** and demonstrating its **reality.** What has been demonstrated has called for **faith** and has been given it. **Now** it becomes a **fact** from which **faith** can no longer be withheld. *T-17.IX.76.4:6*

~ when a situation has been dedicated wholly to **truth, peace** is inevitable. Its attainment is the criterion by which the **wholeness** of the dedication can be safely assumed. *T-19.I.1.1:2*

~ every situation properly perceived becomes an opportunity to heal the **Son of God.** *T-19.I.2.1*

~ each situation that **he thought** before was **means** to justify his **anger** turned to an event which justifies his **love.** *T-25.IV.28.2*

~ it is **impossible** not to use the content of any situation on behalf of what **you** really **teach** and therefore learn. *M-1.5.3*

SLEEP |slēp|

DICTIONARY: *a condition of body and mind such as that which typically recurs for several hours every night, in which the nervous system is relatively inactive, the eyes closed, the postural muscles relaxed, and consciousness practically suspended.*

EGO

~ those who sleep are stupefied, or better, unaware. *T-7.V.33.7*

~ in sleep **you** are **alone,** and your **awareness** is narrowed to yourself. And that is why the nightmares come. **You dream** of isolation because your eyes are closed. **You** do not **see** your brothers, and in the **darkness you** cannot look upon the **light you** gave to them. *T-12.VI.56.4:7*

~ your **Self** seems to sleep, while the **part** of your **mind** that weaves illusions in its sleep appears to be awake. *W-pI.68.3.1*

HOLY SPIRIT; *withdrawing, form of death.*

~ **you have** chosen a sleep in which **you have** had bad dreams, but the sleep is not real, and **God** calls **you** to awake. *T-6.V.50.4*

~ only when **you awaken** joyously **have you** utilized sleep according to the Holy Spirit's **purpose.** *T-8.IX.83.5*

~ sleep is no more a **form** of **death** than **death** is a **form** of unconsciousness. *T-8.IX.83.7*

~ **you will have** no **wish** to sleep but only the **will** to waken and be glad. *T-9.VIII.67.2*

~ sleep is not **death.** What **He** created can sleep, but it cannot die. *T-10.II.13.6:7*

~ even in sleep has **Christ** protected **you**, ensuring the **real world** for **you** when **you** wake. *T-12.VI.57.3*

~ his sleep **will** not withstand the **call** to wake. *T-13.V.44.3*

~ a smile has come to lighten up your sleeping face. The sleep is peaceful **now**, for these are **happy** dreams. *T-27.VIII.74.5:6*

~ what seems to be the **opposite** of **life** is merely sleeping. When the **mind** elects to be what it is not and to assume an alien **power** which it does not **have**, a foreign state it cannot enter, or a false **condition** not **within** its **Source**, it merely seems to go to sleep a while. *W-pI.167.9.1:2*

SON OF GOD   *A Course in Miracles Term*

EGO;   *host*

~ god's Son is indeed in **need** of comfort, for **he** knows not what **he** does, believing his **will** is not his own. The **Kingdom** is his, and yet **he** wanders homelessly. At **home** in **God, he** is lonely, and amid all his brothers, **he** is friendless. *T-10.IV.24.1:3*

~ the Son of God believes that **he** is lost in **guilt, alone** in a dark **world** where **pain** is pressing everywhere upon him from without. *T-13.IV.27.3*

~ **fear** can become so acute that the **sin** is denied the acting out, but while the **guilt** remains attractive the **mind will** suffer and not let go of the **idea** of **sin**. For **guilt** still calls to it, and the **mind** hears it and yearns for it, making itself a willing captive to its sick appeal. **Sin** is an **idea** of **evil** that cannot be corrected and **will** be forever desirable. As an essential **part** of what the **ego** thinks **you** are, **you will** always **want** it. And only an avenger with a **mind** unlike your own could stamp it out through **fear.** *T-19.IV.25.3:7*

~ **he** can **wish** for what would **hurt** him. And **he** has the **power** to think **he** can be **hurt.** *T-25.IV.31.1:2*

~ always in **sickness** does the Son of God attempt to **make** himself his **cause** and not allow himself to be his Father's Son. For this **impossible desire, he** does not believe that **he** is Love's effect and must be **cause** because of what **he** is. *T-28.III.18.1:2*

~ **i have** deluded myself into believing it is possible to imprison the Son of God. *W-pI.57.3.3*

~ for **you** behold the Son of God as but a **victim** to **attack** by fantasies, by dreams, and by illusions **he** has made; yet helpless **he** is in their presence, needful only of **defense** by still more fantasies and dreams by which illusions of his safety comfort him. *W-pI.153.5.2*

~ the Son of God may play **he** has become a **body**, prey to **evil** and to **guilt**, with but a **little life** that ends in **death.** *W-pII.ST251.4.3*

HOLY SPIRIT;   *you*, God's Son, sacred Son of **God**, **host**, *mirror, my* **identity**, *redeemed son of* **man**, **Child** *of* **God**, *Effect, heaven's son.*

~   **god** has only one Son. If all the Souls **God** created are His Sons, then every **Soul** must be an integral **part** of the whole **Sonship**. *T-2.V.101.1:2*

~   the **power** of the Sons of **God** is operating all the **time** because **they** were created as creators. *T-6.II.24.4*

~   because God's equal Sons **have** everything, **they** cannot compete. *T-7.V.28.1*

~   by changing his **mind he** has changed the most powerful device that was ever created for **change**. *T-7.VI.47.6*

~   **grace** is the natural state of every Son of **God**. When **he** is not in a state of **grace**, **he** is out of his natural environment and does not **function** well. Everything **he** does becomes a strain, because **he** was not created for the environment that **he** has made. **He** therefore cannot adapt to it, nor can **he** adapt it to him. *T-7.XII.108.1:4*

~   all God's Sons cannot be recognized through the dominion of one **will** over another. God's Sons are equal in **will**, all **being** the **Will** of their **Father**. *T-8.V.32.7:8*

~   yet their **thought** is so powerful that **they** can even imprison the **mind** of God's Son if **they** so choose. *T-8.VI.48.7*

~   god's Son is one. Whom **God** has joined as one, the **ego** cannot break apart. *T-8.IX.87.3:4*

~   your **acceptance** of **God** in him acknowledges the **love** of **God** which **he** has forgotten. Your recognition of him as **part** of **God** teaches him the **truth** about himself, which **he** is denying. *T-9.IX.77.1:2*

~   god's Son knows no idols, but **he** does know his **Father**. *T-9.IX.79.2*

~   there is no end to **God** and His Son, for **we** are the **universe**. **God** is not incomplete, and **He** is not childless. Because **He** did not **will** to be **alone**, **He** created a Son like Himself. *T-10.II.9.2:4*

~   the Son of **God** has both **Father** and Son because **he** is both **Father** and Son. *T-10.III.16.3*

~   the Son of **God** is **you**. *T-10.IV.23.8*

~   created of **light** and in **light**. The Great **Light** always surrounds **you** and shines out from **you**. *T-10.IV.26.6:7*

~   the **Father** has hidden His Son safely **within** Himself and kept him far away from your destructive thoughts. *T-11.IX.77.2*

~   god's Son is as safe as his **Father**, for the Son knows his Father's protection and cannot **fear**. His Father's **love** holds him in perfect **peace**, and needing **nothing**, **he** asks for **nothing**. *T-11.IX.78.1:2*

~   god's Son can be seen because his **vision** is shared. The **Holy Spirit** looks upon him and sees **nothing** else in **you**. **Guiltless** Son, who did not die because **he** is immortal. *T-11.IX.82.9:11*

~   god's Son is not guilty. **He** deserves only **love** because **he** has given only **love**. **He** cannot be condemned because **he** has never condemned. The **Atonement** is the final **lesson he need** learn, for it teaches him that, never having sinned, **he** has no **need** of **salvation**. *T-11.X.88.3:6*

~   the Son of **God** is **guiltless now**, and the brightness of his purity shines untouched forever in **God's Mind**. God's Son **will** always be as **he** was created. Deny your **world** and judge him not, for his eternal guiltlessness is in the **mind** of his **Father**, and protects him forever. *T-11.X.93.6:8*

~   out of **love he** was created, and in **love he** abides. Goodness and mercy **have** always followed him, for **he** has always extended the **love** of his **Father**. *T-11.X.94.6:7*

~   the Son of **God**, who sleepeth not, has kept **faith** with his **Father** for **you**. There is no road to travel on and no **time** to travel through. For **God** waits not for His Son in **time**, **being** forever unwilling to be without him. *T-11.X.95.2:4*

~   **you** were redeemed with him and **have** never been separated from him. *T-12.II.9.4*

~   for the redeemed son of **man** is the **guiltless** Son of **God**, and to recognize him is your **redemption**. *T-12.II.9.7*

~ only his **love** is real, and **he will** be content only with his **reality**. *T-12.III.18:7*

~ god's **guiltless** Son is only **light**. There is no **darkness** in him anywhere, for **he** is whole. *T-12.VI.52.4:5*

~ god's Son is still as loving as his **Father**. Continuous with his **Father**, **he** has no **past** apart from Him. So **he** has never ceased to be his Father's **witness** and his own. Although **he** slept, **Christ's vision** did not leave him. And so it is that **he** can **call** unto himself the witnesses that **teach** him that **he** never slept. *T-12.VI.57.5:9*

~ **he** is as safe from **pain** as **God** Himself, who watches over him in everything. The **world** about him shines with **love** because **God** placed him in Himself where **pain** is not and **love** surrounds him without end or flaw. Disturbance of his **peace** can never be. In perfect **sanity** he looks on **love**, for it is all about him and **within** him. *T-12.VII.65.2:5*

~ and from this point of safety, **he** looks quietly about him and recognizes that the **world** is one with him. *T-12.VII.65.7*

~ god's Son is not a traveler through outer worlds. However holy his **perception** may become, no **world outside** himself holds his **inheritance**. **Within** himself **he** has no needs. *T-12.VII.71.5:7*

~ thus does the Son of **God give** thanks unto his **Father** for his purity. *T-12.VII.76.9*

~ when **he** has looked **within** and seen the radiance there, **he will remember** how much his **Father** loves him. *T-13.IV.27.4*

~ no **illusion** that **you have** ever held against him has touched his **innocence** in any **way**. His shining purity, wholly untouched by **guilt** and wholly loving, is bright **within you**. *T-13.IV.32.1:2*

~ even the darkest **nightmare** that disturbed the **Mind** of God's sleeping Son holds no **power** over him. **He will** learn the **lesson** of awaking. **God** watches over him, and **light** surrounds him. *T-13.V.43.8:10*

~ **he** cannot separate himself from what is in him. *T-13.V.44.2*

~ no one can **hurt** the Son of **God**. His **guilt** is wholly without **cause**, and **being** without **cause**, cannot **exist**. *T-13.VIII.71.5:6*

~ god's Son **will** always be indivisible. *T-14.VII.71.1*

~ there never was an instant in which God's Son could lose his purity. His changeless state is beyond **time**, for his purity remains forever beyond **attack** and without variability. *T-15.II.15.5:6*

~ a Son of **God** who has been released through the **Holy Spirit** in a **brother**, if the **release** is complete, is always recognized. *T-15.III.19.7*

~ **he** is risen, and **you have** accepted the **cause** of his awakening as yours. *T-17.IX.78.4*

~ his **salvation** is your only **purpose**. *T-17.IX.78.7*

~ no Son of **God** remains **outside** His Fatherhood. *T-18.IX.81.7*

~ the Son of **God** can be mistaken; **he** can deceive himself; **he** can even turn the **power** of his **mind** against himself. But **he** cannot **sin**. There is **nothing he** can do that would really **change** his **reality** in any **way** nor **make** him really guilty. *T-19.III.19.1:3*

~ sometimes a **sin** can be repeated over and over with obviously distressing results but without the **loss** of its appeal. And suddenly **you change** its status from a **sin** to a **mistake**. **Now you will** not repeat it; **you will** merely stop and let it go unless the **guilt** remains. For then **you will** but **change** the **form** of **sin**, granting that it was an **error** but keeping it uncorrectable. This is not really a **change** in your **perception**, for it is **sin** that calls for **punishment**, not **error**. *T-19.IV.27.1:5*

~ **he** started with the sign of victory the **promise** of the **resurrection** already given him. *T-20.II.3.4*

~ **now** is **he** free, unlimited in his **communion** with all that is **within** him. *T-20.III.14.2*

~ the **meaning** of the Son of **God** lies solely in his **relationship** with his **Creator**. *T-20.VII.45.1*

~ the **power** to heal the Son of **God** is given **you** because **he** must be one with **you**. **You** are responsible for how **he** sees himself. And **reason** tells **you** it is given **you** to **change** his whole **mind**, which is one with **you**, in just an instant. *T-21.VII.65.2:4*

~ the Son of **God** is always blessed as one. *T-21.VII.68.1*

~ the Son of **God** retains His Father's **Will**. *T-24.VIII.72.7*

~ the Son of **God** creates to bring him **joy**, sharing his Father's **purpose** in his own **creation** that his **joy** might be increased and God's along with his. *T-25.V.33.7*

~ the Son of **God** cannot be bound by **time** nor place nor anything **God** did not **will**. *T-25.VIII.56.4*

~ and that in **Heaven they** are all the same, without the differences which would **have** made a **hell** of **Heaven** and a **heaven** of **hell**, had such **insanity** been possible. *T-25.VIII.59.6*

~ **nothing** the Son of **God** believes can be destroyed. *T-26.IV.21.1*

~ the Son that **God** created is as free as **God** created him. **He** was reborn the instant that **he** chose to die instead of live. *T-26.VI.40.1:2*

~ god's Son could never be content with less than full **salvation** and escape from **guilt**. For otherwise **he** still demands that **he** must **make** some **sacrifice** and thus denies that everything is his, unlimited by **loss** of any kind. *T-26.VIII.61.4:5*

~ there is no **difference** among the Sons of **God**. *T-26.VIII.66.4*

~ the Son gives fatherhood to his **Creator** and receives the **gift** that **he** has given Him. It is because **he** is God's Son that **he** must also be a **father** who creates as **God** created him. *T-28.III.16.4:5*

~ every aspect of the Son of **God** is just the same as every other **part**. *T-28.V.45.7*

~ god's Son can never **change** by what men made of him. **He will** be as **he** was and as **he** is, for **time** appointed not his destiny nor set the hour of his **birth** and **death**. **Forgiveness will** not **change** him. *T-29.VII.39.11:13*

~ the Son of **Life** cannot be killed. **He** is immortal as his **Father**. What **he** is cannot be changed. **He** is the only **thing** in all the **universe** that must be one. *T-29.VII.39.3:6*

~ what the Son of **God** knew in **creation**, **he** must know again. *T-30.VI.62.5*

~ god's Son is perfect, or **he** cannot be God's Son. *T-30.VII.78.1*

~ god's perfect Son remembers his **creation**. *T-31.I.9.6*

~ **god** has one Son, and **he** is the **resurrection** and the **life**. His **Will** is done because all **power** is given him in **Heaven** and on earth. *W-pI.20.3.6:7*

~ **he** is entitled to everything because it is his birthright as a Son of **God**. *W-pI.37.1.6*

~ a Son of **God** cannot think or speak or act in vain. **He** cannot be **alone** in anything. *W-pI.54.5.3:4*

~ the Son of **God** must be forever free. **He** is as **God** created him, and not what **I** would **make** of him. **He** is where **God** would **have** him be, and not where **I thought** to hold him prisoner. *W-pI.57.3.5:7*

~ the Son of **God** has come in **glory** to redeem the lost, to save the helpless, and to **give** the **world** the **gift** of his **forgiveness**. *W-pI.191.10.3*

~ the Son of **God** deserves your mercy. *W-pI.192.10.2*

~ god's Son can **have** no cares and must remain forever in the **peace** of **Heaven**. *W-pII.255.1.5*

~ **he** is not bound except by his beliefs. *W-pII.277.2.2*

~ the Son of **God** is limitless. There are no limits on his **strength**, his **peace**, his **joy**, or any attributes his **Father** gave in his **creation**. What **he** wills with his **Creator** and Redeemer must be done. His holy **will** can never be denied because his **Father** shines upon his **mind** and lays before it all the **strength** and **love** in earth and **Heaven**. *W-pII.320.1.1:4*

~ the Son of **God** is one in us, and **we** can reach our Father's **Love** through him. *W-pII.ST301.5.6*

~ his Son shares in **creation** and must therefore **share** in **power** to create. *W-pII.ST321.2.3*

~ the Son of **God** is egoless. *W-pII.ST331.3.1*

~ all there is surrounding him is everlasting **peace**, forever conflict-free and undisturbed in deepest silence and tranquility. *W-pII.ST331.3.4*

~ thus does the son of **man** become the Son of **God**. It is not really a change; it is a **change** of **mind**. **Nothing** external alters, but everything internal **now** reflects only the **Love** of **God**. *M-12.2.1:3*

SONG |sôNG|

DICTIONARY: *a short poem or other set of words set to music or meant to be sung.*

EGO

~ there is a tendency, and it is very strong, to hear this song of **death** only an instant, and then dismiss it uncorrected. *P-2.VI.2.1*

~ the willingness to **question** the "**truth**" of the song of **condemnation** must arise. The strange distortions woven inextricably into the **self-concept**, itself but a pseudo-**creation**, **make** this ugly sound seem truly beautiful. "The rhythm of the **universe**," "the herald angel's song," all these and more are heard instead of loud discordant shrieks. *P-2.VI.2.3:5*

HOLY SPIRIT;   *Heaven's melody, song of **Heaven**, song of **freedom**.*

~ every **voice** has a **part** in the song of **redemption**, the hymn of gladness and thanksgiving for the **light** to the **Creator** of **light**. *T-12.VI.5:2.6*

~ not the whole song has stayed with you, but just a **little** wisp of melody, attached not to a person or a place or anything particular. But **you remember** from just this **little part** how lovely was the song, how wonderful the setting where **you** heard it, and how **you** loved those who were there and listened with you. *T-21.II.8.2:3*

~ **you** know the ancient song and know it well. **Nothing will** ever be as dear to **you** as is this ancient hymn [of **love**] the **Son of God** sings to his **Father** still. *T-21.II.11.5:6*

~ **now** the **blind** can **see**, for that same song **they** sing in honor of their **Creator** gives **praise** to them as well. The blindness which **they** made **will** not withstand the **memory** of this song. *T-21.II.12.1:2*

~ the sweetest music—the song it longed to hear since first the **ego** came into your minds. *T-21.V.4.7.2*

~ the song of **Christ** is all there is to hear. *T-24.VI.4.6.8*

~ when **he** hears this song again, **he** knows **he** never heard it not. *T-29.X.6.8.6*

~ those who hear His words **have** heard the song of **Heaven**. *W-p1.198.6.5*

~ his Son gives thanks for his **creation**, in the song of his creating in his Father's **Name**. *S-1.IN.1.6*

~ it is the song that is the **gift**. *S-1.I.3.2*

~ in true **prayer you** hear only the song. *S-1.I.3.4*

~ your song is **part** of the eternal harmony of **love**. *S-3.IV.8.3*

Ego

~ any **part** of the Sonship can believe in **error** or incompleteness if **he** so elects. *T-2.V.103.1*

Holy Spirit; *sum of all the Souls God created, your salvation, your Soul.*

~ sonship is the sum of all the Souls **God** created. *T-1.I.19.2*

~ sonship, which is a state of **completion** and abundance. Whatever is true and real is eternal and cannot **change** or be changed. *T-1.I.68.1:2*

~ the Sonship itself is a perfect **creation**. *T-2.II.40.2*

~ the Sonship in its **oneness** does transcend the sum of its parts. However, this is obscured as long as any of its parts are missing. That is why the **conflict** cannot ultimately be resolved until all the parts of the Sonship **have** returned. Only then can the **meaning** of **wholeness**, in the true **sense**, be fully understood. *T-2.V.102.1:4*

~ the joint **will** of all the Sonship is the only **creator** that can create like the **Father**, because only the complete can think completely, and the thinking of **God** lacks **nothing**. *T-5.VI.57.4*

~ god's extending outward, though not His completeness, is blocked when the Sonship does not communicate with Him as one. *T-6.V.57.7*

~ **you** can appreciate the Sonship only as one. *T-7.VI.53.4*

~ although **you** can **love** the Sonship only as one, **you** can perceive it as fragmented. It is **impossible**, however, for **you** to **see** something in **part** of it that **you will** not attribute to all of it. *T-7.VII.54.1:2*

~ **being** a perfect accomplishment, the Sonship can only accomplish perfectly, extending the **joy** in which it was created and identifying itself with both its **Creator** and its **creations**, knowing **they** are one. *T-7.VII.69.2*

~ only the whole Sonship is worthy to be co-**creator** with **God**, because only the whole Sonship can create like Him. *T-7.XII.112.3*

~ if the Sonship is one, it is one in all respects. *T-9.X.87.2*

~ god gave the Sonship to **you** to ensure your perfect **creation**. This was His **gift**. *T-15.IX.82.1:2*

SOUL [sōl]

Dictionary: *the spiritual or immaterial part of a human being or animal, regarded as immortal.*

Holy Spirit

~ the Soul has not only been fully created but has also been created perfect. There is no emptiness in it. Because of its likeness to its **Creator**, it is creative. *T-2.I.53.3:5*

~ the Soul has been created. *T-2.III.55.2*

~ the Soul is already perfect and therefore does not require **correction**. *T-2.III.61.3*

~ each Soul knows **God** completely. *T-3.VII.59.3*

~ souls cannot clash at all. *T-4.II.12.4*

~ the Soul is far beyond the **need** of your protection or mine. *T-4.II.21.3*

~ **nothing** can reach the Soul from the **ego**, and **nothing** from the Soul can strengthen the **ego** or reduce the **conflict within** it. *T-4.II.8.3*

~ soul cannot perceive and the **ego** cannot know. **They** are therefore not in **communication** and can never be in **communication**. Nevertheless, the **ego** can learn because its maker can be misguided but cannot **make** the totally lifeless out of the **life**-given. The Soul **need** not be taught, but the **ego** must. *T-4.II.8.7:10*

~ the Soul in its **knowledge** is unaware of the **ego**. It does not **attack** it; it merely cannot conceive of it at all. *T-4.III.34.1:2*

~ soul reacts in the same **way** to everything it knows is true and does not respond at all to anything else. Nor does it **make** any attempt to establish what is true. It knows that what is true is everything that **God** created. It is in complete and direct **communication** with every aspect of **creation** because it is in complete and direct **communication** with its **Creator**. *T-4.VIII.96.3:6*

~ the Soul holds everything by **giving** it and thus creates as the **Father** created. *T-5.II.5.8*

~ **self**-fullness is of the Soul, because that is how **God** created it. *T-7.X.91.4*

~ it knows its fullness and cannot conceive of any **part** from which it is excluded. *T-7.X.91.7*

~ every Soul **God** created is **part** of **you** and shares His **glory** with **you**. *T-9.V.33.9*

~ **you** cannot sell your Soul, but **you** can sell your **awareness** of it. **You** cannot perceive your Soul, but **you will** not know it while **you** perceive anything else as more valuable. *T-11.VII.53.6:7*

SOURCE

|sôrs|

Dictionary: *a place, person, or **thing** from which something comes or can be obtained.*

Ego

~ **you** are accustomed to the notion that the **mind** can **see** the source of **pain** where it is not. The doubtful **service** of displacement is to **hide** the real source of your **guilt** and keep from your **awareness** the full **perception** that it is insane. *T-13.IV.20.1:2*

~ **you** are therefore willing with **little** opposition to look upon all sorts of "sources" underneath **awareness**, provided that **they** are not the deeper source to which **they** bear no real **relationship** at all. *T-13.IV.20.4*

Holy Spirit; *God*

~ his **union** with It is the Source of his creating. Apart from this **he** has no **power** to create, and what **he** makes is meaningless. *T-21.III.27.3:4*

~ its Source knows not of incompletion. *T-21.VI.54.6*

~ **where** would the **answer** be but in the Source? *T-21.VI.54.7*

~ your **Identity**, as much a true effect of this same Source as is the **answer**, must therefore be together and the same. the Source of **help**. *T-21.VI.54.9:10*

~ the source of neither **light** nor **darkness** can be found without. *W-pI.73.5.3*

~ **we share** our **life** because **we have** one Source, a Source from Which **perfection** comes to us, remaining always in the holy minds which **He** created perfect. *W-pI.167.12.1*

SPARK

DICTIONARY: *a small fiery particle thrown off from a fire, alight in ashes, or produced by striking together two hard surfaces such as stone or metal.*

EGO

~ do not attribute your **denial** of **joy** to them, or **you** cannot **see** the spark in them that could bring **joy** to **you**. It is the **denial** of the spark that brings depression, and whenever **you see** your brothers without it, **you** are denying **God**. *T-9.XI.94.4:5*

HOLY SPIRIT; *little light, little spark, remaining **call** of **creation**.*

~ all the lamps of **God** were lit by the same spark. It is everywhere, and it is eternal. *T-9.X.91.5:6*

~ in many only the spark remains, for **the Great Rays** are obscured. Yet **God** has kept the spark alive so that the rays can never be completely forgotten. *T-9.X.92.1:2*

~ perceiving the spark **will** heal, but knowing the **light will** create. *T-9.X.92.4*

~ but the spark is still as pure as the great **light**, because it is the remaining **call** of **creation**. Put all your **faith** in it, and **God** Himself **will answer you**. *T-9.X.92.6:7*

~ even the **little** spark in your **mind** is enough to lighten it. *T-10.II.3.6*

~ think like Him ever so slightly, and the **little** spark becomes a blazing **light** that fills your **mind** so that **He** becomes your only Guest. *T-10.III.20.4*

~ for the **little** spark which holds **the Great Rays within** it is also visible. *T-16.VII.6:3.3*

~ the spark of **holiness** must be safe, however hidden it may be, in every **relationship**. *T-17.IV.22.4*

~ **within** the **dream** of bodies and of **death** is yet one theme of **truth**—no more, perhaps, than just a tiny spark, a space of **light** created in the dark, where **God** still shines. *T-29.IV.21.8*

~ this is the spark that shines **within** the **dream**. *T-29.IV.24.6*

SPECIAL

DICTIONARY: *better, greater, or otherwise different from what is usual.*

EGO; *Heaven, triumph.*

~ those who are special must defend illusions against the **truth**. *T-24.II.11.1*

~ specialness not only sets apart but serves as grounds from which **attack** on those who seem "beneath" the special one is "natural" and "just." The special ones feel weak and frail because of differences, for what would **make** them special is their **enemy**. Yet **they** protect its enmity and **call** it "friend." On its behalf **they** fight against the **universe**, for **nothing** in the **world they value** more. *T-24.II.6.4:7*

~ specialness is the great dictator of the wrong decisions. *T-24.II.7.1*

~ the grand **illusion** of what **you** are and what your **brother** is. *T-24.II.7.2*

~ specialness must be defended. Illusions can **attack** it, and **they** do. *T-24.II.7.4:5*

~ specialness is triumph, and its victory is his defeat and shame. *T-24.II.7.8*

~ specialness can never **share**, for it depends on goals that **you alone** can reach. *T-24.II.8.5*

~ specialness always makes comparisons. It is established by a lack seen in another and maintained by searching for and keeping clear in **sight** all lacks it can perceive. *T-24.III.12.2:3*

~ pursuit of specialness is always at the cost of **peace**. *T-24.III.13.1*

~ the pursuit of specialness must bring **you pain**. **Here** is a **goal** that would defeat **salvation** and thus run counter to the **Will** of God. To **value** specialness is to esteem an alien **will** to which illusions of yourself are dearer than the **truth**. *T-24.III.13.7:9*

~ specialness is the **idea** of sin made real. **Sin** is **impossible** even to imagine without this base. For **sin** arose from it out of nothingness; an **evil** flower with no roots at all. **Here** is the **self-made "savior,"** the **"creator"** who creates unlike the **Father** and which made His Son like to itself and not like unto Him. His "special" sons are many, never one, each one in exile from himself and Him of Whom **they** are a **part**. *T-24.III.14.1:5*

~ **they** chose their specialness instead of **Heaven** and instead of **peace** and wrapped it carefully in **sin** to keep it "safe" from **truth**. *T-24.III.14.7*

~ **you** can defend your specialness, but never **will you** hear the **Voice** for God beside it. *T-24.III.16.1*

~ only specialness could **make** the **truth** of God and **you** as one seem anything but **Heaven** and the hope of **peace** at last in **sight**. *T-24.III.22.7*

~ specialness is the seal of treachery upon the **gift** of **love**. Whatever serves its **purpose** must be given to **kill**. No **gift** that bears its seal but offers treachery to giver and receiver. *T-24.III.23.1:3*

~ but seeks for bargains and for **compromise** that would establish **sin** love's **substitute** and serve it faithfully. *T-24.III.23.5*

~ it demands a special place **God** cannot enter and a hiding-place where none is **welcome** but your tiny **self**. **Nothing** is sacred **here** but unto **you** and **you alone**, apart and separate from all your brothers, safe from all intrusions of **sanity** upon illusions, safe from **God**, and safe for **conflict** everlasting. *T-24.III.24.2:3*

~ whatever **form** of specialness **you** cherish, **you have** made **sin**. *T-24.IV.27.1*

~ so does it seem to split **you** off from **God** and **make you** separate from Him as its defender. *T-24.IV.27.4*

~ specialness is a lack of **trust** in anyone except yourself. **Faith** is invested in yourself **alone**. Everything else becomes your **enemy**—feared and attacked, deadly and dangerous, hated and worthy only of **destruction**. Whatever **gentleness** it offers is but deception, but its **hate** is real. In danger of **destruction**, it must **kill**, and **you** are drawn to it to **kill** it first. *T-24.V.34.1:5*

~ specialness is the **function** which **you** gave yourself. It stands for **you alone**, as **self**-created, **self**-maintained, in **need** of **nothing**, and unjoined with anything beyond the **body**. In its eyes, **you** are a separate **universe** with all the **power** to hold itself complete **within** itself, with every entry shut against intrusion and every window barred against the **light**. Always attacked and always furious, with **anger** always fully justified, **you have** pursued this **goal** with **vigilance you** never **thought** to yield and **effort** that **you** never **thought** to cease. *T-24.VII.59.1:4*

~ while it calls to him, **he** hears no other **Voice**. No **effort** is too great, no cost too much, no price too dear to save his specialness from the least slight, the tiniest **attack**, the whispered **doubt**, the hint of **threat**, or anything but deepest reverence. *T-24.VIII.62.5:6*

~ only in **darkness** does your specialness appear to be **attack**. *T-25.VII.49.6*

~ specialness cares not who pays the cost of **sin**. *T-25.IX.74.1*

HOLY SPIRIT; *function you gave yourself, sin made real, seal of treachery, lack of trust.*

~ the **Holy Spirit** knows no one is special. *T-15.VI.49.1*

~ no specialness can offer **you** what **God** has given and what **you** are joined with Him in **giving**. *T-16.V.37.7*

~ **he** is not special, for **He** would not keep one **part** of what **He** is unto Himself, not given to His Son but kept for Him **alone**. And it is this **you** fear, for if **He** is not special, then **He** willed His Son be like Him, and your **brother** is like **you**. Not special, but possessed of everything including **you**. *T-24.III.21.4:6*

404

~ the **death** of specialness is not your **death** but your awaking into **life** eternal. **You** but emerge from an **illusion** of what **you** are to the **acceptance** of yourself as **God** created **you**. *T-24.III.25.4:5*

~ specialness is not the **truth** in **you**. It can be thrown off balance by anything. What rests on **nothing** never can be stable. *T-24.IV.28.4:6*

~ forgive the Holy One the specialness **He** could not **give** and which **you** made instead. *T-24.IV.31.7*

~ the special ones are all asleep, surrounded by a **world** of loveliness **they** do not **see**. *T-24.IV.32.1*

~ your specialness **will** disappear before the **Will** of **God**. *T-24.VII.58.6*

~ the specialness **he** chose to **hurt** himself did **God** appoint to be the **means** for his **salvation** from the very instant that the **choice** was made. *T-25.VII.48.9*

SPECIAL FUNCTION   *Course in Miracles Term*

HOLY SPIRIT;   *call to Him, **treasure house, special form, function**.*

~ such is the Holy Spirit's kind **perception** of specialness—His use of what **you** made, to heal instead of **harm**. To each **He** gives a **special function** in **salvation he alone** can fill—a **part** for only him. Nor is the **plan** complete until **he** finds his **special function** and fulfills the **part** assigned to him to **make** himself complete **within** a **world** where incompletion rules. *T-25.VII.46.1:3*

~ in **light**, **you see** it as your **special function** in the **plan** to save the **Son of God** from all **attack** and let him **understand** that **he** is safe, as **he** has always been and **will** remain in **time** and in **eternity** alike. *T-25.VII.49.7*

~ your **special function** is the **special form** in which the **fact** that **God** is not insane appears most sensible and meaningful to **you**. The content is the same. The **form** is suited to your **special** needs and to the **special time** and place in which **you** think **you** find yourself and where **you** can be free of place and **time** and all that **you** believe must **limit you**. *T-25.VIII.56.1:3*

~ to each his **special function** is designed to be perceived as possible and more and more desired as it proves to him that it is an alternative **he** really wants. *T-25.VIII.58.2*

~ your **special function** is made whole because it shares the **function** of the whole. *T-25.VIII.61.8*

~ your **special function** is a **call** to Him that **He** may smile on **you** whose sinlessness **He** shares. *T-25.IX.75.5*

~ your **special function** shows **you nothing** else but perfect **justice** can prevail for **you**. *T-25.IX.77.3*

~ without your **special function** has this **world** no **meaning** for **you**. *T-26.II.5.2*

~ it is your **special function** to ensure the door be opened that **he** may come forth to shine on **you** and **give you** back the **gift** of **freedom** by receiving it of **you**. *T-26.II.9.2*

~ your **special function** opens wide the door beyond which is the **memory** of His **love** kept perfectly intact and undefiled. *T-26.III.17.4*

~ your **little part** in bringing happiness to all the **world**. *W-pI.95.19.2*

SPECIAL RELATIONSHIP   *A Course in Miracles Term*

EGO;   *continuing hymn of **hate**, unholy **relationship**.*

~ to believe that **special** relationships, with **special love**, can offer **you salvation** is the **belief** that **separation** is **salvation**. *T-15.VI.47.3*

~ because of **guilt**, all **special** relationships **have** some elements of **fear** in them. And this is why **they shift** and **change** so frequently. They are not based on changeless **love alone**. *T-15.VI.48.1:3*

~ **you** but **seek** in them what **you have** thrown away. And through them **you will** never learn the **value** of what **you have** cast aside but what **you** still **desire** with all your hearts. *T-15.IX.80.2:3*

~ **special** relationships, in which **you** are both destroyer and destroyed in **part**, but with the **idea** of **being** able to be neither completely. *T-15.X.98.7*

~ the **special love relationship**, in which the **meaning** of **love** is lost, is undertaken solely to offset the **hate** but not to let it go. *T-16.V.30.3*

~ the **special love relationship** is an attempt to **limit** the destructive effects of **hate** by finding a haven in the storm of **guilt**. It makes no attempt to rise above the storm into the sunlight. On the contrary, it emphasizes **guilt outside** the haven by attempting to build barricades against it and keep **within** them. The **special love relationship** is not perceived as a **value** in itself, but as a place of safety from which hatred is split off and kept apart. The **special love** partner is acceptable only as long as **he** serves this **purpose**. Hatred can enter and indeed is **welcome** in some aspects of the **relationship**, but it is still held together by the **illusion** of **love**. If the **illusion** goes, the **relationship** is broken or becomes unsatisfying on the grounds of disillusionment. *T-16.V.32.1:7*

~ it is certain that those who select certain ones as partners in any aspect of living and use them for any **purpose** which **they** would not **share** with others, are trying to live with **guilt** rather than die of it. This is the **choice they see**. And **love** to them is only an escape from **death**. They **seek** it desperately but not in the **peace** in which it would gladly come quietly to them. And when **they** find the **fear** of **death** is still upon them, the **love relationship** loses the **illusion** that it is what it is not. For then the barricades against it are broken, **fear** rushes in, and hatred triumphs. *T-16.V.33.5:10*

~ the **special love relationship** is an attempt [to bring **love** into **separation**. And, as such, it is **nothing** more than an attempt] to bring **love** into **fear** and **make** it real in **fear**. In fundamental violation of love's **condition**, the **special love relationship** would accomplish the **impossible**. *T-16.V.36.1:3*

~ the **special love relationship** is but a shabby **substitute** for what makes **you** whole in **truth**, not in **illusion**. *T-16.V.37.4*

~ **special** relationships of any kind would hinder God's **completion**. *T-16.V.42.1*

~ involves a great amount of **pain**. Anxiety, **despair**, **guilt**, and **attack** all enter into it, broken into by periods in which **they** seem to be gone. *T-16.VI.43.1:2*

~ **they** are always an **attack** on the **self** to **make** the other guilty. *T-16.VI.43.4*

~ the **special love relationship** is the ego's chief weapon for keeping **you** from **Heaven**. *T-16.VI.44.3*

~ the **special love relationship** is the ego's most boasted **gift**, and one which has the most appeal to those unwilling to relinquish **guilt**. The "dynamics" of the **ego**. *T-16.VI.44.5:6*

~ it is in the **special relationship**, born of the hidden **wish** for **special love** from **God**, that the ego's hatred triumphs. For the **special relationship** is the renunciation of the **love of God** and the attempt to secure for the **self** the specialness which **He** denied. It is essential to the preservation of the **ego** that **you** believe this specialness is not **hell**, but **Heaven**. *T-16.VI.46.1:3*

~ the **special relationship** is a strange and unnatural **ego** device for joining **hell** and **Heaven** and making them indistinguishable. *T-16.VI.48.1*

~ the **special relationship** is the triumph of this **confusion**. It is a kind of **union** from which **union** is excluded, and the basis for the attempt at **union** rests on exclusion. What better example could there be of the ego's maxim, "**Seek** but do not find?" *T-16.VI.48.3:5*

~ the conviction of littleness lies in every **special relationship**, for only the deprived could **value** specialness. The demand for specialness and the **perception** of the giving of specialness as an act of **love** would **make love** hateful. And the real **purpose** of the **special relationship**, in strict accordance with the ego's goals, is to destroy **reality** and **substitute illusion**. *T-16.VI.51.2:4*

~ the **special relationship** is a ritual of **form**, aimed at the raising of the **form** to take the place of **God** at the expense of content. *T-16.VI.54.2*

~ **see** in the **special relationship nothing** more than a meaningless attempt to raise other Gods before Him and by worshiping them to obscure their tininess and His greatness. *T-16.VI.55.3*

~ for the **special relationship** has **value** only to the **ego**. To the **ego** unless a **relationship** has **special value**, it has no **meaning**, and it perceives all **love** as **special**. *T-16.VII.59.2:3*

~ must foster **guilt** and therefore must imprison. *T-16.VII.60.9*

~ the **special relationship** is totally without **meaning** without a **body**. *T-16.VII.61.1*

~ the **special relationship** is a device for limiting your **self** to a **body** and for limiting your **perception** of others to theirs. *T-16.VII.61.4*

~ the **special relationship** which the **ego** seeks does not include even one whole individual. For the **ego** wants but **part** of him and sees only this **part** and **nothing** else. *T-16.VII.62.7:8*

~ without this **illusion**, there can be no **meaning you** would still **seek here**. *T-16.VII.64.7*

~ the **special relationship** is an attempt to reenact the **past** and **change** it. Imagined slights, remembered **pain**, **past** disappointments, perceived injustices, and deprivations all enter into the **special relationship**, which becomes a **way** in which **you seek** to restore your wounded **self-esteem**. *T-16.VII.70.2:3*

~ the **special relationship** takes **vengeance** on the **past**. By seeking to remove **suffering** in the **past**, it overlooks the **present** in its preoccupation with the **past** and its total commitment to it. No **special relationship** is experienced in the **present**. *T-16.VIII.71.1:3*

~ the fantasies it brings to the **special** relationships it chooses in which to act out its **hate** are fantasies of your **destruction**. *T-16.VIII.72.4*

~ in the **special relationship, you** are allowing your **destruction** to be. *T-16.VIII.73.1*

~ in the **special relationship**, which binds **you** to it and would **teach you** that **salvation** is **past** and that **you** must return to the **past** to find **salvation**. *T-16.VIII.73.4*

~ in the **special relationship**, it does not seem to be an acting out of **vengeance** which **you seek**. *T-16.VIII.74.1*

~ the **special relationship** is the acting out of **vengeance** on yourself. *T-16.VIII.74.3*

~ every **special relationship** which **you have** made is a **substitute** for **God's Will** and glorifies yours instead of His because of the **delusion** that **they** are different. *T-17.V.28.6*

~ every **special relationship** which **you have** ever undertaken has as its fundamental **purpose** the aim of occupying your minds so completely that **you will** not hear the **call** of **truth**. In a **sense** the **special relationship** was the ego's **answer** to the **creation** of the **Holy Spirit**. *T-17.V.29.2:3*

~ the **special relationship** has the most imposing and deceptive frame of all the defenses the **ego** uses. Its **thought system** is offered **here**, surrounded by a frame so heavy and so elaborate that the **picture** is almost obliterated by its imposing structure. Into the frame are woven all sorts of fanciful and fragmented illusions of **love**, set with dreams of **sacrifice** and **self**-aggrandizement and interlaced with gilded threads of **self**-**destruction**. The glitter of blood shines like rubies, and the tears are faceted like diamonds and gleam in the dim **light** in which the **offering** is made. *T-17.V.34.1:4*

~ all **special** relationships **have sin** as their **goal**. For **they** are bargains with **reality**, toward which the seeming **union** is adjusted. *T-21.IV.29.1:2*

407

Holy Spirit; *ego device, ritual.*

~ holy Spirit uses **special** relationships, which **you have** chosen to support the **ego**, as a **learning experience** which points to **truth**. *T-15.VI.48.5*

~ he also perceives that **you have** made **special** relationships, which **He** would purify and not let **you** destroy. *T-15.VI.49.2*

~ he can translate them into **holiness** by removing as much **fear** as **you will** let Him. *T-15.VI.49.3*

~ time is kind, and if **you** use it for **reality**, it **will** keep gentle pace with **you** in your transition. *T-16.VII.65.2*

~ he will restore to them the **function** given them by **God**. The **function you have** given them is clearly not to **make happy**. *T-17.V.28.3-4*

~ he does not destroy it nor snatch it away from **you**. [But **He** does use it differently, as a **help** to **make** His **purpose** real to **you**.]Your **special relationship will** remain, not as a **source** of **pain** and **guilt**, but as a **source** of **joy** and **freedom**. *T-18.III.20.5-7*

~ your **special relationship will** be a **means** for undoing **guilt** in **everyone** blessed through your **holy relationship**. It **will** be a **happy dream**, and one which **you will share** with all who come **within** your **sight**. Through it, the **blessing** which the **Holy Spirit** has laid upon it **will** be extended. *T-18.III.21.1-3*

~ love has entered your **special relationship** and entered fully at your weak **request**. *T-18.IX.8.2.1*

~ it is given to **release** and be released from the dedication to **death**. *T-19.V.7.7.1*

~ the **Holy Spirit** must **change** its **purpose** to **make** it useful to Him and harmless unto **you**. *T-21.IV.29.6*

SPIRIT |ˈspirit|

Dictionary: *the nonphysical **part** of a person that is the seat of emotions and character; the **soul**.*

Holy Spirit; *you, altar of **truth**.*

~ his spirit is eternally free. *T-1.I.46.5*

~ a spirit, deathless and without the **promise** of corruption and the stain of **sin** upon **you**. *T-31.VI.6.7.1*

~ **you** are the Spirit lovingly endowed with all your Father's **love** and **peace** and **joy**. **You** are the Spirit which completes Himself and shares His **function** as **Creator**. *W-pI.97.2.2:3*

~ **you** are the Spirit in whose **mind** abides the **miracle** in which all **time** stands still. *W-pI.97.4.1*

~ **you** are the Spirit that abides in Him, and Which calls through His **Voice** to every living **thing**; offers His **sight** to **everyone** who asks; replaces **error** with the simple **truth**. *W-pI.97.5.1*

SPIRITUAL EYE   *A Course in Miracles Term*

Holy Spirit; *mechanism of miracles, **symbol**.*

~ the Spiritual **eye** is the mechanism of miracles, because what It perceives is true. *T-1.I.56.1*

~ it can also separate the true from the false by Its ability to perceive totally rather than selectively. *T-1.I.56.3*

~ the Spiritual **eye**, on the other hand, cannot **see** the building at all because it has perfect **sight**. It can, however, **see** the **altar** with perfect **clarity**. *T-2.II.45.8:9*

~ the Spiritual **eye**, simultaneously weakening the investment in physical **sight**. *T-2.II.48.5*

~ the Spiritual **eye** literally cannot **see error** and merely looks for **Atonement**. All the solutions which the physical eyes **seek** dissolve in its **sight**. The Spiritual **eye**, which looks **within**, recognizes immediately that the **altar** has been defiled and needs to be repaired and protected. Perfectly aware of the right **defense**, It passes over all others, looking **past error** to **truth**. Because of the real **strength** of Its **vision**, It pulls the **will** into Its **service** and impels the **mind** to concur. This reestablishes the true **power** of the **will** and makes it increasingly unable to tolerate **delay**. *T-2.II.49.1:6*

~ spiritual **eye** cannot **see error** and is capable only of looking beyond it to the **defense** of **Atonement**. There is no **doubt** that the Spiritual **eye** does produce extreme discomfort by what it sees. Yet what **man** forgets is that the discomfort is not the final outcome of its **perception**. When the Spiritual **eye** is permitted to look upon the defilement of the **altar**, it also looks immediately toward the **Atonement**. *T-2.III.67.3:6*

~ **nothing** the Spiritual **eye** perceives can induce **fear**. Everything that results from accurate spiritual **awareness** is merely channelized toward **correction**. Discomfort is aroused only to bring the **need** for **correction** forcibly into **awareness**. What the physical **eye** sees is not corrective nor can it be corrected by any device which can be seen physically. As long as a **man** believes in what his physical **sight** tells him, all his corrective **behavior will** be misdirected. *T-2.III.68.1:5*

~ visions are the natural **perception** of the Spiritual **eye**, but **they** are still corrections. The Spiritual **eye** is symbolic and therefore not a device for knowing. It is, however, a **means** of right **perception**, which brings it into the proper domain of the **miracle**. Properly speaking, "a **vision** of **God**" is a **miracle** rather than a **revelation**. The **fact** that **perception** is involved at all removes the **experience** from the realm of **knowledge**. That is why visions do not last. *T-3.V.34.1:6*

STEP |step|

DICTIONARY: *a measure or action, especially one of a series taken in* **order** *to deal with or achieve a particular thing.*

HOLY SPIRIT; *corrective step*

~ the first step toward **freedom** must entail a sorting out of the false from the true. *T-2.VI.109.5*

~ your giant step forward was to insist on a "collaborative venture." *T-4.VIII.91.2*

~ this **little** step, so small it has escaped your notice, is a stride through **time** into **eternity** and beyond all ugliness into beauty that **will** enchant **you** and **will** never cease to **cause you** wonderment at its **perfection**. *T-17.III.8.6*

~ these steps lead **you** from dreams of **judgment** to forgiving dreams and out of **pain** and **fear**. *T-30.I.1.5*

~ each **little** step **will** clear a **little** of the **darkness** away. *W-pI.9.2.5*

STRANGER |ˈstrānjər|

DICTIONARY: *a person whom one does not know or with whom one is not familiar.*

EGO; *brother*

~ **attack** is always made on a stranger. **You** are making him a stranger by misperceiving him so that **you** cannot know him. It is because **you have** made him a stranger that **you** are afraid of him. *T-3.V.36.3:5*

~ **fear** is a stranger to the ways of **love**. Identify with **fear**, and **you will** be a stranger to yourself. *W-pI.160.1.1:2*

HOLY SPIRIT

~ **god** is not a stranger to His Sons, and His Sons are not strangers to each other. *T-3.V.37.1*

- in your **forgiveness** of this stranger, alien to **you** and yet your ancient Friend, lie his **release** and your **redemption** with him. *T-20.II.4.5*

- there is a stranger in him who wandered carelessly into the **home** of **truth**, and who **will** wander off. **He** came without a **purpose**, but **he will** not remain before the shining **light** the **Holy Spirit** offered and **you** accepted. For there the stranger is made homeless and **you** are **welcome**. *T-20.IV.22.3:5*

- his **way** is lost except a **miracle will** search him out and show him that **he** is no stranger **now**. *W-pI.160.6.5*

STRENGTH |streNG(k)TH|

DICTIONARY: *the quality or state of **being** strong.*

EGO;   *arrogance, **threat**, **weakness**.*

- the **ego** teaches that your strength is in **you alone**. *T-8.IV.23.3*

- if **you** are trusting your own strength, **you have** every **reason** to be apprehensive, anxious, and fearful. *W-pI.47.1.1*

- what **we** believe to be our strength is often arrogance. *W-pI.154.1.7*

HOLY SPIRIT;   *sinlessness, **truth** about **you**, true **light**, real strength.*

- the strong do not **attack** because **they see** no **need** to do so. *T-11.VI.43.2*

- the Holy Spirit's **love** is your strength, for yours is divided and therefore not real. *T-11.VI.46.1*

- it is **impossible** to divide your strength between **Heaven** and **hell**, **God** and the **ego**, and **release** your **power** unto **creation**, which is the only **purpose** for which it was given **you**. *T-15.IX.8.8.1*

- for all its might, so great it reaches **past** the stars and to the **universe** that lies beyond them, your **little** faithlessness can **make** it useless if **you** would use the faithlessness instead. *T-17.VIII.70.3*

- those who are strong are never treacherous because **they have** no **need** to **dream** of **power** and to act out their **dream**. *T-21.VIII.72.6*

- his **gentleness** becomes your strength. *T-25.III.19.5*

- replacing all your **weakness** with the strength that comes from **God** and that can never **fail**. *T-31.VIII.91.1*

- it is His strength, not your own, that gives **you power**. *W-pI.42.1.4*

- **god** is indeed your strength. And what **He** gives is truly given. This **means** that **you** can **receive** it any **time** and anywhere, wherever **you** are and in whatever circumstances **you** find yourself. Your passage through **time** and space is not random. **You** cannot but be in the right place at the right **time**. Such is the strength of **God**. Such are His gifts. *W-pI.42.2.1:7*

- the strength of **God** in **you** is successful in all things. *W-pI.47.6.4*

- it is not my own strength through which **I** forgive. It is through the strength of **God** in me, which **I** am remembering as **I** forgive. *W-pI.60.3.1:2*

- realize how great this strength, your doubts would vanish. *W-pI.91.4.4*

- when **you have** felt the strength in **you** which makes all miracles **within** your easy reach, **you will** not doubt. The miracles your **sense** of **weakness** hides **will** leap into **awareness** as **you** feel the strength in **you**. *W-pI.91.4.6:7*

- it is God's strength in **you** that is the **light** in which **you see**, as it is His **Mind** with which **you** think. His strength denies your **weakness**. *W-pI.92.3.1:2*

~ strength overlooks these things by seeing **past** appearances. It keeps its steady gaze upon the **light** that lies beyond them. It unites with **light**, of which it is a **part**. It sees itself. It brings the **light** in which your **Self** appears. In **darkness you** perceive a **self** that is not there. *W-pI.92.4.1:6*

~ strength is the **truth** about **you**. *W-pI.92.5.1*

~ strength comes from **truth** and shines with **light** its **Source** has given it. *W-pI.92.5.2*

~ the **light** of strength is constant, sure as **love**, forever glad to **give** itself away because it cannot **give** but to itself. No one can **ask** in vain to **share** its **sight**, and none who enters its abode can leave without a **miracle** before his eyes and strength and **light** abiding in his heart. *W-pI.92.8.4:5*

~ true **light** is strength, and strength is sinlessness. *W-pI.94.2.1*

~ what **we** think is **weakness** can be strength. *W-pI.154.1.7*

STUDY

|ˈstədē|

DICTIONARY: *the **devotion** of **time** and attention to acquiring **knowledge** on an academic subject, especially by **means** of books.*

EGO

~ the study of the **ego** is not the study of the **mind**. In **fact**, the **ego** enjoys the study of itself and thoroughly approves the undertakings of students who would **analyze** it, approving its importance. Yet **they** but study **form** with meaningless content. For their **teacher** is senseless, though careful to conceal this **fact** behind a lot of words which sound impressive but which lack any consistent **sense** when **they** are put together. *T-14.VI.53.6:9*

SUBSTITUTE

|ˈsəbstəˌt(y)o͞ot|

EGO; *gift*

~ the substitutes for aspects of the **situation** are the witnesses to your lack of **faith**. **They** demonstrate that **you** did not believe that the **situation** and the **problem** were in the same place. The **problem** was the lack of **faith**, and it is this **you** demonstrate when **you** remove it from its **source** and place it elsewhere. *T-17.VII.64.1:3*

~ to substitute is to choose between, renouncing one in favor of the other. For this **special purpose**, one is judged more valuable and the other is replaced by him. The **relationship** in which the substitution occurred is thus fragmented and its **purpose** split accordingly. *T-18.I.1.3:5*

~ substitution is the strongest **defense** the **ego** has for **separation**. *T-18.I.1.6*

~ their **call** is but an echo of the original **error** which shattered **Heaven**. *T-18.I.12.2*

~ it has taken many forms because it was the substitution of **illusion** for **truth**, of fragmentation for **wholeness**. *T-18.II.4.2*

~ that one **error**, which brought **truth** to **illusion**, infinity to **time**, and **life** to **death**, was all **you** ever made. Your whole **world** rests upon it. Everything **you see** reflects it, and every **special relationship** which **you** have ever made is **part** of it. *T-18.II.4.4:6*

~ **have** no substance. **They** fuse and merge and separate in shifting and totally meaningless patterns which **need** not be judged at all. To judge them individually is pointless. Their tiny differences in **form** are no real differences at all. None of them matters. That **they have** in common and **nothing** else. *T-18.II.7.5:10*

~ each substitute **he** may accept as real can but deceive him. *M-16.10.3*

HOLY SPIRIT; *replacement, accept instead, choose between.*

~ to substitute is to accept instead. *T-18.I.1.1*

~ the **Holy Spirit** never uses substitutes. Where the **ego** perceives one person as a replacement for another, the **Holy Spirit** sees them joined and indivisible. **He** does not judge between them, knowing **they** are one. **Being** united, **they** are one because **they** are the same. Substitution is clearly a process in which **they** are perceived as different. One would unite; the other separate. **Nothing** can come between what **God** has joined and what the **Holy Spirit** sees as one. *T-18.I.2.1:7*

~ the one **emotion** in which substitution is **impossible** is **love. Fear** involves substitution by definition, for it is love's replacement. *T-18.I.3.1:2*

~ no substitute can keep **you** from each other. *T-18.II.9.10*

~ sharing and substituting **have nothing** in common in **reality**. *T-18.II.9.2*

~ these gentle sights and sounds are looked on happily and heard with **joy**. **They** are His substitutes for all the terrifying sights and screaming sounds the ego's **purpose** brought to your horrified **awareness**. **They step** away from **sin**, reminding **you** that it is not **reality** which frightens **you** and that the errors which **you** made can be corrected. *T-20.IX.76.5:7*

~ there is no substitute for **peace**. *T-24.I.2.7*

~ nor can **death** be substitute for **life** or **fear** for **love**. *W-pI.110.3.1*

SUFFERING |ˈsəf(ə)riNG|

DICTIONARY: *the state of undergoing **pain**, distress, or hardship.*

EGO

~ suffering is an emphasis upon all that the **world** has done to injure **you**. *T-27.VIII.62.1*

~ no one can suffer if **he** does not **see** himself attacked and losing by **attack**. *T-28.VII.57.5*

~ suffering can never be escaped if **sin** is real. *W-pI.101.3.2*

~ **you** may think it buys **you** something and may still believe a **little** that it buys **you** what **you want**. *W-pI.102.1.2*

~ there can be no **form** of suffering that fails to **hide** an unforgiving **thought**. *W-pI.198.11.1*

HOLY SPIRIT; *request for pain, vain imagining, foolish **wish**.*

~ foolish **wish** with no effects

~ **he** does not **understand** suffering and would **have you teach** it is not understandable. *T-16.I.1.5*

~ suffer, and **you** decided **sin** was your **goal**. *T-21.III.1.7.5*

~ it matters not the **name** by which **you** called your suffering. It is no longer there. *T-27.VII.58.4:5*

~ in your suffering of any kind, **you see** your own concealed **desire** to kill. *T-31.V.57.10*

~ accept not suffering, and **you** remove the **thought** of suffering. Your **blessing** lies on **everyone** who suffers when **you** choose to **see** all suffering as what it is. The **thought** of **sacrifice** gives rise to all the forms that suffering appears to take. *W-pI.187.7.2:4*

~ whatever suffers is not **part** of me. *W-pII.248.1.3*

SUPERCONSCIOUS

DICTIONARY: *transcending human or normal* **consciousness***.*

EGO

~ superconscious was perceived as a **threat**, because **light** does abolish **darkness** merely by establishing the **fact** that it is not there. *T-3.VI.47.1*

~ in its characteristically upside-down way, the **ego** has taken the impulses from the superconscious and perceives them as if **they** arise in the unconscious. The **ego** judges what is to be accepted, and the impulses from the superconscious are unacceptable to it because **they** clearly point to the nonexistence of the **ego** itself. The **ego** therefore experiences **threat** and not only censors but also reinterprets the data. *T-4.IV.45.1:3*

HOLY SPIRIT; *level of the* **mind**

~ the superconscious, which knows, could not be reconciled with this **loss** of **power** because it is incapable of **darkness**. *T-3.VI.46.4*

SURVIVAL

DICTIONARY: *the state or* **fact** *of continuing to live or* **exist***, typically in spite of an accident, ordeal, or* **difficult** *circumstances.*

EGO

~ the "**battle** for **survival**" is **nothing** more than the ego's struggle to preserve itself and its **interpretation** of its own beginning. *T-4.III.35.3*

~ the **God of sickness** obviously demands the **denial** of **health**, because **health** is in direct opposition to its own survival. *T-9.XI.95.2*

~ its survival depends on your **belief** that **you** are exempt from its **evil** intentions. *T-15.VIII.68.4*

SYMBOL

DICTIONARY: *a* **thing** *that represents or stands for something else, especially a material object representing something abstract.*

EGO

~ **man** is very inventive when it comes to twisting symbols around. *T-3.III.16.4*

~ symbols which but represent ideas that cannot be must stand for empty space and nothingness. *T-27.IV.30.6*

~ **you** are each the symbol of your sins to one another, silently, and yet with ceaseless urgency condemning still your **brother** for the hated **thing you** are. *T-31.V.48.8*

~ your **faith** is placed in the most trivial and insane symbols—pills, money, "protective" clothing, "influence," "prestige," **being** liked, knowing the "right" people, and an endless list of forms of nothingness which **you** endow with magical powers. All these things are your replacements for the **Love of God**. All these things are cherished to ensure a **body** identification. **They** are songs of **praise** to the **ego**. *W-pI.50.1.3:6*

~ **you** live by symbols. **You have** made up names for everything **you see**. Each one becomes a separate entity, identified by its own **name**. By this **you** carve it out of **unity**. By this **you** designate its **special** attributes and set it o from other things by emphasizing space surrounding it. This space **you** lay between all things to which **you give** a different **name**—all happenings in terms of place and **time**, all bodies which are greeted by a **name**. *W-pI.184.11:6*

~ and **everyone** who learns to think that it is so accepts the signs and symbols which assert the **world** is real. It is for this **they** stand. **They** leave no **doubt** that what is named is there. It can be seen, as is anticipated. What denies that it is true is but **illusion**, for it is the ultimate **reality**. To **question** it is **madness**; to accept its presence is the proof of **sanity**. *W-pI.184.6.2:7*

HOLY SPIRIT; *name*

~ **i have** made every **effort** to use words that are almost **impossible** to distort, but **man** is very inventive when it comes to twisting symbols around. *T-3.III.16.4*

~ the symbols of **hate** against the symbols of **love** play out a **conflict** which does not **exist**. For symbols stand for something else, and the symbol of **love** is without **meaning** if **love** is everything. *T-16.V.31.1:2*

~ **they** must stand for something other than themselves. Their **meaning** cannot lie in them but must be sought in what **they** represent. And **they** may thus mean everything or **nothing**, according to the **truth** or falsity of the **idea** which **they** reflect. *T-19.V.88.2:4*

~ there is no symbol for totality. *T-27.IV.33.1*

~ symbols which **you** both can **understand**. *T-30.VIII.87.4*

~ through His use of symbols are **we** joined so that **they** mean the same to all of us. *T-30.VIII.88.7*

~ **fear** without symbols calls for no response, for symbols can stand for the meaningless. **Love** needs no symbols, **being** true. *W-pI.161.5.3:4*

~ **they** do not stand for anything at all. *W-pI.184.9.4*

~ **they** become but **means** by which **you** can communicate in ways the **world** can **understand**, but which **you** recognize is not the **unity** where true **communication** can be found. *W-pI.184.9.5*

SYMPTOM |ˈsim(p)təm|

DICTIONARY: *a physical or mental feature that is regarded as indicating a **condition** of disease, particularly such a feature that is apparent to the **patient**.*

EGO

~ every symptom which the **ego** has made involves a **contradiction** in terms. *T-4.II.6.1*

HOLY SPIRIT

~ **you have reason** to **question** the validity of symptom cure, but no one believes that the symptoms can remain if the underlying cause is removed. *T-5.VII.69.5*

~ **fear** is a symptom of your deep **sense** of **loss**. *T-11.III.11.1*

TEACH

|tēCH|

DICTIONARY: *show or explain to (someone) how to do something.*

EGO

~ the deductive approach to **teaching** accepts the generalization which is applicable to all single instances rather than building up the generalization after analyzing numerous single instances separately. *T-3.III.18.6*

~ the **ego** is trying to teach **you** how to **gain** the whole **world** and lose your own **Soul.** *T-11.VII.53.1*

~ the **ego** teaches **you** to **attack** yourself because **you** are guilty, and this must increase the **guilt,** for **guilt** is the result of **attack.** In the ego's **teaching,** then, there is no escape from **guilt.** *T-11.X.99.1:2*

~ the ego's **teaching** produces immediate results because its decisions are immediately accepted as your **choice.** And this **acceptance means** that **you** are willing to judge yourself accordingly. *T-16.IV.22.4:5*

~ what **you have** taught yourselves is such a giant **learning** feat it is indeed incredible. *T-31.I.2.7*

~ while **you fail** to teach what **you have** learned, **salvation** waits and **darkness** holds the **world** in grim imprisonment. *W-pI.153.11.3*

~ such is the **teaching** of the **world.** It is a phase of **learning everyone** who comes must go through. But the sooner **he** perceives on what it rests, how questionable are its premises, how doubtful its results, the sooner does **he question** its effects. **Learning** which stops with what the **world** would teach stops short of **meaning.** In its proper place, it serves but as a starting point from which another kind of **learning** can begin, a new **perception** can be gained, and all the arbitrary names the **world** bestows can be withdrawn as **they** are raised to **doubt.** *W-pI.184.7.1:5*

~ the act of **teaching** is regarded as a **special** activity in which one engages only a relatively small proportion of one's **time.** *M-1.1.4*

HOLY SPIRIT;   *demonstrate, learn, imply a lack.*

~ **you** cannot learn except by **teaching.** *T-5.VI.51.4*

~ **teaching** is done in many ways: by formal **means,** by **guidance,** and above all by example. **Teaching** is therapy because it **means** the sharing of ideas and the **awareness** that to **share** them is to strengthen them. *T-5.VI.53.4:5*

~ **god** does not teach. To teach is to imply a lack, which **God** knows is not there. **God** is not conflicted. Teaching aims at **change,** but **God** created only the changeless. *T-6.V.56.1:4*

~ the **Holy Spirit** teaches **you** to use what the **ego** has made to teach the **opposite** of what the **ego** has learned. *T-7.IV.22.3*

~ only His **teaching will release** your **will** to God's, uniting it with His **power** and **glory** and establishing them as yours. *T-8.IV.17.6*

~ the **Holy Spirit** teaches that **you** cannot lose your **Soul** and there is no **gain** in the **world,** for of itself it profits **nothing.** *T-11.VII.53.2*

~ the undoing of **guilt** is an essential **part** of the Holy Spirit's **teaching.** *T-11.VIII.75.2*

~ it **will** not be possible to exempt yourself from what the **Holy Spirit** wills to teach **you.** *T-13.V.43.5*

~ the **Holy Spirit,** therefore, must begin His **teaching** by showing **you** what **you** can never learn. *T-13.VI.53.1*

~ every **teaching** that points to this points straight to **Heaven** and to the **peace** of God. There is no **pain,** no trial, no **fear** that **teaching** this can **fail** to overcome. The **power** of God Himself supports this **teaching** and guarantees its limitless results. *T-14.I.10.5:7*

~ blessed are **you** who teach with me. *T-14.II.13.1*

~ under the Holy Spirit's **teaching**, all relationships are seen as total commitments, yet **they** do not **conflict** with one another in any **way**. Perfect **faith** in each one for its ability to satisfy **you** completely arises only from perfect **faith** in yourself. *T-15.VI.56.3:4*

~ holy Spirit's **teaching function** to instruct those who believe that **communication** is damnation that **communication** is **salvation**. *T-15.VIII.77.2*

~ "by their fruits ye shall know them, and **they** shall know themselves." For it is certain that **you** judge yourself according to your **teaching**. *T-16.IV.22.2:3*

~ everything the **Holy Spirit** teaches **you** is to remind **you** that **you have** received what **God** has given **you**. *T-16.VIII.77.8*

~ there is no inconsistency in what the **Holy Spirit** teaches. This is the reasoning of the sane. *T-21.V.46.1:2*

~ must It use the **language** which this **mind** can **understand** in the **condition** in which it thinks it is. And It must use all **learning** to transfer illusions to the **truth**, taking all false ideas of what **you** are and leading **you** beyond them to the **truth** that is beyond them. *T-25.II.10.4:5*

~ it is a simple **teaching** in the obvious. *T-31.IV.39.7*

~ teach them by showing them the happiness that comes to those who feel the touch of **Christ** and recognize God's gifts. *W-pI.166.13.5*

~ the **goal** the Holy Spirit's **teaching** sets is just this end of dreams. For sights and sounds must be translated from the witnesses of **fear** to those of **love**. *W-pII.ST281.2.1:2*

~ **you** cannot **give** to someone else, and this **you** learn through **teaching**. **Teaching** is but a **call** to witnesses to attest to what **you** believe. It is a method of conversion. This is not done by words **alone**. Any **situation** must be to **you** a chance to teach others what **you** are and what **they** are to **you**. No more than that, but also never less. *M-I.2.6:11*

~ the verbal content of your **teaching** is quite irrelevant. It may coincide with it or it may not. It is the **teaching** underlying what **you** say that teaches **you**. **Teaching** but reinforces what **you** believe about yourself. Its fundamental **purpose** is to diminish **self doubt**. This does not mean that the **self you** are trying to protect is real. But it does mean that the **self you** think is real is what **you** teach. This is inevitable. There is no escape from it. *M-I.3.4:12*

~ the simplest **level** of **teaching** appears to be quite superficial. It consists of what seem to be very casual encounters. *M-3.2.1:2*

TEACHER

|ˈtēCHər|

DICTIONARY: *a person who teaches, especially in a school.*

EGO; *teacher of* **attack***, poor teacher, poor* **learner***, conflicted* **learner***.*

~ those who believe that **they will** lose their **child** or **pupil** or **patient** if **they** succeed. *T-4.II.11.4*

~ if **you** perceive a teacher as merely a "larger **ego**," **you will** be afraid because to enlarge an **ego** is to increase **separation** anxiety. *T-4.II.12.5*

~ he is concerned with the effect of his **ego** on other egos and therefore interprets their interaction as a **means** of **ego** preservation. *T-4.II.13.2*

HOLY SPIRIT

~ **good** teachers never terrorize their students. To terrorize is to **attack**, and this results in rejection of what the teacher offers. The result is **learning** failure. *T-3.III.21.6:8*

~ **they will** one day no longer **need** him. This is the one real **goal** of the parent, teacher, and **therapist**. *T-4.II.11.2:3*

~ teachers must be **patient** and repeat their lessons until **they** are learned. *T-4.II.14.4*

~ a **good** teacher clarifies his own ideas and strengthens them by **teaching** them. *T-4.II.7.1*

~ a **good** teacher must believe in the ideas which **he** professes, but **he** must meet another **condition**; **he** must also believe in the students to whom **he** offers his ideas. *T-4.II.7.4*

~ a wise teacher teaches through approach, not avoidance. **He** does not emphasize what **you** must avoid to escape from **harm** so much as what **you need** to learn to **have joy**. *T-6.V.59.1:2*

~ all **good** teachers realize that only fundamental **change will** last, but **they** do not begin at that **level**. Strengthening motivation for **change** is their first and foremost **goal**. It is also their last and final one. *T-6.V.71.6:8*

~ one **Child** of God is the only teacher sufficiently worthy to **teach** another. *T-7.VIII.77.1*

~ one Teacher is in all your minds, and **He** teaches the same **lesson** to all. **He** always teaches **you** the inestimable **worth** of every **Son of God**, **teaching** it with infinite **patience** born of the [**love** of Him for whom] **He** speaks. *T-7.VIII.77.2:3*

~ **holy Spirit** shares the **goal** of all **good** teachers, whose ultimate aim is to **make** themselves unnecessary by **teaching** their pupils all **they** know. *T-11.X.89.1*

~ your Teacher came from beyond your **thought system** and so could look upon it fairly and perceive it was untrue. *T-16.IV.21.2*

~ there are two teachers only, who point in different ways. And **you will** go along the **way** your chosen teacher leads. *T-26.VI.30.7:8*

~ the teacher does not **give experience** because **he** did not learn it. It revealed itself to him at its appointed **time**. But **vision** is his **gift**. This **he** can **give** directly, for Christ's **knowledge** is not lost because **He** has a **vision He** can **give** to anyone who asks. The Father's **Will** and His are joined in **knowledge**. *W-pI.158.5.1:5*

~ one wholly perfect teacher whose **learning** is complete suffices. This One, sanctified and redeemed, becomes the **Self** Who is the **Son of God**. **He** who was always wholly **spirit now** no longer sees Himself as a **body** or even as in a **body**. Therefore **He** is limitless. And **being** limitless, His thoughts are joined with God's forever and ever. His **perception** of himself is based upon God's **Judgment**, not His own. Thus does **He share God's Will** and bring His thoughts to still deluded minds. **He** is forever One, because **He** is as **God** created Him. **He** has accepted **Christ**, and **He** is saved. *M-12.1.2:10*

~ **god** has given **everyone** a Teacher Whose wisdom and **help** far exceed whatever contributions an earthly **therapist** can provide. *P-1.1.1.4*

~ no **good** teacher uses one approach to every **pupil**. *P-2.II.7.2*

TEACHER OF GOD   *A Course in Miracles Term*

Ego

~ no **teacher** of God can judge and hope to learn. *M-4.13.11*

~ if **he** argues with his **pupil** about a **magic thought**, attacks it, tries to establish its **error** or demonstrate its falsity, **he** is but witnessing to its **reality**. Depression is then inevitable, for **he** has "proved," both to his **pupil** and himself. *M-18.1.2:3*

~ a major hindrance in this aspect of his **learning** is the **teacher** of God's **fear** about the validity of what **he** hears. *M-21.5.1*

~ when a **teacher** of **God** fails to heal, it is because **he** has forgotten Who **he** is. Another's **sickness** thus becomes his own. In allowing this to happen, **he** has identified with another's **ego** and has thus confused him with a **body**. *M-22.5.1:3*

~ even the most advanced of God's teachers **will give way** to **temptation** in this **world**. *M-23.1.2*

HOLY SPIRIT;   *God's messenger, miracle worker, reminder.*

~ a **teacher** of **God** is anyone who chooses to be one. His qualifications consist solely in this; somehow, somewhere **he** has made a deliberate **choice** in which **he** did not **see** his interests as apart from someone else's. Once **he** has done that, his road is established and his direction is sure. A **light** has entered the **darkness**. It may be a single **light**, but that is enough. **He** has entered an agreement with **God** even if **he** does not yet believe in Him. **He** has become a bringer of **salvation**. **He** has become a **teacher** of **God**. *M-1.1.1:8*

~ **they** come from all over the **world**. **They** come from all religions and from no **religion**. **They** are the ones who **have** answered. *M-1.2.1:3*

~ it does not matter who the **teacher** was before **he** heard the **Call**. **He** has become a **savior** by his answering. **He** has seen someone else as himself. **He** has therefore found his own **salvation** and the **salvation** of the **world**. In his **rebirth** is the **world** reborn. *M-1.3.7:11*

~ **time** has an ending, and it is this that the teachers of **God** are appointed to bring about. For **time** is in their hands. Such was their **choice**, and it is given them. *M-1.4.8:10*

~ and thus **he** who was the **learner** becomes a **teacher** of **God** himself, for **he** has made the one **decision** that gave his **teacher** to him. **He** has seen in another person the same interests as his own. *M-2.5.8:9*

~ the teachers of **God** have no set **teaching level**. *M-3.1.1*

~ in **time**, the **teacher** of **God** seems to begin to **change** his **mind** about the **world** with the single **decision**, and then learns more and more about the new direction as **he** teaches it. *M-3.3.3*

~ god's teachers work at different levels, but the result is always the same. *M-3.3.7*

~ the surface traits of God's teachers are not at all alike. **They** do not look alike to the body's eyes, **they** come from vastly different backgrounds, their experiences of the **world** vary greatly, and their superficial "personalities" are quite distinct. Nor at the beginning stages of their functioning as teachers of **God have they** as yet acquired the deeper characteristics that **will** establish them as what **they** are. **God** gives **special** gifts to His teachers because **they have** a **special role** in His **plan** for **Atonement**. Their specialness is, of **course**, only temporary—set in **time** as a **means** of leading out of **time**. These **special** gifts, born in the **holy relationship** toward which the **teaching-learning situation** is geared, become characteristic of all teachers of **God** who **have** advanced in their own **learning**. In this respect **they** are all alike. *M-4.1.1:7*

~ all other traits of God's teachers **rest** on **trust**. Once that has been achieved, the others cannot **fail** to follow. *M-4.1.1:2*

~ the **peace** of **mind** which the advanced teachers of **God experience** is largely due to their perfect honesty. *M-4.12.1*

~ **they** choose in perfect honesty, sure of their **choice** themselves. *M-4.12.12*

~ there is no challenge to a **teacher** of **God**. Challenge implies **doubt**, and the **trust** on which God's teachers **rest** secure makes **doubt impossible**. Therefore **they** can only succeed. In this, as in all things, **they** are honest. **They** can only succeed because **they** never do their **will alone**. **They** choose for all mankind, for all the **world** and all things in it, for the unchanging and unchangeable beyond appearances, and for the **Son of God** and his **Creator**. *M-4.12.5:10*

~ god's teachers do not judge. *M-4.13.1*

~ no **teacher** of **God** can judge and hope to learn. *M-4.13.11*

~ **trust** remains the bed-rock of the **teacher** of God's whole **thought system**. *M-4.13.6*

419

~ **harm** is **impossible** for God's teachers. **They** can neither **harm** nor be harmed. *M-4.14.1:2*

~ no **teacher** of God but must learn—and fairly early in his training—that harmfulness completely obliterates his **function** from his **awareness**. It **will make** him confused, fearful, angry, and suspicious. It **will make** the Holy Spirit's lessons **impossible** to learn. Nor can God's **Teacher** be heard at all except by those who realize that **harm** can actually achieve **nothing**. No **gain** can come of it. *M-4.14.8:12*

~ god's teachers are wholly gentle. **They need** the **strength** of **gentleness**, for it is in this that the **function** of **salvation** becomes easy. *M-4.15.1:2*

~ the might of God's teachers lies in their **gentleness**, for **they have** understood their **evil** thoughts came neither from God's Son nor his **Creator**. *M-4.15.8*

~ god's teachers **trust** in Him. And **they** are sure His **Teacher** goes before them, making sure no **harm** can come to them. **They** hold His gifts and follow in His **way** because **God's Voice** directs them in all things. **Joy** is their **song** of thanks. And **Christ** looks down on them in thanks as well. His **need** of them is just as great as theirs of Him. How joyous it is to **share** the **purpose** of **salvation!** *M-4.16.9:15*

~ god's teachers **have** learned how to be simple. **They have** no dreams that **need defense** against the **truth**. **They** do not try to **make** themselves. Their **joy** comes from their understanding Who created them. *M-4.17.1:4*

~ no one can become an advanced **teacher** of God until **he** fully understands that defenses are but the foolish guardians of mad illusions. The more grotesque the **dream**, the fiercer and more powerful its defenses seem to be. Yet when the **teacher** of God finally agrees to look **past** them, **he** finds **nothing** was there. Slowly at first, **he** lets himself be undeceived. But **he** learns faster as his **trust** increases. *M-4.17.6:10*

~ the **teacher** of God is generous out of **self**-interest. This does not refer, however, to the **self** the **world** speaks of. The **teacher** of God does not **want** anything **he** cannot **give** away because **he** realizes it would be valueless to him by definition. What would **he want** it for? He could only lose because of it. He could not **gain**. Therefore **he** does not **seek** what only **he** could keep, because that is a guarantee of **loss**. He does not **want** to suffer. Why should he ensure himself **pain**? But **he** does **want** to keep for himself all things that are of **God** and therefore for His Son. These are the things that belong to him. These **he** can **give** away in true generosity, protecting them forever for himself. *M-4.19.1:12*

~ **patience** is natural to the **teacher** of God. All **he** sees is certain outcome, at a **time** perhaps unknown as yet, but not in **doubt**. The **time will** be as right as is the **answer**. And this is true for everything that happens **now** or in the **future**. The **past** as well held no mistakes—**nothing** that did not serve to benefit the **world** as well as him to whom it seemed to happen. Perhaps it was not understood at the **time**. Even so, the **teacher** of **God** is willing to reconsider all his **past** decisions if **they** are causing **pain** to anyone. *M-4.20.2:8*

~ the extent of the **teacher** of God's faithfulness is the measure of his advancement in the **curriculum**. Does **he** still select some aspects of his **life** to bring to his **learning** while keeping others apart? If so, his advancement is limited and his **trust** not yet firmly established. Faithfulness is the **teacher** of God's **trust** in the **word** of **God** to set all things right—not some but all. Generally, his faithfulness begins by resting on just some problems, remaining carefully limited for a **time**. To **give** up all problems to one **Answer** is to reverse the thinking of the **world** entirely. And that **alone** is faithfulness. **Nothing** but that really deserves the **name**. Yet each degree, however small, is **worth** achieving. **Readiness**, as the **text** notes, is not mastery. *M-4.21.1:10*

~ it is the **function** of God's teachers to bring true **learning** to the **world**. Properly speaking it is unlearning that **they** bring, for that is "true **learning**" in the **world**. It is given to the teachers of **God** to bring the glad tidings of complete **forgiveness** to the **world**. Blessed indeed are **they**, for **they** are the bringers of **salvation**. *M-4.25.6:9*

~ the teachers of **God have trust** in the **world**, because **they have** learned it is not governed by the **laws** the **world** made up. It is governed by a **Power** Which is in them but not of them. It is this **Power** that keeps all things safe. It is through this **Power** that the teachers of **God** look on a forgiven **world**. *M-4.3.4:7*

~ not once do the advanced teachers of **God** consider the forms of **sickness** in which their **brother** believes. To do this is to forget that all of them **have** the same **purpose** and therefore are not really different. **They** seek for **God's Voice** in this **brother** who would so deceive himself as to believe God's Son can suffer. And **they** remind him that **he** has not made himself and must remain as **God** created him. **They** recognize illusions can **have** no effect. The **truth** in their minds reaches out to the **truth** in the minds of their brothers, so that illusions are not reinforced. **They** are thus brought to **truth**, and **truth** is not brought to them. So are **they** dispelled, not by the **will** of another but by the **union** of the One **will** with itself. And this is the **function** of God's teachers—to **see** no **will** as separate from their own, nor theirs as separate from God's. *M-5.10.1:9*

~ for those already willing to **change** their **mind** he has no **function** except to rejoice with them, for **they have** become teachers of **God** with him. **He** has, however, a more specific **function** for those who do not **understand** what **healing** is. *M-5.8.4:5*

~ the simple presence of a **teacher** of **God** is a reminder. His thoughts **ask** for the right to **question** what the **patient** has accepted is true. As God's messengers, His teachers are the symbols of **salvation**. They **ask** the **patient** for **forgiveness** for God's Son in his own **name**. They stand for the alternative. With **God's word** in their minds **they** come in benediction, not to heal the sick but to remind them of the remedy **God** has already given them. It is not their hands that heal. It is not their **voice** that speaks the **word** of God. They merely **give** what has been given them. Very gently **they call** to their brothers to turn away from **death**. *M-5.9.2:11*

~ the **teacher** of **God** has seen the **correction** of his errors in the **mind** of the **patient**, recognizing it for what it is. Having accepted the **Atonement** for himself, **he** has also accepted it for the **patient**. *M-6.1.4:5*

~ no **teacher** of **God** should feel disappointed if **he** has offered **healing** and it does not appear to **have** been received. It is not up to him to judge when his **gift** should be accepted. Let him be certain it has been received and **trust** that it **will** be accepted when it is recognized as a **blessing** and not a curse. *M-6.2.7:9*

~ it is not the **function** of God's teachers to evaluate the outcome of their gifts. It is merely their **function** to **give** them. Once **they have** done that, **they have** also given the outcome, for that is **part** of the **gift**. *M-6.3.1:3*

~ for a **teacher** of **God** to remain concerned about the result of **healing** is to **limit** the **healing**. It is **now** the **teacher** of **God** himself whose **mind** needs to be healed. And it is this **he** must facilitate. **He** is **now** the **patient**, and **he** must so regard himself. **He** has made a **mistake** and must be willing to **change** his **mind** about it. **He** lacked the **trust** that makes for giving truly, and so **he** has not received the benefit of his **gift**. *M-7.1.5:10*

~ whenever a **teacher** of **God** has tried to be a **channel** for **healing**, **he** has succeeded. *M-7.2.1*

~ the **teacher** of **God** is a **miracle** worker because **he** gives the gifts **he** has received. Yet **he** must first accept them. **He need** do no more, nor is there more that **he** could do. By accepting **healing**, **he** can **give** it. *M-7.3.3:6*

~ **he** does not **make** his own decisions; **he** asks his **Teacher** for His **answer**, and it is this **he** follows as his guide for action. This becomes easier and easier as the **teacher** of **God** learns to **give** up his own **judgment**. *M-9.2.2:3*

~ god's teachers appear to be many, for that is the world's **need**. Yet **being** joined in one **purpose**, and one **they** share with God. *M-12.2.5:6*

~ their minds are one; their joining is complete. And **God** works through them **now** as One, for that is what **they** are. *M-12.2.8:9*

~ so do God's teachers **need** a body, for their **unity** could not be recognized directly. *M-12.3.8*

~ what makes them God's teachers is their recognition of the proper **purpose** of the **body**. *M-12.4.1*

~ the teachers of **God** appear to **share** the **illusion** of **separation**, but because of what **they** use the **body** for, **they** do not believe in the **illusion** despite appearances. *M-12.4.6*

~ **god's Voice will** tell him when **he** has fulfilled his **role**, just as It tells him what his **function** is. *M-12.5.10*

~ god's teachers choose to look on dreams a while. It is a conscious **choice**. For **they have** learned that all choices are made consciously, with full **awareness** of their consequences. *M-12.6.2:4*

421

~ **awareness** of dreaming is the real **function** of God's teachers. *M-12.6.6*

~ **they** are not deceived by what **they see. They** recognize that to behold a **dream** figure as sick and separate is no more real than to regard it as healthy and beautiful. *M-12.6.8:9*

~ god's teachers can **have** no regret on giving up the pleasures of the **world.** *M-13.4.1*

~ but **time** stands still and waits on the goals of God's teachers. Not one **thought** of **sin will** remain the instant any one of them accepts the **Atonement** for himself. It is not easier to forgive one **sin** than to forgive all of them. The **illusion** of orders of difficulty is an **obstacle** the **teacher of God** must learn to pass by and leave behind. One **sin** perfectly forgiven by one **teacher of God** can **make salvation** complete. *M-14.3.3:7*

~ **he need** merely learn how to approach it, to be willing to go in its direction. **He need** merely **trust** that, if **God's Voice** tells him it is a **lesson he** can learn, **he** can learn it. **He** does not judge it either as hard or easy. His **Teacher** points to it, and **he** trusts that **He will** show him how to learn it. *M-14.4.5:8*

~ to turn **hell** into **Heaven** is the **function** of God's teachers, for what **they teach** are lessons in which **Heaven** is reflected. *M-14.5.9*

~ **he** is set and sees the road on which **he** walks stretch surely and smoothly before him. *M-16.1.10*

~ **he will** be told all that his **role** should be, this day and every day. And those who **share** that **role** with him **will** find him, so **they** can learn the lessons for the day together. Not one is absent whom **he** needs; not one is sent without a **learning goal** already set, and one which can be met that very day. *M-16.1.5:7*

~ god's teachers learn to recognize the forms of **magic** and perceive their meaninglessness. **Fear** is withdrawn from them, and so **they** go. *M-16.11.9:10*

~ **he** cannot claim that title until **he** has gone through the **workbook,** since **we** are **learning within** the framework of our **course.** *M-16.3.7*

~ all that **he** did before in the **name** of safety no longer interests him. For **he** is safe and knows it to be so. **He** has a Guide Who **will** not fail. **He need make** no distinctions among the problems **he** perceives, for **He** to Whom **he** turns with all of them recognizes no **order** of difficulty in resolving them. **He** is as safe in the **present** as **he** was before illusions were accepted into his **mind** and as **he will** be when **he** has let them go. There is no **difference** in his state at different times and different places, because **they** are all one to **God.** This is his safety. And **he** has no **need** for more than this. *M-16.7.2:9*

~ his success depends on his conviction that **he will** succeed. **He** must be sure success is not of him but **will** be given him at any **time,** in any place and circumstance **he** calls for it. There are times his **certainty will** waver, and the instant this occurs **he will** return to earlier attempts to place reliance on himself **alone.** *M-16.8.3:5*

~ the single aim of the **teacher** turns the divided **goal** of the **pupil** into one direction, with the **call** for **help** becoming his one appeal. This then is easily responded to with just one **answer,** and this **answer will** enter the teacher's **mind** unfailingly. From there it shines into his pupil's **mind,** making it one with his. *M-17.3.5:7*

~ **god** sends His teachers. And as **they teach** His lessons of **joy** and hope, their **learning** finally becomes complete. *M-17.8.1:2*

~ **they** bring the **light** of hope from **God** Himself. There is a **way** in which escape is possible. It can be learned and taught, but it requires **patience** and abundant willingness. *M-17.8.2:4*

~ god's teachers' major **lesson** is to learn how to react to **magic** thoughts wholly without **anger.** Only in this **way** can **they** proclaim the **truth** about themselves. Through them, the **Holy Spirit** can **now** speak of the **reality** of the **Son of God. Now He** can remind the **world** of sinlessness, the one unchanged, unchangeable **condition** of all that **God** created. *M-18.2.1:4*

~ **now** is He free to **teach** all minds the **truth** of what **they** are, so **they will** gladly be returned to Him. *M-18.2.6*

~ in **order** to heal, it thus becomes essential for the **teacher** of God to let all his own mistakes be corrected. If **he** senses even the faintest hint of irritation in himself as **he** responds to anyone, let him instantly realize that **he** has made an **interpretation** that is not true. *M-18.5.1:2*

~ the sole responsibility of God's **teacher** is to accept the **Atonement** for himself. *M-18.5.5*

~ **he** overlooks the **mind** and **body**, seeing only the **face of Christ** shining in front of him, correcting all mistakes and **healing** all **perception**. **Healing** is the result of the recognition by God's **teacher** of Who it is that is in **need** of **healing**. *M-22.4.5:6*

~ it is your task to heal the **sense** of **separation** that has made him sick. It is your **function** to recognize for him that what **he** believes about himself is not the **truth**. It is your **forgiveness** that must show him this. *M-22.6.7:9*

~ it is not up to God's teachers to set limits upon Him, because it is not up to them to judge His Son. And to judge His Son is to **limit** his **Father**. Both are equally meaningless. *M-22.7.4:6*

~ no one who has become a true and dedicated **teacher** of **God** forgets his brothers. Yet what **he** can offer them is limited by what **he** learns himself. *M-23.6.6:7*

~ **they** too **have** not attained the necessary understanding as yet, but **they have** joined with others. This is what sets them apart from the **world**. *M-26.1.6:7*

~ **alone they** are **nothing**. But in their joining is the **Power** of **God**. *M-26.1.9:10*

~ sometimes a **teacher** of **God** may **have** a brief **experience** of direct **union** with **God**. *M-26.3.1*

~ **teacher** of **God**, your one assignment could be stated thus: accept no **compromise** in which **death** plays a **part**. *M-27.7.1*

~ god's teachers **have** the **goal** of wakening the minds of those asleep and seeing there the **vision** of Christ's face to take the place of what **they** dreamed. *M-28.6.3*

~ except for God's teachers, there would be no hope of **salvation**, for the **world** of **sin** would seem forever "real." *M-1.5.1*

~ **they** are not perfect or **they** would not be **here**. Yet it is their **mission** to become perfect **here**, and so **they teach perfection** over and over in many, many ways until **they have** learned it. And then **they** are seen no more, although their thoughts remain a **source** of **strength** and **truth** forever. *M-1.5.5*

~ to be a **teacher** of **God**, it is not necessary to be religious or even to believe in **God** to any recognizable extent. It is necessary, however, to **teach forgiveness** rather than **condemnation**. *P-2.II.1.1:2*

TEACHER OF TEACHERS   *A Course in Miracles Term*

HOLY SPIRIT

~ there are those who **have** reached **God** directly, retaining no trace of worldly limits and remembering their own **Identity** perfectly. These might be called the teachers of teachers, because, although **they** are no longer visible, their **image** can yet be called upon. And **they will** appear when and where it is helpful for them to do so. To those to whom such appearances would be frightening, **they give** their ideas. No one can **call** on them in vain. Nor is there anyone of whom **they** are unaware. All needs are known to them, and all mistakes are recognized and overlooked by them. *M-26.2.1:7*

~ **they give** all their gifts to the teachers of **God** who look to them for **help**, asking all things in their **name** and in no other. *M-26.2.9*

~ those who **have** laid the **body** down merely to extend their helpfulness to those remaining behind are few indeed. And **they need** helpers who are still in bondage and still asleep, so that by their awakening can **God's Voice** be heard. *M-26.3.9:10*

TEACHER/STUDENT

see "teacher", "pupil"

EGO

~ at any **time**, the student may disagree with what his would-be **teacher** says about them, and the **teacher** himself is inconsistent in what **he** believes. *M-10.1.8*

HOLY SPIRIT

~ **teacher** and **pupil** are alike in the **learning** process. **They** are in the same **order** of **learning**, and unless **they share** their lessons, **they will** lack conviction. *T-4.II.7.2:3*

~ thus it is that **pupil** and **teacher** seem to come together in the **present**, finding each other as if **they** had not met before. *M-2.4.3*

TEACHING/LEARNING

see "teach", "learning"

EGO

~ the **ego** does not **want** to **teach everyone** all it has learned, because that would defeat its **purpose**. Therefore, it does not really learn at all. *T-7.IV.22.1:2*

~ to **attack** those who **have need** of **teaching** is to **fail** to learn from them. *T-14.II.9.6*

~ the **role** of **teaching** and **learning** is actually reversed in the thinking of the **world**. The reversal is characteristic. It seems as if the **teacher** and the **learner** are separated, the **teacher** giving something to the **learner** rather than to himself. *M-I.1.1:3*

HOLY SPIRIT

~ everything **you teach you** are **learning**. *T-6.IV.44.5*

~ **outside** the **Kingdom teaching** is mandatory, because **learning** is essential. This **form** of the law clearly implies that **you will** learn what **you** are from what **you have** projected onto others and therefore believe **they** are. *T-7.III.14.2:3*

~ when **you teach** anyone that **truth** is true, **you** learn it with him. And so **you** learn that what seemed hardest was the easiest. *T-13.VII.60.1:2*

~ **you will** learn of him exactly what **you** taught. For **you** can **teach** him only that **he** is as **you** would **have** him, and what **you** choose **he** be is but your **choice** for **you**. *T-21.VII.64.3:4*

~ and as **you teach salvation, you will** learn. *W-pI.121.7.6*

~ yet all your **teaching** and your **learning will** be not of **you**, but of the **Teacher** Who was given **you** to show the **way** to **you**. *W-pI.121.8.1*

~ in **order** to **understand** the teaching-**learning plan** of **salvation**, it is necessary to grasp the **concept** of **time** which the **course** sets forth. *M-2.2.1*

~ when **pupil** and **teacher** come together, a teaching-**situation** begins. For the **teacher** is not really the one who does the **teaching**. *M-2.5.1:2*

~ in the teaching-**learning** situation, each one learns that **giving** and **receiving** are the same. The demarcations **they have** drawn between their roles, their minds, their bodies, their needs, their interests, and all the differences **they thought** separated them from one another fade and grow dim and disappear. Those who would learn the same **course share** one interest and one **goal**. *M-2.5.5:7*

~ each teaching-**learning situation** involves a different **relationship** at the beginning, although the ultimate **goal** is always the same—to **make** of the **relationship** a **holy relationship** in which both can look upon the **Son of God** as sinless. There is no one from whom a **teacher of God** cannot learn, so there is no one whom **he** cannot **teach**. However, from a practical point of view, **he** cannot meet **everyone**, nor can **everyone** find him. Therefore, the **plan** includes very specific contacts to be made for each **teacher of God**. *M-3.1.2:5*

~ any **level** of the teaching-**learning situation** is **part** of God's **plan** for **Atonement**. *M-3.3.5*

~ each teaching-**learning situation** is maximal in the **sense** that each person involved **will** learn the most that **he** can from the other person at that **time**. In this **sense**, and in this **sense** only, **we** can speak of levels of **teaching**. Using the term in this **way**, the second **level** of **teaching** is a more sustained **relationship** in which for a **time** two people enter into a fairly intense teaching-**learning situation** and then appear to separate. As with the first **level**, these meetings are not accidental, nor is what appears to be the end of the **relationship** a real end. Again, each has learned the most **he** can at the **time**. *M-3.4.1:5*

~ the third **level** of **teaching** occurs in relationships which, once **they** are formed, are lifelong. These are teaching-**learning** situations in which each person is given a chosen **learning** partner who presents him with unlimited opportunities for **learning**. These relationships are generally few, because their existence implies that those involved **have** reached a stage simultaneously in which the teaching-**learning** balance is actually perfect. This does not mean that **they** necessarily recognize. **They** may even be quite hostile to each other for some **time**, and perhaps for **life**. Yet should **they** decide to learn it, the perfect **lesson** is before them and can be learned. And if **they** decide to learn that **lesson, they** become the saviors of the teachers who falter and may even seem to **fail**. *M-3.5.1:7*

TE MPLE $|'tempəl|$

DICTIONARY: *a building devoted to the worship, or regarded as the dwelling place, of a **God** or Gods or other objects of religious reverence.*

EGO

~ the **altar** disappears, the **light** grows dim, the temple of the Holy One becomes a house of **sin**. And **nothing** is remembered except illusions. *T-23.II.17.3:4*

HOLY SPIRIT; *host, relationship, temple of the living God.*

~ a temple is not a building at all. Its real **holiness** lies in the inner **altar** around which the building is built. The inappropriate emphasis men **have** put on beautiful **church** buildings is a sign of their **fear** of Atonement and their unwillingness to reach the **altar** itself. The real beauty of the temple cannot be seen with the physical **eye**. *T-2.II.45.4:7*

~ "the restoration of the temple." It does not mean the restoration of the building but the opening of the **altar** to **receive** the **Atonement**. This heals the **separation** and places **within man** the one **defense** against all **separation mind**-errors which can **make** him perfectly invulnerable. *T-2.II.46.5:7*

~ the ego's temple thus becomes the temple of the **Holy Spirit**, where **devotion** to Him replaces **devotion** to the **ego**. In this **sense**, the **body** does become a temple to **God**, because His **Voice** abides in it by directing the use to which it is put. *T-8.VII.61.6:7*

~ the temple **you** restore becomes your **altar**, for it was rebuilt through **you**. *T-14.II.14.10*

~ there are no hidden chambers in God's temple. Its gates are open wide to greet His Son. *T-14.III.23.6:7*

~ the temple still is holy, for the Presence that dwells **within** it is **Holiness**. *T-14.V.40.9*

~ in the temple **Holiness** waits quietly for the return of them that **love** it. *T-14.V.41.1*

~ your **relationship** is **now** a temple of **healing**—a place where all the weary ones can come and find **rest**. **Here** is the **rest** that waits for all after the **journey**. *T-19.IV.36.3:4*

~ the Holy Spirit's temple is not a **body**, but a **relationship**. *T-20.VII.49.1*

~ the **Holy Spirit** does not build His temples where **love** can never be. *T-20.VII.49.6*

~ **where you** are the **body** cannot enter, for the **Holy Spirit** has set His temple there. *T-20.VII.51.10*

~ **now** is the temple of the Living **God** rebuilt as **host** again to Him by Whom it was created. *T-26.X.84.1*

TEMPTATION |tem(p)ˈtāSH(ə)n|

DICTIONARY: *a **desire** to do something, especially something wrong or unwise.*

EGO

~ a mad **belief** that God's **insanity** would **make you** sane and **give you** what **you want**. That either **God** or **you** must lose to **madness** because your aims can not be reconciled. *T-25.VIII.62.1:2*

~ what is temptation but a **wish** to **make** illusions real. *T-30.IX.91.1*

~ it is an assertion that some forms of idols **have** a powerful appeal which makes them harder to resist than those **you** would not **want** to **have** reality. Temptation, then, is **nothing** more than this—a **prayer** the **miracle** touch not some dreams but keep their unreality obscure and **give** to them **reality** instead. *T-30.IX.91.3:4*

~ when **he** is tempted, **he** denies **reality**. And **he** becomes the willing slave of what **he** chose instead. *T-30.IX.92.8:9*

~ what is temptation but a **wish** to **make** the wrong **decision** on what **you** would learn and **have** an outcome that **you** do not **want**? It is the recognition that it is a state of **mind** unwanted that becomes the **means** whereby the **choice** is reassessed; another outcome seen to be preferred. *T-31.I.11.1:2*

~ what is temptation but the **wish** to stay in **hell** and **misery**? And what could this **give** rise to but an **image** of yourself that can be miserable and remain in **hell** and torment. *T-31.VII.77.1:2*

~ it always but reflects a **wish** to be a **self** which **you** are not. And from that **wish**, a **concept** rises, **teaching** that **you** are the **thing you wish** to be. It **will** remain your **concept** of yourself until the **wish** that fathered it no longer is held dear. *T-31.VII.79.1:3*

~ temptation has one **lesson** it would **teach** in all its forms wherever it occurs. It would persuade the holy **Son of God** he is a **body**, born in what must die, unable to escape its frailty and bound by what it orders him to feel. It sets the limits on what **he** can do; its **power** is the only **strength he** has; his grasp cannot exceed its tiny reach. *T-31.VIII.83.1:3*

~ what **you** behold as **sickness** and as **pain**, as **weakness** and as **suffering** and **loss** is but temptation to perceive yourself defenseless and in **hell**. *T-31.VIII.92.2*

~ **nothing** the body's eyes seem to **see** can be anything but a **form** of temptation, since this was the **purpose** of the **body** itself. *W-pI.64.2.1*

~ and **you** may find that **you** are tempted still to walk ahead of **truth** and let illusions be your guide. *W-pI.155.9.2*

~ temptation **call** to us to stay and linger in a **dream**. *W-pII.272.2.2*

HOLY SPIRIT; *mad **belief**, attempt to **substitute**.*

~ "lead us not into **temptation**" **means** "do not let us deceive ourselves into believing that **we** can relate in **peace** to **God** or to our brothers with anything external." *T-1.II.104.6*

~ another chance to choose again and let Christ's **strength** prevail in every circumstance and every place **you** raised an **image** of yourself before. *T-31.VIII.88.2*

~ temptation falls away when **we** allow each one **we** meet to save us and refuse to **hide** his **light** behind our grievances. *W-pI.78.12.2*

TEST

DICTIONARY: *take measures to check the quality, performance, or reliability of (something), especially before putting it into widespread use or* **practice**.

HOLY SPIRIT; *test of* **truth**, *test of perfect* **peace**, *"what is it for?"*

~ **you have** one test, as sure as **God**, by which to recognize if what **you** learned is true. If **you** are wholly free of **fear** of any kind, and if all those who meet or even think of **you share** in your perfect **peace**, then **you** can be sure that **you have** learned God's **lesson** and not yours. *T-14.VII.63.1:2*

~ think not **you understand** anything until **you** pass the test of perfect **peace**, for **peace** and understanding go together and never can be found **alone**. *T-14.VII.72.4*

~ leave room for Him, and **you will** find yourself so filled with **power** that **nothing will** prevail against your **peace**. And this **will** be the test by which **you** recognize that **you have** understood. *T-14.VII.75.5:6*

~ the test of everything on earth is simply this: "What is it for?" The **answer** makes it what it is for you. *T-24.VIII.67.1:2*

TEXT

DICTIONARY: *a* **piece** *of written or printed material regarded as conveying the authentic or primary* **form** *of a particular work.*

HOLY SPIRIT

~ a theoretical foundation such as the text is necessary as a background to **make** these exercises meaningful. *W-pI.1.1.1*

~ the text explains that the **Holy Spirit** is the **Answer** to all problems **you have** made. *M-11.3.1*

THE GOLDEN RULE
A Course in Miracles Term

EGO

~ the **illusion** that shallow roots can be deepened and thus made to hold is one of the distortions on which the reversal of the Golden **Rule** rests. *T-1.1.70.4*

HOLY SPIRIT; *rule for appropriate* **behavior**

~ the Golden **Rule** asks **you** to behave toward others as **you** would **have** them behave toward **you**. This **means** that the **perception** of both must be accurate. The Golden **Rule** is the **rule** for appropriate **behavior**. *T-1.1.64.1:3*

THE GREAT RAYS

EGO

~ the Great Rays are obscured. *T-9.X.92.1*

HOLY SPIRIT

~ the Great Rays would establish the total lack of **value** of the **special relationship** if **they** were seen. For in seeing them, the **body** would disappear because its **value** would be lost. And so your whole investment in seeing it would be withdrawn from it. *T-16.VII.61.5:7*

~ **you have** found each other and **will light** each other's way. And from this **light will** the Great Rays extend back into **darkness** and forward unto **God** to shine away the **past** and so **make** room for His eternal Presence, in which everything is radiant in the **light**. *T-18.V.31.6:7*

THE SEPARATED ONES

EGO

~ many Souls offered their efforts on behalf of the separated ones, but **they** could not withstand the **strength** of the **attack** and had to be brought back. Angels came, too, but their protection did not suffice because the separated ones were not interested in **peace**. **They** had already split their minds and were bent on further dividing rather than reintegrating. The levels **they** introduced into their minds turned against each other, and **they** established differences, divisions, cleavages, dispersions, and all the other concepts related to the increasing splits which **they** produced. *T-2.II.38.2:5*

~ not **being** in their right minds, **they** turned their defenses from protection to assault and acted literally insanely. *T-2.II.39.1*

~ **they** cannot believe that a **defense** which cannot **attack** is the best **defense**. *T-2.II.42.4*

~ **they** themselves generally **see** this as a **need** to protect the **body**. *T-2.II.44.5*

~ tendency of the separated ones, who always refuse to consider what **they have** done to themselves. *T-6.II.6.2*

~ all the separated ones **have** a basic **fear** of retaliation and abandonment. This is because **they** believe in **attack** and rejection, so this is what **they** perceive and **teach** and learn. *T-6.V.70.1:2*

THEOLOGIAN

DICTIONARY: *a person who engages or is an expert in theology.*

EGO

~ "i am a miserable sinner and so are **you**." *T-9.IV.20.5*

~ are likely to condemn themselves, **teach condemnation**, and advocate a very fearful solution. Projecting **condemnation** on to **God, they make** Him appear retaliative and **fear** His retribution. *T-9.IV.22.2:3*

~ or like the theologian, by acknowledging **darkness** in yourself and looking for a distant **light** to remove it while emphasizing the distance. *T-9.IV.25.7*

THERAPIST

DICTIONARY: *a person skilled in a particular kind of therapy.*

EGO;   *patient*

~ having made it real, **he** then attempts to dispel its effects by depreciating the importance of the dreamer. This would be a **healing** approach if the dreamer were properly identified as unreal. *T-9.IV.23.3:4*

~ not one of them can cure, and not one of them understands **healing**. At worst, **they** but **make** the **body** real in their own minds, and having done so, **seek** for **magic** by which to heal the ills with which their minds endow it. *P-2.IV.4.2:3*

~ must their cures remain temporary, or another illness rise instead, for **death** has not been overcome until the **meaning** of **love** is understood. *P-2.IV.5.4*

~ the defenses sought for must be magical. **They** must overcome all limits perceived in the **self**, at the same **time** making a new **self-concept** into which the old one cannot return. In a **word**, **error** is accepted as real and dealt with by illusions. *P-2.IV.6.3:5*

~ the therapist is seen as one who is attacking the patient's most cherished **possession**; his **picture** of himself. *P-2.IV.9.5*

~ therapist cannot but be seen as a real **source** of danger, to be attacked and even killed. *P-2.IV.9.6*

~ that many therapists are mad is obvious. *P-2.VII.5.7*

~ those who devote themselves primarily to **healing** of one sort or another as their chief **function**. *P-3.II.1.4*

~ the therapists of this **world** do not expect this outcome, and many of their patients would not be able to accept **help** from them if **they** did. Yet no therapist really sets the **goal** for the relationships of which **he** is a **part**. *P-3.II.5.6:7*

~ some utilize the **relationship** merely to collect bodies to worship at their shrine, and this **they** regard as **healing**. Many patients, too, consider this strange procedure as **salvation**. *P-3.II.9.8:9*

~ the defensive therapist has lost **sight** of the **Source** of his **salvation**. **He** does not **see** and **he** does not hear. *P-3.II.10.2:3*

~ the therapists of this **world** are indeed useless to the world's **salvation**. **They make** demands, and so **they** cannot **give**. *P-3.III.3.1:2*

HOLY SPIRIT;   *saints of God, Holy Spirit, saviors of the world.*

~ the therapist does not heal; **he** lets **healing** be. *T-9.IV.28.1*

~ **he** cannot bring **light** of himself, for **light** is not of him. Yet, **being** for him, it must also be for his **patient**. The **Holy Spirit** is the only therapist. **He** makes **healing** perfectly clear in any **situation** in which **he** is the Guide. The human therapist can only let Him fulfill His **function**. *T-9.IV.28.2:6*

~ the **Holy Spirit** is the only therapist. *T-9.IV.28.4*

~ the therapist is only a somewhat more specialized **teacher of God**. *P-2.I.4.3*

~ **he** learns through **teaching**, and the more advanced **he** is the more **he** teaches and the more **he** learns. But whatever stage **he** is in, there are patients who **need** him just that **way**. *P-2.I.4.4:5*

~ one wholly egoless therapist could heal the **world** without a **word**, merely by **being** there. No one **need see** him or talk to him or even know of his existence. His simple Presence is enough to heal. *P-2.III.3.7:9*

~ the ideal therapist is one with **Christ**. *P-2.III.4.1*

~ **he** must meet **attack** without **attack**, and therefore without **defense**. It is his task to demonstrate that defenses are not necessary, and that **defenselessness** is **strength**. *P-2.IV.10.2:3*

~ the therapist sees in the **patient** all that **he** has not forgiven in himself, and is thus given another chance to look at it, open it to re-evaluation and forgive it. *P-2.VI.6.3*

~ the therapist in no **way** confuses himself with **God**. *P-2.VII.4.1*

~ the advanced therapist in no **way** can ever **doubt** the **power** that is in him. Nor does **he doubt** its **Source**. He understands all **power** in earth and **Heaven** belongs to him because of who **he** is. And **he** is this because of his **Creator**, Whose **Love** is in him and Who cannot **fail**. *P-2.VII.6.2:5*

~ a holy therapist, an advanced **teacher of God**, never forgets one **thing; he** did not **make** the **curriculum** of **salvation**, nor did **he** establish his **part** in it. He understands that his **part** is necessary to the whole, and that through it **he will** recognize the whole when his **part** is complete. *P-3.I.4.1:2*

~ these are therefore "officially" helpers. **They** are devoted to certain kinds of needs in their professional activities, although **they** may be far more able teachers **outside** of them. These people **need** no **special** rules, of **course**, but **they** may be called upon to use **special** applications of the general principles of **healing**. *P-3.II.1.7:9*

~ first, the professional therapist is in an excellent position to demonstrate that there is no **order of difficulty** in **healing**. For this, however, **he** needs **special** training, because the **curriculum** by which **he** became a therapist probably taught him **little** or **nothing** about the real principles of **healing**. In **fact**, it probably taught him how to **make healing impossible**. Most of the world's **teaching** follows a **curriculum** in **judgment**, with the aim of making the therapist a judge. *P-3.II.2.1:4*

~ their **image** remains, because **they have** chosen that it be so. **They** take the place of other images, and **help** with kindly dreams. *P-3.II.7.9:10*

~ most professional therapists are still at the very start of the beginning stage of the first **journey**. *P-3.II.8.5*

~ **he** has chosen a road in which there is great **temptation** to misuse his **role**. This enables him to pass by many obstacles to **peace** quite quickly, if **he** escapes the **temptation** to assume a **function** that has not been given him. To **understand** there is no **order of difficulty** in **healing**, **he** must also recognize the equality of himself and the **patient**. *P-3.II.9.2:4*

~ the defenseless therapist has the **strength of God** with him. *P-3.II.10.2*

~ **they give** because **they have** heard His **Word** and understood it. All that **they need will** thus be given them. *P-3.III.5.6:7*

~ all **they have** comes only from **God**. *P-3.III.5.8*

THERAPIST/PATIENT *see "therapist", "patient"*

Ego

~ whatever resolutions **patient** and **therapist** reach in connection with their own divergent goals, **they** cannot become completely reconciled as one until **they join** with His. *P-2.I.3.6*

~ neither a perfect **therapist** nor a perfect **patient** can possibly **exist**. Both must **have** denied their **perfection**, for their very **need** for each other implies a **sense** of lack. *P-3.II.4.4:5*

Holy Spirit

~ happiness and **peace**. These are the "symptoms" of the ideal **patient-therapist relationship**, replacing those with which the **patient** came to **ask** for **help**. *T-12.II.7.1:2*

~ **they** cannot take more than **he** can **give** for **now**. Yet both **will** find **sanity** at last. *P-2.I.4.6:7*

430

- if **pupil** and **teacher join** in sharing one **goal**, **God will** enter into their **relationship** because **He** has been invited to come in. In the same **way**, a **union** of **purpose** between **patient** and **therapist** restores the place of **God** to ascendance, first through **Christ's vision** and then through the **memory of God** Himself. *P-2.II.5.3:4*

- **now** the extent of their success depends on how much of this potentiality **they** are willing to use. The willingness may come from either one at the beginning, and as the other shares it, it **will** grow. *P-2.III.2.4:5*

- one asks for **help**; another hears and tries to **answer** in the **form** of **help**. *P-2.III.3.4*

- his **knowledge** is reflected in the ideal **patient-therapist relationship**. *P-2.VII.1.13*

- in the end, **everyone** is both. **He** who needs **healing** must heal. *P-2.VII.1.2:3*

- every **therapist** must learn to heal from each **patient** who comes to him. **He** thus becomes his **patient**. *P-2.VII.1.9:10*

- the process that takes place in this **relationship** is actually one in which the **therapist** in his heart tells the **patient** that all his sins **have** been forgiven him, along with his own. *P-2.VII.3.1*

- the therapeutic **relationship** must become like the **relationship** of the **Father** and the **Son**. *P-3.II.5.4*

- no **patient** can accept more than **he** is ready to **receive**, and no **therapist** can offer more than **he** believes **he** has. *P-3.II.6.7*

- the **therapist** repays the **patient** in **gratitude**, as does the **patient** repay him. There is no cost to either. But thanks are due to both, for the **release** from long imprisonment and **doubt**. *P-3.III.4.6:8*

THEY |T Hā|

DICTIONARY: *used to refer to two or more people or things previously mentioned or easily identified.*

EGO

- yet they hear **nothing**. They are lost in dreams of specialness. They **hate** the **call** that would **awaken** them, and they curse **God** because **He** did not **make** their **dream reality**. *T-24.IV.32.3:5*

- as long as they believe they are in bodies, where they think they are **He** cannot be. And so they carry Him unknowingly and do not **make** Him manifest. And thus they do not recognize Him where **He** is. The son of **man** is not the risen **Christ**. *T-25.I.2.3:6*

- and so they **fear** the **Holy Spirit** and perceive the "wrath" of **God** in Him. *T-25.IX.68.2*

- they do believe that **Heaven** is **hell** and are afraid of **love**. And deep suspicion and the chill of **fear** comes over them when they are told that they **have** never sinned. Their **world** depends on sin's stability. *T-25.IX.68.5:7*

- so do they think the **loss** of **sin** a curse. *T-25.IX.69.1*

- their helplessness and **weakness** represents the grounds on which they justify his **pain**. The constant sting of **guilt he** suffers serves to prove that **he** is slave but they are free. *T-27.III.21.3:4*

- stability to those who are confused is meaningless, and **shift** and **change** become the law on which they predicate their lives. *T-29.III.15.6*

- they were not free from bitter cost and joyless consequence. *T-30.VI.65.12*

- if they believe they **need** anything from a **brother**, they **will** recognize him as a **brother** no longer. And if they do this, a **light** goes out even in **Heaven**. *P-3.III.5.9:10*

~ they **want** for **nothing**. Sorrow of any kind is inconceivable. Only the **light** they **love** is in **awareness**, and only **love** shines upon them forever. It is their **past**, their **present**, and their **future** always the same, eternally complete, and wholly shared. They know it is **impossible** their happiness could ever suffer **change** of any kind. *T-23.V.54.2:6*

THING

|THiNG|

DICTIONARY: *an inanimate material object as distinct from a living sentient* ***being***.

EGO; *shadows of a **decision** already made, replacements.*

~ each has imprisoned **you** with **laws** as senseless as itself. **You** are not bound by them. Yet to **understand** that this is so, **you** must first realize **salvation** lies not there. While **you** would **seek** for it in things that **have** no **meaning**, **you** bind yourself to **laws** that **make** no **sense**. Thus do **you seek** to prove **salvation** is where it is not. *W-pI.76.1.2:6*

~ of **service** for a while and fit to serve, to keep its usefulness while it can serve, and then to be replaced for greater **good**. *W-pII.293.2.14*

~ a neutral thing does not **see death**, for thoughts of **fear** are not invested there, nor is a mockery of **love** bestowed upon it. Its neutrality protects it while it has a use. And afterwards, without a **purpose**, it is laid aside. It is not sick or old or **hurt**. It is but functionless, unneeded and cast off. *W-pII.293.2.9:13*

HOLY SPIRIT; *gift of **God**, lessons **God** would **have** me learn, Echoes of the **Voice** of **God**.*

~ **you see** no neutral things because **you have** no neutral thoughts. *W-pI.17.1.2*

~ unbind your **mind** from **little** things the **world** sets forth to keep **you** prisoner there. **Value** them not, and **they will** disappear. Esteem them, and **they will** seem real to **you**. *W-pI.129.5.5:7*

~ all things are valuable or valueless, worthy or not of **being** sought at all, entirely desirable or not **worth** the slightest **effort** to obtain. *W-pI.133.13.1*

~ things but represent the thoughts that **make** them. *W-pI.187.2.3*

THOUGHT

|THôt|

DICTIONARY: *an **idea** or opinion produced by thinking or occurring suddenly in the **mind**.*

EGO; *illusions, meaningless thoughts, **conflict** thoughts, **attack** thoughts, irrational thought, thought disorder.*

~ everything **you** think that is not through the **Holy Spirit** is lacking. *T-5.VI.57.5*

~ irrational thought is a thought disorder. *T-5.VII.68.1*

~ **you have** experienced lack of competition among your thoughts, which, even though **they** may **conflict**, can occur to **you** together and in great numbers. **You** are so used to this that it can **cause you little** surprise. *T-14.VI.48.6:7*

~ yet **you** are also used to classifying some of your thoughts as more important, larger or better, wiser or more productive and valuable than others. And this is true about the thoughts which cross the **mind** of those who think **they** live apart. For some are reflections of **Heaven**, while others are motivated by the **ego**, which but seems to think. The result is a weaving, changing pattern which never rests and is never still. It shifts unceasingly across the mirror of your **mind**, and the reflections of **Heaven** last but a moment and grow dim as **darkness** blots them out. Where there was **light**, **darkness** removes it in an instant, and alternating patterns of **light** and **darkness** sweep constantly across your minds. *T-14.VI.49.1:6*

~ **you have** no basis at all for ordering your thoughts. *T-14.VI.50.7*

~ **you** believe that it is possible to harbor thoughts **you** would not **share** and that **salvation** lies in keeping your thoughts to yourself **alone**. For in private thoughts, known only to yourself, **you** think **you** find a **way** to keep what **you** would **have alone** and **share** what **you** would **share**. *T-15.V.41.3:4*

~ **you** could not recognize your "**evil**" thoughts as long as **you see value** in **attack**. **You will** perceive them sometimes, but **will** not **see** them as meaningless. And so **they** come in fearful **form**, with content still concealed, to shake your sorry **concept** of yourself and blacken it with still another "**crime**." *T-31.VII.69.1:4*

~ **they** represent such a mixture that, in a **sense**, none of them can be called "**good**" or "bad." This is why **they** do not mean anything. *W-pI.4.1.6:7*

~ none of them represents your real thoughts, which are **being** covered up by them. The "**good**" ones of which **you** are aware are but shadows of what lies beyond, and shadows **make sight difficult**. The "bad" ones are blocks to **sight** and **make** seeing **impossible**. **You** do not **want** either. *W-pI.4.2.3:6*

~ it is because the thoughts **you** think **you** think appear as images that **you** do not recognize them as **nothing**. **You** think **you** think them, and so **you** think **you see** them. This is how your "seeing" was made. This is the **function you have** given your body's eyes. *W-pI.15.1.1:4*

~ there is no more **self**-contradictory **concept** than that of "idle thoughts." *W-pI.16.2.1:2*

~ the **cause** of the **world you see** is **attack** thoughts. *W-pI.23.2.1*

~ uneasiness, depression, **anger, fear,** worry, **attack,** insecurity, and so on. Whatever **form they** take, **they** are unloving and therefore fearful. And so it is from them that **you need** to be saved. *W-pI.39.6.2:4*

~ unreal thoughts that cover the **truth** in your **mind**. *W-pI.45.8.1*

~ **i have** no private thoughts. Yet it is only private thoughts of which **I** am aware. They do not **exist**, and so they mean **nothing**. *W-pI.52.6.1:3*

~ insane thoughts are upsetting. **They** produce a **world** in which there is no **order** anywhere. *W-pI.53.3.1:2*

~ whatever **I see** reflects my thoughts. It is my thoughts which tell me where **I** am and what **I** am. The **fact** that **I see** a **world** in which there is **suffering** and **loss** and **death** shows me that **I** am seeing only the representation of my insane thoughts and am not allowing my real thoughts to cast their beneficent **light** on what **I see**. *W-pI.53.6.1:3*

~ whatever **form** such thoughts may take, **they have** no **meaning** and no **power**. *W-pI.Rev II.3.5*

~ an unforgiving thought is one which makes a **judgment** that it **will** not raise to **doubt**, although it is not true. The **mind** is closed and **will** not be released. The thought protects **projection**, tightening its chains so that distortions are more veiled and more obscure, less easily accessible to **doubt**, and further kept from **reason**. *W-pII.ST221.2.1:3*

~ an unforgiving thought does many things. In frantic action, it pursues its **goal**, twisting and overturning what it sees as interfering with its chosen path. Distortion is its **purpose** and the **means** by which it would accomplish it as well. It sets about its furious attempts to smash **reality**, without concern for anything that would appear to pose a **contradiction** to its point of view. *W-pII.ST221.3.1:4*

HOLY SPIRIT; *images, reflections,* **communication,** *loving thoughts, real thoughts.*

~ the **truth** is that there are no "idle" thoughts. All thinking produces **form** at some **level.** *T-2.V.92.3:4*

~ the **will** to **share** them is their **purification.** *T-5.VI.56.9*

~ your thought was created by Him. *T-5.VII.68.2*

~ its **power** is not of your making. Your ability to direct your thinking as **you will** is **part** of its **power.** *T-7.VII.55.5:6*

~ thought cannot be made into flesh except by **belief,** since thought is not physical. Yet thought is **communication,** for which the **body** can be used. *T-8.VII.59.4:5*

~ every loving thought that the **Son of God** ever had is eternal. Those which his **mind** perceived in this **world** are the world's only **reality.** **They** are still perceptions because **he** still believes that **he** is separate. Yet **they** are eternal because **they** are loving. And **being** loving, **they** are like the **Father** and therefore cannot die. *T-10.VIII.70.1:5*

~ **he will** heal every **little** thought which **you have** kept to **hurt you** and cleanse it of its littleness, restoring it to the **magnitude** of **God.** *T-12.III.17.6*

~ the thoughts which the **Mind** of God's Son projects **have** all the **power** that **he** gives to them. The thoughts **he** shares with **God** are beyond his **belief,** but those **he** made are his beliefs. And it is these, and not the **truth,** that **he** has chosen to defend and **love. They will** not be taken from him. But **they** can be given up by him, for the **Source** of their undoing is in him. *T-13.VI.51.3:7*

~ in these loving thoughts is the **spark** of beauty hidden. *T-17.IV.20.5*

~ no thought but has the **power** to **release** or **kill.** And none can leave the thinker's **mind** or leave him unaffected. *T-21.VIII.84.7:8*

~ for **God** and His beloved Son do not think differently. And it is the agreement of their thought that makes the Son a co-**creator** with the **mind** Whose **Thought** created him. *T-25.VIII.53.2:3*

~ every thought extends because that is its purpose, **being** what it really is. *T-27.III.25.1*

~ thoughts are not born and cannot die. **They share** the attributes of their **creator,** nor **have they** a separate **life** apart from his. The thoughts **you** think are in your **mind,** as **you** are in the **mind** Which thought of **you.** *T-30.IV.43.5:7*

~ thoughts seem to come and go. Yet all this **means** is that **you** are sometimes aware of them and sometimes not. An unremembered thought is born again to **you** when it returns to your **awareness.** Yet it did not die when **you** forgot it. It was always there, but **you** were unaware of it. *T-30.IV.44.1:5*

~ everything **you see** is the result of your thoughts. There is no **exception** to this **fact.** Thoughts are not big or **little,** powerful or weak. **They** are merely true or false. Those which are true create their own likeness. Those which are false **make** theirs. *W-pI.16.1.2:7*

~ every thought **you have** makes up some segment of the **world you see.** *W-pI.23.1.4*

~ **you** think with the **Mind** of **God.** Therefore **you share** your thoughts with Him, as **He** shares His with **you.** **They** are the same thoughts because **they** are thought by the same **Mind.** To **share** is to **make** alike or to **make** one. Nor do the thoughts **you** think with the **Mind** of **God** leave your **mind,** because thoughts do not leave their **source.** Therefore your thoughts are in the **Mind** of **God,** as **you** are. **They** are in your **mind** as well, where **He** is. As **you** are **part** of His **Mind,** so are your thoughts **part** of His thoughts. *W-pI.45.2.1:8*

~ under all the senseless thoughts and mad ideas with which **you have** cluttered up your **mind** are the thoughts which **you** thought with **God** in the beginning. **They** are there in your **mind now,** completely unchanged. **They will** always be in your **mind,** exactly as **they** always were. *W-pI.45.9.1:3*

~ my real thoughts are the thoughts I think with **God.** *W-pI.51.5.3*

434

~ **i have** real thoughts as well as insane ones. **I** can therefore **see** a **real world** if **I** look to my real thoughts as my guide for seeing. *W-pI.53.2.3:4*

~ **neutral thoughts** are **impossible**, because all thoughts **have power**. They **will** either **make** a false **world** or lead me to the real one. But thoughts cannot be without effects. *W-pI.54.2.1:3*

~ my thoughts cannot be neither true nor false. They must be one or the other. What **I see** shows me which **they** are. *W-pI.54.2.5:7*

~ if **I have** no private thoughts, **I** cannot **see** a private **world**. *W-pI.54.4.1*

~ my real thoughts, which **share** everything with everybody. As my thoughts of **separation call** to the **separation** thoughts of others, so my real thoughts **awaken** the real thoughts in them. And the **world** my real thoughts show me **will** dawn on their **sight** as well as mine. *W-pI.54.4.4:6*

~ my loving thoughts **will** save me from this **perception** of the **world** and **give** me the **peace** God intended me to **have. I have** no thoughts **I** do not **share** with **God. I have** no thoughts apart from Him because **I have** no **mind** apart from His. As **part** of His **Mind**, my thoughts are His and His thoughts are mine. *W-pI.55.3.5:8*

~ your **Self** retains its thoughts, and **they** remain **within** your **mind** and in the **Mind** of God. *W-pI.96.8.1*

~ one Thought, completely unified, **will** serve to unify all thought. This is the same as saying one **correction will** suffice for all **correction** or that to forgive one **brother** wholly is enough to bring **salvation** to all minds. *W-pI.108.5.1:2*

~ it is not a thought which judges an **illusion** by its size, its seeming gravity, or anything that is related to the **form** it takes. It merely focuses on what it is and knows that no **illusion** can be real. *W-pI.140.6.6:7*

~ evaluate each thought that comes to **mind**, remove the elements of dreams, and **give** them back to **you** as clean ideas that do not contradict the **Will** of God. *W-pI.151.13.4*

~ **give** Him your thoughts, and **He will give** them back as miracles which joyously proclaim the **wholeness** and the happiness **God** wills His Son as proof of His eternal **Love**. And as each thought is thus transformed, it takes on **healing power** from the **Mind** Which saw the **truth** in it and failed to be deceived by what was falsely added. *W-pI.151.14.1:2*

~ a thought is in the **mind**. It can be then applied as **mind** directs it. But its origin is where it must be changed if **change** occurs. *W-pI.167.3.3:5*

~ for **honest** thoughts, untainted by the **dream** of worldly things **outside** yourself, become the holy messengers of **God** Himself. *W-pI.188.6.6*

~ **they** lead **you** back to **peace** from where **they** came but to remind **you** how **you** must return. They heed your Father's **Voice** when **you** refuse to listen. And **they** urge **you** gently to accept His **word** for what **you** are instead of fantasies and shadows. They remind **you** that **you** are the co-**creator** of all things that live. For as the **peace** of **God** is shining in **you**, it must shine on them. *W-pI.188.7.2:6*

~ **we have** betrayed them, ordering that **they** depart from us. *W-pI.188.8.5*

~ wash them clean of strange desires and disordered wishes. *W-pI.188.8.6*

~ there is no thought that **will** not **gain** thereby in **power** to **help** the **world**, and none which **will** not **gain** in added gifts to **you** as well. *W-pI.199.5.3*

~ **you have** been given them in perfect **trust**, in perfect **confidence** that **you** would use them well, in perfect **faith** that **you** would **see** their messages and use them for yourself. *W-pI.Rev III.7.1*

~ **they will** not come from **you alone**, for **they will** all be shared with Him. *W-pI.Rev IV.9.2*

~ permit no idle thought to go unchallenged. *W-pI.Rev VI.7.2*

~ his thoughts **have** lit the **darkness** of our minds. His **Love** has called to us unceasingly since **time** began. *W-pII.1.8.4:5*

THOUGHT SYSTEM

EGO;   *ego's **thought** system, chaotic **thought** system, delusional **thought** system, world's **thought** system.*

~   the ego's whole **thought** system blocks **extension** and thus blocks your only **function**. It therefore blocks your **joy**, and that is why **you** perceive yourselves as unfulfilled. *T-7.X.93.7:8*

~   a **thought** system which has become so twisted and so complex that **you** cannot **see** that it **means nothing**. He merely looks at its foundation and dismisses it. But **you**, who cannot **undo** what **you have** made [nor escape the heavy burden of its dullness that lies upon your minds], cannot **see** through it. It deceives **you** because **you** chose to deceive yourselves. *T-13.VI.53.2:5*

~   the **thought** system which the **special relationship** protects is but a system of delusions. *T-17.V.32.1*

~   the whole **thought** system of the **ego** lies in its gifts. *T-17.V.37.8*

HOLY SPIRIT;   *His **thought** system, unified **thought** system, **light**.*

~   every system of **thought** must **have** a starting point. It begins with either a making or a creating, a **difference** which **we have** discussed already. Their resemblance lies in their **power** as foundations. Their **difference** lies in what rests upon them. Both are cornerstones for systems of **belief** by which men live. *T-3.IX.72.1:5*

~   the **light will** shine from the true Foundation of **Life**, and your own **thought** system **will** stand corrected. It cannot stand otherwise. *T-3.IX.80.3:4*

~   every thought system has internal consistency. *T-4.III.37.1*

~   **you** cannot retain **part** of a **thought** system, because it can be questioned only at its foundation. And this must be questioned from beyond it, because, **within** it, its foundation does stand. *T-9.VI.44.4:5*

~   the **Holy Spirit** judges against the **reality** of the ego's **thought** system merely because **He** knows its foundation is not true. Therefore, **nothing** that arises from it **means** anything. *T-9.VI.44.6:7*

~   a very different **thought** system and one with **nothing** in common with yours. *T-16.IV.21.3*

~   **thought** systems are but true or false, and all their attributes come simply from what **they** are. *T-17.IV.25.6*

~   there are only two **thought** systems, and **you** demonstrate that **you** believe one or the other is true all the **time**. From your demonstration, others learn and so do **you**. *M-1.2.2:3*

THREAT

|THret|

DICTIONARY: *a statement of an intention to inflict **pain**, injury, damage, or other hostile action on someone in retribution for something done or not done.*

EGO

~   the **ego**, which judges only in terms of threat or non-threat to itself. *T-4.VI.70.3*

~   **ego** does not recognize the real **source** of its perceived threat. *T-4.VII.83.1*

~   individual egos perceive different kinds of threat which are quite specific in their own **judgment**. *T-4.VIII.95.5*

~   that the **ego** is aware of threat, but does not **make** distinctions between two entirely different kinds of threat to its existence. *T-9.VII.50.2*

~   when it experiences threat, its only **decision** is whether to **attack now** or to withdraw to **attack later**. If **you** accept its offer of **grandiosity**, it **will attack** immediately. If **you** do not, it **will** wait. *T-9.VII.50.4:6*

~   harmony is threat. *T-10.VI.53.6*

- the **ego** is hyperalert to threat. *T-17.V.31.1*

- **pain**, illness, **loss**, age, and **death** seem to threaten me. *W-pI.56.2.2*

- a **sense** of threat is an **acknowledgment** of an inherent **weakness**, a **belief** that there is danger which has **power** to **call** on **you** to **make** appropriate **defense**. *W-pI.135.2.3*

- evaluates a threat, decides escape is necessary, and sets up a series of defenses to reduce the threat that has been judged as real. *W-pI.136.4.1*

- threat brings **anger**, **anger** makes **attack** seem reasonable, honestly provoked, and righteous in the **name** of **self defense**. *W-pI.153.2.2*

- the **sense** of threat the **world** encourages is so much deeper and so far beyond the frenzy and intensity of which **you** can conceive that **you have** no **idea** of all the devastation it has wrought. **You** are its slave. **You** know not what **you** do in fear of it. **You** do not **understand** how much **you have** been made to **sacrifice** who feel its iron grip upon your heart. *W-pI.153.4.3:6*

- the **ego**, under what it sees as threat, is quick to cite the **truth** to save its lies. *W-pI.196.2.2*

HOLY SPIRIT

- no real threat is involved anywhere. *T-1.I.29.6*

- above all are all things welcoming, for threat is gone. *M-4.24.6*

THRONE |THrōn|

DICTIONARY: *a ceremonial chair for a sovereign, bishop, or similar figure.*

EGO

- **chaos** sits in triumph on His throne. *W-pI.136.10.3*

- **sickness** is a method, conceived in **madness**, for placing God's Son on his Father's throne. *M-5.2.7*

HOLY SPIRIT

- throne of **God today**, the **quiet** place **within** the **mind** where **He** abides forever in the **holiness** which **He** created and **will** never leave. *W-pI.125.4.3*

TIME |tīm|

DICTIONARY: *the indefinite continued progress of existence and events in the **past**, **present**, and **future** regarded as a whole.*

EGO; *a waste, effort dissipated, downward spiral, phase of what does **nothing**, sleight of hand, trick, vast **illusion**, mad **belief**, belief, **ego concept**, **veil** of time, **enemy**, meaningless **defense**.*

- time can waste as well as be wasted. *T-1.I.87.4*

- time is a **belief** of the **ego**, so the lower **mind**, which is the ego's domain, accepts it without **question**. *T-5.V.37.4*

- the ego's time is borrowed from your **eternity**. *T-9.III.17.4*

- while time lasts in your minds, there **will** be choices. Time itself was your **choice**. *T-9.XI.106.5:6*

~ the **ego**, on the other hand, regards the **function** of time as one of extending itself in place of **eternity**, for like the **Holy Spirit**, the **ego** interprets the **goal** of time as its own. The continuity of **past** and **future** under its direction is the only **purpose** the **ego** perceives in time, and it closes over the **present** so that no **gap** in its own continuity can occur. Its continuity, then, would keep **you** in time, while the **Holy Spirit** would **release you** from it. *T-12.IV.31.1:3*

~ **you** would destroy time's continuity by breaking it into **past**, **present**, and **future** for your own purposes. *T-12.VI.48.5*

~ the making of time to take the place of timelessness lay in the **decision** to be not as **you** were. Thus, **truth** was made **past**, and the **present** was dedicated to **illusion**. And the **past**, too, was changed and interposed between what always was and **now**. *T-14.V.38.7:9*

~ the **ego**, which uses time to support its **belief** in **destruction**. The **ego**, like the **Holy Spirit**, uses time to convince **you** of the inevitability of the **goal** and end of **teaching**. *T-15.I.2.6:7*

~ the **ego** is an ally of time, but not a friend. *T-15.II.3.1*

~ time, according to its **teaching**, is **nothing** but a **teaching** device for compounding **guilt** until it becomes all-encompassing and demands **vengeance** forever. *T-15.II.8.7*

~ time is cruel in the ego's hands. *T-17.IV.18.2*

~ **nothing** is ever lost but time, which in the end is [**nothing**. It] is but a **little** hindrance to **eternity**, quite meaningless to the real **Teacher** of the **world**. *T-26.VI.31.1*

~ and all of time is but the mad **belief** that what is over is still **here** and **now**. *T-26.VI.42.4*

~ **you make** strange use of it, as if the **past** had caused the **present**, which is but a consequence in which no **change** can be made possible because its **cause** has gone. *T-28.II.6.4*

~ old ideas about time are very **difficult** to **change** because everything **you** believe is rooted in time and depends on your not **learning** these new ideas about it. *W-pI.7.8.1*

~ time becomes a **future** emphasis to be controlled by **learning** and **experience** obtained from **past** events and previous beliefs. *W-pI.135.16.3*

~ for it lets **you** think what **God** has given **you** is not the **truth** right now. *W-pI.136.14.2*

~ time but seems to go in one direction. *W-pI.158.3.5*

~ time is a trick—a sleight of hand, a vast **illusion** in which figures come and go as if by **magic**. *W-pI.158.4.1*

~ it dreams of time—an **interval** in which what seems to happen never has occurred, the changes wrought are substanceless, and all events are nowhere. *W-pI.167.9.3*

~ **god** holds your **future** as He holds your **past** and **present**. **They** are one to Him, and so **they** should be one to **you**. Yet in this **world** the temporal progression still seems real. And so **you** are not asked to **understand** the lack of sequence really found in time. **You** are but asked to let the **future** go and place it in God's hands. And **you will see** by your **experience** that **you have** laid the **past** and **present** in His hands as well because the **past will** punish **you** no more and **future** dread **will now** be meaningless. *W-pI.194.4.1:6*

~ time, with its illusions of **change** and **death**, wears out the **world** and all things in it. *M-1.4.7*

HOLY SPIRIT; *eternity, friend, teaching device, now, illusion, corrective device.*

~ the **purpose** of time is to enable **man** to learn to use it constructively. Time is thus a **teaching** device. *T-1.I.15.2:3*

~ the **acceptance** of the **Atonement** by **everyone** is only a matter of time. In **fact**, both time and matter were created for this **purpose**. *T-2.II.47.1:2*

~ time is essentially a device by which all **compromise** in this respect can be given up. It seems to be abolished by degrees because time itself involves a **concept** of intervals which do not really **exist**. The faulty use of **creation** made this necessary as a corrective device. *T-2.V.100.2:4*

- the **purpose** of time is solely to "**give** him time" to achieve this **judgment**. It is his own perfect **judgment** of his own **creations**. *T-2.VI.III.5:6*

- time is under my direction, but Timelessness belongs to **God alone**. In time **we exist** for and with each other. In Timelessness **we** coexist with **God**. *T-3.II.10.5:7*

- always has no direction. Time seems to go in one direction, but when **you** reach its end, it **will** roll up like a long carpet which has spread along the **past** behind **you** and **will** disappear. *T-11.X.91.3:4*

- the **Holy Spirit** interprets time's **purpose** as rendering the **need** for it unnecessary. Thus does **He** regard the **function** of time as temporary, serving only His **teaching function**, which is temporary by definition. His emphasis is therefore on the only aspect of time which can extend to the infinite, for **now** is the closest approximation of **eternity** which this **world** offers. *T-12.IV.30.1:3*

- if **you** accept your **function** in the **world** of time as **healing**, **you will** emphasize only the aspect of time in which **healing** can occur. *T-12.IV.32.2*

- time **will** be as **you** interpret it, for of itself it is **nothing**. *T-12.IV.32.6*

- time can **release** as well as imprison, depending on whose **interpretation** of it **you** use. *T-12.VI.48.1*

- **he** does not **see** time as **you** do. And each **miracle He** offers **you** corrects your use of time and makes it His. *T-14.VII.69.10:11*

- no cares, no worries, no anxieties, but merely to be perfectly **calm** and **quiet** all the time? Yet that is what time is for—to learn just that and **nothing** more. *T-15.I.1.1:2*

- the **Holy Spirit** uses time in His own **way** and is not bound by it. *T-15.I.2.3*

- time is inconceivable without **change**. *T-15.II.11.1*

- your illusions of time **will** not prevent the timeless from **being** what it is nor **you** from experiencing it as it is. *T-16.VIII.76.5*

- it is kind when used for **gentleness**. *T-17.IV.18.2*

- only the timeless must remain unchanged, but everything in time can **change** with time. *T-22.III.18.8*

- everything in time can **change** with time. *T-22.III.18.8*

- time **you** made, and time **you** can command. **You** are no more a slave to time than to the **world you** made. *T-22.III.23.7:8*

- no trace of anything in time can long remain in minds that serve the timeless. *T-22.VII.56.8*

- the time **he** chooses can be any time, for **help** is there, awaiting but his **choice**. *T-25.IV.28.1*

- all time becomes a **means** to reach a **goal**. *T-25.IV.31.8*

- while in time, there is still much to do. *T-25.VII.48.1*

- time lasted but an instant in your **mind**, with no effect upon **eternity**. *T-26.VI.32.3*

- for time and space are one **illusion** which takes different forms. If it has been projected beyond your minds, **you** think of it as time. The nearer it is brought to where it is, the more **you** think of it in terms of space. *T-26.IX.68.3:5*

- time is as neutral as the **body** is except in terms of what **you see** it for. *T-26.IX.70.7*

- an unused **interval** of time not seen as spent and fully occupied, becomes a silent invitation to the **truth** to enter and to **make** itself at home. *T-27.IV.32.1*

- regularity in terms of time is not the ideal requirement for the most beneficial **form** of **practice** in **salvation**. It is advantageous, however, for those whose motivation is inconsistent and who remain heavily defended against **learning**. *W-pI.95.6.2:3*

~ the minutes which **you give** are multiplied over and over, for the **miracle** makes use of time but is not ruled by it. *W-pI.97.3.3*

~ the **miracle** in which a minute spent in using these ideas becomes a time which has no length and which has no end. *W-pI.97.4.1*

~ in timelessness **you rest**, while time goes by without its touch upon **you**, for your **rest** can never **change** in any **way** at all. *W-pI.109.5.2*

~ time is the great **illusion**; it is **past** or in the **future**. *W-pI.131.7.3*

~ time is an **illusion**. *W-pI.136.14.1*

~ the thoughts of **God** are quite apart from time. For time is but another meaningless **defense you** made against the **truth**. *W-pI.136.14.3:4*

~ yet time has still one **gift** to **give** in which true **knowledge** is reflected in a **way** so accurate its **image** shares its unseen **holiness**; its likeness shines with its immortal **love**. *W-pI.158.11.2*

~ **he** recognized all that time holds and gave it to all minds that each one might determine from a point where time has ended when it is released to **revelation** and **eternity**. *W-pI.169.7.5*

~ for time has lost its hold upon the **world**. *W-pI.191.10.2*

~ **i have** conceived of time in such a **way** that I defeat my aim. If **I** elect to reach **past** time to timelessness, I must **change** my **perception** of what time is for. Time's **purpose** cannot be to keep the **past** and **future** one. The only **interval** in which I can be saved from time is **now**. *W-p2.308.1.1:4*

~ time really, then, goes backward to an instant so ancient that it is beyond all **memory** and **past** even the possibility of remembering. Yet because it is an instant that is relived again and again and still again, it seems to be **now**. *M-2.4.1:2*

~ one instant out of time can bring time's end. *M-15.3.7*

~ the saving of time is an essential early emphasis which, although it remains important throughout the **learning** process, becomes less and less emphasized. At the outset, **we** can safely say that time devoted to starting the day right does indeed save time. *M-16.3.3:4*

~ the **Holy Spirit** uses time as **He** thinks best, and **He** is never wrong. *P-1.1.5.5*

~ in time no **effort** can be made in vain. *P-2.V.7.2*

TODAY |təˈdā|

DICTIONARY: *this **present** day.*

HOLY SPIRIT;   *now, **time** of **grace**, **special** dedication, day of **peace**.*

~ this is the day of **peace**. *W-pI.109.4.1*

~ today is set by **Heaven** Itself to be a **time** of **grace** for **you** and for the **world**. *W-pI.131.18.3*

~ it is a **time** of **special** celebration. For today holds out the instant to the darkened **world** where its **release** is set. The day has come when sorrows pass away and **pain** is gone. The **glory** of **salvation** dawns today upon a **world** set free. *W-pII.241.1.2:5*

~ **give** this day to Him and there **will** be no **fear** today because the day is given unto **Love**. *W-pII.274.2.2*

~ it is this **serenity we seek**, unclouded, obvious, and sure today. *W-pII.300.1.4*

- today **I** can forget the **world I** made. Today **I** can go **past** all **fear** and be restored to **love** and **holiness** and **peace**. Today **I** am redeemed and born anew into a **world** of mercy and of care; of loving kindness and the **peace** of **God**. W-pII.306.1.2:4

- there is no room for anything but **joy** and thanks today. W-pII.340.2.2

TRAITOR

|ˈtrādər|

DICTIONARY: *a person who betrays a friend, country, principle, etc.*

EGO;   *God*

- the **ego** is not a traitor to **God** to Whom treachery is **impossible**, but it is a traitor to **you** who believe **you have** been treacherous to your **Father**. T-11.VIII.75.1

- **god** is denied, confused with **fear**, perceived as mad, and seen as traitor to Himself. W-pI.190.3.2

TRANSLATOR

|ˈtransˌlādər|

DICTIONARY: *a person who translates from one **language** into another, especially as a profession.*

HOLY SPIRIT;   *Holy Spirit*

- a **good** translator, although **he** must alter the **form** of what **he** translates, never changes the **meaning**. In **fact**, his whole **purpose** is to **change** the **form** so that the original **meaning** is retained. The **Holy Spirit** is the translator of the **Laws** of **God** to those who do not **understand** them. **You** could not do this yourselves, because conflicted minds cannot be faithful to one **meaning** and **will** therefore **change** the **meaning** to preserve the **form**. T-7.III.15.3:6

- **he** translates only to preserve the original **meaning** in all respects and in all languages. Therefore, **He** opposes differences in **form** as meaningful, emphasizing always that these differences do not matter. T-7.III.16.2:3

- **he** translates what **you have** made into what **God** created. T-9.III.11.3

- **he** gently translates **hell** into **Heaven**. T-15.III.17.7

TRANSPORTATION

|ˌtran(t)spərˈtāSH(ə)n|

DICTIONARY: *the action of transporting someone or something or the process of **being** transported.*

HOLY SPIRIT

- this feeling of liberation far exceeds the **dream** of **freedom** sometimes experienced in **special** relationships. It is a **sense** of actual escape from limitations. T-18.VII.58.9:10

- if **you will** consider what this "transportation" really entails, **you will** realize that it is a sudden unawareness of the **body** and a joining of yourself and something else in which your **mind** enlarges to encompass it. It becomes **part** of **you** as **you** unite with it. And both become whole as neither is perceived as separate. What really happens is that **you have** given up the **illusion** of a limited **awareness** and lost your **fear** of **union**. The **love** that instantly replaces it extends to what has freed **you** and unites with it. And while this lasts, **you** are not **uncertain** of your **Identity** and would not **limit** it. **You have** escaped from **fear** to **peace**, asking no questions of **reality** but merely accepting it. **You have** accepted this instead of the **body** and **have** let yourself be one with something beyond it simply by not letting your **mind** be limited by it. T-18.VII.59.1:8

~ the "something" can be anything and anywhere—a sound, a **sight**, a **thought**, a **memory**, and even a general **idea** without specific reference. Yet in every case, **you** joined it without reservation because **you love** it and would be with it. And so **you** rush to meet it, letting your limits melt away, suspending all the "**laws**" your **body** obeys and gently setting them aside. *T-18.VII.60.3:5*

~ there is no violence at all in this escape. The **body** is not attacked, but simply properly perceived. It does not **limit you** merely because **you** would not **have** it so. **You** are not really "lifted out" of it; it cannot contain **you**. **You** go where **you** would be, gaining, not losing, a **sense** of **self**. In these instants of **release** from physical restrictions, **you experience** much of what happens in the **holy instant**; the lifting of the barriers of **time** and space, the sudden **experience** of **peace** and **joy**, and, above all, the lack of **awareness** of the **body** and of the questioning whether or not all this is possible. *T-18.VII.61.1:6*

~ it is possible because **you want** it. The sudden expansion of the **self** which takes place with your **desire** for it is the irresistible appeal the **holy instant** holds. It calls to **you** to be yourself **within** its safe embrace. There are the **laws** of **limit** lifted for **you**, to **welcome you** to openness of **mind** and **freedom**. Come to this place of refuge, where **you** can be yourself in **peace**. Not through **destruction**, not through a "breaking out," but merely by a **quiet** "melting in." For **peace will join you** there simply because **you have** been willing to let go the limits **you have** placed upon **love** and joined it where it is and where it led **you** in **answer** to its gentle **call** to be at **peace**. *T-18.VII.62.1:7*

TREASURE

|ˈtreZHər|

DICTIONARY: *a very valuable object.*

EGO; *little treasure, trifling treasures.*

~ **death** is your treasure. *T-11.V.41.4*

~ he would **sacrifice** his own **identity** with everything to find a **little** treasure of his own. *T-26.VIII.58.2*

HOLY SPIRIT; *God's treasure, treasure of **God**, His treasure, treasure of **salvation**, father's treasure.*

~ where your heart is, there is your treasure also. *T-2.II.18.2*

~ your **function** is to add to God's treasure by creating yours. *T-8.VI.47.1*

~ nor is the treasure less as it is given out. *T-25.X.79.5*

~ but when **you have** received, **you will** be sure **you have** the treasure **you have** always sought. *W-pI.165.5.3*

~ a treasure his so great that everything the **world** contains is valueless before its **magnitude**. *W-pI.166.5.5*

~ a treasure his so great that everything the **world** contains is valueless before its **magnitude**. *W-pI.166.5.5*

TREASURE HOUSE

A Course in Miracles Term

EGO

~ **treasure** house barren and empty with an open door inviting everything that would disturb your **peace** to enter and destroy. *T-24.V.37.6*

HOLY SPIRIT; *gift, God's **treasure** house.*

~ it can become a **treasure** house as rich and limitless as **Heaven** itself. *T-26.II.5.3*

~ this is the Holy Spirit's single **gift**—the **treasure** house to which **you** can appeal with perfect **certainty** for everything that can contribute to your happiness. *W-pI.159.6.1*

~ my **treasure** house is full, and angels watch its open doors that not one **gift** is lost and only more are added. Let me come to where my treasures are and enter in where **I** am truly **welcome** and at **home** among the gifts that **God** has given me. *W-pII.316.1.4:5*

~ god's **treasure** house can never be empty. And if one **gift** were missing, it would not be full. Yet is its fullness guaranteed by **God**. *M-6.4.8:10*

TRUST |trəst|

DICTIONARY: *firm **belief** in the reliability, **truth**, ability, or **strength** of someone or something.*

EGO

~ **being** the **part** of your **mind** which does not believe it is responsible for itself and **being** without allegiance to **God**, the **ego** is incapable of trust. *T-7.VIII.79.1*

~ whenever **they** trust themselves, **they will** not learn. *T-14.IV.72.2*

~ trust not your **good** intentions. **They** are not enough. *T-18.V.33.1:2*

~ **you** cannot believe that trust would settle every **problem now**. *T-26.IX.69.3*

~ nor does **he** trust the "**good**" in anyone, believing that the "bad" must lurk behind. *T-31.VII.68.7*

~ it is not by trusting yourself that **you will gain confidence**. *W-pI.47.6.3*

HOLY SPIRIT

~ my trust in **you** is greater than yours in me at the moment, but it **will** not always be that way. *T-4.VII.89.1*

~ no one obeys gladly a guide **he** does not trust, but this does not mean that the guide is untrustworthy. In this case, it always **means** that the follower is. However, this too is merely a matter of his own **belief**. Believing that **he** can betray, **he** believes that everything can betray him. *T-7.XI.104.1:4*

~ **you will** not know the trust **I have** in **you** unless **you** extend it. You **will** not trust the **guidance** of the **Holy Spirit** or believe that it is for **you** unless **you** hear it in others. *T-8.XI.112.5:6*

~ my trust in **you** is without **limit** and without the **fear** that **you will** hear me not. *T-13.IV.33.5*

~ your **present** trust in Him is the **defense** which promises a **future** undisturbed, without a trace of sorrow and with **joy** which constantly increases as this **life** becomes a **holy instant**, set in **time** but heeding only **immortality**. *W-pI.135.20.1*

~ his trust has made your pathway certain and your **goal** secure. *W-pI.155.13.6*

~ god's trust in **you** is limitless. *W-pI.166.1.2*

~ trusting your brothers is essential to establishing and holding up your **faith** in your ability to transcend **doubt** and lack of sure conviction in yourself. *W-pI.181.1.1*

~ this is the foundation on which their ability to fulfill their **function** rests. *M-4.3.1*

~ the trust on which God's teachers **rest** secure makes **doubt impossible**. *M-4.12.6*

~ trust remains the bed-rock of the **teacher** of God's whole **thought system**. *M-4.13.6*

~ **he** learns faster as his trust increases. *M-4.17.10*

TRUTH

DICTIONARY: *that which is true or in accordance with **fact** or **reality**.*

EGO; *error*

~ **you** believe that in the presence of truth **you will** turn on yourself and destroy yourself. *T-12.II.8.6*

~ so fearful has the truth become to **you** that unless it is weak and **little**, [and unworthy of **value**,] **you** would not dare to look upon it. *T-16.VI.53.2*

~ **you** are denying truth, and so are making yourself unable to **make** the simple * **choice** between truth and **illusion, God** and **fantasy**. *T-16.VI.56.3*

~ **you** learn to deal with **part** of truth in one **way** and in another **way** the other **part**. To **fragment** truth is to destroy it by rendering it meaningless. *T-17.II.4.3:4*

~ **you** are still convinced your understanding is a powerful contribution to the truth and makes it what it is. *T-18.V.39.5*

~ **belief** that truth may be the **enemy you** yet may find. *T-21.VIII.76.6*

~ the truth is hidden deep **within** under a heavy cloud of insane thoughts, dense and obscuring, yet representing all **you see**? *W-pI.41.4.2*

~ truth and **illusion** cannot be reconciled, no matter how **you** try, what **means you** use. *W-pI.96.2.1*

~ truth is eclipsed by **fear**, and what remains is but imagined. *W-pI.130.3.3*

~ truth cannot come where it could only be perceived with **fear**, for this would be the **error** truth can be brought to illusions. Opposition makes the truth unwelcome, and it cannot come. *W-pI.138.2.4:5*

~ it is concealed behind a vast array of choices which do not appear to be entirely your own. *W-pI.152.4.3*

~ **i have** disowned the truth. *W-pII.248.1.1*

~ finding truth unacceptable, the **mind** revolts against truth and gives itself an **illusion** of victory. *M-8.2.6*

~ who is unaware of truth must look upon illusions. *M-17.4.11*

~ truth becomes diminutive and meaningless. *M-18.3.5*

HOLY SPIRIT; *God, God's **creation**, love, **savior**, great wings of **truth**, absence of **illusion**.*

~ truth is always abundant. *T-1.I.58.4*

~ truth overcomes all **error**. This **means** that if **you** perceive truly, **you** are canceling out misperceptions in yourself and in others simultaneously. *T-3.IV.29.4:5*

~ truth can only be known. All of it is equally true, and knowing any **part** of it is to know all of it. *T-3.VII.58.3:4*

~ truth is beyond your ability to destroy but entirely **within** your grasp. It belongs to **you**, because **you** created it. It is yours because it is a **part** of **you**, just as **you** are **part** of **God** because **He** created **you**. *T-5.VI.46.4:6*

~ truth is without illusions and therefore **within** the **Kingdom**. *T-6.V.94.1*

~ **nothing** that is true needs to be explained. *T-7.II.6.4*

~ truth can only be recognized and **need** only be recognized. *T-7.V.33.1*

~ if truth is total, the untrue cannot **exist**. *T-7.VII.63.2*

~ truth is **God**. *T-7.X.100.4*

~ together **we** can meet its conditions, but truth **will** dawn upon **you** of itself. *T-8.VI.51.6*

~ the **function** of truth is to collect data which are true. *T-8.VIII.76.7*

~ in the presence of truth, there are no unbelievers and no sacrifices. *T-8.X.99.3*

~ truth does not vacillate; it is always true. *T-9.VII.54.2*

~ truth is not obscure nor hidden, but its obviousness to **you** lies in the **joy you** bring to its witnesses, who show it to **you**. *T-9.VII.55.3*

~ truth is indivisible. *T-9.VII.58.1*

~ is whole and cannot be known by **part** of a **mind**. *T-9.X.86.7*

~ truth lies only in the **present**, and **you will** find it if **you seek** it there. **You have** looked for it where it is not and therefore **have** not found it. Learn, then, to **seek** it where it is, and it **will** dawn on eyes that **see**. *T-12.VI.49.4:6*

~ truth comes of its own **will** unto its own. When **you have** learned that **you** belong to truth, it **will** flow lightly over **you** without a **difference** of any kind. For **you will need** no **contrast** to **help you** realize that this is what **you want**, and only this. *T-13.V.40.5:7*

~ it is this reconciliation with truth, and only truth, in which the **peace** of **Heaven** lies. *T-13.V.46.5*

~ the truth is true. **Nothing** else matters, **nothing** else is real, and everything beside it is not there. *T-13.VII.58.1:2*

~ **you will love** it because **you will understand** it. *T-13.VII.58.7*

~ like **you**, the **Holy Spirit** did not **make** truth. Like **God**, **He** knows it to be true. **He** brings the **light** of truth into the **darkness** and lets it shine on **you**. *T-13.VII.59.1:3*

~ with truth before **you**, **you will** not look back. *T-13.VII.61.5*

~ the quietness of its simplicity is so compelling that **you will** realize it is **impossible** to deny the simple truth. *T-13.VII.63.5*

~ it can be neither lost nor sought nor found. It is there, wherever **you** are, **being within you**. Yet it can be recognized or unrecognized, real or false to **you**. If **you hide** it, it becomes unreal to **you** because **you** hid it and surrounded it with **fear**. *T-14.IV.25.2:5*

~ truth does not struggle against ignorance. *T-14.IV.28.6*

~ there is no **substitute** for truth. *T-14.IV.36.1*

~ merely by **being** what it is does truth **release you** from everything that it is not. *T-14.V.40.1*

~ truth is so far beyond **time** that all of it happens at once. For as it was created one, so its **oneness** depends not on **time** at all. *T-15.III.16.9:10*

~ **you will** yield to its compelling **attraction**. *T-16.III.16.9*

~ truth must be recognized if it is to be distinguished from **illusion**. *T-16.V.36.1*

~ truth has no **meaning** in **illusion**. The frame of reference for its **meaning** must be itself. *T-17.II.5.2:3*

~ truth asks **nothing**. Let it enter, and it **will call** forth and secure for **you** the **faith you need** for **peace**. But rise **you** not against it, for against your opposition it cannot come. *T-17.IX.75.5:7*

~ truth calls for **faith**, and **faith** makes room for truth. *T-17.VIII.72.4*

~ truth extends inward, where the **idea** of **loss** is meaningless and only increase is conceivable. *T-18.II.6.3*

~ the truth **will** save **you**. *T-18.II.7.1*

~ truth has rushed to meet **you** since **you** called upon it. *T-18.IV.25.7*

~ truth **will** stay forever. *T-19.II.15.5*

~ truth is the absence of **illusion**. *T-19.II.5.8*

~ truth is restored to **you** through your **desire**, as it was lost to **you** through your **desire** for something else. *T-20.IX.67.2*

~ truth is constant and implies a state where vacillations are **impossible**. *T-21.VIII.81.5*

~ truth is the **opposite** of illusions because it offers **joy**. *T-22.III.17.1*

~ in truth **you** stand together with **nothing** in between. *T-22.VI.47.2*

~ truth stands radiant, apart from **conflict**, untouched and **quiet** in the **peace** of God. *T-23.II.13.10*

~ truth does not fight against illusions, nor do illusions fight against the truth. *T-23.II.13.3*

~ the truth arises from what **He** knows. *T-24.I.2.9*

~ this is the only "cost" of truth: **you will** no longer **see** what never was, nor hear what makes no sound. *T-24.III.17.4*

~ it gives no different messages and has one **meaning**. *T-24.III.18.4*

~ truth is not frail. Illusions leave it perfectly unmoved [and undisturbed]. *T-24.IV.28.2:3*

~ yet to the dedication to the truth as **God** established it no **sacrifice** is asked, no strain called forth, and all the **power** of **Heaven** and the might of truth itself is given to provide the **means** and guarantee the goal's accomplishment. The truth is simple—it is one, without an **opposite**. *T-24.VII.60.5:6*

~ truth must be revealed to **you** because **you** know not what it is. *T-25.X.78.9*

~ the truth is in your **memory**. *T-26.VIII.63.1*

~ and truth **will** be revealed to **you** who chose to let love's symbols take the place of **sin**. *T-27.VII.61.6*

~ truth has left no room for them in any place or **time**. For it fills every place and every **time** and makes them wholly indivisible. *T-28.VI.52.5:6*

~ the truth in **you** remains as radiant as a star, as pure as **light**, as **innocent** as **Love** Itself. *T-31.VI.67.8*

~ the **light** of truth is in us, where it was placed by **God**. *W-pI.72.10.1*

~ to recognize the **light** of truth in us is to recognize ourselves as **we** are. *W-pI.72.10.4*

~ the truth of what **you** are calls on the **strength** in **you** to bring to your **awareness** what the **mistake** concealed. *W-pI.91.8.5*

~ truth is a **savior** and can only **will** for happiness and **peace** for **everyone**. It gives its **strength** to **everyone** who asks, in limitless supply. It sees that lack in anyone would be a lack in all, and so it gives its **light** that all may **see** and benefit as one. Its **strength** is shared that it may bring to all the **miracle** in which **they will** unite in **purpose** and **forgiveness** and in **love**. *W-pI.92.6.1:4*

~ it **will** bring your **mind** from **conflict** to the **quiet** fields of **peace**. *W-pI.97.1.4*

~ appearances cannot withstand the truth. *W-pI.99.16.2*

~ truth **will** correct all errors in your **mind** which tell **you you** could be apart from Him. *W-pI.107.11.1*

~ truth which **will** envelop **you** and **give you peace** so deep and tranquil that **you will** return to the familiar **world** reluctantly. *W-pI.107.13.1*

~ when truth has come, all **pain** is over, for there is no room for transitory thoughts and dead ideas to linger in your **mind**. Truth occupies your **mind** completely, liberating **you** from all beliefs in the ephemeral. **They have** no place because the truth has come, and **they** are nowhere. **They** cannot be found, for truth is everywhere forever **now**. When truth has come, it does not stay a while to disappear or **change** to something else. It does not **shift** and alter in its **form**, nor come and go and go and come again. It stays exactly as it always was, to be depended on in every **need** and trusted with a perfect **trust** in all the seeming difficulties and the doubts that the appearances the **world** presents engender. **They will** merely blow away when truth corrects the errors in your **mind**. *W-pI.107.4.2:9*

~ when truth has come, it harbors in its wings the **gift** of perfect constancy and **love** which does not falter in the face of **pain** but looks beyond it, steadily and sure. *W-pI.107.6.1*

~ **here** is the **gift** of **healing**, for the truth needs no **defense**, and therefore no **attack** is possible. *W-pI.107.6.2*

~ truth does not come and go nor **shift** nor **change**, in this **appearance now** and then in that, evading capture and escaping grasp. It does not **hide**. It stands in open **light**, in obvious accessibility. It is **impossible** that anyone could **seek** it truly and would not succeed. *W-pI.107.7.1:4*

~ **give** truth its due, and it **will give you** yours. **You** were not meant to suffer and to die. Your **Father** wills these dreams be gone. Let truth correct them all. *W-pI.107.8.2:5*

~ no one can **fail** who asks to reach the truth. *W-pI.131.11.1*

~ in truth is **innocence** the only **thing** there is. *W-pI.134.10.3*

~ truth is God's **creation**, and to pardon this is meaningless. All truth belongs to Him, reflects His **laws** and radiates His **Love**. *W-pI.134.2.4:5*

~ it does not **make** appeal to might nor triumph. It does not command obedience nor **seek** to prove how pitiful and futile are your attempts to **plan** defenses which would alter it. Truth merely wants to **give you** happiness, for such its **purpose** is. *W-pI.136.13.2:4*

~ it knows with perfect **certainty** that what **God** wills for **you** must be received. *W-pI.136.13.5*

~ truth has a **power** far beyond **defense**, for no illusions can remain where it has been allowed to enter. And it comes to any **mind** that would lay down its arms and cease to play with folly. It is found at any **time**—**today**, if **you will** choose to **practice** giving **welcome** to the truth. *W-pI.136.15.1:3*

~ and truth **will** come, for it has never been apart from us. *W-pI.136.16.1*

~ for truth is true and **nothing** else is real. *W-pI.138.4.5*

~ there is no **contradiction** to the truth. *W-pI.138.4.7*

~ but the truth cannot be learned but only recognized. In recognition its **acceptance** lies, and as it is accepted, it is known. *W-pI.138.5.2:3*

~ truth must be all-inclusive if it be the truth at all. *W-pI.152.2.6*

~ truth cannot **have** an **opposite**. *W-pI.152.3.4*

~ **nothing** but the truth is true, and what is false is false. *W-pI.152.3.7*

~ but truth is humble in acknowledging its mightiness, its changelessness, and its eternal **wholeness**—all-encompassing, God's perfect **gift** to His beloved Son. *W-pI.152.9.3*

~ for as truth goes before us, so it goes before our brothers who **will** follow us. *W-pI.155.11.6*

~ the truth that walks before us **now** is one with Him and leads us to where **He** has always been. *W-pI.155.12.7*

~ truth must be true throughout if it be true. It cannot contradict itself nor be in parts **uncertain** and in others sure. *W-pI.156.2.2:3*

~ truth is His **message**; truth His **teaching** is. His are the lessons **God** would **have** us learn. *W-pI.193.15.5:6*

~ no one can **hide** forever from a truth so very obvious that it appears in countless forms. *W-pI.193.7.4*

~ is free, and what is bound is not a **part** of truth. *W-p2.278.1.5*

~ **loss** is not **loss** when properly perceived. **Pain** is **impossible**. There is no grief with any **cause** at all. And **suffering** of any kind is **nothing** but a **dream**. Such is the truth—at first to be but said and then repeated many times and next to be accepted as but partly true with many reservations. Then to be considered seriously more and more, and finally accepted as the truth. *W-pII.284.1.1:6*

~ truth undoes its **evil** dreams by shining them away. Truth never makes **attack**. It merely is. And by its presence is the **mind** recalled from fantasies, awaking to the Real. **Forgiveness** bids this presence enter in and take its rightful place **within** the **mind**. *W-pII.332.1.2:6*

~ and truth can be but filled with **knowledge** and with **nothing** else. *W-pII.ST251.1.8*

~ truth can come only where it is welcomed without **fear**. *M-12.3.7*

~ either truth is apparent or it is not. It cannot be partially recognized. Who is unaware of truth must look upon illusions. *M-17.4.9*

~ truth neither moves nor wavers nor sinks down to **death** and dissolution. *M-27.7.6*

UNCERTAIN

|ˌənˈsərtn|

DICTIONARY: *not able to be relied on; not known or definite.*

EGO

~ uncertainty merely **means** that **you** do not know. *T-3.V.30.4*

~ **he** is therefore incapable of **knowledge, being** uncertain. *T-3.VI.38.4*

~ a separated or divided **mind** must be confused; it is uncertain by definition. *T-3.VI.41.5*

~ all uncertainty comes from a totally fallacious **belief** that **you** are under the coercion of **judgment**. *T-3.VIII.63.4*

~ as long as **you** remain uncertain, it can be only because **you have** not given complete **release**. *T-15.III.19.9*

~ what **he** is uncertain of, **God** cannot **give**. For **he** does not **desire** it while **he** remains uncertain. *T-21.IX.88.8:9*

~ only uncertainty can be defensive. And all uncertainty is **doubt** about yourself. *T-22.VI.47.9:10*

~ a **mistake** about your **will** and what **you** really are. *T-26.VIII.58.8*

~ uncertainty about what **you** must be is **self**-deception on a scale so vast its **magnitude** can hardly be conceived. *W-pI.139.2.5*

~ **you have** been weak at times, uncertain in your **purpose** and unsure of what **you** wanted, where to look for it, and where to turn for **help** in the attempt. *W-pI.185.10.5*

~ the functions which the **world** esteems are so uncertain that **they change** ten times an hour at their most secure. *W-pI.186.10.4*

~ uncertainty is not **love** but **fear** and therefore **hate**. *M-7.2.5*

HOLY SPIRIT; *doubt, fear.*

~ **god** does not **change** His **Mind** about you, for **He** is not uncertain of Himself. *T-9.VIII.61.1*

~ uncertainty was brought to **certainty** so long ago that it is hard indeed to hold it to your heart as if it were before **you** still. *T-26.VI.33.5*

UNDERSTAND

|ˌəndərˈstand|

DICTIONARY: *perceive the intended **meaning** of (words, a **language**, or speaker).*

EGO; *confusion born of error, powerful contribution to the **truth.***

~ **you will** not know how to respond to what **you** do not understand. *T-16.II.5.6*

~ **you** think your lack of understanding is a **loss** to **you,** and so **you** are unwilling to believe that what has happened is true. *T-16.III.14.1*

~ **you** are still convinced your understanding is a powerful contribution to the **truth** and makes it what it is. *T-18.V.39.5*

~ and **you seek** to be content with sighing and with "reasoning" **you** do not understand it **now** but **will** some day. And then its **meaning will** be clear. This is not **reason,** for it is unjust and clearly hints at **punishment** until the **time** of liberation is at hand. *T-26.IX.74.6:8*

~ **you** do not understand how what **you** see arose to meet your **sight**. For if **you** did, it would be gone. *T-31.VI.64.6:7*

~ our understanding is so limited that what **we** think **we** understand is but **confusion** born of **error**. *W-pI.192.7.9*

HOLY SPIRIT; *appreciation, consistence, your **inheritance**, **light**.*

~ understanding is beyond **perception** because it introduces **meaning**. It is, however, below **knowledge** even though it can grow towards it. *T-5.VI.44.4:5*

~ the incredible cannot be understood, because it is unbelievable. *T-7.IX.89.5*

~ understanding **means consistence** because **God means consistence**. *T-7.VI.46.5*

~ understanding is **appreciation**, because what **you** understand **you** can identify with, and by making it **part** of **you**, **you have** accepted it with **love**. *T-7.VI.49.6*

~ understanding is your **inheritance**. *T-10.VIII.76.6*

~ **nothing you** understand is fearful. *T-14.III.16.2*

~ **peace** and understanding go together and never can be found **alone**. Each brings the other with it, for it is the law of **God they** be not separate. **They** are **cause** and effect, each to the other, so where one is absent the other cannot be. *T-14.VII.72.4:6*

~ understanding is in **you**, and from it **peace** must come. *T-14.VII.74.8*

~ understanding is of the **mind** and only of the **mind**. *T-15.VII.63.5*

~ **you** do not understand what **you** accepted, but **remember** that your understanding is not necessary. All that was necessary was merely the **wish** to understand. That **wish** was the **desire** to be holy. *T-18.IV.27.11:13*

~ **you need** understand **nothing**. *T-18.V.39.6*

~ the understanding which **you need** comes not of **you** but from a larger **Self**, so great and holy that **He** could not **doubt** His **innocence**. *T-25.IX.75.4*

~ his understanding **will** be yours. *T-25.IX.75.6*

~ understanding **will** naturally come to lighten every corner of the **mind** which has been cleared of the debris that darkens it. *W-pI.9.2.5*

~ **everyone** must **share** in my understanding, which is the **gift** of **God** to me and to the **world**. *W-pI.58.5.4*

UNDO

[ən'do͞o]

DICTIONARY: *cancel or reverse the effects or results of (a previous action or measure).*

HOLY SPIRIT

~ regression is an **effort** to return to your own original state. It can thus be utilized to restore, rather than to go back to the less mature. *T-2.II.32.1:2*

~ the **Holy Spirit** has the task of undoing what the **ego** has made. *T-5.V.36.6*

~ the undoing is necessary only in your **mind** so that **you** cannot project falsely. *T-6.V.84.5*

~ undoing is indirect, as **doing** is. *T-13.VI.52.3*

~ undoing is for unreality. *T-14.V.39.9*

~ **you will** go through this last undoing quite unharmed and **will** at last emerge as yourself. *T-16.V.31.3*

~ with each **step** in His undoing is the **separation** more and more undone and **union** brought closer. *T-17.IV.21.2*

~ prepare **you now** for the undoing of what never was. *T-18.VI.41.1*

~ undoing is not your task, but it is up to **you** to **welcome** it or not. *T-21.III.23.5*

451

~ yet true undoing must be kind. And so the first replacement for your **picture** is another **picture** of another kind. *T-27.IV.32.7:8*

~ **salvation** is undoing. *T-31.VI.63.1*

~ the recognition that **you** do not **understand** is a prerequisite for undoing your false ideas. *W-pI.9.1.4*

UNFAIR

| ˌənˈfer|

DICTIONARY: *not based on or behaving according to the principles of equality and **justice**.*

EGO

~ **you** cannot be unfairly treated. The **belief you** are is but another **form** of the **idea you** are deprived by someone not yourself. *T-26.XI.87.2:3*

~ **projection** of the **cause** of **sacrifice** is at the root of everything perceived to be unfair and not your just deserts. *T-26.XI.87.4*

~ **you** think your **brother** is unfair to **you** because **you** think that one must be unfair to **make** the other **innocent**. *T-26.XI.89.1*

~ if **you** are unfairly treated, **he** must suffer the unfairness that **you see.** *T-27.I.1.6*

~ what to **you** has been unfair **will** come to him in righteousness. *T-27.I.2.4*

~ pardon is unfair. *T-27.III.14.2*

HOLY SPIRIT

~ it is **impossible** the **Holy Spirit** could **see** unfairness as a resolution. To Him, what is unfair must be corrected because it is unfair. *T-25.X.80.4:5*

~ to **hurt** God's Son must be unfair and therefore is not so. *T-26.III.13.9*

UNFORGIVENESS

A Course in Miracles Term

EGO

~ there remains an unforgiveness hiding in the **mind** which sees the **pain** through eyes the **mind** directs. *W-pI.193.11.4*

~ when an unforgiveness is not recognized, the **form** it takes seems to be something else. *P-2.VI.4.5*

~ **sickness** takes many forms, and so does unforgiveness. The forms of one but reproduce the forms of the other, for **they** are the same **illusion**. So closely is one translated into the other, that a careful **study** of the **form** a **sickness** takes **will** point quite clearly to the **form** of unforgiveness that it represents. *P-2.VI.5.1:3*

~ only **forgiveness** heals an unforgiveness, and only an unforgiveness can possibly **give** rise to **sickness** of any kind. *P-2.VI.5.5*

UNHEALED

DICTIONARY: *not yet healed.*

EGO

~ the unhealed cannot pardon. For **they** are the witnesses that pardon is **unfair**. **They** would retain the consequences of the **guilt they** overlook. *T-27.III.14.1:3*

HOLY SPIRIT

~ **he** would not leave one **source** of **pain** unhealed nor any **image** left to **veil** the **truth**. *T-31.VIII.8.7:3*

UNHEALED HEALER   *A Course in Miracles Term*

EGO

~ the **unhealed healer** wants **gratitude** from his brothers, but **he** is not grateful to them. This is because **he** thinks **he** is giving something to them and is not receiving something equally desirable in return. His **teaching** is limited, because **he** is **learning** so **little**. His **healing lesson** is limited by his own ingratitude, which is a **lesson** in **sickness**. *T-7.VI.4.7:4*

~ **he** is trying to **give** what he has not received. *T-9.IV.20.4*

~ all **unhealed** healers follow the ego's **plan** for **forgiveness** in one **form** or another. *T-9.IV.22.1*

~ **nothing** real has happened to the **unhealed healer**, and **he** learns from his own **teaching**. *T-9.IV.24.5*

~ because his **ego** is involved, it always attempts to **gain** some support from the **situation**. Seeking to get something for himself, the **unhealed healer** does not know how to **give** and consequently cannot **share**. He cannot correct because **he** is not working correctively. **He** believes that it is up to him to **teach** the **patient** what is real, but **he** does not know it himself. *T-9.IV.25.1:4*

~ all "**unhealed** healers" **make** this fundamental **confusion** in one **form** or another, because **they** must regard themselves as **self**-created rather than **God**-created. This **confusion** is rarely if ever in **awareness**, or the **unhealed healer** would instantly become a **teacher of God**, devoting his **life** to the **function** of true **healing**. Before **he** reached this point, **he thought he** was in charge of the therapeutic process and was therefore responsible for its outcome. His patient's errors thus became his own failures, and **guilt** became the cover, dark and strong, for what should be the **Holiness of Christ**. *P-2.VII.4.2:5*

~ no **unhealed healer** can be wholly sane. *P-2.VII.5.8*

~ the **unhealed healer** cannot but be fearful of his patients, and suspect them of the treachery **he** sees in him. He tries to heal, and thus at times **he** may. But **he will** not succeed except to some extent and for a **little** while. **He** does not **see** the **Christ** in him who calls. What **answer** can **he give** to one who seems to be a **stranger**; alien to the **truth** and poor in wisdom, without the **God** who must be given him? *P-2.VII.7.3:7*

~ the **unhealed healer** may be **arrogant**, selfish, unconcerned, and actually dishonest. **He** may be uninterested in **healing** as his major **goal**. *P-3.II.3.2:3*

~ only an **unhealed healer** would try to heal for money, and **he will** not succeed to the extent to which **he** values it. Nor **will he** find his **healing** in the process. *P-3.III.2.1:2*

HOLY SPIRIT;   *therapist*

~ the **unhealed healer** obviously does not **understand** his own vocation. *T-7.VI.39.5*

UNION

DICTIONARY: *the action or **fact** of joining or **being** joined.*

EGO

~ in any union with a **brother** in which **you seek** to lay your **guilt** upon him or **share** it with him or perceive his own, **you will** feel guilty. *T-13.IV.22.1*

~ when two individuals **seek** to become one, **they** are trying to decrease their **magnitude**. Each would deny his **power**, for the separate union excludes the **universe**. Far more is left **outside** than would be taken in. For **God** is left without and **nothing** taken in. *T-16.VII.62.2:5*

~ the attempt at union becomes a **way** of excluding even the one with whom the union was sought. For it was formed to get him out of it and **join** with fantasies in uninterrupted "bliss." *T-17.IV.19.3:5*

HOLY SPIRIT;   *truth, gift, gift of union.*

~ in union, everything that is not real must disappear, for **truth** is union. *T-14.IV.24.5*

~ when two or more **join** together in searching for **truth**, the **ego** can no longer defend its lack of content. The **fact** of union tells them it is not true. *T-14.VI.54.6:7*

~ if one such union were made in perfect **faith**, the **universe** would enter into it. *T-16.VII.62.6*

~ **sin will** not prevail against a union **Heaven** has smiled upon. *T-19.IV.35.3*

~ his real **relationship** is one of perfect union and unbroken continuity. *T-20.VII.45.5*

~ how **little** stands between **you** and your **awareness** of your union. *T-22.VI.49.1*

~ **nothing** can be caused without some **form** of union, be it with a **dream** of **judgment** or the **Voice** for **God**. *T-30.II.31.4*

UNITY

DICTIONARY: *the state of **being** united or joined as a whole.*

EGO

~ **we** cannot be united in **crucifixion** and in **death**. *T-20.II.3.1*

HOLY SPIRIT;   *Son of God*

~ for there is **peace**, and nowhere else can **peace** be sought and found. *T-3.VI.38.9:10*

~ the unity that specialness denies **will** save them all, for what is one can **have** no specialness. *T-26.VIII.66.5*

~ uniting with a brother's **mind** prevents the **cause** of **sickness** and perceived effects. *T-28.IV.29.5*

~ yours is the unity of all **creation**. Your perfect unity makes **change** in **you impossible**. *W-pI.95.1.3:4*

~ unity **alone** is not a **thing** of dreams. *M-12.6.10*

UNIVERSE

DICTIONARY: *all existing matter and space considered as a whole; the cosmos. The universe is believed to be at least 10 billion **light** years in diameter and contains a vast number of galaxies; it has been expanding since its **creation** in the Big Bang about 13 billion years ago.*

EGO

~ **you** are a separate universe with all the **power** to hold itself complete **within** itself, with every entry shut against intrusion and every window barred against the **light**. *T-24.VII.59.3*

~ deny your own **Identity**, and **you** assail the universe **alone**, without a friend, a tiny particle of dust against the legions of your enemies. *W-pI.191.3.2*

HOLY SPIRIT; *Himself*

~ the **laws** of the universe do not permit **contradiction**. *T-10.II.8.5*

~ there is no end to **God** and His Son, for **we** are the universe. *T-10.II.9.2*

~ the universe of **love** does not stop because **you** do not **see** it. *T-10.II.9.7*

~ this universe, **being** of **God**, is far beyond the petty sum of all the separate bodies **you** perceive. For all its parts are joined in **God** through **Christ**, where **they** become like to their **Father**. *T-15.IX.82.5:6*

~ one instant spent together restores the universe to both of you. *T-18.VIII.67.3*

~ no accident nor chance is possible **within** the universe as **God** created it, **outside** of which is nothing. *T-21.III.17.4*

~ the universe is one. *T-22.VII.62.10*

~ **you have** the right to all the universe. *T-25.IX.77.1*

~ the universe remains unheeding of the **laws** by which **you thought** to govern it. *W-pI.136.12.2*

~ decide but to accept your rightful place as co-creator of the universe, and all **you** think **you** made **will** disappear. *W-pI.152.8.3*

~ the **Light** in **you** is what the universe longs to behold. *W-pI.156.5.1*

~ the universe consists of **nothing** but the **Son of God** who calls upon his **Father**. *W-pI.183.12.4*

~ what your inward **vision** looks upon is your **perception** of the universe. *W-pI.188.5.7*

UNKNOWING

DICTIONARY: *lack of **awareness** or **knowledge**.*

EGO

~ it is not possible to convince the unknowing that **they** know. *T-14.IV.26.1*

HOLY SPIRIT

~ to **God**, unknowing is **impossible**. It is therefore not a point of view at all but merely a **belief** in something that does not **exist**. It is only this **belief** that the unknowing **have**, and by it **they** are wrong about themselves. **They have** defined themselves as **they** were not created. Their **creation** was not a point of view, but rather a **certainty**. Uncertainty brought to **certainty** does not retain any conviction of **reality**. *T-14.IV.26.5:10*

~ his gentle **Voice** is calling from the known to the unknowing. *W-pI.186.13.1*

VALUE

DICTIONARY: *the regard that something is held to deserve; the importance, **worth**, or usefulness of something.*

EGO

~ when **you** do not value yourself, **you** become sick. *T-9.IX.79.5*

~ no one would choose to let go what **he** believes has value. *T-15.VIII.67.3*

~ all things **you seek** to **make** your value greater in your **sight limit you** further, **hide** your **worth** from **you**, and add another bar across the door that leads to true **awareness** of your **Self**. *W-pI.128.3.3*

~ a temporary value is without all value. *W-pI.133.7.2*

HOLY SPIRIT

~ values are relative, but **they** are powerful because **they** are mental judgments. *T-7.VIII.74.4*

~ your value is in **God's Mind** and therefore not in yours **alone**. *T-9.VII.57.7*

~ **you** did not establish your value, and it needs no **defense**. **Nothing** can **attack** it or prevail over it. It does not vary. It merely is. *T-9.VII.58.2:5*

~ my value of **you** can heal **you** because the value of God's Son is one. *T-9.IX.79.5*

~ your **choice** is determined by what **you** value. *T-9.XI.107.3*

~ as **self**-value comes from **self-extension**, so does the **perception** of **self**-value come from the **projection** of loving thoughts outward. *T-11.VII.55.5*

~ what is not real cannot be seen and has no value. **God** could not offer His Son what has no value, nor could His Son **receive** it. *T-11.IX.81.7:8*

~ when **we** are all united in **Heaven**, **you will** value **nothing** that **you** value **here**. For **nothing** that **you** value **here you** value wholly, and so **you** do not value it at all. Value is where **God** placed it, and the value of what **God** esteems cannot be judged, for it has been established. It is wholly of value. It can merely be appreciated or not. To value it partially is not to know its value. In **Heaven** is everything **God** valued and **nothing** else. *T-13.V.37.1:7*

~ value always lies in joint **appreciation**. *T-14.III.16.8*

~ what **you** value, **you will** keep. *T-16.VII.61.3*

~ for what **you** value **you make part** of **you** as **you** perceive yourself. *W-pI.128.3.2*

~ your values are determiners of this, for what **you** value **you** must **want** to **see**, believing what **you see** is really there. No one can **see** a **world** his **mind** has not accorded value. And no one can **fail** to look upon what **he** believes **he** wants. *W-pI.130.1.4:6*

~ **time** can never take away a value that is real. *W-pI.133.7.3*

VAULT

vôlt

DICTIONARY: *a large room or chamber used for storage, especially an underground one.*

EGO

~ committed to its vaults, the history of all the body's **past** is hidden there. *T-28.II.5.7*

~ in these shrouded vaults are all his sins and yours preserved and kept in **darkness** where **they** cannot be perceived as errors, which the **light** would surely show. *T-31.V.48.6*

VEIL

DICTIONARY: *a **thing** that conceals, disguises, or obscures something.*

EGO;   *fantasies, dark veil, veil of **time**, veil of ugliness, fragile veil, heavy veil, veil of **fear**, veil of **sin**, veil of specialness, veil of ignorance, veil of old ideas, veil of your **grievances**, veil of **guilt**, veil across the **face of Christ**, **world** of idols.*

~ heavy veils of **guilt within** which the **Son of God** has hidden himself from his own **sight**. *T-14.II.8.5*

~ this is the darkest veil, upheld by the **belief** in **death** and protected by its **attraction**. The dedication to **death** and to its sovereignty is but the solemn **vow**, the **promise** made in **secret** to the **ego** never to lift this veil, not to approach it nor even to suspect that it is there. This is the **secret bargain** made with the **ego** to keep what lies beyond the veil forever blotted out and unremembered. *T-19.V.92.1:3*

~ either **alone will see** it as a solid block, nor realize how thin the drapery that separates **you now**. *T-22.V.40.4*

~ standing before the veil, it still seems **difficult**. *T-22.V.44.5*

~ veil of specialness that hides the **face of Christ** from him, and **you** as well. *T-24.VII.54.5*

~ the veil of ignorance is drawn across the **evil** and the **good**. *T-31.VI.64.8*

HOLY SPIRIT;   *veil of **light***

~ there is no veil the **love** of God in us together cannot lift. *T-16.V.42.9*

~ the fourth **obstacle** to be surmounted hangs like a heavy veil before the **face of Christ**. Yet as His face rises beyond it, shining with **joy** because **He** is in His Father's **Love**, **peace will** lightly brush the veil aside and run to meet Him and to **join** with Him at last. For this dark veil, which seems to **make** the **face of Christ** Himself like to a leper's and the bright rays of His Father's **love** which **light** His face with **glory** appear as streams of blood, fades in the blazing **light** beyond it when the **fear** of **death** is gone. *T-19.V.91.1:3*

~ what attracts **you** from beyond the veil is also deep **within you**, unseparated from it and completely one. *T-19.V.96.7*

~ no one can stand before this **obstacle alone**, for **he** could not **have** reached thus far unless his **brother** walked beside him. *T-19.V.98.2*

~ no one would dare to look on it without complete **forgiveness** of his **brother** in his heart. *T-19.V.98.3*

~ together **we will** disappear into the Presence beyond the veil, not to be lost, but found; not to be seen, but known. *T-19.V.108.1*

~ and so **you** stand, **here** in this holy place, before the veil of **sin** that hangs between **you** and the **face of Christ**. *T-22.V.40.1*

~ how beautiful the **sight you** saw beyond the veil which **you will** bring to **light** the tired eyes of those as weary **now** as once **you** were. *T-22.V.41.6*

~ this veil **you** lift together opens the **way** to **truth** to more than **you**. *T-22.V.43.4*

~ it is no solid wall. And only an **illusion** stands between **you** and the holy **Self you share**. *T-22.V.44.7:8*

~ no more a veil can banish what it seems to separate nor darken by one whit the **light** itself. *T-29.IX.54.8*

~ behind every veil **I have** drawn across the face of **love**, its **light** remains undimmed. *W-pI.56.5.2*

~ as the veil of your grievances is lifted, **you** are released with him. *W-pI.69.1.3*

~ in **time** there can be a great lag between the **offering** and the **acceptance** of healing. This is the veil across the **face of Christ**. *P-3.II.10.9:10*

VENGEANCE

|ˈvenjəns|

DICTIONARY: *punishment inflicted or retribution exacted for an injury or wrong.*

EGO

~ demands vengeance forever. *T-15.II.8.7*

~ vengeance becomes your **substitute** for **Atonement**, and the escape from vengeance becomes your **loss**. *T-16.VIII.74.7*

~ to the **world**, **justice** and vengeance are the same. *T-25.IX.65.2*

~ vengeance without **love** has gained in **strength** by **being** separate and apart from **love**. *T-25.IX.71.3*

~ having projected his **anger** onto the **world**, **he** sees vengeance about to strike at him. *W-pI.22.1.2*

~ the **world you see** is a vengeful **world**, and everything in it is a **symbol** of vengeance. *W-pI.23.3.1*

~ **now** is vengeance all there is to **wish** for. *W-pI.195.3.2*

HOLY SPIRIT

~ vengeance cannot be shared. **Give** it therefore to the **Holy Spirit**, who **will undo** it in **you** because it does not belong in your **mind**. *T-5.VIII.76.4:5*

~ the **past** is gone, and with its passing the drive for vengeance has been uprooted and has disappeared. *T-16.VIII.72.4*

~ vengeance is alien to **God's Mind** because **He** knows of **justice**. To be just is to be fair and not be vengeful. Fairness and vengeance are **impossible**, for each one contradicts the other and denies that it is real. *T-25.IX.67.1:3*

~ it is **impossible** the **Son of God** could merit vengeance. *T-25.IX.75.1*

~ **problem** solving cannot be vengeance, which at best can bring another **problem** added to the first, in which the murder is not obvious. *T-25.X.82.2*

~ vengeance must **have** a focus. *T-27.VIII.65.6*

~ vengeance is not **part** of **love**. *W-pI.190.3.5*

VICTIM

|ˈviktəm|

DICTIONARY: *a person harmed, injured, or killed as a result of a crime, accident, or other event or action.*

EGO; *brother, I, victim of **sacrifice**, victim of **attack**, victim to a **dream**.*

~ a victim of **sacrifice**, justified in sacrificing others. *T-15.XI.105.2*

~ the **laws** of **sin** demand a victim. *T-25.IX.65.3*

~ **he** is the victim of this "something else," a **thing outside** himself for which **he** has no **reason** to be held responsible. **He** must be **innocent** because **he** knows not what **he** does, but what is done to him. *T-27.VIII.62.4:5*

~ **he** must **see** it in another's hand if **he** would be a victim of **attack he** did not choose. And thus **he** suffers from the wounds a knife **he** does not hold has made upon himself. *T-27.VIII.65.8:9*

~ helpless **he** stands, a victim to a **dream** conceived and cherished by a separate **mind**. *T-27.VIII.69.4*

~ thus does **he fear** his own **attack** but sees it at another's hands. As victim, **he** is **suffering** from its effects but not their cause. **He** authored not his own **attack**, and **he** is **innocent** of what **he** caused. *T-28.III.22.7:9*

HOLY SPIRIT

~ in forgiving dreams is no one asked to be the victim and the sufferer. *T-28.III.20.2*

~ **you** are not the victim of the **world you see** because **you** invented it. *W-pI.32.1.2*

VIGILANCE

DICTIONARY: *the action or state of keeping careful watch for possible danger or difficulties.*

EGO

~ by deciding against your **reality**, **you have** made yourself vigilant against **God** and His **Kingdom**. And it is this vigilance that makes **you** afraid to **remember** Him. *T-9.IX.73.5:6*

HOLY SPIRIT

~ consider how much vigilance **you have** been willing to exert to protect your **ego** and how **little you have** been willing to expend to protect your higher **mind**. *T-4.IV.55.3*

~ vigilance is not necessary for **truth**, but it is necessary against illusions. *T-6.V.93.7*

~ your vigilance against this **sickness** is the **way** to heal it. *T-6.V.94.6*

~ vigilance does require **effort**, but only to **teach you** that **effort** itself is unnecessary. *T-6.V.95.5*

~ vigilance has no place at all in **peace**. It is necessary against beliefs which are not true and would never **have** been called upon by the **Holy Spirit** if **you** had not believed the untrue. *T-7.VII.61.5:6*

~ while **you** believe that two totally contradictory **thought** systems **share truth**, your **need** for vigilance is apparent. *T-7.VII.63.5*

~ the alertness of the **ego** to the errors which other egos **make** is not the kind of vigilance the **Holy Spirit** would **have you** maintain. *T-9.I.1.1*

~ all your striving must be directed against littleness, for it does require vigilance to protect your **magnitude** in this **world**. *T-15.IV.25.4*

VISION

DICTIONARY: *the faculty or state of **being** able to **see**.*

EGO; *enemy, double vision.*

~ all vision starts with the perceiver who judges what is true and what is false. And what **he** judges false **he** does not **see**. *T-12.VII.63.3:4*

~ when vision is denied, **confusion** of **cause** and effect becomes inevitable. *T-21.III.25.1*

HOLY SPIRIT; *way to You, Christ's vision, vision of Christ, His vision, savior's vision, vision of sinlessness, real vision, perfect vision, single vision, **gift**, **miracle**, **bridge**, holy ground.*

~ a Vision **will** correct the **perception** of everything **you see**. *T-11.IX.80.3*

~ the Holy Spirit's vision is merciful. *T-12.III.17.2*

~ vision depends on **light**. *T-12.V.41.1*

~ and with this vision of the **truth** in them came all the beauty of the **world** to shine upon them. *T-12.V.44.7*

~ the **light** of perfect vision is freely given as it is freely received and can be accepted only without **limit**. *T-12.VI.51.4*

~ it has been given **you** to **see** no thorns, no strangers, and no obstacles to **peace**. *T-20.III.11.2*

~ your vision has become the greatest **power** for the undoing of **illusion** that **God** Himself could **give**. *T-20.III.11.5*

~ in our vision **will** be no illusions—only a pathway to the open door of **Heaven**. *T-20.III.12.8*

~ vision adapts to **wish**, for **sight** is always secondary to **desire**. *T-20.VIII.62.6*

~ for vision, like relationships, has no **order**. **You** either **see** or not. *T-20.VIII.62.8:9*

~ vision is learned from Him Who would **undo** your **teaching**. His vision cannot **see** the **body** because it cannot look on **sin**. And thus it leads **you** to **reality**. *T-20.VIII.65.4:6*

~ vision **will** come to **you** at first in glimpses, but **they will** be enough to show **you** what is given **you** who **see** your **brother sinless**. *T-20.IX.67.1*

~ vision would not be necessary had **judgment** not been made. *T-20.IX.67.5*

~ vision is freely given to those who **ask** to **see**. *T-20.IX.68.10*

~ there is no **problem**, no event or **situation**, no perplexity that vision **will** not solve. All is redeemed when looked upon with vision. For this is not your **sight**, and brings with it the **laws** beloved of Him Whose **sight** it is. *T-20.IX.71.7:9*

~ everything looked upon with vision falls gently into place according to the **laws** brought to it by His **calm** and certain **sight**. The end for everything **He** looks upon is always sure. For it **will** meet His **purpose**, seen in unadjusted **form** and suited perfectly to meet it. Destructiveness becomes benign, and **sin** is turned to **blessing** under His gentle gaze. *T-20.IX.72.1:4*

~ vision sets all things right, bringing them gently **within** the kindly sway of Heaven's **laws**. *T-20.IX.73.2*

~ vision is the **means** by which the **Holy Spirit** translates your nightmares into **happy** dreams; your wild hallucinations that show **you** all the fearful outcomes of imagined **sin** into the **calm** and reassuring sights with which **He** would replace them. *T-20.IX.76.4*

~ everything looked upon with vision is healed and holy. **Nothing** perceived without it **means** anything. *T-21.I.1.10:11*

~ vision shows **you** where to go. *T-21.II.4.5*

~ recognition comes of vision and suspended **judgment**. *T-21.III.23.3*

~ in this **change** is room made **way** for vision. Vision extends beyond itself, as does the **purpose** which it serves and all the **means** for its accomplishment. *T-21.VI.58.5:6*

~ constant vision can be given only those who **wish** for constancy. *T-21.VIII.84.4*

~ only your vision can convey to **you** what **you** can **see**. It reaches **you** directly without a **need** to be interpreted to **you**. *T-22.II.9.4:5*

~ vision cannot damn, but only bless. *T-22.III.23.4*

~ and gladly is His vision given to anyone who is but willing to **see** his **brother sinless**. *T-22.III.28.2*

~ the beginning of a vision that has **meaning**. Vision is **sense**, quite literally. If it is not the body's **sight**, it must be understood. For it is plain, and what is obvious is not ambiguous. It can be understood. *T-22.IV.29.6:10*

~ vision's fundamental law: **you see** what **you** believe is there, and **you** believe it there because **you want** it there. *T-25.IV.23.3*

~ in this single vision does **he** see the **face of Christ** and understands **he** looks on **everyone** as **he** beholds this One. *T-31.VII.75.6*

461

~ vision can but represent a **wish**, because it has no **power** to create. Yet it can look with **love** or look with **hate**, depending only on the simple **choice** of whether **you** would **join** with what **you see** or keep yourself apart and separate. *T-31.VII.79.5:6*

~ this a vision is which **you** must **share** with **everyone you see**, for otherwise **you will** behold it not. *T-31.VIII.93.7*

~ recognizing that your **mind** has been merely blank, rather than believing that it is filled with real ideas, is the first **step** to opening the **way** to vision. *W-pI.8.3.3*

~ our **decision** to see is all that vision requires. *W-pI.20.3.1*

~ in your determination to **see** is vision given **you**. *W-pI.20.3.8*

~ vision already holds a replacement for everything **you** think **you see now**. *W-pI.23.4.4*

~ real vision is not limited to concepts such as "near" and "far." *W-pI.30.4.1:2*

~ real vision is not only unlimited by space and distance, but it does not depend on the body's eyes at all. The **mind** is its only **source**. *W-pI.30.4.3:4*

~ **everyone** gains through your holy vision. It signifies the end of **sacrifice** because it offers **everyone** his full due. *W-pI.37.1.4:5*

~ vision is my greatest **need**. *W-pI.56.3.1*

~ **christ's vision** is His **gift**, and **He** has given it to me. *W-pI.59.3.3*

~ yet the vision of **Christ** has been given me to replace them. It is through this vision that **I** choose to **see**. As **I** look upon the **world** with the vision He has given me, **I remember** that **I** am His Son. *W-pI.59.4.6:8*

~ miracles and vision necessarily go together. *W-pI.91.1.1*

~ vision sees beyond appearances to that same **truth** in **everyone** and everything there is. *W-pI.109.2.4*

~ perfect vision which **will** heal all the mistakes that any **mind** has made at any **time** or place. It is enough to heal the **past** and **make** the **future** free. It is enough to let the **present** be accepted as it is. It is enough to let **time** be the **means** for all the **world** to learn escape from **time** and every **change** that **time** appears to bring in passing by. *W-pI.110.2.2:5*

~ this **you will** never **teach**, for **you** attained it not through **learning**. *W-pI.157.9.3*

~ by the holy gifts **we give**, **Christ's vision** looks upon ourselves as well. *W-pI.158.11.4*

~ yet there is a vision which the **Holy Spirit** sees because the **mind** of **Christ** beholds it too. *W-pI.158.5.6*

~ our concern is with **Christ's vision**. This **we** can attain. *W-pI.158.6.6:7*

~ **christ's vision** has one law. It does not look upon a **body** and **mistake** it for the Son whom **God** created. It beholds a **light** beyond the **body**, an **idea** beyond what can be touched, a purity undimmed by errors, pitiful mistakes, and fearful thoughts of **guilt** from dreams of **sin**. It sees no **separation**. And it looks on **everyone**, on every **circumstance**, all happenings, and all events without the slightest fading of the **light** it sees. *W-pI.158.7.1:5*

~ **christ's vision** is a **miracle**. It comes from far beyond itself, for it reflects eternal **love** and the **rebirth** of **love** which never died but has been kept obscure. **Christ's vision** pictures **Heaven**, for it sees a **world** so like to **Heaven** that what **God** created perfect can be mirrored there. *W-pI.159.3.1:3*

~ **christ's vision** is the **miracle** in which all miracles are born. It is their **source**, remaining with each **miracle you give** and yet remaining yours. It is the bond by which the giver and receiver are united in **extension here** on earth as **they** are one in **Heaven**. *W-pI.159.4.1:3*

~ in **Christ's vision** is his loveliness reflected in a **form** so holy and so beautiful that **you** could scarce refrain from kneeling at his feet. *W-pI.161.9.3*

~ **christ's vision** has restored your **sight** by salvaging your **mind**. *W-pI.162.4.5*

~ your vision, given **you** from far beyond all things **within** the **world**, looks back on them in a new **light**. And what **you see** becomes the **healing** and **salvation** of the **world**. The valuable and valueless are both perceived and recognized for what **they** are. *W-pI.164.6.2:4*

~ it is not **difficult** to look **within**, for there all vision starts. There is no **sight**, be it of dreams or from a truer **source**, that is not but the **shadow** of the seen through inward vision. There **perception** starts, and there it ends. *W-pI.188.2.5:7*

~ through **Christ's vision we** behold a **world** beyond the one **we** made and take that **world** to be the full replacement of our own. *W-pII.1.6.4*

~ **christ's vision** looks through me **today**. His **sight** shows me all things forgiven and at **peace** and offers this same vision to the **world**. *W-pII.291.1.1:2*

~ **i** can obscure my holy **sight** if **I** intrude my **world** upon it. Nor can **I** behold the holy sights **Christ** looks upon unless it is His vision that **I** use. *W-pII.304.1.1:2*

~ who uses but **Christ's vision** finds a **peace** so deep and **quiet**, undisturbable and wholly changeless that the **world** contains no counterpart. Comparisons are still before this **peace**. And all the **world** departs in silence as this **peace** envelops it and gently carries it to **truth**, no more to be the **home** of **fear**. For **Love** has come and healed the **world** by giving it Christ's **peace**. *W-pII.305.1.1:4*

~ it can offer me a day in which **I see** a **world** so like to **Heaven** that an ancient **memory** returns to me. *W-pII.306.1.1*

~ **christ's vision** does not use your eyes, but **you** can look through His and learn to **see** like Him. *S-2.1.6.4*

VOICE |vois|

DICTIONARY: *the sound produced in a person's larynx and uttered through the mouth, as speech or **song**.*

EGO;   *hallucination, ego's voice.*

~ the ego's voice is an hallucination. *T-8.I.3.1*

~ voice of the **ego**, which tells **you** that **you have** been treacherous to **God** and therefore deserve **death**. *T-11.VIII.75.3*

~ the **shadow** voices do not **change** the **laws** of **time** or of **eternity**. **They** come from what is **past** and gone and hinder not the true existence of the **here** and **now**. *T-26.VI.41.1:2*

HOLY SPIRIT;   *gentle voice, Holy Spirit's voice.*

~ the Voice of the **Holy Spirit** is the **call** to **Atonement** or the restoration of the integrity of the **mind**. *T-5.IV.20.4*

~ the Voice of the **Holy Spirit** does not command, because it is incapable of arrogance. It does not demand, because it does not **seek** control. It does not overcome, because it does not **attack**. It merely reminds. It is compelling only because of what it reminds **you** of. It brings to your **mind** the other **way**, remaining **quiet** even in the midst of the turmoil **you have** made for yourselves. *T-5.IV.24.1:6*

~ the Voice for **God** is always **quiet**, because it speaks of **peace**. Yet **peace** is stronger than **war** because it heals. *T-5.IV.24.7:8*

~ listening to one voice **means** the **will** to **share** the voice in **order** to hear it yourself. *T-5.VI.52.3*

~ his Voice reminds **you** always that all hope is yours, because of His care. *T-5.IX.90.6*

~ his Voice **will teach you** how to distinguish between **pain** and **joy** and **will** lead **you** out of the **confusion** which **you have** made. *T-7.XI.105.10*

~ the Holy Spirit's Voice is as loud as your willingness to listen. It cannot be louder without violating your **will**, which the **Holy Spirit** seeks to free but never to command. *T-8.VIII.78.7:8*

~ a Voice **will answer** every **question you ask**. *T-11.IX.80.3*

~ every voice has a **part** in the **song** of **redemption**, the hymn of gladness and thanksgiving for the **light** to the **Creator** of **light**. *T-12.VI.52.7*

~ his appointed Voice, Which silences the thunder of the meaningless and shows the **way** to **peace** to those who cannot **see**. *W-pI.106.2.1*

~ **he** needs your voice to speak to them. *W-pI.106.5.5*

~ in **everyone** and everything, His Voice would speak to **you** of **nothing** but your **Self** and your **Creator**. *W-pI.151.12.3*

~ whatever your appointed **role** may be, it was selected by the Voice for God, Whose **function** is to speak for **you** as well. *W-pI.154.2.1*

~ it is this Voice which speaks of **laws** the **world** does not obey, which promises **salvation** from all **sin**, with **guilt** abolished in the **mind** that **God** created **sinless**. *W-pI.154.4.2*

~ voice for **God** assuring **you** that He has judged **you** as the Son **He** loves. *W-pII.347.2.2*

VOW |vou|

DICTIONARY: *a solemn **promise**.*

EGO;   *solemn vow, **secret** vow.*

~ c is but the solemn vow, the **promise** made in **secret** to the **ego** never to lift this **veil**, not to approach it nor even to suspect that it is there. *T-19.V.92.2*

~ **nothing** is safe from its **attack**, and it is safe from **nothing**. It **will** forever more be unforgiving, for that is what it is—a **secret** vow that what **God** wants for **you will** never be and that **you will** oppose His **Will** forever. *T-24.IV.29.5:6*

~ his **secret** vows are powerless before the **Will** of **God**, whose promises **he** shares. And what **he** substitutes is not his **will**, who has made **promise** of himself to **God**. *T-28.VII.59.8:9*

VULNERABILITY |ˈvəln(ə)rəb(ə)l|

DICTIONARY: *susceptible to physical or emotional **attack** or **harm**.*

EGO;   *argument*

~ as long as their **sense** of vulnerability persists, **they** should be preserved from even attempting miracles. *T-2.III.62.7*

~ the vulnerable are essentially miscreators because **they** misperceive **creation**. *T-2.V.95.6*

~ the body's vulnerability is its own best argument that **you** cannot be of God. *T-4.VI.71.2*

~ its own profound **sense** of vulnerability renders it incapable of **judgment** except in terms of **attack**. *T-9.VII.50.3*

HOLY SPIRIT

~ vulnerability or **invulnerability** is the result of your own thoughts. *W-pI.26.4.1*

WANT

DICTIONARY: *have a **desire** to possess or do (something); **wish** for.*

EGO

~ what **you** want in yourself, **you will make** manifest by **projection**, and **you will** accept it from the **world** because **you** put it there by wanting it. *T-11.VIII.67.5*

~ when **you** think **you** are projecting what **you** do not want, it is still because **you** do want it. *T-11.VIII.68.1*

~ what **you** want to be is what **you** think **you** are. Therefore, what **you** want to be determines every response **you make**. *T-7.VIII.72.7:8*

~ offer to the **Holy Spirit** everything **you** do not want. **He** knows what to do with it. *T-11.III.23.1:2*

~ when **you** want only **love you will see nothing** else. *T-11.VIII.69.1*

~ what **you** think is real **you** want and **will** not let it go. *T-19.IV.26.7*

~ wishful thinking is how the **ego** deals with what it wants to **make** it so. There is no better demonstration of the **power** of wanting, and therefore of **faith**, to **make** its goals seem real and possible. **Faith** in the unreal leads to adjustments of **reality** to **make** it fit the **goal** of **madness**. *T-21.III.24.1:3*

~ **reason** assures **you Heaven** is what **you** want, and all **you** want. *T-21.VII.66.5*

~ **everyone will receive** what **he** requests. But **he** can be confused indeed about the things **he** wants, the state **he** would attain. *W-pII.339.1.5:6*

HOLY SPIRIT

~ the **power** of your wanting must first be recognized. **You** must accept its **strength** and not its **weakness**. **You** must perceive that what is strong enough to **make** a **world** can let it go and can accept **correction** if it is willing to **see** that it was wrong. *T-21.III.18.8:10*

~ i want all of **Heaven** and only **Heaven**, as **God** wills me to **have**. *W-pI.89.5.5*

WAR

DICTIONARY: *a state of competition, **conflict**, or hostility between different people or groups.*

EGO

~ every response to the **ego** is a **call** to war, and war does deprive **you** of **peace**. *T-8.I.3.7*

~ no one sees himself in **conflict** and ravaged by a cruel war unless **he** believes that both opponents in the war are real. *T-13.IV.35.2*

~ the war against yourself was undertaken to **teach** the **Son of God** that **he** is not himself and not his Father's Son. For this, the **memory** of his **Father** must be forgotten. *T-23.II.11.3:4*

~ war is the **condition** in which **fear** is born and grows and seeks to dominate. *T-23.II.18.4*

~ your choosing it has given it all the **reality** it seems to **have**. *T-24.II.3.6*

HOLY SPIRIT

~ war is division, not increase. *T-5.IV.24.9*

~ the war is between forces that are real and unreal powers. *T-13.IV.35.4*

~ **you** are but trying to escape a bitter war from which **you have** escaped. The war is gone. *T-13.IV.36.2:3*

- yet as **you** made not **freedom**, so **you** made not a war that could endanger **freedom**. **Nothing** destructive ever was or **will** be. The war, the **guilt**, the **past** are gone as one into the unreality from which **they** came. *T-13.IV.36.6:8*

- the **means** of war are not the **means** of peace, and what the warlike would **remember** is not **love**. War is **impossible** unless **belief** in victory is cherished. *T-23.II.7.3:4*

- the war against yourself is but the **battle** of two illusions, struggling to **make** them different from each other in the **belief** the one which conquers **will** be true. There is no **conflict** between them and the **truth**. Nor are **they** different from each other. *T-23.II.12.1:3*

- the meeting of illusions leads to war. *T-23.II.18.2*

- there is no war without **attack**. *T-23.IV.46.13*

- war, the **substitute** for peace. *T-24.II.3.5*

WAY |wā|

DICTIONARY: *a **course** of travel or route taken in **order** to reach a place.*

EGO;   *ego's way*

- **you see** it as the road to **hell** instead of looking on it as a simple way, without a **sacrifice** or any **loss**, to find yourself in **Heaven** and in **God**. *T-29.III.10.4*

HOLY SPIRIT;   *God's way, His way **quiet** way.*

- the way is not hard, but it is very different. *T-10.IV.26.1*

- the way to **truth** is open. *T-16.V.42.10*

- this is the way to **Heaven** and to the **peace** of **Easter**, in which **we join** in glad **awareness** that the **Son of God** is risen from the **past** and has awakened to the **present**. *T-20.III.14.1*

- the **quiet** way is open. *T-21.V.48.8*

- your way is decided. There **will** be **nothing you will** not be told if **you** acknowledge this. *T-22.V.39.4:5*

- **you** cannot lose your way because there is no way but His and nowhere can **you** go except to Him. *T-26.VI.38.8*

- **will** the way be made serene and simple in the rising up to waking and the ending of the **dream**. *T-28.IV.28.5*

- the way **will** open if **you** believe that it is possible. *W-pI.41.7.4*

- god's way is sure. *W-pI.53.5.4*

- its simplicity avoids the snares the foolish convolutions of the world's apparent reasoning but serve to **hide**. *W-pI.189.6.4*

- the way is simple. *W-pI.192.9.3*

WE |wē|

DICTIONARY: *used by a speaker to refer to himself or herself and one or more other people considered together.*

EGO;   *sinners*

- we are lost in mists of shifting dreams and fearful thoughts, our eyes shut tight against the **light**, our minds engaged in worshipping what is not there. *W-pI.192.7.10*

467

HOLY SPIRIT; *God's children, joint will of the Sonship, Sons of God Himself, Your Son, the on of God, holy messengers of God, the universe, one.*

~ our **creations** are as holy as we are, and we are the Sons of **God** Himself and therefore as holy as **He** is. *T-8.VI.50.1*

~ we **will** restore to **you** the **peace** of **mind** that we must find together. *T-12.VII.75.4*

~ we **need** only **call** to **God** and all temptations disappear. Instead of words, we **need** but feel His **Love.** Instead of **prayer,** we **need** but **call** His **Name.** *W-pII.I.10.2:4*

~ we can **fail** in **nothing.** *W-pI.124.1.3*

~ what we are cannot be judged. We stand apart from all the judgments which the **world** has laid upon the **Son of God.** *W-pI.125.3.2:3*

~ we **have** a **mission here.** We did not come to reinforce the **madness** which we once believed in. *W-pI.139.8.3:4*

~ it is more than just our happiness **alone** we came to **gain.** What we accept as what we are proclaims what **everyone** must be along with us. *W-pI.139.8.6:7*

~ as we were, so are we **now** and **will** forever be. *W-pI.167.12.2*

~ we are the **Son of God.** There is no **fear** in us, for we are each a **part** of **Love** Itself. *W-pII.240.1.7:8*

~ in **God** are we secure. *W-pII.244.2.3*

~ holy indeed are we because our **Source** can know no **sin.** And we who are His Sons are like each other and alike to Him. *W-pII.260.2.2:3*

~ we save the **world** when we are joined. For in our **vision** it becomes as holy as the **light** in us. *W-pII.313.2.5:6*

~ we **will** be told exactly what **God** wills for us each **time** there is a **choice** to **make.** And **He will** speak for **God** and for your **Self,** thus making sure that **hell will** claim **you** not and that each **choice you make** brings **Heaven** nearer to your reach. *W-pII.E.5.2:3*

~ in **peace** we **will** continue in His **way** and **trust** all things to Him. In **confidence** we wait His answers, as we **ask** His **Will** in everything we do. He loves God's Son as we would **love** him, and **He** teaches us how to behold him through His eyes and **love** him as **He** does. *W-pII.E.6.2:4*

~ we can do **God's Will** and **join** together in its holy **light.** *W-pII.ST301.5.5*

~ we are **creation**—we the Sons of **God.** We seem to be discrete and unaware of our eternal **unity** with Him. Yet back of all our doubts, **past** all our fears, there still is **certainty.** *W-pII.ST321.4.1:3*

~ the **truth** of what we are is not for words to speak of nor describe. Yet we can realize our **function here,** and words can speak of this and **teach** it, too, if we exemplify the words in us. *W-pII.ST351.2.5:6*

~ we are the bringers of **salvation.** We accept our **part** as saviors of the **world,** which through our joint **forgiveness** is redeemed. And this, our **gift,** is therefore given us. We look on **everyone** as brothers and perceive all things as kindly and as **good.** We do not **seek** a **function** that is **past** the gates of **Heaven. Knowledge will** return when we **have** done our **part.** We are concerned only with giving **welcome** to the **truth.** *W-pII.ST351.3.1:7*

~ ours are the eyes through which **Christ's vision** sees a **world** redeemed from every **thought** of **sin.** Ours are the ears that hear the **Voice** of **God** proclaim the **world** as **sinless.** Ours the minds which **join** together as we bless the **world.** And from the **oneness** that we **have** attained we call to all our brothers, asking them to **share** our **peace** and consummate our **joy.** *W-pII.ST351.4.1:4*

~ we are the holy messengers of **God** who speak for Him, and carrying His **word** to **everyone** whom **He** has sent to us, we learn that it is written on our hearts. And thus our minds are changed about the aim for which we came and which we **seek** to serve. We bring glad tidings to the **Son of God,** who **thought he** suffered. **Now** is **he** redeemed. And as **he** sees the gate of **Heaven** stand open before him, **he will** enter in and disappear into the Heart of **God.** *W-pII.ST351.5.1:5*

~ we **have** been saved from wrath because we learned we were mistaken. *W-pII.ST361.5.5*

468

WEAKNESS

DICTIONARY: *the state or* **condition** *of lacking* **strength**.

EGO;   *the dark,* **strength**, *his* **strength**.

~ the **ego** cannot tolerate **ego** weakness either without ambivalence because it is afraid of its own weakness as well as the weakness of its chosen **home**. When it is threatened, the **ego** blocks your natural impulse to **help**, placing **you** under the strain of divided **will**. *T-4.IX.104.2:3*

~ those who **see** themselves as weakened do **attack**. *T-7.VII.66.1*

~ weakness is frightening. *T-7.XI.103.3*

~ before the **idea** of **attack** can enter your **mind**, **you** must **have** perceived yourself as weak. Because **you** had attacked yourself and believed that the **attack** was effective, **you** behold yourself as weakened. No longer perceiving yourself and all your brothers as equal and regarding yourself as weaker, **you** attempt to "equalize" the **situation you have** made. **You** use **attack** to do so because **you** believe that **attack** was successful in weakening **you**. *T-11.VI.43.3:6*

~ someone must always lose if **you** perceive yourself as weak. *T-15.VII.58.4*

~ to weaken is always to **attack**. *T-16.I.2.5*

~ all **sense** of weakness is associated with the **belief** that **you** are a **body**, a **belief** that is mistaken and deserves no **faith**. *W-pI.91.12.3*

~ it is your weakness that sees through the body's eyes, peering about in **darkness** to behold the likeness of itself—the small, the weak, the sickly and the dying, those in **need**, the helpless and afraid, the **sad**, the poor, the starving, and the joyless. These are seen through eyes which cannot **see** and cannot bless. *W-pI.92.3.3:4*

~ weakness is an **idol** falsely worshiped and adored that **strength** may be dispelled and **darkness rule** where **God** appointed that there should be **light**. *W-pI.92.5.1*

~ weakness reflects the **darkness** of its maker. It is sick and looks on **sickness**, which is like itself. *W-pI.92.5.2:3*

~ weakness, which looks in **darkness**, cannot **see** a **purpose** in **forgiveness** and in **love**. It sees all others different from itself and **nothing** in the **world** that it would **share**. It judges and condemns but does not **love**. In **darkness** it remains to **hide** itself and dreams that it is strong and conquering, a victor over limitations that but grow in **darkness** to enormous size. It fears and it attacks and hates itself, and **darkness** covers everything it sees, leaving its dreams as fearful as itself. No miracles are **here**, but only **hate**. It separates itself from what it sees, while **light** and **strength** perceive themselves as one. *W-pI.92.7.1:7*

HOLY SPIRIT;   *idol falsely worshiped,* **illusion**.

~ to weaken is to **limit** and impose an **opposite** that contradicts the **concept** which it attacks. And by this does it **join** to the **idea** a something it is not and **make** it unintelligible. *T-27.IV.29.7:8*

~ tolerance for weakness **will** enable us to overlook it, rather than **give** it **power** to **delay** our **learning**. *W-pI.95.10.1*

WELCOME

DICTIONARY: *greet (someone arriving) in a glad, polite, or friendly* **way**.

HOLY SPIRIT;   *gentle welcome, joyous welcome.*

~ god's welcome waits for us all, and **He will** welcome us as **I** am welcoming you. *T-8.VI.42.4*

~ where **I** am made welcome, there **I** am. *T-19.V.55.6*

~ i am made welcome in the state of **grace**, which **means you have** at last forgiven me. *T-19.V.56.1*

WHOLENESS

|ˈhōlnəs|

DICTIONARY: *the state of forming a complete and harmonious whole;* **unity**.

EGO; *enemy, seeming wholeness.*

HOLY SPIRIT; *perceptual content of miracles, God's Wholeness,* **sanity**, *His Wholeness.*

~ the full **appreciation** of its **self**-fullness makes selfishness **impossible** and **extension** inevitable. *T-7.X.94.6*

~ wholeness is for all. *T-8.VI.42.1*

~ the **power** of wholeness is **extension**. *T-8.VII.68.7*

~ wholeness heals because it is of the **mind**. *T-8.IX.82.1*

~ wholeness is indivisible, but **you** cannot learn of your wholeness until **you see** it everywhere. *T-9.V.34.6*

~ every aspect is the same, perceived in the same **light** and therefore one. *T-13.II.5.3*

~ **we** are made whole in our **desire** to **make** whole. *T-18.IV.30.4*

~ infinity cannot be understood by merely counting up its separate parts. . *T-27.VI.53.8*

~ wholeness has no **form** because it is unlimited. *T-30.IV.40.2*

~ more than whole is meaningless. *T-30.IV.42.4*

~ what is whole can **have** no missing parts that **have** been kept **outside**. *T-30.VII.77.4*

~ those who **see** themselves as whole **make** no demands. *W-pI.37.2.7*

~ wholeness is immortal. It remains forever and forever like its **Creator, being** one with Him. *M-19.4.4:5*

WILL

|wil|

DICTIONARY: *expressing a strong intention or assertion about the* **future**.

EGO; *effort*

~ the misuse of will engenders a **situation** which in the extreme becomes altogether intolerable. **Pain** thresholds can be high, but **they** are not limitless. *T-2.II.48.1:2*

~ if **you** will to separate yourself from **God**, that is what **you** will think others are **doing** to you. *T-7.VIII.79.5*

~ divided wills do not communicate because **they** speak for different things to the same **mind**. This loses the ability to communicate simply because confused **communication** does not mean anything. *T-8.X.95.1:2*

~ to will contrary to **God** is wishful thinking and not real willing. *T-10.VI.44.3*

~ your will speaks against your **learning**, as your **learning** speaks against your will, and so **you** fight against **learning** and succeed, for that is your will. *T-11.VI.50.4*

~ to **give** this **sad world** over and exchange your errors for the **peace** of **God** is but your will. *T-12.VII.64.6*

~ this other will, which seems to tell **you** what must happen, **you** gave **reality**. *T-21.III.22.4*

~ a tiny willingness, a nod to **God**, a greeting to the **Christ** in **you**, **you** find a burden wearisome and tedious, too heavy to be borne. *T-24.VII.60.4*

~ yet it is up to us when this is reached—how long **we** let an alien will appear to be opposing His. And while **we** think this will is real, **we** will not find the end **He** has appointed as the outcome of all problems **we** perceive, all trials **we see**, and every **situation** that **we** meet. *W-pII.292.1.3:4*

HOLY SPIRIT; *"price" of the Kingdom, Spirit, His Life, your salvation, your will, mechanism of decision.*

~ the real **meaning** of "are of one kind," which was mentioned before, is "are of one **mind** or will." When the will of the **Sonship** and the **Father** are one, their perfect accord is **Heaven**. *T-2.II.21.8:9*

~ when the will is really free, it cannot miscreate because it recognizes only **truth**. *T-2.II.22.7*

~ the **light** is in it because it does not oppose the Will of **God**. It is not **Heaven**, but the **light** of **Heaven** shines on it. *T-2.IV.72.6:8*

~ a state in which **you** bring your will under my **guidance** without much conscious **effort**, but this implies habit patterns which **you have** not developed dependably as yet. **God** cannot **ask** more than **you** will. The **strength** to do comes from your own undivided will to do. *T-2.IV.80.4:6*

~ instead of, "**Seek** ye first the **Kingdom** of Heaven" say, "Will ye first the **Kingdom** of Heaven," and **you have** said, "I know what I am, and I will to accept my own **inheritance**." *T-3.VIII.71.8:9*

~ in the holy state, the will is free in the **sense** that its creative **power** is unlimited, but **choice** itself is meaningless. *T-5.IV.22.9*

~ will itself is an **idea** and is therefore strengthened by **being** shared. *T-5.V.35.6*

~ what **you** will, **you** expect. *T-5.VIII.70.4*

~ to will with **God** is to create like Him. *T-7.II.4.5*

~ **god** wills. **He** does not **wish**. Your will is as powerful as His because it is His. *T-7.X.91.1:3*

~ the **Holy Spirit** opposes any imprisoning of the will of a **Son of God**, knowing that the will of the Son is the Father's. *T-8.III.11.3*

~ your will is in your nature and therefore cannot go against it. *T-8.III.9.9*

~ the will of **Father** and of the Son are one together by their **extension**. *T-8.IV.18.1*

~ your will is the **means** by which **you** determine your own **condition**, because will is the mechanism of **decision**. It is the **power** by which **you** separate or **join** and **experience pain** or **joy** accordingly. *T-8.V.31.2:3*

~ this will is invincible, because it is undivided. The undivided will of the **Sonship** is the perfect **creator**, **being** wholly in the likeness of **God**, whose Will it is. *T-8.V.36.4:5*

~ willing is **salvation** because it is **communication**. *T-8.X.94.6*

~ the will to **receive** is the will to accept. *T-9.V.32.6*

~ **god** willed to create, and your will is His. It follows, then, that **you** will to create since your will follows from His. And **being** an **extension** of His Will, yours must be the same. *T-10.II.11.7:9*

~ your will is His **Life**, which **He** has given to **you**. *T-10.II.13.5*

~ your willingness **need** not be **perfect**, because His is. *T-10.III.21.6*

~ **spirit** is will, and will is the "price" of the **Kingdom**. *T-11.V.42.4*

~ for it is your will to learn aright, and **nothing** can oppose the Will of God's Son. *T-11.VI.52.6*

~ the **Holy Spirit** wills only this, for sharing the Father's **love** for His Son, **He** wills to remove all **guilt** from his **mind** that **he** may **remember** his **Father** in peace. *T-11.X.89.2*

~ willingness is signified by **giving**. *T-12.VI.56.2*

~ will was given them because it is holy and will bring to them all that **they need**, coming as naturally as **peace** that knows no limits. There is **nothing** their wills will not provide that offers them anything of **value**. Yet because **they** do not **understand** their will, the **Holy Spirit** quietly understands it for them and gives them what **they** will without **effort**, strain, or the **impossible** burden of deciding what **they want** and **need alone**. *T-13.VIII.74.2:4*

~ the **release** from littleness in the **mind** of the **host** of **God** depends on willingness and not on **time**. *T-15.V.39.3*

~ it is your will to be in **Heaven**, where **you** are complete and **quiet** in such sure and loving relationships that any **limit** is **impossible**. *T-15.IX.89.3*

~ your willingness **need** not be complete because His is perfect. It is His task to atone for your unwillingness by His perfect **faith**, and it is His **faith you share** with Him there. *T-16.VII.69.4:5*

~ offer Him a **little** willingness to let Him remove all **fear** and hatred and to be forgiven. *T-18.VI.42.5*

~ no mad **desire**, no trivial impulse to forget again, no stab of **fear**, nor the cold sweat of seeming **death** can stand against your will. *T-19.V.96.6*

~ your willingness to let illusions go is all the **Healer** of God's Son requires. *T-28.V.46.8*

~ unless **you** do your will, **you** are not free. *T-30.III.34.4*

~ it is not your will to **hate** and be a prisoner to **fear**, a slave to **death**, a **little** creature with a **little life**. Your will is boundless. *T-30.III.35.3:4*

~ he would but keep your will forever and forever limitless. *T-30.III.36.5*

~ it is by your will the **world** is given **freedom**. Nor can **you** be free apart from Him Whose holy will **you share**. *T-30.III.37.3:4*

~ your will is universal, **being** limitless. And so it has no **form** nor is content for its expression in the terms of **form**. *T-30.IV.38.2:3*

~ your will is granted. *T-30.IV.42.10*

~ he is delivered from illusions by his will and but restored to what **he** is. *T-30.V.56.12*

~ there is no living **thing** which does not **share** the universal will that it be whole and that **you** do not leave its **call** unheard. *T-31.I.9.1*

~ my will is His, and **I** will place no other Gods before Him. *W-pI.53.6.6*

~ beyond all my insane wishes is my will united with the Will of my **Father**. *W-pI.56.5.3*

~ he will **answer you** in proportion to your willingness to hear His **Voice**. *W-pI.71.12.2*

~ yet the **light** which shines upon this **world** reflects your will, and so it must be in **you** that **we** will look for it. *W-pI.73.5.1*

~ your will is free, and **nothing** can prevail against it. *W-pI.73.9.2*

~ your will remains your **teacher**, and your will has all the **strength** to do what it desires. *W-pI.91.5.4*

~ having joined your will with His this day, what **you** are asking must be given **you**. *W-pI.157.4.2*

~ **god** gives but to unite. To take away is meaningless to Him. And when it is as meaningless to **you, you** can be sure **you share** one will with Him, and He with **you**. And **you** will also know **you share** one will with all your brothers, whose intent is yours. *W-pI.185.13.2:5*

~ your will has **power** over all fantasies and dreams. **Trust** it to **see you** through and carry **you** beyond them all. *W-pI.Rev II.3.7:8*

~ what happens is what **I desire**. What does not occur is what **I** do not **want** to happen. *W-pII.253.1.3:4*

~ a state where conflict cannot come because **we join** our holy will with God's in recognition that **they** are but one. *W-pII.307.2.1*

~ because your will is free, **you** can accept what has already happened at any **time you** choose, and only then will **you** realize that it was always there. *M-2.3.5*

WISH |wiSH|

DICTIONARY: *a **desire** or hope for something to happen.*

EGO; *tiny **illusion**, microscopic remnant of the **belief** in **sin**, **little** wish, **little** insane wish, feather of a wish, **ego** wish, **idol** wish, savage wish, hidden wish.*

~ wishes are not facts by definition. To wish is to imply that willing is not sufficient. Yet no one believes that what is wished is as real as what is willed. *T-3.VIII.71.5:7*

~ the ego's wishes do not mean anything, because the **ego** wishes for the **impossible**. *T-7.XI.102.9*

~ your lack of **faith** in the **power** that heals all **pain** arises from your wish to retain some aspects of **reality** for **fantasy**. *T-17.II.3.3*

~ your wish to **make** another **world** that is not real remains with **you**. *T-18.III.19.1*

~ for your wish to **make** destructive what cannot destroy can **have** no real effect at all. *T-18.VII.53.4*

~ this **little** wish, uprooted and floating aimlessly, can land and settle briefly upon anything, for it has no **purpose now**. *T-19.V.46.2*

~ **now** it is aimless, wandering pointlessly, causing no more than tiny interruptions in love's appeal. *T-19.V.46.4*

~ feather of a wish, this tiny **illusion**, this microscopic remnant of the **belief** in **sin**, is all that remains of what once seemed to be the **world**. It is no longer an unrelenting barrier to **peace**. Its pointless wandering makes its results appear to be more erratic and unpredictable than before. *T-19.V.47.1:3*

~ it is **nothing** in itself and stood for **nothing** when **you** had greater **faith** in its protection. *T-19.V.48.5*

~ the fixed and unchangeable dedication to **sin** and its results. *T-19.V.46.3*

~ his wish is law unto him, and **he** obeys. *T-24.VIII.62.2*

~ any wish that seems to go against His **Will** has no foundation in the **truth**. *T-26.VIII.51.11*

~ in every wish to **hurt**, **he** chooses **death** instead of what his **Father** wills for him. *T-26.VIII.63.6*

~ the wish to be unfairly treated is a **compromise** attempt that would combine **attack** and **innocence**. *T-27.I.1.1*

~ if **you** can be **hurt** by anything, **you see** a **picture** of your **secret** wishes. *T-31.V.57.8*

~ it is but a wish, insane and meaningless, to **make** yourself a **thing** which **you** are not. *T-31.VII.81.1*

~ **we** had a wish that **God** would **fail** to **have** the Son whom He created for Himself. **We** wanted **God** to **change** Himself and be what **we** would **make**. *W-pII.9.1:2*

~ the ego's fundamental wish is to replace **God**. In **fact**, the **ego** is the physical embodiment of this wish. For it is this wish which seems to surround the **mind** with a **body**, keeping it separate and **alone** and unable to reach other minds except through the **body** which was made to imprison it. *W-pI.72.2.1:3*

~ ego's idle wishes, out of which **darkness** and nothingness arise. The **will you share** with **God** has all the **power** of **creation** in it. The ego's idle wishes are unshared and therefore **have** no **power** at all. Its wishes are not idle in the **sense** that **they** can **make** a **world** of illusions in which your **belief** can be very strong. But **they** are idle indeed in terms of **creation**. **They make nothing** that is real. *W-pI.73.1.2:7*

~ **they** become the middlemen the **ego** employs to traffic in grievances and stand between your **awareness** and your brothers' **reality**. Beholding them, **you** do not know your brothers nor your **Self**. *W-pI.73.2.3:4*

~ it is only the wish to deceive that makes for **war**. *M-4.12.2*

HOLY SPIRIT

~ what **you** wish is true for **you**. Nor is it possible that **you** can wish for something and lack **faith** that it is so. Wishing makes real, as surely as does **will** create. The **power** of a wish upholds illusions as strongly as does **love** extend itself, except that one deludes; the other heals. *T-24.VI.40.6:9*

~ **nothing** is harmful or beneficent apart from what **you** wish. It is your wish that makes it what it is in its effects on **you**. Because **you** chose it as a **means** to **gain** these same effects, believing them to be the bringers of rejoicing and of **joy**. *T-25.V.33.3:5*

~ the wish to **see** calls down the **grace** of **God** upon your eyes and brings the **gift** of **light** that makes **sight** possible. *T-25.VII.44.7*

~ yet is this wish in line with Heaven's state and not in opposition to **God's Will**. Although it falls far short of giving **you** your full **inheritance**, it does remove the obstacles which **you have** placed between the **Heaven** where **you** are and recognition of where and what **you** are. *T-26.VIII.55.1:2*

~ what **you** wish is given **you** to see. *T-27.III.19.8*

~ no idle wishes can detain us nor deceive us with an **illusion** of **strength**. *W-pI.73.9.4*

~ **we** would wish for **nothing** else, for **nothing** else belongs to us in **truth**. *W-pI.104.7.3*

WITHIN

|wə'THin|

DICTIONARY: *inside (something).*

EGO

~ **you** do not know how to look within yourself, for **you** do not believe your **home** is there. *T-11.V.40.4*

~ loudly the **ego** tells **you** not to look inward, for if **you** do, your eyes **will light** on **sin**, and **God** will strike **you blind**. *T-21.V.42.3*

~ the search implies **you** are not whole within and **fear** to look upon your devastation and prefer to **seek outside** yourself for what **you** are. *T-29.VIII.46.6*

HOLY SPIRIT

~ and as **you** manifest it, **you will see** it both without and within, for **you will see** it without because **you** saw it first within. Everything **you** behold without is a **judgment** of what **you** beheld within. *T-11.VIII.73.2:3*

~ within **you** is everything **you** taught. *T-16.IV.24.4*

~ within yourselves **you love** each other with a perfect **love**. **Here** is holy ground in which no substitution can enter and where only the **truth** about each other can abide. **Here you** are joined in **God**, as much together as **you** are with Him. The original **error** has not entered **here**, nor ever **will**. **Here** is the radiant **truth** to which the **Holy Spirit** has committed your **relationship**. *T-18.II.9.3:7*

~ the **holiness** that leads us is within us, as is our **home**. *T-20.III.13.5*

~ within **you** there is a Force which no illusions can resist. *T-22.VI.49.4*

~ there is One within **you** Who is right. *T-27.VI.51.6*

~ **god** dwells within, and your **completion** lies in Him. *T-29.VIII.48.3*

~ **peace** comes from deep within myself. *W-pI.57.6.1*

WITNESS

DICTIONARY: *a person who sees an event, typically a crime or accident, take place.*

EGO;   *sin's witnesses*

~ those who **want** the **ego** are predisposed to defend it. Therefore, their **choice** of witnesses should be suspect from the beginning. The **ego** does not **call** upon witnesses who would disagree with its case. *T-8.VIII.74.1:3*

~ when the **ego** calls on a witness, it has already made the witness an ally. *T-8.VIII.74.6*

~ deny a **brother here**, and **you** deny the witnesses to] your fatherhood in **Heaven**. *T-13.II.9.3*

~ the **world you see** is but the idle witness that **you** were right. This witness is insane. **You** trained it in its testimony, and as it gave it back to **you**, **you** listened and convinced yourself that what it saw was true. *T-21.III.19.1:3*

~ a sick and **suffering you** but represents your brother's **guilt**—the witness which **you** send lest **he** forget the injuries **he** gave from which **you** swear **he** never **will** escape. *T-27.II.4.3*

~ these are the witnesses that are called forth to be believed and lend conviction to the system **they** speak for and represent. And each has many voices, speaking to your **brother** and yourself in different tongues. *T-27.II.7.4:5*

~ these are not sins, but witnesses unto the strange **belief** that **sin** and **death** are real. *T-27.II.9.1*

~ sin's witnesses hear but the **call** of **death**. *T-27.VII.55.11*

~ each one seems different because it has a different **name**, and so it seems to **answer** to a different sound. *T-27.VII.55.5*

~ the witnesses of **sin** are all alike. **Call pleasure pain**, and it **will hurt**. **Call pain** a **pleasure**, and the **pain** behind the **pleasure will** be felt no more. Sin's witnesses but **shift** from **name** to **name**, as one steps forward and another back. *T-27.VII.55.6:9*

~ **fear** is witness unto **death**. *T-27.VII.58.7*

~ the **laws** of **sin have** different witnesses with different strengths. And **they** attest to different sufferings. *T-27.VII.59.4:5*

~ the witnesses to **sin** all stand **within** one **little** space. *T-27.VIII.67.9*

~ for eyes and ears are senses without **sense**, and what **they see** and hear **they** but report. It is not **they** that hear and **see**, but **you**, who put together every jagged **piece**, each senseless scrap and shred of evidence, and **make** a witness to the **world you want**. *T-28.VI.51.6:7*

~ the witnesses it sends to prove to **you** its **evil** is your own are false and speak with **certainty** of what **they** do not know. *W-pI.151.6.2*

~ idle witnesses, which merely bear false witness to God's Son. *W-pI.151.7.2*

HOLY SPIRIT

~ everything **you** perceive is a witness to the **thought system you want** to be true. *T-10.VI.58.3*

~ they **will** not deny the **truth** in **you** because **you** looked for it in them and found it there. *T-12.VI.51.6*

~ **you will remember** Him as **you call** forth the witnesses to His **creation**. Those whom **you** heal bear witness to your **healing**, for in their **wholeness you will see** your own. *T-12.VI.53.1:2*

~ those who accept **love** of **you** become your willing witnesses to the **love you** gave them, and it is they who hold it out to **you**. *T-12.VI.56.3*

~ **you** are the witnesses to the Fatherhood of **God**, and **He** has given **you** the **power** to create the witnesses to yours, which is as His. *T-13.II.9.2*

~ **you will** be sure because the witness to Him **will** speak so clearly of Him that **you will** hear and **understand**. *T-15.III.19.12*

~ his witnesses, who bring **you** the glad tidings **He** has come. *T-16.III.16.5*

~ witnesses to your **teaching have** gathered to **help you** learn. Their **gratitude** has joined with yours and God's to strengthen your **faith** in what **you** taught. For what **you** taught is true. *T-16.IV.26.4:6*

~ with them **you** must learn that **you** but taught yourself and learned from the conviction **you** shared with them. *T-16.IV.26.8*

~ and **you will see** the witness to the **choice you** made and learn from this to recognize which one **you** chose. *T-21.I.2.6*

~ just one witness is enough if **he** sees truly. Simple **justice** asks no more. *T-25.IX.74.2:3*

~ a witness unto his sinlessness and not his **sin**. *T-25.IX.75.8*

~ the **power** of witness is beyond **belief** because it brings conviction in its wake. The witness is believed because **he** points beyond himself to what **he** represents. *T-27.II.4.1:2*

~ god's Witness sees no witnesses against the **body**. *T-27.VII.57.1*

~ the **miracle** the witness unto **life**. *T-27.VII.58.7*

~ your dreams are witnesses to his, and his attest the **truth** of yours. *T-28.V.42.5*

~ what **I see** witnesses to what **I** think. *W-pI.54.3.1*

~ witnesses that show me the thinking of the **world** has been changed. *W-pI.54.6.2*

~ each day, each hour, every instant, **I** am choosing what **I want** to look upon, the sounds **I want** to hear, the witnesses to what **I want** to be the **truth** for me. *W-pII.271.1.1*

WORD |wərd|

DICTIONARY: *a single distinct meaningful element of speech or writing, used with others (or sometimes **alone**) to **form** a sentence.*

HOLY SPIRIT;   *symbols, symbols of symbols, twice removed from **reality**.*

~ beneath your words is written the word of **God**. *W-pI.12.8.7*

~ word which lifts the **veil** which lies upon the earth and wakes all those who **sleep** and cannot **see**. *W-pI.106.5.3*

~ to say these words is **nothing**. But to mean these words is everything. *W-pI.185.1.1:2*

~ these words do not **request** another **dream** be given us. **They** do not ask for **compromise** nor try to **make** another **bargain** in the hope that there may yet be one which can succeed where all the **rest have** failed. To mean these words acknowledges illusions are in vain, requesting the eternal in the place of shifting dreams which seem to **change** in what **they** offer, but are one in nothingness. *W-pI.185.7.4:6*

~ his words **will** work. His words **will** save. His words contain all hope, all **blessing** and all **joy** that ever can be found upon this earth. His words are born in **God**, and come to **you** with Heaven's **love** upon them. Those who hear His words **have** heard the **song** of Heaven, for these are the words in which all **will** merge as one at last. And as this one **will** fade away, the word of **God will** come to take its place, for it **will** be remembered then and loved. *W-pI.198.6.1:6*

~ the **truth** bestows these words upon your **mind** that **you** may find the key to **light** and let the **darkness** end. *W-pI.198.9.2*

~ in these words is all there is and all that there **will** be throughout all **time** and in **eternity**. *W-pII.ST361.6.5*

~ strictly speaking, words play no **part** at all in **healing**. The motivating factor is **prayer**, or asking. What **you** ask for, **you receive**. But this refers to the **prayer** of the heart, not to the words **you** use in praying. Sometimes the words and the **prayer** are contradictory; sometimes **they** agree. It does not matter. **God** does not **understand** words, for **they** were made by separated minds to keep them in the **illusion** of **separation**. Words can be helpful, particularly for the beginner, in helping concentration and facilitating the exclusion or at least the control of extraneous thoughts. Let us not forget, however, that words are but symbols of symbols. **They** are thus twice removed from **reality**. *M-21.1.1:10*

~ as symbols, words **have** quite specific references. Even when **they** seem most abstract, the **picture** that comes to **mind** is apt to be very concrete. Unless a specific referent does occur to the **mind** in conjunction with the word, the word has **little** or no practical **meaning** and thus cannot **help** the **healing** process. The **prayer** of the heart does not really **ask** for concrete things. It always requests some kind of **experience**, the specific things asked for **being** the bringers of the desired **experience** in the **judgment** of the asker. The words, then, are symbols for the things asked for, but the things themselves but stand for the experiences which are hoped for. *M-21.2.1:6*

~ there are many who must be reached through words, **being** as yet unable to hear in silence. The **teacher of God** must, however, learn to use words in a new **way**. Gradually, **he** learns how to let his words be chosen for him by ceasing to decide for himself what **he will** say. *M-21.4.3:5*

~ the **teacher of God** accepts the words which are offered him and gives as **he** receives. **He** does not control the direction of his speaking. **He** listens and hears and speaks. *M-21.4.7:9*

~ judge not the words that come to **you**, but offer them in **confidence**. **They** are far wiser than your own. God's teachers **have God's word** behind their symbols. And **He** Himself gives to the words **they** use the **power** of His **Spirit**, raising them from meaningless symbols to the **call** of **Heaven** itself. *M-21.5.6:9*

WORKBOOK

|'wərk,boŏk|

DICTIONARY: *a student's book containing **instruction** and exercises relating to a particular subject.*

HOLY SPIRIT

~ the workbook is divided into two sections, the first dealing with the undoing of what **you see now** and the second with the restoration of **sight**. *W-pI.I.3.2*

WORLD

|wərld|

DICTIONARY: *the earth, together with all of its countries, peoples, and natural features.*

EGO; *parody of God's* **creation***, World: a natural grand division,* **battleground***, a dismal alcove, endless circle of* **despair***, unreal world, delusional* **system***,* **idol***, world of* **illusion***, hallucination,* **dream***, false* **projection***, the world of accusation, dark world of* **misery***, world of ambiguity,* **shadow** *world, insane world, vengeful world, world of shadows,private world,* **symbol** *of* **punishment***,* **judgement** *on yourself, petulant device,* **witness***,* **picture***, world of* **time***.*

~ the world is very tired, because it is the **idea** of weariness. *T-5.IV.28.6*

~ the **ego** made the world as it perceives it. *T-5.V.42.4*

~ the world of the **ego** is—**nothing**. It has no **meaning**. It does not **exist**. *T-7.VII.66.4:6*

~ the world goes against your nature, **being** out of accord with **God's laws**. The world perceives orders of difficulty in everything. *T-7.XII.107.4:5*

~ a world that does deny itself everything. It does this simply by dissociating itself from everything. *T-8.V.26.1:2*

~ an **illusion** of isolation, maintained by **fear** of the same loneliness which is its **illusion**. *T-8.V.26.3*

~ the world is the **belief** that **love** is **impossible**. *T-8.V.28.1*

~ the world can add **nothing** to the **power** and the **glory** of **God** and His holy Sons, but it can **blind** the Sons to the **Father** if **they** behold it. *T-8.VI.42.6*

~ **you have** made many ideas which **you have** placed between yourselves and your **Creator**, and these beliefs are the world as **you** perceive it. **Truth** is not absent **here**, but it is obscure. *T-10.VIII.72.4:5*

~ **you** are at odds with the world as **you** perceive it because **you** think it is antagonistic to **you**. *T-11.IV.31.1*

~ **you have** no control over the world **you** made. *T-11.IV.33.3*

~ the world **you** made is therefore totally chaotic, governed by arbitrary and senseless "laws," and without **meaning** of any kind. For it was made out of what **you** do not **want**, projected from your **mind** because **you** were afraid of it. *T-11.IV.33.5:6*

~ yet this world is only in the **mind** of its maker along with his real **salvation**. *T-11.IV.34.1*

~ what **you** made of it is not its **reality**, for its **reality** is only what **you** gave it. *T-11.VIII.70.3*

~ the unreal world is a **thing** of **despair**, for it can never be. *T-11.IX.83.3*

~ the world **you see** is the delusional system of those made mad by **guilt**. *T-11.X.86.2*

~ this world is the **symbol** of **punishment**, and all the **laws** which seem to govern it are the **laws** of **death**. *T-11.X.86.4*

~ this world is a **picture** of the **crucifixion** of God's Son. *T-11.X.88.1*

~ in this strange world which **you have** made, the **Son of God** has sinned. *T-11.X.90.1*

~ **you** think **you have** made a world which **God** would destroy; and by loving Him, which **you** do, **you** would throw this world away, which **you** would. Therefore, **you have** used the world to cover your **love**, and the deeper **you** go into the blackness of the ego's foundation, the closer **you** come to the **love** that is hidden there. And it is this that frightens **you**. *T-12.III.14.4:6*

~ each one peoples his world with figures from his individual **past**, and it is because of this that private worlds do differ. *T-12.V.34.1*

~ **sight** of it is costing **you** a different kind of **vision**. *T-12.VII.60.1*

~ it is old and tired and ready to return to dust even as **you** made it. This aching world has not the **power** to touch the living world at all. **You** could not **give** it that, and so although **you** turn in sadness from it, **you** cannot find in it the road that leads away from it into another world. *T-12.VII.61.5:7*

~ in your world **you** do **need** things because it is a world of scarcity in which **you** find yourself because **you** are lacking. *T-12.VII.68.3*

~ yet in this world, your **perfection** is unwitnessed. **God** knows it, but **you** do not, and so **you** do not **share** His **witness** to it. Nor do **you witness** unto Him. *T-13.II.10.1:3*

~ **nothing** in this world can **give** this **peace**, for **nothing** in this world is wholly shared. *T-13.V.38.1*

~ the **logic** of the world must therefore lead to **nothing**, for its **goal** is **nothing**. *T-13.VI.49.6*

~ this is an insane world. *T-13.VI.50.3*

~ everything in this world is **little** because it is a world made out of littleness in the strange **belief** that littleness can content **you**. *T-15.IV.22.4*

~ in the world of scarcity, **love** has no **meaning**, and **peace** is **impossible**. For **gain** and **loss** are both accepted, and so no one is aware that perfect **love** is in him. *T-15.VII.60.2:3*

~ bleak world of **illusion**, where **nothing** is certain, and where everything fails to satisfy. *T-16.V.38.4*

~ for this world is the **opposite** of **Heaven**, **being** made to be its **opposite**, and everything **here** takes a direction exactly **opposite** of what is true. *T-16.VI.45.2*

~ here, where the **illusion** of **love** is accepted in love's place, **love** is perceived as **separation** and exclusion. *T-16.VI.45.4*

~ in the mad world **outside you, nothing** can be shared but only substituted. *T-18.II.9.2*

~ a world, clearly **within** your **mind**, that seems to be **outside**. *T-18.III.18.3*

~ the **ego** made its world on **sin**. Only in such a world could everything be upside-down. This is the strange **illusion** which makes the **clouds** of **guilt** seem heavy and impenetrable. The solidness this world's foundation seems to **have** is found in this. *T-19.III.22.1:4*

~ a world of murder and **attack** through which **you** thread your timid **way** through constant dangers, **alone** and frightened, hoping at most that **death will** wait a **little** longer before it overtakes **you** and **you** disappear. *T-20.IV.19.2*

~ the world **you see** is but a **judgment** on yourself. It is not there at all. Yet **judgment** lays a sentence on it, justifies it, and makes it real. Such is the world **you** see—a **judgment** on yourself and made by **you**. This sickly **picture** of yourself is carefully preserved by the **ego**, whose **image** it is and which it loves, and placed **outside you** in the world. *T-20.IV.20.2:6*

~ this world is merciless, and were it **outside you, you** should indeed be fearful. *T-20.IV.20.8*

~ the world the **ego** looks upon is like itself. *T-20.IV.21.2*

~ **you** made it up. *T-20.IX.73.4*

~ those who seem to walk about in it, to **sin** and die, **attack** and murder and destroy themselves, are wholly unreal. *T-20.IX.73.5*

~ if **you** think the world **you** made has **power** to **make you** what it wills, **you** are confusing Son and **Father**, effect and **Source**. *T-21.III.26.5*

~ this shifting world which has no **meaning** in **reality**. *T-24.V.39.2*

~ to the world, **justice** and **vengeance** are the same. *T-25.IX.65.2*

~ world, which is but shadows of all that is really happening **within** yourself. *T-25.IX.75.3*

~ here, where the **laws** of **God** do not prevail in perfect **form**. *T-25.VII.47.1*

~ this world is not your **home**; its **laws** are not imposed on you; its values are not yours. *T-25.VII.48.5*

~ nor can the basis of a world **He** did not **make** be firm and sure as **Heaven**. *T-25.VIII.51.2*

~ not one **Thought** of His makes any **sense** at all **within** this world. And **nothing** that the world believes as true has any **meaning** in His **Mind** at all. *T-25.VIII.52.3:4*

~ this world is meaningless because it rests on **sin**. *T-25.VIII.53.9*

~ in this world, it seems that one must **gain** because another lost. *T-25.VIII.60.2*

~ **you will see nothing** attached to anything beyond itself. All seeming entities can come a **little** nearer or go a **little** farther off but cannot **join**. *T-26.I.1.7:8*

~ in this world, there are no simple facts because what is the same and what is different remain unclear. *T-26.IV.21.6*

~ there is no basis for **choice** in this complex and over-complicated world. For no one understands what is the same and seems to choose where no **choice** really is. *T-26.IV.23.1:2*

~ anything in this world that **you** believe is **good** and valuable and **worth** striving for can **hurt you** and **will** do so. Not because it has the **power** to **hurt**, but just because **you have** denied it is but an **illusion** and made it real. *T-26.VII.44.1:2*

~ this world is an attempt to prove your **innocence** while cherishing **attack**. Its failure lies in that **you** still feel guilty, though without understanding why. *T-26.VIII.59.4:5*

~ it is not **will** for **life**, but **wish** for **death** that is the motivation for this world. Its only **purpose** is to prove **guilt** real. No worldly **thought** or act or feeling has a motivation other than this one. *T-27.II.7.1:3*

~ it looks as if the world were hurting **you**. And so it seems as if there is no **need** to go beyond the obvious in terms of **cause**. *T-27.VIII.64.6:7*

~ a timelessness in which is **time** made real; a **part** of **God** which can **attack** itself; a separate **brother** as an **enemy**; a **mind within** a **body**, all are forms of circularity whose ending starts at its beginning, ending at its **cause**. The world **you see** depicts exactly what **you thought you** did. Except that **now you** think that what **you** did is **being** done to **you**. The **guilt** for what **you thought** is **being** placed **outside** yourself and on a guilty world which dreams your dreams and thinks your thoughts instead of **you**. *T-27.IX.83.1:4*

~ the world but demonstrates an ancient **truth**—**you will** believe that others do to **you** exactly what **you** think **you** did to them. But once deluded into blaming them, **you will** not **see** the **cause** of what **they** do because **you want** the **guilt** to **rest** on them. *T-27.IX.84.1:2*

~ this world is causeless, as is every **dream** that anyone has dreamed **within** the world. No plans are possible and no design exists that could be found and understood. *T-28.III.20.5:6*

~ what is the world except a **little gap** perceived to tear **eternity** apart and break it into days and months and years? *T-28.IV.34.4*

~ this world is but the **dream** that **you** can be **alone** and think without affecting those apart from **you**. *T-28.VIII.64.2*

~ on **confusion** has this world been based, and there is **nothing** else it rests upon. Its basis does not **change**, although it seems to be in constant **change**. *T-29.III.15.3:4*

~ **you give** it goals it does not **have**, and thus do **you** decide what it is for. *T-29.VIII.49.2*

~ this world of idols is a **veil** across the **face of Christ** because its **purpose** is to separate your **brother** from yourself. A dark and fearful **purpose**. *T-29.IX.55.1:2*

~ its **form** is nowhere, for its **source** abides **within** your **mind**, where **God** abideth not. *T-29.IX.55.3*

~ **here** the deathless come to die, the all-encompassing to suffer **loss**, the timeless to be made the slaves of **time**. **Here** does the changeless **change**, the **peace** of God, forever given to all living things, **give way** to **chaos**, and the **Son of God**, as perfect, **sinless** and as loving as his **Father**, come to **hate** a **little** while, to suffer **pain**, and finally to die. *T-29.IX.57.3:4*

~ here, it is **thought** that understanding is acquired by **attack**. *T-30.VI.58.1*

~ it is a place where **choice** among illusions seems to be the only **choice**. And **you** are in control of outcomes of your choosing. Thus **you** think **within** the narrow band from **birth** to **death** a **little time** is given **you** to use for **you alone**, a **time** when **everyone** conflicts with **you**, but **you** can choose which road **will** lead **you** out of **conflict** and away from difficulties which concern **you** not. *T-31.IV.33.3:5*

~ all its roads but lead to disappointment, nothingness, and **death**. There is no **choice** in its alternatives. *T-31.IV.34.3:4*

~ the world was made that problems could not be escaped. Be not deceived by all the different names its roads are given. They have but one end. And each is but the **means** to **gain** that end, for it is **here** that all its roads **will** lead, however differently **they** seem to start, however differently **they** seem to go. Their end is certain, for there is no **choice** among them. All of them **will** lead to **death**. *T-31.IV.34.6:11*

~ to **see** a guilty world is but the sign your **learning** has been guided by the world, and **you** behold it as **you see** yourself. *T-31.V.57.6*

~ a world of **separation**, unrelated things, and happenings that **make** no **sense** at all. *T-31.VI.63.2*

~ so is all the world perceived as treacherous and out to **kill**. *T-31.VI.66.10*

~ but because it is meaningless, **you** are impelled to write upon it what **you** would **have** it be. *W-pI.12.8.4*

~ the world **you see** has **nothing** to do with **reality**. It is of your own making, and it does not **exist**. *W-pI.14.1.4:5*

~ the world **you see** is a vengeful world, and everything in it is a **symbol** of **vengeance**. *W-pI.23.3.1*

~ **you see** the world which **you have** made, but **you** do not **see** yourself as the **image**-maker. **You** cannot be saved from the world, but **you** can escape from its **cause**. This is what **salvation means**, for where is the world **you see** when its **cause** is gone? *W-pI.23.4.1:3*

~ in this world, **you** believe **you** are sustained by everything but God. *W-pI.50.1.2*

~ what is producing this world is insane, and so is what it produces. *W-pI.53.2.2*

~ the world **I see** is hardly the representation of loving thoughts. It is a **picture** of **attack** on everything by everything. It is anything but a **reflection** of the **Love** of **God** and the **love** of His Son. It is my own **attack** thoughts which **give** rise to this **picture**. *W-pI.55.3.1:4*

~ all my hopes and wishes and plans appear to be at the mercy of a world **I** cannot control. *W-pI.56.2.3*

~ the world **I see** attests to the fearful nature of the **self-image I have** made. *W-pI.56.3.2*

~ the world **I see** holds my fearful **self-image** in place, and guarantees its continuance. *W-pI.56.4.1*

~ the **purpose** of the world **you see** is to obscure your **function** of **forgiveness** and provide **you** with a justification for forgetting it. It is the **temptation** to abandon **God** and His Son, taking on a physical **appearance**. *W-pI.64.1.2:3*

~ idle wishes and grievances are partners or co-makers in picturing the world **you see**. The wishes of the **ego** gave rise to it, and the ego's **need** for grievances, which are necessary to maintain it, peoples it with figures that seem to **attack you** and **call** for "righteous" **judgment**. *W-pI.73.2.1:2*

~ complexities the world has spun of fragile cobwebs. *W-pI.122.6.7*

~ what the world believes was made to **hide** love's **meaning** and to keep it dark and **secret**. There is not one principle the world upholds but violates the **truth** of what **love** is, and what **you** are as well. *W-pI.127.5.2:3*

~ each **thing you value here** is but a **chain** that binds **you** to the world, and it **will** serve no other end but this. *W-pI.128.2.1*

~ **nothing** is **here** to cherish. **Nothing here** is **worth** one instant of **delay** and **pain**, one moment of uncertainty and **doubt**. *W-pI.128.4.2:3*

~ the world **you see** is merciless indeed, unstable, cruel, unconcerned with **you**, quick to avenge, and pitiless with **hate**. It gives but to rescind and takes away all things that **you have** cherished for a while. No lasting **love** is found, for none is **here**. This is the world of **time**, where all things end. *W-pI.129.2.3:6*

~ yet searching is inevitable **here**. For this **you** came, and **you will** surely do the **thing you** came for. *W-pI.131.4.1:2*

~ strange world **you** made and all its ways—its shifting patterns and **uncertain** goals, its painful pleasures, and its tragic joys. *W-pI.131.8.1*

~ there is no world because it is a **thought** apart from **God** and made to separate the **Father** and the Son and break away a **part** of **God** Himself and thus destroy His **wholeness**. *W-pI.132.14.1*

~ **you have** enslaved the world with all your fears, your doubts and miseries, your **pain** and tears, and all your sorrows press upon it and keep it a prisoner to your beliefs. **Death** strikes it everywhere because **you** hold the bitter **thought** of **death within** your **mind**. The world is **nothing** in itself. Your **mind** must **give** it **meaning**. And what **you** behold upon it are your wishes, acted out so **you** can look on them and think them real. *W-pI.132.4.1:5*

~ there are no satisfactions in the world. *W-pI.133.3.1*

~ all its structures, all its thoughts and doubts, its penalties and heavy armaments, its legal definitions and its codes, its ethics and its leaders and its Gods, all serve but to preserve its **sense** of **threat**. For no one walks the world in armature but must **have** terror striking at his heart. *W-pI.135.3.2:3*

~ **nothing** the world believes is true. It is a place whose **purpose** is to be a **home** where those who claim **they** do not know themselves can come to **question** what it is **they** are. *W-pI.139.6.6:7*

~ **god** made it not. *W-pI.152.6.2*

~ **you** who feel threatened by this changing world, its twists of fortune and its bitter jests, its brief relationships and all the "gifts" it merely lends to take away again. *W-pI.153.1.1*

~ the world provides no safety. It is rooted in **attack** and all its "gifts" of seeming safety are illusory deceptions. It attacks and then attacks again. No **peace** of **mind** is possible where danger threatens thus. *W-pI.153.1.2:5*

~ the world gives rise but to defensiveness. *W-pI.153.2.1*

~ the world is an **illusion**. Those who choose to come to it are seeking for a place where **they** can be illusions and avoid their own **reality**. *W-pI.155.2.2:3*

~ this world is not the **Will** of **God**, and so it is not real. *W-pI.166.2.2*

~ this world **you** seem to live in is not **home** to **you**. And somewhere in your **mind you** know that this is true. A **memory** of **home** keeps haunting **you**, as if there were a place that called **you** to return, although **you** do not recognize the **Voice** nor what it is the **Voice** reminds **you** of. Yet still **you** feel an alien **here**, from somewhere all unknown. **Nothing** so definite that **you** could say with **certainty you** are an exile here. Just a persistent feeling, sometimes not more than a tiny throb, at other times hardly remembered, actively dismissed, but surely to return to mind again. *W-pI.182.1.1:6*

~ a world in which **forgiveness** shines on everything and **peace** offers its gentle **light** to **everyone** is inconceivable to those who **see** a world of hatred, rising from **attack**, poised to avenge, to murder and destroy. *W-pI.189.3.5*

~ the world may seem to **cause you pain**. And yet the world, as causeless, has no **power** to **cause**. As an effect, it cannot **make** effects. As an **illusion** it is what **you will**. Your idle wishes represent its pains. Your strange desires bring it **evil** dreams. Your thoughts of **death** envelop it in **fear**, while in your kind **forgiveness** does it live. *W-pI.190.7.1:7*

482

~ it cannot **have reality** because it never was created. *W-pI.200.7.3*

~ not one **thing** in this world is true. It does not matter what the **form** in which it may appear. It witnesses but to your own illusions of yourself. *W-pII.240.1.3:5*

~ **death** and sorrow are the certain lot of all who come **here**. For their joys are gone before **they** are possessed, or even grasped. *W-pII.300.1.1:2*

~ the world was made as an **attack** on **God**. It symbolizes **fear**. *W-pII.ST241.2.1:2*

~ the world was meant to be a place where **God** could enter not and where His Son could be apart from Him. **Here** was **perception** born, for **knowledge** could not **cause** such insane thoughts. But eyes deceive, and ears hear falsely. **Now** mistakes become quite possible, for **certainty** has gone. *W-pII.ST241.2.3:6*

~ your world is seen through eyes of **fear** and brings the witnesses of terror to your **mind**. *W-pII.ST291.1.3*

~ the world is very tired **now**. It is old and worn and without hope. *M-1.4.4:5*

~ the world of **time** is the world of **illusion**. What happened long ago seems to be happening **now**. Choices made long since appear to be open, yet to be made. *M-2.3.1:3*

~ the world's training is directed toward achieving a **goal** in direct opposition to that of our **curriculum**. The world trains for reliance on one's **judgment** as the criterion for maturity and **strength**. *M-9.2.5:6*

~ the world **you see** cannot be the world **God** loves. *M-11.1.6*

HOLY SPIRIT; *"external **reality**", **illusion, treasure house**, new world, God's world.*

~ the physical world exists only because **man** can use it to correct his unbelief, which placed him in it originally. *T-1.I.93.1*

~ the world was made as "a natural grand division," or a projecting outward of **God**. *T-2.I.11.3*

~ the world, in the original connotation of the term, included both the proper **creation** of **man** by **God** and the proper **creation** by **man** in his right **mind**. *T-2.I.12.1*

~ a **means** of **healing** the **separation**. *T-2.II.51.5*

~ "and **God** so loved the world that **He** gave His only begotten Son that whosoever believeth in Him shall not perish, but **have** eternal **life**" needs only one slight **correction** to be entirely meaningful in this context. It should read, "**He** gave it to His only begotten Son." *T-2.V.100.5:7*

~ the world is not left by **death** but by **truth**, and **truth** can be known by all those for whom the **Kingdom** was created and for whom it waits. *T-3.IX.80.11*

~ the ability to accept **truth** in this world is the perceptual counterpart of creating in the **Kingdom**. *T-9.IX.70.3*

~ your **mind** is capable of creating worlds, but it can also deny what it creates, because it is free. *T-9.XI.101.7*

~ the end of the world is not its **destruction**, but its translation into **Heaven**. *T-10.VIII.75.3*

~ **love**, which is the world's **reality**. *T-11.III.13.1*

~ the only **thing** of **value** in it is whatever **part** of it **you** look upon with **love**. This gives it the only **reality** it **will** ever have. *T-11.VII.55.2:3*

~ a world that cannot die. *T-11.VIII.76.6*

~ this other world is bright with **love**, which **you have** given it. And **here will** everything remind **you** of your **Father** and His Holy Son. **Light** is unlimited and spreads across this world in **quiet joy**. *T-12.VI.55.6:8*

~ **you** cannot **see** both worlds, for each of them involves a different kind of seeing and depends on what **you** cherish. The **sight** of one is possible because **you have** denied the other. Both are not true, yet either one **will** seem as real to **you** as the amount to which **you** hold it dear. And yet their **power** is not the same because their real **attraction** to **you** is unequal. *T-12.VII.60.2:5*

~ the **real world** has the **power** to touch **you** even **here** because **you love** it. *T-12.VII.62.1*

~ the one **you** made is false. *T-12.VII.62.4*

~ the world can **give you** only what **you** gave it, for **being nothing** but your own **projection**, it has no **meaning** apart from what **you** found in it and placed your **faith** in. *T-13.III.13.1*

~ **you see** the world **you value**. *T-16.VII.61.8*

~ forgiven world, the **Son of God** is lifted easily into his **home**. And there **he** knows that **he** has always rested there in **peace**. *T-17.III.12.4:5*

~ in this world it is **impossible** to create, yet it is possible to **make happy**. *T-17.V.28.1*

~ here, **you** are "**free**" to **make** over whatever seemed to **attack you** and **change** it into a tribute to your **ego**, which was outraged by the "**attack**." *T-18.III.14.5:6*

~ the world **will** be transformed before your **sight**, cleansed of all **guilt** and softly brushed with beauty. *T-19.V.54.2*

~ the world contains no **fear** which **you** laid not upon it. *T-19.V.54.3*

~ **you make** the world and then adjust to it, and it to **you**. Nor is there any difference between yourself and it in your **perception**, which made them both. *T-20.IV.18.6:7*

~ it is a **picture** of what **you** think **you** are, of how **you see** yourself. *T-20.IV.19.4*

~ the world the holy **see** is one with them. *T-20.IV.21.2*

~ the world the holy **see** is beautiful because **they see** their **innocence** in it. **They** did not tell it what it was; **they** did not **make** adjustments to fit their orders. *T-20.IV.21.3:4*

~ the world **you** look on is the **answer** that it gave **you**, and **you have** given it **power** to adjust the world to **make** its **answer** true. *T-20.IV.24.3*

~ it is the **witness** to your state of **mind**, the **outside picture** of an inward **condition**. *T-21.I.1.5*

~ the world **you see** but shows **you** how much **joy you have** allowed yourself to **see** in **you** and to accept as yours. And if this is its **meaning**, then the **power** to **give** it **joy** must lie **within you**. *T-21.I.2.7:9*

~ it is irrelevant to how it happens but not to why. **You have** control of this. And if **you** choose to **see** a world without an **enemy** in which **you** are not helpless, the **means** to **see** it **will** be given **you**. *T-21.VIII.80.2:4*

~ in kind **forgiveness will** the world sparkle and shine and everything **you** once **thought sinful now will** be reinterpreted as **part of Heaven**. *T-23.I.6.4*

~ forget not that the **healing** of God's Son is all the world is for. That is the only **purpose** the **Holy Spirit** sees in it and thus the only one it has. *T-24.VII.52.1:2*

~ it is given **you** to be beyond its **laws** in all respects, in every **way**, and every circumstance. *T-24.VII.52.5*

~ this world has much to offer to your **peace** and many chances to extend your own **forgiveness**. Such its **purpose** is to those who **want** to **see peace** and **forgiveness** descend on them and offer them the **light**. *T-25.IV.29.6:7*

~ the Maker of the world of **gentleness** has perfect **power** to offset the world of violence and **hate** that seems to stand between **you** and His **gentleness**. *T-25.IV.30.1*

~ another world perceived. And one in which **nothing** is contradicted that would lead the **Son of God** to **sanity** and **joy**. **Nothing** attests to **death** and cruelty, to **separation**, and to differences. For **here** is everything perceived as one, and no one loses that each one may **gain**. *T-25.VIII.54.1:4*

~ it can become a **treasure house** as rich and limitless as **Heaven** itself. No instant passes **here** in which your brother's **holiness** cannot be seen. *T-26.II.5.3:4*

~ where **sin** once was perceived **will** rise a world which **will** become an **altar** to the **truth**. *T-26.V.29.1*

~ the world is fair because the **Holy Spirit** has brought **injustice** to the **light within**, and there has all unfairness been resolved and been replaced with **justice** and with **love**. *T-26.XI.90.4*

~ a dying world asks only that **you rest** an instant from **attack** upon yourself, that it be healed. *T-27.VI.47.7*

~ thus is your **healing** everything the world requires that it may be healed. It needs one **lesson** which has perfectly been learned. *T-27.VI.49.1:2*

~ when **you** forgive the world your **guilt, you will** be free of it. Its **innocence** does not demand your **guilt**, nor does your guiltlessness **rest** on its sins. *T-27.IX.89.11:12*

~ this world was over long ago. The thoughts that made it are no longer in the **mind** that **thought** of them and loved them for a **little** while. *T-28.I.1.6:7*

~ the world is neutral, and the bodies which still seem to move about as separate things **need** not be feared. And so **they** are not sick. *T-28.III.25.6:7*

~ the world **you see** does not **exist** because the place where **you** perceive it is not real. *T-28.VI.53.2*

~ **change** is the only **thing** that can be made a **blessing here**, where **purpose** is not fixed, however changeless it appears to be. *T-29.VII.40.3*

~ the world becomes a place of hope because its only **purpose** is to be a place where hope of happiness can be fulfilled. And no one stands **outside** this hope because the world has been united in **belief** the **purpose** of the world is one which all must **share** if hope be more than just a **dream**. *T-30.VI.58.7:8*

~ not yet is **Heaven** quite remembered, for the **purpose** of **forgiveness** still remains. Yet **everyone** is certain **he will** go beyond **forgiveness**, and **he** but remains until it is made perfect in himself. **He** has no **wish** for anything but this. And **fear** has dropped away because **he** is united in his **purpose** with himself. *T-30.VI.59.1:4*

~ the **Holy Spirit** looks upon the world as with one **purpose**, changelessly established. *T-30.VIII.82.4*

~ no **situation** can affect its aim but must be in accord with it. *T-30.VIII.82.5*

~ a world in which there is no **fear** and everything is lit with hope and sparkles with a gentle friendliness. *T-31.I.8.1*

~ the world can **teach** no images of **you** unless **you want** to learn them. *T-31.V.59.1*

~ the world is harmless in your **sight**. *T-31.VI.66.6*

~ then is the world forgiving, for **you have** forgiven it its trespasses and so it looks on **you** with eyes that **see** as yours. *T-31.VI.66.8*

~ so the world is seen as stable, fully worthy of your **trust**; a **happy** place to **rest** in for a while, where **nothing need** be feared but only loved. *T-31.VI.67.2*

~ it needs the **light**, for it is dark indeed. *T-31.VII.82.2*

~ a world whose loveliness can yet be so intense and so inclusive it is but a **step** from there to **Heaven**. *T-31.VIII.93.5*

~ the world is meaningless in itself. *W-pI.12.1.4*

~ actually, a meaningless world is **impossible**. *W-pI.13.1.2*

~ every **thought you have** makes up some segment of the world **you see**. *W-pI.23.1.4*

~ it is incapable of **change** because it is merely an effect. *W-pI.23.2.4*

~ your inner and outer worlds, which are actually the same. *W-pI.32.2.1*

~ as the world I **see** arises from my thinking errors, so **will** the **real world** rise before my eyes as I let my errors be corrected. *W-pI.54.2.4*

~ the world I **see** can **change** as well. *W-pI.54.3.5*

485

~ the world is really a place where **he** can be set free. *W-pI.57.4.4*

~ a place where the **Son of God** finds his **freedom**. *W-pI.57.4.5*

~ **peace**, not **war**, abides in it. *W-pI.57.5.2*

~ **peace** also abides in the hearts of all who **share** this place with me. *W-pI.57.5.3*

~ the world I look upon has taken on the **light** of my **forgiveness** and shines **forgiveness** back at me. *W-pI.57.6.2*

~ to the **Holy Spirit**, the world is a place where **you** learn to forgive yourself what **you** think of as your sins. In this **perception**, the physical **appearance** of **temptation** becomes the spiritual recognition of **salvation**. *W-pI.64.2.3:4*

~ your **picture** of the world can only mirror what is **within**. *W-pI.73.5.2*

~ **you** can look upon it **now** as if **you** never saw it before. **You** do not know yet what it looks like. **You** merely wait to **have** it shown to **you**. *W-pI.75.7.4:6*

~ this world **will change** through **you**. No other **means** can save it. *W-pI.125.2.1:2*

~ the world that seems to hold **you** prisoner can be escaped by anyone who does not hold it dear. *W-pI.127.7.4*

~ the only **purpose** worthy of your **mind** this world contains is that **you** pass it by, without delaying to perceive some hope where there is none. *W-pI.128.2.3*

~ your whole perspective on the world **will shift** by just a **little** every **time you** let your **mind** escape its chains. The world is not where it belongs. *W-pI.128.7.3:4*

~ it is **impossible** to **see** two worlds which **have** no overlap of any kind. **Seek** for the one; the other disappears. But one remains. **They** are the range of **choice** beyond which your **decision** cannot go. *W-pI.130.5.2:5*

~ the world **you see** is proof **you have** already made a **choice** as all-embracing as its **opposite**. *W-pI.130.6.2*

~ the one **you see** is quite consistent from the point of view from which **you see** it. It is all a **piece** because it stems from one **emotion** and reflects its **source** in everything **you see**. *W-pI.130.6.4:5*

~ the world **you see** before **you** in the **light** reflects the **truth you** knew and did not quite forget in wandering away in dreams. *W-pI.131.16.3*

~ but the world cannot dictate the **goal** for which **you** search unless **you give** it **power** to do so. *W-pI.131.4.3*

~ there is no world apart from your ideas because ideas leave not their **source**, and **you** maintain the world **within** your **mind** in thought. *W-pI.132.11.3*

~ there is no world apart from what **you wish**, and herein lies your ultimate **release**. **Change** but your **mind** on what **you want** to **see**, and all the world must **change** accordingly. *W-pI.132.5.3:4*

~ what is true in God's **creation** cannot enter **here** unless it is reflected in some **form** the world can **understand** For it is **we** who **make** the world as **we** would **have** it. *W-pI.138.2.3*

~ it welcomes **you**, rejoices that **you** came, and sings your praises as it keeps **you** safe from every **form** of danger and of **pain**. It offers **you** a warm and gentle **home** in which to stay a while. It blesses **you** throughout the day and watches through the night as silent guardian of your holy **sleep**. It sees **salvation** in **you** and protects the **light** in **you** in which it sees its own. It offers **you** its flowers and its snow in thankfulness for your benevolence. *W-pI.189.2.2:6*

~ yet is the world of hatred equally unseen and inconceivable to those who feel God's **Love** in them. Their world reflects the quietness and **peace** that shines in them, the **gentleness** and **innocence they see** surrounding them, the **joy** with which **they** look out from the endless wells of **joy within**. What **they have** felt in them **they** look upon and **see** its sure **reflection** everywhere. *W-pI.189.4.1:3*

~ the world **you see** does **nothing**. It has no effects at all. It merely represents your thoughts. And it **will change** entirely as **you** elect to **change** your **mind** and choose the **joy of God** as what **you** really **want**. *W-pI.190.6.1:4*

~ in **error** it began. But it **will** end in the **reflection** of his **holiness**. *W-pI.191.12.2:3*

~ **now** is there silence all around the world. **Now** is there stillness where before there was a frantic rush of thoughts that made no **sense**. **Now** is there tranquil **light** across the face of earth, made **quiet** in a dreamless sleep. And **now** the **word** of **God alone** remains upon it. Only that can be perceived an instant longer. Then are symbols done and everything **you** ever **thought you** made completely vanished from the **mind** which **God** forever knows to be His only Son. *W-pI.198.13.1:6*

~ this world is not where **you** belong. **You** are a **stranger here**. But it is given **you** to find the **means** whereby the world no longer seems to be a **prison** house for **you** or anyone. *W-pI.200.4.3:5*

~ for **you** must **change** your **mind** about the **purpose** of the world if **you** would find escape. *W-pI.200.5.2*

~ yet can **he** learn to look on it another **way** and find the **peace** of **God**. *W-pI.200.7.6*

~ if **I** so choose, **I** can depart this world entirely. It is not **death** which makes this possible, but it is **change** of **mind** about the **purpose** of the world. *W-pII.226.1.1:2*

~ but if **I** see no **value** in the world as **I** behold it, **nothing** that **I want** to keep as mine or search for as a **goal**, it **will** depart from me. *W-pII.226.1.4*

~ the world becomes a place of **joy**, abundance, **charity**, and endless **giving**. It is **now** so like to **Heaven** that it quickly is transformed into the **Light** that it reflects. *W-pII.249.1.5:6*

~ **i see** the world in the celestial **gentleness** with which **creation** shines. There is no **fear** in it. *W-pII.265.1.4:5*

~ **god's** world is **happy**. Those who look on it can only add their **joy** to it and bless it as a **cause** of further **joy** in them. **We** wept because **we** did not **understand**. But **we have** learned the world **we** saw was false, and **we will** look upon God's world **today**. *W-pII.301.2.1:4*

~ from new **perception** of the world there comes a **future** very different from the **past**. The **future now** is recognized as but **extension** of the **present**. **Past** mistakes can cast no shadows on it, so that **fear** has lost its idols and its images, and **being** formless, it has no effects. *W-pII.314.1.1:3*

~ earth is **being** born again in new **perception**. *W-pII.ST231.4.5*

~ the world is false **perception**. It is born of **error**, and it has not left its **source**. It **will** remain no longer than the **thought** which gave it **birth** is cherished. When the **thought** of **separation** has been changed to one of true **forgiveness will** the world be seen in quite another **light**, and one which leads to **truth**, where all the world must disappear and all its errors vanish. **Now** its **source** has gone, and its effects are gone as well. *W-pII. ST241.1.1:5*

~ for **we** who made it must behold it through the eyes of **Christ**, that what was made to die be restored to Everlasting **Life**. *W-pII.ST241.5.5*

~ the world must be looked at differently if His promises are to be accepted. What the world is, is but a **fact**. **You** cannot choose what this should be. But **you** can choose how **you** would **see** it. Indeed, **you** must choose this. *M-11.1.8:12*

~ it is not the world that makes **peace** seem **impossible**. It is the world **you see** that is **impossible**. *M-11.4.4:5*

~ yet has God's **Judgment** on this distorted world redeemed it and made it fit to **welcome peace**. And **peace** descends on it in joyous **answer**. **Peace now** belongs **here**, because a **thought** of **God** has entered. *M-11.4.6:8*

~ no one who has escaped the world and all its ills looks back on it with **condemnation**. *M-13.4.5*

~ the world **will** end in an **illusion**, as it began. Yet **will** its ending be an **illusion** of mercy. The **illusion** of **forgiveness**, complete, excluding no one, limitless in **gentleness**, **will** cover it, hiding all **evil**, concealing all **sin**, and ending **guilt** forever. So ends the world that **guilt** had made, for **now** it has no **purpose** and is gone. *M-14.1.2:5*

~ until **forgiveness** is complete, the world does **have** a **purpose**. It becomes the **home** in which **forgiveness** is born and where it grows and becomes stronger and more all embracing. **Here** is it nourished, for **here** it is needed. *M-14.2.1:3*

~ the world **will** end when all things in it **have** been rightly judged by His **judgment**. The world **will** end with the benediction of **holiness** upon it. When not one **thought** of sin remains, the world is over. It **will** not be destroyed nor attacked nor even touched. It **will** merely cease to seem to be. *M-14.2.8:12*

~ the world **will** end when its **thought system** has been completely reversed. Until then, bits and pieces of its thinking **will** still seem sensible. The final **lesson** which brings the ending of the world cannot be grasped by those not yet prepared to leave the world and go beyond its tiny reach. *M-14.4.1:3*

~ the world **will** end in **joy** because it is a place of sorrow. When **joy** has come, the **purpose** of the world has gone. The world **will** end in **peace** because it is a place of **war**. *M-14.5.1:3*

~ the world **will** end in laughter because it is a place of tears. *M-14.5.5*

~ in **blessing** it departs, for it **will** not end as it began. *M-14.5.8*

~ without the **idea** of **death**, there is no world. *M-27.6.3*

WORTH

DICTIONARY: *the **value** equivalent to that of someone or something under consideration; the **level** at which someone or something deserves to be valued or rated.*

EGO

~ all things **you seek** to **make** your **value** greater in your **sight limit you** further, hide your worth from **you**. *W-pI.128.3.3*

~ the worthless offer **nothing**. **Certainty** of worth cannot be found in worthlessness. *W-pI.128.4.4:5*

HOLY SPIRIT

~ your worth is beyond **perception** because it is beyond **doubt**. *T-3.VII.60.7*

~ your worth is not established by your **teaching** or your **learning**. Your worth was established by **God**. *T-4.II.14.1:2*

~ once again—**nothing you** do or think or **wish** or **make** is necessary to establish your worth. *T-4.II.14.6*

~ "as ye sow, so shall ye reap" merely **means** that what **you** believe to be worth cultivating **you will** cultivate in yourself. Your **judgment** of what is worthy makes it worthy for **you**. *T-5.VIII.76.1:2*

~ his own worth is beyond anything **he** can **make**. *T-7.XII.108.8*

~ it is not our **part** to judge our worth. *W-pI.154.1.5*

YOU

DICTIONARY: *used to refer to the person or people that the speaker is addressing.*

EGO; *ego,* **body,** *miserable sinner,* **shadow,** *idolaters, prisoner,* **enemy,** *destroyer, dreamer of the* **world** *of dreams, dreamer,* **dream,** *babies, images of your own* **creation,** *a poor* **teacher** *and a poor* **learner, home** *of* **evil, darkness** *and* **sin, sin,** *what you made.*

~ you believe that you are responsible for what you do but not for what you think. *T-2.IV.73.6*

~ you are much too tolerant of **mind** wandering, thus passively condoning its miscreations. *T-2.IV.75.9*

~ you do not guard your thoughts carefully except for a small **part** of the day and somewhat inconsistently even then. *T-2.V.93.6*

~ you are placing your **belief** in the unreal. *T-3.VIII.62.8*

~ you cannot create and are filled with **fear** about what you **make.** *T-3.IX.77.9*

~ you do not **see.** *T-9.V.34.3*

~ you cannot triumph, but you are exalted. And in your exalted state, you **seek** others like you and rejoice with them. *T-9.VII.54.8:9*

~ you do not know the **meaning** of anything you perceive. Not one **thought** you hold is wholly true. *T-10.VIII.76.1:2*

~ you **have** projected outward what is antagonistic to what is inward, and therefore you would **have** to perceive it this **way.** *T-11.IV.31.3*

~ what you **have** made invisible is the only **truth,** and what you **have** not heard is the only **answer.** *T-11.IX.80.4*

~ believing you are no longer you, you do not realize that you are failing yourself. *T-12.I.2.6*

~ you **have** handled this **wish** to **kill** yourself by not knowing who you are and identifying with something else. You **have** projected **guilt** blindly and indiscriminately, but you **have** not uncovered its **source.** *T-12.II.5.4:5*

~ you associate **love** with **weakness** and hatred with **strength,** and your own real **power** seems to you as your real **weakness.** *T-12.III.13.2*

~ you can accept **insanity** because you made it, but you cannot accept **love** because you did not. *T-12.III.15.1*

~ for your individual **death** is more valued than your living **oneness,** and what is given you is not so dear as what you made. You are more afraid of **God** than of the **ego,** and **love** cannot enter where it is not **welcome.** But hatred can, for it enters of its **will** and cares not for yours. *T-12.III.15.3:5*

~ you believe that **attack** is your **reality** and that your **destruction** is the final proof that you were right. *T-12.IV.24.5*

~ **within** you is not what you believe is there and what you put your **faith** in. *T-13.III.18.6*

~ you whose minds are darkened by **doubt** and **guilt.** *T-13.V.39.1*

~ if you decide to **have** and **give** and be **nothing** except a **dream,** you must direct your thoughts unto oblivion. *T-13.VI.50.1*

~ you who **have** thrown your selves away and valued **God** so **little.** *T-14.I.2.3*

~ you **have** taught yourselves how to imprison the **Son of God,** a **lesson** so unthinkable that only the insane, in deepest **sleep,** could even **dream** of it. *T-14.VII.59.2*

~ you **will see** safety in **guilt** and danger in **communication.** *T-15.VIII.76.3*

~ you believe that it is possible to be **host** to the **ego** or hostage to **God.** This is the **choice** you think you **have,** and the **decision** which you believe that you must **make.** *T-15.X.95.8:9*

~ your brothers and your **Father have** become very fearful to you. And you would **bargain** with them for a few **special** relationships in which you think you **see** some scraps of safety. *T-15.XI.10.3:4*

~ you do not know what **healing** is. *T-16.I.3.3*

~ you **have** never tried to solve anything yourself and been successful. *T-16.III.19.5*

~ you sought a blackness so complete that you could **hide** from **truth** forever in complete **insanity**. *T-18.IV.24.5*

~ you **have** paid very dearly for your illusions, and **nothing** you **have** paid for brought you **peace**. *T-19.V.64.1*

~ you are indeed afraid to look **within** and **see** the **sin** you think is there. *T-21.V.41.3*

~ you **see** yourself as vulnerable, frail, and easily destroyed and at the mercy of countless attackers more powerful than you. *T-22.VII.60.6*

~ anyone who still retains one unlearned **lesson** in his **memory**, one **thought** with **purpose** still **uncertain**, or one **wish** with a divided aim. *T-24.VIII.68.5*

~ you **have hurt** yourself and made your **Self** your "**enemy**." *T-25.VI.38.4:5*

~ you are like to one who still hallucinates but lacks conviction in what **he** perceives. *T-26.VI.40.7*

~ and so you **see** yourself deprived of **light**, abandoned to the dark, unfairly left without a **purpose** in a futile **world**. *T-26.XI.90.3*

~ what are you who live **within** the **world** except a **picture** of the **Son of God** in broken pieces. *T-28.IV.34.5*

~ what is real and what is but **illusion** in yourself you do not know and cannot tell apart. *T-28.V.38.10*

~ you came to die. *T-29.VIII.47.2*

~ you **will attack** what does not satisfy, and thus you **will** not **see** you made it up. You always fight illusions. *T-30.V.49.1:2*

~ you believe you **want disaster** and disunity and **pain**. *T-31.I.11.3*

~ you can be neither blamed for what you are, nor can you **change** the things it makes you do. *T-31.V.48.7*

~ you **will** not perceive that you can interact but with yourself. *T-31.V.57.5*

~ you are too inexperienced as yet to avoid a tendency to become pointlessly preoccupied. *W-pI.4.5.4*

~ you do not think of **light** in terms of **strength** and **darkness** in terms of **weakness**. *W-pI.92.1.2*

~ you think you are the **home** of **evil**, **darkness**, and **sin**. You think if anyone could **see** the **truth** about you **he** would be repelled, recoiling from you as if from a poisonous snake. You think if what is true about you were revealed to you, you would be struck with **horror** so intense that you would rush to **death** by your own hand, living on after seeing this **being impossible**. *W-pI.93.1.1:3*

~ you believe that you **have** changed yourself already. You **see** yourself as a ridiculous parody on God's **creation**—weak, vicious, ugly and **sinful**, miserable and beset with **pain**. *W-pI.95.1.5:6*

~ you are lost and do not know yourself while **He** is unacknowledged and unknown. *W-pI.110.9.5*

~ you look for permanence in the impermanent, for **love** where there is none, for safety in the midst of danger, **immortality within** the **darkness** of the **dream** of **death**. *W-pI.131.1.2*

~ if you let your **mind** harbor **attack** thoughts, yield to **judgment**, or **make** plans against uncertainties to come, you **have** again misplaced yourself, and made a bodily **identity** which **will attack** the **body**, for the **mind** is sick. *W-pI.136.21.2*

~ you **have** sought to be both weak and bound because you feared your **strength** and **freedom**. *W-pI.196.9.7*

~ you think you made a place of safety for yourself. You think you made a **power** that can save you from all the fearful things you **see** in dreams. It is not so. Your safety lies not there. What you **give** up is merely the **illusion** of protecting illusions. And it is this you **fear**, and only this. *M-16.6.3:8*

HOLY SPIRIT;   *I, Spirit, co-creator with God, part of His Mind, mind, in Mind, purely mind, idea, love, reality, God, God and Him together, God's messenger, His messenger, one with God, His Son, what God created, the work of God, Son of God, God's Son, His beloved Son, Child of God, His gifts, God's Will, One Self, Kingdom of God, Kingdom of Heaven, part of God, My Son, the Son He loves, light, miracle, mirrors of truth, light of the world, aspect of knowledge, witnesses to the Fatherhood of host, most holy Self, your brother's savior, part of me, saviors of the world, His home, Self.*

~ your **creation** by **God** is the only foundation which cannot be shaken because the **light** is in it. Your starting point is **truth**, and you must return to this beginning. *T-3.IX.79.1:2*

~ your **worth** is beyond **perception** because it is beyond **doubt**. *T-3.VII.60.7*

~ you cannot be attacked; **attack** has no justification; and you are responsible for what you believe. *T-6.I.2.2*

~ you who are co-creators with Him extend His **Kingdom** forever and beyond **limit**. *T-7.II.5.4*

~ **god** Himself created you—in understanding, in **appreciation**, and in **love**. *T-7.VI.50.1*

~ you are **part** of Him Who is all **power** and **glory** and are therefore as unlimited as **He** is. *T-8.III.14.7*

~ you are the **treasure** of **God**. *T-8.VI.46.5*

~ you are not of yourselves. *T-8.VII.58.2*

~ your **learning** is the result of what you taught them. What you **call** upon in them, you **call** upon in yourself. And as you **call** upon it in them, it becomes real to you. *T-9.V.33.2:4*

~ you are "always," in His Mind and with a **mind** like His. *T-9.V.37.3*

~ you cannot be anywhere except in the **Mind** of **God**. *T-9.VII.52.5*

~ you are altogether irreplaceable in the **Mind** of **God**. No one else can fill your **part** of it, and while you leave your **part** of it empty, your eternal place merely waits for your return. *T-9.VII.57.1:2*

~ **being** in **God**, you encompass everything. *T-9.VIII.61.7*

~ you are at **home** in **God**, dreaming of exile but perfectly capable of awakening to **reality**. *T-9.VIII.65.3*

~ you were created through His **laws** and by His **Will**, and the manner of your **creation** established you as creators. *T-9.X.89.6*

~ you are not sick, and you cannot die. But you can confuse yourself with things that do. *T-9.XI.100.3:4*

~ wholly without **sin**, wholly without **pain**, and wholly without **suffering** of any kind. *T-9.XI.101.5*

~ infinity is meaningless without you, and you are meaningless without **God**. *T-10.II.9.1*

~ you who **share** God's **Being** with Him could never be content without **reality**. *T-11.IX.83.4*

~ you are not **guiltless** in **time**, but in **eternity**. You **have** "sinned" in the **past**, but there is no **past**. *T-11.X.91.1:2*

~ you are immortal because you are eternal. *T-11.X.96.6*

~ you, then, are saved because God's Son is **guiltless**. And **being** wholly pure, you are invulnerable. *T-11.X.99.7:8*

~ you dwell not **here**, but in **eternity**. You travel but in dreams while safe at **home**. *T-12.VII.76.6:7*

~ **within** you is the holy sign of perfect **faith** your **Father** has in you. *T-13.III.19.1*

~ you cannot be as you believed you were. Your **guilt** is without **reason**, because it is not in the **Mind** of **God** where you are. *T-13.IV.29.6:7*

~ **praise** be unto you who **make** the **Father** one with His own Son. *T-13.IV.34.1*

~ you are blessed indeed. Yet in this **world**, you do not know it. *T-13.VI.47.1:2*

~ you who belong to the First **Cause**, created by Him like unto Himself and **part** of Him, are more than merely **guiltless**. *T-13.IX.8.7.1*

~ you are where you **have** forever been and **will** forever be. *T-15.III.18.2*

~ you are of your **Father**. *T-15.IV.31.7*

~ you are an **idea**. And like Him, you can **give** yourself completely, wholly without **loss**, and only with **gain**. *T-15.VII.59.5:6*

~ **god** and the **power** of God **will** take their rightful place in you, and you **will experience** the full **communication** of ideas with ideas. *T-15.VII.64.6*

~ for you **will see** the **Son of God**. You **will** behold the beauty which the **Holy Spirit** loves to look upon and which **He** thanks the **Father** for. *T-17.III.7.6:7*

~ in you there is no **separation**. *T-18.II.9.10*

~ you are surrounded only by Him. *T-18.VII.58.6*

~ the sun and ocean are as **nothing** beside what you are. *T-18.IX.77.2*

~ in neither sun nor ocean is the **power** that rests in you. *T-18.IX.77.4*

~ you who were prisoners in **separation** are **now** made free in Paradise. *T-20.IV.26.6*

~ you did not create yourself. *T-21.III.26.1*

~ this **part** has seen your **brother** and recognized him perfectly since **time** began. And it desired **nothing** but to **join** with him and to be free again, as once it was. It has been waiting for the **birth** of **freedom**, the **acceptance** of **release** to come to you. *T-21.V.45.1:3*

~ you who complete **God's Will** and are His happiness, whose **will** is powerful as His, a **power** that is not lost in your illusions. *T-21.IX.89.1*

~ how thankful **will they** be to **see** you come among them, **offering** Christ's **forgiveness** to dispel their **faith** in **sin**. *T-22.V.41.7*

~ what you bring is your remembrance of everything that is eternal. *T-22.VII.56.7*

~ **nothing** around you but is **part** of you. *T-23.I.6.1*

~ what you **remember** is a **part** of you. For you must be as **God** created you. *T-23.II.13.1:2*

~ you dwell in **peace** as limitless as its **Creator**, and everything is given those who would **remember** Him. *T-23.II.16.6*

~ you are not **special**. *T-24.III.15.1*

~ you are alike to **God** as **God** is to Himself. *T-24.III.21.3*

~ you are not **within** a **body**. What is **within** you cannot be **outside**. *T-25.I.1.3:4*

~ you are the **means** for God—not separate nor with a **life** apart from His. *T-25.II.7.1*

~ you **need** no **forgiveness**, for the wholly pure **have** never sinned. *T-25.III.21.2*

~ you can come their **rest**. From you can rise a **world they will** rejoice to look upon and where their hearts are glad. In you there is a **vision** which extends to all of them and covers them in **gentleness** and **light**. *T-25.V.34.3:5*

~ in the sunlight you **will** stand in **quiet**, in **innocence**, and wholly unafraid. *T-25.V.35.7*

~ in you is all of **Heaven**. *T-25.V.36.1*

~ you **have** the right to all the **universe**—to perfect **peace**, complete deliverance from all effects of **sin**, and to the **life** eternal, joyous and complete in every **way**, as **God** appointed for His holy Son. *T-25.IX.77.1*

~ you **have power** to save the **Son of God** because his **Father** willed that it be so. And in your hands does all **salvation** lie, to be both offered and received as one. *T-26.VIII.64.5:6*

~ you are wrong, but there is One **within** you Who is right. *T-27.VI.51.6*

~ thus are you the one decider of your destiny in **time**. *T-27.VIII.70.3*

~ you cannot do his **part**, but this you do when you become a passive figure in his **dream** instead of dreamer of your own. *T-28.V.41.3*

~ you are free of **pain** and **sickness**, **misery** and **loss**, and all effects of hatred and **attack**. *T-29.III.12.6*

~ you cannot **see** your Guest, but you can **see** the gifts **He** brought. *T-29.III.14.6*

~ you are saved. *T-29.IV.24.7*

~ the changelessness of **Heaven** is in you. *T-29.VI.32.1*

~ you were not born to die. *T-29.VII.41.1*

~ what shares in all **creation** cannot be content with small ideas and **little** things. *T-30.IV.39.11*

~ you but behold your **Self** in what you see. *T-30.IX.94.8*

~ you can not escape from what you are. *T-31.IV.42.8*

~ you are worthy that your **will** be done! *T-31.VI.67.9*

~ you are as **God** created you. *T-31.VIII.92.1*

~ you are not the **victim** of the **world** you **see** because you invented it. You can **give** it up as easily as you made it up. You **will see** it or not **see** it, as you **wish**. While you **want** it, you **will see** it; when you no longer **want** it, it **will** not be there for you to **see**. *W-pI.32.1.2:5*

~ you are holy because your **mind** is **part** of God's. And because you are holy, your **sight** must be holy as well. *W-pI.36.1.2:3*

~ deep **within** you is everything that is perfect, ready to radiate through you and out into the whole **world**. *W-pI.41.2.3*

~ you can never be deprived of your perfect **holiness** because its **Source** goes with you wherever you go. You can never suffer because the **Source** of all **joy** goes with you wherever you go. You can never be **alone** because the **Source** of all **life** goes with you wherever you go. **Nothing** can destroy your **peace** of **mind** because **God** goes with you wherever you go. *W-pI.41.3.1:4*

~ you cannot **see** apart from **God** because you cannot be apart from **God**. Whatever you do, you do in Him because whatever you think, you think with His **Mind**. If **vision** is real, and it is real to the extent to which it shares the Holy Spirit's **purpose**, then you cannot **see** apart from **God**. *W-pI.43.3.1:3*

~ there is a place in you where the **strength** of God abides. *W-pI.47.8.6*

~ you are the **light** of the world. *W-pI.61.10.1*

~ you who **have** the **power** to bring **peace** to every **mind**! *W-pI.63.1.1*

~ the **Son of God** looks to you for his **redemption**. It is yours to **give** him, for it belongs to you. *W-pI.63.2.2:3*

~ you are entitled to **peace today**. *W-pI.80.3.1*

~ you are what **God** created or what you made. One **Self** is true; the other is not there. *W-pI.93.11.1:2*

~ you are as pure and holy as you were created, and that **light** and **joy** and **peace** abide in you. *W-pI.93.4.1*

~ your **image** of yourself cannot withstand the **Will** of **God**. You think that this is **death**, but it is **life**. You think you are destroyed, but you are saved. *W-pI.93.4.2:4*

~ you are and **will** forever be exactly as you were created. **Light** and **joy** and **peace** abide in you because **God** put them there. **Here** you are. This is you. And **light** and **joy** and **peace** abide in you because this is so. *W-pI.93.7.6:10*

~ you stand in **light**, strong in the sinlessness in which you were created and in which you **will** remain throughout **eternity**. *W-pI.94.2.6*

~ you are one **within** yourself and one with Him. *W-pI.95.1.2*

~ you are One **Self**, united and secure in **light** and **joy** and **peace**. You are God's Son, One **Self** with one **Creator** and one **goal**—to bring **awareness** of this **oneness** to all minds, that true **creation** may extend the Allness and the **Unity** of **God**. *W-pI.95.16.2:3*

~ you are One **Self**, complete and healed and whole, with **power** to lift the **veil** of **darkness** from the **world** and let the **light** in you come through to **teach** the **world** the **truth** about itself. You are One **Self**, in perfect harmony with all there is and all that there **will** be. You are One **Self**, the holy **Son of God**, united with your brothers in this **Self**, united with your **Father** in His **Will**. *W-pI.95.17.1:3*

~ you are the **Spirit** lovingly endowed with all your Father's **love** and **peace** and **joy**. You are the **Spirit** which completes Himself and shares His **function** as **Creator**. *W-pI.97.2.2:3*

~ you are the **Spirit** in whose **mind** abides the **miracle** in which all **time** stands still. *W-pI.97.4.1*

~ you are the **Spirit** that abides in Him, and Which calls through His **Voice** to every living **thing**; offers His **sight** to **everyone** who asks; replaces **error** with the simple **truth**. *W-pI.97.5.1*

~ god's **peace** and **joy** are yours. *W-pI.105.1.1*

~ you are not made of flesh and blood and bone but were created by the **self**-same **thought** which gave the **gift** of **life** to Him as well. *W-pI.107.10.2*

~ you **call** to all to **join** you in your **rest**, and **they will** hear and come to you because you **rest** in **God**. **They will** not hear another **voice** but yours because you gave your **voice** to **God** and **now** you **rest** in Him and let Him speak through you. *W-pI.109.4.5:6*

~ in Him you **have** no cares and no concerns, no burdens, no anxiety, no **pain**, no **fear** of **future**, and no **past** regrets. *W-pI.109.5.1*

~ you are changeless, for the Son **He** loves is changeless as Himself. *W-pI.123.3.2*

~ you **have** a **function** in **salvation** to fulfill. *W-pI.123.3.4*

~ for what you are is what **He** is. *W-pI.127.4.3*

~ you do not **want** illusions. *W-pI.130.8.2*

~ you **will** find **Heaven**. Everything you **seek** but this **will** fall away, yet not because it has been taken from you. It **will** go because you do not **want** it. *W-pI.131.6.2:4*

~ you remain as **He** created you. *W-pI.136.14.5*

~ only **acceptance** can be asked of you, for what you are is certain. It is set forever in the holy **Mind** of **God** and in your own. It is so far beyond all **doubt** and **question**. *W-pI.139.7.2:4*

~ as **God** created you, you must remain unchangeable with transitory states by definition false. And that includes all shifts in feeling, alterations in conditions of the **body** and the **mind**, in all **awareness**, and in all response. This is the all-inclusiveness which sets the **truth** apart from falsehood, and the false kept separate from the **truth** as what it is. *W-pI.152.5.1:3*

~ there is a **way** of living in the **world** that is not **here**, although it seems to be. You do not **change** **appearance**, though you smile more frequently. Your forehead is serene; your eyes are **quiet**. *W-pI.155.1.1:3*

~ you are entrusted with the world's **release** from **pain**. *W-pI.166.14.6*

~ **god** has entrusted all His gifts to you. *W-pI.166.15.3*

~ from you **salvation** radiates with gifts beyond all measure, given and returned. *W-pI.188.4.2*

~ you who perceive yourself as weak and frail, with futile hopes and devastated dreams, born but to die, to weep, and suffer **pain**, hear this: all **power** is given you in earth and **Heaven**. There is **nothing** that you cannot do. You play the game of **death**, of **being** helpless, pitifully tied to dissolution in a **world** which shows no mercy to you. Yet when you accord it mercy **will** its mercy shine on you. *W-pI.191.11.1:4*

~ you are God's Son. In **immortality** you live forever. *W-pI.199.8.1:2*

~ you are His Son, completing His **extension** in your own. *W-pI.Rev V.12.5*

~ you do not walk **alone**. God's angels hover close and all about. His **Love** surrounds you, and of this be sure: that **I will** never leave you comfortless. *W-pII.E.6.5:7*

~ you **have** been called by **God**, and you **have** answered. *M-13.6.7*

~ few **have** heard it as yet, and **they** can but turn to you. There is no other hope in all the **world** that **they** can **trust**. There is no other **voice** in all the **world** that echoes God's. *M-13.6.9:11*

~ you are His **completion** and His **Love**. *M-29.7.1*

~ whatever you may think about yourself, whatever you may think about the **world**, your **Father** needs you and **will call** to you until you come to Him in **peace** at last. *S-3.IV.10.7*

AFTERWORD

Thank you for reading this book. If your heart guides you to share it or our other books with your relations and/or to leave feedback on Amazon, we would be deeply grateful. Also, your comments and suggestions will help us to improve the clarity of our publications and will thus be gifts to us and all our readers. Circulating your loving thoughts throughout the world will uplift and empower many.

All digital versions of our books are free on Amazon's Kindle and on Smashwords and Lulu. We invest all of the revenue generated from the sale of printed versions into translating our books into multiple languages.

As long as you keep an open mind, this book will help you sort out what is true from what is false. We hope you generalize these ideas and integrate them into the present moment—you are entitled to experience a state of unlimited inner radiance in a joyous, heart-centered life.

WORKS CITED

New Oxford Dictionary, Second Edition. New York, New York: Oxford University Press. 2005. Print.

Schucman, Helen. *A Course in Miracles Original Edition.* Omaha, Nebraska. Course in Miracles Society. 2011. ebook.

Wierix, Hieronymus. *The Throne of Mercy.* 1578. Engraving. Philadelphia Museum of Art. Philadelphia, Pennsylvania.

BIOGRAPHY

The details of our lives are quite inconsequential.
All that need be known is that a tranquil mind has been achieved.

ISBN 978-164516410-4

Made in the USA
Columbia, SC
20 November 2022

71488615R10280